ORGANIZATIONS, POLICY,

AND THE

NATURAL ENVIRONMENT

*Institutional and
Strategic Perspectives*

ANDREW J. HOFFMAN

MARC J. VENTRESCA

Editors

STANFORD UNIVERSITY PRESS
Stanford, California 2002

Stanford University Press

Stanford, California

© 2002 by the Board of Trustees of the
Leland Stanford Junior University

Printed in the United States of America
on acid-free, archival-quality paper.

Library of Congress Cataloging-in-Publication Data

Organizations, policy, and the natural environment :
institutional and strategic perspectives / Andrew J. Hoffman and
Marc J. Ventresca, editors.
      p.   cm.
Includes index.
    ISBN 0-8047-4195-6 (cloth : alk. paper) — ISBN 0-8047-4196-4
(pbk. : alk. paper)
    1. Green movement. 2. Pressure groups. 3. Environmental
policy. I.
Hoffman, Andrew J., date   II. Ventresca, Marc J.
    JA75.8 .O74 2002
    333.7—dc21

2002001105

Original Printing 2002

Last figure below indicates year of this printing:

11   10   09   08   07   06   05   04   03   02

Designed by James P. Brommer

Typeset by G & S Typesetters, Inc. in 10/13 Minion

CONTENTS

TABLES

FIGURES

FOREWORD

John W. Meyer
Stanford University

The studies in this book show how organizations, including national states, adapt to the pressures and rules of the modern environmental movement, and try to change or manage these rules. Andy Hoffman and Marc Ventresca have put together a most impressive set of studies covering many fronts. Their collaborators discuss the nature of environmental policy pressures and the varied responses of different types of organizations in different types of countries. They are concerned with the conditions under which organizations produce purely symbolic as opposed to more implemented responses, and the attempts of organizations to create and perhaps manipulate the environmental rules under which they are to function.

In the background, and central to the driving forces faced by both modern organizations and the researchers here, is a social movement of great urgency and impact. In the last three or four decades, "the environment" has come to be a main focus of attention in all leading countries and in world society as a whole. Public concern with the topic has a number of properties that make it both powerful and pervasive.

First, environmental concerns are matters both of social organization and of an embedded culture and set of meanings. We talk differently about the air, water, earth, and biosystem than we used to, and perceive many detailed problems and crises. Large numbers of new social organizations arise focusing on these problems: public and private structures that did not exist a few years ago. Local organizations question water quality, national organizations track wildlife declines, and many international organizations call attention to widespread problems (Chapter 2).

Second, the new patterns of talk and organization occur at every level of social life from the most local to the most global. The concerns at each level are often integrated with those at other levels. So people with reasonable skills at public talk can now quickly see the problems of the local stream as linked to global problems of water pollution, or hot days as instances of the greenhouse effect. Similarly, local environmental organizations are linked in networks to national and global ones. The local air reflects a world problem, and the world problem is shown to be a problem of local air.

Third, the whole system of discourse and organization takes a universal and global turn. We are all given more and more reasons to be concerned with, and feel entitled and obligated to be concerned with, environmental events everywhere else. The rain forest is a property of the world, not just (for example) Brazil. Wherever you travel in the modern world, you are likely to find at least some recognition of the universal problems and issues involved. An endangered species is endangered for all of us. More directly, worldwide interdependencies are involved in flows of disease-carrying dust, genetic material, species invasions, and so on. We have the right and obligation to complain about any problem anywhere, and to complain in general and universal scientific terms.

Fourth, the problems of the natural environment, though specific and technical and disparate in character, fall under a general rubric. They reflect a broad and integrated set of problems and crises: an overall moral confrontation. Thus the term "environment" reflects a highly general and highly codified frame within which an enormous number of specific issues can be tightly fit. In a technical sense this is not obviously true; many environmental problems could be seen in isolation. But "the environment" is not a technical matter. It is a global frame for understanding. Urban sprawl around one city can now be seen as a multidimensional assault on the whole ecosystem.

An enormously expanded institution full of meanings and organizations has come into place. The natural environment, as interpreted in the scientific language of the new culture by the new organizational system, is now a codified part of the social environment within which we all live.

This book is about the impact of this great institutional system on the public and private organizations that make up so much of modern social life. It is about whether and how organizations come to terms with the new pressures and rules. It is about how and when they feed back and modify the rapidly evolving controls and rules making up the new environmental regime.

The book contains academic analyses of the ways modern organizations adapt to and modify their wider social environment—in this case, those components of the social environment that celebrate and regulate the natural environment. The writers are following the tradition called institutional analysis: the line of thought, in modern organization theory, that emphasizes the breadth of interdependence of organizations with their social settings. In this tradition, organizations are not only involved in some exchanges (such as of resources or products) with the social world around them: they are created and legitimated by this world, and their identities depend on it. On the other side, they make strenuous and sometimes successful efforts, not only to do business within their contexts, but to build and change the fundamental rules by which they themselves live.

This intellectual tradition turns out to be especially useful in analyzing the interrelations of organizations with modern environmentalism, as this book convincingly demonstrates. Fundamentally, this is because the modern movement concerned with the natural environment is a very broad cultural force changing the rules defining public and private actors, including all sorts of organizations. Thus new rules regulating, say, air pollution, are not simply matters of technical costs or exchanges. They have a broad moral and cultural character, activating fundamental rights and obligations that are supposed to be part of the identity of all of us. Thus they penetrate modern organizations' technical transactions, but also the broader moral obligations that are to determine what organizations do or don't do. There's a difference between charging too much for a product and poisoning the local water supply.

The authors of the chapters in this book understand and share that vision. They understand that the natural environment is in crisis on many fronts. Many changes, and much adaptation, are desperately needed. So the research questions here have a moral and policy urgency. But this is true of the organizations they study, too. The crucial character of environmental crises and problems is taken for granted here. It pervades the thinking of researchers, organizations, and most readers. The urgency involves the questions researchers ask and the ways organizations tend to relate to environmental pressures. Important themes of the studies in this book follow:

- Organizations confront an environmental system defined in terms of objective scientific laws, studies, and measures (Chapters 2 and 5).

- There is a tendency to respond to environmental regulation with symbolic conformity (Chapters 6–9, 11). This kind of conformity is practically required, may be highly rewarded, and may in the long run be consequential (Chapters 8 and 9). The fears that organizational responses are *only* symbolic are endemic—both in the research community represented here, and in the wider world. Throughout this book, questions of overall effectiveness of environmental regulation recur. Partly this reflects uncertainty about effective implementation. But it also reflects the shared urgency associated with constantly expanding perceptions of environmental problems and crises. Today, pictures of environmental problems expand faster than any set of possible solutions.

- Countries differ not only in how they respond to the pressures of modern environmentalism, but in the organizational forms of their responses. More corporatist (that is, European) responses involve more effective cooperation (Chapters 15 and 18). Market society and the adversarial polity (as in the United States) may produce more response (Chapters 7 and 16), but market rationality may distort the formulation of environmental problems (Chapters 5 and 14).

- Industries and ecological settings differ in how much impact environmental pressures have (Chapters 3 and 6). In high-impact industries, stabilized and codified responses may be more likely—but this does not mean the responses are homogeneous (Chapter 6).

- There is much variation among organizations in their response to environmental regulation (Chapters 6, 7, 10–13, 17). Sometimes organizations feel obliged to stick with their old organizational fields, with their customary arrangements and accounts (Chapters 4, 14, 15). The researchers tend to see fields that work by negotiation as more effective than those that work through adversarial or competitive arrangements (but see Chapter 16).

- Finally, a dominant theme throughout the studies in this book is that organizations try to affect environmental rules that regulate them. There is much institutional entrepreneurship, and active management of the regulatory world around focal organizations. The authors here reject the common picture of organizations as passive instruments of a dominating external control system. They see organizations as trying to lead the wider polities in which they are embedded with various mixtures of vision, self-interest, and self-protection (Chapters 7, 10–12, 14–15, and 17–18). There is, on one hand, a tendency to fear the influence of dominating large corporations over environmental regulations. But in the studies here, on the other hand, this is balanced by a picture of organizations that are involved in long-term cooperative arrangements. The question of who is co-opting whom is left partially open. No simple account of dominance is plausible. In the complex pattern of relationships and the context of rapidly expanding perceptions of environmental problems, yesterday's solutions may come to be seen, today, as sellouts.

But the common framework is clear. It is shared by most researchers, readers, and the general public. It involves a vision: the natural environment is filled with overwhelming problems and crises that must be solved by extant organizations (and new ones). The fear that these organizations will not try to deal with these problems, or will try to minimize or evade the problems, is part of public discourse. It is a force leading to constant organizational expansion in the modern system, as organizations come to terms with expanding pressures.

None of us are in the best position to assess the overall effectiveness of contemporary efforts at environmental regulation. But this book makes it clear that the environmental movement has had enormous impact on modern organizations. Everywhere the researchers look, they find organizations trying to deal with new pressures: structuring symbolic and implemented conformity, manipulating the regulations they face, trying to find forms for incorporating environmental concerns, and implementing reinterpreted external controls. None of this may work well, but note what the researchers do not find: they do not find organizational systems that simply ignore the whole business: the cultural changes and organizational pressures have built the problematic "natural environment" into issues in the social environment with which every organization must try to deal.

PREFACE

For ten days in January 1969, the Union Oil Company's Platform A spilled an estimated 3.25 million gallons of thick crude oil into the Santa Barbara Channel on the coast of Southern California. By mid-May, the slick had covered virtually the entire city coastline, as well as most of the coastlines of Ventura and Santa Barbara Counties (Scheffer, 1991). This event became a lightning rod and turning point in environmental policy and activism in the United States (Dowie, 1995). In trying to understand the policy issues in this environmental disaster—how it happened, how it was resolved, and with what consequences—we could focus on many dimensions. We could assess the toxicity of the crude oil that was leaked; the ecological damage the oil imposed on fish and plant species along the fragile coastline; the economic impact of this ecological damage on the tourism industry that had become the economic base of the region; the political interests at work in mobilizing resources for the cleanup, or other similarly important concerns. These are well-debated topics, structured as analytic problems by technical, legal, and economic approaches to environmental policy issues.

But standard approaches in policy studies often neglect the organizational component. They give explanatory primacy to malfunctions in technological systems while focusing less on the complex, contingent organizational processes at play (Beamish, 2001; Perrow, 1984; Vaughan, 1996). They focus on the aggregate of political interests as decision drivers rather than on the decision processes distributed across complex social fields and bureaucratic arrangements (Espeland, 1998). They seek the sources of accountability in the intentional and interested actions of individual firms or agencies, with less regard to the contributing sources of standard organizational practices, industry-level beliefs, or the guiding legacy of regulatory models (such as "command and control").

The case of the Santa Barbara oil spill is instructive for exploring organizational issues. Molotch (1970) uses this case to move away from technological and economic accounts to understand why this oil spill, rather than one of the many other (and larger) spills that had occurred worldwide, garnered such national attention. Like Molotch, we are making socially, politically, and institutionally based arguments to understand environmental problems and solutions. But we consider the *field-level processes* by which *collective rationalities* shape meaning and action around the enactment of an event like this. We use the term "field-level" activities to describe organizational and institutional dynamics in order to emphasize the level of analysis and types of processes involved. Molotch, for example, argued that to understand the Santa Barbara oil spill we need to begin with a focus on the social class and status of the residents of Santa Barbara. In his study, political interests, class resources, and social networks account for why such an unusually high level of field-level debate occurred and then turned into policy action of equally unusual speed and scope. The Nixon administration imposed a moratorium on California offshore development, temporarily shutting it down. Cleanup efforts were impressively extensive for their day. And the legacy of this spill continues thirty years later, fueling opposition to proposed drilling in the potentially lucrative reserves of the Alaskan tundra (Yergin, 1991). In the end, more than oil leaked from Union Oil's Platform: "a bit of truth about power in America spilled out along with it" (Molotch, 1970: 131).

We propose the intertwining of social and political processes with technical and economic dynamics as a preferred research stance. As such, the intended audience for this book is twofold, reflecting both a theoretical and empirical focus. One set of readers at whom the book is directed are organizational and management scholars working within the tradition of the institutional analysis of organizations and policy. The others are environmental scholars interested in management and policy. Providing a useful synthesis of theory and empirical setting that is novel to both sets of readers, the studies in this volume apply a set of analytic lenses grounded in field-level organization and institutional approaches as they probe for answers to how environmental policy and practices get shaped, are spread, are contested, and have consequences. Similarly, we see the interplay of organizations, policy, and the natural environment as a critical empirical domain for understanding central paradoxes in policy studies, sharpening the analytic insights of recent institutional and strategic theories of organizations, and building awareness about the interface of the social and natural environments. Situated at this intersection, the chapters in this volume contribute to discussion about how organizational approaches to environmental issues can inform key research concerns such as the sources of organization-level policies and practices, the dynamics of policy systems and wider organizational fields, and the institutional framing of the natural environment and its interplay within society and specific industrial sectors.

To date, the research insights of the organizational sciences are little evident in the policy study of environmental issues. This absence is the focus of several recent challenges by senior scholars. Gladwin (1993) called attention to this missing contribution by calling for an application of organizational theory to the study of corporate environmental management. He argued that "sociological theory pertaining to organizations holds the greatest promise for improving our understanding of how greening works . . . [because they focus] on basic characteristics of organizational participants, goals, social structure, technology and external environment, at different levels of analysis" (p. 47). Where Gladwin sought to provoke contributions from outside the field, Stern and Barley (1996) directed an internal challenge to research colleagues, arguing for an engagement of classic concerns from organizational theory to issues of broad social relevance, such as the environment. They argued that most academic contributions to such issues presently come from the disciplines of economics and law. But these disciplines focus narrowly on overly rational conceptions and coercive mechanisms for identifying and solving key issues of public concern, approaches that neglect systemic organizational contexts that establish parameters for individual choice and action.

This book is an answer to the call of such scholars. The chapters discuss a variety of environmental issues and report evidence on the dynamics of social structure and organizational processes in identifying, shaping, and resolving them.

A focus on organizational processes leads to new types of questions and analytical concerns regarding previously addressed environmental issues. For example, why did the Love Canal disaster of 1978 become a national emergency—ultimately precipitating the legislation of the Comprehensive Environmental Response, Compensation and Liability Act (CERCLA) or Superfund law—and not any of the other 10,000 hazardous waste dumpsites across America? Love Canal was a catastrophe, but it wasn't the worst hazardous waste site in the country, in New York State, or even in Niagara County (Keating and Russell, 1992). Why do we devote such enormous attention and money to cleaning up hazardous waste sites when the U.S. Environmental Protection Agency's own internal technical studies show that other issues such as ground-level radon and acid rain present greater threats to human health and the environment? Why have corporations begun to develop formal mechanisms at the firm- and industry-levels for self-enforcement on certain environmental issues even when government has yet to act? Why have global problems such as ozone depletion and global climate change displaced more local problems such as groundwater contamination and urban waste disposal as priorities for governments, the press, and the mainstream environmental movement?

These form an important category of questions for understanding the full dimensions of environmental problems and solutions. Although the immediate answers to such questions are generally local and technological, more basic issues lie in the cultural and institutional context of environmental decision making. Rather than asking about the technical sources of environmental pollution, we need to ask how environmental problems are conceived and framed. This line of questioning will lead to further questions about why environmental problems persist and, more important, how solutions are fashioned in response. This will lead us to questions of values, norms, politics, and power. And to probe at this level of analysis, we need to consider the different constituencies that have a stake in particular environmental problems and the domains in which they interact. This is an area that is gaining increasing attention from scholars focused on environmental issues within the fields of management, sociology, policy, and political science (Buttel, 1987; Hannigan, 1995; Shrivastava, 1995; MacNaughten and Urry, 1998; Becker and Jahn, 1999; Starik and Marcus, 2000).

Varied in theoretical and empirical approach, the chapters in this volume emphasize five themes. The *first* is the focus on organizational structures and actions in relation to the natural environment. But more than focusing on any single organization in isolation, these studies develop arguments about how field-level distributions of resources and meanings guide collective understanding and beliefs about the nature of environmental problems and their solutions. The focus is on political and institutional mechanisms and empirical studies that feature attention to local, organizational, national, and global processes. The *second* is the inclusion of the natural environment as a "participant" in field-level policy processes, a critical and distinct element in institutional analyses. The presence and influence of the natural environment in this way poses novel kinds of practical and theoretical research issues for organizational studies. The chapters deal with these issues in ways that help define new research directions. The *third* is the theoretical application of organizational studies to the empirical domain of environmental issues as generative for both organization theory and environmental studies. Our goal is to bring together theory and research that charts a distinctive analytic point of view regarding the complex analytical and practical tasks in the study of environmental policy and corporate environmental action. The *fourth* is the commitment to ground studies of environmental policy in rigorous, empirical, and disciplinary research, a clear statement about the value of basic organization and social science research studies on complicated, contested contemporary issues. This can help counter the appearance to some that studies in this domain are "advocacy."

The *fifth* and final theme is that the research reported in this book treats institutions and organizations as a relevant level of analysis for these types of issues. For although technological and economic activity may be proximate factors in environmentally destructive behavior, the chapters focus on the sources and structure of collective rationality, framing processes, and social and political institutions that embed those technical and economic factors (Bazerman and Hoffman, 1999; Dacin, Ventresca, and Beal; 1999; Hirsch, 1986). Our critical questions are not about technology per se, but about how organizational and institutional processes shape its development, interpret its impact on the natural environment, and enact organizational and institutional changes to resolve it. We use the research in this book as a basis to develop an argument for studies based on analytic attention to field-level processes and organizational mechanisms.

ACKNOWLEDGMENTS

This book is the culmination of work presented at a Kellogg Environmental Research Center (KERC)–sponsored conference at Northwestern University April 28–30, 2000. We would like to thank Max Bazerman for initial support of the project through generous KERC grants and for his own energies and long-term interest in bringing institutional arguments and behavioral theories into dialogue with environmental policy issues. We also owe substantial thanks to Dean Donald Jacobs at the Kellogg School of Management for enabling us to host the conference at the James C. Allen Center and for making available all manner of resources to bring together the contributors to this book for initial discussion and exciting exchange of ideas. Our home departments at Boston University and Kellogg, respectively, provide intellectual environments conducive to this sort of cross-disciplinary and integrative work. David Messick, director of the Ford Motor Company Center for Global Citizenship, and Daniel Diermeier, acting director, provided generous support, especially the expertise of key staffers: Susan Rees was indispensable in helping to coordinate the conference, and both she and Andrew Marfia worked the technological wonders of maintaining the OPNE web page. Andy Marfia also provided sustained, excellent staff work through the completion of the book. The Allen Center staff, in particular Carol Rose, displayed their usual excellence in making the conference occur in that most conducive venue.

Other colleagues played an early, important role in reading and commenting on draft chapters. They include James Gillespie, Michael Johnson-Cramer, Don Moore, Amit Nigam, Naomi Olson, and Trex Proffitt. Their efforts improved the chapters and also helped us as we structured the conference sessions. In addition, Naomi Olson and Wendy Espeland offered useful counsel as we developed the final structure of the book. Naomi Olson and Susan Martenson provided expert editorial services at key moments in the completion of the book. We thank them all.

Senior acquisitions editor Bill Hicks, assistant editors Sumathi Raghavan and Kate Wahl, and production editor David Horne from Stanford University Press deserve special thanks in supporting the work of the authors and us in helping to bring the volume to fruition in the form you now hold. We are particularly pleased that the papers for this conference evolved through three rounds of feedback and revision with few ever materializing in paper form. Through our web page and e-mail correspondence, this "virtual" editing process was one of the most resource-minimizing conferences with which we've ever been involved. Thanks to all the authors for making this possible.

Andrew J. Hoffman
Boston, Massachusetts

Marc J. Ventresca
Evanston, Illinois

REFERENCES

Bazerman, Max, and Andrew J. Hoffman. 1999. "Sources of Environmentally Destructive Behavior: Individual, Organizational and Institutional Perspectives." *Research in Organizational Behavior,* 21: 39–79.

Beamish, Thomas. 2001. *Silent Spill: The Organization of Industrial Crisis,* Cambridge, MA: MIT Press.

Becker, Egon, and Thomas Jahn, eds. 1999. *Sustainability and the Social Sciences: A Cross-Disciplinary Approach to Integrating Environmental Considerations into Theoretical Reorientation.* Paris: UNESCO.

Buttel, Frederick. 1987. "New Directions in Environmental Sociology." *Annual Review of Sociology,* 13: 465–488.

Dacin, Tina M., Marc J. Ventresca, and Brent Beal. 1999. "The Embeddedness of Organizations: Research Dialogue and Directions." *Journal of Management,* 25(3): 317–356.

Dowie, Mark. 1995. *Losing Ground: American Environmentalism at the Close of the Twentieth Century.* Cambridge, MA: MIT Press.

Espeland, Wendy Nelson. 1998. *The Struggle for Water: Politics, Rationality, and Identity in the American Southwest.* Chicago: University of Chicago Press.

Gladwin, Thomas. 1993. "The Meaning of Greening: A Plea for Organizational Theory." In Fischer and Schott, eds., *Environmental Strategies for Industry: International Perspectives on Research Needs and Policy Implications,* pp. 37–62. Washington, DC: Island Press.

Hannigan, John. 1995. *Environmental Sociology: A Social Constructionist Perspective.* London: Routledge.

Hirsch, Paul. 1986. "From Ambushes to Golden Parachutes: Corporate Takeovers as an Instance of Cultural Framing and Institutional Integration." *American Journal of Sociology,* 91(4): 800–837.

Keating, Brian, and Dick Russell. 1992. "EPA Yesterday and Today." *E Magazine,* July/Aug.: 30–37.

MacNaughten, Phil, and John Urry. 1998. *Contested Natures.* Thousand Oaks, CA: Sage.

Molotch, Harvey. 1970. "Oil in Santa Barbara and Power in America." *Sociological Inquiry,* 40: 131–144.

Perrow, Charles. 1984. *Normal Accidents: Living With High Risk Technologies,* New York: Basic Books.

Scheffer, Victor. 1991. *The Shaping of Environmentalism in America.* Seattle: University of Washington Press.

Shrivastava, Paul. 1995. "The Role of Corporations in Achieving Ecological Sustainability." *Academy of Management Review,* 20(4): 936–960.

Starik, Mark, and Alfred Marcus. 2000. "Introduction to the Special Research Forum on the Management of Organizations in the Natural Environment: A Field Emerging from Multiple Paths, with Many Challenges Ahead." *Academy of Management Journal,* 43(4): 539–546.

Stern, Robert, and Steven Barley. 1996. "Organizations and Social Systems: Organization Theory's Neglected Mandate." *Administrative Science Quarterly,* 41(1): 146–162.

Vaughan, Diane. 1996. *The Challenger Launch Decision: Risky Technology, Culture, and Deviance at NASA.* Chicago: University of Chicago Press.

Yergin, Daniel. 1991. *The Prize.* New York: Touchstone.

ABOUT THE CONTRIBUTORS

The Editors

ANDREW J. HOFFMAN is assistant professor of organizational behavior at the Boston University School of Management. He is the author of *Competitive Environmental Strategy: A Guide to the Changing Landscape* (2000, Island Press) and *From Heresy to Dogma: An Institutional History of Corporate Environmentalism* (2001, Stanford University Press: originally published in 1997 by New Lexington Press), which was awarded the 2001 Rachel Carson Prize from the Society for Social Studies of Science. He is editor of *Global Climate Change: A Senior-Level Dialogue* (1998, New Lexington Press). His research deals with the nature and dynamics of change within institutional and cultural systems. He applies that research toward understanding the cultural and managerial implications of environmental protection for industry.

MARC J. VENTRESCA is assistant professor of management and organizations at the Kellogg School of Management, assistant professor of sociology (by courtesy), and research associate at the Institute for Policy Research, all at Northwestern University. Recent publications include *Constructing Markets and Industries* (2002, Elsevier Science), edited with Joe Porac; *Social Structure and Organization Revisited,* edited with Michael Lounsbury (2002, JAI Press); and articles in the *Socioeconomic Review, American Behavioral Scientist,* and *Journal of Management* on studies of institutional change processes in environmental policy and on embeddedness and organizations. He specializes in the study of organizations, industries, and entrepreneurial activity, with focus on industry emergence and organizational change. Current projects highlight the interplay of institutions, organizations, conflict, and policy in the global exchange–traded financial markets industry.

The Contributors

PRATIMA BANSAL is an assistant professor of general management at the Richard Ivey School of Business at the University of Western Ontario. She coedited *Business and the Natural Environment* (1997, Butterworth-Heinemann) with Elizabeth Howard and has published in the *Academy of Management Journal*, *Academy of Management Executive,* and other academic and professional journals. Her research interests are centered primarily in the application of institutional theory and strategic management perspectives to corporate environmental management.

MICHAEL L. BARNETT is a Ph.D. candidate in the management department at the Stern School of Business at New York University. His dissertation work explores when, why, and how self-interested firms engage in collective industry-level activities in lieu of firm-level competitive pursuits, and how firms dynamically balance competitive and collective interests to construct competitive advantage.

MAX H. BAZERMAN is the Jesse Isador Straus professor of business administration at the Harvard Business School. He has authored or coauthored more than 120 articles and has authored, coauthored, or coedited nine books, including *You Can't Enlarge the Pie* (2001, Basic Books, in press), *Smart Money Decisions* (1999, Wiley), *Judgment in Managerial Decision Making* (2002, Wiley, now in its fifth edition), *Cognition and Rationality in Negotiation* (1991, Free Press, with M. Neale), and *Negotiating Rationally* (1992, Free Press, with M. Neale). Bazerman's research focuses on decision making, negotiation, and the natural environment.

JEFFREY W. BERNICKE is a Ph.D. candidate in corporate strategy at the University of Michigan Business School. His dissertation investigates the effects of performance and organizational structure on the search activities in firms. His research interests are in the areas of organizational change, innovation, and environmental management.

MAGALI DELMAS is assistant professor of business strategy at the Donald Bren School of Environmental Science and Management at the University of California, Santa Barbara. She is investigating the interaction between environmental regulation and firms' innovative strategies. She has been analyzing the effect of regulatory and technological uncertainty on the organization of the waste management and nuclear industries in Europe and the United States. She is currently analyzing how alternative policy instruments to command and control regulation, such as self-regulation and voluntary agreements, could have an impact on firms' innovative strategies and competitive advantage.

JOHN R. EHRENFELD retired in April 2000 as director of the MIT Program on Technology, Business, and Environment. He is executive director of the International Society of Industrial Ecology. He is author or coauthor of more than two hundred papers, books, reports, and other publications, and is associate editor of the *Journal of Industrial Ecology* and a member of the editorial advisory board of *Environmental Science & Technology*. His research examines the way businesses manage environmental concerns, seeking models leading to organizational and technological changes to improve sustainable practices. In October 1999, the World Resources Institute honored him with a lifetime achievement award for his academic accomplishments in the field of business and environment. He received the Founders Award for Distinguished Service from the Academy of Management's Organization and Natural Environment Division in August 2000.

WENDY NELSON ESPELAND is associate professor of sociology at Northwestern University. She is the author of *The Struggle for Water: Politics, Rationality, and Identity in the American Southwest* (1998, University of Chicago Press), which was awarded the 2000 Rachel Carson Prize from the Society for Social Studies of Science, the Louis Brownlow Book Award from the National Academy of Public Administration, and the Book Award from the Culture Section of the American Sociological Association. She is currently serving as a consulting editor for the *American Journal of Sociology*. Her areas of interest include environmental politics, organizations, culture, and law.

LINDA C. FORBES is assistant professor of management at Marist College. Her interests include cultural studies and organizational symbolism, environmental philosophy, and varieties of qualitative inquiry. Her current work draws on symbolic organization theory as a framework for analyzing contemporary responses to flexible forms of organizing and for analyzing the greening of organizational cultures. She is a feature editor for the journal *Organization & Environment,* where she recently published an archives feature, "John Muir's Message: An Introduction to Our National Parks." She lives in the Hudson River valley of New York state and is an avid hiker.

DAVID JOHN FRANK is associate professor of sociology at Harvard University. He has published on global environmentalism in *Social Forces, International Organization, Sociological Inquiry,* and most recently in the *American Sociological Review.* Future projects on global environmentalism include investigations of the relationship between the proliferation of environmental policies and improvements in environmental quality, and the determinants of environmental values.

HEATHER GERACI is a Ph.D. candidate in organizational behavior at Cornell University's Industrial and Labor Relations School. Her research interests include the study of institutional change and professions. Currently she is studying how competing institutional logics shaped women's access to the profession of law in the late nineteenth and early twentieth centuries.

STUART L. HART is professor of strategic management and director of the Sustainable Enterprise Initiative at the University of North Carolina's Kenan-Flagler Business School. He has published over forty papers and authored or edited four books. His article "Beyond Greening: Strategies for a Sustainable World" won the McKinsey Award for Best Article in the *Harvard Business Review* for 1997. His research interests center on strategy innovation and change. He is particularly interested in the implications of environmentalism and sustainable development for corporate and competitive strategy.

ANN HIRONAKA is an assistant professor in the Department of Sociology at the University of Minnesota. Her main research interest is the study of conflict and institutional mechanisms in the context of war and ethnic identity. A second major research interest is on the effects of the global environmental regime on national environmental policies, which has led to publications in the *American Sociological Review* and *International Organization.*

JENNIFER A. HOWARD-GRENVILLE is assistant professor of organizational behavior at the Boston University School of Management. She is interested in how companies adapt to and create their changing environments and studies the role of culture and institutional processes in constraining or advancing this adaptation process. She has a particular interest in understanding how corporate culture informs an organization's perception of the natural environment and has carried out an ethnographic study at a major semiconductor manufacturer to examine this issue.

P. DEVEREAUX JENNINGS is an associate professor in the faculty of commerce at the University of British Columbia, Vancouver. He is currently an "action editor" for the *Academy of Management Review* and is one of the founding editors of *Strategic Organization!* His areas of research interest are organizations and the natural environment, organizational geography, and comparative human resource management systems—primarily from an institutional and political approach.

JOHN M. JERMIER is professor of organizational behavior and environmental science and policy at the University of South Florida, Tampa. He is founding editor (with Paul Shrivastava) and current editor of the journal *Organization & Environment: International Journal for Ecosocial Research* and also serves on the editorial review boards of *Organization Science* and *Leadership Quarterly.* Most of his research has focused on developing critical perspectives in organizational studies with emphasis on research philosophy and methodology. He has published his work in a variety of journals including *Academy of Management Journal, Academy of Management Review, Administrative Science Quarterly, Journal of Management, Organization Science,* and *Organization Studies.* His most recent project is a book chapter (coauthored with Linda Forbes) titled "Organizational Greening: Critical Issues."

ANDREW A. KING is assistant professor of management and operations management at the Stern School of Business at New York University. He is the founder and coordinator of Business and Environment at Stern. He was the 1999 AT&T Fellow for Industrial Ecology, and his thesis was awarded the Zannetos Thesis Prize. He currently directs an EPA-funded research effort on how voluntary agreements influence environmental performance.

MICHAEL J. LENOX is assistant professor of management at the Stern School of Business at New York University. He studies the economics of organization with an interest in the role of incentives and information on the rate and direction of innovation within firms. He has an applied interest in understanding under what circumstances firms pursue innovative activities that have a public-goods spill-over—in particular, innovations that benefit the natural environment.

PETER LEVIN is a Ph.D. candidate in sociology at Northwestern University. His research focuses on the cultural and social elements of economic markets. His dissertation is an ethnographic examination of futures trading in face-to-face and electronic trading organizations.

DAVID L. LEVY is associate professor of management at the University of Massachusetts, Boston. His research examines the intersection of business strategy and politics in the development of environmental policy. In the last few years, he has studied responses to climate change by U.S. and American multinational corporations in the oil and automobile industries. Dr. Levy has also undertaken research projects in cooperation with the OECD, the UN Centre for Transnational Corporations, and the U.S. EPA. He is currently researching the potential for renewable energy, as a source of energy and economic development, in Massachusetts.

MICHAEL LOUNSBURY is assistant professor at the School of Industrial and Labor Relations and Department of Sociology at Cornell University. His research, which focuses on the social construction of economic practices, has been published in journals such as *Administrative Science Quarterly, Academy of Management Journal, American Behavioral Scientist,* and *Strategic Management Journal.* His environment-related research has concentrated mainly on understanding the origins of the contemporary recycling industry.

MARTIN L. MARTENS is a Ph.D. candidate in the faculty of commerce at the University of British Columbia and an assistant professor at Concordia University. His research interests are entrepreneurial risk and strategy in initial public offerings, organizational cognition, neo-institutional theory and the natural environment, and Sir Ernest Shackleton's Endurance expedition.

PETER J. MENDEL is an associate behavioral scientist at RAND, a social and policy research institute in Santa Monica, California. He is coauthor of *Institutional Change and Healthcare Organizations: From Professional Dominance to Managed Care* (2000, University of Chicago Press), which received the Max Weber Award for best scholarly book in organizational sociology from the American Sociological Association. His interests focus on the comparative analysis of institutions and organizations, including the global diffusion of modern management and organizational reforms. Mendel earned his Ph.D. and M.A. degrees in sociology at Stanford University and received his B.A. degree in industrial relations from Cornell University.

MARK B. MILSTEIN is a Ph.D. candidate in strategic management at the University of North Carolina, Chapel Hill. His research interests include organizational strategies for sustainable development, organizational change, industry transformations, and innovation. His current research examines how top management team decision-making processes affect the exploratory and exploitative nature of organizational responses to strategic issues.

CALVIN MORRILL is professor of sociology at the University of California, Irvine (with courtesy appointments in the Department of Criminology, Law & Society and the Graduate School of Management). He is the author of *The Executive Way: Conflict Management in Corporations* (1995, University of Chicago Press), which won the 1997 Distinguished Scholarship Award from the Pacific Sociological Association and was selected as a 1995 "Best Nonfiction Book" by the *Chicago Tribune*; coauthor of *Codes of Conflict: Youth Culture and Violence in a Multiethnic High School* (forthcoming, University of Chicago Press) and coeditor of *Personal Relationships in Public Contexts: Studies in Relational Ethnography* (forthcoming, University of California Press). His interests span law and society, organizational conflict and change, sociology of culture, sociology of youth, and social network analysis.

YIORGOS MYLONADIS is assistant professor at the London Business School. His research aims at answering the question "Where do strategies come from?" and he is particularly interested in the conditions that enable learning to take place within and among organizations. His latest project is on "Firm Factories"—the global venture communities in which new firms get insight, resources, and guidance to develop into high-valuation propositions.

JASON OWEN-SMITH is an assistant professor of organizational studies and sociology at the University of Michigan. He completed his dissertation, a multi-method examination of the causes and consequences of increased science and engineering commercialization at research intensive universities, at the University of Arizona Department of Sociology in August 2000.

WENDY J. PENNER is a private consultant in Williamstown, Massachusetts. Her research examines businesses' responses to issues of environmental quality. She has worked at the Center for Ecological Technology in Western Massachusetts to implement waste reduction programs for businesses, including reuse of industrial waste, purchasing recycled products, and recycling of conventional and construction waste.

HANNAH C. RILEY is a Ph.D. candidate in the Negotiation, Organizations and Markets unit at Harvard Business School. Her dissertation research focuses on gender as a social phenomenon in negotiation. She has conducted field research on corporations' management of multiparty environmental conflicts.

SANDRA ROTHENBERG is assistant professor of organizational behavior at the Rochester Institute of Technology's College of Business. Her research focuses on environmental management within the automobile industry, where her interests have included corporate environmental strategy and management, lean manufacturing and environmental performance, regulation and technical innovation, international environmental management, worker participation, and environmental activism within firms.

M. ANJALI SASTRY is assistant professor of management in the system dynamics group at the MIT Sloan School of Management. Her research investigates organizational change from a variety of perspectives, including computer simulation, system dynamics, and feedback thinking. Her recent research includes imprinting in organizations, path dependence, punctuated change, organizational learning, and the pacing of change in organizations.

EVAN SCHOFER is an assistant professor in the Department of Sociology at the University of Minnesota. His research looks at the expansion of education and science, and their effects on the economy, environmental activity, and the political systems of nations. He has coauthored several papers on the rise and expansion of the global environmental movement. Additionally, he is working on a research project investigating the causes of cross-national variation in civil society.

W. RICHARD (DICK) SCOTT is professor emeritus of sociology at Stanford University with courtesy appointments in the Schools of Business, Education, and Medicine. His research interests focus on the relation between organizations and their environments, with his more recent work focusing on institutional environments. His two most recent books are *Institutional Change and Healthcare Organizations* (2000, University of Chicago Press), coauthored with Martin Ruef, Peter Mendel, and Carol Caronna; and *Institutions and Organizations* (2001, revised edition, Sage).

ANN TERLAAK is a Ph.D. candidate in environmental management at the Donald Bren School of Environmental Science and Management at the University of California Santa Barbara. Her dissertation investigates the diffusion of Environmental Voluntary Agreements and the effects of the agreements on firms' performance.

JOHN G. TROAST JR. is director of policy at the Department of Economic Development for the Commonwealth of Massachusetts. His research interests include business and government policy formulation, large multiparty negotiations, and strategy and public management. Jack has twenty years of experience in the public, private, and nonprofit sectors and has conducted mediation and conflict resolution training for professionals and students in a variety of settings.

RONIT WAISMEL-MANOR is a Ph.D. candidate at the School of Industrial and Labor Relations at Cornell University and a predoctoral fellow at the Cornell Employment and Family Careers Institute. She is interested in the study of institutional and organizational change, especially as it relates to work and family.

ANNE S. YORK is assistant professor of business administration at the Kenan-Flagler Business School at the University of North Carolina, Chapel Hill. She is the coeditor (with Richard D'Aveni and Arie Lewin) of *Managing in Times of Disorder* (1998, Sage) and has been guest editor of special issues of *Organization Science* (Hypercompetition) and *Academy of Management Journal* (Management of Organizations in the Natural Environment). Her research involves strategies for managing change and improving the corporate performance of firms in primarily mature, commodity-based industries, including the impact of vertical integration, diversification, the natural environment, and global exporting.

PAUL A. ZANDBERGEN is assistant professor in environmental planning at the University of Florida. He does research on watershed management and water quality indicators, teaches courses in Geographic Information Systems (GIS), environmental planning, and water resources, and consults around the world on watershed management projects.

ORGANIZATIONS, POLICY,

AND THE

NATURAL ENVIRONMENT

1 INTRODUCTION

Andrew J. Hoffman and Marc J. Ventresca

Organizations, Policy, and the Natural Environment recasts standard approaches to corporate environmentalism and environmental policy studies in light of recent developments in organization theory and institutional analysis. We draw on the empirical case of the natural environment to redirect theoretical emphases in institutional theory and highlight organizational field-level analysis and the linkage between social meaning and social structures within policy worlds. The book introduces a new category of research questions and approaches them from the intersection of environmental policy studies, sociology of the environment, and management and organization theory. These questions are both theoretical and substantive, making use of a current, contested policy domain to enrich and extend theory in organizational sociology and strategy.

What is at stake here? Issues of environmental sustainability, management, and corporate environmentalism are high on the global policy agenda today. They are of concern to specialty researchers, policy makers, business executives, and others (Becker and Jahn, 1999; Rothenberg, 2002). Consider the developments that have brought these issues into policy dialogue: validation of early claims by then-unknown authors and scientists sounding alarms about the fate of the planet (such as Carson, 1962); the rise of recycling and struggles over political economy and alternative technologies (Weinberg, Pellow, and Schnaiberg, 2000; Karnoe and Garud, 2002; Lounsbury, Ventresca, and Hirsch, forthcoming); complex struggles over public infrastructures and the environment (Espeland, 1998); local social movements' expanding concern about "global" environmental issues (Dunlap, 1991; Meyer and others, 1997); and the growing number of multinational corporations that are making environmental issues central to corporate strategy (Hoffman, 1997, 2000; Hart, 1997).

Environmental issues and the policy initiatives related to them have altered basic political, economic, and social institutions that organize the operation of industrial and market economies today. The empirical studies in this book analyze how this happens—how institutions define environmental problems, devise plausible solutions, and impede or foster implementation. Moving beyond arguments grounded in economic, legal, or technical studies, the arguments developed in this book treat this complex evolution of ideas, resources, social structures, and practices as an *organizational* process that takes shape in broader, increasingly institutionally structured policy fields.

The case of corporate environmentalism provides an example of how the very conception of policy issues evolves over time through interested actions (Hoffman, 1997; Prakash, 2000). In the 1970s, corporations viewed environmentalism as an external threat to established business practices and profits. But, through a decades-long process that included changes in influential actors, the redefinition of the role of government, the rise of related social movements, court battles and legislative activity, and much public attention, environmentalism has emerged as a routine strategic consideration of major corporations. Over the course of roughly three decades, norms for corporate environmental practice have radically changed. National governments enacted myriad environmental regulations. The United Nations established global treaties on environmental issues such as endangered species protection, toxic chemical controls, hazardous waste shipments, pesticide use, tropical timber management, and global climate change. Trade agreements made by the World Trade Organization, the North American Free Trade Agreement, and the European Union address a wide range of environmental issues. The insurance, banking, and investor communities include environmental concerns in their underwriting, loan granting, and investment procedures. And new forms of industrywide programs (such as the Chemical Manufacturers Association Responsible Care Program), environmental management standards (such as ISO14001 and EMAS), performance reporting procedures (such as environmental annual reports), and staffing objectives (such as environmental vice presidents and the inclusion of environmentalists on boards of directors) are increasingly commonplace.

This complex array of organizational initiatives is marked by and proceeds in part because of conflicting logics and meaning systems, heterogeneous governance arrangements, and a plurality of types of actors. For example, issues of environmental protection are contested among a wide range of interested parties, both public and private, and including both collective and individual persons (Mac-Naughten and Urry, 1998). This makes corporate environmental management issues a strategic research area for organizational scholars trying to understand change processes that span "levels of analysis" and the complex social systems in which they occur.

In this chapter, we introduce the organizational and field-level approach developed in this book. We join recent work on field-level analysis with analytic problems of environmental policy and management to illustrate the usefulness of an organizational approach. We discuss how taking an organization and field-level approach can illuminate the emergence and significance of "policy theories" (Weiss, 1998) that define issues in particular ways, elucidating the roles of ambiguity, expertise, and contested natures in policy problems, their proposed solutions, and possible interventions. We contrast our approach with other disciplinary approaches commonly used to study environmental issues, and track the history and tensions in two specific legacy research domains, sociology of the environment and environmental management, to examine the benefits of specialty research subfields. We suggest six new research directions exemplified by the work in this book. We close by introducing the key arguments and findings in the chapters, and discuss their contributions to organizational, policy, and environmental research. Overall, we use the empirical cases in the chapters to inform redirections in institutional theories of organization and to highlight opportunities for policy studies of this tradition.

THE INTELLECTUAL FOUNDATION OF THE BOOK

This book presents a framework and empirical studies grounded in institutional theories of organization (Powell and DiMaggio, 1991; Scott, 1991, 1995) to examine the interplay of organizations, policy, and the natural environment. Our analytic stance starts with four premises. (1) Policy issues and the broader fields of expertise and activity that form around them are organizational productions (Beamish, 2001; Egri and Pinfield, 1994; Hoffman and Ventresca, 1999; Meyer and Rowan, 1977). (2) The social worlds that help to stabilize and make policy issues recognizable are complex systems of organized activity shaped not only by expertise, technology, and scientific activity but also by social processes of identity construction, negotiation, and control (Becker, 1982; Clarke, 1995; Espeland, 1998; Haas, 1990). (3) Changes in the scale and scope of environmental issues and the policy communities involved, especially as they involve shifts from local to global activity, merit direct analytic attention and pose challenges to standard approaches in policy studies (Frank, Hironaka, and Schofer, 2000; Liberatore, 1991). (4) We offer the book in part to suggest that contested nature of environmental issues, coupled with changes in the scale and scope of governance, invite institutional and organizational analysis to complement other research approaches (Hoffman, 2001; Jennings and Zandbergen, 1995; Starik and Marcus, 2000).

Recent initiatives in corporate alliances and strategies illustrate these premises. They provide evidence of activity occurring outside the boundary of any one organization and beyond conventional regulatory activity. Much of this activity is occurring at a global level, that is, among organizational actors working across national boundaries, authorized to act by transnational authority, and actively creating policy venues external to any one country's laws and regulations. Consider the following examples of field-level debate among heterogeneous organizational actors:

- In 2000, seven multinational companies (DuPont, Shell, Alcan Aluminum, BP, SuncorEnergy, Pechiney, and Ontario Power Generation) joined in a partnership with the environmental group Environmental Defense to voluntarily reduce the emissions of greenhouse gases even though the Kyoto Treaty that mandates the reductions was not ratified.

- Also in 2000, fifty multinational corporations joined forces with activist groups, labor unions, and the United Nations by signing a global compact on environmental protection and human rights. Signatories included executives from companies such as DaimlerChrysler, Nike, Royal Dutch Shell, Bayer, and Unilever as well as activist groups such as the World Wildlife Fund and Amnesty International.

- In 1992, the Geneva-based International Standards Organization began developing ISO14001, a voluntary set of standards to promote the adoption of corporate environmental responsibility into corporate management systems worldwide. Representatives from companies such as IBM, Eastman Kodak, and British Telecom established specifications and guidelines. Now ISO certification is necessary to do business in certain multinational markets (such as the European Union). By late 1998, more than 5,500 organizations had been certified to ISO 14001.

- In 1990, the Chemical Manufacturers' Association (CMA) recognized that all its member companies share a common reputation on the environment and instituted a program called Responsible Care that bound its 170 members to a set of ten principles designed to improve environmental performance. After Responsible Care was unveiled, similar programs emerged in other industries such as petroleum, printing, textiles, paper, lead, and automobiles. Like Responsible Care, they are built on the belief that the environmental reputation of a single company is dependent on the reputation of the entire industry.

These examples provide evidence of coordination and cooperation at the global field level. Some represent novel coalitions, forging new kinds of industry relationships in the service of governing environmental issues. Moreover, they provide new organizational venues for the collective definition of key problems and solutions in a way that redefines the community of relevant policy actors (Haas, 1990; Haas, Keohane, and Levy, 1993). These developments also highlight why organization theory and field-level perspectives are especially timely and should usefully extend studies of organizational strategy to consider the processes by which collective notions of rationality form (DiMaggio and Powell, 1983; Galvin, 2002; Hoffman, 1997; Jennings, Martens, and Zandbergen, Chapter 3; Rosenkopf, Metiu, and George, 2001; Scott, 1983). This style of analysis shows how new forms of legal, political, social, and economic institutions mediate between organizational and societal expectations regarding what is legitimate practice with respect to the environment. In this book, we examine such organizational and institutional processes as they affect policy formation, implementation, and consequences.

ARGUMENTS: FIELD-LEVEL INSTITUTIONS AND COLLECTIVE RATIONALITY

Research in organizational and management sociology emphasizes attention to field-level systems and their institutional and cultural features, the "vertical" aspects of social organization, an approach that distinguishes a field-level analysis from an industry focus or a corporate demography approach (Fligstein, 2001). An organizational field is "a community of organizations that partake of a common meaning system and whose participants interact more frequently and fatefully with one another than with actors outside the field" (Scott, 1995: 56). A field is an empirical trace, and may include constituents such as government actors, critical exchange partners, intermediaries in the value chain, professional and trade associations, policy entrepreneurs, regulatory bodies, and organized public opinion evident in consumer or other organized interests—all constituencies that interact and contend in the definition of the broader field logics, governance institutions, and activity (Fligstein, 1996; Scott, 1991; McDonough, Ventresca, and Outcalt, 2000). But more than just a collection of influential organizations, a field comprises common channels of dialogue and discussion focused on central policy issues (Hoffman, 1999).

Scott (2001) identifies three basic models (or "pillars") of institutions that undergird conceptions of a field: cognitive, normative, and regulative. Each is grounded in different (disciplinary) assumptions about what institutions are and how they affect organizational behavior and activity. They range from conceptions of explicit, direct provision of incentives for action to tacit processes embodied in taken-for-granted assumptions (Zucker, 1983). These three analytic conceptions offer distinct vantage points for exploring institutional processes at work in a particular empirical case. Each has practical value for understanding the institutional framing of policy issues and for informing organizational analysis (Hoffman and Ventresca, 1999). Each provides metatheoretical descriptions of collective reality for the organization—explanations of what is and what is not, what can be acted upon and what cannot. Finally, each opens further analytic questions about the cross-effects among these three source mechanisms of institutional effects. As institutional arrangements emerge, contend, become stable, and change, the proximate field of structured activity comprises both sources of empowerment by providing alternative conceptions of action and sources of control by limiting options for consideration (Jepperson, 1991; Fligstein, 1992).

By highlighting field-level approaches, the chapters chart synergies between organizational and environmental studies, a redirection of the core "pillars" approach to institutional analysis, and an alternative to the aspiration of a distinct, separate subfield of environmental scholarship. We view environmentalism and the accompanying policy debates as a domain of conflict among ideologies. A shift in these ideologies is manifest in the shifts in roles, meaning systems, and dominant logics. Thus at the core, this book treats these shifts as social contests among competing field-level constituencies. Broad issues of environmental protection, generally of environmental quality and social interests, are neither socially nor politically separable from constituting the policy theories that shape them, nor are they made tractable by technical analysis alone. "The question must always be asked, for whom and from whom is [the environment] being protected?" (Schnaiberg, 1980: 5).

This book introduces a synthesis of ideas that cross the theoretical domain of institutional and cultural analyses with the empirical domain of environmental issues as they relate to organization studies, strategy, and management. This makes explicit opportunities to specify institutional and social processes that configure organizational structures and policy, taking advantage of environmental management as a critical empirical site. The field-level focus directs attention to three aspects of field situation: to shifts in ideologies and cultural logics that specify conditions of feasibility and what is imaginable; to the governance arrangements that establish regulatory possibilities and implementation; and to the changing role and authority of actors who struggle, negotiate, and redefine the terms of policy issues in these fields (Scott, 1994; 2001; Hoffman and Ventresca, 1999).

This book focuses deliberately on the field level in order to emphasize the analytic value-added, in contrast to other directions in institutional theories of organization that underspecify field elements and mechanisms. Field-level analysis provides us with tools and concepts with which to examine institutional mechanisms that influence organizational structures, strategies, and policies. In their classic paper on mechanisms of organizational change, DiMaggio and Powell (1983) argued that organizational analysts could garner new insights by paying attention to the "collective rationality" of organizational fields. This argument summarized and introduced a longer tradition of field-level analysis among organization theorists (Mohr, 2002). DiMaggio and Powell argued that from the early years of the twentieth century, new forms of political authority (especially nation-states and government in general) and new sources of expertise (especially modern professions and other knowledge-intensive occupations) played a basic role in driving changes in organizational structures and strategies. In particular, they argued that the activities of states and professions supplanted efficiency or market-based drivers of organizational change, and that variation in the social structure of organizational fields provides a better-specified account of the sources of organization-level change. This was not a normative position, but rather an effort to theorize in behavioral terms the changing drivers of organizational structure and policy.

But much recent empirical analysis has underspecified or simply neglected the import of institutional processes by which collective rationality forms within organizational fields, focusing instead on outcomes. This is unfortunate, both for theory development and the misrecognized empirical insights possible from this vantage point. DiMaggio, reflecting on "what theory is not" (1995) suggested that core institutional claims in the 1983 paper have suffered asymmetric attention:

> Somewhat to my surprise . . . papers . . . cited our paper as support for the proposition that all organizations become like all others, regardless of field. Somehow the network argument that we authors regarded as so central had been deleted in the paper's reception. Within a few more years, the paper had turned into a kind of ritual citation, affirming the view that, well, organizations are kind of wacky, and (despite the presence of "collective rationality" in the paper's subtitle) people are never rational (DiMaggio, 1995: 395).

We refocus on the "collective rationality" of organizational fields—the structured and collectively held systems of meaning that inform field-level sources, mechanisms, and effects for organizations and other social actors. We highlight theoretical and empirical processes of change and conflict at the level of fields, organizations, and practices (DiMaggio, 1995; Greenwood and Hinings, 1996). Further, this book focuses on the dynamics that shift social structures, create new realities for organizations, and redefine the basic resource context. Table 1.1 summarizes some of the key redirections that expand the elements of environmental and field-level analysis offered in this volume.

This focus begins with a move away from assessments of individual rationality or action to investigate how collective rationality comes to provide fundamental sources and motivations for those actions. Collective notions of what is appropriate corporate behavior emerge and evolve through field-level debate. The focus on debate, dialogue, and conflict among field-level actors is an important direction for this research stream and is refocusing analysts on the dynamics of field-level collective rationality—its sources, mechanisms by which it changes, and its effects on organizational actors and policy (Proffitt, 2001). This line of inquiry is critical for understanding how conceptions of environmental issues are created and how those conceptions result in individual and organizational action which may conflict with environmental interests (Bazerman and Hoffman, 1999; Clark and Jennings, 1997). In particular, institutional and organizational analysis seeks to understand the cultural and social sources of policy models and conventions (Dobbin, 1994; Guillén, 1994), and to explain how ideas and beliefs about organizational strategies and practice become standard and spread in highly structured fields of activity (Edelman, 1990; Guthrie and Roth, 1999; Washington and Ventresca, 2001). Its focus is on the dynamics by which the natural environment is defined and enacted through relevant social and institutional structures of information and attention (Hoffman and Ocasio, 2001). These are typically collective orders, and the evolution in these policy regimes and governance arrangements is an important direction for this area of research (Haas, 1990; Meyer and others, 1997).

The chapters in this book also move away from a focus on outcomes of stability, inertia, and convergence as central and defining of institutional analysis, to instead consider the linkages between field-level processes and heterogeneity of organizational structures, strategy and activity, and outcomes. Much empirical work in the institutional analysis tradition has treated increased homogeneity among organization structures and practices as evidence of a "master hypothesis" of isomorphism, that is, change processes that lead toward sameness in structures. Similarly, heterogeneity of form and practice is often treated as evidence that counters

Table 1.1

Expanding the Elements of Environmental and Field-Level Analysis

Element	Current View	Expanded View
Level of analysis	Organization-level activity	Field-level activity
Market activity	Rationally directed	Politically inflected
Fields	Centered on common technology and markets	Centered around issues of debate
	Domains of stability	Domains of contest, conflict, and change
Institutions	Things	Processes and mechanisms
	Constraints	Opportunities *and* constraints
	Cognitive	Cognitive *and* political
Central organizing concept	Isomorphism	Collective rationality
Institutions and organizations	Separate levels of analysis	Linked levels of analysis
Field/organization interface	Unidirectional from field to organization	Dual-directional between field and organization
	Uniform across organizational contexts	Affected by organizational filtering and enactment processes
Organizational activity	Defined by field-level activity	Negotiated with field-level constituents
	Strategically inert	Strategically active
	Scripted	Entrepreneurial
	Homogeneous	Heterogeneous
Institutional change	Undeveloped	Open to entrepreneurial influence

the claims of institutional theories of organization (Kraatz and Zajac, 1996). But this master hypothesis view and focus on particular outcomes can deflect attention from the specification of collective rationality, contending logics, and mechanisms that result in structured heterogeneity in a field (DiMaggio and Powell, 1983; Washington and Ventresca, 2001).

To redress this situation, the chapters that follow move away from simple *outcomes* of institutional processes, to focus on origins, structured heterogeneity, and institutional *mechanisms,* all embedded in field-level contexts. They provide evidence from varied cases to examine these issues. The effort here is to reconnect analysis to the field-level processes by which collective rationality is arbitrated, channeled, and formed (Espeland, 1998). They focus on institutional *processes* or mechanisms, rather than on institutions as *things.* They illuminate field-level debates that highlight how institutional arrangements, although sometimes stable, are not inert. They extend continuities between the rich legacy of institutional sociology that precedes this volume, contemporary research directions, and the insights from environmental issues as an empirical discipline. They move beyond notions of institutions as barriers, as always taken for granted and as leading toward isomorphism, to reincorporate field-level dynamics, collective rationality within these fields, and the behavior of individual organizations as integral parts of these processes. They show how field-level processes and mechanisms comprise opportunities for change as well as sources of stability.

Efforts to bridge field- and organization-level analysis have taken several forms. Some recent scholarly strategies focus on restoring power and agency to institutional accounts by inserting a rational choice conception of agency or an instrumental and material view of power into institutional arguments. Not surprisingly, this returns a version of resource dependence views to institutional analysis, where "legitimacy" is the resource being struggled over. These arguments are often weakened by their underspecification of field-level processes. Others have begun to argue that individual firms can respond strategically to institutional pressures (Oliver, 1991) or may strategically influence the process of institutional change (Lawrence, 1999). In these cases, the organization and the field are treated as separate and distinct. The firm responds to institutional pressures rather than interacting with them. In fact, we speculate that the conception of "pressures" itself may be misdirected (Washington and Ventresca, 2001). DiMaggio and Powell based the study of collective rationality in organizational fields in a social network approach that emphasizes power and the distribution of material resources combined with a social cognition approach concerned with broad public categories of meaning (DiMaggio, 1995). As a result, we find that other kinds of mechanisms adapted from research on conflict—negotiation and social cognition, for example—may be more useful in specifying these processes than the somewhat general pressures formulation consistent with early conceptions of open systems and organizational environments.

One persisting criticism of institutional theories of organization focuses on how the arguments address change processes (DiMaggio, 1988; Brint and Karabel, 1991; Hirsch and Lounsbury, 1997; Perrow, 1986), but chapters in this book address this by linking institutional change processes with the behavior of specifically powerful organizations. Some organizations are more effective at producing desired social outcomes than others. These organizations can have disproportionate size or legitimacy that allow them to dictate the actions of others and shape social fields (Fligstein, 1991), or have distinctive social capital (Coleman, 1988) such that they can influence the formation and evolution of field-level dynamics. The chapters in this volume consider the institutional context of resources and the particular skill set and strategy that can be employed by institutional entrepreneurs (Fligstein, 1997).

Locating organizations in fields of activity animated by competing institutional arrangements helps to link micro and macro levels of analysis (Hoffman, 2001). Collective rationality is an animated process that takes form across several levels. Few institutional analyses fully connect the influence of institutional fields to culture and practice on the organizational level. Most research analyzes dynamics in terms of field-level change, not individual response. We underscore the linkages between organizational culture and societal institutions, urging a conversation between these two, often separate, literatures. This follows early institutionalist insights that "we have come to label the present perspective, for better or worse, as an institutionalist model, although we hope that 'culture' eventually can be reclaimed by macro-sociology" (Thomas and others, 1987: 7). Some chapters in this book suggest that to understand firm heterogeneity within an institutional context, organization-level analysis complements and extends field-level analysis; the value of such dual specification is clear—directly redressing the oversocialized view (Granovetter, 1985) that would depict recipients of field-level influence as a homogenous collection of organizational actors, each behaving according to a social script designed by the social environment.

But more important, the interaction between firm and field is not unidirectional nor is it apart from interpretation and enactment processes. The work in this book incorporates concerns for sense making and issue interpretation by field-level constituents (Dutton and Dukerich, 1991; Hoffman and Ocasio, 2001). Field influences are not uniformly understood by participants within the field; organization-level dynamics can filter and alter institutional demands. Further, the research here describes how organizations might transmit their interests back to the field. Organization reputations, identities, and images are pliable concepts, shaped by the perception of players within the field and shaping the field (Douglas, 1986; March and Olsen, 1989). With the linkage of organizational and cultural dynamics created, opportunities for strategic action within a field become vivid, leading some chapter authors to develop the notion of the institutional or cultural entrepreneur (DiMaggio, 1988; Fligstein, 1997; Zucker, 1988).

ENVIRONMENTAL ISSUES AND ORGANIZATIONAL STUDIES: DISTINCTIVE FIELD-LEVEL AND INSTITUTIONAL ELEMENTS

We are convinced that the intersection of business and the natural environment is an especially timely and useful domain for organizational analysis of field-level dynamics and policy. Overall, environmental issues are tough policy issues that are shaped by contending ideologies, defined by much ambiguity about causal linkages and consequences, and driven by increasingly well-organized constituencies and stakeholders. The definition of the issue, the provision of its solutions, and the modes of policy intervention applied vary and are contested (Weiss, 1998). Moreover, the scientific and technical base of evidence regarding these processes is often thin or debated. Even where clear evidence is available, political processes reshape available repertoires of intervention (Douglas and Wildavsky, 1982). In these ways, environmental issues are similar to other social, technical, and economic policy issues.

The environmental domain shares features with social policy sectors such as education and health care and with other social issues confronting corporations, such as the social responsibility of business, labor relations, and the presumed tradeoff of efficiency and social effectiveness (Wade-Benzoni and Bazerman, 1999). But environmental issues are also marked by technical and economic components that make them more akin to consumer demand, material processing, or competitive strategy. This combination of social and technical elements makes environmental issues distinctive. And it makes the environmental domain both especially difficult and especially useful as an empirical site of organizational research. In this section we explore the distinctiveness of environmental policy and management issues through (a) the kind and variety of field-level constituencies engaged in debate and (b) the institutional elements that emerge from that debate.

The Field-Level Constituency Invoked by Environmental Issues

We begin by discussing the range of actors that can be thought of as constituencies for relevant policies and practices. Social movements and government actors have been prominent constituencies in the development of environmentalism and environmental policy issues. The field of actors relevant for environmental issues has shifted in recent years, however, to include more prominent business interests and also more organized interests at the transnational level (Brulle, 2000; Hoffman, 1997; 2000). The primary early linkage in environmental issues between social movement activism and regulatory or judicial activism is common with other issues such as gender equity or civil rights—constituency groups lobby for social change and make claims in standard and organized venues across society. These movements connect the values of their cause with their personal identity, creating a value resonance that is a potent force for social change. The activist organizations have little material stake in organizational output yet influence that output through ideological activism, driving change in the norms, values, and beliefs of organizational systems.

However, the composition of field-level constituencies around the environmental issue is less well-defined than that of some other policy issues with strong social movement stakeholders. Whereas other public issues have a more clearly specified constituency, membership in the environmental movement cannot be specified by demographics, class position, or other familiar sources of identity (Beck, 1992; Egri and Pinfield, 1994). Environmentalism has no single demographic or well-structured political constituency among proponents or opponents of particular environmental policy initiatives. In fact, opposition to environmentalism on the grounds of threatened material interests or aversion to state intervention would be easier to explain than environmental advocacy (Buttel, 1992). A high-quality environment tends to be a public good, which when achieved cannot be denied, even to those who resist environmental reforms. So firms concerned with corporate environmental responses are left to decide who is a legitimate representative for environmental concerns, beyond those addressed by basic regulatory compliance.

Field-level environmental constituencies are often organized environmental nonprofit groups. But the contested nature of many environmental policy issues and solutions also means that they attract a wide range of field-level supporters, including employee groups, labor unions, community groups, consumers, environmental activists, investors, insurers, the government, industry competitors, and even internal managers (Hoffman, 2000; Morrison, 1991). In addition, environmental issues also make visible two distinctive field-level actors.

The first is decidedly nonsocial, for there is the environment itself to contend with. The prominence and effect of environmental change acts as a unique form of pressure, placing demands on social, political, economic, and technical institutions that are distinct from other demands the corporation faces. Conditions such as species extinction, acid rain, the ozone hole, fisheries collapse, and others focus attention without warning, imposing demands for action and change. Although open to social interpretation and enactment (Hoffman and Ocasio, 2001), environmental events nonetheless provoke organizational and institutional resources and attention.

The second distinct field-level participant is the social constituent who is not yet social. Environmental issues (such as ozone depletion, species extinction, and global warming) raise basic issues of intergenerational goods, boundaries, and resource claims (Wade-Benzoni, 1996). The vast geographic scales and time horizons involved to preserve the long-term viability of the ecosystem on the behalf of future generations are difficult to represent adequately in policy discussions. As future generations cannot express their interests in social debates, their needs are open to social interpretation and enactment by cultural and institutional entrepreneurs, much like the interpretation of environmental events. The inclusion of these two unconventional actors expands the range of field-level participation and creates greater challenges for both organizational actors and researchers.

The Institutional Elements of Environmental Issues

The emergent and evolving interests within field-level debates over the meaning of environmentalism result in the continuing redefinition in its form and focus (Hoffman, 1997; 1999). The recurring entry of new field constituents leads to the kind of sustained support that environmental issues have received over the past forty years. For example, when conservation groups and a wilderness ideology prevailed in the early part of the century, environmental policy issues were cast primarily in terms of managing natural resources for social benefit. As modern environmental activists entered the policy space in the 1960s, the ideologies shifted along with the social organization of the field, and the priority became the protection of natural ecosystems. With the entry of employee and community groups in the 1970s and 1980s, the issues focused on workplace safety and community "right-to-know" laws. In the mid-1980s, insurers prompted an integration with risk management. In the early 1990s, investor groups brought a challenge to the core firm strategies and objectives; and the growing influence of customers in the late 1990s turned attention to a redefinition of product development. (These latter developments reflect the growing attention to sustainability.)

The introduction of each of these new field-level constituents changes the kinds of challenges and responses made on organizational structures and internal conceptions of the organization's purpose. Issues of environmental policy and environmental management are mediated by the culture and norms of this diverse set of field-level constituents. More important, given the ideological and technological nature of the environmental issue coupled with the diversity of field-level governance arrangements and systems of meaning and actors, the meaning and value of the environment is contested through what may be termed "institutional war" (White, 1992).

The systemic and technical features of environmental issues directly challenge core strategy and production processes—how organizations obtain and handle raw materials, produce goods and services, dispose of production byproducts, and handle produced goods once consumed. Over the past three decades, the technological demands of corporate environmental responsibility have shifted from removing visible contaminants from effluent streams to removing concentrations in the parts per billion and parts per trillion range. Beyond process emissions, environmental issues also mandate changes in the content of product development. Legal environments have evolved to mandate the public disclosure of emission levels and product contents as well as the potential health effects of these chemicals, creating daunting technological challenges for the firm (Hoffman and Ehrenfeld, 1998).

The effects of these demands are not unitary. Importantly, they span many industry and policy fields. Some industries, such as oil and chemicals, face greater challenges in measuring and controlling environmental impacts. Within industries, different companies face different challenges in developing new products, processes, or raw materials in the face of environmental considerations. The technical challenges of environmentalism add a new dimension to the strategic landscape, one that may decide which firms succeed and which ones fail. Field-level responses to environmental issues can cause the elimination of entire product markets, as occurred with CFCs and DDT. They can also cause the formation of new markets, as they did for Freon substitutes in the wake of the 1987 worldwide ban on CFC production.

Often, firms are required to collect data, initiate change, and develop an understanding of their processes and products in ways outside the scope of traditional conceptions of corporate or business strategy. Institutional and field-level processes can then transform the boundaries and structures of the organization, change the scope of business decisions, and alter the relevant constituents involved in what were once considered internal decisions. Engineering calculations may now consider analyses of the social, political, economic, and cultural contexts. Concepts such as waste minimization, pollution prevention, and product stewardship find their way into all aspects of operations, from process design to product development.

Beyond conceptions of technology, environmentalism also challenges economic conceptions of the firm (Christensen, Craig, and Hart, 2001). Unlike social issues that deal with equity and the fair distribution of opportunity and wealth, environmental issues increasingly affect basic business economics, effectively redefining the conceptions of production in industry (Hoffman and Ehrenfeld, 1998). Field-level demands from the changing constituencies of environmental issues have redefined fundamental economic models of consumption and production, resulting in a net change in efficiency. For example, a recent debate has emerged over the economic impact of climate change controls. Some estimates predict a drain on U.S. Gross National Product (GNP) of as much as 3.5 percent if aggressive emission reduction targets are set. Others estimate that modest controls on greenhouse gas emissions would not damage the economy, as the world has significant opportunities to control emissions by making its energy systems and automobiles more efficient. This more efficient use of energy could increase GNP by 1 or 2 percent (Hoffman, 1998).

In essence, field-level processes for environmental protection are altering the institutions that define the core objectives of the firm and the basic conceptions of production. Shareholder equity may remain the single most important criterion for corporate survival. Yet environmental concerns may change the understanding of what is equitable for the shareholder. The "rules of the game" (Friedman, 1970: 126) have changed such that managers act in the best interests of their investors by considering environmental protection in their decisions. Today, executives from corporations such as Ford, BP Amoco, DuPont, Bristol-Myers Squibb, Johnson & Johnson, and Monsanto actively espouse the benefits of proactive environmental management while instituting programs for community relations, product stewardship, pollution prevention, and environmental leadership, all in the name of increasing corporate competitiveness and shareholder equity. These institutional changes represent an evolution of organizational purpose and boundaries that make environmental issues distinct as an empirical topic for organizational inquiry.

How does this matter for research? We suggest that environmental issues have much in common with other contested policy domains that make them difficult to study and that reinforce persisting policy struggles and debates about means, ends, and appropriate interventions. We also argue that distinctive field-level constituencies and resulting institutional elements make environmental issues different from many other policy domains. Thus researchers on organizations, policy, and the natural environment encounter both advantages and challenges.

OTHER DISCIPLINARY APPROACHES TO ORGANIZATIONS AND THE NATURAL ENVIRONMENT

The study of the natural environment and society lies at a distinct juncture of the physical and the social sciences, both of which seek to understand the behavior of natural ecosystems either as separate entities or in relation to social systems. The only way to understand these systems as separate entities is through chemistry, toxicology, biology, physics, entomology, and other hard sciences. In fact, the study of the environment has been on the agenda of the modern physical sciences so long that boundary-spanning research specialties such as environmental engineering and ecology are now recognized areas of research and professional standing.

Industrial ecology provides another boundary-spanning discipline that offers an alternative to a fragmented view of environmental problems and solutions, instead focusing on the system as a whole. Using natural ecosystems as its model (Friedman, 2000), industrial ecology highlights transformational change in local, regional, and global material and energy flows, the components of which are products, processes, industrial sectors, and economies. It promotes efficient resource use by reducing environmental burdens throughout the total material cycle. This cycle consists of a continuous feedback loop, with materials and energy flowing between natural and industrial systems in three stages: extraction of natural materials that are converted into raw materials and mechanical energy; working them into useable and saleable products; and distributing them to be consumed, used, and disposed of by consumers. Developed largely by engineers, the central unit of analysis in industrial ecology is that of industrial organizations within broad-scale systems of facilities, regions, industries, and economies. The discipline seeks to reduce the environmental burden of that system through broad-scale changes (Environmental Protection Agency, 2000). The systemic unit of analysis is the technical "ecology" of the industrial enterprise, but industrial ecology is silent with regard to "social ecology."

Attention to the natural environment in the social sciences has spanned new research traditions and professional infrastructure but fewer established cross-disciplinary research fields. Specialty subfields do focus on environmentalism and environmental policy concerns in economics (Baumol and Blinder, 1985; Cropper and Oates, 1992; Tietenberg, 1992; Hahn and Stavins, 1991), philosophy and ethics (Eliot and Gore, 1983; Hargrove, 1989; Holmes, 1988); law (Hoban and Brooks, 1996; Revesz, 1997), and business history (Cronon, 1991; Hays, 1998; McGurty, 1997; Rosen, 1995, 1997; Rosen and Sellers, 1999). Each investigates the linkages between social and environmental systems in its own characteristic idiom of research questions, designs and evidence, and policy implications. Each also has a vocabulary for connecting disciplinary standards, research, and policy and practice issues. In each, leading-edge scholars try to take advantage of the distinct features of environmentalism as a theoretical and empirical pivot for further research. Next we consider in more detail two research streams proximate to the approach we develop—environmental sociology and environmental management.

Perspectives from Environmental Sociology

Organizational and sociological study of the interaction between the natural environment and social organization and behavior dates at least from the early 1970s, coinciding with the emergence of environmental activism and social movements in the United States, Europe, and elsewhere (Laclau and Mouffe, 1985). This is evident in the activity of professional associations, intellectual organizing, and specialty journals.[1] By the late 1980s, reviews of the field identified five areas of scholarship in environmental sociological (Buttel, 1987): (1) the new ecological paradigm; (2) environmental attitudes, values, and behaviors; (3) the environmental movement; (4) technological risk and risk assessment; and (5) the political economy of the environment and environmental politics. By the mid-1990s, two core issues were at the center of the sociological agenda (Hannigan, 1995): the causes of environmental destruction and the rise of environmental consciousness and movements. The field is now addressing these key themes from a social constructionist approach that focuses on the "social, political and cultural processes" by which environmental issues, problems, and solutions are given attention and defined (Hannigan, 1995: 30).

A perennial tension seems to exist between the goal of fostering research in the subfield and the professional project of defining a distinct stand-alone empirical field of research. For example, Catton and Dunlap's (1980) New Ecological Paradigm—the shift away from anthropocentric (human-centered) to ecocentric thinking (humans are one of many species inhabiting the earth)—is a central, influential theoretical insight of environmental sociology. Yet this argument has generated less research interest outside the specialty field (Hannigan, 1995). Beck's

(1992) *Risk Society,* on the other hand, has had considerable impact beyond the subfield, perhaps because it approaches the subject of environmental risks from a more established tradition dealing with the macro-sociology of social change (Lash and Wynne, 1992) rather than from the subfield-specific concerns of environmental sociology. The differential impact of these two strategies highlights the tensions over the value-added creation of distinct specialty fields versus remaining engaged with established disciplinary approaches.

Perspectives from Environmental Management

Scholars in management schools have also entered this research domain. An international group of scholars, the Greening of Industry Network (GIN), was formed in 1989. It produced one of the first collections of research in environmental management. GIN participants argued that "most regulation has not been based on a solid understanding of how industrial firms operated" and that future advances in environmental policy required an appreciation for the "intradynamic and interdynamic processes" of organizational learning that incorporate an awareness for how "various groups both inside and outside the firm conjointly shape its behavior and strategy" (Fischer and Schott, 1993: 372).

This first initiative to build a research community among management scholars was followed by the formation of the Management Institute for Environment and Business (MEB, now a division of the World Resources Institute) in 1990 and the establishment of the Organizations and the Natural Environment (ONE) special interest group of the Academy of Management in 1994. To support this burgeoning research area, special issues on the natural environment and organizations have appeared in the *Academy of Management Review* (1995), *American Behavioral Scientist* (1999), *Business History Review* (1999), and *Academy of Management Journal* (2000). Further, academic journals dedicated to the interface between managerial action and environmental protection also emerged in the 1990s, including *Business Strategy & the Environment* and *Organization & Environment.*

The corpus of research parallels developments in environmental sociology. For example, one common theme has been the shift from an anthropocentric to ecocentric perspective similar to the New Ecological Paradigm (Colby, 1991; Gladwin, Kennelly, and Krause, 1995; Purser, Park, and Montuori, 1995). But the primary focus of this research domain is on the behavior of the firm, management research, and management education. Further, much of this research has been normative in focus, focusing on understanding and predicting why and how corporations "can take steps forward toward [being] environmentally more sustainable" (Starik and Marcus, 2000: 542). Some researchers have focused on the implications of the shift to an ecocentric perspective for organizations (and corporations in particular) (Starik and Rands, 1995; Shrivastava, 1995). Others have considered how to merge existing concerns for economic competitiveness with environmental demands to gain market advantage (Schmidheiny, 1992; Smart, 1992; Porter and van der Linde, 1995; Stead and Stead, 1995; Roome, 1998; Sexton and others, 1999).

Moving to a multilevel analysis, some of this research has focused on why firms respond to ecological issues by analyzing both individual and organization level variables (Hart, 1995; Lawrence and Morell, 1995; Lober, 1996). Individual level variables of concern have included management leadership styles (Egri and Herman, 2000) and individual interpretation and intention (Ramus and Stegner, 2000; Flannery and May, 2000). Organizational variables studied have included identity and environmental interpretation (Sharma, 2000) and organizational culture (Hunt and Auster, 1990; Roy, 1991). Other scholars focus on the role of organizational clusters or fields as determinants of corporate environmental behavior (Jennings and Zandbergen, 1995; King and Lenox, 2000; Bansal and Roth, 2000).

An underlying tension parallels that within environmental sociology—the question of whether the goal of this group of researchers is to create a distinct specialty field of management inquiry. Some have argued that academic research in the "organizations and natural environment area" is based on a vision of practice and policy based on new values, attitudes, and behaviors (Starik and Marcus, 2000). Others consider this an empirical domain into which existing theory can be applied. These are fruitful tensions about intellectual and professional strategies.

WHY YOU SHOULD READ THIS BOOK

Table 1.1 reports key features of field-level analysis and the redirection of research questions of organization theory, environmental management, and policy that a field perspective makes possible. We have organized the empirical chapters in six sections that provide substance to these new directions. The chapter authors report empirical research on a variety of organizational processes and institutional mechanisms that shape possibilities for organizational structure, culture, and action in broad fields of activity and policy process. They analyze issues at the level of the company, trade association, industry, regional regulation, federal regulation, transnational comparisons, international standards, and society. The empirical cases include recycling, global climate change, acid rain, solid waste management, oil spills, dam building, and endangered species protection. They employ disciplinary foundations including organization theory, management studies, sociology, international regime studies, psychology, political science, and the social studies of science and technology. And the research deals with a range of policy and management issues such as corporate environmental reporting, voluntary agreements, industry/government collaboration, environmental impact assessments, emissions trading schemes, open-sourcing environmental policy, regulatory enforcement, and proactive environmental strategy.

Institutional Origins: Competing Frameworks and Logic

A central theme of this book is that environmental issues are a domain in which logics and ideologies compete for meaning and legitimacy. The first four chapters chart ways that plural and contested logics inform strategy, policy, and organizational actions. The environmental issues make vivid why contending logics and ideologies matter and how systems of meaning ground large-scale structures and local action; the routinely contested nature of such frameworks and logics over time and across settings; the specification of variations in policy and practice that result, and the value of research into the organizational origins and sources of available models of environment and action.

Frank (Chapter 2) investigates the fates of two historically available "global" conceptions of the environment—one justifying nature protection in moral terms, one in rational scientific terms. Despite considerable support for the moral model from the late nineteenth century, Frank finds that the growth of a rationalized global culture reinforces central assumptions of the scientific model of an ecosystem. This scientific model of nature protection is that which most organizations and policies embody today as a core conception of the interface of social and natural environment.

Jennings, Martens, and Zandbergen (Chapter 3) offer a grounded case study countering Frank's chapter. They focus on the administrative politics of environmental enforcement in the Lower Fraser Basin (LFB) of British Columbia. They develop a close empirical study of "complications in policy compliance" that highlights the organizational processes and institutional mechanisms that explain the substantial variations in enforcement intensity under a common regulatory regime. Jennings and colleagues show that provincial politics, variations in local geography, resources for regulatory agents in each district, the nature of the environmental issue, and characteristics of the regulated organizations (such as being large, in primary manufacturing, having multiple units, and having a resource permit) provide the basis for heterogeneous outcomes in enforcement practice.

Morrill and Owen-Smith (Chapter 4) develop a narrative theory of organizational field development, showing how narratives are cultural resources that contribute to the creation (and change) of institutional fields. They analyze three cases of environmental dispute resolution—the Storm King Mountain hydroelectric plant, river management in the Snoqualmie River Valley, and the Santa Barbara oil spill—to identify narratives consistent with technocratic, pluralist, and communitarian collective action frames. They suggest further that the narrative styles that institutional entrepreneurs use affect the enactment of these collective action frames, in turn shaping the emergence of environmental conflict resolution strategies. This chapter contributes a novel research strategy with which to study institutional change, macro-micro linkages, and narrative approaches to field heterogeneity.

Levin and Espeland (Chapter 5) report on the creation of markets for sulfur dioxide (SO_2) pollution under the 1990 Amendments to the Clean Air Act. The authors highlight the cultural, cognitive, and organizational work needed to create and sustain these markets, which they refer to as the work and politics of "commensuration." They explain how commensuration, the transforming of qualitative distinctions into quantitative ones through a common metric, was crucial for turning SO_2 into a commodity amenable to marketization. But commensuration creates some forms of knowledge while obscuring others. This chapter identifies the complex institutional activity requisite for making such marketizing projects feasible. It also attends to the persisting dilemmas and contradictions in such policy initiatives.

Beyond Isomorphism: Structural Variation and Collective Rationality

Studies of institutional isomorphism occupy much research attention, often to the neglect of more textured conceptions of the structuring of organizational fields and the research on the collective rationality that precedes change processes, such as isomorphism. This section emphasizes the analytic and practical value of focusing on the dynamics of collective rationality and the sources of structured variation. These four chapters make this point by reconsidering the causal linkage between the degree and form of collective rationality in a field, available level and type of change mechanisms, and outcomes such as homogeneity of structures and strategies.

Milstein, Hart, and York (Chapter 6) examine standard mechanisms of institutional change, presenting evidence that coercive pressure on companies to improve their environmental performance can result in industry and firm-level variations in environmental strategies, rather than isomorphism. The findings come from a comparative study that uses a subset of S&P 500 companies in the Interfaith Center on Corporate Responsibility Company Environmental Profiles

Directory (IRRC, 1992). The authors compare one industry under heavy coercive pressure (chemicals) to another under lighter pressure (computers) to show how environmental strategies (emissions, spills, and compliance efforts) vary more in highly coercive than lightly coercive environments. This chapter challenges the baseline model of institutional isomorphism by pointing out the interplay of organization and policy mechanisms. This is a task the other three chapters in the section extend by highlighting institutional processes occurring in complex structured policy fields and recognizing several outcome types as institutional effects.

Levy and Rothenberg (Chapter 7) develop "institutional embeddedness of strategy," and provide a detailed discussion of cross-national variation in policy styles among auto companies. The authors examine differences in strategic responses between auto companies in the United States and Europe toward the environmental issue of global climate change. They argue that top management definitions of corporate strategic interests develop from culturally variable attitudes to the particular environmental issue, the prospects for an appropriate technological response, anticipations concerning consumer responses, and expected policy responses. Firm interests are constituted in the context of a firm's structures and sense-making frameworks and in interactions with a wider field of industry associations, universities, the media, and national and international governance structures. Their model of institutional change underscores the importance of local histories and experiences in shaping corporate strategic issue definition and responses.

Forbes and Jermier (Chapter 8) start with insights from organizational culture frameworks, including symbolic organization theory, to elaborate how and why organizations adopt green ceremonial facades. The chapter scrutinizes the contemporary trend toward proactive environmental management by addressing the limits and opportunities of culture-based strategies. The chapter acknowledges reasons to be skeptical about voluntary initiatives to promote organizational greening, but contends that seemingly surface compliance and ceremonial actions might become steps taken along the path toward authentic organizational change.

Hironaka and Schofer (Chapter 9) develop central theoretical and conceptual issues about the decoupled features of regulation in policy systems, using the case of the origins, spread, and effects of NEPA (National Environmental Policy Act), which are mandated environmental impact assessment reports. This chapter suggests that decoupling the intent and practice of Environmental Impact Assessments (EIAs) may be a result of technical and practical challenges to performing high-quality assessments that include fundamental factors such as a lack of resources, lack of organizational capacity, and multiple organizational goals. The chapter argues for a more basic insight about organizations and policy systems: that this variance and decoupling, the perceived failures of EIAs, is also evidence of more basic effects of the EIA legislation that includes putting environmental policies on national agendas, creating nodes for environmental protest by citizens and international organizations to occur, and increasing overall environmental awareness.

Institutional Processes of Negotiation and Narrative

The key construct of "institutionalization" suffers from underspecification in much contemporary research. Organizational studies of policy have long pointed to the variety of political struggles and negotiations that shape outcomes at each stage in the policy process. The chapters in this section use negotiation and narrative approaches to engage standard views of institutional process with research on conflict, discourse, and firm- and issue-specific initiatives in shaping policy. These chapters explore how organizations inject their interests and identities back into a broader organizational field, presenting this process in the idiom of contemporary theories of negotiation and dispute resolution.

Troast, Hoffman, Riley, and Bazerman (Chapter 10) discuss the tactics used by a specific firm in its attempts to negotiate a Habitat Conservation Plan, an emergent form of regulatory compliance, as a point of access linking field-level and negotiations arguments. This chapter combines institutionalist insights about socially skilled actors and core claims from negotiation studies to give practical shape to what institutional entrepreneurs do in the policy process. With the growing emphasis in institutional theory on conflict, contestation, and change, negotiation research is a natural complement. Conversely, the authors illustrate how institutional theory can inform the negotiation literature by offering a broader framework for the social context of negotiating processes. This cross-fertilization also provides a nice contrast between a positive and a more prescriptive scientific orientation—institutionalism versus negotiation research, respectively—and a useful avenue for the former to provide tools for policy analysis.

Sastry, Bernicke, and Hart (Chapter 11) discuss attempts by the Monsanto Company to project an image to a broader organizational field through the content of its annual Corporate Environmental Reports (CERs) during the 1990s. The authors find that the thematic content of the reports during this time period shifts from specific "integrationist" promises to reduce pollution in the first half of the 1990s, to a more open-ended "anticipatory" orientation in the late 1990s. They argue that Monsanto's response to institutional pressures was not simply a one-shot or mechanical decoupling of the institutional and technical domains, but rather involved redefining process goals and structural arrangements. During this period, Monsanto reframed its earlier goals to reduce pollution emissions by 90 percent when it could not achieve reductions and spun off its chemical producing divisions into an autonomous corporation during the late 1990s.

Howard-Grenville (Chapter 12) turns the focus to industry-level analysis—to the attempts by the semiconductor manufacturing industry sector to develop new rules for reduction of PFC emissions (a global warming gas) in response to pressures from broader field-level constituencies. Where Chapter 11 focuses on corporate-initiatives to manage identity in a wider policy field, Howard-Grenville focuses on industry collective efforts. This chapter describes how actors and their interpretations of the central issues changed over time, resulting in changes in the visible trappings of institutionalization—rules and structures. Two different mechanisms of institutional evolution are identified: the transfer or reframing of core ideas, and the broadening and deepening of institutional rules and structures. She argues that the power of individual actors to influence institutional outcomes is contextually contingent. This reinforces the policy insight that efforts to influence institutions for environmental protection need to take into account a broader political economy of issues including topics indirectly related to environmental impact.

Field-Level Analyses

Field-level analyses promote attention to the social and cognitive structuring of policy fields. To date, much field-level analysis focuses on broad social structures and interdependencies. From the original arguments in Bourdieu (1983; 1987) and DiMaggio and Powell (1991), both contradictory logics and more local contexts are crucial in the ways that fields matter for firm structures and strategies. The three chapters in this section highlight field dynamics on three levels. These chapters challenge future researchers to specify field-level structures and processes more specifically and to recognize the multiple dimensions along which fields take form. Also, they extend the standard framework of field elements (logics, governance arrangements, and actors) to include intermediate institutions and the salience of local sense-making activity.

Bansal and Penner (Chapter 13) investigate interpretations of the recycled newsprint issue by four newspaper publishers in Michigan. The authors identify the regional networks within the recycled newsprint field, emphasizing how local meaning frames and enactment processes affect the variable social definition of the recycled newsprint issue. They find that feasibility, importance, and organizational responsibility for recycling account for variation in organizational responses. Because the four newspapers operated under common regulatory and normative conditions, this chapter points to ways that cognitive models of institutions can help in explaining differences in organizational behavior. The chapter connects arguments from cognitive strategy theory on issue interpretations to institutional analysis in order to explain heterogeneity in firm responses.

Lounsbury, Geraci, and Waismel-Manor (Chapter 14) argue and present evidence for how discourse and symbolic activity help construct new field-level elements and centralize solid waste management practices. They report original data on the varied actors whose testimony at formative Congressional hearings in 1969 and 1970 helped shape the consensus meaning of alternative recycling technologies, incineration, and solid waste management. They show that even though a broad consensus emerged in the 1970s that gave primacy to incineration as the preferred solution for solid waste management, evidence such as content and participant analysis of Congressional testimony argues that recycling practices appeared to be an equally viable solution to field participants at the time. The chapter reports that field-level discourse shapes policy and practice outcomes, in this case by supporting a market efficiency logic that shaped preferences for alternative technical solutions.

Delmas and Terlaak (Chapter 15) discuss national variations in field structures and processes that affect the configuration of Voluntary Environmental Agreements (VEAs) between government and industry in the United States and the Netherlands. They distinguish two types of VEAs: negotiated agreements that provide regulatory flexibility in exchange for "beyond compliance" environmental performance, and public voluntary programs that provide other incentives such as R&D subsidies, technological assistance, or other help that has a positive effect on a firm's reputation in exchange for improved environmental performance. The authors show how fragmentation and open access in policy making hamper the implementation of VAs by creating uncertainties about government commitment to these agreements. A national culture marked by consensual policy making is also important to smooth the development of such negotiated agreements. When these two conditions are not met, voluntary programs to encourage best practices become the more viable solution to provide incentives for firms to improve their performance beyond existing regulation. The chapter extends the focus on United States experiences with regulation to include comparative evidence.

Governance and Regulatory Structures

In this section, three chapters explore distinctly different notions of governance and control in light of institutions and policy. Each of the chapters explores how the traditional roles of players within a policy field are shifting and, as a result, how the locus of control for industry action changes.

Mylonadis (Chapter 16) argues that attempts to regulate the natural environment are limited by current institutional arrangements. In these arrangements, the government actors have a well-defined set of concerns evident in regulation, and firms are faced with the difficult task of conforming to these regulatory regimes. This "regulate what you know" strategy solves the problem of ambiguity over how and what to regulate, but has other costs: flexibility may be curtailed in favor of known (though perhaps suboptimal) solutions to environmental dangers. Drawing on models from other knowledge-intensive organizing contexts, Mylonadis argues that an "open-source" approach to environmental regulation that recognizes ambiguity in both environmental objectives and methodologies would potentially improve both the efficiencies of firms and the quality of the natural environment.

King, Lenox, and Barnett (Chapter 17) bring the discussion to the industry level and show how trade associations are becoming a source of organizational control. They introduce the idea that difficulties in information processing can cause the public to ascribe the same reputation to all firms in an industry. When stakeholders can sanction firms individually or collectively but cannot distinguish their relative performance, firms face a collective problem of "reputation commons." The authors contend that the strategic response to such a commons is likely to be different from strategies used to resolve resource commons problems. They argue that the intangible nature of reputation allows firms to reason with the resource either to distinguish (and thus privatize) their reputation or to reduce the likelihood of stakeholder sanction. The chapter explores some individual and collective strategies for resolving a reputation commons problem.

Mendel (Chapter 18) discusses international collective policy fields, analyzing how the growth of International Standards Organizations tools like ISO 9000 and ISO 14001 are subsuming national and regional forms of control by standardizing process evaluation of management worldwide. Mendel argues that in a global society in which it may be difficult to legislate and enforce technical criteria, standards regimes represent a unique form of social coordination and governance. ISO offers managerial accreditation systems for organizational actors using process standards, in contrast to conventional product or technical requirements, which has made ISO an attractive policy and control strategy to organizations in many countries and industries. The chapter discusses institutional and market sources in the diffusion of these international standards.

Closing Commentary

In this final section, short essays by senior commentators John Ehrenfeld and W. Richard Scott outline key observations, concerns, and encouragement for future research directions at the intersection of organizations, policy, and the natural environment. Ehrenfeld (Chapter 19) emphasizes institutional arguments in the broad sense of Giddens's work and speech act theory, and he emphasizes a focus on language, control, and action. He charts continuing challenges for institutional analysis in the context of both academic research and policy. Scott (Chapter 20) restates the importance of field-level analysis for studies of policy and organizations, and the opportunities for research in environmental management in the traditions of organization and the natural environment, environmental sociology, and linked approaches to contribute to new theoretical directions in institutional analysis.

CONCLUSION

This book treats the natural environment as a domain of activity and attention shaped by institutional and organizational processes, one in which contested ideologies, resources, and identities come to be refocused, redefined, and distributed (Espeland, 1998; Hoffman, 1997). In that spirit, the chapters span emerging perspectives from organization theory and management, sociology, international regime studies, and the social studies of science and technology. We see a synergy among this integration of theoretical fields both among each other and as they interconnect with the empirical domain of the natural environment. We hope this book helps to inform you about the genesis and diffusion of institutional beliefs, their connection to the natural environment, and theoretical models available for explaining both. The chapters suggest ways that discipline-based studies of environmental management and corporate environmentalism can inform each other and offer a point of departure for continuing studies of organizations, policy, and the natural environment.

NOTES

1. By the mid-1970s, the American Sociological Association, the Rural Socio-logical Association, and the Society for the Study of Social Problems had all established sections related to environmental sociology (Dunlap and Catton, 1979). To provide an outlet for this growing volume of research, special journal issues were devoted to environmental sociology: *Sociological Inquiry* (1983), *Annual Review of Sociology* (1979, 1987), *Journal of Social Issues* (1992), *Qualitative Sociology* (1993), *Social Problems* (1993), *Canadian Review of Sociology and Anthropology* (1994) (Hannigan, 1995). Schools increasingly posted position announcements in environmental sociology, and numerous research centers and institutes have been established, including targeted funding for dissertations and some postdoctoral funding such as the NSF program initiatives in the early 1990s on global environmental change.

REFERENCES

Bansal, Pratima, and Kendall Roth. 2000. "Why Companies Go Green: A Model of Ecological Responsiveness." *Academy of Management Journal* 43(4): 717–736.

Baumol, William, and Alan Blinder. 1985. *Economics: Principles and Policy.* San Diego: Harcourt Brace Jovanovich.

Bazerman, Max, and Andrew J. Hoffman. 1999. "Sources of Environmentally Destructive Behavior: Individual, Organizational and Institutional Perspectives." *Research in Organizational Behavior,* 21: 39–79.

Beamish, Thomas. 2001. "Environmental Hazard and Institutional Betrayal: Lay-Public Perceptions of Risk in the San Luis Obispo County Oil Spill." *Organization & Environment,* 14(1): 5–33.

Beck, Ulrich. 1992. *Risk Society: Towards a New Modernity.* London: Sage.

Becker, Egon, and Thomas Jahn, eds. 1999. *Sustainability and the Social Sciences: A Cross-Disciplinary Approach to Integrating Environmental Considerations Into Theoretical Reorientation.* Paris: UNESCO.

Becker, Howard S. 1982. *Art Worlds.* Berkeley: University of California Press.

Bourdieu, Pierre. 1983. "The Field of Cultural Production, or the Economic World Reversed." *Poetics,* 12(Nov.): 311–356.

Bourdieu, Pierre. 1987. "The Force of Law: Toward a Sociology of the Juridical Field." *Hastings Journal of Law,* 38: 209–248.

Brint, Steven, and Jerome Karabel. 1991. "Institutional Origins and Transformations: The Case of American Community Colleges." In Walter W. Powell and Paul J. DiMaggio, eds., *The New Institutionalism in Organizational Analysis,* 337–360. Chicago: University of Chicago Press.

Brulle, Robert J. 2000. *Agency, Democracy, and Nature.* Cambridge, MA: MIT Press.

Buttel, Frederick. 1987. "New Directions in Environmental Sociology." *Annual Review of Sociology* 13: 465–488.

Buttel, Frederick. 1992. "Environmentalism: Origins, Processes, and Implications for Rural Social Change." *Rural Sociology,* 57(1): 14.

Carson, Rachel. 1962. *Silent Spring.* Boston: Houghton-Mifflin.

Catton, William, and Riley Dunlap. 1980. "A New Ecological Paradigm for Post-Exuberant Sociology." *American Behavioral Scientist,* 20(1): 15–47.

Christensen, Clark, T. Craig, and Stuart Hart. 2001. "The Great Disruption." *Foreign Affairs,* 80(2): 80–95.

Clark, Vivien, and P. Devereaux Jennings. 1997. "Talking About the Natural Environment: A Means for Deinstitutionalization." *American Behavioral Scientist,* 40(4): 454–464.

Clarke, Adele E. 1995. "Research Materials and Reproductive Science in the United States, 1910–1940." In S. Leigh Star, ed., *Ecologies of Knowledge: Work and Politics in Science and Technology.* Albany, NY: State University of New York Press.

Colby, Michael. 1991. "Environmental Management in Development: The Evolution of Paradigms." *Ecological Economics,* 3: 193–213.

Coleman, James. 1988. "Social Capital in the Creation of Human Capital." *American Journal of Sociology,* 94(Suppl.): 95–120.

Cronon, William. 1991. *Nature's Metropolis: Chicago and the Great West.* New York: Norton.

Cropper, Maureen, and Wallace Oates. 1992. "Environmental Economics: A Survey." *Journal of Economic Literature,* 30:675–740.

DiMaggio, Paul. 1988. "Interest and Agency in Institutional Theory." In Lynne Zucker, ed., *Institutional Patterns and Organizations,* 3–21. Cambridge, MA: Ballinger.

DiMaggio, Paul. 1995. "Comments on What Theory Is Not." *Administrative Science Quarterly,* 40: 391–397.

DiMaggio, Paul, and Walter W. Powell. 1983. "The Iron Cage Revisited: Institutional Isomorphism and Collective Rationality in Organizational Fields." *American Sociological Review,* 48: 147–160.

DiMaggio, Paul, and Walter W. Powell. 1991. "Introduction." In Walter W. Powell and Paul J. DiMaggio, eds., *The New Institutionalism in Organizational Analysis*, 1–40. Chicago: University of Chicago Press.

Dobbin, Frank. 1994. *Forging Industrial Policy: The United States, Britain, and France in the Railway Age.* Cambridge: Cambridge University Press.

Douglas, Mary. 1986. *How Institutions Think.* Syracuse, NY: Syracuse University Press.

Douglas, Mary, and Aaron B. Wildavsky. 1982. *Risk and Culture.* Berkeley: University of California Press.

Dunlap, Riley. 1991. "Trends in Public Opinion Toward Envronmental Issues: 1965–1990." *Society and Natural Resources,* 4: 285–312.

Dunlap, Riley, and William Catton. 1979. "Environmental Sociology." *Annual Review of Sociology,* 5: 243–273.

Dutton, Jane, and Janet Dukerich. 1991. "Keeping an Eye on the Mirror: Image and Identity in Organizational Adaptation." *Academy of Management Journal,* 34(3): 517–554.

Edelman, Lauren. 1990. "Legal Environments and Organizational Governance: The Expansion of Due Process in the American Workplace." *American Journal of Sociology,* 95: 1401–1440.

Egri, Carolyn, and Susan Herman. 2000. "Leadership in the North American Environmental Sector: Values, Leadership Styles, and Contexts of Environmental Leaders and Their Organizations." *Academy of Management Journal,* 43(4): 571–604.

Egri, Carolyn, and Lawrence T. Pinfield. 1994. "Organizations and the Biosphere: Ecologies and Environments." In S. R. Clegg, C. Hardy, and W. R. Nord, eds., *Handbook of Organization Studies.* Thousand Oaks, CA: Sage.

Eliot, Robert, and Arran Gore, eds. 1983. *Environmental Philosophy: A Collection of Readings.* University Park: Pennsylvania State University Press.

Environmental Protection Agency. 2000. *Industrial Ecology and EPA: Report on the EPA Industrial Ecology Workshop,* internal memo, Workshop Organizing Committee, US Environmental Protection Agency, February 7.

Espeland, Wendy Nelson. 1998. *The Struggle for Water: Politics, Rationality, and Identity in the American Southwest.* Chicago: University of Chicago Press.

Fisher, Kurt, and Johan Schot, eds. 1993. *Environmental Strategies for Industry: International Perspectives on Research Needs and Policy Implications.* Washington, DC: Island Press.

Flannery, Brenda, and Douglas May. 2000. "Environmental Ethical Decision Making in the US Metal-Finishing Industry." *Academy of Management Journal,* 43(4): 642–662.

Fligstein, Neil. 1991. "The Structural Transformation of American Industry: An Institutional Account of the Causes of Diversification in the Largest Firms: 1919–1979." In Walter W. Powell and Paul J. DiMaggio, eds. *The New Institutionalism in Organizational Analysis.* Chicago: University of Chicago Press, 311–336.

Fligstein, Neil. 1992. "Bank Control, Owner Control or Organizational Dynamics: Who Controls the Large Modern Corporation?" *American Journal of Sociology,* 98(2): 280–307.

Fligstein, Neil. 1996. "Markets as Politics: A Political Cultural Approach to Market Institutions." *American Sociological Review,* 64(4): 656–673.

Fligstein, Neil. 1997. "Social Skill and Institutional Theory." *American Behavioral Scientist,* 40(4): 397–405.

Fligstein, Neil. 2001. *The Architecture of Markets: An Economic Sociology of 21st Century Capitalist Societies.* Princeton: Princeton University Press.

Frank, David John, Ann Hironaka, and Evan Schofer. 2000. "The Nation-State and the Natural Environment Over the Twentieth Century." *American Sociological Review,* 65: 96–116.

Friedman, Milton. 1970. "The Social Responsibility of Business Is to Increase Its Profits." *New York Times Magazine,* Sept. 13: 32–33, 122, 124, 126.

Friedman, Robert. 2000. "When You Find Yourself in a Hole, Stop Digging." *Journal of Industrial Ecology,* 3(4): 15–19.

Galvin, Tiffany. 2002. "Examining Institutional Change: Evidence from the Founding Dynamics of U.S. Health Care Interest Associations." *Academy of Management Journal,* 46.

Gladwin, Thomas, James Kennelly, and Tara-Shelomith Krause. 1995. "Shifting Paradigms for Sustainable Development: Implications for Management Theory and Research." *Academy of Management Review,* 20(4): 874–907.

Granovetter, Mark. 1985. "Economic Action and Social Structure: The Problem of Embeddedness." *American Journal of Sociology,* 91: 481–510.

Greenwood, Royston, and C. R. Hinings. 1996. "Understanding Radical Organizational Change: Bringing Together the Old and the New Institutionalism." *Academy of Management Review,* 21(4): 1022–1054.

Guillén, Mauro. 1994. *Models of Management: Work, Authority, and Organization in a Comparative Perspective,* Chicago: University of Chicago Press.

Guthrie, Doug, and Louise Roth. 1999. "The States, Courts, and Maternity Leave Policies in the US: Specifying Institutional Mechanisms." *American Sociological Review,* 64: 41–63.

Haas, Peter. 1990. *Saving the Mediterranean: The Politics of International Environmental Cooperation.* New York: Columbia University Press.

Haas, Peter, Robert Keohane, and Marc Levy, eds. 1993. *Institutions for the Earth: Sources of Effective International Environmental Protection.* Cambridge, MA: MIT Press.

Hahn, Robert, and Robert Stavins. 1991. "Incentive-Based Environmental Regulation: A New Era from an Old Idea." *Ecology Law Quarterly,* 18(1): 1–42.

Hannigan, John. 1995. *Environmental Sociology: A Social Constructionist Perspective.* London: Routledge.

Hargrove, Eugene. 1989. *Foundations of Environmental Ethics.* Englewood Cliffs, NJ: Prentice Hall.

Hart, Stuart. 1995. "A Natural-Resource Based View of the Firm." *Academy of Management Review,* 20(4): 986–1014.

Hart, Stuart. 1997. "Beyond Greening: Strategies for a Sustainable World." *Harvard Business Review,* Jan.–Feb.: 66–76.

Hays, Samuel. 1998. "The Future of Environmental Regulation." In Samuel P. Hays and Joel A. Tarr, eds., *Explorations in Environmental History: Essays,* 109–114. Pittsburgh, PA: University of Pittsburgh Press.

Hirsch, Paul, and Michael Lounsbury. 1997. "Ending The Family Quarrel: Toward a Reconciliation of 'Old' And 'New' Institutionalisms." *American Behavioral Scientist,* 40(4): 406–418.

Hoban, Thomas, and Richard Brooks. 1996. *Green Justice: The Environment and the Courts.* Boulder, CO.: Westview Press.

Hoffman, Andrew J. 1997. *From Heresy to Dogma: An Institutional History of Corporate Environmentalism.* San Francisco: New Lexington Press. Reprinted by Stanford University Press, 2001.

Hoffman, Andrew J., ed. 1998. *Global Climate Change: A Senior Level Dialogue at the Intersection of Economics, Strategy, Technology, Science, Politics and International Negotiation,* San Francisco: New Lexington Press.

Hoffman, Andrew J. 1999. "Institutional Evolution and Change: Environmentalism and the US Chemical Industry." *Academy of Management Journal,* 42(4): 351–371.

Hoffman, Andrew J. 2000. *Competitive Environmental Strategy: A Guide to the Changing Business Landscape.* Washington, DC: Island Press.

Hoffman, Andrew J. 2001. "Linking Organizational and Field-Level Analyses: The Diffusion of Corporate Environmental Practice." *Organization & Environment,* 14(2): 133–156.

Hoffman, Andrew J., and John Ehrenfeld. 1998. "Corporate Environmentalism, Sustainability and Management Studies." In N. Roome, ed., *Environmental Strategies for Industry: The Future of Corporate Practice,* 55–73. Washington, DC: Island Press.

Hoffman, Andrew J., and William Ocasio. 2001. "Not All Events Are Attended Equally: Toward a Middle-Range Theory of Industry Attention to External Events." *Organization Science,* 12(4): 414–434.

Hoffman, Andrew J., and Marc J. Ventresca. 1999. "The Institutional Framing of Policy Debates: Economics Versus the Environment." *American Behavioral Scientist,* 42(8): 1368–1392.

Holmes, Rolston. 1988. *Environmental Ethics.* Philadelphia: Temple University Press.

Hunt, Christopher, and Ellen Auster. Winter 1990. "Proactive Environmental Management: Avoiding the Toxic Trap." *Sloan Management Review:* 7–18.

Jennings, P. Devereaux, and Paul Zandbergen. 1995. "Ecologically Sustainable Organizations: An Institutional Approach." *Academy of Management Review,* 20(4): 1015–1052.

Jepperson, Ronald. 1991. "Institutions, Institutional Effects, and Institutionalism." In Walter W. Powell and Paul J. DiMaggio, eds., *The New Institutionalism in Organizational Analysis.* Chicago: University of Chicago Press: 143–163.

Karnoe, Peter, and Raghu Garud. 2002. "Path Creation and Dependence in the Danish Wind Turbine Field." In Marc J. Ventresca and Joseph Porac, eds., *Constructing Industries and Markets.* London: Elsevier Science, Ltd.

King, Andrew, and Michael Lenox. 2000. "Industry Self-Regulation Without Sanctions: The Chemical Industry's Responsible Care Program." *Academy of Management Journal,* 43(4): 698–716.

Kraatz, Matthew, and Edward Zajac. 1996. "Exploring the Limits of the New Institutionalism: The Causes and Consequences of Illegitimate Organizational Change." *American Sociological Review,* 61: 812–836.

Laclau, Ernesto, and Chantal Mouffe. 1985. *Hegemony and Socialist Strategy: Towards a Radical Democratic Politics.* London: Verso.

Lash, Scott, and Brian Wynne. 1992. "Introduction." In Ulrich Beck, ed., *Risk Society: Towards a New Modernity:* 1–8. London: Sage.

Lawrence, Anne, and David Morell. 1995. "Leading-Edge Environmental Management: Motivation, Opportunity, Resources and Processes." In James Post, ed., *Research in Corporate Social Performance and Policy,* 99–126. Greenwich, CT: JAI.

Lawrence, Thomas. 1999. "Institutional Strategy." *Journal of Management,* 25(2): 161–188.

Liberatore, Angela. 1991. "Problems of Transnational Policymaking: Environmental Policy in the European Community." *European Journal of Political Research,* 19: 281–305.

Lober, Douglas. 1996. "Evaluating the Environmental Performance of Corporations." *Journal of Managerial Issues* 8(2): 184–205.

Lounsbury, Michael, Marc J. Ventresca, and Paul Hirsch. Forthcoming. "Social Movements, Field Frames, and Industry Emergence: A Cultural-Political Perspective on U.S. Recycling." *Socio-Economics Review,* 1(1).

MacNaughten, Phil, and John Urry. 1998. *Contested Natures.* Thousand Oaks, CA: Sage.

March, James, and Johan Olsen. 1989. *The Organizational Basis of Politics.* New York: MacMillan.

McDonough, Patricia M., Marc J. Ventresca, and Charles Outcalt. 2000. "Field of Dreams: Organizational Field Approaches to Understanding the Transformation of College Access, 1965–1995." *Higher Education: Handbook of Theory and Research,* 15: 371–405.

McGurty, Eileen Maura. 1997. "From NIMBY to Civil Rights: The Origins of the Environmental Justice Movement." *Environmental History,* 2:301–323.

Meyer, John W., and Brian Rowan. 1977. "Institutional Organizations: Formal Structure as Myth and Ceremony." *American Journal of Sociology,* 83: 340–363.

Meyer, John W., David Frank, Anne Hironaka, Evan Schofer, and Nancy Tuma. 1997. "The Structuring of the World Environmental Regime, 1870–1990." *International Organization,* 51(4): 623–651.

Mohr, John. 2002. "Implicit Terrains: Meaning, Measurement, and Spatial Metaphors in Organizational Theory." In Marc J. Ventresca and Joseph Porac, eds., *Constructing Industries and Markets.* London: Elsevier Science, Ltd.

Morrison, Catherine. 1991. *Managing Environmental Affairs: Corporate Practices in the US, Canada and Europe.* New York: The Conference Board.

Oliver, Christine. 1991. "Strategic Responses to Institutional Processes." *Academy of Management Review,* 16: 145–179.

Perrow, Charles. 1986. *Complex Organizations: A Critical Essay.* 3rd Ed. New York: McGraw Hill.

Porter, Michael, and Claas van der Linde. 1995. "Green and Competitive: Ending the Stalemate." *Harvard Business Review,* Sept.–Oct.: 120–134.

Powell, Walter, and Paul DiMaggio. 1991. *The New Institutionalism in Organizational Analysis.* Chicago: University of Chicago Press.

Prakash, Aseem. 2000. *Greening the Firm: The Politics of Corporate Environmentalism.* New York: Cambridge University Press.

Proffitt, Trexler W. 2001. *Ideology and Field Rationalization: Shareholder Activism.* Unpublished dissertation, Northwestern University.

Purser, Ronald, Changkil Park, and Alfonso Montuori. 1995. "Limits to Anthropocentrism: Toward an Ecocentric Organization Paradigm." *Academy of Management Review,* 20(4): 1053–1089.

Ramus, Catherine, and Ulrich Stegner. 2000. "The Roles of Supervisory Support Behaviors and Environmental Policy in Employee 'Ecoinitiatives' at Leading Edge European Companies." *Academy of Management Journal,* 43(4): 605–626.

Revesz, Richard L. 1997. *Foundations of Environmental Law and Policy.* New York: Oxford University Press.

Roome, Nigel, ed. 1998. *Sustainability Strategies for Industry: The Future of Corporate Practice.* Washington DC: Island Press.

Rosen, Christine Meisner. 1995. "Businessmen Against Pollution in Late Nineteenth Century Chicago." *Business History Review,* 71(Fall): 351–397.

Rosen, Christine Meisner. 1997. "Industrial Ecology and the Greening of Business History." *Business and Economic History,* 26: 123–137.

Rosen, Christine Meisner, and Christopher C. Sellers. 1999. "The Nature of the Firm: Towards an Ecocultural History of Business." *Business History Review,* 73(Winter): 577–600.

Rosenkopf, Lori, Anca Metiu, and Varghese George. 2001. "From the Bottom Up? Technical Committee Activity and Alliance Formation." *Administrative Science Quarterly,* 46(4).

Rothenberg, Lawrence S. 2002. *Environmental Choices: Policy Responses to Green Demands.* Congressional Quarterly Press.

Roy, Manik. 1991. "Pollution Prevention, Organizational Culture and Social Learning." *Environmental Law,* 22: 188–251.

Schmidheiny, Stephan. 1992. *Changing Course.* Cambridge, MA: MIT Press.

Schnaiberg, Alan. 1980. *The Environment: From Surplus to Scarcity.* New York: Oxford University Press.

Scott, W. Richard. 1983. "Network, Cultural, and Historical Elements of Environments." In John Meyer and W. Richard Scott, eds., *Organizational Environments: Ritual and Rationality,* 63–95. Beverly Hills, CA: Sage.

Scott, W. Richard. 1991. "Unpacking Institutional Arguments." In Walter W. Powell and Paul DiMaggio, eds., *The New Institutionalism In Organizational Analysis,* 164–182. Chicago: University of Chicago Press.

Scott, W. Richard. 1994. "Conceptualizing Organizational Fields: Linking Organizations and Societal Systems." In Hans-Ulrich Derlien, Uta Gerhardt, and Fritz Sharpf, eds. *System Rationalitat und Partialinteresse,* 203–221. Baden-Baden: Nomos Verlagsgesellschaft.

Scott, W. Richard. 1995. *Institutions and Organizations.* London: Sage.

Scott, W. Richard. 2001. *Institutions and Organizations,* 2nd edition. Thousand Oaks, CA: Sage.

Scott, W. Richard, and John W. Meyer. 1991. "The Organization of Societal Sectors: Propositions and Early Evidence." In Walter W. Powell and Paul J. DiMaggio, eds., *The New Institutionalism in Organizational Analysis,* 108–140. Chicago: University of Chicago Press.

Sexton, Ken, K. Alfred Marcus, William Easter, and Timothy Burkhardt, eds. 1999. *Better Environmental Decisions: Strategies for Governments, Businesses and Communities.* Washington, DC: Island Press.

Sharma, Sanjay. 2000. "Managerial Interpretations and Organizational Context as Predictors of Corporate Choice of Environmental Strategy." *Academy of Management Journal,* 43(4): 681–697.

Shrivastava, Paul. 1995. "The Role of Corporations in Achieving Ecological Sustainability." *Academy of Management Review,* 20(4): 936–960.

Smart, Bruce. 1992. *Beyond Compliance.* Washington, DC: World Resources Institute.

Starik, Mark, and Alfred Marcus. 2000. "Introduction to the Special Research Forum on the Management of Organizations in the Natural Environment: A Field Emerging from Multiple Paths, with Many Challenges Ahead." *Academy of Management Journal,* 43(4): 539–546.

Starik, Mark, and Gordon Rands. 1995. "Weaving an Integrated Web: Multilevel and Multi-system Perspectives of Ecologically Sustainable Organizations." *Academy of Management Review,* 20(4): 908–935.

Stead, W. Edward, and Jean Stead. 1995. *Management for a Small Planet.* London: Sage.

Thomas, George, John Meyer, Francisco Ramirez, and John Boli. 1987. *Institutional Structure: Constituting State, Society, and the Individual.* Newbury Park, CA: Sage.

Tietenberg, Thomas. 1992. *Environmental and Natural Resource Economics.* New York: Harper Collins, 3rd edition.

Wade-Benzoni, Kimberly. 1996. *Intergenerational Justice: Discounting, Reciprocity, and Fairness as Factors That Influence How Resources Are Allocated Across Generations.* Northwestern University, Evanston, IL: Unpublished dissertation.

Wade-Benzoni, Kimberly, and Max Bazerman, eds. 1999. Special Issue: "Barriers to Wiser Agreements Between Environmental and Economic Concerns." *American Behavioral Scientist,* 42(8), May.

Washington, Marvin, and Marc J. Ventresca. 2001. *Institutional Support for the Incorporation of Emerging Strategies: Three Field-level Mechanisms in U.S. Higher Education.* Working paper, Kellogg School of Management.

Weiss, Janet. 1998. "Theoretical Foundations of Policy Intervention." In H. George Fredrickson and Jocelyn M. Johnston, eds. *Public Management Reform and Innovation,* 37–69. Birmingham: University of Alabama Press.

Weinberg, Adam S., David N. Pellow, and Allan Schnaiberg. 2000. *Urban Recycling and the Search for Sustainable Community Development.* Princeton, NJ: Princeton University Press.

White, Harrison. 1992. *Identity and Control: A Structural Theory of Social Interaction.* Princeton, NJ: Princeton University Press.

Zucker, Lynne. 1983. "Organizations as Institutions." In Samuel B. Bacharach, ed., *Research in the Sociology of Organizations: Organizational Politics,* 1–47. Greenwich, CT: JAI.

Zucker, Lynne. 1988. "Where Do Institutional Patterns Come From? Organizations as Actors in Social Systems." In Lynne Zucker, ed., *Institutional Patterns and Organizations: Culture and Environment,* 23–49. Cambridge, MA: Ballinger.

I

INSTITUTIONAL ORIGINS: COMPETING FRAMEWORKS AND LOGICS

2

THE ORIGINS QUESTION:
BUILDING GLOBAL INSTITUTIONS
TO PROTECT NATURE

David John Frank

Global institutional theorists have increasingly turned their attention from diffusion to the question of origins. Analyses of the rise of specific global institutions, such as schools (Ramirez and Boli, 1987) and nation-states (Meyer, Boli, Thomas, and Ramirez, 1997), as well as broad considerations of institutional origins (Boli and Thomas, 1999; Meyer 1994; Meyer, Boli, and Thomas, 1987), are prolific in the recent literature. The core focus of this work is on the world frame itself; its core argument is that change and expansion in the world frame (that is, in the culture and organization of world society) give rise to new and expanded global institutions.

From this work, this chapter draws general themes, discussing their application to nature protection. In particular, it compares the fates of two models of nature protection, one humanitarian and one scientific. In the early twentieth century, the humanitarian model provided the dominant rationale for nature protection in the world, but it did not fare well over time. Changes in the wider world frame increasingly favored the alternative scientific model, and it quickly went on to become more legitimate and authoritative. The scientific model presented a version of "nature protection" that was extensively rationalized and universalized and thus better suited to a world constituted around progress and equality (Meyer, Boli, and Thomas, 1987). The comparison between scientific and humanitarian models unearths the root characteristics of "environmentalism" as we know it today and in the process reveals the cultural foundations on which stand the great majority of current organizations and policies (Frank, 1997; Weiss, 1999).

ALTERNATIVE MODELS OF NATURE PROTECTION

By the early twentieth century, nature protection was already a common concern in the Western world. Both citizens and states were mobilized across borders around a wide variety of related issues, from the decimation of songbird populations to the mistreatment of draught horses. By far the majority of these activities were humanitarian in focus—marked by compassion and sympathy and centered on preserving the right place of humanity in the organic moral community.

In the course of industrialization and urbanization, the balance of the nature-culture dyad was seen to have been upset (Jasper and Nelkin, 1992). As one observer wrote:

> [W]hen the iron axe and the steel plough came into use, and population steadily increased, the conflict [between nature and culture] became so fatal in its effects on nature that man began to consider the outcome. Man's dominion over nature was not an unmixed blessing, and in the course of the conflict, much of value was irretrievably lost. Present day nature protection is, accordingly, the natural reaction against the one-sided materialistic developments of the last decades. It directs its activity against all needless destruction and unreasonable prodigality in land cultivation, and works for the preservation of natural beauty, virgin landscapes, and natural objects of unusual significance (Brouwer, 1938: 7–8).

Notice the qualities—beauty, virginity, and unusual significance—on the wane in the machine age.

To reequilibrate balance between nature and culture, there appeared on one hand mobilization to return humans to their right place *in* nature. Urbanization had drawn people in unprecedented numbers to live in the new industrial cities—sites of "filth, ruin, and uninhabitleness," too far from the restorative vigor of field and stream (Engels, 1978: 584). Organizations and policies arose to pull people back into purifying intercourse with nature. These included the International Friends of Nature, founded in 1895 in Vienna, which sought, by promotion of "the hike," to entice urbanites back into wild settings, where nature's tonic might cleanse their city-stained souls.

Also developed were protective activities to restore the moral rightness of human behavior *toward* nature. This issue arose especially in relation to the new-found power of technology and industry. Although from the humanitarian perspective, nature (creation) might be used to benefit humanity, humanity's superior position carries with it responsibility—to respect and care for nature, and to harbor it from abuse (Pepper, 1984). And abuse was seen to occur more routinely when humanity's god-given superiority was fortified with the powers of technology and industry. Recognition of this danger generated protective efforts, such as the Nordic Society Against Painful Experimentation on Animals, founded in 1882, and the International Union and People's League Against Vivisection, founded in Paris in 1900. The two organizations had the objective of saving animals from abandonment and vivisection (medical research on living animals): the latter reported saving 818 animals in the year 1906. The same reasons mobilized the Society for the Preservation of the Wild Fauna of the Empire in London in 1903. It aimed to safeguard wildlife from extermination—an increasing concern with rising gun ownership—through measures to interest the public and governments in wildlife preservation (see Hornaday, 1913).

When regarded from the vantage point of twenty-first century global environmentalism, these early humanitarian efforts at "nature protection" are striking in their sentimentality. Their central thrust involves the preservation of a god-given moral order and community. With urbanization and industrialization, humans were seen to have lost touch with and to threaten the natural creation. The harm that followed was harm—mainly, at least—to human souls: the protection of a spiritual order was at issue, not the protection of a physical system, and it gave impetus to considerable international organization and activity.

In contrast to the relatively high levels of international mobilization to protect the *moral* integrity of the human-nature relationship in the early twentieth century, social activities to protect its *physical* integrity were scarcely evident. Although Malthus, Darwin, and others had already gone far in building the now-dominant model of physical interdependencies—with humanity and nature interlocked in a life-sustaining web—little in the way of international organization or policy had followed.

The activities that did treat nature as a physical entity or system at the time were only peripherally concerned with nature protection: mainly they were interested in nature qua nature, bounded from humanity. For example, the International Ornithological Committee, founded in 1884, aimed to study the anatomy, migration, biology, and protection of birds in their natural habitat, as well as issues of breeding and domestication. The loops of vitality integrating the feathered vertebrates with *Homo sapiens,* however, remained mostly unconstructed. Other scientific organizations operated in similar fashion: nature remained mostly external and separated from humanity.

Indeed, the systematic evidence from the period, although thin, suggests a strong predominance of humanitarian rationales for nature protection (Table 2.1). Of the six nature-protection organizations listed in the 1929 League of Nations

Table 2.1
Nature Protection Organizations Listed in the League of Nations *Handbook of International Organizations, 1929* (and 1931 supplement)

The International Humanitarian Bureau of Animal Lovers
Founded 1928
Objective: The Bureau, with which hundreds of societies have associated themselves, is a world-center for the dissemination of information relating to the treatment of animals, legislation, propaganda and united action for reform. It works to promote international co-operation and has been established with the object of showing that humane education and the protection of animals are integral parts of the movement for international peace and progressive civilization. It seeks to introduce into schools the teaching of humanitarian principles and practice as part of their curriculum.

International Bureau of Societies for the Protection of Animals and Anti-Vivisection Societies
Founded 1925
Objective: To ensure that animals are treated in accordance with the higher rules of kindness and humanity; to study and promote such legislative and other measures as can be taken in this direction; to examine and compare the methods adopted for the purpose in the various countries, and to bring them into line with one another when this is possible and desirable; to create the necessary public opinion in the various countries for the achievement of these aims.

International Committee for Bird Preservation
Founded 1922
Objective: To stimulate interest in all countries for a more adequate protection of wild bird-life.

International Union and People's League Against Vivisection
Founded 1900
Objective: To endeavor to obtain legislative and executive powers by means of petitions, requests, etc. for the suppression of vivisection: to form by every possible legal means a body of opinion strong enough to draw the attention of the public authorities to the danger to the progress of national morals represented by the cruel practices of vivisection; to make known by press publicity or any other means the horrible tortures inflicted on animals and to put a stop to them.

International Legal Committee for the Protection of Animals
Objective: To make a study of the laws, conventions and regulations relative to the protection of animals; to put forward suggestions for their improvement and to give free legal advice to societies for the protection of animals.

International Office for the Protection of Nature
Founded 1928
To collect from all over the world documents, as correct and complete as possible, which directly or indirectly touched on the question of the protection of nature. On behalf of public administration, scientific societies and all who are interested, the Office tries to circulate, by means of publication, its most important texts and documents. The Office also contributes to the centralization of work done all over the world for the preservation of scenery and natural wealth.

Handbook of International Organizations, three have unequivocal moral foundations (and in fact are indexed under the heading Humanitarianism, Religion and Morals). These are the International Humanitarian Bureau of Animal Lovers, the International Bureau of Societies for the Protection of Animals and Anti-Vivisection Societies, and the International Union and People's League Against Vivisection. The other three organizations—the International Committee for Bird Preservation, the International Legal Committee for the Protection of Animals, and the International Office for the Protection of Nature—are more difficult to peg given the information available, but they appear to contain at least some humanitarian elements.[1]

Here then lie the theoretical and substantive problems. On the one hand, there is a version of "nature protection" that depicts the human-nature relationship in terms of an organic community and promotes nature protection for the moral well-being of humanity. In the early twentieth century, it had more adherents, more organizations, and more elite European support than the scientific alternative. Yet it faded into the background over the twentieth century. On the other hand, there is a version of "nature protection" that depicts the human-nature relationship as an interdependent physical system and promotes nature protection for the physical sustenance of humanity. In the early twentieth century, it had only scattered support, almost entirely from scientific professionals. Yet it went on to develop into what is today one of the very most central of all global institutions—forming an extraordinarily dense node of global understandings, organizations, policies, and activities (Haas and Sundgren, 1993; Meyer, Frank, Hironaka, Schofer, and Tuma, 1997; Wapner 1996).[2]

Why did the scientific version of nature protection prevail over the humanitarian one? That is the question addressed here. The answer, I believe, has to do with changes in world society itself: they are changes in the cultural and organizational frame that give rise (and fall) to the various versions of nature protection. This process of selection and its outcome have extensive implications for contemporary organization and policy. Had the humanitarian version continued to dominate the world stage, much of what we currently take for granted as nature protection would be off the global agenda. Likewise, at least some of what global authorities fail to consider would be central.

Accordingly I compare the humanitarian and scientific versions of nature protection as they pass through the three main stages[3] of global institutionalization: change in the world culture, change in the world organization, and change in nation-state polities (see Figure 2.1). Also, this chapter recapitulates and summarizes some of what is known about the origins of global institutions generally.

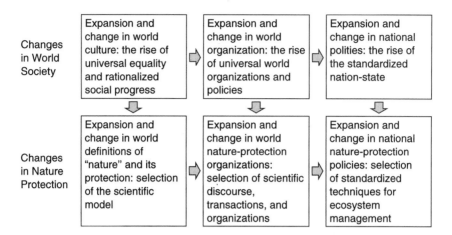

	Expansion and change in world culture: the rise of universal equality and rationalized social progress	Expansion and change in world organization: the rise of universal world organizations and policies	Expansion and change in national polities: the rise of the standardized nation-state
Changes in World Society			

	Expansion and change in world definitions of "nature" and its protection: selection of the scientific model	Expansion and change in world nature-protection organizations: selection of scientific discourse, transactions, and organizations	Expansion and change in national nature-protection policies: selection of standardized techniques for ecosystem management
Changes in Nature Protection			

Figure 2.1   Changes in the Global Institutionalization of Nature Protection over the Twentieth Century

CHANGES IN THE WORLD CULTURE

First, there have been many changes in the wider world culture. With modernity's steady rise, what had been more segmented and hierarchical turned increasingly inclusive and universalistic; and what had been tied to traditional (often religious) orders became increasingly tied to rationalized progress (Boli and Thomas, 1999). A spectrum of indicators embodies the cultural shifts, the rise and globalization of the university prominent among them. Such transformations in the framework of meaning altered the criteria for measuring truth and goodness and thus privileged and gave rise to universalized (increasingly one and the same) and rationalized (increasingly hitched to human purpose) entities. Regarding nature protection, the wider world cultural shift heavily favored the scientific model over the humanitarian: the former involves a more universalized and rationalized version of "nature protection" (see Morrill and Owen-Smith, Chapter 4).

To be specific, the scientific model presents a universalized nature insofar as it is abstracted and lawlike. In the scientific view, the rhinoceroses populating Africa and Asia are seen as the same species of entity; the photosynthesis occurring in Brazil's rain forest and Siberia's tundra are known as the same category of process; and the food chain linking aardvarks to termites and grizzlies to salmon are identified as the same kind of relationship. In scientific terms, the generic features of natural phenomena come to the fore, unrestricted by local peculiarities or geopolitical boundaries.

Universalism is prominent in the scientific model of nature protection in a second sense, too—in the extensive interconnectedness of the natural entity. The linkages are partly historical—in the origin of planet Earth and the origin of life, in the single shared landmass (the supercontinent Pangaea) and the single shared evolution. And the ties are partly present day—in the panoply of biogeochemical processes connecting, for example, mosquito deaths to human deaths (in the famous case, DDT kills mosquitoes and thus geckos and thus cats, thereby allowing the proliferation of rats, which carry bubonic plague to humans—Ehrlich and Ehrlich, 1983), linking South Pacific volcanoes to Alaskan cloud cover, and tying aerosols in Chicago to skin cancer in Tasmania. The connective loops permeating the scientific model are seemingly endless, sometimes spectacularly remote, and in aggregate they present a nature literally universal in scope.

Third, the scientific model embodies a universalized nature in the sense that it bridges the chasm separating humans from the rest of the natural world. In the Judeo-Christian and Islamic traditions, at least, this chasm is infinite: humans alone are created in the image of God, and humans alone have potential for the afterlife. From the scientific point of view, however, the radical divide becomes a more routine division: Humans represent an advanced stage of the evolutionary process, but not another order of being entirely. To scientists, humans are one with the rest of nature, a species known as *Homo sapiens,* joined to the single natural entity and encompassed by the single natural system.

Altogether, the scientific model presents nature as a universal ecosystem—law-like, global, and integrated with humanity (see for example Thomas, 1983). Somewhat the opposite characteristics apply to the humanitarian model, which focuses on the particular aspects of a local nature (its unique beauties, its inimitable wonders), distinct from and even opposed to humanity. In this way, the scientific model of nature protection better articulated with the rising world culture of universalism and equality, and it thrived over time better than the humanitarian alternative prevalent in late-nineteenth- and early-twentieth-century Europe.

The scientific model enjoyed further advantages in the rising world culture in its extensive rationalization, in which nature is implicated in a panoply of systematic functions in the routine operations of society. Narrowly, rationalization involves commodification (and thus commensuration—see Chapter 5). For example, in the scientific frame, various seed-bearing plants, such as corn, can be labeled "crops," to be sold on regular markets in manifold forms (on the cob, in cans, frozen, ground into meal, and so on). But commodification is only the tip of the iceberg. The larger process involves the almost unlimited incorporation and absorption of "natural resources" into the collective good: nature becomes increasingly subordinated to the purposes of, and utilized as a support system for, the expanded society. For example, a simple tree becomes, from the scientific standpoint, timber for construction, pulp for paper, and the bearer of fruit—attached not only to markets, that is, but also to nation-building and the pursuit of progress generally.

More broadly still, in the scientific rubric of the natural ecosystem, nature has life-sustaining capacities. Scientists forge (or in the usual argot "discover") an enormous array of relationships in which nature provides not only the raw materials for profit and progress but also for human life itself. In myriad processes—such as respiration, in which the human body engages in a ceaseless exchange of gases with its environment—humanity's utter dependence on nature is established: Any disruption of the sustaining cycles threatens the most basic conditions of human *being*. Here is a rationalization even more extensive than the previous one, in which all of nature (even once menacing processes, such as forest fires) provides human life support.

These two dimensions of rationalization reinforce more than contradict each other (Schnaiberg and Gould, 1994). Taken together, they contribute to the presentation of the entity "nature as an ecosystem," with vast utility for the progress of human society. By contrast, the humanitarian model provides moral and aesthetic benefits to humanity, but nothing so all-important as life support. Accordingly, the scientific model of nature protection enjoyed selection advantages in the rising world culture, and thus became increasingly dominant.

The general idea, then, is that changes in the wider world culture selected out one model of nature protection over another. As the dominant global culture came to emphasize universal equality and rationalized progress as basic goals and measuring sticks, the scientific version of nature protection grew in influence.

CHANGES IN THE WORLD ORGANIZATION

Changes in the world culture—in the meaning system, that is—are just the first stage in global institutionalization, and thus in distinguishing the respective fates of the ecosystem and humanitarian candidate. Changes in world polity—that is, in the organizational system—must follow if candidate institutions are to take root. And on the universalized and rationalized foundations laid by scientists, this is exactly what happened around the scientific model of nature protection. Over the twentieth century an enormous wave of international organization occurred (see Meyer, Frank, Hironaka, Schofer, and Tuma, 1997).

The overall organizational upswell followed from a cultural imperative. If nature was an entity with global (and even universal) dimensions, and if nature was useful even to the point of providing the basic stuff of human life, then world-level social organization aimed at regulating and protecting the human-nature relationship was essential. Anything less would be irresponsible (or ignorant or foolish, as social-movement activists claimed), at least in the modern world, where humans are vested with control over their own fates. The same could not be said for global institutionalization of nature protection based on the humanitarian logic, because it emerged from the first stage of global institutionalization only weakly universalized and rationalized, the humanitarian model had little capacity to generate international organization in this second stage (see Frank, 1997).

As it got stitched into the societal action system, the general mission of nature protection became operationalized in highly specific, recipe-like ways. Species protection came to mean parks, waste reduction came to mean recycling, and overpopulation came to mean contraception. In some cases, the relationship of the "solution" to the "problem" was tenuous: many kinds of recycling, for example, produce at least as much waste as they save. But the recipes became fixed, in organizational aims, treaty provisions, and other ways, and their effectiveness remained mostly unexamined. Thus arose an ever-growing (rarely shrinking) laundry list of nature-protection action plans.

These plans nearly always place responsibility for action in the hands of nation-states. This is logical. Even in a world of transnational corporations, intergovernmental organizations, and international associations, nation-states remain the lead actors on the global stage. This does not mean that nation-states alone make things happen. But it does mean that when other entities make things happen, they do so at the pleasure of nation-states. It remains legitimate, in other words, for nation-states to curtail the activities of the other entities (and many do so), but the reverse is not true: A nation-state legitimately may place limits on a transnational corporation, for example, but not vice versa. Thus when it comes to ecosystem protection, nearly all global action plans focus first on the specification of the proper conduct, the correct organization, and the right regulatory structure *of nation-states.*

All this implies a typical sequence of shifts in the world polity (Meyer, Frank, Hironaka, Schofer, and Tuma, 1997). The first distillation of world-cultural changes comes in the form of international nongovernmental organizations (Boli and Thomas, 1999). These are almost coterminous with world-cultural changes: they represent associations of professionals, experts, and other agents of the collective good. And by the argument presented here, their distillation from the world culture almost must be first among the world-polity changes. The disinterestedness and universalism of posture that characterize agents of the collective good are key to the success of candidate global institutions. Too early an association with particular national or other interests limits a candidate's generalizability.

As their main agenda, associations of generalized others seek to script the actions of nation-states, and to do so fairly and equally. Thus a buildup of international nongovernmental organizations leads to a proliferation of intergovernmental transactions—usually first in the form of conferences and then later in conventions, agreements, and treaties (Frank, 1999). Typically, the various intergovernmental transactions seek to specify general standards of conduct, to be observed by all nation-states alike (Haas and Sundgren, 1993). Their virtue—that which deepens the roots of incipient institutions—is their uniformity: they promote global institutions by concretizing expectation schemes for the whole population of nation-states.

In turn, the various intergovernmental transactions spur the formation of more permanent intergovernmental organizations. Almost by definition, these organizations are direct outcomes of international conventions, agreements, or treaties. In one sense, most intergovernmental organizations are powerless: rarely can they force nation-states to do much. But informally, through social more than political-legal mechanisms, intergovernmental organizations exert the deepest sort of power. By establishing the parameters of reality—the entities that exist, their characteristics and relationships—the formal international sector constitutes the basic possibilities for action.

The logic of this sequence, from international nongovernmental organizations to intergovernmental transactions to intergovernmental organizations, corresponds to shifts from the cognitive to the normative and then to the active. The cognitive—the reality established by generalized others—suggests the normative—that which should be done based on that which is. And the normative in turn promotes the active—that which can be done as a subset of that which should be.

Because the creation model had weak cognitive foundations—it was too attached to particular religious beliefs, themselves too deeply associated with European culture to serve as a global-institutional springboard—the changes that followed in the world polity were also weak. Some international nongovernmental organizations did arise, such as the previously mentioned International Union and People's League Against Vivisection and the International Friends of Nature. And a few conferences and treaties followed, including the 1900 Convention for the Preservation of Wild Animals, Birds, and Fish in Africa and the 1979 European Convention for the Protection of Animals from Slaughter. But very little permanent intergovernmental organizing occurred, and all the polity changes remained largely confined to Europe. The humanitarian candidate for global institutionalization failed, in other words, to generate much in the way of world-polity change, and thus it faltered on the road to global institutionalization.

By contrast, the ecosystem model, as I have shown, was much more consistent with values of rationalization and universalization, and thus much better positioned to promote and sustain world-polity changes. Many prominent international nongovernmental organizations arose around the ecosystem model, including the International Union for the Conservation of Nature in 1948, which later joined forces with the World Wildlife Fund formed in 1971. These organizations promoted an enormous rise in intergovernmental transactions: from informal exchanges of diplomatic notes to more formal conferences and agreements. The best known of these are undoubtedly the United Nations Conference on the Human Environment, held in Stockholm in 1972, and the United Nations Conference on Environment and Development, held in Rio de Janeiro in 1992. And then appeared the enduring intergovernmental organizations, epitomized by the United Nations Environment Programme, formed in 1972 to oversee and coordinate the range of human interactions with the natural environment worldwide.

The general idea here is that global institutionalization involves transformations first in the world culture and next in the world polity. Together these changes set the stage for the final step in global institutionalization—the reconstitution of national polities.

CHANGES IN NATIONAL POLITIES

The last fork to separate the scientific from humanitarian candidates for global institutionalization comes at the level of nation-states. Given successful world-cultural changes, in which candidate institutions become rationalized and universalized, and given successful world-polity changes, in which candidate institutions were written into the expectation schemes of official intergovernmental organizations, nation-states open up to the possibility of deep constitutional transformation. Such changes did not occur around the humanitarian model of the human-nature relationship; only a few national polities accommodated it. By contrast, national polity changes around the ecosystem model occurred in spades (Frank, Hironaka, and Schofer, 2000a). This is true in good measure because science and scientists, much more than humanitarians and humanitarianism, are housed in a worldwide organizational system—universities and schools (Ramirez and Boli, 1987). This allows scientific claims with regards to nature to find harbor in local organizational structures with exceptional rapidity.

In the first place, national-polity changes involve the implementation of laws and policies. The international sector is focused on the nation-state as the lead global actor, and thus it produces models defining what a legitimate nation-state is and does. This definitional work is done with the direct participation of nation-states (represented on intergovernmental bodies), and thus nation-states are often quick to take on the expected characteristics. Doing so may mean passing new regulations, appropriating new funds, accepting new goals, or simply confirming existing policy.

Of course, not all nation-states change equally deeply or rapidly. Those that are more embedded in the world polity generally will be faster to the line than others (Frank and others, 2000a). This is true both because the more embedded nation-states are more likely to have supplied or influenced the shape of candidate institutions in the first place, and also because the more embedded nation-states are most thoroughly linked to the conduits that transmit rationales for the benefits of reformation. Once the most embedded nation-states enact a new model, others are usually quick to follow.

In the case of the humanitarian, creation-based models of nature protection, only a few state policies and laws came into being, and these did so mostly in Europe. The world cultural and political structure was too weak to support more. The various anticruelty statutes passed in the late nineteenth century are perhaps the most prominent of these national polity changes: they embodied the notion that humans have a moral obligation to be kind to all God's creatures. By contrast, ecosystem-based candidate models of nature protection engendered a very wide variety of policies and laws, spread very broadly around the world. Its world cultural and political structure was very strong, resulting in a great deal of isomorphism and much explicit standardization (see Mendel, Chapter 18). Provisions to protect plant and animal biodiversity and to promote clean air and water are just a few of the polity changes that have occurred in virtually every nation-state on earth (see, for example, Hironaka and Schofer, Chapter 9).

National parks provide an interesting case in point. Originally established around the humanitarian rationale, parks were intended to preserve the awesome evidence of God's handiwork in nature. Yosemite was protected not as a biodiversity hotspot—it is not—but rather because it has breathtaking scenery. In this guise, national parks arose in many European countries and colonies, but the innovation spread little further. It was not until much later, when the concept of the national park was reconstituted around the ecosystem rationale, with an emphasis on the protection of habitats and species, that parks diffused worldwide. Only in the latter form did parks have the necessary world-cultural and world-political leverage to promote general national-polity changes.

On the heels of state laws and policies come changes in society itself, both in the form of social movements and in the form of individual beliefs and values. This imagery of downward penetration is somewhat contrary to many orthodox sociological depictions, and it may not well describe the workings of a powerful liberal polity such as that of the United States. But on reflection and as a general matter, it is clear that many societal changes, both in social movements and in individual beliefs and values, are composed of global materials (Frank, Hironaka, and Schofer, 2000b). How might a person in rural Brazil come to believe that "ozone depletion" is a significant and serious problem (see Dunlap, 1994)? Only through an elaborate process of education and inculcation, based in the global scientific imageries. How might impoverished Sumatran villagers come to organize social protests against the clearcut policies of a repressive state and powerful transnational corporations (Kamieniecki, 1993)? Only with the elaborate sponsorship of externally legitimated parties. This is not to say that once in place, individuals and social movements do not themselves propel change in national polities: certainly they do. It is merely to say that in relation to global institutions, the catalysts for the formation of social movements and the seeds for the transformation of individual beliefs and values come mostly from the world culture and polity.

Because the humanitarian model faltered on each of the earlier steps toward global institutionalization, it also faltered in inspiring societal changes. In only a few countries did social movement organizations arise around moral aspects of the human-nature relationship, and in only a few countries are individuals characterized by related beliefs and values. (The "hike," for example, in which humans seek the restorative tonic of nature, is surprisingly unknown as a recreational activity outside the Western countries.) On the other hand, a welter of social-movement organizations arose around the ecosystem candidate of the human-nature relationship: the United Nations Environment Programme maintains relations with 10,000 such organizations worldwide. And individual beliefs and values on ecosystem questions are much too uniformly supportive, even across widely disparate countries, to imagine anything other than a global process putting them in place (see Dunlap, 1994).

In sum, in the wake of world-cultural and -polity changes, national polities also changed, first at the level of state laws and policies and then at the level of social movements and individual beliefs and values. Once these final pieces were set in place, the process of institutionalizing "global environmentalism" was complete.

CONCLUSION

The story remains unfinished in one very important sense. It does not say whether all the world-cultural, world-political, and national-political changes actually make any difference. Do global institutions matter?

In one very important sense, they do. They establish parameters of legitimacy within which organizations and policies—at the global, national, and local levels—arise and operate. For example, once there is an international treaty calling attention to transboundary air pollution, efforts to mitigate such pollution, whether it is between the United States and Canada or between Long Island and Albany, are much easier to promote. By the same token, aspects of "nature protection" that do not have the cover of global institutionalization are often vulnerable to attack. The fact that animal rights, for example, are *not* included on the global-institutional agenda means that animal rights are often considered illegitimate.

But there is another sense in which the question—do global institutions matter?—is more typically asked, and that is in regard to environmental quality. In the case at hand, global institutions would matter if the natural environment is better off than it would be absent the global institution. Although it is exceedingly difficult to gather systematic data on this issue—too many variables affect the quality of the natural environment—one thing seems clear. Even weak, poorly implemented institutions for the protection of nature are likely to be better than no institutions. An intergovernmental body that is able to spur just one of its members to establish a fisheries-management policy is better than no intergovernmental body at all. A clean-water law, if implemented only 10 percent of the time, is better than no clean-water law. And an individual belief in the relationship between electricity usage and global warming, even if the belief causes just one light per week to be turned off, is better than no such belief. Global institutions are almost certainly not effective *enough,* but neither are they likely to be totally ineffective.

The origins of global institutions lie clearly in world culture. When the agents of the collective good—the generalized others who serve as the high priests of the world culture—are able to universalize and rationalize raw materials, the process of global institutionalization is set in motion.

NOTES

1. Although scientific nature-protection organizations are absent from the *Handbook* at this time, scientific nature-*study* organizations are not. Several, such as the International Entomological Society, appear.

2. Evidence from international environmental treaties shows the same pattern. See Frank, 1997.

3. The word "stage" too strongly implies a time sequence; the alternative "dimension" implies none at all. I prefer "stage," but with the caveat that the implied time sequencing is neither inevitable nor unidirectional.

REFERENCES

Boli, John, and George M. Thomas, eds. 1999. *Constructing World Culture: International Nongovernmental Organizations Since 1875.* Stanford, CA: Stanford University Press.

Brouwer, G. A. 1938. *The Organisation of Nature Protection in the Various Countries.* Cambridge, MA: American Committee for International Wild Life Protection.

Dunlap, Riley E. 1994. "International Attitudes Towards Environment and Development." In Helge Ole Bergesen and Georg Parmann, eds., *Green Globe Yearbook,* 115–26. Oxford: Oxford University Press.

Ehrlich, Paul, and Ann Ehrlich. 1983. *Extinction: The Causes and Consequences of the Disappearance of Species.* New York: Ballantine.

Engels, Frederick. 1978. "Working-Class Manchester." In Robert C. Tucker, ed., *The Marx-Engels Reader,* 579–585. New York: Norton.

Frank, David John. 1997. "Science, Nature, and the Globalization of the Environment, 1870–1990." *Social Forces,* 76: 409–435.

Frank, David John. 1999. "The Social Bases of Environmental Treaty Ratification, 1900–1990." *Sociological Inquiry,* 69 (Fall): 523–550.

Frank, David John, Ann Hironaka, and Evan Schofer. 2000a. "The Nation-State and the Natural Environment over the Twentieth Century." *American Sociological Review,* 65: 96–116.

Frank, David John, Ann Hironaka, and Evan Schofer. 2000b. "Environmentalism as a Global Institution" (response). *American Sociological Review* 65 (Feb.): 122–127.

Haas, Peter M., and Jan Sundgren. 1993. "Evolving International Environmental Law: Changing Practices of National Sovereignty." In Nazli Choucri, ed., *Global Accord: Environmental Challenges and International Responses,* 401–429. Cambridge, MA: MIT Press.

Hornaday, William T. 1913. *Our Vanishing Wild Life: Its Extermination and Preservation.* New York: New York Zoological Society.

Jasper, James M., and Dorothy Nelkin. 1992. *The Animal Rights Crusade: The Growth of a Moral Protest.* New York: The Free Press.

Kamieniecki, S., ed. 1993. *Environmental Politics in the International Arena.* Albany: State University of New York.

Meyer, John W. 1994. "Rationalized Environments." In W. R. Scott and John W. Meyer, eds., *Institutional Environments and Organizations,* 28–54. Newbury Park, CA: Sage.

Meyer, John W., John Boli, and George M. Thomas. 1987. "Ontology and Rationalization in the Western Cultural Account." In George M. Thomas, John W. Meyer, Francisco O. Ramirez, and John Boli, eds., *Institutional Structure: Constituting State, Society, and the Individual,* 12–38. Newbury Park, CA: Sage.

Meyer, John W., John Boli, George M. Thomas, and Francisco O. Ramirez. 1997. "World Society and the Nation-State." *American Journal of Sociology,* 103: 144–181.

Meyer, John W., David John Frank, Ann Hironaka, Evan Schofer, and Nancy Brandon Tuma. 1997. "The Structuring of a World Environmental Regime, 1870–1990." *International Organization,* 51: 623–651.

Pepper, David. 1984. *The Roots of Modern Environmentalism.* London: Croom Helm.

Ramirez, Francisco O., and John Boli. 1987. "The Political Construction of Mass Schooling: European Origins and Worldwide Institutionalization." *Sociology of Education,* 60: 2–17.

Schnaiberg, Allan, and Kenneth Alan Gould. 1994. *Environment and Society: The Enduring Conflict.* New York: St. Martin's.

Thomas, Keith Vivian. 1983. *Man and the Natural World.* New York: Pantheon.

Wapner, Paul. 1996. *Environmental Activism and World Civic Politics.* Albany: State University of New York Press.

Weiss, Janet A. 1999. "Theoretical Foundations of Policy Intervention." In H. George Frederickson and Jocelyn M. Johnston, eds., *Public Management Reform and Innovation: Research, Theory, and Application* 37–69. Tuscaloosa: University of Alabama Press.

3

COMPLICATIONS IN COMPLIANCE:

VARIATION IN ENVIRONMENTAL

ENFORCEMENT IN BRITISH COLUMBIA'S

LOWER FRASER BASIN, 1985-1996

P. Devereaux Jennings, Paul A. Zandbergen,
and Martin L. Martens

Social and ecological systems must be more tightly coupled if the health of the biosphere is to be improved. So goes the argument of several well-known ecological thinkers and activist organizations (Laszlo and others, 1977; Daly and Cobb, 1994; Gladwin, 1992; Meadows, 1992; Suzuki, 1997). Broadly speaking, this normative position also has theoretical and empirical support from organization theory, particularly from the institutional perspective (Friedland and Alford, 1991; Jepperson, 1991; Meyer and Scott, 1983). But recent new institutional research also suggests that compliance with state directives and coercive pressure is more complicated than the general theories about organizations and institutions might predict. First, at the level of the nation-state, countries may not have equally strong policy regimes and regulatory mechanisms (Dobbin, 1994; Meyer and Scott, 1983; North, 1990; North and Thomas, 1973). Second, within a state, the regulatory domain governing the environment may not be well-developed or as affected by state strength as are other domains, making coercive pressures weaker (Burstein, 1990; Dobbin and Sutton, 1998; Laumann and Knoke, 1987). Third, within a regulatory system, the legal system or profession may influence the enforcement of laws and standards, creating a mediating effect of compliance (Abbott, 1988; Dobbin, 1994; Suchman and Edelman, 1996). Fourth, the compo-

This research was carried out under the SSHRC's Program for Eco-Research, from 1994 through 1998. We would like to thank the members of the University of British Columbia's Eco-Research Group, anonymous reviewers at the *Academy of Management Journal*, and participants in the Organizations, Policy, and Natural Environment (OPNE) Conference for their earlier comments and ideas that have been incorporated in this chapter. Special thanks go to Emese Kiss for her help in the last phase of data collection.

nents in the regulatory system and its subsystems are likely to be loosely coupled, making systems-level outcomes unpredictable (Hironaka and Schofer, Chapter 9; March and Olsen, 1976; March, 1989; Thompson, 1967). Finally, a policy domain or regulatory system may be subject to different political regimes or modes of understanding over time (such as cognitive, regulative, and normative modes), and these modes may be somewhat independent of modes in operation elsewhere in the regulatory system or state (Hoffman, 1997; 1999; Hoffman and Ventresca, 1999; Powell and DiMaggio, 1991; Scott, 1995).

One important complication that has not been elaborated upon much in new institutional research into regulatory systems is the role of *enforcement* in compliance, especially as it relates to environmental compliance outside the United States. To our knowledge, only Edelman, Pettersen, Chambliss, and Erlanger (1991) have begun to look at this issue. They examine the different roles human resources (HR) officers take in four organizational case studies of HR practices involving EEO/AA legislation. No one, to our knowledge, has examined how environmental enforcement fits into the regulatory domain. This chapter examines this question by examining variations in environmental enforcement in British Columbia's Lower Fraser Basin (LFB), a region in a well-developed, non-U.S. state—Canada (Lipset, 1960; Inkeles and Smith, 1974; Meyer, 1983). To document variations in enforcement, we focus on rates of environmental charges for noncompliance with water-related legislation from 1985 through 1996, a time following the establishment of most of the important water-related laws and the local regulatory machinery. We use piecewise exponential rate models (Blossfeld and Rohwer, 1995; Tuma and Hannan, 1984) of an organization's risk of being charged in a given year to demonstrate the effects of political changes, spatial differences across three enforcement districts, and a few important organizational characteristics that are associated with noncompliance.

THE NEW INSTITUTIONAL PERSPECTIVE ON REGULATORY SYSTEMS AND ENFORCEMENT

Formally speaking, "compliance" refers to a regulated actor following the explicit and implicit laws, rules, and standards in a regulatory system (Environment Canada, 1998; Wilson, 1989). Compliance is shaped by the regulatory framework or system against which it may be evaluated. That system can include guiding policies, bureaucrats who help develop and interpret policies, and routines and actors who apply them to regulated actors (Downs, 1967; Krasner, 1983; North, 1990;

Wilson, 1989). The system has multiple levels, from the policy level down to a technical issues level and to actors most involved in operationals level; in this the system consists primarily of the field of regulated actors. Compliance occurs when the policy and rules are followed by the regulated organizations in an acceptable manner, as determined by bureaucrats and based on information received from operational agents.

A key space or domain for compliance within this regulatory system exists at the intersection of the system and the regulated field—the *domain of enforcement*. This domain includes the agents who monitor the regulated entities, detect noncompliance, and apply sanctions, and it includes everything and everyone formally in the purview of the regulatory system. If monitored activities are within the standards of the regulatory system, then the regulated field is compliant and its activities are legitimate. But if they are outside the standards, then their activities are noncompliant, the actors involved are deemed illegitimate, and the field's legitimacy as a whole is threatened. The daily struggle of the regulatory system is to minimize noncompliance, whereas the struggle of the field is to maximize freedom for its activities without losing legitimacy. This interplay creates a dynamic around enforcement that makes compliance somewhat problematic.

In older institutional theory, the key factor for understanding this dynamic was the existence of credible threat or application of formal sanctions (North, 1990; Williamson, 1985). That implied an analytical focus on the power of enforcing agencies and their actual sanctions. But at a deeper level, such threats and sanctions depend on having a state in which the regulatory system has embedded, legitimately, the sanctions and threats and that controls the means of power. That is, sanctions depend on state militaries, paramilitaries, and police. Legitimacy combined with force creates "coercive pressure" (DiMaggio and Powell, 1983).

Once a regulatory system creates standards or rules with the state's approval, coercive pressure will guarantee compliance by a field within low but acceptable limits. If you define compliance as consisting of zero actions being found as out of noncompliance (and hence sanctioned), you would expect that following the passage of a new law or standard, the number of sanctions applied would rise to match the field's rate of noncompliance but that as time passed both would drop dramatically in tandem. The picture would be of a geometrically decreasing rate of noncompliance and sanctions.

However, a number of new institutionalists (Friedland and Alford, 1991; Hoffman and Ventresca, 1999; Meyer and others, 1994) have argued that the older institutional view of the regulatory system fails to include underlying interest groups and political cultures that might strongly influence enforcement. Research and theory have shown that the political culture of the regulatory system shapes the creation and interpretation of regulatory policy over time (Edelman, 1992; Dobbin, 1994; Frank, 1997). Sets of understandings and interpretations of issues are likely to develop around interests and past activities. A consistent pattern of understanding and application of policy creates a "regime." In the case of enforcement, some regimes are more flexible in their interpretation and application than others, with implications for the enforcement domain. Political cultures that are more liberal, and technical bureaucrats who feel negotiation is better than direct orders in enforcement, will have different effects on enforcement than will conservatives and bureaucrats believing in aggressive enforcement. Having one form of regime versus another changes what is considered an acceptable level of compliance with rules.

Furthermore, new institutionalists have documented the heterogeneity of organizational activities in fields and change in the compositions of these activities over time (Cliff, 2000; Strang and Meyer, 1994). Both such heterogeneity and change over time have effects on the types of structures that arise and the legitimacy of activities in the field (Fligstein, 1991; Greenwood, Suddaby, and Hinings, 2001). By implication, a change in the demographic makeup of a field, and the spatial heterogeneity of an organizational field, should affect monitoring and sanctioning of field member activities.

The combined effects of changes in the regulatory system and changes in the activities of the organizational field may encourage swings in enforcement rates. For instance, rates of noncompliance and enforcement may not always follow a geometrically decreasing curve, but sometimes a sine wave pattern—a cyclical pattern of increasing and decreasing as enforcement regimes in a larger regulatory system change (Lawrence, Winn, and Jennings, 2001).

Environmental Enforcement as a Domain

The environmental domain is one arena in which cyclical patterns of enforcement are particularly likely. Like other enforcement domains, the natural environment is an area in most developed states and has a formal regulatory system in charge of policy creation and interpretation and application (Frank, 1997; Laumann and Knoke, 1987). In addition, most nation-states tend to incorporate the machinery for regulation into a few closely related organizations that are in charge of a wide variety of environmental laws. Similarly to police forces, environmental agencies tend to have enforcement branches with conservation officers (COs) who enforce these laws, at times drawing on local police.

In addition, and in contrast to some other enforcement domains, the environmental domain often requires active negotiation by actors in the regulatory system and organizational field as to the boundaries and indicators of each (Hironaka and Shofer, Chapter 9; Jennings, Zandbergen, and Clark, 1999). Furthermore, because environmental enforcement involves both social and ecological components, these two dimensions often delimit enforcement (Jennings and Zandbergen, 1995). For instance, an enforcement subdomain may be defined in relation to a regional ecosystem that is naturally bounded by mountains and rivers and with social and political boundaries that roughly match the natural ones. Or it may be built around a type of community that has become somewhat sustainable in a particular locale (King, 1995). Enforcement in the regions is determined jointly by the needs of the local ecosystem for sustainability, part of which can be documented by ecologists, and by the demands of the social system for efficient regulation. In many local domains, conservation officers do not act as police officers or as military personnel, but as conservation biologists and stewards who negotiate local standards.

ONE CASE OF ENVIRONMENT ENFORCEMENT
WATER REGULATION IN THE LOWER FRASER
BASIN OF BRITISH COLUMBIA

To detail our argument about enforcement as a domain and how sanctions work over time within it, we examine environmental enforcement in one case: that of water regulation in the Lower Fraser Basin (LFB) in British Columbia, one of Canada's eight provinces. Figure 3.1 shows the local enforcement domain of the LFB. The LFB constitutes the lower one-third of British Columbia; it is geographically bounded but still diverse, and it contains the majority of organizations in the province (80,000 or so). The British Columbia Ministry of Environment, Lands, and Parks (BCMOELP) divides up the province into different enforcement "regions," each of which is a different "district" for enforcement.

Four acts make up the bulk of water regulation and law that influence this domain: the Water Act (WA), the Fisheries Act (FA), the Waste Management Act (WMA), and the Pesticides Control Act (PCA). The two federal acts, the FA and WA, are the oldest, but were substantially modified in the 1970s. In the early 1980s, the WMA was created by the Province, along with a new set of agencies and enforcement principles for water management. The PCA was added in 1988, partly as an elaboration of key elements of the WMA for the agricultural sector. Therefore, the water-related laws and the regulatory machinery for them have remained

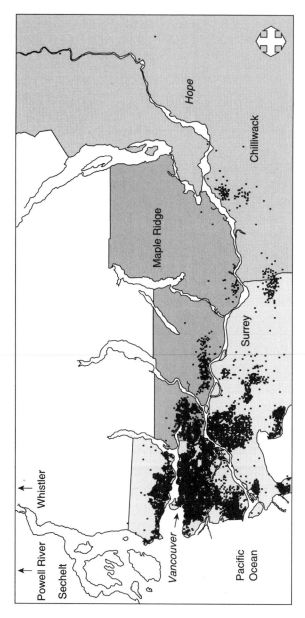

Figure 3.1 Enforcement Districts and Presence of Organizations in the Lower Fraser Basin

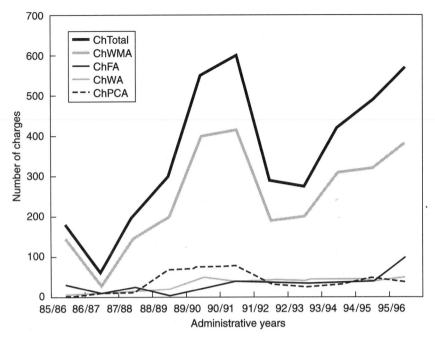

Figure 3.2   Selected Environmental Charges in British Columbia, 1985–1996

Note: Ch = number of legal charges brought against companies under four acts, WMA = Waste Management Act; FA = Fisheries Act; WA = Water Act; PCA = Pesticides Control Act.

relatively constant (compared to laws for forest practices, wildlife, or air quality) from 1983 through 1996, the period under consideration.

Figure 3.2 shows the variations in the charges against LFB companies under water-related acts from 1985 through 1996. The total number of charges accelerates, then drops, then accelerates, then levels—creating almost two full oscillating cycles of charges. The first oscillation lasts from 1985 to 1991, and the second from at least 1991 to 1996. Two changes in two other indicators of enforcement, the number of hours spent enforcing all environmental acts and the strongest of the Acts that existed throughout the same time period (the WMA), roughly parallel the pattern for total charges. Although the LFB was growing during this time period, suggesting that the number of charges might increase in parallel, the rate of growth in the agency does not match the rate of growth in charges, the latter being much steeper. In addition, the charge rate oscillates, which is not explained just by the number of regulated actors in the system or by growth in the system itself. What, then, explains these variations in charges?

EXPLAINING VARIATIONS IN
ENVIRONMENTAL ENFORCEMENT

Changing Policy and Enforcement Regimes

Changes in enforcement regimes should affect changes in enforcement rates. An enforcement regime is the result of the interaction between the policy approach and the monitoring and control exercised by the regulators in a domain. A strong enforcement regime for environmental issues is one in which the policy approach is liberal (pro-environmental) and monitoring and control are quite active. A moderately strong regime is one in which the policy is more conservative, but the monitoring and control are active. A somewhat weaker regime is one in which the policy regime is more liberal, but monitoring and control are passive. And the weakest regime is one in which policy is conservative (not environmental) and the monitoring and control are passive.

For instance, in the United States a moderately strong enforcement regime prevailed in the early 1970s under a conservative government but with the new EPA in place; but that regime was considerably weaker in the mid-1980s under a conservative government that was busy trying to dismantle key pieces of enforcement machinery in the EPA and putting discretionary monies into sinkholes such as the Superfund. As evidence, a geometric increase in lawsuits occurred from 1970 to 1978, followed by a slight dip, then a rise, then a drop again in the mid-1980s (Hoffman, 1997: 88–91).

In Canada, the enforcement regimes for water regulation are more local in nature. Even though Canada is a well-developed nation-state (Lipset, 1960; Inkeles and Smith, 1974; Meyer, 1983), Canada's Environmental Protection Act (CEPA) is much weaker than the U.S. National Environmental Protection Act (NEPA) and similar legislation in other countries. CEPA was passed in 1989 to supplement and coordinate existing legislation (Dorsey, 1991b; Rankin, 1991; Thompson, McConnell, and Huestis, 1993). But in fact it gave the provinces and provincial laws more influence over water regulation and enforcement (Dorsey and Ruggeberg, 1989; Rankin and Finkle, 1983), which makes focusing on provincial level variations in enforcement critical.

The Effects of Regimes in B.C.

In British Columbia in the 1980s, a conservative (Tory) government was in control. Its formal opposition party, the NDP (National Democratic Party), was explicitly associated in the press and in political campaigns with unionism and environmentalism (Dyck, 1995). And starting in the mid-1980s, federal and provincial regulators were increasingly active in their approaches to environmental issues (Dorsey, 1991a; Huestis, 1993; Jennings and Zandbergen, 1995). Joint provincial-federal programs were developed in 1985 to handle noncompliance and pollution problems in a number of industries. These multistage programs had an enormous effect for several years, one documented by a three-case study of industries in British Columbia (Krahn, 1998). In 1987 and 1988, the fourth stage of the antisapstain and the pulp and paper program began, one that involved the imposition of charges, fines, and possibilities of business closures, causing firms to begin to comply (Krahn, 1998: 19). This period corresponds to the first wave of increased enforcement of environmental laws shown in Figure 3.2.

But this aggressive enforcement effort eventually ran afoul of the conservative government: in mid-1990 the conservatives vetoed legislation strengthening water-related measures, putting a brake on some of the administrative fervor for cleaning up industries and waterways (Dyck, 1995). At the same time, the head of this party, Bill Vander Zalm, was under pressure to resign due to improprieties, and a new election was on the horizon within a year. The decreased period of enforcement activity shown in Figure 3.2 corresponds to this time period.

In the fall of 1991 there was an election, and a new, more liberal government took power at the provincial level and immediately signaled its willingness to increase enforcement activities and to demand more than voluntary compliance. This new government wanted to distance itself from the former conservative party that had ruled the province for most of the two previous decades, and it wanted to address a local and international perception that the province lacked state-of-the art environmental technology and standards. The focus of the new government was on forest-related matters: it developed the Forest Practice Code legislation that was eventually passed in 1995. In the area of water quality and pollution, its plan was to extend the funding of programs like FBMP and FREMP out more years and to modestly increase the number of conservation officers in the LFB districts (BCMOELP 1997; BCMOELP 1999).

However, in 1994 the leader of the new party and the Forest Practice Code initiative, Premier Mike Harcourt, like Vander Zalm before him, had to resign due to some improprieties in his party. He was replaced in the next year by a premier who was more concerned about jobs for union members and who portrayed environmental regulation as a constraint on the industries that employed them. Ironically, during the time when the liberal government was in power in the province and concerned with the environment, the federal government and the Canadian people became less interested in social programs and initiatives like the environment (Blake, 1996). Instead, the attention was on balancing jobs and environmental conservation and reducing the federal deficit. The legal policy instruments encouraged in the 1980s were still being used, but the administration of the laws and the pursuit of enforcement by the federal groups became less aggressive, partly because departments like DFO were cut back and reorganized a number of times during this period. The outcome was a more passive stance toward enforcement in the 1994–96 period, but under the aegis of a liberal regime (Dyck, 1995).

To summarize and simplify this complex historical picture about policy and enforcement regimes, one might say that the earliest period under study was defined by a conservative policy, starting with passive but ending with increasingly active enforcement. The second period was characterized by conservative policy administered by an embattled government yet with aggressive enforcement, but near election time enforcement activities dropped dramatically. The third period, beginning just after the election, is defined by a liberal policy with increasingly active enforcement—but in selected environmental areas. And the fourth period is one of liberal policy with somewhat passive enforcement. In other words:

> *Hypothesis 1: Due to changes in policy regimes, the rates of enforcement were highest in Period 3 (1991–1994), then Period 2 (1988–1991), followed by Period 4 (1994–1996), and lowest in Period 1 (1985–1988).*

Spatial Differences and Heterogeneity of Organizational Activities in the Field

Policy and its enforcement should vary across social and political boundaries within domains. Strang and Meyer (1994) demonstrated in their study of school districts that the history and demographics of districts may make them more likely to adopt or resist new practices (also see Baron, Mittman, and Newman, 1991). In the case of the environment, initiatives are pursued within defined administrative and ecosystem boundaries. Highly urbanized districts face different problems than do less urbanized districts. For instance, the former have a much denser set of organizations to monitor, and a much higher likelihood of non-point pollution because of runoff from paved areas. The types of remediation that can be done in an urban area are also quite different from the rural area. It is difficult to turn the city back into countryside (Zandbergen, 1999).

Within the regional ecosystem defined by the LFB, there is one highly urban, enforcement district (Surrey), one suburban district (Maple Ridge), and one rural district (Chilliwack). Variation exists across districts in terms of their budgets, officers, and the profile of the organizations being monitored. In 1995, the Surrey district contained over 65,000 organizations of all sizes, many involved in service businesses; the Maple Ridge district had just over 10,000, with a mix of industries;

and the Chilliwack district had the remaining 6,000 or so firms, many directly or indirectly involved in agriculture (Jennings, Zandbergen, and Clark, 1999). Along with the administrative office, monitoring groups, and local volunteers, the Surrey district has had an average of six conservation officers; the Maple Ridge, four; and Chilliwack, two full-time and one part-time officers. Based on these rates of resource allocation, we might expect the most rural district, Chilliwack, to have the highest enforcement rates per organization.

But there is a deeper policy issue that may shape district enforcement levels. In the 1980s, following the 1970s Fraser River projects and the Waste Management Act's passage, the focus in the LFB was on cleaning up industrial areas affecting waterways (Dorsey, 1976; 1991a). In the mid-1990s, the focus in the LFB appeared to shift somewhat toward agricultural issues, such as runoff and aquifer pollution (Lavkulich, Hall, and Schreier, 1999). These issues are more rural in nature. The suburban district is a mix of urban and rural areas. One might expect that the suburban district would be affected by both tendencies in policy and have its own unique issues around expansion onto agricultural reserves. But one might also argue that it will not be as heavily affected as the other districts given its different mix of organizations. The main contrast is thus between the urban and rural districts:

Hypothesis 2: Rates of enforcement will be higher in the rural than the urban enforcement district.

Rates of enforcement within an enforcement subdomain should also vary with the types of organizations being monitored and controlled. Not only is the sheer number of organizations being monitored (that is, in a district) important, but also the types of activities of these organizations make a difference for their likelihood of being charged. In this case, we are concerned with the actual establishment of an organization in the LFB, for it is the establishment that is monitored and fined by the regulatory agency.

There are two ways of assessing the activities of establishments: one in terms of more observable regulations and resources and activities in the regulatory system (an older institutional view), and one in terms of the less observable activities that help guarantee legitimacy and negotiate understanding in the system (the newer institutional view). The amount of pollution that an establishment produces is a critical consideration in whether it will be charged for an environmental offense. However, as regulators lack direct indicators of pollution intensity, given how much variation there is in types of pollution, systematic monitoring information, and the large number of establishments, the scale of operation can act as a proxy for the amount of pollution activity (Kolluru, 1994; Porter and van der Linde,

1995; Schmidheiny, 1992). In addition, from the older institutional point of view, large establishments that cause a lot of pollution may be more valuable enforcement targets, because they are more visible. Prosecuting them sends observable signals to others in the system that pollution is *not* okay (BCMOELP, 1997; Krahn, 1998).

However, from the new institutional point of view, a large establishment is concerned with legitimacy and being caught polluting can damage the establishment's standing in the local community as well as it legitimacy with regulators (Scott, 1995; Scott, Meyer, and associates, 1994). Large establishments depend more on their standing and legitimacy than do smaller ones, and large establishments know that they are more visible (Meyer and Scott, 1983; Scott, 1995), so they should try harder not to pollute. Hoffman (1997; 1999) suggests that many such establishments are adopting more advanced environmental management systems and the philosophy of strategic environmental management in order to clean up their acts.

On balance, it seems that from within the intersection of the regulatory system and the organizational field, size is more representative of scale of pollution and visibility of signal to the other establishments than of how concerned an establishment will be with not polluting. This is particularly true if other measures about reputation, such as membership in environmental associations, are considered, as they are below. In other words, we expect:

Hypothesis 3: Rates of enforcement will be higher against larger establishments.

Similarly, being an older establishment and/or being a manufacturing establishment should lead to higher rates of enforcement. Age and manufacturing are proxies for older technology and technologies that involve more pollution. Besides being more likely to have older technologies, older establishments are better known to the regulatory institutions and thus monitoring their behavior may be easier. By the same token, establishments in heavy manufacturing, mining, and agriculture are often monitored by the Ministry because they are the sources of many of the substances listed in the water quality standards, such as dioxin, lead, arsenic, and PCPs (Dorsey, 1991a; Hall, Schreier, and Brown, 1991). More permits are also issued in this sector (Dorsey and Ruggeberg, 1989). In fact, studies have shown that older establishments in heavy manufacturing tend to be prosecuted relatively more often for pollution (Brander, 1995; Hoffman, 1997).

Hypothesis 4: Rates of enforcement will be higher against older establishments.

Hypothesis 5: Rates of enforcement will be higher for establishments in primary manufacturing than for those in secondary manufacturing, and lowest for those in nonmanufacturing sectors.

Establishments that are part of multiunit firms may also experience different rates of environmental enforcement than do single-unit firms, even when controlling for size and industrial variation. We operationalize as a multiunit operation, a firm with two or more plants and a headquarters unit. From an institutional theory point of view, the existence of multiple branch plants means that there is less monitoring in each plant and thus a greater chance that operations in one unit might fail, causing pollution, and that this pollution might be detected. New institutional theorists might predict that a branch plant would be less tied to the local community and we expect less concerned with local legitimacy. We expect this to be particularly true when the headquarters unit is outside of the LFB or British Columbia. Research on plant location has documented the higher rates of plant closure and community impact of branch plants (Erickson, 1980). In either case we would expect that:

Hypothesis 6: Rates of enforcement will be higher for branch plants than for locally owned and/or operated establishments.

Headquarters of a multiunit establishment located in the LFB may also experience different rates of environmental enforcement than single-unit, locally owned and operated establishments. From an institutional standpoint, the strategic planning and responsibility for the establishment is located in the headquarters and whenever there is ambiguity about who should be cited for an environmental offense, the top managers will be the default. The law does hold managers and directors of companies liable, lending some support for this view (Dorsey, 1991a). From a new institutional point of view, the headquarters is concerned with the image and legitimacy of the establishment. Headquarters units are likely to take more responsibility, and if there are production operations at the headquarters site, then these operations are more likely to be in compliance than more distant operations. Both viewpoints have merits in terms of how headquarters might be evaluated in the enforcement subdomain. Therefore, we argue that:

Hypothesis 7: Rates of enforcement will be different for headquarters of multiunit firms than for locally owned and/or operated establishments.

A final consideration is that some establishments are allowed through the regulatory vehicle of a "resource use permit" to use more resources and to create more waste than others. The Ministry keeps track of these establishments and they in turn keep track of their resource use and waste generation. From the point of view of the regulator, if an establishment has a permit, it is more likely to be monitored by the agents of the Ministry. On the one hand, this may make the establishment more conscientious and thus less likely to be noncompliant; on the other hand, because more monitoring is occurring, it may mean that the establishment is more likely to be charged. Even if the monitoring rates are low, if an establishment is caught violating its permit, it may be more likely to be charged because it should have been in compliance.

Within the subdomain of enforcement, we think that having a resource use permit simply means that the resource covered by the standards and the legislation of the system is in heavy use and that pollution is more likely—and hence so is a fine. Permits are signals to enforcement officers that establishments need extra attention, thus:

Hypothesis 8: Rates of enforcement will be higher for establishments with resource use permits.

A final, important consideration is whether an organizational employee is a member of a professional environmental association. If so, he or she may respond differently to pressures for compliance than someone who is not. New institutional theory maintains that professional associations act as independent bodies that enhance mimetic and normative forces, and even help block coercive ones (Powell and DiMaggio, 1991; Scott, 1995). Having a representative of the organization as a member in an environmental association may provide it with more expertise to address its environmental problems. It may also increase the normative pressure to conform to professional norms or association standards.

Dobbin and Sutton (1998) and Edelman (1990; 1992) have argued that professional associations may have mediating effects on important institutional outcomes. Their studies of legal professionals in the adoption of HR departments and practices show that having a legal professional may actually substitute for an HR department, depressing the rate of department adoption or practice use. However, employing a member of an environmental association should not have the same impact as having an environmental lawyer on retainer. It does not bring the legal field into action and barely activates the field of environmental specialists on the establishment's behalf. We feel, then, that there will be mostly a main and not mediating effect in this case:

Hypothesis 9: Rates of enforcement will be lower against companies that employ a member or are members of a locally recognized environmental association.

METHODOLOGY FOR ASSESSING ENFORCEMENT VARIATION AND ITS SOURCES

To test our hypotheses, we collected episode data on enforcement, as well as some panel data on government changes, enforcement districts, and organizational characteristics in the LFB. In addition, we interviewed enforcement officials in the Ministry in 1995 and 1999 about enforcement policies and practices during the 1980s and 1990s, and we interviewed other selected members of the organizational field about environmental management during the same years. We analyzed the longitudinal data with event history models and used the interview data as anecdotal material whenever we felt it fit.

Sample

Our sample consists of all firms in the LFB that existed from 1984 to 1996 ($N = 58,172$). We used 1994 data collected by Contact Target Marketing Service on all registered establishment in the LFB's municipalities ($N = 85,443$) and selected only establishments that were at least ten years old for the study. Although the surviving population differs in size from the full population, t-tests on comparable variables showed no major differences. Both samples are characterized by a high number of small organizations, primarily in nonmanufacturing and with private ownership.

Rates of enforcement came from a number of small data sets on enforcement actions per year (about 300 per year) collected by the B.C. Ministry of the Environment. The 1980s data were available in hard copy by administrative year (July 1–June 30) and had to be collected in the provincial capitol, integrated into a larger data set, and matched with the data on existing firms. Charges against individuals were not included in the analysis, only those against companies. In the case of multiunit organizations, we recorded only offenses against the subunit whenever possible. If it was not clear which subunit had been charged, we recorded the charge against the headquarters. Most firms consisted of only one establishment, most multiunit firms had only two or three branches, and few establishments incurred more than one charge in a single year.

Variables

The main dependent variable is being charged or not during an administrative year (Table 3.1). "Charged" refers to legal charges laid by BCMOELP under the Water Act (WA), the federal Fisheries Act (FA), the Waste Management Act (WMA), and the Pesticide Control Act (PCA). These four water-related acts, like a number of other water-related standards and laws, overlap and are often used in conjunction. Hence, we code whether or not a company was charged under any one of them in a given year as a "charge." There are 634 such charges in our eleven-period data set (see Table 3.1).

The periods in the analyses were created based on the historical record, encoded in Hypothesis 1, and on visual examination of Figure 3.2. The first period is from 1985/86 through 1987/88; the second period is from 1988/89 through 1990/91; the third period is from 1991/92 through 1993/94; and the fourth period is from 1994/95 through 1995/96. The first is labeled as "conservative, passive," the second as "conservative, aggressive," the third as "liberal, aggressive," and the fourth as "liberal, passive." Note that the regime labels and the tendencies that they capture do not exactly match the oscillations found in Table 3.1. The figure might lead us to believe that a much more passive enforcement system was at work during the 1991–93 period than the case history of the system actually demonstrates.

The enforcement districts in the analyses are based on Hypothesis 2. We coded districts as urban or suburban, with rural districts as the omitted baseline. The urban district refers to the Surrey enforcement area, which includes Vancouver, Burnaby, Richmond, and Surrey. The suburban district includes Langley, Delta, and parts of Surrey, Maple Ridge, and Coquitlam. The rural district includes Abottsford, Chilliwack, Matsqui, and areas surrounding Hope. The boundaries for these districts did not change substantially in the 1985–96 period, although there was one unit, "Industrial Investigations," associated with the Surrey office and one associated with the Maple Ridge office, and the latter unit was closed in the late 1990s. The data for these units were rolled into the offices in question.

The independent variables for the organizational characteristics are quite similar, with the addition of a few covariates. Size is operationalized as the number of employees at a location. Contact Marketing categorized this data in groups of 1–10, 10–20, 20–50, 50–100, 100–250, 250–500, and 500+ employees. We used the midpoint of the size classes to create an interval level variable. The average size of firms was eleven persons. Industry refers to being in primary, secondary, or tertiary industries, where primary refers to agriculture, mining, and construction, sec-

Table 3.1

Frequencies, Means, Standard Deviations, and Correlations
for Selected Determinants of Environmental Enforcement

Variables	Frequency (Number)	Means (Standard Deviation)	Correlation with Being Charged
Charged vs. not charged	(634) 1%		
Period			
Conservative, passive:			
1985/86–1987/88	(6) 1%		
Conservative, aggressive:			
1988/89–1990/91	(190) 30%		
Liberal, aggressive:			
1991/92–1993/94	(262) 41%		
Liberal, passive:			
1993/94–1995/96	(176) 28%		
Nonrural district			
Urban district	(47,743) 82.1%		−.040**
Suburban district	(6,790) 11.7%		.038***
Organization			
Organizational size		11.23 (39.01)	.088***
Organizational age		21.18 (24.80)	.012***
Primary manufacturing	(9,582) 16.5%		−.004
Secondary manufacturing	(18,538) 31.9%		.077***
Branch plant	(14,345) 24.7%		.118***
Headquarters	(2,621) 4.5%		.012***
Permit	(626) 1%		.392***
Environmental association	(595) 1%		.276***

$N = 58,172$ firms existing in Lower Fraser Basin 1984–96.
$*p \leq .10$ $**p \leq .05$ $***p \leq .01$

ondary to manufacturing and heavy utilities, and tertiary to all other industries—mostly services. Producing in a tertiary industry is the omitted category in all analyses. As expected, the bulk of organizations are in services. The establishment type refers to being a local firm, a branch plant, or a headquarter with branch plants in the LFB and elsewhere. A dummy variable is constructed for the analyses with being a locally owned and operated company as the omitted category. About a third of companies are nonlocal branch plants. Age is the number of years from date of incorporation to 1995. Having a resource use permit refers to having a water permit on file with the Ministry of Environment for at least one year, 1984–96, based on 1999 data of all permits and permit dates provided by the Ministry. Few companies have a water permit (626 in Table 3.1). Being a member of an environmental association refers to being registered in 1999 by one of four known environmental associations that have some representatives in British Columbia: the Canadian Environmental Industry Association-B.C. Chapter (CEIA-BC), the Industrial, Commercial, Institutional Environmental Managers Association (ICIEMA), the Canadian Environmental Certificates Approval Board, and the Canadian Water Resources Association. Data from the last two groups was eventually dropped because they are new associations. Again, the rates here are low ($N = 595$ in Table 3.1).

Methods of Analysis

Dobbin and Sutton (1998) and Edelman (1990; 1992) in their studies of the evolution of HR policy and practices employ event history models to determine whether variation is more strongly associated with time periods, types of states, or time periods. We follow a similar strategy. Like the other authors, we use piecewise, exponential hazard rate models (Allison, 1984; Cox, 1972; Blossfeld and Rohwer, 1995; Tuma and Hannan, 1984) to estimate effects of the determinants on charges. In the piecewise exponential model, the hazard rate is a function of time periods and proportional covariates:

$$r_{(jk)}(t) = \exp[a_1^{(jk)} + A^{(jk)}a^{(jk)}], \text{ if } \tau_1 < \epsilon < \tau_{(l+1)} \qquad (Eq.\ 1)$$

where $r_{(jk)}(t)$ is the transition rate, and for each transition (j,k), $a_1^{(jk)}$ is the constant coefficient associated with the lth time period, $A^{(jk)}$ is the (row) vector of covariates, and $a^{(jk)}$ is an associated vector of coefficients assumed not to vary across the periods (Blossfeld and Rohwer, 1995: 111–117). We also employ exponential models with period-specific effects to capture the impact of constant covariates within each of the four time periods in question. This model is a slightly more general model than the one in Equation 1, where t varies only within each time period and not for all.

Maximum likelihoods are shown in the tables to assess the overall fit of the model, based on -2 x loglikelihood having a chi-squared distribution with N degrees of freedom (N = difference between the prior and the next model). Student t-tests are used to examine the significance of specific coefficients. However, we have selected what amount to the known population of surviving firms from 1985–96, so it might be argued that all the coefficients are significant, even if some have more variation around their estimates than others.

RESULTS

The Effects of Regimes and Enforcement Districts

Table 3.2 shows the exponential models for being charged, with pieces for the time period for enforcement regimes. We step in the regime periods and then district characteristics to test our argument about the existence and operation of this sub-domain. The third column has the full model to see if the subdomain's effects are robust and as direct as we have argued. All three models in Table 3.2 show significant effects for the pattern we expected, providing strong support for Hypothesis 1: enforcement regimes have different effects which, over time, create cyclical variations in enforcement.

More specifically, we argue that the second and third period would exhibit most enforcement activity, followed by the fourth and then the first periods. The results show that the third period has the highest rates (least impact) of being charged, followed by the second and fourth and then by the first period. Period 1 (1985/86–1987/88) is one of policy development under a conservative local government and with a weak enforcement tradition, whereas Period 2 (1988/89–1990/91) is one with focused policy implementation and enforcement, particularly in the pulp and paper industry. Period 3 (1991/92–1993/94) is one of a liberal government with strong policy and increasingly strong enforcement in the last year and a half of the period. Period 4 (1994/95–1995/96) is one of instability. The enforcement rates remained somewhat high but leveled. In part, this is due to a provincial change in government (again!) and to a freeze, then a cut, in resources available to the Ministry.

As we argued in Hypothesis 2, the policy domain of enforcement also appears to have a spatial component. Table 3.2 shows that enforcement varies by district, with lower rates of enforcement occurring in the urban district relative to the omitted baseline, the rural Chilliwack enforcement area. No effect is found for enforcement in the suburban district versus the rural one. The results support the argument that resources for enforcement per regulated organization were quite low in the urban area and the argument that rural issues came to dominate the focus of enforcement in the basin in the 1990s.

Although the piecewise model supports the hypothesized period and spatial effects, analysts may find it hard to accept the claim that these effects are actually indicators of changes in the enforcement subdomain, one driven by a great deal of provincial policy development and implementation. Many researchers would need more evidence. Table 3.3 offers additional supporting evidence in the form

Table 3.2
Piecewise Exponential ML Estimates of the Determinants of Being Charged

Variables	Periods	Periods and Districts	Periods, Districts, Organization
Period			
Conservative, passive:			
1985/86–1987/88	−9.872*** (.408)	−9.491*** (.427)	−11.620*** (.446)
Conservative, aggressive:			
1988/89–1990/91	−6.821*** (.0725)	−6.439*** (.1445)	−8.536*** (.194)
Liberal, aggressive:			
1991/92–1993/94	−6.494*** (.062)	−6.111*** (.140)	−8.150*** (.189)
Liberal, passive:			
1993/94–1995/96	−7.177*** (.075)	−6.794*** (.146)	−8.691*** (.193)
Nonrural district			
Urban district		−.577*** (.140)	−.6631*** (.144)
Suburban district		.312** (.155)	.1925 (.158)
Organization			
Organizational size			.0024*** (.0003)
Organizational age			.0049*** (.0015)
Primary manufacturing			.9838*** (.139)
Secondary manufacturing			1.1223*** (.1094)
Branch plant			1.6966*** (.1097)
Headquarters			1.2245*** (.1849)
Permit			2.7532*** (.1052)
Environmental association			1.4457*** (.1443)
Log-likelihood	−4,953.96***	−4,913.07***	−3,847.978***
Degrees of freedom	(4)	(6)	(14)

Note: All models use 12 periods with 634 events across the periods with the total number of spells of 58,172. The constant in the model is constrained to zero, and the log-likelihood of the constant's model is −5,071.12.

$*p \leq .10$ $**p \leq .05$ $***p \leq .01$

of time period models for being charged (Blossfeld and Rohwer, 1995: 115). If there is a dynamic going on within the enforcement subdomain, then we might also anticipate that the various enforcement regimes will have different influences on the impact of enforcement districts and organizational characteristics. In Table 3.3, we see that being in a particular period does influence the pattern of effects. Being in an urban versus a rural district has the strongest effect in Periods 3 and 4, and being in a suburban district has positive effects in the late 1980s but negative effects in the 1990s. It appears that the urban district was "where the action was" in the 1980s, whereas the rural districts were where the action was in the 1990s. The variation over time is greater for district characteristics than most organizational characteristics. Most organizational characteristics, except age, appear to have a uniformly positive effect on enforcement. We discuss these effects in more detail soon, but the point here is that the elements of enforcement domain do indeed vary over time and have documented effects. This supports the claim that environmental enforcement is a subdomain.

When we interviewed conservation officers in 1995 and in 1997, we found that they were aware of some shifts in focus and some policy changes over the years. The chief conservation officer (CO) for the LFB in the early 1990s noted that there was a large concern with agricultural runoff and with specific farms that could not be named at the time (BCMOELP, 1997). When asked about increases in enforcement, the chief CO agreed that the Ministry had spent a lot of time in the late 1980s and early 1990s investigating pulp and paper and chemical firms. In the words of the CO, "It was a blitz." But neither the older nor newer officer acknowledged changes in the provincial capital, or changes in parties, as having had a direct effect on their enforcement practice. The most they would say was that if someone phoned in from higher in the Ministry with a particular issue, often one hot off the front page of the newspaper, they would probably have to move investigations around to place that issue forward in the queue. Such was the case with wildlife enforcement in 1994–95 (BCMOELP, 1997), and, more recently, with mushroom composting and Burns Bog (BCMOELP, 2000).

The Effects of Heterogeneous Organizational Activities

When considering the regime and district effects explicitly—that is, the context of enforcement—what are the effects of organizational characteristics on being charged for an environmental offence? In Table 3.2, we see that, as predicted by Hypotheses 3–7, being large and old and in manufacturing (primary or secondary), being multiunit (a branch or headquarters), and requiring a resource permit

Table 3.3
Piecewise Exponential ML Estimates of the Determinants of Being Charged by Time Period

Variables	1985/86– 1987/88	1988/89– 1990/91	1991/92– 1993/94	1994/95– 1995/96
Constant	−27.7244	−9.578***	−7.7435***	−8.4752***
	(75.3601)	(.3892)	(.2731)	(.3655)
Urban district	7.9085	−.2503	−.9772***	−.8663***
	(70.4398)	(.2911)	(.2112)	(.2692)
Suburban district	8.4740	.8852***	−.4603**	−.5997**
	(70.3561)	(.2936)	(.2480)	(.3236)
Organizational size	.0048***	.0009	.0040***	.0008
	(.0020)	(.0008)	(.0005)	(.0010)
Organizational age	−.0141***	.0109***	−.0079***	−.0057*
	(.0290)	(.0023)	(.0029)	(.0039)
Primary manufacturing	8.3664	.1628	1.5254***	1.6834***
	(27.0137)	(.2861)	(.2215)	(.3051)
Secondary manufacturing	7.6628	1.0072***	1.4809***	1.5217***
	(27.0165)	(.1796)	(.1751)	(.2744)
Branch plant	−1.6042	2.1842***	1.7652***	.5517***
	(1.1855)	(.2580)	(.1642)	(.2272)
Headquarters	−1.6076***	2.0887***	.7374***	1.0936***
	(1.7448)	(.3449)	(.3209)	(.3222)
Permit	5.3345***	4.1446***	−.1753	3.4616***
	(.1123)	(.1612)	(.2416)	(.2098)
Environmental association	.6562	−11.4195	2.8678***	2.8738***
	(1.3150)	(49.3741)	(.1581)	(.2162)
Log-likelihood (total)	−3,511.954**			
Degrees of freedom	(44)			

*$p \leq .10$ **$p \leq .05$ ***$p \leq .01$

all have a positive effect on the likelihood of being charged from 1985–96. This supports the claims that size, age, industry, configuration, and resource use are visible signals and proxies for actual resources flows when seen from the policy subdomain. These elements tend to be monitored and controlled, even if in other fields they might actually be proxies for legitimacy, especially for firms that have experience with handling pollution, such as those dealing in the environmental management field (Hoffman, 1997; Lex and Jennings, 1998).

However, contrary to our prediction in Hypothesis 8, being a member of an environmental association does not decrease the likelihood of being charged for an environmental offense—it increases it. A cynic might say that environmental associations mean little and are just covers for polluters. But new institutional theory has consistently shown the positive impact of professions and professional associations on organizational outcomes, so this explanation cannot be accepted without question. One possibility is that the environmental associations are not that professional, but this is unlikely given the very formal designation of the associations by federal and provincial bodies and given the "blue chip" membership list of many of them. Another possibility is that the impact of the associations on practice may not have occurred yet. Perhaps in most cases professionals begin to make a difference only in places where they are first really needed. This is a possibility, because two of the four associations had to be dropped from our data sources for being too new, and the other two were established only in the early 1990s.

Table 3.3 shows the effects of organizational characteristics over time. We find that the effect of organizational signifiers in the system may change, but they do not appear to have changed much between 1985 and 1996. Whenever effects are registered, they tend to be positive. Being large, in manufacturing, in a multiunit firm, having a resource permit, and belonging to an environmental association increase the likelihood of being charged. Being an older firm tends to increase charges only in Period 2, but actually decreases them in Periods 1, 3, and 4. We do not have a good theoretical explanation based on the regimes or nature of the variable to explain this. However, given the time-related character of this variable, we think it is worth exploring as a time-dependent covariate. It may be better recoded as a more explicit set of categories for very old versus moderately old versus younger firms, because our argument is that age is a signal in the subdomain and we could actually try to see if there is a discrete element to that variable.

Nevertheless, one question worth pondering is whether organizational characteristics should show more variation across enforcement regimes than they do. If an enforcement regime is "passive and conservative," then the view of the regulated members of that domain might differ from their views when it is "active and liberal." In our interviews, we asked how conservative officers view organizations and how firms respond to their investigations. One CO said, "It doesn't matter: we're coming in to get our information whether they want us or not." That person related a story of how a firm tried to stonewall and the firm's manager was very surprised to see the CO back a day or two later with a court order to seize documents. But another CO also noted that "there are good firms and bad firms." She felt particularly bad about having to charge a good firm twice, a couple of years apart, because "you could see that they were trying."

In other words, there is some anecdotal evidence that people in the enforcement agency conceptualized firms in different ways even though they claimed they didn't negotiate and treated all companies the same way. But there was little evidence of a conscious reconceptualization of the role of firms in the system. Instead, officers wrestled more with their own roles and activities within their agency. Some COs expressed interest in having the enforcement branch join the policing unit; others acknowledged that conservationists had their own ethic and the movement was best left under the Ministry of Environment. In a sense, this reinforces the view that environmental enforcement is a unique subdomain, one that reflects a broader set of tensions but one with its own systematic sets of effects.

IMPLICATIONS

In this chapter we reported large variations in enforcement intensity that tracks variations in enforcement regimes (Edelman, 1992; Dobbin and Sutton, 1998). We also demonstrated spatial variation in these enforcement effects (Haveman, 1995; Wade, Swaminathan, and Saxon, 1998; Strang and Meyer, 1994). Finally, we found that, in the context of the enforcement regime, organizational characteristics (such as size) act as consistent indicators of environmental enforcement intensity. These are important complications in the compliance process.

We also confirmed three complications with compliance found by other institutional researchers: first, a state may be relatively well developed but may not have well-articulated environmental policies and regulation and enforcement systems (Dobbin and Sutton, 1998; Edelman, 1990; 1992; Meyer and Scott, 1983); second, within the environmental domain of a state, enforcement may be weaker and less systematic than enforcement in other policy-making and regulatory domains (Burstein, 1990; Dobbin and Sutton, 1998; Knoke and Laumann, 1987); third, components of a regulatory system and its subsystems, such as enforcement, are likely to be loosely coupled, making systems-level outcomes less predictable (Hironaka and Schofer, Chapter 9; March and Olsen, 1976; March, 1989; Thompson, 1967).

These results for enforcement, taken jointly, suggest that a policy domain or regulatory system may reflect deeper understandings and interpretation of regulation, an understanding that changes over time. For instance, enforcement may appear to be more cognitive, normative, and regulative (rule-following) during different time periods (Powell and DiMaggio, 1991; Scott, 1995). In our longitudinal data on British Columbia, we found evidence that a normative mode of regulation was becoming more regulative and coercive over time, even if there was still a lot of variation in the regulatory side and the cognitive views of the system were still being worked out. This is in contrast to the finding of Hoffman (1997; 1999) for the United States, which showed cognitive understanding to be superceded by regulative rather than normative standards in the period between 1970 and 1993. Finally, while there is still some evidence that a normative regime exists in some areas of water management, we did not find that it had an impact on professional associations when it comes to regulatory outcomes. Perhaps this is not due to errors in the data or the coding of the variable, but may be due to a lag effect that has not yet appeared. For example, associations and organizations present in the Lower Fraser Basin take them seriously, but being a member of an association has not yet had an impact on the firm. But we do not think it is just a matter of time. In the United States, it appears that the dominant logic or regime had to become more regulative as a whole and then moved toward a normative mode before professional associations could make a difference in strategic environmental management (Hoffman, 1999). Similar shifts in regimes and understandings have been shown by Frank (2001) and Hironaka and Schofer (Chapter 9) to lay the groundwork for professional effects. Once such shifts occur, we have little doubt that the large volume and variety of environmental professionals who live and work in the Lower Fraser Basin will have a more noticeable impact on enforcement.

Implications for Institutional Theory and the Natural Environment

Our results and the patterns they uncover and confirm have some broader implications for both old and new institutional theory (Hirsch and Lounsbury, 1997). Whereas institutional economists such as North (1990; North and Thomas, 1973) have discussed the powers of the state and use of coercive force by agents across economies, they should incorporate enforcement procedures more directly in their historical studies of regulatory systems if they wish to elaborate on the importance of enforcing contracts. Although new institutional sociologists interested in policy regimes, regulatory systems, and their effects acknowledge their importance, they need to incorporate the role of the enforcement process more explicitly into compliance and isomorphism (Dobbin, 1994; Dobbin and Sutton, 1994; Edelman, 1990, 1992; Edelman and others, 1991; Meyer and Scott, 1983; Scott, Meyer, and associates, 1994). If a policy regime is strong and regulatory machinery is elaborate, but enforcement weak, then noncompliance may increase. The consequence is, despite apparent coercive pressure, that only moderate isomorphism may occur in the field.

In the case of new institutional work on the natural environment, our work questions this assumption by showing that enforcement activity—that cognitive regimes are replaced by regulative (Hironaka and Schofer, Chapter 9; Hoffman, 1997. 1999; Hoffman and Ventresca, 1999). Canada is moving toward more of a regulatory regime characterized by higher rates of enforcement during the last fifteen years—away from a more normative and conciliatory approach of earlier periods. It may be that the locus of action or level of analysis for this pattern of replacement of regimes is not only at the national but the international level. On the one hand, the increasing rationalization and legalization found around the world may have unifying, isomorphic effects on all of the member communities of the polity (Frank, 2001; Meyer and Scott, 1983; Meyer and others, 1994). Most countries then will experience an increase in regulation. On the other hand, there may only be a country-to-country diffusion effect of policy regimes (Hironaka and Schofer, Chapter 9). If so, Canada would be highly influenced by its trade with, and social and cultural proximity to, America. The normative models for professional environmental management would become increasingly important. Still, under either the world polity or the national diffusion type of model, any normative and cognitive shifts in policy within Canada are likely to be built on increasingly elaborate regulatory regimes for environmental policy.

Finally, the context for assessing environmental processes is strongly influenced by the mode or regime that the investigator perceives to be in operation. In our study, the boundaries of the natural system are contiguous with the boundaries defined by the regulatory system (at three levels of analysis—the local, the provincial, and the federal). Within this bounded system, investigators have shown that water quality and riparian health have generally decreased over the last twenty years (Lavkulich and others, 1999; Rees and Wackernagel, 1994, 1999; Zandbergen, 1999; but see BCMOELP, 2000). If a different regime were operating and used

COMPLICATIONS IN COMPLIANCE | 83

to define the boundaries of the natural system, then the complications in compliance would become even more complex and the outcomes more difficult to assess. Ultimately, trying to examine the effects of these fluctuating systems on ecological outcomes as regimes cycle and trying to build some form of control and feedback across them is the real complication of compliance.

REFERENCES

Abbott, Andrew. 1988. *The System of Professions: An Essay on the Division of Expert Labor.* Chicago: University of Chicago Press.

Allison, Paul. 1984. *Event History Analysis: Regression for Longitudinal Event Data.* Newbury Park, CA: Sage.

Baron, James N., Brian Mittman, Andrew Newman. 1991. "Targets of Opportunity: Organizational and Environmental Determinants of Gender Integration Within the California Civil Service, 1979–1985." *American Journal of Sociology,* 96: 1362–1401.

BCMOELP. 1997. Author interviews with senior conservation officers and Deputy Director of Environmental Enforcement. British Columbia Ministry of Environment, Lands, and Parks, Enforcement Branch.

BCMOELP. 1999. British Columbia Ministry of Environment, Lands, and Parks. Homepage and historical overview of enforcement in British Columbia. www.gov.bc.ca/elp/. Viewed March, 2000.

BCMOELP. 2000. Author interviews with senior conservation officers. British Columbia Ministry of Environment, Lands, and Parks, Enforcement Branch.

Blake, Donald. 1996. "B.C. Political Culture." In R. K. Carty, ed. *Politics, Policy, and Government in British Columbia.* Vancouver: University of British Columbia Press.

Blossfeld, Hans, and Gert Rohwer. 1995. *Techniques of Event History Modelling: New Approaches to Causal Analysis.* Mahwah, NJ: Erlbaum.

Brander, James A. 1995. *Government Policy Towards Business.* Toronto: Wiley.

Burstein, Paul. 1990. "Intergroup Conflict, Law, and the Concept of Labor Market Discrimination." *Sociological Forum,* 5: 459–476.

Cliff, Jennifer. 2000. "Following Versus Breaking with Precedent: Organizational Conformity and Deviation in the British Columbia Legal Profession." Unpublished Dissertation: University of British Columbia.

Cox, Richard. 1972. "Regression Models and Life Rate Tables." *Journal of the Royal Statistical Society,* Series B, 34: 187–202.

Daly, Herman E., and John J. Cobb, Jr. 1994. *For the Common Good: Redirecting the Economy Toward Community, the Environment and a Sustainable Future.* (2nd ed.). Boston: Beacon Press.

DiMaggio, Paul, and Walter W. Powell. 1983. "The Iron Cage Revisited: Institutional Isomorphism and Collective Rationality in Organizational Field." *American Sociological Review,* 48: 147–160.

DiMaggio, Paul, and Walter W. Powell. 1991. "Introduction." In Walter W. Powell and Paul J. DiMaggio, eds., *The New Institutionalism in Organizational Analysis.* Chicago: University of Chicago Press, 1–40.

Dobbin, Frank R. 1994. *Forging Industrial Policy: The United States, Britain, and France in the Railway Age.* New York: Cambridge University Press.

Dobbin, Frank R., and John Sutton. 1998. "The Strength of a Weak State: The Rights Revolution and the Rise of Human Resources Management Divisions." *American Journal of Sociology,* 104: 441–476.

Dorsey, Anthony. 1976. *The Uncertain Future of the Lower Fraser.* Vancouver: Westwater Research Centre, University of British Columbia.

Dorsey, Anthony, ed. 1991a. *Water in Sustainable Development: Exploring Our Common Future in the Fraser River Basin.* Vancouver: Westwater Research Centre, University of British Columbia.

Dorsey, Anthony, ed. 1991b. *Perspectives on Sustainable Development in Water Management: Towards Agreement in the Fraser River Basin.* Vancouver: Westwater Research Centre, University of British Columbia.

Dorsey, Anthony, and Harriet I. Ruggeberg. 1989. "Facilitator's Summary Report, National Workshop on State of the Environmental Reporting." Victoria, BC.

Downs, Anthony. 1967. *Inside Bureaucracy.* Boston: Little, Brown.

Dyck, Richard. 1995. *Provincial Politics in Canada: Towards the Turn of the Century.* 3rd Edition. Scarborough, Ontario: Prentice Hall, Canada.

Edelman, Lauren. 1990. "Legal Environments and Organizational Governance: The Expansion of Due Process in the American Workplace." *American Journal of Sociology,* 95: 1401–1440.

Edelman, Lauren. 1992. "Legal Ambiguity and Symbolic Structures: Organizational Mediation of Civil Right Laws." *American Journal of Sociology,* 97: 1531–1576.

Edelman, Lauren B., Stephen Petterson, Elizabeth Chambliss, and Howard S. Erlanger. 1991. "Legal Ambiguity and the Politics of Compliance: Affirmative Action Officers' Dilemma." *Law and Policy,* 13: 73–97.

Environment Canada, Commission for Environmental Cooperation. 1998. *1998 North American Annual Report on Environmental Enforcement.* Ottawa: Government of Canada. www.ec.gc.ca/enforce/cec98

Erickson, Rodney A. 1980. "Corporate Organization and Manufacturing Branch Plant Closure in Nonmetropolitan Areas." *Regional Studies,* 14: 491–502.

Fligstein, Neil. 1991. "The Structural Transformation of American Industry: An

Institutional Account of the Causes of Diversification in the Largest Firms, 1919–1979." In Walter W. Powell and Paul J. DiMaggio, eds., *The New Institutionalism in Organizational Analysis,* 311–336. Chicago: University of Chicago Press.

Frank, David J. 1997. "Science, Nature, and the Globalization of the Environment, 1870–1990." *Social Forces,* 76: 409–435.

Frank, David J. 2001. "The Origins Question: Building Global Institutions to Protect Nature." In Andrew Hoffman and Marc Vantresca, eds., *Organizations, Policy, and the Natural Environment: Institutional and Strategic Perspectives.* Stanford, CA: Stanford University Press.

Friedland, Roger, and Robert Alford. 1991. "Bringing Society Back In: Symbols, Practices, and Institutional Contradictions." In Walter W. Powell and Paul J. DiMaggio, eds., *The New Institutionalism in Organizational Analysis,* 232–266. Chicago: University of Chicago Press.

Greenwood Royston, Roy Suddaby, and C. R. Hinings. 2001. "Theorizing Change: The Role of Professional Associations in the Transformation of Institutionalized Fields." *Academy of Management Journal,* forthcoming.

Gladwin, Thomas N. 1992. *Building the Sustainable Corporation: Creating Environmental Sustainability and Competitive Advantage.* Washington, D.C.: Island Press.

Hall, Ken J., Hans Schreier, and Sandra Brown. 1991. "Water Quality in the Fraser River Basin." In Anthony Dorsey, ed., *Water in Sustainable Development: Exploring Our Common Future in the Fraser River Basin,* 41–75. Vancouver: Westwater Research Centre, University of British Columbia.

Haveman, Heather. 1995. "The Demographic Metabolism of Organizations: Industry Dynamics, Turnover, and Tenure Distributions." *Administrative Science Quarterly,* 40: 586–618.

Hirsch, Paul M., and Michael Lounsbury. 1997. "Ending the Family Quarrel: Towards a Reconciliation of 'Old' and 'New' Institutionalism." *American Behavioral Scientist,* 40(4): 406–418.

Hoffman, Andrew J. 1997. *From Heresy to Dogma: An Institutional History of Corporate Environmentalism.* San Francisco: New Lexington Press.

Hoffman, Andrew J. 1999. "Institutional Evolution and Change: Environmentalism and the U.S. Chemical Industry." *Academy of Management Journal,* 42: 351–371.

Hoffman, Andrew J., and Marc J. Ventresca. 1999. "The Institutional Framing of Policy Debates: Economics versus the Environment." *American Behavioral Scientist,* 42: 1368–1392.

Huestis, Lynne B. 1993. In Geoffrey Thompson, Moria L. McConnel, and Lynne

B. Heustis, eds., *Environmental Law and Business in Canada,* 243–274. Aurora, ON: Canada Law Book.

Inkeles, Alex, and David Smith. 1974. *Becoming Modern.* Cambridge, MA: Harvard University Press.

Jennings, P. Devereaux, and Paul A. Zandbergen. 1995. "Ecologically Sustainable Organizations: An Institutional Approach." *Academy of Management Review,* 20: 1015–1052.

Jennings, P. Devereaux, Paul A. Zandbergen, and Vivien Clark. 1999. "Organizations and Ecosystem Sustainability: An Institutional Study of Water Quality in the Lower Fraser Basin." In Mike Healey, ed., *Seeking Sustainability of the Lower Fraser Basin,* 64–105. Vancouver: University of British Columbia Press.

Jepperson, Ronald. 1991. "Institutions, Institutional Effects, and Institutionalization." In Walter W. Powell and Paul J. DiMaggio, eds., *The New Institutionalism in Organizational Analysis,* 143–163. Chicago: University of Chicago Press.

King, Andrew. 1995. "Avoiding Ecological Surprise: Lessons from Long-Standing Communities." *Academy of Management Review,* 20: 961–985.

Knoke, David, and Edward Laumann. 1987. "The Social Organization of National Policy Domains: An Exploration of Some Structural Hypotheses." In Peter V. Marsden and Nan Lin, eds., *Social Structure and Network Analysis,* 255–270. Beverly Hills, CA: Sage.

Kolluru, Rao V., ed. 1994. *Environmental Strategies Handbook: A Guide to Effective Policies and Practices.* New York: McGraw Hill.

Krahn, Peter K. 1998. "Enforcement Versus Voluntary Compliance: An Examination of the Strategic Enforcement Initiatives Implemented by the Pacific and Yukon Regional Office of Environment Canada, 1983–1998." Department of Environment, Fraser River Action Plan: Regional Action Report, 98–102.

Krasner, Steven, ed. 1983. *International Regimes.* Ithaca, NY: Cornell University Press.

Laszlo and others. 1977. *Goals for Mankind.* New York: Signet.

Laumann, Edward, and David Knocke. 1987. *The Organizational State: Social Choice in National Policy Domains.* Madison: University of Wisconsin Press.

Lavkulich, Les, Ken Hall, and Hans Schreier. 1999. "Land and Water Interactions: Present and Future." In Mike Healey, ed., *Seeking Sustainability in the Lower Fraser Basin: Issues and Choices,* 170–201. Vancouver, BC: Institute for Resources and the Environment, Westwater Research.

Lawrence, Thomas, Monika Winn, and P. Devereaux Jennings. 2001. "Power and the Temporal Dynamics of Institutional Change." *Academy of Management Review,* 26(4): 624–644.

Lex, Charlotte, and P. Devereaux Jennings. 1998. "Environmental Management—Fad or Form? Arguments from Fashion and Neo-Institutional Theory." Presented at the Academy of Management Conference, San Diego, CA.

Lipset, Seymour Martin. 1960. *Political Man: The Social Bases of Politics.* Garden City, NY: Anchor.

March, James G. 1989. *Rediscovering Institutions: The Organizational Basis of Politics.* New York: Wiley.

March, James G., and Johan Olsen. 1976. *Ambiguity and Choice in Organizations.* Bergen, Norway: Universitetsforlaget.

Meadows, Donella. 1992. *Beyond the Limits: Confronting Global Collapse, Envisioning a Sustainable Future.* Post Mills, VT: Chelsea Green.

Meyer, John W. 1983. "Centralization of Funding and Control in Educational Governance." In John W. Meyer and W. Richard Scott, eds., *Organizational Environments: Ritual and Rationality,* 179–198. Beverly Hills, CA: Sage.

Meyer, John W., and W. Richard Scott. 1983. *Organizational Environments: Ritual and Rationality.* Beverly Hills, CA: Sage.

Meyer, John W., W. Richard Scott, David Strang, and Andrew Creighton. 1994. "Bureaucratization Without Centralization: Changes in the Organizational System of U.S. Public Education, 1940–80." In W. Richard Scott and John Meyer, eds., *Institutional Environments and Organizations: Structural Complexity and Individualism,* 179–206. Thousand Oaks, CA: Sage.

North, Douglass. 1990. *Institutions, Institutional Change and Economic Performance.* Cambridge, UK: Cambridge University Press.

North, Douglass, and Richard Thomas. 1973. *The Rise of the Western World: A New Economic History.* Cambridge, UK: Cambridge University Press.

Porter, Michael, and Claas van der Linde. 1995. "Green and Competitive: Ending the Stalemate." *Harvard Business Review,* 73: 120–133.

Powell, Walter, and Paul J. DiMaggio, eds. 1991. *The New Institutionalism in Organizational Analysis.* Chicago: University of Chicago Press.

Rankin, Murray. 1991. "Despoiling a River: Can the Law Help to Sustain the Fraser River?" In Anthony Dorsey, ed., *Perspectives on Sustainable Development in Water Management: Towards Agreement in the Fraser River Basin,* 391–416. Vancouver: Westwater Research Centre, University of British Columbia.

Rankin, Murray, and Peter Finkle. 1983. "The Enforcement of Environmental Law: Taking the Environment Seriously." *UBC Law Review,* 17: 34–57.

Rees, William E., and Mathis Wackernagel. 1994. "Ecological Footprints and Appropriated Carrying Capacity: Measuring the Natural Capital Requirements of the Human Economy." In A.M. Janson and others, eds., *Investing in Nat-*

ural Capital: The Ecological Economics Approach to Sustainability. Washington, DC: Island Press.

Rees, William E., and Mathis Wackernagel. 1999. "Our Ecological Footprint: Where on Earth is the Lower Fraser Basin?" In Michael Healey, ed., *Seeking Sustainability in the Lower Fraser Basin: Issues and Choices,* 202–236. Vancouver, BC: Institute for Resources and Environment, Westwater Research.

Schmidheiny, Stephen. 1992. *Changing Course: A Global Business Perspective on Development and the Environment.* Cambridge, MA: MIT Press.

Scott, W. Richard. 1995. *Institutions and Organizations.* Thousand Oaks, CA: Sage.

Scott, W. Richard., John W. Meyer, and associates, eds. 1994. *Institutional Environments and Organizations: Structural Complexity and Individualism.* Thousand Oaks, CA: Sage.

Strang, David, and John W. Meyer. 1994. "Institutional Conditions for Diffusion." In W. Richard Scott, John W. Meyer, and Associates, eds., *Institutional Environments and Organizations: Structural Complexity and Individualism,* 100–112. Thousand Oaks, CA: Sage.

Suchman, Mark, and Lauren Edelman. 1996. "Legal-Rational Myths: The New Institutionalism and the Law and Society Tradition." *Law and Social Inquiry,* 21: 903–941.

Suzuki, David. 1997. *The Sacred Balance: Rediscovering Our Place in Nature.* Vancouver, BC: Greystone Books.

Thompson, Geoffrey, Moria L. McConnell, and Lynne B. Huestis. 1993. *Environmental Law and Business in Canada.* Aurora, Ontario: Canadian Law Books, Inc.

Thompson, James. 1967. *Organizations in Action.* New York: McGraw-Hill.

Tuma, Nancy B., and Michael Hannan. 1984. *Social Dynamics: Models and Methods.* New York: Academic Press.

Wade, James, Anand Swaminathan, and Michael Scott Saxon. 1998. "Normative and Resource Flow Consequences of Local Regulations in the American Brewing Industry, 1845–1918." *Administrative Science Quarterly,* 43: 905–935.

Williamson, Oliver E. 1985. *The Economic Institutions of Capitalism: Firms, Markets, Relational Contracting.* New York: Free Press.

Wilson, James Q. 1989. *Bureaucracy: What Government Agencies Do and Why They Do It.* New York: Basic Books.

Zandbergen, Paul A. 1999. *Urban Watershed Assessment: Linking Watershed Health Indicators to Management.* CD-ROM Dissertation for Institute of Resources and Environment, University of British Columbia.

4

THE EMERGENCE OF ENVIRONMENTAL CONFLICT RESOLUTION: SUBVERSIVE STORIES AND THE CONSTRUCTION OF COLLECTIVE ACTION FRAMES AND ORGANIZATIONAL FIELDS

Calvin Morrill and Jason Owen-Smith

Storytelling is the lifeblood of social interaction. Whether at home, on the street, or in a workplace, people tell stories to entertain or persuade, to inform or exonerate, and to render meaningful the events of their lives. But storytelling is also central to larger social institutions. Stories lie at the heart of institutional persistence, development, and change. This is especially true in the complex and sometimes murky organizational infrastructure at the interface between the social and natural environments. Nearly forty years ago, for example, Rachel Carson's *Silent Spring* helped subvert existing assumptions about environmental degradation with vivid stories about the consequences of pesticides. Ultimately, her stories became a clarion call for an environmental movement that begat a vast regulatory architecture.

New stories continue to inform the negotiated and contested development of environmentally related organizations and institutions. Some of these stories embed site-specific environmental disasters, such as nuclear accidents (Three Mile Island) or chemical spills (Love Canal), in the failures of regulatory structures and markets. Other stories focus on environmental problems that affect vast expanses of territory (such as ground water pollution and water table depletion in the American Southwest) and implicate failures of both public and private organizations.

Portions of this paper were presented at the "Special Session on Cultural Boundaries in Theory and Practice: Implications for Social Change" during the annual meeting of the American Sociological Association in Washington, D.C. in August 2000. We thank Jennifer Howard-Grenville, Andy Hoffman, Mark Jacobs, Marc Schneiberg, and Marc Ventresca for helpful comments. Parts of the data collection for this chapter were supported by a Research Fellowship for the first author in the Environmental Conflict Resolution Program, Udall Center for Studies in Public Policy, University of Arizona.

Still other stories focus on the failures of traditional institutions and forms of dispute resolution to handle the seemingly intractable conflicts that arise from competing claims on the natural environment. These narratives not only recount particular cases, but contribute to the collective development and legitimacy of an ensemble of practices known as "environmental conflict resolution" (ECR).

Generally speaking, ECR refers to techniques that fall outside adjudication, administrative actions, executive orders, or legislation, and include such processes as mediation, arbitration, or community consensus building (Emerson, 1996).[1] It shares many features with Alternative Dispute Resolution (ADR), but key ECR practitioners have sought to differentiate themselves from the larger field of ADR because they specialize in environmental matters. Over the past twenty years, ECR has been applied to hundreds of disputes involving land, air, water, and endangered species. Aspects of ECR (especially mediation) are now a part of the official repertoire of techniques used with federal and local governmental agencies in the regulation of industrial pollutants, the management of wilderness areas, and land-use conflicts (Bingham, 1986; Blackburn and Bruce, 1995; Fox, 1995; Jacobs, 1995; O'Leary, 1999).

In this chapter, we open a new analytic front in cultural institutional analysis by exploring the role of political narratives in constituting and developing ECR as a field. Although cultural institutionalists have long acknowledged the importance of symbols in institutional change and construction (see Friedland and Alford, 1991; Lounsbury, Geraci, and Waismel-Manor, Chapter 14), little systematic attention has been devoted to political narratives that provide compelling mechanisms for embedding and constituting political concepts in broad cultural contexts. We focus on "subversive stories" that undermine existing institutions by highlighting their failures through dramatizations of particular events in specific locales (Ewick and Silbey, 1995).

For a story to be subversive, storytellers must move beyond the local and link elements of their narratives to broader social discourses that evince underlying institutional logics, definitions of institutional failure, conceptions of alternative practices and emergent fields, and images of advocates ("heroes") and opponents ("villains"). Subversive storytellers thus lay bare linkages between local and broader social institutions. As they become highly stylized in their portrayal of alternative practices and possibilities, subversive stories feed into collective action frames (Snow and Benford, 1992) that institutional entrepreneurs use to mobilize constituencies and resources to reconfigure existing institutions and carve out new social terrains (DiMaggio, 1991; Fligstein, 2001; Rao, Morrill, and Zald, 2000).

In the next sections, we outline the theoretical foundations of our approach and then illustrate our arguments with the emergence of ECR. Specifically, we recount three key subversive stories that fed into collective action frames for ECR. We then briefly discuss how frames matter in terms of practice and collective action within the nascent ECR field. Finally, we close with a series of emergent questions for future research suggested by our work.

A NARRATIVE PERSPECTIVE ON INSTITUTIONAL CHANGE

Institutions and Fields

Institutions comprise taken-for-granted premises that enable patterns of human activity to be organized, made sense of, and navigated (Scott, 1995). If institutions provide cultural and cognitive backdrops for action, "fields" embed institutional premises in bounded social domains where individual and collective players strategically orient themselves toward one another and negotiate meanings for their actions (Fligstein, 2001; Dacin, Ventresca, and Beal, 1999). Fields achieve "relative independence from external constraints" through the construction of distinctive symbolic, technical, and moral boundaries relative to other organized practices (Ferguson, 1998: 597; Moore, 1973). More concretely, fields encompass expertise and legitimacy, interpersonal and organizational networks, hierarchical relationships, distributions of material resources, and internal "rules of the game" (Dezalay and Garth, 1996: 16; Bourdieu and Wacquant, 1992: 94–100). Some professional fields, such as law, medicine, or engineering, have an expressly normative character (Abbott, 1988); others organize more diffuse practices such as culinary styles or self-help therapies (Ferguson, 1998). Whatever their substantive foci, fields matter because they influence collective rationality, individual and group identity, state (regulatory and legal) structures, and organizational forms (Meyer and Rowan, 1978; DiMaggio, 1991). Indeed, fields are so far-reaching that some institutionalists provocatively claim that much contemporary "social change" is really the reconfiguration of fields (Fligstein, 2001). If so, two questions become crucial for contemporary institutional analyses: *When do fields change? How do fields change?*

Opportunity Structures, Collective Action, and Skilled Players

Explanations for the timing of field-level change often turn to collective action and social movement theory to identify "opportunity structures" that enable individual and collective players to build and alter fields. Opportunity structures are alterations in the configuration of state authority, elite alignments, cultural traditions, and other social arrangements that affect the possibilities for and outcomes of collective action (Tilly, 1978; McAdam, McCarthy, and Zald, 1996; Gamson and Meyer, 1996; Meyer and Staggenborg, 1996). Such opportunities arise from the interplay of external crises and internal contradictions in fields and institutions (Fligstein, 1996; Clemens, 1997; Levin and Espeland, Chapter 5).

To explain the process of change, institutionalists have turned to two increasingly convergent theoretical streams within the collective action/movements literature: the social psychology of collective action and analyses of institutional entrepreneurship. The social psychology of collective action touches on a broad range of issues concerned with beliefs, values, and ideologies. However, a central focus is on micromobilization: why and how people become involved in collective action or, more abstractly, the link between broad sociocultural processes and self- and collective identities (Gamson, 1992: 55). The linchpin of this perspective borrows from Erving Goffman's work on frames and framing processes. Frames enable individuals to "locate, perceive, and identify" events and contexts within their own lives (Goffman, 1974: 21). Collective action frames emerge interactively through political contestation to provide interpretive bridges between individual consciousness and social movements. Frames enable people to make sense of collective problems and possible solutions while providing vocabularies of motive to legitimize collective action (Snow and Benford, 1992).

Crucial for a frame is its "resonance" or, in plainer terms, whether it has staying power and efficacy on the political landscape. Frames manifest themselves in ways of talking about movements, conceptual templates for structuring social movement organizations, slogans, strategies, and goals. Social movements can become associated with particular frames as illustrated by ethnic- and gender-based movements associated with a civil rights frame that locates injustice in violations of due process and solutions in legal protection.

Frames do not develop by themselves from organic, mystical processes; they require real people in interaction and conflict to formulate, contest, modify, and deploy them. Moreover, frames do not emerge from thin air. They are cobbled together from existing cultural traditions and social discourses. Only certain actors can produce frames that resonate with participants and constituencies. Frame development, then, suggests the critical role of "projective" agency by key players who actively engage in the improvisational and future-oriented meaning work necessary to construct collective action frames (Emirbayer and Mische, 1998: 983–991; Joas, 1993). Such action can be interest driven or motivated by normative commitments to particular practices or discourses.

Institutional analysts increasingly identify frame construction with skilled institutional entrepreneurs who are socially positioned to access relevant cultural, material, and organizational resources (Fligstein, 2001). But institutional entrepreneurs are not the sole contributors to collective frame building; rank-and-file participants, media actors, opposition groups (including governmental agents engaged in social control), and public audiences all participate in the interactive milieus and social networks out of which frames emerge (Hilgartner and Bosk, 1988). Yet institutional entrepreneurs play key roles by coloring, sharpening, and disseminating frames. Such players are not merely scripted dupes, but can "driv[e] and sometimes even reshap[e]" collective action frames, which in turn can powerfully affect efforts to change or construct new fields and institutions (Creed and Scully, 1998).

Neglected in this discussion, however, is the crucial step of how frames are actually constructed. We know who, what, and why, but not how. This processual question, we maintain, is vitally important for fleshing out theoretical explanations of field change. We believe that political narratives—stories that relate to collective issues, problems, troubles, failures, and injustices—provide foundational building blocks for collective action frames.

Stories and Narrative Styles

Stories have several attributes that facilitate their contribution to collective action frames. First, narratives are among the most pervasive and common forms of human communication (Riessman, 1993). Second, everyday stories can be highly accessible as they approximate lived experience. Most plots unfold in time sequences that can mirror actual events. This means, among other things, that stories are often easier to remember than are other forms of communication. However, as in lived experience, not all stories flow in neat sequences. Nor do stories always reflect experience in a perfect way. Rather, stories enable people to represent various realities, while helping to constitute those realities. Third, narratives can generate affective commitments. Storytellers and audiences can develop emotional identifications with the twists and turns of a plot, as well as with its characters. Finally, stories can function differently according to the intents, social power, and skill of their tellers and the contexts in which they are told. Stories are mutable; their contents and implications can change even as they retain many of their original elements (Ewick and Silbey, 1995; see also Schank, 1990).

Whether a story is written formally (as an essay or a book) or told informally during the course of everyday interaction, storytellers typically find their authorial voices by tacitly or explicitly drawing upon taken-for-granted conventions called "narrative styles" (Morrill and others, 2000). Narrative styles operate as higher-order cultural "tool kits" (Swidler, 1986) from which authors draw substantive imageries, ways of lending coherence and meaning to plots, and accenting devices.

Storytellers can draw on archetypal narrative styles that appear in many western and nonwestern societies, such as tragedy, comedy, romanticism, or satire (White, 1973). They also can use styles that appear in particular historical time periods (Van Maanen, 1988) or from particular identity groups, such as Native American tribes (Cornell, 2000) or urban youth gangs (Cintron, 1997); formal organizations, including private corporations (Morrill, 1995) and public policy agencies (Roe, 1994; Czarniawska, 1997); or social movements (Gamson, 1992). However, not all narrative styles are equally accessible to all storytellers. Social resources of various kinds can stratify access to styles. Moreover, part of being a skilled political storyteller is knowing where to look for narrative styles relevant to particular audiences (see Edelman, 1967: 130–151).

Aside from drawing from archetypal and particularized styles, skilled political storytellers draw from narrative styles that flow from long-standing political discourses deeply rooted in their cultures and societies. Williams and Matheny (1995) identify three such discourses in American society: a "technocratic" discourse that emphasizes efficiency, trained expertise, and the scientific model in governance (see also Frank, Chapter 2); a "pluralistic" discourse that focuses on the representation and balancing of collective interests in governance institutions; and a "communitarian" discourse that privileges contextuality and local concerns in geographically bounded communities.

Stories constructed using narrative styles drawn from these discourses evince many of the same flash points of debate and contestation that the discourses themselves manifest. In this sense, political narrative styles and the stories associated with them become a core currency of standing, competition, and opposition among those in political conflict. Broad political narrative styles can be found in specific collective action frames. Technocratic narratives have become associated with frames accenting the reform of governmental inefficiencies; the pluralistic style is a mainstay of contemporary civil rights frames; and the communitarian style informs grassroots stories and collective action frames about community control and autonomy.

Subversive stories link particular problems with broad social institutions (Ewick and Silbey, 1995) through the mechanism of narrative style. In this way, stories that initially seem like the misfortunes of a single locale or even a single individual can become a part of the "hidden transcript" of resistance among the oppressed or disenfranchised (Scott, 1990). In the shadows, individuals in interpersonal exchanges or small, localized gatherings can share subversive stories, thus nurturing them through retellings, while their low visibility protects both the stories and the storytellers. Even in this guise, subversive stories can begin to delegitimize existing institutions and destabilize field boundaries by calling into question institutions' abilities to satisfactorily manage the dramatic events recounted. Subversive stories thus carry with them normative elements by tacitly suggesting that existing arrangements should be changed.

Subversive Stories and Collective Action Frames

At any point in history, countless subversive stories may exist in a society. In the crux of opportunity structures, however, stories topically related to crises can emerge into the light of day—through personal communications and retelling at gatherings where the less powerful meet to share their stories. Under these conditions, subversive tales become more collective and contentious vis-a-vis existing institutions and powerful players. Subversive stories also become more clearly associated with political narrative styles as storytellers accent particular language, imagery, and interests.

Institutional entrepreneurs—either the originators of stories or actors who swoop in and synthesize narratives already in play—transform subversive stories into collective action frames via "theorization" (Strang and Meyer, 1994), which itself entails three processes: conceptualization, elaboration, and generalization. Conceptualization occurs as the elements that form the logical underpinnings of stories are identified. For example, a story about an African American being refused service at a restaurant can be conceptualized in terms of racism and violations of legally guaranteed civil rights. Elaboration refers to the development and articulation of conceptual elements from a story (that is, spelling out what constitutes racial injustice in the preceding story). Finally, generalization refers to demonstrations of a story's applicability across contexts. These processes can occur in "bottom-up" or "top-down" fashions. From the bottom up, subversive storytellers cobble together collective action frames from a mix of stories and styles. Here, key actors' and constituencies' interests start out murky, but telling and retelling subversive tales helps constitute and articulate collective interests and strategies. A top-down process, by contrast, occurs when institutional entrepreneurs with articulated interests assemble subversive stories into collective action frames or flesh out nascent frames borrowed from adjacent fields of collective action.

The role of subversive stories is not limited to frame construction. Subversive stories remain in constant dialogue with collective action frames. As new stories are added to the canon of a social movement, they can modify frames and feed into "frame disputes" within social movements (Benford, 1993). In their relationships to both existing institutions and challengers, subversive stories explicitly raise the issue of power, specifically, "*whose narrative gains currency*" and "*who gets to narrate who*" (emphasis in the original; Cornell, 2000: 11).[2]

To recap the argument advanced in this section:

(1) Crises and internal contradictions in existing fields create opportunity structures for collective action aimed at institutional and field change.

(2) Opportunity structures are necessary, but not sufficient for collective action. Sufficiency results from micromobilization efforts by institutional entrepreneurs who actively work to develop collective action frames and activist networks.

(3) Subversive stories vividly dramatize local events that point to failures and crises of social institutions and fields. Such narratives draw on political narrative styles that are useful for cobbling together collective action frames.

We illustrate these propositions by exploring three key subversive stories in the rise of American ECR and the collective action frames with which they are currently associated.

A TALE OF THREE SUBVERSIVE STORIES: STORM KING, SNOQUALMIE, AND SANTA BARBARA

Each of the subversive stories discussed in this section critique the same target, environmental litigation, but in very different ways: as inefficient (the technocratic critique expressed through Storm King), as incapable of managing the political complexities of environmental disputes (the pluralist critique represented in Snoqualmie), or as unresponsive to local community concerns (the communitarian critique conveyed in Santa Barbara).[3]

Storm King and the Crisis of Environmental Litigation

In 1962, residents and weekenders with resort homes along New York's Hudson River Highlands became concerned about the aesthetic impact of Consolidated Edison's proposed hydroelectric plant at the base of Storm King Mountain. Con Ed planned to remove a portion of Storm King Mountain to build the plant and a water reservoir that would provide additional water when auxiliary power was needed for peak demand. The dispute over Storm King caught fire when the Federal Power Commission (FPC) granted Con Ed a construction license in late 1963 (Talbot, 1972). Together with local opponents, a coalition of hiking, garden, environmental, and outdoor sporting clubs formed the Scenic Hudson Preservation Conference in 1964 and succeeded in attracting high-profile support from concerned government officials (such as Robert Kennedy), celebrities (such as Pete Seeger, Aaron Copeland, and James Cagney), and national environmental organizations (such as the Sierra Club and Audubon Society). In 1965, the Conference challenged the FPC's granting of the construction license in the Second Circuit of Appeals. The court held that the Conference had legal standing to protect Storm King's natural beauty under the Federal Power Act and that the FPC had not adequately considered the "need for preserving the area's unique beauty and historical significance, which the Federal Power Act required" ("Calm After the Storm," 1981: 10074). The Court further instructed the FPC to reopen hearings on the matter.

Following the Second Circuit's decision, the case wound its way along a complex path through federal and state courts, commissions, and agencies until 1979 when Russell Train, former administrator of the EPA and president of the World Wildlife Fund, volunteered his services as a mediator. Four other utility firms, four public agencies, and dozens of environmental and recreational groups who supported the Scenic Hudson Preservation Conference had joined the case in the nearly two decades since it began. Train mediated a settlement among all the parties, which stipulated that Con Edison would surrender its license to build the plant and donate a 500-acre site on Storm King for park use. In return, the Conference agreed to discontinue all litigation against the utilities and drop their demands that Con Ed and other utilities modify all their existing open-cycle plants to closed-cycle operations by installing cooling towers ("Calm After the Storm," 1981: 10076).

The important legal finding from Storm King—that parties can bring suit "to protect the aesthetic, conservation, and recreational interests in an area"—resulted in an "environmental litigation explosion" in the 1970s and 1980s (Hyatt, 1995). During the mid-1980s, Rick Sutherland, the former executive director of the Sierra Club Legal Defense Fund, argued that "litigation is the most important thing the environmental movement has done over the past fifteen years" (Turner, 1988: 26). Such litigation came from several sources: the EPA, which was charged with enforcing many of the environmental protection and pollution-related laws passed by Congress; grass-roots environmental groups and communities that used the courts to fight corporate polluters, developers, and governmental agencies who failed to comply with environmental impact requirements; and private corporations that filed countersuits against those who opposed their operations on environmental bases (Hyatt, 1995). Although no one is certain of the number of environmental suits filed during the 1970s and 1980s, there is little question that many professionals involved with environmental regulation and litigation perceived a crisis in the courts as they handled the influx of environmental suits (Mays, 1988; Percival, 1992).

In the aftermath of the mediated settlement in 1980, the Storm King story focused on the success of mediation at resolving a seemingly intractable dispute. Listen to this environmental mediator talk about how Russell Train told the story of Storm King:

> For the people involved, it was a story of good and evil. Each side told horror stories about the evil the other side had done or wanted to do. The way he [Train] told it, the utilities and the Storm King preservation coalition [Scenic Hudson Preservation Conference] had been in conflict for so long, they had both lost sight of what it was they were fighting about. But it was more than the parties involved being screwed up; the litigation process was screwed up and wasteful. All the litigation, with its combativeness, helped create the ill will that everyone had for each other and kept the dispute from being resolved. Everything was so adversarial and there was no one to turn to except hired-gun lawyers who kept pushing, pushing, pushing. The case would never have resolved without mediation.

Here the focus of Storm King shifts from the parties' failure to keep the real issues in sight to institutional failures that limited the efficiency of litigation.

Train's success and the lengthy legal ordeal that led up to it formed the basis for a Storm King narrative that called into question the effectiveness of environmental litigation to solve environmental conflict. Although Train did not write his story in memoirs or professional essays, he operated as an early institutional entrepreneur for ECR through his connection to federal- and state-level policy circles. His social ties to these elite contexts ensured that broad, face-to-face networks of environmental lawyers, administrators at the state and federal levels (especially those in the EPA), and corporate counsel and top managers heard and retold the story of Storm King (Train, 1993). The story they heard subverted environmental litigation even as it highlighted mediation as a way to efficiently settle environmental disputes. This efficiency focus linked the Storm King story with the broad technocratic narrative style.

The link to the technocratic style and consequent move toward a Storm King-based frame for ECR occurred with the publication of a 1981 comment in the *Environmental Law Reporter* (a publication read by virtually all environmental lawyers and professionals). The piece officially summed up the Storm King settlement and its general implications for environmental litigation and ECR. Its author (unnamed by convention) indicted formal litigation as "burdensome" and "one of the least efficient and effective means of obtaining relief" and proclaimed that "[m]ediation . . . is emerging as one promising method of conflict resolution" ("Calm After the Storm," 1981: 10074). Six years later, the EPA's chief administrator, Lee M. Thomas, issued a memorandum that urged the use of ECR techniques for environmental disputes involving EPA offices. Thomas drew explicitly from the technocratic style in laying out the problems with litigation and the benefits of mediation, and used Storm King as a prime example of success (Mays, 1988). By 1987, a technocratic ECR frame—informed by Storm King—was in play at the highest levels of public environmental management.

Snoqualmie

As Storm King snowballed with new issues and disputants in the 1970s, another ECR subversive story emerged about the Snoqualmie River Valley in the Pacific Northwest. The Snoqualmie joins with the Snohomish River to form a natural bracket around the Seattle metropolitan area. The three forks of the Snoqualmie flow from steep alpine valleys into a middle river valley modestly populated by two towns, and then on to a lower valley densely filled by farms. In the wake of a serious flood in 1959, the local county enlisted the U.S. Army Corps of Engineers to develop plans for a flood control dam that could protect homes and agricultural businesses in both the middle and lower valleys. The farmers supported the resultant plan, while a coalition of environmental and community groups opposed the dam in the belief it would spur "urban sprawl . . . [and would] interrupt a free flowing river" (Cormick, 1976: 220). Coalitions of farmers, environmentalists, and residents pushed the plan back and forth between threatened litigation and various state agencies until the governor vetoed it in 1973, calling for public hearings on the plan. The hearings dragged on for months, further polarizing farmers, residents, environmentalists, and the Corps of Engineers. In early 1974, Gerald Cormick, then the director of the University of Washington's Environmental Mediation Project (EMP), contacted the governor's office and the Corps to inquire whether they would agree to his and a colleague's intervention into the conflict as mediators. Both parties consented and the governor officially appointed Cormick and his colleague as mediators in late 1974.

Cormick came to the dispute with a background in labor mediation and strong links to the Ford Foundation, which funded the EMP. As a result of his connections to Ford, he also knew about conflict management models from the "racial" mediation programs Ford had funded in the 1960s that attempted to resolve urban tensions among ethnic groups and fed into the community meditation movement (see Morrill, 2002). This background set the stage for Cormick's approach to the dispute, which began with assessments of the social, political, and economic "interests" that needed to be represented in the conflict resolution process and the differential social power among the parties (Cormick, 1982). Through a lengthy interviewing process, Cormick and colleagues from the EMP uncovered the "core group" of decision makers in the Snoqualmie river valley, among them farmers, environmentalists, home owners, and representatives from the Corps, county, and state. By mid-1974, Cormick began meeting as a mediator with the core group on a regular basis. By December of 1974, the parties reached an agreement that provided for a multipurpose set of flood controls on the Snoqualmie, including a flood control dam on the upper part of the river, a basin planning council to coordinate planning for the entire river basin, and an interim committee with wide citizen participation to implement the agreement (Cormick, 1992).

Unlike Russell Train, who largely told the Storm King story in his personal network and left its public dissemination to others, Cormick began to publicly tell the Snoqualmie story almost as soon as the agreement was struck. He first told it through presentations and meetings at conferences (especially meetings of the National Association of Environmental Professionals; NAEP), and then through a series of scholarly and practitioner-oriented articles. Regardless of the medium, Cormick emphasized the politics of the Snoqualmie conflict resolution process, especially the deadlocks, impasses, and breakthroughs. He also emphasized how litigation could not have achieved a multifaceted agreement because it could not adequately handle the complexity of the case. Nor could litigation create sustainable, collaborative dispute "solutions" (Cormick, 1976, 1980). Listen to this environmental mediator, from an interview with the first author, discuss one of Cormick's early conference presentations on Snoqualmie:

> He liked to tell a story about the aftermath of the Snoqualmie agreement. I think it was 1975. Before much of the agreement could be implemented, a flood hit the valley that damaged a lot of houses and farms. Right after the flood, you could see a lot of environmentalists out there with generators helping dairy farmers with their milking. Before the mediation, these guys were at each others throats. Now they helped each other out. If they had gone to court, they would never heard each other's voices or interests. Snoqualmie wasn't only about getting something done more efficiently because the things Cormick described sounded like it [the conflict resolution process] was pretty rocky at points; it was about getting peoples' interests on the table; creating a solution to the conflict that could balance those interests in a sustainable way.

This recounts Cormick's (1976, 1980) earliest writings. In them, Cormick uses the 1975 flood to illustrate how the Snoqualmie mediation created a foundation of trust among valley residents that could sustain collaborative planning in the valley—an outcome, Cormick argued, that could not have occurred in court or through traditional public hearings.

Cormick's Snoqualmie story exhibits strong links with the pluralist narrative style. In some of his pieces he argues that Snoqualmie illustrates ECR's contribution to a "democratic society," noting that "political power is a route to social participation and change" (1980: 33). In other pieces, he contends that ECR can balance and represent political interests in environmental disputes (Cormick, 1992). As a result, Snoqualmie subverts environmental litigation less through demonstrations of legal inefficiencies (the central subversive theme in Storm King) than through the court's ineffectiveness at managing politics and balancing interests in a complex environmental dispute. Although Cormick retained the labels of "mediation" and "mediator" in his tellings, he broadened the purposes and goals of ECR beyond settlement to include collaborative planning and facilitated problem solving (Cormick, 1982). By emphasizing the importance of obtaining political support from governmental elites, Cormick underscored the importance of political power in ECR. He illustrates a shift from story to frame carried by a storyteller turned institutional entrepreneur, who generalized his tale by linking it with broad pluralist attempts to effect social change through ECR.

Santa Barbara

From one perspective, the story of Santa Barbara, California, does not seem like an ECR story. High-profile ECR entrepreneurs did not intervene in or mediate the dispute; nor did they spin the story through elite networks or widely read publications. But the ECR story of Santa Barbara diffused through social networks of community and grassroots activists up and down the Pacific coast, and more recently through the Internet to far-flung communities around the world.

Storytellers mark the beginning of the Santa Barbara narrative at January 29, 1969, when a Union Oil Company platform six miles off the Santa Barbara coast suffered a "blowout" while it was pumping natural gas out of a well. Initial efforts to cap the blowout created further leaks and ruptures on the ocean floor that ultimately released 200,000 gallons of crude oil into the Santa Barbara Channel. For eleven days, workers struggled to cap the leaks. Meanwhile, an 800-square-mile slick hit the beaches of Santa Barbara and the Santa Barbara Channel Islands. The impact was almost immediate on sea life, as thousands of sea birds, seals, dolphins, tidal plants, and animals died as a result of ingesting or coming into contact with the oil. The community response to the spill was also immediate; thousands of Santa Barbara County residents banded together to try to save the wildlife and coastline. Much of their efforts involved transporting afflicted sea life (especially birds) to "treatment centers" where the oil on them could be washed. For larger creatures who could not be moved, volunteers washed them on the beach. And the beach itself was washed a few feet at time by removing and diluting oil (Easton,

1972). Of the community response to the oil spill, nature writer John McKinney wrote: "I had been impressed by the way energetic college students, shopkeepers, surfers, parents with their kids, all joined the beach clean-up. I saw a Montecito [a wealthy town a few miles south of Santa Barbara] society matron transporting oily birds in her Mercedes" (1995: 136).

In the weeks and months that followed, a multiagency investigation discovered that Union Oil's rig ruptured due to inadequate protective casings, which the U.S. Geological Survey had permitted the company to use. Because the rig stood more than three miles offshore, it escaped regulation by California's stringent codes and inspections. The focus of the dispute over the spill centered on who should pay for the cleanup, how the communities affected should be compensated, and what measures should be put into place to prevent or lessen the effects of a future spill (Steinhart, 1972; Molotch, 1970). A long-time environmental activist living in Santa Barbara at the time of the spill recounts how the dispute evolved at the local level:

> Everybody was filing lawsuits against everybody else. There was one story about a guy out in Isla Vista [the college town north of Santa Barbara adjacent to the University of California, Santa Barbara campus] who was trying to file a suit on behalf of some seals out on Devereaux Point [near the university]. Nobody thought that the lawsuits would do any good. Union Oil's president got quoted in the newspaper saying that it [the spill] wasn't a big deal because nobody got killed—I guess he counted the 50,000 sea birds and other animals as nobodies. Bud Bottoms had already organized GOO [Get Oil Out] and other community groups started to get into the act. Some of the national environmental organizations, like the Sierra Club, got involved.

Eventually, Union Oil spent millions of dollars in its cleanup efforts, and millions more flowed to local fishing-based businesses for losses they incurred and to local communities in legal settlements (Steinhart, 1972). But disputes over the spill did not end with the legal settlements because the damage continued to affect Santa Barbara and nearby communities well beyond the 1970s to the present. The story of the damage done to Santa Barbara by Union Oil also continued to be told, but with an added twist. In the 1980s, so argues this environmental activist/mediator, the Santa Barbara story began to be about ECR:

> What Santa Barbara meant to a lot of us was that conflict resolution didn't only have to occur at the mediator's table . . . or the courtroom. Conflict resolution needs to occur in somebody's living room, on the beach, or on a website when people become aware and work together. In fact, maybe it shouldn't occur at a bargaining table at all. Hell, all of this stuff really happens in communities, not in some office somewhere.

This speaker implies that the Santa Barbara tale is really an amalgam of stories about community empowerment, each spun at public protests, meetings, town halls, direct mailings, word-of-mouth, and, increasingly in the 1990s, on websites with hypertext links to other organizations. GOO, for example, recounts its ongoing "consciousness raising" public protests about oil company operations on its website. The Santa Barbara Wildlife Care Network (SBWCN), to cite another example, devotes part of its website to "success stories" that recount how SBWCN volunteers working with other grassroots groups save particular animals who have been adversely affected by pollution. Even oil companies spin their own community-oriented stories with their "Clean Seas" website. Clean Seas is an oil-industry-funded organization operating three ocean-going "clean up" vessels (dubbed, without a hint of irony, Mr. Clean, Mr. Clean II, and Mr. Clean III) that can participate in cleanups when spills occur along the coastlines of Santa Barbara and nearby counties. As a group, the GOO, SBWCN, and Clean Seas websites contain perhaps the most subversive ECR stories of all. The Santa Barbara stories question not only the efficacy of traditional environmental conflict resolution but also conventional ECR techniques including the field's centerpiece, mediation. Thus, the ECR frame that emerged from the Santa Barbara stories links with the communitarian narrative style and its focus on local empowerment and support networks within and across communities.

HOW FRAMES MATTER: ECR PRACTICE AND COLLECTIVE ACTION

During the past two decades, institutional entrepreneurs conceptualized, elaborated, and generalized the three stories recounted above into explicit collective action frames. Top EPA personnel continue to be closely involved in the development and deployment of the technocratic frame both within the EPA and in the emerging ECR field (Mays, 1988). More recently, top corporate managers from firms closely regulated by the EPA (especially chemical firms) and environmental lawyers have become involved in efforts to mobilize support for ECR from a technocratic perspective.[4] Snoqualmie became the basis for Cormick's initial development of the pluralistic ECR frame. Other practitioner/entrepreneurs, such as Lawrence Susskind, Howard Bellman, and James Laue have conceptualized and articulated this frame through conference and workshop presentations, and through their publications (such as Bellman, Sampson, and Cormick, 1982; Susskind, Bacow, and Wheeler, 1983; Susskind, McKearnan, and Thomas-Larmer, 1999; and Laue, 1988). Perhaps because of its diffuse nature, typified by the Santa

Barbara story, the communitarian frame has few large sponsors (Williams and Matheny, 1995). But it has blossomed in hundreds of locales and can now be found easily on grassroots organizations' websites. Table 4.1 summarizes the components of each ECR collective action frame.

Each of these frames has exerted considerable influence in the emergent ECR field, which, at this writing, is quite heterogeneous and contested with regards to norms of practice and collective action. Practitioners, entrepreneurs, and organizations draw on the technocratic frame to champion more formalized and settlement-oriented mediation processes of mediation and procedures that efficiently approximate court procedures, such as arbitration, minitrials, or private judging. Key in these procedures is providing information and choice sets to disputants that will lead to settlement (Mays, 1988; Hyatt, 1995). By contrast, the pluralist frame leads to less structured and more open-ended citizen participation as captured by facilitated problem solving, negotiated rule making, and collaborative planning. Disputants are assumed to have conflicting interests, although individual players may not always be able to articulate their interests before entering into an ECR process. Thus, an important part of pluralistic ECR focuses on the identification and development of interests on the way to finding consensus among conflicting parties (Susskind, McKearnan, and Thomas-Larmer, 1999; Cormick, 1992). Finally, the communitarian frame is associated with processes that fit less easily within the bailiwick of most ECR techniques. The goal of communitarian ECR is to repair tears in the social fabric by building networks of cooperation among communities and other players.

The practices associated with these frames continue to contend with more orthodox dispute settlement (such as litigation and regulatory procedures). Adherents of technocratic and pluralist ECR face opposition from within the federal government (especially from Department of Justice lawyers who fear the liability and procedural implications of ECR for environmental law) and grassroots environmentalists (who fear that professional ECR will either "sell out" to corporate and governmental interests in the name of compromise or simply does not have the enforcement bite of hard-edged legislation and adjudication). Communitarian ECR has experienced the most opposition from federal agencies, who fear that community-based ECR will interfere with the enforcement of broad-based standards.

Aside from conflict between ECR and external players, there is also considerable contestation among adherents to various ECR frames. Some of the conflict manifests itself as conflict over the appropriateness and effectiveness of modal practices. Proponents of technocratic ECR, for example, call into question the ef-

Table 4.1

Components of Collective Action Frames for Environmental Conflict Resolution

Components	Technocratic	Pluralistic	Communitarian
Key subversive story	Storm King	Snoqualmie	Santa Barbara
Underlying logic	Efficiency Trained expertise	Pluralism Balancing power	Holism Contextuality
Existing institutional failures	Inefficient	Unrepresentative	Fragmenting
Expert underpinnings	Environmental law Science and engineering Bureaucratic regulation	Labor relations	Local knowledge Helping professionals Eco-science
Disputes	Lack of expert information	Conflicting interests	Tear in community fabric
Disputants	Uninformed actors	Interest-bearing actors	Situated actors
ECR	Efficient settlement technique	Participatory mechanism	Mechanism of community empowerment and linkage with natural environment
Modal practices	Mediation Arbitration Mini trial/private judging	Facilitated problem solving Negotiated rule making Collaborative planning	Networks of cooperation between communities and other relevant actors
Evaluation	Cost-benefit analysis	Scope of participation	Community health Self-determination
Associated ECR collective action	Professionalization Insinuation into government agencies	Professionalization Restructuring public decision making	Direct action and protest
Principal advocates	Environmental lawyers Chemical corporations EPA administrators	Mediators Institutional environments	Community activists State agencies

Table 4.1
(*continued*)

Components	Technocratic	Pluralistic	Communitarian
Principal opponents	U.S. Justice Department Grassroots environmentalists	Grassroots environmentalists	Federal agencies
Principal audiences	State courts Federal judges	Federal agencies (sans EPA) State agencies	Diffuse collectivities Grassroots environmentalists

fectiveness of more open-ended pluralistic and communitarian ECR. A high-ranking administrator from a large Western state commented in an interview with the first author that some disputants, especially in the corporate world and among large ranching interests, ". . . want settlements. They don't want to sit around and talk forever and plan for all of the contingent problems that could arise or get in bed with a thousand little community interests. They want to know that this particular dispute is off the table and that they can move on unimpeded with their business."

Other forms of contention appear in the kinds of collective action associated with each frame. Both technocratic and pluralistic frames dominate the discourse about practice and collective action spearheaded by the primary ECR professional organization, SPIDR. From the standpoint of these frames, building ECR is a professional project with different, albeit potentially complementary, trajectories. Technocratic professionalization has meant the insinuation of ECR into state-level and federal courts (including administrative courts) in which ECR stands as an alternative to adjudication (Collins, 1990; Jacobs, 1995). Such insinuation has occurred in two ways, first through the recruitment of judges, lawyers, and other court personnel into state and national professional organizations, and second through uniform rules and memoranda either requiring or strongly suggesting ECR (especially mediation) for particular classes of disputes. Pluralistic ECR efforts have been more radical in attempting to restructure dispute-related and other administrative decision making. Professionalized ECR proponents have led the charge to encourage administrative personnel to be trained in ECR techniques and to develop freestanding ECR departments within all administrative agencies as part of the comprehensive Administrative Dispute Resolution Act of 1990, which sought to overturn "the overjudicalization of administrative processes" (Bingham and Wise, 1996). At the same time, as ECR collective action related to the technocratic and pluralistic frames has occurred primarily in and around state organizations, communitarian activists have been busy building networks within and across communities. Here, ECR collective action often takes the form of coalition building by grassroots organizations who have negotiated working agreements among themselves and, in some cases, across the political divide to state-level agencies and private corporations.

The influence and use of ECR frames also can be seen in the most important institutional ECR entrepreneur on the contemporary scene: the U.S. Institute for Environmental Conflict Resolution, founded and led by Kirk Emerson. Funded by a congressional act in 1998 but located outside the Beltway in Tucson, Arizona, the Institute's stated mission is to "assist parties in resolving environmental conflicts around the country that involve federal agencies or interests" (see the website located at http://ecr.gov.about.htm). Because many environmental disputes involve public lands, the Institute's activities extend across wide domains. In the mid-1990s, Senator John McCain, a friend of the late representative and environmental champion Morris Udall, crossed party lines to draft legislation for a federal clearing house for environmental disputes. McCain drew on the technocratic frame to sell ECR in conservative circles by arguing its "risk management" benefits to the federal government, and drew on the pluralistic and communitarian frames to attract liberal and environmentally minded congressional supporters by claiming ECR could balance complex political interests expressed in environmental disputes at the same time as it met community needs.

From the outset the Institute was intended to function outside traditional governmental channels but within the "federal family" of administrative agencies. Emerson's strategy has been to operate the Institute as a "broker" organization by employing multiple ECR frames to build constituencies within and across multiple audiences (just as McCain had successfully done in Congress), link networks of practitioners outside and within the federal government, and create normative boundaries of ECR expertise and practice. During the past three years, the Institute engaged in ECR interventions in fourteen states and nationally through several web-based applications.

The use of multiple frames can be seen in the ECR definition located on the Institute's home page. The definition includes references to how ECR can "save time and avoid many of the costs of traditional legal proceedings" (technocratic frame); provide "opportunities . . . for all groups affected by proposed federal policies or actions in participating in their formulation, revision, or implementation" (pluralistic frame); and facilitate "community-based collaborations" (communitarian frame). The Institute, working with personnel from the EPA and nongovernmental ECR practitioners, has created a national roster of ECR professionals with the explicit goal of "advanc[ing] the interests of the growing field of dispute resolution." The Institute is also creating a web-based archive of ECR cases, which will document the successes of ECR across a broad range of environmental contexts. If the Institute is successful at using multiple ECR frames and strategies to legitimize and institutionalize ECR, it will emerge as a key organizational player within the ECR field, which in turn will carry important implications for the stratification of the field in terms of practices and practitioners.

CONCLUSION

We have explored the linkages between political storytelling, the production of collective action frames, and the rise of ECR in the United States during the 1960s and 1970s. We organized our analysis around the argument that collective action frames facilitate the mobilization efforts of institutional entrepreneurs to create ECR as a set of recognized practices in a variety of contexts and to the emergence of ECR as a nascent, albeit highly contested, heterogeneous field. Key in these processes were three subversive stories—Storm King, Snoqualmie, and Santa Barbara—that supplied vivid dramatizations of the courts' failures to manage environmental disputes and, through the processes of conceptualization, generalization, and elaboration, led to the development of ECR collective action frames.

Beyond providing some analytic purchase on the origins of ECR as a field, we believe that several useful implications flow from our narrative approach. First, our approach expands the research strategies available for studying institutional change. Standard research strategies for studying social change from an institutionalist perspective typically rely on the covariance of factors rather than the processes that underlie or shape institutional effects (Schneiberg and Clemens 2002; Scott 1995). Our approach, by contrast, focuses on the *processual* production of ideational factors in institutional change, especially the processes by which collective action frames are constructed and deployed. In so doing, it is consistent with collective action approaches that regard meaning work by movement participants and broader social constituents as significant for institutional change (Benford and Snow, 2000; Clemens and Cook, 1999).

Our narrative approach also provides a window to top-down and bottom-up interactions that link the microlevel with broader social phenomena. Specifically, we draw attention to how stories come to be instantiated with elements drawn from higher-order cultural models (narrative styles), which in turn can have significant influence on meso-level phenomena, such as the evolution of collective interests and rationality within institutional fields (for example, the desirability or costs associated with particular strategies or resources).

Moreover, our approach can supplement existing strategies for analyzing the textured nature of structural variation and power within fields (see, for example, Milstein, Hart, and York, Chapter 6; Levy and Rothenberg, Chapter 7). Specifically, narrative analysis provides a basis for examining symbolic—especially discursive—variation within emergent and established fields. Questions such as which stories have currency and legitimacy, which stories have disappeared from common parlance, or which subversive stories make it from the backstage to the frontstage, all provide clues to the constitution of a field and its continued power dynamics.

This chapter only scratches the surface of how political stories operate in the construction of collective action frames and institutional change, as well as the role of institutions, more generally, in the management of the natural environment. Future research should consider a number of important questions. How do particular types of narratives function in historical context? All of the stories explored here emerged during the turbulent 1960s and 1970s, which was a period of intense social movement activity and widely circulated subversive stories about a broad range of social institutions. Indeed, the cultural climate during this period among some social audiences was particularly welcoming to protest and subversion (see Snow and Benford, 1992). Given this context, one could argue that the three ECR stories faced less repression than they would have experienced had they emerged in a less politically volatile period. Clearly, for example, Storm King and its technocratic frame meshed well with legal concerns about court efficiency. Under what conditions does this relationship hold? Was technocratic discourse viewed as less threatening and therefore more attractive by elites and government officials given the contentious state of American politics at the time? When will a story told using the communitarian or pluralist style be most effective in mobilizing efforts?

The issue of context also suggests the role that geographical region or state could play in the production of subversive stories. All three of the stories we considered emanated from states (New York, Washington, and California) that are among the most progressive in the United States regarding environmental regulation and legal administration. In other words, how do the cultural, political, and legal climates of states affect the production, resonance, and role of subversive stories in institutional change?

Other questions suggested by our research concern the structuring of political narratives by each other and by institutional crises. Is there a kind of path dependency when one narrative or narrative style precedes another? Are some frames easier than others to switch to and from? With regard to crises, the crisis of environmental litigation could be said to be one of sociopolitical legitimacy in the legal system rather than of market failure. Does the type of institutional crisis affect the production and subsequent impact of subversive stories? How can we theorize institutional crises and their relationships to political opportunities for change? Relevant to institutional entrepreneurship, our analysis points toward the importance of the positioning and types of actors involved. Storm King and Snoqualmie illustrate elite-spun subversive stories in that both Russell Train and Gerald Cormick were embedded in elite networks. Santa Barbara, by contrast, represents a "bottom-up" subversive story largely spun by non-elites. What kinds of social locations are most conducive to institutional entrepreneurship? Under what conditions does elite subversion occur? Under what conditions can subordinate subversive stories feed into change efforts directed at organizational fields and institutions? How does the "routinization" of entrepreneurship occur such that charismatic individuals give way to collective entrepreneurs (such as the U.S. Institute)?

Taken as a whole, this chapter provides some purchase on Aldrich's (1999: 332) invitation to study key "agents in action," who are highly influential in the often "disorderly" process of organizational and institutional emergence. As Aldrich (1999: 1000) notes, stories can provide effective ways for entrepreneurs to communicate their vision of a new organization or community of practice during the process of emergence. Subversive stories are potentially powerful tools for the institutional entrepreneur, for they offer ways to think and communicate about alternative realities long before the problems associated with existing realities and the possibilities for change have been fully articulated in collective action frames. As a result, subversive stories are not only an important symbolic resource used to construct frames, but also can operate as anticipatory socialization to prepare audiences for collective frames once they are constructed. Subversive stories thus provide an important analytic linchpin between skilled actors, collective action and efficacy, broad cultural discourses, and the construction of new institutional arrangements.

NOTES AND REFERENCES

NOTES

1. Although part of the business of this chapter is to examine the various meanings given to ECR techniques by different constituencies, it might be useful to provide some preliminary working definitions at the outset. In a widely known definition, Lon Fuller (1971) argues that mediation involves a neutral third party who facilitates joint decision making by disputants, but who does not have the authority to pronounce outcomes. Other techniques discussed within the auspices of ECR include collaborative group planning, facilitated community problem solving, public consensus building (all of which are less settlement oriented and can occur with or without specific disputes present); arbitration (adjudicatory-like procedures without the direct enforcement powers of a court); early neutral evaluation (in which a third party evaluates the merits of a case prior to it going through a more formal procedure); mini-trials and private judging (trial-like procedures conducted by private parties); and hybrids, such as "med-arb" (in which the third party is authorized to act as an arbitrator if impasse is reached during mediation). For further background discussions on ECR and the wider field of alternative dispute resolution (ADR), see Menkel-Meadow (1997); Moore (1973).

2. Political narratives are not limited to stories that challenge existing institutions and fields; within established fields, subversive stories can function constitutively by exemplifying the "truth" of already "successful" frames. When constitutive stories reinforce taken-for-granted assumptions they become "hegemonic tales" (Ewick and Silbey, 1995; Clemens and Cook, 1999). Hegemonic tales reify the symbolic, technical, and moral boundaries of fields. As such, they stifle alternatives by representing certain events as part of the natural order. Under these conditions, critiques become difficult to imagine and, when presented, may even be incomprehensible to audiences steeped in contradictory hegemonic tales. Stories thus can control as well as subvert.

3. The ECR case sections are derived from several data sources collected between 1996 and 1999: (1) essays and first-hand accounts written by key players in the Snoqualmie and Storm King cases; (2) in-depth interviews of key ECR players (n = 11) at the regional and national conferences for the Society for Professionals in Dispute Resolution (SPIDR) meetings of the Environmental and

Public Sector of SPIDR, and ECR conferences sponsored by the Udall Center for Studies in Public Policy; (3) multiday observation of planning meetings (n = 3) for the United States Institute of Environmental Conflict Resolution and at other meetings (n = 4) of key players in the ECR field; and (4) information from Internet websites associated with key organizations (such as SPIDR and the Institute) and from individual players in the field.

4. See, for example, the panel discussion reproduced from the 1999 Environmental and Public Policy Sector conference on SPIDR's website at http://www.spidr.org/envpol/

REFERENCES

Abbott, Andrew. 1988. *The System of the Professions.* Chicago: University of Chicago Press.

Aldrich, Howard. 1999. *Organizations Evolving.* Thousand Oaks, CA: Sage.

Bellman, Howard S., Cynthia Sampson, and Gerald Cormick. 1982. *Using Mediation When Siting Hazardous Waste Management Facilities: A Handbook.* Washington, DC: U.S. Environmental Protection Agency.

Benford, Robert D. 1993. "Frame Disputes Within the Nuclear Disarmament Movement." *Social Forces,* 71: 677–701.

Benford, Robert D., and David A. Snow. 2000. "Framing Processes and Social Movements: An Overview and Assessment." *Annual Review of Sociology,* 26: 611–639.

Bingham, Gail. 1986. *Resolving Environmental Disputes: A Decade of Experience.* Washington, DC: The Conservation Foundation.

Bingham, Lisa B., and Charles R. Wise. 1996. "The Administrative Dispute Resolution Act of 1990: How Do We Evaluate Its Success." *Journal of Public Administration Research and Theory,* 6: 383–414.

Blackburn, J. Walton, and Willa Bruce. 1995. *Mediating Environmental Conflicts: Theory and Practice.* Westport, CT: Quorum Books.

Bourdieu, Pierre, and Loic J. D. Wacquant. 1992. *An Invitation to Reflexive Sociology.* Chicago: University of Chicago Press.

"Calm After the Storm: Grandmother of Environmental Lawsuits Settled by Mediation." *Environmental Law Reporter,* 1981, 11, 10074–10077.

Carson, Rachel. 1962. *Silent Spring.* Boston: Houghton Mifflin.

Cintron, Ralph. 1997. *Chero Ways, Gang Life, and Rhetorics of the Everyday.* Boston: Beacon Press.

Clemens, Elisabeth S. 1997. *The People's Lobby: Organizational Innovation and the Rise of Interest Group Politics in the United States, 1890–1925.* Chicago: University of Chicago Press.

Clemens, Elisabeth S., and James M. Cook. 1999. "Politics and Institutionalism: Explaining Durability and Change." *Annual Review of Sociology,* 25: 441–466.

Collins, Richard C. 1990. "The Emergence of Environmental Mediation." *Virginia Environmental Law Journal,* 104: vi–x.

Cormick, Gerald W. 1976. "Mediating Environmental Controversies: Perspectives and First Experience." *Earth Law Journal,* 2: 215–221.

Cormick, Gerald W. 1980. "The 'Theory' and Practice of Environmental Mediation." *The Environmental Professional,* 2: 24–33.

Cormick, Gerald W. 1982. "Intervention and Self-Determination in Environmental Disputes: A Mediator's Perspective." *Resolve,* 3: 3–7.

Cormick, Gerald W. 1992. "Environmental Conflict, Community Mobilization and the 'Public Good.'" *Studies in Law, Politics, and Society,* 12: 309–329.

Cornell, Stephen. 2000. "That's the Story of Our Life." In Paul R. Spickard and W. Jeffrey Burroughs, eds., *We Are a People: Narrative and Multiplicity in the Construction of Ethnic Identity,* 41–53. Philadelphia: Temple University Press.

Creed, W. E. Douglas, and Maureen A. Scully. 1998. "Switchpersons on the Tracks of History: Situated Agency and Contested Legitimacy in the Diffusion of Domestic Partner Benefits." Paper presented at the annual meetings of the Academy of Management, San Diego, CA.

Czarniawska, Barbara. 1997. *Narrating the Organization: Dramas of Institutional Identity.* Chicago: University of Chicago Press.

Dacin, M. Tina, Marc J. Ventresca, and Brent D. Beal. 1999. "The Embeddedness of Organizations: Dialogue and Directions." *Journal of Management,* 25: 317–356.

Dezalay, Yves, and Bryant G. Garth. 1996. *Dealing in Virtue: International Commercial Arbitration and the Construction of a Transnational Legal Order.* Chicago: University of Chicago Press.

DiMaggio, Paul J. 1991. "Constructing an Organizational Field as a Professional Project: U.S. Art Museums, 1920–1940." In Walter W. Powell and Paul J. DiMaggio, eds., *The New Institutionalism in Organizational Analysis.* Chicago: University of Chicago Press.

DiMaggio, Paul J., and Walter W. Powell. 1983. "The Iron Cage Revisited: Institutional Isomorphism and Collective Rationality in Organizational Fields." *American Sociological Review,* 48: 147–160.

DiMaggio, Paul J., and Walter W. Powell. 1991. "Introduction." In Walter W. Powell and Paul J. DiMaggio, eds., *The New Institutionalism in Organizational Analysis,* 1–38. Chicago: University of Chicago Press.

Easton, Robert Olney. 1972. *Black Tide: The Santa Barbara Oil Spill and Its Consequences.* New York: Delacorte.

Edelman, Murray. 1967. *The Symbolic Uses of Politics.* Urbana: University of Illinois Press.

Emerson, Kirk. 1996. "A Critique of Environmental Dispute Resolution Research." Unpublished paper available from the Udall Center for Studies in Public Policy, University of Arizona.

Emirbayer, Mustafa, and Ann Mische. 1998. "What Is Agency?" *American Journal of Sociology,* 103: 962–1023.

Ewick, Patricia, and Susan S. Silbey. 1995. "Subversive Stories and Hegemonic Tales: Toward a Sociology of Narrative." *Law & Society Review,* 29: 197–226.

Ferguson, Priscilla Parkhurst. 1998. "A Cultural Field in the Making: Gastronomy in 19th Century France." *American Journal of Sociology,* 104: 597–641.

Fligstein, Neil. 1996. "Markets as Politics: A Political-Cultural Approach to Market Institutions." *American Sociological Review,* 61: 656–673.

Fligstein, Neil. 2001. "Social Skill and the Theory of Fields." *Sociological Theory,* 19: 105–125.

Fox, Kelly. 1995. "Survey Tracks Use of ADR for Environmental Disputes." *Corporate Legal Times,* April, 13–14.

Friedland, Roger, and Robert R. Alford. 1991. "Bringing Society Back In: Symbols, Practices, and Institutional Contradictions." In Walter W. Powell and Paul J. DiMaggio, eds., *The New Institutionalism in Organizational Analysis,* 232–263. Chicago: University of Chicago Press.

Fuller, Lon. 1971. "Mediation—Its Forms and Functions." *Southern California Law Review,* 44: 305–339.

Gamson, William A. 1992. "The Social Psychology of Collective Action." In Aldon D. Morris and Carol McClung Madler, eds., *Frontiers in Social Movement Theory.* New Haven, CT: Yale University Press.

Gamson, William A., and David S. Meyer. 1996. "Framing Political Opportunity." In Doug McAdam, John D. McCarthy, and Mayer N. Zald, eds., *Comparative Perspectives on Social Movements: Political Opportunities, Mobilizing Structures, and Cultural Framings,* 275–290. Cambridge, England: Cambridge University Press.

Goffman, Erving. 1974. *Frame Analysis.* New York: Harper & Row.

Hilgartner, Stephen, and Charles L. Bosk. 1988. "The Rise and Fall of Social Problems: A Public Arenas Model." *American Journal of Sociology,* 94: 53–78.

Hyatt, William H. 1995. "Taming the Environmental Litigation Tiger." *Journal of Environmental Regulation,* 5: 91–98.

Jacobs, Joel S. 1995. "Compromising NEPA? The Interplay Between Settlement Agreements and the National Environmental Policy Act." *Harvard Environmental Law Review,* 19: 113–156.

Joas, Hans. 1993. *Pragmatism and Social Theory.* Chicago: University of Chicago Press.

Laue, James H. 1988. *Using Mediation to Shape Public Policy.* San Francisco: Jossey-Bass.

Mays, Richard H. 1988. "Alternative Dispute Resolution and Environmental Enforcement: A Noble Experiment or a Lost Cause?" *Environmental Law Reporter,* 18: 10087–10097.

McAdam, Doug, John D. McCarthy, and Mayer N. Zald. 1996. "Opportunities, Mobilizing Structures, and Framing Processes: Toward a Synthetic Comparative Perspective on Social Movements." In Doug McAdam, John D. McCarthy, and Mayer N. Zald, eds., *Comparative Perspectives on Social Movements: Political Opportunities, Mobilizing Structures, and Cultural Framings,* 1–20. Cambridge, England: Cambridge University Press.

McKinney, John. 1995. *A Walk Along Land's End: Discovering California's Unknown Coast.* San Francisco: HarperCollins West.

Menkel-Meadow, Carrie. 1997. "What Will We Do When Adjudication Ends? A Brief Intellectual History of ADR." *UCLA Law Review,* 44: 1613–1630.

Meyer, David S., and Suzanne Staggenborg. 1996. "Movements, Counter Movements and the Structure of Political Opportunity." *American Journal of Sociology,* 101: 1628–1660.

Meyer, John W., and Brian Rowan. 1978. "Institutionalized Organizations: Formal Structure as Myth and Ceremony." *American Journal of Sociology,* 83: 340–363.

Molotch, Harvey. 1970. "Oil in Santa Barbara and Power in America." *Sociological Inquiry,* 40: 131–144.

Moore, Sally Falk. 1973. "Law and Social Change: The Semi-Autonomous Social Field as an Appropriate Subject of Study." *Law & Society Review,* 8: 719–746.

Morrill, Calvin. 1995. *The Executive Way: Conflict Management in Corporations.* Chicago: University of Chicago Press.

Morrill, Calvin. 2002. "Institutional Change Through Interstitial Emergence: The Growth of Alternative Dispute Resolution in American Law, 1965–1995." In Walter W. Powell and Daniel L. Jones, eds., *How Institutions Change.* Chicago: University of Chicago Press, forthcoming.

Morrill, Calvin, Christine Yalda, Madelaine Adelman, Michael Musheno, and Cindy Bejarano. 2000. "Telling Tales in School: Youth Culture and Conflict Narratives." *Law & Society Review,* 34: 521–566.

O'Leary, Rosemary. 1999. *Managing for the Environment: Understanding the Legal Organizational and Policy Challenges.* San Francisco: Jossey-Bass.

Percival, Robert V. 1992. "The Ecology of Environmental Conflict: Risk, Uncertainty and the Transformation of Environmental Policy Disputes." *Studies in Law, Politics, and Society,* 12: 209–246.

Rao, Hayagreeva, Calvin Morrill, and Mayer N. Zald. 2000. "Power Plays: Social Movements, Collective Action, and New Organizational Forms." *Research in Organizational Behavior,* 22: 237–282

Reissman, Catherine Kohler. 1993. *Narrative Analysis.* Thousand Oaks, CA: Sage.

Roe, Emery. 1994. *Narrative Policy Analysis: Theory and Practice.* Durham, NC: Duke University Press.

Schank, Roger C. 1990. *Tell Me a Story: A New Look at Real and Artificial Memory.* New York: Scribner's.

Schneiberg, Marc, and Elisabeth S. Clemens. 2002. "The Typical Tools for the Job: Research Strategies in Institutional Analysis." In Walter W. Powell and Daniel L. Jones, eds., *How Institutions Change.* Chicago: University of Chicago Press, forthcoming.

Scott, James C. 1990. *Domination and the Arts of Resistance: Hidden Transcripts.* New Haven, CT: Yale University Press.

Scott, W. Richard. 1995. *Institutions and Organizations.* Beverly Hills, CA: Sage.

Snow, David A., and Robert D. Benford. 1992. "Master Frames and Cycles of Protest." In Aldon D. Morris and Carol McClung Mueller, eds., *Frontiers in Social Movement Theory,* 33–155. New Haven, CT: Yale University Press.

Steinhart, Carol E. 1972. *Blowout: A Case Study of the Santa Barbara Oil Spill.* North Scituate, MA: Duxbury Press.

Strang, David, and John W. Meyer. 1994. "Institutional Conditions for Diffusion." In W. Richard Scott, John W. Meyer, and Associates, eds., *Institutional Environments and Organizations: Structural Complexity and Individualism,* 100–112. Thousand Oaks, CA: Sage.

Susskind, Lawrence, Lawrence S. Bacow, and Michael Wheeler. 1983. *Resolving Environmental Regulatory Disputes.* Cambridge, MA: Schenkman.

Susskind, Lawrence, Sarah McKearnan, and Jennifer Thomas-Larmer. 1999. *The Consensus Building Handbook: A Comprehensive Guide to Reaching Agreement.* Thousand Oaks, CA: Sage.

Swidler, Ann. 1986. "Culture in Action: Symbols and Strategies." *American Sociological Review,* 51: 273–286.

Talbot, Allan R. 1972. *Power Along the Hudson: The Storm King Case and the Birth of Environmentalism.* New York: Dutton.

Tilly, Charles. 1978. *From Mobilization to Revolution.* Reading, MA: Addison-Wesley.

Train, Russell. 1993. *EPA History Program Oral History Interview.* Washington, DC: U.S. EPA.

Turner, Tom. 1988. "The Legal Eagles." *The Amicus Journal,* 10(1): 25–37.

Van Maanen, John. 1988. *Tales from the Field: On Writing Ethnography.* Chicago: University of Chicago Press.

White, Hayden. 1973. *Metahistory.* Baltimore: Johns Hopkins University Press.

Williams, Bruce A., and Albert R. Matheny. 1995. *Democracy, Dialogue, and Environmental Disputes: The Contested Languages of Social Regulation.* New Haven, CT: Yale University Press.

5 | POLLUTION FUTURES:

COMMENSURATION, COMMODIFICATION,

AND THE MARKET FOR AIR

Peter Levin and Wendy Nelson Espeland

Carlton Bartels,* a successful broker with the behemoth brokerage company Cantor Fitzgerald, is on the phone with a promising client. "The market has been down a bit," he tells him. "I think it's a buying opportunity." Bartels gazes out his window in the World Trade Center at the hazy air that obscures his view of uptown Manhattan. "It looks like a beautiful day to sell pollution," he says (Kranish, 1999).

Bartels is one of a small but growing number of traders with an unusual specialty. Where others might work in stocks, bonds, or futures in everything from pork bellies to oil, Bartels sells what amounts to a right to pollute. For him, a typical trade might involve selling permits to emit 10,000 tons of sulfur dioxide (SO_2). Sulfur dioxide, along with nitrogen oxides, is a main component of acid rain. Permits to emit SO_2 are one of a range of environmental "economic instruments" that Cantor Fitzgerald brokers.[1] Permits can also be purchased at an annual auction organized by the EPA under the auspices of the Chicago Board of Trade. Environmental groups have bought a few permits in order to retire them, but the annual auction, like the trades negotiated by brokers at Cantor Fitzgerald, is dominated by

Thanks to conference participants and to Bruce Carruthers, Anita Engels, Andy Hoffman, Marc Milstein, Tom Tietenberg, Marc J. Ventresca, and especially Arthur Stinchcombe and Mitchell Stevens, for detailed comments. We are grateful for financial support from the Dispute Resolution Research Center at Northwestern University. The second author is also grateful for generous support from the Russell Sage Foundation, assistance from Mariam Manichaikul and Nicole Radmore, and for the enduring warmth of the Lochinvar Society.
*Carlton Bartels, age 44, was one of almost 3,000 people killed in the September 11, 2001 terrorist attack on the World Trade Center, where Cantor Fitzgerald was located. This article was written before the attack. After weighing whether to keep his account in the article, we decided that editing out the existence of the victims does not do justice to the lives they led.

utility companies. Two kinds of allowances are traded: "spot" allowances, available for use immediately, and "future" allowances, which can be used seven years after the purchase date.

The buying and selling of permits to pollute is a dramatic new approach to environmental protection. The Acid Rain Program is part of the sweeping changes ushered in by the Clean Air Act Amendments of 1990. The amendments enlarged and codified earlier efforts to reduce air pollution by "harnessing market forces" (Stavins, 1998b: 1). These included "emission reduction credits" for firms reducing pollution below allowable levels, and banking procedures that would allow firms to "save" their pollution credits for future use (Tietenberg, 1997: 2–4). These early experiments yielded mixed results. After decades of lobbying and debate, the 1990 Amendments provided the political and legal impetus that ushered in a new regulatory regime.[2] Title IV of the Amendments created "the first large-scale, long-term" market in tradable emission permits (Ellerman and others, 2000: 3). In doing so, it supplemented traditional forms of regulation known as "command and control" with what have become known as "market-based" or "cap-and-trade" solutions to regulating air quality.

The command-and-control approach to air-quality regulation imposes ambient air quality standards on all polluters, requiring them to conform to these standards or face mandatory remediation requirements. By contrast, under a cap-and-trade program, polluting firms are allocated pollution "allowances" annually, with the aggregate number of allowances capped to ensure that pollution is gradually reduced. Firms may either reduce their emissions or purchase additional allowances on the open market, so long as at the end of the year their total emissions equal their allowances. Unused allowances can be sold on the open market or "banked" for future use. The market-based approach effectively creates a market in pollution by turning emissions into a scarce, fungible commodity (Tietenberg, 1985). In this chapter we use the creation of a market in air pollution as a case for investigating the institutional work of implementing markets as policy tools.

One image of markets sees them as the spontaneous outcome of individual decision making. Markets reflect the cumulative decisions of rational, decentralized individuals who, within the limits of their resources, maximize their individual utilities (Knight, [1921] 1985). A different view emerges from more sociological approaches to markets. These approaches understand markets as socially constructed institutions, the culmination of complex and varied social processes (Weber, 1978: 63–211, 311–355; Barber, 1977; Zelizer, 1989). Scholars in this tradition often stress how markets are embedded in social relations (Granovetter, 1985). They show, for example, how social networks affect the performance of markets (Uzzi,

1996), the distinctive subcultures of "market-makers" (Abolafia, 1996), the ways markets are used to express political partisanship (Carruthers, 1996), or how appeals to markets legitimate social inequality (Nelson and Bridges, 1999). This work depicts markets as more heterogeneous and political, and less self-regulating and spontaneous, than the markets described in most economic textbooks.

We build on this sociological approach to markets by examining the role of commensuration in the social construction of a commodity. We focus on how prices become attached to air pollution. Prices, as an expression of value, depend on transforming emissions into comparable, standardized commodities; doing so, in turn, depends on our being able to conceive of the environment as composed of discrete, measurable objects. Commensuration, the transformation of qualitative relations into quantities on a common metric, is central to both of these processes. Commensurative practices are fundamental for making markets.

Commensuration is a complex social process. It often requires vast resources, elaborate coordination, and diligent and imaginative labor. Because of the scale and complexity involved, commensuration, especially that which undergirds markets, is often a state project. Failing to appreciate how much work and creativity this takes risks minimizing a key role that states (or other large social institutions) play in creating the infrastructure for markets. Such neglect makes it easier to conceive of markets as more autonomous and easier to enact than they are; it also perpetuates the misperception that markets and states are antithetical or competing modes of organizing. States often help construct, whether legally or metrologically, the commodities that markets distribute and the conditions that make prices seem legitimate.

We analyze here the significance of commensuration in the creation of the futures market in air pollution, highlighting the crucial role the state plays in creating and coordinating the various kinds of commensuration required. We disclose the different dimensions of commensuration and how their salience changes over time. We conclude by describing some ideological implications of minimizing the importance of commensuration, and its effects, in markets.

MARKETS AS THEORIES OF THE WORLD

Market-based solutions have become an increasingly popular policy option for addressing all kinds of social problems. As part of a broader movement of privatization since the early 1980s, an appreciation of markets as an effective tool for improving public policy has moved from "intellectual fringe" to the center in policy debates (Lounsbury, Geraci, and Waismel-Manor, Chapter 14). Increasingly, regulators and legislators agree with J. H. Dales' conclusion that "if it is feasible to establish a market to implement a policy, no policy-maker can afford to do without one" (Dales, 1968, cited in Ellerman and others, 2000: v). In environmental regulation, the SO_2 trading program has become the model for market-based solutions. In addition to being used to regulate acid rain, lead, and ozone-depleting gases, they are also being applied to auto emissions, water pollutants, and fishing and water rights.[3] The stature of the SO_2 program is such that, in 1999, the EPA renamed its "Acid Rain Division" the "Clean Air Markets Division."

An institutional approach to studying this policy shift challenges what is emerging as the new conventional wisdom in regulation: that markets as effective and fair policy instruments are limited only by minor technical problems or by politics. In nature, air pollution does not appear as a fungible, tradable commodity. To see it as such requires elaborate human interventions. The market in air pollution, like all markets, was an organized activity. It required the coordinated labor of thousands of people, the mobilization of vast and disparate technical and cultural resources, and layers of commensurative practices. Institutional approaches highlight the work that other perspectives assume, including the question of how "problems" get defined as such, and how they become relegated to particular fields.

Examining the institutional bases for command-and-control and market-based regulation requires that we appreciate the cultural, political, and economic aspects of policy. Policies are implicit "theories of the world," predicated on assumptions about how the world works (Hoffman and Ventresca, 1999; Majone, 1981: 25; Stinchcombe, 1974, 1990). These assumptions shape where attention is directed, how problems, solutions, and their causal connections get defined, and who participates in creating and implementing policy. Public policies embody ideas about the relationship between the state and societal conditions that identify and classify social conditions as dependent variables and government actions as independent variables, and the causal relations between them (Feigenbaum, Henig, and Hamnett, 1998: 116–117). In this view, making policy is a more complex and institutionalized process than simply deciding which alternative to implement.

As theories of the world, market-based approaches should be evaluated not only as successes or failures, but also for their symbolic and cultural effects (Hironaka and Schofer, Chapter 9). This is particularly true at the intersection of policy and markets, since market logic is often used to challenge state intervention (Lounsbury, Geraci, and Waismel-Manor, Chapter 14). Market logic also has influenced prevailing theories that explain what motivates people, how they make rational decisions, and how they value things (Anderson, 1993: xi–xii). Markets offer powerful models for organizing behavior. They can change the way politics is conducted. When schoolchildren hold bake sales in order to buy and retire pollution allowances, this form of political engagement contrasts sharply with more traditional actions such as political protests, letter writing, or energy conservation campaigns. As generic vehicles for satisfying wants, markets define rationality in terms of the evaluation of outcomes, and place cash values on people's wants.

As Johannes Berger (1994: 790) summarizes, "The central message of environmental economics is: environmental use poses an allocation problem." Currently, three principles inform market-based approaches to environmental policy: first, environmental problems are defined in terms of the *absence* of markets in environmental goods; second, resolving environmental problems depends on *extending* markets (or the logic of the marketplace) to environmental goods; and third, environmental values can be made *commensurate* with all other values and preferences. This last idea logically links to the first two, because creating or simulating a market requires that environmental goods be treated as commodities with precise prices.

Concern with how to properly value the environment is a relatively recent issue in economics (O'Connor and Spash, 1999: 1–2). The main emphasis of value theory in economics has traditionally been on the quantity and pricing of "produced wealth"—goods or services that are created for exchange in markets. The nonproduced "free gifts of nature" that are the raw materials and pre-conditions for productive wealth (air, water, soil, and sun) typically have been treated as exogenous givens in economic analyses that focused on produced wealth. Broad public attention to environmental degradation has prompted economists to revise this emphasis in order to incorporate the impact of economic activity on our environment. This has entailed a shift in the image of nature from that of an exogenous, "free gift," to that of a precisely valued resource, expanding the conception of an "optimum" to include the harm associated with economic production, and theorizing environmental damages as "negative externalities."

A negative externality occurs when an activity has a third-party effect that harms someone's ability to satisfy her preferences that has not been taken into account in market exchanges. In such a case, prices do not capture the social costs of production (Coase, 1960). Air pollution is a standard example of a negative externality. The pollutants emitted by Midwestern utility companies are a primary source of the acid rain that damages forests in the northeastern United States and southeastern Canada.[4] In the absence of government regulation, these companies treated air as a free good and simply released their wastes into the atmosphere. This practice adversely affects those who were not a party to the market transaction but who must nevertheless breathe or otherwise contend with its effects. In the past, utilities have not taken into account the "full" costs associated with their pollution, which means that they produce more than the economically "optimal" amount of pollution (Baumol and Oates, 1979: 71–79).

Once pollution is defined as a negative externality, its solution seems obvious: internalize the externalities. There are several ways of doing so. One approach would impose a corrective tax on those who produce the externality. Another entails constructing shadow prices for environmental goods by devising strategies for determining what people would pay for them if there were a market, and by incorporating these into cost-benefit analyses of proposed policies.[5] A third approach involves creating new markets by extending property rights to environmental goods. This was the approach taken in Title IV of the Clean Air Act. Firms now have incentives to reduce pollution because they must acquire pollution allowances before they can increase production, and because they can sell allowances they do not use. But this process of internalization is more than a simple economic act of assigning prices to an already existing—though undervalued—commodity. It is an organizational and cultural feat, requiring substantial investments in identifying (and sometimes creating) new actors, credible forms of knowledge, and measurement regimes (Callon, 1998). And it requires commensuration.

The assumptions behind market-based approaches seem straightforward and appealing. They define a problem and offer a solution. But just what is at stake with the theory of the world underlying market-based approaches to public policy? Some scholars dispute a view of markets as a simple, general, or neutral model for distributing scarce resources or for organizing and understanding human behavior. Before saying more about the role that commensuration plays in establishing markets and the implications of this, we should explain what we mean by commensuration and why some are wary of markets as policy tools.

COMMENSURATION AS A SOCIAL PROCESS[6]

Commensuration is a process for comparing and integrating different objects and practices. It constructs relations among disparate things by uniting them based on their shared relationship to a third thing—a metric. Common products of commensurative processes include votes, standardized test scores, rankings, opinion polls, batting averages, and cost-benefit ratios. In markets, prices and quantities are the most prominent forms of commensuration.

Commensuration transforms qualitative differences into quantitative ones, where the difference between things is subsumed and expressed as magnitude. By emphasizing differences in magnitude, and by obscuring differences or similarities along other dimensions (such as form, history, geographical contexts), commensuration directs attention in patterned ways. For example, this emphasis on magnitude facilitates stratification in the form of hierarchical rankings. We get used to thinking about the world in terms of precise, hierarchical distinctions, such that someone is thought of as the second-best rebounder or in the top 3 percent of her class.

Commensuration systematically organizes and discards information. It simplifies complex cognitive tasks in two general ways: by reducing *how much* information we have to pay attention to, and by *integrating into one, comprehensive form,* information that was originally produced in many different forms. Numbers that are the culmination of commensurative processes (such as prices) are highly portable and easy to compare. The simplification that commensuration produces also facilitates control. Simplification is a fundamental feature of state domination (Scott, 1998: 2–3). Commensuration, as one prominent form of simplification, renders complex, heterogeneous relations more legible and more available for scrutiny. Such legibility makes it easier to manipulate and "manage" people and objects, and is a prerequisite for regulation.

Commensuration is a powerful means of classifying the world. It is radical for its capacity to create new objects or subjects. "Futures options" are new objects that emerge from commensuration in the form of prices, standardized grading, precise measurement regimes, and careful bookkeeping. As Marc Ventresca (1995) has argued, "citizens," as a meaningful category, and "nation states," as reified social entities, depend on the commensuration of disparate peoples that a census produces. Whatever arbitrariness characterized the origins of these classifications, once they become inscribed in law, enshrined in politics, routinized in organizations, or taken for granted in culture, their influence is profound and hard to dislodge. These few examples suggest how commensuration can, as Theodore Porter has shown (1995: 41–45), refashion the world.

Commensuration is also radical for what it renders invisible or irrelevant. When so much public policy relies on cost-benefit analyses as a means of evaluating alternatives, things without market prices or things for which it is hard to establish prices often disappear from analysis. The symbolic value of something, the moral implications of action, the importance of something whose value is defined against market values (that is, sacred or incommensurable things), or value that is explicitly derived from the location of some activity outside of markets, get ignored (Waring, 1988; Espeland, 1998).

Part of the appeal of commensurative practices is that they seem to offer a technical solution to a core problem in politics: how to adjudicate between people's conflicting values. If all values can be expressed according to the same metric, commensuration can turn complex decisions into simple choices that hinge on selecting the biggest number. As expressions of value, the relationship that commensuration constructs and expresses between things is fundamentally relative: the value of something is always determined in relation to other things as expressed on a metric. This means that commensuration cannot accommodate particular forms of value: absolute or intrinsic value, value that is defined as "priceless," or sacred values which cannot legitimately be expressed in terms of tradeoffs or in relation to other valued things. But commensuration as a form of value integration is just *one* of its core dimensions.

Not all commensuration integrates value, nor is it always directly linked to markets. The extent to which commensuration is a strategy for measuring or classifying specific characteristics or practices more accurately—what might be called "technical commensuration"—is a second core dimension. For example, a sophisticated system for precisely measuring the speed of sprinters is a technical refinement that does not commensurate values. The use of electronic photo finish cameras, electronic guns, or reaction time equipment are devices for measuring time more precisely and for linking it more tightly to the relevant behavior. These commensurative practices establish precise relationships between all participants in the race and make it possible to compare their performances with past and future races (that use similar strategies and equipment).

A third crucial dimension of commensuration might be termed "cognitive commensuration." Often a more tacit cultural accomplishment, it involves reclassifying the world in terms of categories that align more closely with the new metrics. These new classifications influence what we notice. They draw attention toward relationships that are expressed as numbers, and they divert attention from unquantified qualities. For example, Werner Sombart (1953: 38) has argued that the idea of capital as an entity emerged from the development of double-entry bookkeeping, a system for commensurating values as debt and credit. As a way to conceptualize financial relationships, capital obscures the social dimensions and idiosyncratic characteristics of economic exchange. This mode of understanding investment focuses more attention on profits and losses than on, say, distributional effects or personal ties.

To understand the effects of commensuration, it is crucial to appreciate the relative distinctiveness and significance of these three core dimensions. In many examples of commensuration, especially if institutionalized, all three dimensions will be present to varying degrees. Sorting out their relative significance is an important empirical task. In markets, commensuration is the process by which value is constructed and represented. Commensuration is necessary for creating prices among different, intangible things. In efficient markets, prices are the main focus in buying and selling. But prices as forms of value integration depend on these other dimensions of commensuration. Appreciating how these dimensions build on and reinforce each other is key for grasping the significance of commensuration.

Technical commensuration is often a prerequisite for markets because it helps construct commodities as standardized objects distinguishable mainly by price. As Carruthers and Stinchcombe (1999: 353–4) have argued, the liquidity of a market depends heavily on the standardization and homogenization of commodities. Commensuration is crucial for making objects seem alike enough such that traders can focus exclusively on price. This standardization is fundamentally a "social and cognitive achievement," because lots of people (buyers, sellers, brokers, and various intermediaries) have to be convinced that the commodities that get defined as equivalent really are the same. Commensuration plays a key role in convincing people of this. It helps create what Porter (1995: 45) calls "public information," knowledge that transcends the particular experiences of those who use it. For traders, such public information permits them to focus almost exclusively on movements in price; they can buy and sell commodities they never see, or even commodities that do not yet exist—futures.[7]

The dimensions of commensuration that matter the most will vary. Sometimes commensurative efforts will emphasize integrating values or creating more precise measures, or achieving conceptual clarity. Precise measures may make it easier to turn objects into commodities, even if that is not what they were designed to do. For example, accurate, reliable race results standardize and summarize performances, but they do not integrate disparate values. Nevertheless, the capacity to credibly establish Marion Jones as the "fastest woman in the world" is crucial for efforts to transform her reputation into a marketable commodity. And once we understand athletic achievement as a commodity, we may be less inclined to think of excellence as intrinsically valuable.

Commensuration creates and unmakes important social categories, changes what we pay attention to and how we compare things, and alters the way we conduct politics and express our values. New markets offer a good site for investigating the stakes of commensuration. As they are not fully institutionalized, it is easier to expose the conditions and consequences of commensuration. The vast resources that commensuration requires, the way it disciplines the actions of broad networks of people, accumulates new constituencies that become committed to its use, and creates new ways of interpreting the world, are all characteristics of commensuration that are easier to discern before it is naturalized. In subsequent sections, we offer examples of some of these characteristics of commensuration as they apply to the emerging markets in air pollution.

CRITIQUES OF MARKET MODELS

Although market-based approaches are spreading quickly, not all scholars are convinced that these are appropriate or just policy responses. One deep disagreement some scholars have with market approaches is over the monistic theory of value that they imply. They argue that we value different kinds of goods differently, and this is important for how we create and sustain social relationships. Many market-based approaches presume that people value as self-interested individuals whose well-being is expressed primarily as consumers in a market; and that individuals have exclusive rights to their instrumentally valued resources. This view of valuing cannot account for modes of valuing in which people are not reacting as consumers of goods (Sagoff, 1988); nor can it accommodate the prevalence or the importance of pluralistic modes of valuing, where what matters is not only what or how much someone values something, but also the form in which that value is expressed. The importance of preserving "distinct spheres" (Waltzer, 1983) or "domains of cultural practices" (Keat, 1993), of "incommensurable values" (Raz, 1986; Anderson, 1993; O'Neil, 1993; Espeland, 1998) or "inalienable goods" (Radin, 1996) is difficult to reconcile within a market framework. These modes of valuing are crucial for understanding how we create identities, invest in people and places, and create distinctive and meaningful moral boundaries.

Another criticism of using markets as models for how to distribute goods is that markets are hardly neutral vehicles. The philosopher John O'Neil (1993: 175) argues that the realization of environmental goods is incompatible with using markets to allocate most resources, because markets respond only to preferences that can be expressed through acts of buying and selling. People who are "inarticulate"—the poor, who "sell cheap," future generations, whose preferences may be radically different from our own, and nonhumans—are badly represented in markets.

Some have criticized taking the preferences of individuals as the starting point of markets, where ends and ideals are treated as wants. The market is not conceived as something that cultivates certain wants but as a neutral mediator of these, according to criteria of efficiency that exclude judgments about the appropriateness of wants (O'Neil, 1998: 20). As Elizabeth Anderson (1993: 194) explains, "Markets are responsive only to given wants, without evaluating the reasons people have for wanting the goods in question, which may be based on ideals or principles. By using market valuations to guide public policies, cost-benefit analyses assume that ideals, needs, and principles have no distinctive role to play with regard to safety and the environment." This view, when applied to the realm of public policy, neglects the importance of deliberation for challenging, or justifying, preferences.

Mark Granovetter (1985: 484) argues that part of the scholarly allure of markets is that when they are conceptualized as mechanisms for efficiently allocating scarce resources, they "remove the problem of order" from the analysis. This is important for several reasons. First, if markets appear to be self-regulating, scholars will neglect the institutional and cultural work that is required for markets to work. Failing to appreciate this work leaves a big hole in our understanding of markets. And this hole has important ideological implications. To the extent that this work remains an invisible feature of regulation, markets appear easier to enact than they are. Furthermore, since these commensurative practices are typically performed by the state, their invisibility perpetuates an inaccurate image of a deep divide between "markets" and "government intervention." This depiction is especially pronounced in debates about regulation.

One way that commensurative practices contribute to the appearance of markets as self-regulating is by the way they either constrain human agency or divert attention from the underlying work involved. An example of the former is how commensuration makes possible the algorithms that are the basis for mechanical stock trading. The computer programs devised for mechanical trading are obviously the product of human actors but once created, these programs can, in effect, "vote stocks" in ways that sharply curtail human discretion and intervention in the financial markets.

Commensuration distracts us from noticing our agency, partly because of the simplification it produces. The integration and reduction of information that commensuration accomplishes results in "uncertainty absorption" (March and Simon, 1958). The caveats, local knowledge, assumptions, and tenuousness that inform and characterize the production of information are often extruded in the process of commensuration. This produces numbers that seem more "robust" the further removed they are from their production. The portability of numbers, their capacity to transcend easily institutional, cultural or geographical domains, fur-

ther diminishes an appreciation of the agency involved in commensuration by eas-
ing the removal of numbers from their productive contexts. The impersonal quality of numbers that devolves from this is, of course, crucial for their authority.

Another way that commensuration disrupts our consciousness of agency is that
the impersonality and objectivity it confers makes it easier to reify markets. At the
same time that commensuration erases our own agency, it helps to construct the
market as an "actor" and market forces as autonomous. By simultaneously dis-
tancing and solidifying complex interactions into something we objectify as "the
market," we are able to think and speak of markets as if they were actors doing
things: we refer to how markets value goods, respond to events, or discipline firms.
This form of reification is ideologically significant. As Robert Nelson and William
Bridges (1999) have shown, gender discrimination is justified by appeals to "market forces" in external labor markets in ways that neglect the selective attention
that people pay to different parts of markets.

RADICAL REGULATION: THE CREATION
OF TRADABLE POLLUTION

Before market-based approaches, the standard ways to regulate and monitor air
pollution were known collectively as "command-and-control" regulation. This
form of regulation required individual emissions sources to conform to performance standards and imposed particular abatement methods on polluting firms.
The EPA created standards establishing targets that defined the maximum allowable concentration of a particular pollutant in the ambient air or water. To reach
these targets, ceilings were imposed on the specific sites where pollutants were dis-
charged. In highly polluted areas where it was hard to meet the ambient standards,
or for new polluters, the technologies that best reduced pollutants were imposed.
The guidelines regulating older plants in less polluted areas were less strict than for
new entrants or those in highly polluted areas.

Command-and-control regulations conceptualized the relationship between
industry and government as antagonistic, with industry attempting to skirt rules
imposed by government agencies (Hoffman and Ventresca, 1999: 1375–1376).
This approach fixed limits on pollutants and required firms to implement specific
remediation technologies, such as installing "scrubbers" or burning coal that contains less sulfur.[8] In doing so, these regulations forced firms to shoulder similar
shares of the regulatory burden, despite differences in relative costs across firms for
doing so (Stavins 1998b). Differences in the location of power plants, how they
were designed, or how heavily they were used all affected how hard and expensive

it was for a given unit to meet standards or incorporate abatement methods. After stricter standards were imposed on new emitters, there were strong incentives to retain old units. Polluters sometimes responded to this regulation by fighting the imposed standards in court, persuading legislators to grant them exemptions, or refusing to comply.

Under Title IV of the 1990 amendments to the Clean Air Act, polluters have been allocated allowances, based on prior pollution levels, that amount to a property right.[9] Allowances grant their holder the right to pollute, measured in tons of SO_2 emitted into the atmosphere. Polluting companies are required to turn in allowances equal to the amount of sulfur dioxide they emitted over the past year, as certified by approved emissions measurements. Firms whose emissions exceed their allowances are heavily penalized for not complying: $2,000 per ton over their allotted allowance limit plus a reduction in their allowance allocation for the following year. Conversely, if a firm's emissions are below their total number of allowances, it can sell its excess allowances or "bank" them for future use. The total number of allowances is capped to ensure the reduction by 8.9 million tons annually by 2000. After the initial allocation of allowances, the EPA holds back a number of reserve allowances by buying from each source 2.8 percent of their allotment. The EPA then auctions off this pool of permits through the Chicago Board of Trade.

The creation of tradable permits in air pollution differs fundamentally from command-and-control regulation. Moving to tradable allowances in SO_2 emissions transformed the unit of analysis from individual polluting firms to an aggregated and abstracted conception of pollution, from rates to absolutes. Rather than requiring each firm to reduce their emissions rate by 5 percent, for example, the EPA focuses now on reducing overall emissions for the United States. This shifted the regulatory burden from the government to polluting firms. Firms now must "pay for" their air emissions and can choose from varied strategies for eliminating excess pollution.

Market-based regulation also shifts the locus of discretion for remediation of pollution. In the past the EPA required individual polluters to install specific pollution reduction technologies. Now, how firms achieve these reductions is up to them. Because the EPA is no longer concerned with *how* firms meet their pollution cap requirement, firms now have incentives to adopt cheaper and more effective pollution-control technologies (Stavins, 1998b: 3). One option includes buying allocations from another firm instead of reducing one's own emissions. This means that the most drastic reductions in pollution could be done at the plants where it is the cheapest to do so. Plants where the cost of abatement is higher could be offset by buying extra allocations on the open market. This equalizes the marginal costs for firms to reduce pollution.

HOW THE MARKET IS COMMENSURATED

The commensuration needed to create pollution permits required the mobilization of organizations and legions of actors with various expertise and authority. Lawyers and legislators created the legal infrastructure. Economists provided theoretical justifications and technical expertise. Engineers designed the emissions monitoring equipment and the technology that made it possible for utilities to adapt boilers designed for high-sulfur coal to switch to lower-sulfur bituminous coal. Brokerage firms publicize and legitimize the market. And the EPA managed and implemented the changes, which entailed an elaborate administrative process of making and modifying rules, monitoring compliance, and organizing the annual auction. The commensuration these actors accomplished included the parsing of air pollution into discrete, quantifiable elements that could be measured (its technical dimension), creating the vehicles for attaching prices to pollutants and for monitoring these prices (value integration), and the tacit commensuration of polluters, pollutants, time, and space (its cognitive dimension).

Technical Commensuration

Trading emissions requires that buyers and sellers see pollution as standardized units of some scarce resource. The shift in units of analysis from rates to aggregate pollution, which was crucial for creating this conception of pollution, was accomplished largely through the development of a rigorous emissions monitoring system. The EPA was primarily responsible for designing and implementing this "continuous emissions monitoring system" (CEMS). The CEMS program was the culmination of years of EPA administrative rulemaking.[10] Rulemaking, the core of administrative law, is the arduous process by which federal agencies make, revise, and in some cases adjudicate rules. Rulemaking involves highly standardized procedures for publishing proposed rule changes in the federal register, soliciting comments from interested parties on the proposed changes, responding to comments, and publishing the final rules (Lubbers, 1998). There are dozens of rules that regulate CEMS. The "Final Rules" regulating the use of CEMS were issued on January 11, 1993. Since then, largely in response to industry concerns, they have been revised many times.

CEMS measures pollutants emitted into the atmosphere in exhaust gases from combustion or other industrial processes. CEMS approximate continuous measurements of emissions by extrapolating from separate measures taken at least every fifteen minutes. It includes an array of technical devices that are installed on smokestacks to sample, analyze, and record data emissions. CEMS include monitors for concentrations of SO_2, and NO_x, as well as diluent (diluting) gases such as oxygen and carbon dioxide, volumetric flow and opacity monitors, and a computer-based data acquisition and handling system (DAHS) for recording and performing calculations with the data provided by the various monitoring devices.

Detailed procedures govern the certification, use, and testing of this CEMS technology (U.S. EPA, 2000). These procedures coordinate and regulate hundreds of tasks. For example, they include precise instructions on how to calibrate equipment, test for errors, calculate missing data estimates, calculate average emissions for each pollutant, keep and maintain records, and standardize the reporting of emissions data. The Field Manual summarizing the guidelines for complying with the CEMS is nearly 200 pages long and includes a glossary that meticulously defines key terms and units.[11]

To illustrate the complexity of this regulation, consider how one small technical problem was redressed. The EPA required daily calibration error tests of the entire monitoring system while units were operating. A problem arose in conducting these online calibration tests because some units are used only during peak demand. Operating these units solely for purposes of performing calibration tests produces additional pollution. As some monitoring systems adjust for variations in temperature and pressure, these systems do not require that units be operating in order to produce accurate calibration tests. The EPA agreed that it was ill-advised to fire up units just for testing. After studying the issue, it issued a proposed revision to the original rule to allow firms with monitoring systems that work off-line to occasionally perform off-line calibration tests. To do so, a firm must pass a performance test demonstrating the validity of its off-line calibration measures, and perform an online test within 26 hours.

To enact this revision, the EPA first responded to written and oral comments (which are carefully documented and cited) by participants. It then proposed a new revision that included the problem, a discussion of alternative solutions, the designated solution, and a rationale for why it was selected. It published this proposed revision in the Federal Register, solicited comments, and eventually promulgated the final, new rule (Federal Register, 61: 225, Nov. 20, 1996). All this bureaucratic work was needed to smooth one wrinkle in the CEMS regulation.

The fungibility of pollutants as commodities hinged on people's faith that one ton of SO_2 in Chicago was really equal to a ton of SO_2 in New York. Standardized measures help produce these equivalencies and help reassure traders and regulators alike of the legitimacy of this equivalency. The technical commensuration accomplished in this synchronization of software, hardware, and bureaucratic rule-making transformed smoke from smokestacks into a meticulously tracked quantity. It is through such scrutiny and calibration that amorphous pollution is made discrete and real.

Value Commensuration

Value commensuration occurs when prices are attached to allowances. Although technical commensuration standardizes allowances, more work is needed to establish their value as prices. The 1990 Amendments allow for two mechanisms of "price discovery": private markets and an annual auction. The auction was added during legislative debate to assuage fears about irrational hoarding and guarantee that allowances would be available for new firms (Ellerman and others, 2000: 169).

The statute provided limited guidance about how the EPA should implement the auction. It stipulated only that the auctions be conducted annually, that they be open to any person, and that there be no minimum reserve price. This left the EPA with broad responsibility and latitude in organizing the auction. The EPA first selected an organization to oversee the bidding—the Chicago Board of Trade—and then had to create the contracts that eventually established their relationship with it. The agency established rules for opening an account, certifying authorized bidders and acceptable forms of payment. It created a schedule for the auction and deadlines for entertaining bids. The agency had to determine what *form* the auction would take. After much debate, it selected a "discriminatory" auction design where allowances are allocated to winning bidders at the prices that they bid rather than at a uniform clearing price (Joskow, Schmalensee, and Bailey, 1996: 5). The EPA also had to decide how to publicize the auction results (where, what form, and what information to provide) and notify the winners. Finally, it needed to create a process for maintaining accurate records of the results for each auction. For each of these activities, the EPA had to write guidelines that delegated responsibility for these tasks and issue instructions for how they would be executed.

Although creating the institutions necessary for value commensuration involves complex bureaucratic labor, this work is largely invisible to traders (and most other people). Although the process of valuing permits in an auction appears straightforward, it is predicated on elaborate state intervention. The outcome of these interventions was that allowances became a kind of currency with which firms (and, now, nonpolluting participants) could "buy" the right to pollute. The value of this currency was created through rules and regulations that effectively conferred legitimacy by creating conditions of scarcity and liquidity.

Cognitive Commensuration

Once allowances and the credibility of their prices have been established, commensurative effects arise. These largely tacit cognitive effects become part of the institutional logic that shapes the way we understand the natural environment. They follow from applying the abstract logic of markets to a particularized natural world; for most "established" commodities, they are taken for granted. In the market for acid rain permits, these institutional effects include the commensuration of polluters: the object of commodification, time, and space.

The creation of an emissions market changed the unit of analysis for measuring and controlling pollution. The unit shifted from the rates produced by individual firms to aggregate levels of pollution. This turned SO_2 from something that a particular firm emitted into a fraction of some aggregate standard. In doing so, the link between the firm that emitted SO_2 and the SO_2 itself was transformed. The salient characteristic of the SO_2 was no longer who produced it—which made it distinctive—but rather how much of it was in relation to the total number of pollution permits in the market.

This creation of what might be called "abstract polluters" is similar to state interventions directed toward "abstract citizens" rather than discrete persons (Scott, 1998: 345–347). A firm that emits two thousand tons of SO_2 in Los Angeles has become equivalent, in the eyes of the EPA, to a firm that emits one ton of SO_2 in South Carolina, so long as both hold the requisite number of allowances. The EPA no longer focuses on the specific emission practices of individual firms, and it no longer dictates to firms how they should clean up their emissions. All that matters now is whether a firm's annual production of pollution equals its annual allowances. Other distinctive characteristics of a firm—its size, the amount of pollution it emits, its location, or even the source of its allowances—became irrelevant when compliance was defined this way.[12] This was one step in producing fungible pollution, and it encouraged what amounted to a tacit commensuration of polluters.

The market in air pollution commensurates pollutants. The use of tradable allowances to control pollution creates standardized air and uniform pollutants. It also constructs "new relationships" among pollutants. One way it does this is by neglecting the interactive effects of chemical pollutants. For example, SO_2 causes acid rain in conjunction with other chemical compounds. Treating these components as discrete entities in separate markets obscures the fact that SO_2 becomes something new when it is combined with other chemicals. Early proposals for global expansion of a market in greenhouse gases, for instance, treat each of the six ozone-depleting chemicals that cause global warming as interchangeable. Reducing any one of these six gases is considered equivalent to any other, even though their effects are interactive rather than additive (Kruger and Dean 1997).

Treating air pollution as commodity futures further commensurates time. Acid rain allowances systematically create conditions under which a ton of SO_2 emitted in 2001 is made exactly equal to a ton of SO_2 emitted in 2011, 2061, or 2101. It is true that the chemical composition of sulfur dioxide will not change, but the social meaning and environmental impact of a ton of sulfur dioxide might change dramatically over time. Changes in world population, declining or increasing interest in environmental issues, or technological advances may change how a ton of sulfur dioxide affects the future. The creation of a standardized, quantifiable air pollution allowance ignores potential changes across time by fixing the present meaning of SO_2 emissions into the future.

Finally, air pollution markets facilitate a form of spatial commensuration. Because the purpose of the air pollution market is to reduce the overall aggregate of emissions in the United States, a ton of emissions anywhere in the country "counts" the same as any other ton.[13] In the United States, however, atmospheric airsheds shift in predicable patterns, such that pollution emitted in Illinois or Ohio will typically wind up in New York or Connecticut. Long Island Lighting Company (LILCO) was recently pressured by New York to stop selling its excess allowances on the open market. Midwestern companies buying these futures could pollute over their own allotted amount and still comply with the EPA by submitting a larger number of allowances. The wind would then blow the pollution back over the Adirondack and Catskill mountains, where concentrated SO_2 levels continue their damage (Hernandez, 1998). The influence of weather patterns and distinctive ecological systems that mark regional boundaries, however, become irrelevant in the face of an institutionalized logic that treats emissions as a continuous and commensurate variable. Allowances free emissions from their spatial context in ways that make any unit of space equivalent to any other from the standpoint of air pollution.

The tacit commensuration of polluters, pollution, time, and space that is encouraged by a shift to market-based regulation subtly alters some of the basic categories we use to interpret policy. In helping to induce a new cognitive framework for understanding pollution and its regulation, the various kinds of commensuration that are enacted create new objects (allowances and homogenous pollutants) and new actors who are the subject of regulation (anonymous firms with greater discretion). It also changes the role of the regulator from enforcer of specific remediation measures to facilitator of markets. Collectively, these shifts have altered the meaning of pollution and regulation.

EFFECTS OF POLLUTION ALLOWANCES

So what have been the effects of all this commensuration, of commodifying air pollution? Most scholars agree that the market-based approach worked as intended. In reducing aggregate SO_2 and minimizing regulatory costs, the Acid Rain Program has been successful. It has reduced the costs of regulation by approximately $225 million to $375 million annually (Schmalensee and others, 1998). Utilities have used the flexibility this program offers in deciding to switch fuel, buy or trade allowances, install scrubbers, and selectively operate their units. This flexibility has saved them money. Over the past decade, the total amount of SO_2 emissions dropped from about 10.5 million tons in 1985 to 5.3 million tons in 1998 (U.S. EPA, 1999).[14] In 1995, the first year of compliance, SO_2 emissions for electric utilities fell by 39 percent, 3.4 million tons below the levels required by Title IV. Most of these reductions occurred in the Midwest. Furthermore, there has been 100 percent compliance by firms, no lawbreaking, little litigation, and virtually no exemptions granted: a remarkable record. Also, many of those who initially opposed market-based programs (legislators, bureaucrats, emitting firms, and many environmental groups) have been mollified (Stavins, 1998a).

Nevertheless, despite impressive reductions in SO_2 it is still too early to determine the effects of these on the ecological problems associated with acid rain. Because so many factors influence the deposition of acids—wind, the length of time pollutants are in the atmosphere, the form in which they return to earth—understanding the implications of reducing SO_2 on air, aquatic life, forests, and soil is extremely difficult. Over the past fifteen years, sulfate concentrations seem to have declined in some places (State College, Pennsylvania), remained stable in others (Adirondack lakes), and increased in others (Shenandoah National Park). Although the effects of this general reduction in SO_2 may become clearer over time, so far reductions have not significantly improved the ecological problems associated with acid rain (U.S. NAPAP, 1996).

The commodification of air pollution is ongoing and sometimes unstable. As we have argued, one key effect of commensuration is the way it highlights some features of social life while masking others. The market approach obscures regional differences in the distribution of air pollution. The case of New York State is instructive. New York's participation in the market for air pollution is complicated for two reasons. First, it contains an ecosystem environmentally sensitive to acid rain, the Adirondack mountains. Estimates of the percentage of lakes in the region that would become acidified by 2040 range between 43 and 50 percent (U.S. GAO, 2000). Second, the Adirondacks are located downwind from the Midwest, which emits more SO_2 pollution than any other region of the United States (U.S. GAO, 2000). In an approach that distributes the marginal costs of pollution abatement across all market participants, New York loses. In May 2000, New York passed a bill that would constrain the sale of SO_2 allowances to out-of-state power plants and businesses. Under this law, plants selling credits to states that may send pollution back over New York would be fined the price of the allowance, eliminating the incentive to sell these allowances to Midwestern state plants.[15] This amounts to reasserting regional distinctiveness in reaction against the commensuration of space.

CONCLUSION

Commensuration facilitates transformations of all sorts. It turns qualities into quantities, heterogeneous goods into homogenous ones, messy complexity into straightforward hierarchy. A key mechanism in the structure of markets, it helps change intangible things, like pollution, into commodities. It eases the move toward markets as policy tools. Understanding how commensuration does this is an empirical question. It requires that we appreciate how different dimensions of commensuration build on and interact with one another. Technical commensuration helps construct credible prices. The simplification that it accomplishes, and the standard, comparable objects that it produces, erase the distinctiveness and quiets the "noise" that might divert attention from price.

Commensuration also transforms in broader, more inchoate ways. It subverts boundaries, displaces categories, and disrupts settled ways of seeing and doing. Commensuration helps change air pollution from a social problem to a technical problem. It shapes what we notice. People understand prices as proxies for value. But the technical commensuration that makes prices possible is less visible. For example, the significance of a shift in unit of analysis from parts per million to a percentage of aggregate tonnage is hard to assess. We relegate both the task and its assessment to experts and regulators. In doing so, it is easy to miss the relationship between prices and data, measurements and markets, and the crucial role that states play in mediating these. If we fail to see the connections between value, technical, and cognitive modes of commensuration, we risk missing the ideological implications of the divisions we erect: between public values and private technique, politics and science, states and markets. We may not fully appreciate the transforming potential of the "technical" label.

Roger Friedland and Robert Alford (1991) have observed that institutions, as modes of action and symbolic structures, develop distinctive "institutional logics" that shape how they value things and what they do. Where the projects of states involve the rationalization of work and the expression of values as rules, the logic of the market entails commodification, with value expressed as price. Commensuration is a vehicle for projecting market logic onto states. So, for example, when New York State tries to limit the fungibility of air pollution allowances, it is seen not as enacting environmental protection but as interfering with interstate commerce (Hernandez, 2000).

Commensuration is no simple task, and it is important to appreciate the work it entails. Commensuration requires disciplinary work that coordinates actions across vast regions and varied institutional domains. To ensure that the person charged with recording the SO_2 emissions from a plant in Ohio is measuring exactly the same thing as someone in Nevada, it was necessary for the EPA to devise an elaborate monitoring system.

Commensuration requires cognitive work. It creates new modes of classification as it renders old ones obsolete. Commensuration produces the units that allow us to conceive of air pollution as a discrete, fungible thing. This conception of air pollution threatens our image of air as a collective good, as exogenous or as intangible. In shifting the unit of analysis, commensuration depersonalizes, blurring the link between polluter and pollution. The tacit commensuration of time and space obscures regional and temporal distinctiveness.

Commensuration involves cultural work, as moral boundaries and cultural frames are redefined. In this case, commensuration helps transform what had long been interpreted as a social problem into a commodity. The relevance of culpability recedes when efficiency and technical criteria dominate the discussion; as the legitimacy of the marketplace envelops pollution and as norms give way to prices, politics appears as science (Habermas, 1970). This reinforces the hegemony of market values as the dominant mode of valuing, and threatens the legitimacy of other ways of valuing people and places.

Commensuration also undermines the integrity of nature. Its wholeness is compartmentalized to create an image of nature as discrete bundles of resources, objects of manipulation. In this sense, commensuration can become a powerful force for reproducing and strengthening the "tyranny of instrumental reason" (Horkheimer, [1947] 1977; Horkheimer and Adorno, [1944] 1972). Viewed in these terms, nature is understood one-dimensionally. It is a resource whose only value is as an object of domination (Worster, 1985: 56). The role of nature is reduced to servicing our needs and enhancing our power.

The success of market-based approaches in reducing SO_2 has had two broad effects. It has bolstered the status of markets as a policy tool, which has been interpreted by many as the triumph of markets over state regulation. This conclusion oversimplifies the crucial part played by the state in providing the legal, bureaucratic, and technical foundation for markets: states are often responsible for producing the metrics that sustain markets.

A second effect of the success of market approaches is that it has mobilized vast constituencies for the products of commensuration. Brokers, lawyers, economists, engineers, politicians, and even some environmental groups have become invested in the use and spread of market models. It is hard to quibble with the value of dramatic reductions in SO_2. It is also impressive that the cost of complying with environmental regulation has been substantially reduced. The market has proven to be a powerful mechanism for regulating emissions. But as we celebrate the success of the SO_2 program and its expansion, we should be mindful that, as theories of the world, the effects are broader than imagined.

Efforts to generalize broadly from the success of the SO_2 program are risky. As David Miliband (1993) suggests, "The important point is that there are different sorts of market economy, not simply more or less marketised ones." Administrative design matters, and the payoff, like the devil, is in the details. Ten years of revisions and fine-tuning have shown that market making is a protracted endeavor, and that markets are idiosyncratic in ways that are hard to discover. For example, greenhouse gases such as carbon dioxide are emitted from many different sources scattered all over the world, often in minute amounts. Efforts to measure these consistently and precisely would be a monumental task (Ellerman and others, 2000: 321).

A second concern about markets is the extent to which they deemphasize distributive effects. Creating a commodity out of air pollution obviates regional distinctions and attention to both ecologically sensitive areas and economically vulnerable populations. In a market-based program in Los Angeles, manufacturers used credits for pollution from mobile sites (cars) to offset pollution at stationary refineries. This reduced a source of emissions dispersed throughout a region while concentrating pollution in the poor neighborhoods near the refineries (Tietenberg, 1997: 22–23).

A third issue associated with generalizing too broadly stems from deeper concern about preserving pluralistic modes of valuing. To the extent that market models drive out other ways of valuing nature or other social goods, politics become narrower and more restrictive. Politics is misunderstood as the aggregation of consumer preferences and not as the process by which citizens deliberate public judgments about what is valuable (Sagoff, 1988). Noninstrumental values, personal experience with and knowledge of particular places, some ethical claims, and some forms of politics become less relevant. Social practices and cultural boundaries that are sustained by treating them as inalienable or incommensurable are subverted. Our role as consumers overwhelms other ways of understanding ourselves, whether as citizens in a broad sense, caretakers of future generations, or stewards of the earth.

Finally, however tempting it may be to try to replicate successes, the achievements of the SO_2 market should not be translated too crudely into the triumph of markets over states. First, markets depend heavily on states, especially for the commensuration that makes possible coordination and monitoring. Second, if the triumph of markets is used to justify privatization and cutting state services, this will have dramatic distributional effects. The poor and the powerless will suffer.

Such a shift would upset political balances, because states are accountable to different constituencies in different ways than are markets. The ability to express interests in the marketplace is heavily skewed to the wealthy and powerful. Even if the value of markets as policy tools would ultimately remain subject to electoral politics, the terms of politics would shift in ways that reflect the logic of the marketplace (O'Neil, 1993). If we conceive of citizens as hedonistic, well-being as the satisfaction of wants, nature as a scarce resource, rationality as maximizing individual utility, and pollution as an externality, the market is already deeply present in our debates.

The movement from scrubbers to permits, from regulators to brokers, is a striking realignment in regulation. Institutional theory, with its emphasis on symbolic frameworks and their constitutive effects, offers one valuable guide for analyzing how policies, as theories of the world, move among arenas and across constituencies. When the stakes are high and their effects enduring, as they are in the realm of environmental policy, understanding the emergence and diffusion of such changes is important knowledge. It is critical that we understand how trading pollution became Carlton Bartels's business, and ours.

NOTES

1. Other tradable allowances include Greenhouse Gas reductions, NO_x (nitrous oxides) allowances, and RTCs and REMs that are regional air pollution credits in California and Illinois.

2. The 1990 Clean Air Act Amendments (Public Law 101–549), some 800 pages long, revises the 1970 Clean Air Act. Title IV establishes the emissions market, but the law also includes other forms of regulation.

3. As Ellerman and others (2000: 315) conclude, "The experience thus far with Title IV clearly establishes that large-scale tradable-permit programs can work more or less as textbooks describe."

4. In 1985, electric utilities accounted for 70 percent of SO_2 emissions. 96 percent of this total was from coal-fired units and the remaining 4 percent from oil-fired units (Ellerman and others, 2000: 5).

5. Several methods exist for calculating shadow prices. The "travel price method" estimates how much people would pay to visit some natural site. Hedonic pricing estimates the value of some environmental amenity by correlating some environmental good or bad with variations in the actual market values of something like a house. Contingent valuation uses surveys to determine what people would pay to improve the environment or how much compensation they would require for some environmental damage or risk (O'Connor and Spash, 1999: 7–8).

6. This section relies on Espeland and Stevens (1998).

7. William Cronon (1991: 97–147) provides a superb account of the emergence of the first futures market, documenting the work, organizations, and technological innovations required to turn grain from the distinctive property of individual farmers into anonymous commodities bought and sold by anonymous traders.

8. Scrubbing and switching fuel remain the main methods for reducing SO_2 rates. Market-based approaches allow utilities to decide which methods to deploy. Scrubbing is the generic term for desulfurizing flue gas. It entails installing facilities to reduce the SO_2 emitted from a smoke stack by a chemical reaction with limestone or other base reagents as the exhaust passes up the stack. For a medium-sized generating unit, installing scrubbers would cost about $125 mil-

lion. Although they require a large initial investment, scrubbers are relatively cheap to operate. Low-sulfur fuel costs more but requires no capital outlay (Schmalensee and others, 1998: 55; Ellerman and others, 2000:126–127).

9. Allowances were supposedly allocated based on "past fossil fuel consumption" and the rates required by law (U.S. EPA, 1990). The actual process of handing out permits was more complicated. Initial allocations were giveaways, which favored existing firms over new ones (Tietenberg, 1997: 16; Joskow and Schmalensee, 1998).

10. During the debate over the 1990 Amendments, the need for new measurement techniques for emissions was controversial (Ellerman and others, 2000: 248). Industry argued that imposing continuous emissions measures was expensive and unnecessary. Conventional methods for estimating emissions were based on sampling fuel input, something that utilities did routinely to verify the quality of the fuel they were buying. Because accurate methods for establishing the sulfur content for fuel were already used, these could easily be used to estimate the emissions that would result from burning them. Environmentalists did not trust industry to estimate their own emissions, so to assuage their concerns CEMS was adopted instead. CEMS also made it easier for the EPA to administer compliance.

11. In addition to developing a credible way to measure emissions, the EPA also had to devise its Allowance Tracking System. This complex computer-based system creates and tracks allowance accounts for all generating units and for any party that buys an allowance. Much like a checking account in a bank, "deposits" and "withdrawals," or use and trading of allowances, are carefully monitored (Ellerman and others, 2000: 6, 9). Unlike bank balances, however, the EPA's database allows participants and third parties to track the number of allowances in any parties' account at a particular time. Allowances as "objects" do not exist apart from the EPA's tracking records.

12. Of course, a firm's distinctiveness becomes salient again if it fails to comply. Not complying re-creates distinctiveness by imposing penalties on particular firms.

13. Many argue that the efficiency of markets depends partly on the absence of regulatory restrictions imposed on them (Carruthers and Stinchcombe, 1999: 353). The SO_2 market is notably free of restrictions, and one crucial aspect of this lack of constraint is that allowances can be traded nationally (Ellerman and others, 2000: 167–168).

14. Not all of this is attributable to the Title IV program. Declining transportation costs have lowered the costs of switching to higher quality coal. Even when controlling for this, Ellerman and others (2000: 141–166) conclude that

the reductions caused by trading are substantial. Trading permits have lowered emissions levels more than any other regulatory provisions associated with the Clean Air Act.

15. New York Governor George Pataki's office, 5/24/00 press release.

REFERENCES

Abolafia, Mitchel Y. 1996. *Making Markets: Opportunism and Restraint on Wall Street.* Cambridge, MA: Harvard University Press.

Anderson, Elizabeth. 1993. *Value in Ethics and Economics.* Cambridge, MA: Harvard University Press.

Barber, Bernard. 1977. "Absolutization of the Market: Some Notes on How We Got from There to Here." In Gerald Dworkin, Gordon Bermant, and Peter Brown, eds., *Markets and Morals,* 15–31. Washington, DC: Hemisphere Publishing.

Baumol, William J., and Wallace E. Oates. 1979. *Economics, Environmental Policy, and the Quality of Life.* Englewood Cliffs, NJ: Prentice-Hall.

Berger, Johannes. 1994. "The Economy and the Environment." In Neil J. Smelser and Richard Swedberg, eds., *The Handbook of Economic Sociology,* 766–797. Princeton, NJ: Russell Foundation and Princeton University Press.

Callon, Michel. 1998. "An Essay on Framing and Overflowing: Economic Externalities Revisited by Sociology." In Michel Callon, ed., *The Laws of the Market,* 244–269. Oxford: Blackwell.

Carruthers, Bruce G. 1996. *City of Capital.* Princeton, NJ: Princeton University Press.

Carruthers, Bruce G., and Arthur L. Stinchcombe. 1999. "The Social Structure of Liquidity: Flexibility, Markets, and States." *Theory and Society,* 28: 353–382.

Coase, Ronald. 1960. "The Problem of Social Cost." *Journal of Law and Economics,* 3: 1–44.

Cronon, William. 1991. *Nature's Metropolis: Chicago and the Great West.* New York: Norton.

Dales, J. J. 1968. *Pollution, Property & Prices: An Essay in Policy-making and Economics.* Toronto: University of Toronto Press.

Ellerman, A. Denny, Paul L. Joskow, Richard Schmalensee, Juan-Pablo Montero, and Elizabeth M. Bailey. 2000. *Markets for Clean Air: The U.S. Acid Rain Program.* Cambridge: Cambridge University Press.

Espeland, Wendy Nelson. 1998. *The Struggle for Water: Politics, Rationality, and Identity in the American Southwest.* Chicago: University of Chicago Press.

Espeland, Wendy Nelson, and Mitchell L. Stevens. 1998. "Commensuration as a Social Process." *Annual Review of Sociology,* 24: 313–343.

Federal Register. 1996, November 20. "Acid Rain Program; Continuous Emission Monitoring Rule Technical Revisions; Final Rule." 40 CFR Part 75. Volume 61 (225): 59141–59166.

Feigenbaum, Harvey, Jeffrey Henig, and Chris Hamnett. 1998. *Shrinking the State: The Political Underpinnings of Privatization.* Cambridge: Cambridge University Press.

Friedland, Roger, and Robert R. Alford. 1991. "Bringing Society Back In: Symbols, Practices, and Institutional Contradictions." In Walter W. Powell and Paul J. DiMaggio, eds., *The New Institutionalism in Organizational Analysis,* 232–263. Chicago: University of Chicago Press.

Granovetter, Mark. 1985. "Economic Action and Social Structure: The Problem of Embeddedness." *American Journal of Sociology,* 91: 481–510.

Habermas, Jürgen. 1970. "Technology and Science as Ideology." In Jeremy J. Shapiro, trans., *Towards a Rational Society,* 81–122. Boston: Beacon Press

Hernandez, Raymond. 1998. "Lilco Is to Stop Selling Credits to Upwind Polluters." *New York Times.* April 30; p. B1.

Hernandez, Raymond. 2000. "Pataki Signs 2 Measures Seeking to Curb Pollution." *New York Times.* May 25, 2000; p. A27.

Hoffman, Andrew J., and Marc J. Ventresca. 1999. "The Institutional Framing of Policy Debates: Economics Versus the Environment." *American Behavioral Scientist,* 42(8): 1368–1392.

Horkheimer, Max [1947] 1977. *Critique of Instrumental Reason.* New York: Continuum.

Horkheimer, Max, and Theodore Adorno. [1944] 1972. *Dialectics of Enlightenment.* Trans. John Cummings. New York: Seabury Press.

Joskow, Paul L., and Richard Schmalensee. 1998. "The Political Economy of Market-Based Environmental Policy: The U.S. Acid Rain Program." *Journal of Law and Economics XLI:* 37–83.

Joskow, Paul L., Richard Schmalensee, and Elizabeth Bailey. 1996. "Auction Design and the Market for Sulfur Dioxide Emissions." Working paper 96007. Center for Energy and Environmental Policy Research, MIT.

Keat, Russell. 1993. "The Moral Boundaries of the Market." In Colin Crouch and David Marquand, eds., *Ethics and Markets,* 6–20. Oxford: Blackwell Publishers.

Knight, Frank. [1921] 1985. *Risk, Uncertainty, and Profit.* Chicago: University of Chicago Press.

Kranish, Michael. 1999. "The Politics of Pollution." *Boston Globe.* Feb. 8, 16.

Kruger, Joseph, and Melanie Dean. 1997. "Looking Back on SO2 Trading: What's Good for the Environment Is Good for the Market." *Public Utilities Fortnightly,* 135(15): 30–37.

Lubbers, Jeffrey S. 1998. *A Guide to Federal Agency Rulemaking.* Chicago: American Bar Association.

Majone, Giandomenico. 1981. "Policies as Theories." In Irving Louis Horowitz, ed., *Policy Studies Review Annual,* v. 5, 15–26. Beverly Hills, CA: Sage.

March, James G., and Herbert A. Simon. 1958. *Organizations.* New York: Wiley.

Milliband, David. 1993. "The New Politics of Economics." In Colin Crouch and David Marquand, eds., *Ethics and Markets,* 21–30. Oxford: Blackwell.

Nelson, Robert, and William Bridges. 1999. *Legalizing Gender Inequality: Courts, Markets, and Unequal Pay for Women in the United States.* Cambridge: Cambridge University Press.

O'Connor, Martin, and Clive Spash, eds. 1999. *Valuation and the Environment: Theory, Methods and Practice.* Cheltenham, U.K.: Edward Elgar.

O'Neil, John. 1993. *Ecology, Policy and Politics.* London: Routlege.

O'Neil, John. 1998. *The Market: Ethics, Knowledge and Politics.* London: Routledge.

Porter, Theodore M. 1995. *Trust in Numbers: The Persuit of Objectivity in Science and Public Life.* Princeton, NJ: Princeton University Press.

Radin, Margaret. 1996. Contested Commodities. Cambridge, MA: Harvard University Press.

Raz, Joseph. 1986. *The Morality of Freedom.* Oxford: Oxford University Press.

Sagoff, Mark. 1988. *The Economy of the Earth.* Cambridge: Cambridge University Press.

Schmalensee, Richard, Paul L. Joskow, A. Denny Ellerman, Juan Pablo Montero, and Elizabeth M. Bailey. 1998. "An Interim Evaluation of Sulfur Dioxide Emissions Trading." *Journal of Economic Perspectives,* 12(3): 53–68.

Scott, James C. 1998. *Seeing Like a State: How Certain Schemes to Improve the Human Condition Have Failed.* New Haven, CT: Yale University Press.

Sombart, Werner. 1953. "Medieval and Modern Commercial Enterprise." In Frederic C. Lane and Jelle Riemersma, eds., *Enterprise and Secular Change,* 25–40. Homewood, IL: Irwin.

Stavins, Robert N. 1998a. "What Can We Learn from the Grand Policy Experiment? Lessons from SO2 Allowance Trading." *Journal of Economic Perspectives,* 12(3): 69–88.

Stavins, Robert N. 1998b. "Market-Based Environmental Policies." Discussion paper 98–26. Washington, DC: Resources for the Future, March.

Stinchcombe, Arthur. 1974. *Creating Efficient Industrial Administrations.* New York: Academic Press.

Stinchcombe, Arthur. 1990. *Information and Organizations.* Berkeley: University of California Press.

Tietenberg, Thomas H. 1985. *Emissions Trading: An Exercise in Reforming Pollution Policy.* Washington, DC: Resources for the Future, Inc.

Tietenberg, Thomas H. 1997. "Tradable Permits and the Control of Air Pollution in the United States." Written for the 10th anniversary jubilee edition of the *Zeitschrift für Angewandte Umweltforschung.*

United States Environmental Protection Agency. 1990. *Clean Air Act Amendments of 1990: Detailed Summary of Titles.* U.S. EPA: November 30.

United States Environmental Protection Agency. 1999. *1998 Compliance Report: Acid Rain Program.* U.S. EPA-430-R-99-010: July.

United States Environmental Protection Agency. 2000. *Continuous Emissions Monitoring (CEMS) Field Audit Manual.* Washington, DC: EPA. Web address: http://www.epa.gov/airmarkt/monitoring/auditmanual/index.html.

United States General Accounting Office. 2000. *Acid Rain: Emissions Trends and Effects in the Eastern United States.* GAO/RCED-00-47: March.

United States National Acid Precipitation Assessment Program. 1996. Biennial Report to Congress: An Integrated Assessment: May.

Uzzi, Brian. 1996. "The Sources and Consequences of Embeddedness for the Economic Performance of Organizations: The Network Effect." *American Sociological Review,* 61: 674–698.

Ventresca, Marc. 1995. "When States Count: Institutional and Political Dynamics in Modern Census Establishment." Unpublished Ph.D. Dissertation, Department of Sociology, Stanford University.

Waltzer, Michael. 1983. *Spheres of Justice.* New York: Basic Books.

Waring, Marilyn. 1988. *If Women Counted: A New Feminist Economics.* San Francisco: Harper and Row.

Weber, Max. 1978. *Economy and Society.* Berkeley, CA: University of California Press.

Worster, Donald. 1985. *Rivers of Empire: Water, Aridity, and the Growth of the American West.* New York: Pantheon.

Zelizer, Viviana. 1989. "Beyond the Polemics of the Market: Establishing a Theoretical and Empirical Agenda." *Social Forces,* 3: 614–634.

II

BEYOND ISOMORPHISM: STRUCTURAL VARIATION AND COLLECTIVE RATIONALITY

6

COERCION BREEDS VARIATION: THE DIFFERENTIAL IMPACT OF ISOMORPHIC PRESSURES ON ENVIRONMENTAL STRATEGIES

Mark B. Milstein, Stuart L. Hart, and Anne S. York

The concept of isomorphism has been used to explain the similarity of form or archetype among organizations. DiMaggio and Powell (1983) suggest that three different pressures—coercive, mimetic, and normative—cause firms to become more homogenous, or isomorphic, over time, limiting their opportunities and actions. Researchers considering organizations and the natural environment have used these pressures to explain the convergence of attitudes regarding environmental strategies among or within firms (Hoffman, 1997; Jennings and Zandbergen, 1995).[1]

Prior research on environmental strategies has helped point out how isomorphic pressures have or will influence organizational acceptance of environmental agendas. However, consideration of isomorphic pressures within the context of organizations and the natural environment has, for the most part, been limited to the context of a single firm or industry (Hoffman, 1997; 1999) or as a catalyst for consensus around the issue of sustainable development (Jennings and Zandbergen, 1995). As yet, little attempt has been made to understand how isomorphic pressures may differ across industries, explore whether there are differential effects that stem from the three types of isomorphic pressure, or consider how isomorphic pressures may affect a firm's ability to realize superior financial performance from environmental strategies.

In a study using data of multiple firms and industries contained in the Investor Responsibility Research Center's (IRRC) 1992 Corporate Environmental Profiles, we obtained unexpected results that suggested all isomorphic pressures may *not* lead to homogeneity among firms. Despite predictions of isomorphism to the contrary, firms in an industry with strong coercive pressures displayed *more* variation in environmental strategy than did firms in an industry with weaker coercive pressures. The fact that coercive pressures may not lead to homogeneity among firms caused us to reexamine assumptions regarding the effects isomorphic pressures have on firm actions.

We draw greater distinction between the different pressures assumed to lead to isomorphism. It may be that although the dynamics of mimetic and normative pressures lead to isomorphic outcomes, coercive pressures may be responsible for differentiation among firms. Implications for the conceptualization of the effects of industry isomorphic pressures on firm environmental strategies are explored and propositions concerning the relationship between environmental strategies and financial performance as moderated by isomorphic pressures are developed.

THEORETICAL BACKGROUND

Institutional Isomorphism

Firms do not exist in a vacuum. They are embedded within an inescapable web of relationships, constraints, and expectations imposed upon them by actors both inside and outside the firm. The interconnectedness of organizations within their institutional environment causes some sets of firms to become more similar over time. As a population of firms becomes more defined and established, rational actors' actions cause the firms within it to become less distinct (DiMaggio and Powell, 1983).

Tests of homogeneity, or isomorphism, were originally applied to structures and practices within organizations (Meyer and Rowan, 1977; Tolbert and Zucker, 1983). More recently, however, researchers have applied tests to a variety of strategies, including acquisition, diversification, and financing (Deephouse, 1996). The forces that lead to isomorphism have been found to transcend cultural and political boundaries, affecting variance above and beyond that explained by economic variables (Dacin, 1997).

DiMaggio and Powell (1983) proposed three main institutional pressures that lead to isomorphism: coercive, mimetic, and normative. Coercive forces originate from entities external to a population of firms. They may be in the form of persuasion, force, or collusion. Typically, coercive pressures are conceived as government regulation, public opinion, or lawsuits (Dacin, 1997; Siegel, Agrawal, and Rigsby, 1997). Coercive mechanisms are important because they confer legitimacy on organizations and industries, allowing them to exist and operate (Deephouse, 1996).

Whereas coercive mechanisms are imposed from outside firm boundaries, mimetic pressures originate from among the members of a group as standard responses to uncertainty. Such uncertainty might pertain to ambiguous goals, technologies, or environments (Siegel, Agrawal, and Rigsby, 1997). In uncertain environments, firms attempt to reduce search costs by imitating other organizations (Cyert and March, 1963). Firms tend to imitate large, profitable firms they perceive as successful within their industry (Haveman, 1993). Within an industry, isomorphism results as newcomers try to be more like their successful seniors (Siegel, Agrawal, and Rigsby, 1997). It may also develop as laggards attempt to catch up to first-movers and industry leaders (Tolbert and Zucker, 1983). Mimetic forces have led to changes within hospitals, governments, corporations, HMOs, and the savings and loan industry (Haveman, 1993). Once locked into place, however, mimetic forces can favor inertia or resistance to change (Hannan and Freeman, 1984).

Finally, normative pressures—industry standards, best practices, and conventional wisdom—originate from university and professional networks that attempt to normalize a given field by setting clearer boundaries and providing more standardized, routinized conditions associated with a given profession. Universities help to provide the cognitive basis on which professional norms are established, whereas networks and trade associations help to confer common career titles and paths that make transactions more parsimonious (Siegel, Agrawal, and Rigsby, 1997). Normative mechanisms also provide a more homogenous pool of individuals who can fill similar positions, perform similar functions, and communicate through a similar vocabulary (DiMaggio and Powell, 1983).

Isomorphic pressures are not the same for all industries. The degree to which isomorphic pressures are manifested varies over time, by level of analysis, over ecological and economic forces, as well as other sources of institutional expectations (Dacin, 1997). Researchers have not yet considered in any detail the variation of institutional pressures' effects that may affect organizations in different ways (Dacin, 1997).

Institutional Isomorphism and Environmental Strategies

Institutional theory has been used as a theoretical framework for explaining the adoption of similar environmental practices and attitudes among firms (Jennings and Zandbergen, 1995; Hoffman, 1997; 1999). Jennings and Zandbergen (1995) theorized that environmental sustainability might only be achieved through institutional mechanisms. Considering the relative impact of DiMaggio and Powell's three types of isomorphic pressure, Jennings and Zandbergen (1995: 1031) suggest, "In the case of ecology, the main reason for adopting practices within both societal and organizational fields has been direct or indirect coercion. . . ." They hypothesize that as coercive pressure increases, so does the likelihood that a population of firms will adopt the form or structure of a practice. However, because enforcement efforts leave few incentives for firms to adopt mandated activities in ways more suitable to their particular needs, the value of adoptions diminishes across organizations. In the absence of direct coercive pressure, Jennings and Zandbergen (1995: 1033) suggest that normative and mimetic pressures play a more significant role in the diffusion of environmental practices. For example, organizations may seek value simply from copying the behavior of firms that appear to be garnering success from environmental practices.

Jennings and Zandbergen's work was one of the first to apply institutional theory to environmental management, but it was limited solely to theory building. Hoffman (1997; 1999) also used institutional theory to take a detailed empirical look at organizational attitudes toward environmental issues. Hoffman's analysis was important because it proposed the role institutional theory has in explaining the adoption of environmental management and tested those assertions. Hoffman's analyses considered how different institutional pressures shape the perception and acceptance of environmental management within firms. Using both a detailed case study and later a larger single industry sample, he traced, over a period of decades, how coercive, followed by normative and mimetic, forces caused organizational actors first to reject and later to embrace the natural environment as a strategic issue. Key findings were that institutional forces can be used for strategic gain and that institutionalism may cause a change in corporate attitudes toward environmental issues, ultimately driving a transformation in the way corporations perceive such issues. Hoffman also broke new ground by demonstrating that the institutional pressures companies face do not remain constant over time. His findings, however, are limited to the workings and metamorphosis of a single company and industry; they do not necessarily generalize across multiple industries. In addition, his research question focused on institutional pressures that might cause firms within an industry to adopt similar practices, rather than investigating firms' strategic responses to different sources of isomorphic pressure.

Each of these studies suggest a differential, temporal characteristic inherent in the three isomorphic pressures within the context of environmental issues, with coercive pressures having the earliest, strongest effect on populations of firms. Indeed, the coercive pressure on firms to behave in environmentally sound ways is tremendous. A variety of external pressures coalesce to influence the development of environmental strategies within firms (Henriques and Sadorsky, 1996). Legislators, lobbyists, the courts, activists, and everyday consumers define the institutional boundaries of the firm through regulations, protests, lawsuits, political lobbying, or direct negotiation.

Coercive forces are strong because they directly affect organizational legitimacy. Legitimacy—the validity external actors confer on firms—is a force that can determine organizational survival (Aldrich and Fiol, 1994; Hunt and Aldrich, 1998; Rao, 1994). Society bestows upon both the individual firm and the collective industry a license to exist and operate (Korten, 1995). To avoid regulations and intensive public scrutiny, corporations are willing to respond to the demands placed on it by a variety of stakeholders. Despite the best intentions of some organizations, when a single organization within an industry violates social and political norms, all organizational actors within the industry may suffer negative consequences as stakeholder anger is broadly applied to a perceived group of similar firms. Such collective effects are strongest when stakeholders lack information on the differential effect of each firm's actions and impose unilateral sanctions on firms regardless of their individual performance (King, Lenox, and Barnett, Chapter 17).

Two competing arguments can be made regarding the effects of coercive pressures on firms that share a common reputation. From an isomorphic perspective, coercive pressures, like regulations and public opinion, will cause firms to conform to a limited set of strategic options. When organizations are forced to follow similar strategies, it becomes more difficult for them to differentiate themselves. Thus, in and of themselves, coercive pressures can be a formidable force for producing isomorphism in observed environmental strategies.

Based on that argument, when isomorphic pressures are strong in an industry, we might expect to see low variation in environmental strategies across firms as the opportunities and abilities for divergence from desired or expected behaviors are limited or discouraged. Organizations adopt a narrow range of practices because firms that deviate are punished. On the other hand, when coercive pressures in an industry are relatively weak, theory dictates that environmental strategies among firms will be more heterogeneous.

But from a strategic perspective, in industries where strong negative common reputational effects persist, a firm may be better off differentiating itself from its fellow group members and assuring that stakeholder sanctions are levied on those firms that deserve them. Coercive mechanisms may offer firms that can comply more quickly and/or cheaply a unique opportunity and public forum for overcoming the effects of a negative common reputation. Under strong, negative coercive pressures an industry may exhibit high variation in environmental strategies across firms, due to firms' differential resource endowments and the greater value attached to divergence from a negative common reputation. On the other hand, firms in an industry characterized by weak coercive pressures may pursue more homogeneous strategies, due to the lack of value derived from achieving a differential position in the minds of stakeholders.

Firms with existing resources that are complementary to those needed to achieve desired cost advantages are more likely to successfully implement such practices and thus take advantage of the differential positioning than firms without such complementary resources (Christmann, 2000). Because these complementary resources are a function of the firm's underlying corporate strategy and are not directly related to a specific environmental issue, such resource endowments would vary across firms (Teece, 1987). Firms' structures, histories, and network of relationships shape their attitudes about environmental science, anticipated consumer and policy responses (Bansal and Penner, Chapter 13; Levy and Rothenberg, Chapter 7). Such attitudes affect whether firms view coercive mechanisms as strategic opportunities or threats, which in turn influence organizations' strategic responses (Dutton and Duncan, 1987).

In the following section, we describe an exploratory study conducted to gain insight into the relationship between isomorphism and environmental management by examining whether various levels of isomorphic pressures result in expected variation in environmental strategies.

EXPLORATORY STUDY

Sample

To understand whether strong coercive pressures suppress the variation in environmental strategies in an industry, we used data contained in the 1992 Corporate Environmental Profiles Directory compiled by the Investor Responsibility Research Center (IRRC), which contains compliance data for the years 1987 through 1989. In 1988, firms were required to begin reporting legal toxic waste emissions under the Emergency Planning and Community Right to Know Act (EPCRA). We chose to use 1989 data in order to try and maximize coercive pressures for a set of firms. In 1988 toxic emissions data were released to the public for the first time. By 1989, an unanticipated result of EPCRA was that pressure on firms from stakeholders to address these emissions was increasing. Thus, by 1989 firms would have confronted particularly strong coercive pressures.

The IRRC Directory contains information on environmental liabilities, compliance, and practices for each of the companies included in the Standard & Poor's (S&P) 500. Information is collected from government agencies, corporations, and the media. The database was chosen for two reasons. First, it contains various information related to environmental activities, including environmental capital expenditures, hazardous waste cleanup responsibilities, toxic chemical releases, reported spills, compliance data, environmental staffing data, corporate policies, environmental audit information, environmental communications, environmental achievements, and environmental projects which can be used as measures for both coercive pressures and environmental strategies. Second, the database includes the five hundred companies that constitute the S&P 500, a sample of firms that are a representative cross section of domestic U.S. corporate activity. A subsample of these IRRC firms was chosen, representing two industries exhibiting relatively high and low degrees of coercive pressure from external entities regarding the environment. Chemicals, forest products, oil and gas, and electric utilities were all considered for the high coercive pressure sample. Low coercive pressure possibilities included the computer, financial services or insurance industries, retailing companies, apparel manufacturers, restaurants, and grocery stores.

We chose the chemicals and computer industries for three reasons. First, we wanted to ensure that both industries were similarly and significantly affected by environmental regulations. As collections of material-intensive manufacturers who use toxic inputs, both chemical companies and computer firms have compliance issues related to air, water, and ground waste pertaining to the nine major U.S. federal environmental statutes[2] considered by the IRRC Company Profiles. We also wanted to choose industries with as wide a range of firms as possible represented in the IRRC database, in order to increase the statistical power of our analysis. Finally, and most important, the two sets of firms provide significant contrasts in terms of their degree of coercive pressure, due not only to the very real differences in the relative magnitude of and uncertainties associated with potential environmental damage but also to the public perception that stems from such differences.

Chemical firms have a complex history. Over the past fifty years, chemicals have revolutionized the way people live. Fertilizers and pesticides aided the post-war agricultural boom, helping to feed a growing world and contributing to the lowest food prices in history. In addition, chemical compounds have produced a myriad of convenience products from synthetic fibers to clear plastic wrap for food. At the same time, chemicals are associated with the horrors of war in Southeast Asia, burning rivers, and toxic dumps. Over the past few decades, consumers have become more wary and suspicious of chemical firms and their products. Older and larger chemical manufacturers may be subject to higher degrees of regulatory oversight and enforcement, due to their history and degree of past pollution and the use of older equipment and practices (Jennings, Martens, and Zandbergen, Chapter 3). All of these forces contribute to not only a more coercive environment, but also a more negative common reputation (King, Lenox, and Barnett, Chapter 17). Conversely, the computer industry is not as widelyassociated with negative environmental issues, despite the chemicals and vast amounts of water they consume in their production process. Instead, computer firms are perceived as a clean vanguard of technology and a key driver of economic activity. These differences in industry characteristics have resulted in very different pressures stemming from legislators, the courts, activists, consumers, and the public at large.

In order to determine which firms to include in the sample, primary SIC codes, the S&P Classification System, and industry segment data available on COMPUSTAT were examined to derive sets of similar firms. Within the IRRC directory, individual profiles indicate a firm's primary industry as determined by the December 1989 S&P 500 list. The IRRC classified twenty companies as either Chemical or Chemical (Diversified) and fourteen companies as Computer Systems. However, of these thirty-four companies, profitability information for two of the chemical companies and one of the computer firms was not available on COMPUSTAT and thus they were omitted from the sample. Further examination of SIC codes revealed several firms that were not classified by S&P in either the chemical or computer industries did share primary SIC codes with the rest of the firms in the sample. Thus, three firms were added to the chemical industry subgroup and one firm was added to the computer subgroup to form a final sample of thirty-five firms: twenty-one chemical firms and fourteen computer firms.

Measures

The IRRC directory was not created to explicitly measure types of isomorphic pressures or environmental strategies. Nonetheless, we believe the directory contains data that can be used as reasonable proxies for measures in an exploratory study.

Coercion. Several measures were used to measure coercive pressure at the industry level. Each measure was chosen for its ability to represent pressure placed on an industry by external observers or stakeholders. To this extent, three broad categories of measures were identified within the IRRC data: penalties, lawsuits, and public relations. For each of the coercive measures, individual firm data were aggregated and compared at the industry level.

Penalties can be conceived as a proxy for coercive pressure because they are an indication of when firms fail to adhere to desired public policies. The more an industry as a whole fails to achieve those goals, the more the firms in that industry are subject to regulatory attention. The IRRC Directory contains the number of Superfund sites, RCRA corrective actions, and RCRA denials for each firm in 1989. RCRA corrective actions represent the number of company facilities at which the Environmental Protection Agency (EPA) required an RCRA facility investigation be undertaken to assess the presence of chemicals at a facility that may require environmental cleanup activities as a condition of its RCRA permit (IRRC, 1992: 18). RCRA denials represent the number of times the EPA denied the company a RCRA permit to operate a facility that treats, stores or disposes of hazardous waste (IRRC, 1992: 18).

It is important to note that both Superfund and RCRA cleanup liabilities do not necessarily represent illegal activity by a corporation. Much of the cleanup responsibility that applies to corporations centers on remediation of past activities that were legal at the time they were conducted. Nonetheless, they are good proxies for coercive pressure because they can indicate the degree to which outside entities pay attention to and restrict the current activities of a corporation. The IRRC notes that the magnitude of government penalty assessments represents the opinion of the responsible government authority on the severity of an environmental violation (IRRC, 1992: 7). Thus, the attention bestowed on an industry due to violation of government statutes could reasonably represent coercive pressure exerted on that industry.

Lawsuits were used as another proxy for coercive pressure because they indicate the degree to which lawyers, regulators, and other external stakeholders concerned with firm behavior are watching an industry. The IRRC directory contains information on the number of lawsuits facing individual companies brought on by federal, state, and local governments. According to the IRRC (1992: 10) companies are required to report individual environmental enforcement proceedings that are expected to cost more than $100,000 and environmental litigation that may have a material financial impact on firm operations. When no lawsuits were disclosed in the company profiles, it was assumed the firm was not facing any material challenges.

Finally, firm actions can cause widespread public attention, both positive and negative. Crises and environmental awards can serve to diminish or increase a firm's reputation. Taken together, they may lead to either a positive or negative public perception for a given industry that affects the operations of all of the firms within that industry. Soderstrom, Ilinitch, and Thomas's (1998) Black-Eye effect, coded on a scale from $+2$ to -2, was used to measure positive or negative public perceptions related to an industry.[3] Negative public perception would be related to higher coercive pressures. On the other hand, indifferent or positive public perception would be related to weaker coercive pressures.

The 1992 IRRC profiles include activities more recent than the 1987 to 1989 period reflected in the compliance data. To root the measure in 1989 data, Black-Eye values assigned by Soderstrom, Ilinitch, and Thomas that depended completely on non-1989 information were erased or adjusted to reflect 1989-only information. Next, major newspapers dating from January 1, 1989 to December 31, 1989 were searched for the following string of keywords using Lexis-Nexis: "EPA, Justice Department, environmental, environmentalists, fines, rewards, spills." When no articles related to a company appeared in the search, the company was given a Black-Eye value of 0. When articles for the companies were obtained, they were reviewed for content. The variable Black-Eye was then coded for values ranging from $+2$ to -2, following the procedure described by Soderstrom, Ilinitch, and Thomas (1998). Any discrepancy between the values that remained from Soderstrom's list and that derived from the keyword search were resolved by comparing the information in the News & Notes section for that company with the contents of the newspaper articles and adjusted accordingly.

Environmental Strategy. Three categories of measures are used to reflect individual firm environmental strategies: emissions, compliance with regulations, and spills/accidents, each normalized for size. To implement environmental strategies, firms must choose capital investments that limit or remove environmental impacts. Although the IRRC data do not look directly at the environmental attributes of individual products produced by each firm, low emissions indicate that a firm may have invested in technologies to remove or reduce toxic materials from its production process. The IRRC's emissions efficiency index is a ratio of legal toxic emissions (in pounds) to firm revenues for U.S. manufacturing facilities owned by a company and its subsidiaries.

Compliance is a suitable proxy for a firm's environmental strategy because environmental strategies are, to some extent, an attempt to reduce exposure to regulatory pressures. When firms incur penalties, this can be attributed to a strategy to comply with regulatory requirements. The IRRC notes that penalties paid for noncompliance with environmental laws also can be viewed as an inexact proxy for the level of effort, and associated expense, that a company must devote to meet the common standards of environmental performance set by U.S. law for companies operating in a particular industry (IRRC, 1992: 7–8). The IRRC compliance index-penalty information normalized by size is meant to compare the historical ability of firms to meet national standards and comply with applicable environmental laws at all U.S. facilities.

Finally, spills were used as a proxy for environmental strategies because firms can take action to reduce or remove toxic materials from their production processes and reduce the possibility that accidents or spills will expose them to unnecessary liabilities. Because information on spills and releases is estimated or self-reported, the IRRC chooses not to normalize the information because it is considered less reliable than other information contained in the profiles. Nonetheless, because firms have an opportunity to review and comment on IRRC profiles before they are publicly released, and because the IRRC takes those comments into consideration and publishes them in a separate appendix, we believe that the information contained in them is suitable for normalization. No firms in the directory's appendix had contentions regarding spill data contained in the report.

Because we are interested in the *variation* of environmental strategies, the measures reflect deviation from group means. Thus, for each of the three measures, observed values were subtracted from the mean for each industry. The absolute value of that number was then summed and used to calculate a mean for the variation in environmental strategy for chemical and computer firms, respectively. The correlations associated with the environmental strategy measures and the coercion measures ranged from .10 to .24, with none significant at the .10 level or above.

Results

To explore whether coercive pressures were associated with homogeneity in environmental strategies, tests of means were conducted using an independent samples t-test in SPSS Version 8.0. Means for the measures of coercion and variation in environmental strategies are shown in Table 6.1. All mean values for coercion were in the expected direction. That is, chemical firms received less favorable publicity (lower values for the Black-Eye effect) and had more Superfund sites, RCRA actions, and RCRA denials than computer firms. Furthermore, differences between the means for the two industries were significant at the $p < .05$ level, leading us to conclude that the chemical industry operated under higher coercive pressures and that the computer industry operated under lower coercive pressures.

Additionally, the average variances from the industry mean for emissions, compliance, and spills normalized by firm size for firms in the chemical industry were

Table 6.1

Differences in Industry Means of Coercive Pressures and Strategic Responses

PRESSURE/RESPONSE	Mean (Standard Deviation)		t-TEST
	CHEMICAL INDUSTRY[a]	COMPUTER INDUSTRY[b]	
Black-eye effect	−1.00 (0.63)	0.29 (0.49)	−4.86**
Total Superfund sites	22.91 (12.78)	3.29 (4.42)	5.33**
RCRA actions	9.36 (9.04)	1.57 (3.36)	2.87**
RCRA denials	0.82 (1.08)	0.00[c] (—)	2.26*
Government lawsuits	0.91 (1.04)	0.29 (0.49)	2.13*
Emissions efficiency	6.44 (8.33)	0.06 (0.04)	3.52**
Compliance efficiency	11.62 (9.29)	5.12 (7.80)	2.24*
Spills	56.45 (49.64)	0.09 (0.15)	5.20**

[a] $n = 21$
[b] $n = 14$
[c] RCRA denials were constant for firms in the computer industry.
*$p < .05$ **$p < .01$

significantly *larger* than for those in the computer industry. Thus, our results seem to support the notion that high strategic variance is observed among a set of firms in an industry with significantly higher coercive pressures, while low strategic variance is observed among firms in an industry with lower coercive pressures.

IMPLICATIONS FOR THEORY DEVELOPMENT

In this final section, we explore the implications of our findings for theory development concerning the relationship between institutional pressures, environmental strategies, and firm performance. We contend that if coercive institutional pressures increase the heterogeneity of strategic responses, then strategic choice may play a more important role than previously thought in such environments, particularly in terms of firm performance.

If, as has been argued in the past, strong institutional environments constrict strategic variance in a population of firms, then we would logically conclude that deviating firms would be penalized for their divergence from the group mean. Such environments, theorized to reward homogeneity with legitimacy, exact a toll for heterogeneity. Paradoxically, however, an industry filled with firms following similar environmental strategies presents few opportunities for achieving abnormal returns. Any environmental strategies that prove profitable would be quickly diffused via normative mechanisms, copied via mimetic responses, or imposed by coercion. If variation among firms for environmental strategies is low or nonexis-

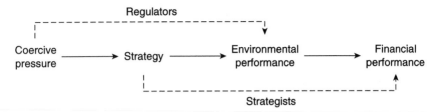

Figure 6.1 Regulatory versus Strategic Perspectives on the Effect of Coercive Pressures on Firm Performance

tent, it is statistically impossible for the environmental strategy variable to explain differences in firm performance. On the other hand, if we observe more strategic variation in the face of certain isomorphic pressures, which was the case in this study regarding coercive pressures, we must consider whether some of those pressures might directly or indirectly lead to heterogeneity in firm performance.

Consider different perspectives for viewing the manner in which coercive pressures may affect firm performance (Figure 6.1). From a public policy perspective, external entities impose rules and regulations to evoke a standardized, desired behavioral response from a set of firms. The particular skills or capabilities that enable or retard a firm's ability to achieve the desired response are not of primary concern. For regulators or public policy makers, attention is focused on applying pressure and achieving a minimum level of desired environmental performance. That is, the political process yields regulations meant to elicit a level of environmental performance that is minimally acceptable to the broadest group of stakeholder interests, even if some stakeholders may feel that the regulations go too far in restricting firms while others may feel that regulations do not go far enough.

Thus strategy is only considered to the extent that firm behaviors meet a set of actions believed to lead to desired environmental performance. Failure to meet minimum standards results in punishment and loss of legitimacy. Those outcomes are assumed to evoke desired firm behaviors (that is, environmental performance). Proactive behavior—behavior beyond the specified minimum—exists only as a positive externality of the regulatory framework imposed by regulatory agencies that ensure compliance with set standards.

Next, consider a strategic perspective incorporating strategic choice for achieving superior financial performance (Child, 1972; Porter, 1990; Rumelt, 1974). Theory suggests that successful firms are able to tailor their strategies to their operating environments (Donaldson, 1987; Oliver, 1990; Venkatraman, 1989), as well as to employ existing resources in new settings (Christmann, 2000; Teece, 1987). Environmental strategies may provide a way for firms to realize improved financial performance by applying such complementary and proprietary skills, resources, and capabilities to environmental issues (Hart, 1995; Porter, 1991; Porter and van der Linde, 1995).

Numerous environmental strategies and best practices are available to today's manager, beginning with end-of-pipe solutions (pollution control) to pollution prevention and product stewardship, and ultimately working toward strategies for sustainable development (Hart, 1997). The fundamental question—under which conditions do these environmental strategies successfully lead to improved performance?—is not yet clearly understood.

Some conventional managerial wisdom holds that environmental strategies have a negative relationship with organizational performance (Friedman, 1970; Haveman and Christainsen, 1981; Portney, 1994; Walley and Whitehead, 1994). Empirical studies both in the United States (Diltz, 1995; Hamilton, Jo, and Statman, 1993; Jaggi and Freedman, 1992; Morais, 1995) and Europe (Mallin, Saadouni, and Briston, 1995) have failed to find evidence that firms adopting environmental strategies enjoy significant performance advantages over rivals who do not.

Recently, some strategists have argued that environmental strategies are a way for firms to gain first mover advantage (Porter, 1990, 1991; Porter and van der Linde, 1995; Christmann, 2000). According to this logic, environmental capabilities, like other firm-specific resources, become embedded, difficult to copy, and a source of competitive advantage (Hart, 1995; Russo and Fouts, 1997; Sharma and Vredenburg, 1998). It has been shown that operational improvements can lead to more complex, environmentally benign products, processes, and services which lower overall firm costs and improve profitability within a year of implementation (Hart and Ahuja, 1996).

Lack of convincing empirical evidence of the relationship between environmental strategies and financial performance may be due to insufficient consideration of the circumstances under which that link exists. The assumption that appropriate environmental technologies coupled with the appropriate environmental management system leads to organizational improvement is mistakenly based on simple anecdotes that have ignored the how and the why of environmental strategies (Newton and Harte, 1997). Firms will capture cost advantages from environmental best practices only when they have existing complementary resources that enable them to do so (Christmann, 2000). The adoption of environmental policies by firms should not be undertaken without the explicit consideration of individual firms' operating environments, needs, and capabilities (Rondinelli and Vastag, 1996).

Isomorphic pressures may be one such contingency. In the face of coercive pressures that are stronger in some industries than in others, firms with different complementary resource profiles often have a choice as to how they will respond to a rule or regulation. Additionally, because the financial cost of not complying with regulations and laws in terms of fines and penalties can be a relatively small percentage of the cost of complying in such industries, firms may have more latitude regarding their environmental strategies. Thus, we find that even within the same industry, firms will decide to exceed, meet, fight, or ignore coercive goals, depending on their relative capabilities and the differential cost of each option (Engelberg, 1995).

The case of Arco's response to California's 1989 clean air regulation provides an example of how strategic heterogeneity can enable firms to gain differential competitive advantage. Over a period of years dating back to the development of the trans-Alaska pipeline in the 1970s, the company differentiated itself with respect to environmental issues so that by 1989 it was significantly ahead of the rest of the industry in meeting the new standards. Its proprietary gasoline formula allowed Arco to break ranks with other oil companies that staunchly opposed alternative fuels and become the strongest performing oil company of that period (Grover, Cahan, Finch, and Maremont, 1990).

As with the results that we have presented, this example suggests that despite theoretical claims to the contrary, strong coercive pressures might actually lead to variation not only in firm strategies but also in firm performance. Coercive pressures may encourage managers to pursue different environmental strategies based on existing complementary resources that result in performance variations. Thus:

Proposition 1: A significant relationship between a firm's environmental strategy and its performance will be observed when coercive pressures are strong because those pressures will elicit strategic variation that can be linked to resource and ultimately performance differences.

If coercive pressures lead to strategic variation, then what forces might influence popular and managerial opinion that greater isomorphism is occurring in environments with strong institutional pressures? We believe that mimetic and normative pressures are driving this perceived isomorphism.[4] Although coercive forces may cause firms to consider substantively different strategic responses based both on how they interpret the issues and on their unique endowments of complementary resources, mimetic and normative forces may raise an overall industry reputation and confer legitimacy across a wider group of firms. Such forces can result in superficial responses from firms that look similar through the adoption of standardized practices such as environmental auditing, producing corporate environmental reports, hiring corporate environmental officers and so forth. These sorts of activities may blunt substantive strategic differences among firms and make the environmental strategy-performance link more difficult to establish. For instance, first movers enact a given strategy because they hope to benefit from a match of operating context and firm skills or capabilities. Laggards then enact the same strategy because they hope to enjoy the same benefits realized by the first movers. The net result is that all firms appear similar; they all appear to be following the same strategy. That similarity may confer legitimacy, but it will not be associated with variation in performance. On average the laggards will not be able to successfully implement the strategy, due to their lack of complementary resources (Christmann, 2000). When firms mimic the actions and strategies of their competitors, they reduce variation observed in an industry. The lack of variation in strategies precludes a causal relationship to financial performance. Simply put, without variation in the explanatory variable, we cannot explain variation in the outcome variable.

The logic applies to normative pressures as well. When an industry imposes a set of standards on itself or forces its members to adopt the same set of environmental principles, strategic variation is removed from the equation. An absence of variation in environmental strategies cannot be responsible for variation in firm performance. Consider the Chemical Manufacturing Association's (CMA) Responsible Care program. In response to several environmental disasters in the 1980s (such as spills and dumping), public pressure was mounting on the chemical industry for change in operating procedures. Some advocated much heavier regulatory pressure to instigate the change. Leading firms in the industry realized that their ability to operate was being compromised, and they moved to form a set of binding environmental principles to which member firms would have to adhere if they were to enjoy membership in the CMA. However, there has been no observable economic benefit stemming from the program for member firms (King and Lenox, 2000). Instead, benefits associated with the program have accrued to the largest member firms that first established the program who have succeeded in reestablishing legitimacy for their industry in the face of a disastrous public relations crisis. Thus:

> *Proposition 2: Mimetic and normative pressures cause firms to look similar, but the effect is superficial because they remove variation in observed strategy, thus precluding a significant direct link between environmental strategy and performance.*

DISCUSSION AND POLICY IMPLICATIONS

The purpose of this chapter is to reexamine the relationship between isomorphism and environmental strategies in light of findings from an exploratory study that found high strategic variation in an industry with strong isomorphic pressures. We offer propositions that draw a clearer distinction between the differential effects of isomorphic pressures. Furthermore, we suggest how those differential effects might affect the relationship between industry isomorphic pressures, environmental strategies, and firm performance.

In our model, coercive pressures exert a negative influence on isomorphism and strategic homogeneity. As coercive mechanisms increase, isomorphic pressure falls, and variation in firm environmental strategies increase, thus allowing for variation in overall firm performance. On the other hand, when mimetic and normative pressures increase, isomorphic pressure also rises and variation in environmental strategies is reduced or eliminated, precluding significant effects on performance.

Our use of comparison industries provides a larger sample size than has been used in past research as a vehicle for examining differences and similarities across industries to gain a better understanding of the effects of different isomorphic pressures. Results support the proposition that as a catalyst for strategic variation, environmental regulations can improve competitiveness (Porter and van der Linde, 1995) but within an environmental context, previously hypothesized effects of institutional isomorphism may in fact be driven by mimetic and normative pressures. Thus our study suggests that future research should include the specific type of institutional pressure being exerted when examining the relationship between environmental strategy and firm performance.

No doubt the conclusions reached here would be better supported by a study that used more sensitive measures for the variables in question. The measures employed are simplified proxies for institutional pressure and individual firm environmental strategies. Attempts to operationalize institutional theory are difficult, and there have been relatively few attempts to do so in the past. Better results might be obtained using data derived from measures designed to more directly represent the constructs of interest. Surveys might better ascertain the coercive pressures on organizations by directly measuring stakeholder attention focused on a set of industries, the perceived degree to which a set of industries are susceptible to environmental problems, the degree to which these problems are being addressed, and the methods by which firms are perceived to be handling their environmental challenges. Interviews with firm executives and other stakeholders might provide a clearer understanding of the environmental challenges facing firms, how firms attempt to meet those challenges, and whether organizational agendas are being driven from inside the firm or by outside stakeholders.

Future studies would also benefit from longitudinal data. The data used for this study were for 1989, an important time in environmental regulation, but it would be interesting to see what results are obtained using more recent IRRC data. Besides providing an opportunity to confirm the results found in this study, additional data would allow for an analysis over a period of time during which firms have been particularly active in developing environmental strategies. Furthermore, although the 1992 IRRC Directory was the first attempt to collect data related to firms' environmental activities, that data is not complete. Subsequent directories are more complete in the information they seek to gather and could allow for an analysis of isomorphic effects over a larger period. Finally, the industries examined in our exploratory study represent only a subset of possible industries. Future studies would benefit from looking at additional industries to determine if observed trends generalize across other industries with varying levels of isomorphic pressure.

The policy implications of this study suggest that firm managers and environmental policymakers employ different models to realize goals based on behaviors that do not necessarily achieve the desired results of either group. Policy makers impose rules and regulations to exert pressure on firms to meet a set of minimum standards of behavior. Differential behavior is not explicitly encouraged, even though firms will act so that they rely on firm-specific complementary resource endowments to realize superior environmental and financial performance. This may be why the imposition of regulations seems to elicit a variety of substantive strategic responses, whereas industry standards and best practices tend to make firms simply appear more similar.

NOTES

1. To clarify a potentially confusing point, for the duration of this piece, the term "environmental strategy" shall refer to those strategies of the firm that address ecological issues pertaining to air, water, soil, and the like. Similarly, the word "environment" is used to refer to natural biotic systems. Finally, the terms "institutional environment" and "operating environment" are used to describe organizational contexts.

2. The statutes are the Resource Conservation and Recovery Act (RCRA), Clean Air Act (CAA), Clean Water Act (CWA), Safe Drinking Water Act (SDWA), Toxic Substances Control Act, Federal Insecticide Fungicide and Rodenticide Act (TSCA/FIFRA), Occupational Safety and Health Act (OSHA), Atomic Energy Act (AEA), and Mining Safety and Health Act (MSHA).

3. The measure is based on information contained in the News & Notes section of Company Profiles that detail environmental enforcement actions and other financially relevant environmental incidents of the company in question. The section contains both negative information related to enforcement action and positive information related to awards or recognition firms may receive. We thank Soderstrom, Ilinitch, and Thomas for providing us access to their original codes.

4. Preliminary examination of the data available in the Company Profiles on mimetic and normative pressures suggested results that behaved differently than those observed for coercive pressures, leading the authors to think further about the relationship between mimetic and normative pressures and financial performance. However, much of the data available in the Company Profiles was missing, yielding too small a sample size to render any meaningful statistical analyses for this study.

REFERENCES

Aldrich, Howard E., and C. Marlene Fiol. 1994. "Fools Rush In? The Institutional Context of Industry Creation." *Academy of Management Review,* 19: 645–670.

Child, John. 1972. "Organization Structure, Environment, and Performance: The Role of Strategic Choice." *Sociology,* 6: 2–22.

Christmann, Petra. 2000. "Effects of Best Practices of Environmental Management on Cost Advantage: The Role Of Complementary Assets." *Academy of Management Journal,* 43: 663–680.

Cyert, Richard M., and James G. March. 1963. *A Behavioral Theory of the Firm.* Englewood Cliffs, NJ: Prentice-Hall.

Dacin, M. Tina. 1997. "Isomorphism in Context: The Power and Prescription of Institutional Norms." *Academy of Management Journal,* 40: 46–81.

Deephouse, David. L. 1996. "Does Isomorphism Legitimate?" *Academy of Management Journal,* 39: 1024–1039.

Diltz, J. David. 1995. "The Private Cost of Socially Responsible Investing." *Applied Financial Economics,* 5: 69–77.

DiMaggio, Paul J., and Walter W. Powell. 1983. "The Iron Cage Revisited: Institutional Isomorphism and Collective Rationality in Organizational Fields." *American Sociological Review,* 48: 147–160.

Donaldson, Lex. 1987. "Strategy and Structural Adjustment to Regain Fit and Performance: In Defense of Contingency Theory." *Journal of Management Studies,* 24: 1–24.

Dutton, Jane, and Robert B. Duncan. 1987. "The Creation of Momentum for Change Through the Process of Strategic Issue Diagnosis." *Strategic Management Journal,* 8: 279–295.

Engelberg, S. 1995. "Tall timber and the E.P.A." *New York Times* (May 21): Section 3-1.

Friedman, Milton. 1970. "The Social Responsibility of Business Is to Increase Profits." *New York Times Magazine* (Sept. 13): 32–33 and 122–126.

Grover, Ronald, Vicky Cahan, Peter Finch, and Mark Maremont. 1990. "Lod Cook: Mixing Oil and PR." *Business Week* (Oct. 8): 110.

Hamilton, Sally, Hoje Jo, and Meir Statman. 1993. "Doing Well While Doing Good? The Investment Performance of Socially Responsible Mutual Funds." *Financial Analysts Journal* (Nov./Dec.): 62–66.

Hannan, Michael T., and John H. Freeman. 1984. "Structural Inertia and Organizational Change." *American Sociological Review* 49: 149–164.

Hart, Stuart. 1995. "A Natural Resource Based View of the Firm." *Academy of Management Review,* 20: 986–1014.

Hart, Stuart. 1997. "Beyond Greening: Strategies for a Sustainable World." *Harvard Business Review,* 75: 66–76.

Hart, Stuart, and Guatam Ahuja. 1996. "Does It Pay to Be Green? An Empirical Examination of the Relationship Between Emission Reduction and Firm Performance." *Business Strategy and the Environment,* 5: 30–37.

Haveman, Heather A. 1993. "Follow The Leader: Mimetic Isomorphism and Entry into New Markets." *Administrative Science Quarterly,* 38: 593–627.

Haveman, Robert H., and Gregory B. Christainsen. 1981. "Environmental Regulations and Productivity Growth. In Henry M. Peskin, Paul Portney, and Allen Kneese, eds., *Environmental Regulation and the U.S. Economy,* 55–76. Washington, DC: Resources for the Future.

Henriques, Irene, and Perry Sadorsky. 1996. "The Determinants of an Environmentally Responsive Firm: An Empirical Approach." *Journal of Environmental Economics and Management,* 30: 381–395.

Hoffman, Andrew J. 1997. *From Heresy to Dogma: An Institutional History of Corporate Environmentalism.* San Francisco: New Lexington.

Hoffman, Andrew J. 1999. "Institutional Evolution and Change: Environmentalism and the U.S. Chemical Industry." *Academy of Management Journal,* 42: 351–371.

Hunt, Courtney S., and Howard E. Aldrich. 1998. "The Second Ecology: Creation and Evolution of Organizational Communities." *Research in Organizational Behavior,* 20: 267–301.

IRRC. 1992. *Corporate Environmental Profiles Directory.* Washington, DC: Investor Responsibility Research Center.

Jaggi, Bikki, and Martin Freedman. 1992. "An Examination of the Impact of Pollution Performance on Economic and Market Performance: Pulp and Paper Firms." *Journal of Business Finance and Accounting,* 19: 697–713.

Jennings, P. Devereaux, and Paul A. Zandbergen. 1995. "Ecologically Sustainable Organizations: An Institutional Approach." *Academy of Management Review,* 20: 1015–1052.

King, Andrew, and Michael Lenox. 2000. "Industry Self-Regulation Without Sanctions: The Chemical Industry's Responsible Care Program." *Academy of Management Journal,* 43: 698–716.

Korten, David C. 1995. *When Corporations Rule the World.* West Hartford, CT: Kumarian Press.

Mallin, Christopher A., Brahim Saadouni, and Richard J. Briston. 1995. "The Financial Performance of Ethical Investment Funds." *Journal of Business Finance and Accounting,* 22: 483–496.

Meyer, John W., and Brian Rowan. 1977. "Institutional Organizations: Formal Structure as Myth and Ceremony." *American Journal of Sociology,* 83: 340–363.

Morais, Richard C. 1995. "Feel-Good Investing." *Forbes* (Dec. 18): 84.

Newton, Tim, and George Harte, G. 1997. "Green Business: Technicist Kitsch?" *Journal of Management Studies,* 34: 75–98.

Oliver, Christine. 1990. "Determinants of Interorganizational Relationships: Integration and Future Directions." *Academy of Management Review,* 15: 241–265.

Porter, Michael. 1990. *The Competitive Advantage of Nations.* New York: The Free Press.

Porter, Michael. 1991. "America's Green Strategy." *Scientific American* (April): 168.

Porter, Michael, and Claas van der Linde. 1995. "Green and Competitive: Ending the Stalemate." *Harvard Business Review,* 5: 120–134.

Portney, Paul. 1994. "Does Environmental Policy Conflict with Economic Growth?" *Resources* (Spring): 21–23.

Rao, Hayagreeva. 1994. "The Social Construction of Reputation: Certification Contests, Legitimation, and the Survival of Organizations in the American Automobile Industry, 1895–1912." *Strategic Management Journal,* 15: 29–44.

Rondinelli, Dennis A., and Gyula Vastag. 1996. "International Environmental Standards and Corporate Policies: An Integrative Framework." *California Management Review,* 39: 106–122.

Rumelt, Richard. 1974. *Strategy, Structure and Economic Performance.* Boston: Graduate School Business Administration, Harvard University.

Russo, Michael V., and Paul A. Fouts. 1997. "A Resource-Based Perspective on Corporate Environmental Performance and Profitability." *Academy of Management Journal,* 40: 534–559.

Sharma, Sanjay, and Harrie Vredenburg. 1998. "Proactive Corporate Environmental Strategy and the Development of Competitively Valuable Organizational Capabilities." *Strategic Management Journal,* 19: 729–753.

Siegel, Philip H., Surendra Agrawal, and John T. Rigsby. 1997. "Organizational and Professional Socialization: Institutional Isomorphism in an Accounting Context." *Mid-Atlantic Journal of Business,* 33: 49–68.

Soderstrom, Naomi, Anne Y. Ilinitch, and Tom E. Thomas. 1998. "Measuring Corporate Environmental Performance." *Journal of Accounting and Public Policy,* 17: 383–408.

Teece, D. J. 1987. "Profiting from Technological Innovation: Implications for Integration, Collaboration, Licensing, and Public Policy." In D. J. Teece, ed., *The Competitive Challenge: Strategies for Industrial Innovation and Renewal,* 185–219. Cambridge, MA: Ballinger.

Tolbert, Pamela S., and Lynne G. Zucker. 1983. "Institutional Sources of Change in the Formal Structure of Organizations: The Diffusion of Civil Service Reform, 1880–1935." *Administrative Science Quarterly,* 28: 22–39.

Venkatraman, N. 1989. "The Concept of Fit in Strategy Research: Toward a Verbal and Statistical Correspondence." *Academy of Management Review,* 14: 423–444.

Walley, Noah, and Bradley Whitehead. 1994. "It's Not Easy Being Green." *Harvard Business Review,* 3: 46–52.

7

HETEROGENEITY AND CHANGE IN ENVIRONMENTAL STRATEGY: TECHNOLOGICAL AND POLITICAL RESPONSES TO CLIMATE CHANGE IN THE GLOBAL AUTOMOBILE INDUSTRY

David L. Levy and Sandra Rothenberg

The formulation of strategy is generally treated as a rational process of matching corporate capabilities to market demands. But this does not always account well for the heterogeneity observed in corporate strategies toward complex environmental issues such as climate change. In this chapter, we propose that strategy is often developed in light of expectations and assumptions concerning a firm's internal competencies and the external market and nonmarket environments. These expectations, we propose, are shaped by institutional forces at multiple levels, including the firm, the national industry, the global industry, and the specific environmental issue. In particular, we argue that collective interpretations about the nature of and solutions to climate change constitute important drivers of strategy, and these collective interpretations are molded and contested within institutional fields.

In addition to providing a fresh perspective on corporate environmental strategy, this chapter makes a number of contributions to institutional theory. First, we reject a strict dichotomy between the influence of the institutional environment and the competitive environment, as corporate perceptions of market trends are themselves subject to institutional construction. Second, we argue that tensions and political contestation across the complex terrain of interpenetrating and nested fields give rise to heterogeneity and change as integral features of institutional fields rather than difficulties to be explained away. Finally, we suggest that

The authors gratefully acknowledge financial support for this project from the Global Environmental Assessment Project, Kennedy School of Government, Harvard University, and the Consortium on Environmental Challenges, Massachusetts Institute of Technology.

the institutionalization of specific notions of economic interest is closely related to the institutionalization of particular perspectives on environmental science.

Automobile companies exhibit considerable variation in their strategic responses to climate change. U.S. companies responded relatively early to the issue, aggressively challenged the need for emission controls, and have invested in a range of long-term technological approaches to emission reductions without committing to production vehicles. European companies, by contrast, have been less engaged in public debates about climate science, have accommodated regulatory demands for significant emission reductions, and have invested in more incremental, short-term improvements to conventional internal combustion engine technology. The different economic and market environments in each region offer only a partial explanation for these divergent strategic responses. There are also differences within regions; Ford, for example, has been more outspoken than General Motors (GM) against mandatory emission controls. We argue that these strategic differences can largely be explained in terms of the construction of perceptions of economic interests, which occurs in particular institutional contexts.

In the theoretical section of this chapter, we outline three primary mechanisms by which institutional processes might lead to heterogeneity rather than conformity. We then describe the strategic responses of the automobile industry in the United States and Europe to the climate change debate, and analyze these responses in light of the theoretical issues discussed earlier. We conclude with a discussion of the dynamics of institutional change and highlight some issues for future research.

METHOD

We adopt a case study approach to explore the climate strategies of the two major American automobile manufacturers, GM and Ford, and two European companies, Daimler-Chrysler and Volkswagen. The auto industry is significant because of its contribution to greenhouse gas (GHG) emissions and its political salience in the global warming debate. Moreover, the industry's stance on the issue is less obviously determined by economic circumstances than is the case in the coal or renewable energy sectors. As a result, managers have a degree of strategic discretion and institutional pressures are more likely to be prominent. The responses in the United States and Europe are sufficiently distinct to provide a basis for examining the reasons for this variation.

Data were collected from a series of interviews in the United States and Europe with twenty-four senior managers in companies, industry associations, government agencies, and environmental nongovernmental organizations (NGOs). Interviews were conducted with a cross section of firm employees, including environmental staff and those in strategy, product development, marketing, and R&D. Some interviews, particularly with ex-employees that focused on more historical data, were performed over the phone using a semistructured interview format. For additional information on industry involvement with climate policy, records of industry comments on the Intergovernmental Panel on Climate Change (IPCC) Second Assessment Report were reviewed in their entirety.

THEORETICAL BACKGROUND

Institutional theory suggests that corporate perspectives on climate change are likely to be premised upon views of climate science, expectations of regulatory responses, and the market potential for mitigation technologies. These perspectives are mediated by the institutional environment, including competitors, industry associations, consumers, NGOs, regulatory agencies, and the media (DiMaggio, 1988; Powell and DiMaggio, 1991; Scott and Meyer, 1994). The application of the institutional approach to strategy builds on the idea that markets are socially constructed and embedded within broader political and cultural structures (Callon, 1998; Granovetter, 1985). Eisenhardt and Brown (1996: 187), in a study of a technology-based firm, concluded that "the firm's strategy was critically shaped by the institutional context of industry fads that came and went over time." Overall, however, the institutional approach is not well developed in the strategy literature.

Oliver (1997) contends that uncertainty increases the influence of the institutional environment and reduces the impact of economic and competitive factors (the "task environment"). Given the high level of uncertainty concerning climate science, technological and market developments, and policy responses, car makers cannot easily make a rational, objective calculus of their economic interests and appropriate strategic responses, and might therefore be more subject to institutional pressures. The sharp distinction between institutional and economic explanations breaks down, however, under closer examination. A more useful theoretical approach avoids this dualism and recognizes that economic calculations of interests always embody assumptions that are more or less certain and are constructed in broader social contexts (Callon, 1998). The problem is not that investment decisions are taken under conditions of risk, for which many techniques exist (Dixit and Pindyck, 1994); rather, planning scenarios contain assumptions and predictions about research and development costs, technological developments, consumer behavior, competitors' reactions, and regulatory responses that are shaped by organizational fields and are not stable over time. Indeed, we encountered firms with very different market perceptions which, nevertheless, held their respective views with some conviction.

Institutional theory generally predicts convergence, or isomorphism, among organizational actors, though several writers have recognized the need to account for heterogeneity and institutional change. According to Oliver (1996: 171), "firm heterogeneity is explained, at least in part, by variation in the degree of connectedness between firms and their institutional environment." It has also been argued that weak institutional fields, which exert little pressure on firms, will also give rise to heterogeneity (Scott and Meyer, 1991). These views presume that the institutional environment is fixed and static, and that organizations only vary in their degree of embeddedness and conformity with it.

Extant accounts of institutional change point to substantial disruptions or shocks in the external environment (Fligstein, 1991; A. Hoffman, 1999), or to changes in the balance of power among field actors (Greenwood and Hinings, 1996; Oliver, 1992). The problem with the exogenous approach is that it ignores the potential for dynamics to be driven endogenously, and, indeed, for such endogenous change to affect the external environment. But the endogenous approach is also problematic, as it does not explain the change in the balance of power, which is itself a function of the specific configuration of an organizational field.

Here we offer a perspective in which multiple sets of practices and discourses coexist and compete across an untidy and ill-defined terrain of overlapping and nested institutional fields, giving rise to endogenous dynamics. Three specific arguments are developed to account for heterogeneous corporate perceptions and strategic responses. First, institutional discourses and practices do not pass undisturbed across organizational boundaries. Each company interprets the institutional environment through a unique lens, a product of its history, organizational culture, and market positioning. A history of conflictual relations with regulatory agencies or of unsuccessful ventures with low-emission technologies, for example, predicts how its external discourses and practices are imported and rearticulated.

Second, organizations often operate within multiple, overlapping institutional fields, belonging to various industry associations or national cultural and regulatory contexts, creating divergent pressures (Alexander, 1996; D'Aunno and Sutton, 1991; Holm, 1995; Kempton and Craig, 1993). Ford, for example, until the end of 1999 was a member of the Global Climate Coalition (GCC), the leading industry association opposed to mandatory curbs on emissions of greenhouse gases.

General Motors also was a member of the GCC, but it joined an initiative of the World Resources Institute called "Safe Climate, Sound Business," putting it in touch with other companies more open to change on the issue. Both companies have subsidiaries in Europe exposed to very different political and cultural institutional environments. Instead of a unitary field with a monolithic set of practices and discourses, organizations are thus situated in complex, fragmented fields with imprecise boundaries, providing repertoires of practices and discourse within which they can exercise some agency and choice.

A third explanation for heterogeneity is that even a single organizational field can sustain multiple competing discursive forms. The global automobile industry can be considered to be a single organizational field with nested national subfields. Scott (1994: 206) has argued that institutional fields are less defined by their geographic boundaries and more by cultural and functional boundaries: "Organizations are in the same field if they take one another into account, regardless of the geographic propinquity. In this way, the field conception emphasizes the possible importance of distant, nonlocal connections among organizations." By this reasoning, the emerging climate change regime itself constitutes an organizational field at the issue level, with intense and frequent interactions among various actors, which intersects with the industry field. Environmental NGOs and fossil fuel companies compete for institutional legitimacy and influence in the issue-level field, with neither group achieving complete domination of the field. Diversity in an organizational field can thus result from the interaction of related subfields, enabling ideas and practices to migrate across porous and ambiguous field boundaries and challenge established forms. Bansal and Penner (Chapter 13) describe how the use of recycled newsprint varies in the publishing industry, and is related to differing management perspectives on the feasibility and importance of recycling. These divergent perspectives derive, in turn, from the managers' experiences in other social and cultural contexts.

Competing perspectives on the costs and value of environmental management provide another example of competing discourses. Many companies still adhere to the traditional notion that environmental regulations are inherently costly, but many others are embracing the discourse and practices of environmental management, termed "eco-modernism" by Hajer (1995), which asserts that incorporating environmental concerns into business strategy can generate "win-win" outcomes. As Milstein, Hart, and York point out (Chapter 6), these competing claims cannot be resolved through empirical analysis and are perhaps better viewed as alternative ideologies or discourses (Rothenberg and Zyglidopoulos, 2001; Levy,

1997). In the climate case, the Global Climate Coalition has advocated the more traditional discourse while the Pew Center for Global Climate Change has argued the more optimistic "win-win" approach.

These three explanations for heterogeneity are derived from viewing institutionalization as an ongoing but incomplete *process* (DiMaggio, 1988), during which an organizational field can sustain more than one set of practices and norms. The process is never complete because of the "leakage" of competing institutional forms from related fields and because subordinate institutional behaviors are rarely extinguished entirely, instead remaining active in the margins. Scott (1994) has observed that a single dominant belief system often exists along with a number of secondary or subordinate belief sets. Social movement theory has noted a similar phenomenon in broader social spheres, by which subordinate groups maintain skeletal organizational forms and sustain their ideologies in "abeyance structures," providing the seeds of change when conditions are ripe (Laraña, Johnston, and Gusfield, 1994).

Heterogeneity and change are thus intrinsically linked. The presence of multiple competing institutional forms generates a dynamic process of institutionalization. In turn, this dynamic process, seeded by the emergence of new forms from adjoining fields and the resurgence of previously marginalized practices, ensures that no single institutional form achieves complete domination. Dynamics and instability can therefore be endogenous to a fragmented system of overlapping and porous fields.

STRATEGIC RESPONSES TO CLIMATE CHANGE IN THE UNITED STATES AND EUROPE

Background

Controls on emissions of carbon dioxide (CO_2), released from the combustion of fossil fuels and the main contributor to global warming, would threaten oil and coal companies, as well as industries dependent on these fuels, particularly transportation and electric utilities. In addition, higher energy prices would raise input costs for a range of energy-intense products (Mansley, 1995). Investments in R&D for low-GHG products and processes appear highly risky at this stage, and technologies associated with low-emission automotive products and processes will require radically new capabilities that threaten to undermine industry incumbents (Anderson and Tushman, 1990).

U.S.-based fossil-fuel-related industries responded relatively early to the climate issue, providing time and organizational resources to develop an effective political strategy against emission controls. On the organizational level, the three major U.S. automobile companies, as well as the American Automobile Manufacturers Association (AAMA) worked largely through the GCC, which was formed in 1990 and represented about 40 companies and industry associations in energy related sectors. Although the GCC was initially a U.S.-based organization focused on domestic lobbying, a number of U.S. subsidiaries of European multinationals also joined and the GCC quickly rose to be the most prominent voice of industry in the international negotiations.

A key component of the GCC's political strategy has been to engage in a public debate over the science of climate change (Boyle, 1998; Leggett, 2000). As part of this campaign, the GCC criticized the review process for the Second Assessment Report (SAR) of the Intergovernmental Panel on Climate Change (IPCC), the group of more than 1000 international scientists charged with assessing the current state of knowledge concerning climate change (Edwards and Schneider, 1997; Gelbspan, 1997; Intergovernmental Panel on Climate Change, 1995). The GCC also emphasized the economic cost of emission controls and commissioned a series of economic studies from a number of consulting organizations (Montgomery, 1995).

The lobbying efforts of U.S. industries were successful in securing political allies in Congress, making Senate ratification of Kyoto a very dim prospect. Federal funding for climate research has been constrained, and the U.S. State Department opposed mandatory international GHG emission controls until 1996. Even after the United States accepted the principle of an international protocol at the Geneva negotiations in July 1996, it advocated no more than a freeze on emissions at 1990 levels, whereas the European Union was pushing for a 15 percent reduction below those levels.

The technological strategies of U.S.-based auto companies were primarily geared toward addressing local air quality, which could be addressed through catalytic converters rather than higher fuel efficiency. The companies were also investing in a range of alternative fuel programs for fleet vehicles. By the late 1980s, any technological improvements on the fuel efficiency front were being more than offset by increasing weight of vehicles and larger engine sizes (Stoffer, 1997). One effort to improve fuel economy was the Partnership for a New Generation of Vehicles (PNGV), launched in 1993 with substantial federal funding and the participation of the three U.S. manufacturers. The objective of this venture was to produce a car that did not sacrifice the capacity, safety, range, power, or comfort of a conventional large vehicle. The assumption that consumers would not compromise traditional attributes of cars placed a heavy burden on radical innovation in motive technologies and in light-weight materials. The U.S. industry response to climate change could be characterized as a long-term hedging strategy based on the development of radical and expensive technological options without committing large sums to a production vehicle.

Far from having political allies, European firms found themselves in a context in which politicians were looking to the auto industry for substantial early-emission reductions. Germany, with a well-organized green political party, had unilaterally committed to significant GHG reductions during the Framework Convention on Climate Change (FCCC) negotiations in Berlin in 1994 and had pushed the German auto industry association, the Automobile Industry Association of Germany (VDA), into a "voluntary" agreement to reduce CO_2 emissions from new cars by 25 percent. Concerned that these constraints might affect the competitiveness of its national automobile companies, Germany then pushed the European Union to adopt similar measures.

The EU was sensitive to charges that it talked a tough game but lacked the will to implement anything. The European Commission introduced a proposal to reduce average new-car CO_2 emissions from 186 grams/km to 120 g/km by 2005 (equivalent to about 45 mpg). The European Parliament called for even stricter limits, with a figure of 90 g/km being mentioned. European automobile companies avoided direct challenges to the scientific need for GHG controls, with various managers calling any such effort "futile" and "inappropriate." After three years of negotiations, in 1998 the European Automobile Industry Association (ACEA) accepted a voluntary agreement to reduce emissions to 140 g/km by 2008. The agreement included Ford and GM's European subsidiaries, but not Japanese manufacturers (Bradsher, 1998a).

European companies have responded to these pressures by introducing very light-weight cars such as Daimler-Chrysler's SMART car, and investing substantial amounts in a range of technologies from diesel to fuel cells. Daimler has aggressively pursued fuel cell technology, investing $320 million in the Canadian company Ballard in April 1997, and has announced plans for a limited commercial launch by 2004 (P. Hoffman, 1999). European efforts emphasized short- to medium-term emission reductions through weight and size reduction and incremental technological improvements.

The Timing and Context of Climate Change as a Strategic Concern

The U.S. automobile industry responded much earlier to the climate issue than did their counterparts in Europe. Research divisions at Ford and GM had been aware of the issue since the late 1970s, but managers and scientists at both companies recalled James Hansen's testimony before the U.S. House Energy Committee in June 1988 as the catalyst that catapulted climate change onto corporate radar screens, gaining the attention of the mass media and senior management (Edwards and Lahsen, forthcoming). Ford's climate specialist described his shock at how quickly "climate went from zero to sixty," and the company began sending a representative to IPCC meetings, taking a lead role in reviewing chapters of the IPCC's Second Assessment Report on behalf of the GCC and the AAMA.

It is notable that the U.S. automobile companies paid much more attention to the national media and political events in Washington, D.C. than to the development of scientific concern around greenhouse gases. The President's Science Advisory Committee had discussed greenhouse gases and climate as far back as 1965, and in the early 1970s, two major scientific studies put climate firmly on the U.S. policy agenda (Edwards and Lahsen, forthcoming). Awareness of the issue did not penetrate to boardroom level, however. Surprisingly, none of the managers interviewed recalled the June 1988 Toronto Conference on the Changing Atmosphere, which called for a 20 percent cut in greenhouse gas emissions by 2005, despite the fact that Detroit is closer to Toronto than to Washington, D.C.

Without Hansen's Congressional testimony during a hot summer as a stimulus, European industry did not pay serious attention to the issue until the summer of 1992. Interviewees from European companies mentioned the UNCED conference in Rio de Janeiro as the crucial event that spurred corporate attention. By this time, the Second Assessment Report (SAR) of the IPCC was already under way, leaving little room for European industry involvement.

Corporate responses were also conditioned by the existing regulatory context. In the United States, the primary concern for many years had been local air quality. U.S. industry was already subject to CAFE standards under the Clean Air Act, and the California Air Review Board (CARB) was mandating zero emission vehicles in the longer term. Initially, U.S.-based companies understood climate change as a continuation of this pressure, thus not requiring a major strategic change in direction. As GM's former vice president for research, Robert Frosch, explained, the initial reaction to climate change from product developers was "we're already running as fast as we can in that direction." Helen Petrauskas, a Ford vice president, concurred: "Climate did not require a step function change in strategy."

Over a period of time, companies came to appreciate that many technological approaches involved tradeoffs. Electric vehicles, for example, can account for substantial indirect emissions depending on the fuel mix and efficiency of electricity generation. Similarly, the introduction of catalytic converters in the early 1980s caused a noticeable decrease in fuel efficiency. It was not easy, however, for American companies to shift their technology strategies toward carbon reduction, because the fragmented regulatory system was still ratcheting up controls on non-GHG emissions while paying no attention to CO_2.

In Europe, by contrast, preexisting environmental concerns about automobiles were more aligned with the strategic challenge of climate change. Instead of a focus on local air quality, concerns about resource depletion and congestion had led to policies such as high fuel prices and investments in public transportation that reduced fuel consumption and vehicle use overall. European innovation efforts were therefore already more directed toward fuel efficiency, and companies were more aware of potential challenges to the private automobile in the broader transportation system.

The Political Environment in the Unites States and Europe

The Congressional hearings on climate change exemplified the adversarial, legalistic courtroom style through which the scientific basis for regulation is developed and contested in the United States (Edwards and Lahsen, forthcoming; Gelbspan, 1997). This contrasts sharply with the approach found in Europe, and particularly in Germany, which is often characterized as more integrated and consensual (Jasanoff, 1991). The governance structures in the United States cause companies engaged in contested policy arenas to make their case in a vociferous and public manner. As GM's Frosch put it, "The Hill works by compromise, so you need to go to the extreme. The more strident one side gets, the more the other side must. It ends up completely polarized." Helen Petrauskas commented, "It doesn't help to have politicians saying that people are dying in Chicago in a heat wave because of climate change. We are forced to be strident to counter that misinformation."

U.S. companies tended to be wary of international regulatory initiatives over which they had little control (Levy and Egan, 1998), whereas European car companies welcomed harmonized emissions regulations at the regional level. A Ford Europe manager explained: "Both the Commission and industry did not want to have a patchwork of regulations and standards. At the end of the eighties, the emissions situation was a strategic nightmare. We wanted harmonization, because otherwise we face the nightmare of managing product mix by country."

As a result of the political and cultural environment in Europe, challenging the scientific basis for regulation was seen as futile. An official with the German environmental ministry said:

> It's not like the United States. Here the companies make some comments in presentations or interviews, but nothing serious because they know public opinion

would be against them. If they would argue in the way they do in the States, it would create an image disaster.

Perhaps reflecting a more general cynicism about business influence in Europe, a representative with the VDA, the German auto industry association, commented that "if the auto industry were to support a specific study, the people would think that scientists were bought by industry and they would not believe them." Regarding negotiations with the EU over automobile emissions of CO_2, a manager in a European subsidiary of a U.S.-based company commented that:

> My boss in Detroit said we should argue about the science and the economics. It was an education process to get them on board. We had to explain that it's not constructive to challenge the science in Europe if we want to influence the debate. Here, the IPCC reports are accepted without question by policymakers. We would be thrown out of the room if we challenged them.

A Ford Europe executive with experience in the United States pointed to differences in the political process that led to this outcome:

> You have to understand the process by which the 120 g/km target entered the debate. In the U.S. there is a long period for public input and delay, and economic interests can be balanced against environmental concerns. Here, there is little balance or accountability. The 120 target was proposed by the EU Environmental Council, which consists of only the environmental ministers of member states. We said that they needed to talk to the economics, finance and labor ministers, but the environmental ministers have power to initiate legislation on their own. The Environmental Council simply said 'this is the target', and other ministers were cut out of the loop. The Environmental Council then tasked the Commission to develop a strategy to achieve the 120 target. The Directorates General for Energy and Industry had little influence.

These negotiations also highlighted the difference between the technocratic policy process in the United States and the lack of technical capacity of the EU institutions. Policy battles in the United States were waged on the basis of detailed technical studies. In Europe, the Commission's demand for a 120g/km standard was not based on any analysis of technical feasibility, environmental need, or economic costs. ACEA commissioned a report from the consultants A. D. Little, which provided technical justification for the industry's position that the target was not feasible in the time frame. One executive summed up the Commission's reaction to the A.D. Little analysis as, "a very nice report, but what are you going to do about the 120 target?"

Perspectives on Climate Science

Most descriptions of industry's challenge to climate science present them as cynical manipulations of the public discourse (Gelbspan, 1997; Leggett, 2000). While there clearly has been a strategic component to corporate political activities in this arena, it is argued here that skeptical perspectives on climate science became institutionalized in the automobile companies, particularly those based in the United States, and these perspectives in turn contributed toward the constitution of perceptions of strategic interest. In other words, perspectives on climate science and economic interests are mutually constitutive.

Ford's Trotman and Chrysler's Eaton were especially vociferous in the early 1990s, through speeches and editorials, in castigating concerns about climate change and emphasizing the high cost of precipitate action in the face of uncertainty. Our interviews revealed that these views were not just those of top management, but had permeated throughout various departments and management levels. One manager at Ford commented, "We have followed the science as a company and we would like to see more science and less hot air! What we'd like to see is good science driving good policy."

Generally, less skepticism concerning climate science was evident among the European companies; a few managers expressed skeptical views, but acknowledged that the debate had moved beyond science. One reason for this might be the different sources of information used by European and U.S. companies. U.S. companies tended to rely on American scientists, including quite a few skeptics. The German car manufacturers primarily relied on German scientists, especially from the Wuppertal Institute, but had also invited in people from Greenpeace, from the German environmental ministry, and Amory Lovins from the Rocky Mountain Institute, an ardent supporter of technological solutions to environmental problems. European companies generally lacked internal scientists who were directly engaged with atmospheric science. Nevertheless, both Volkswagon and Daimler maintained close contacts with local university scientists.

Despite their adherence to the scientific norms of objectivity and independence, the internal scientists in the United States tended toward the skeptical end of the spectrum of legitimate opinion among respected climate scientists (Morgan and Keith, 1995). They all interpreted scientific uncertainties in a conservative manner, viewing them as a rationale for further research rather than seeing the potential for climate shocks from positive feedback or threshold effects. They pointed to the long time frame of atmospheric accumulation of GHGs as a comfortable margin of time for reducing uncertainty rather than an urgent reason for early precautionary action. These conservative viewpoints appear to be constituted in a subtle process of negotiation with dominant corporate perspectives. As GM's Frosch expressed, "There is social pressure. They are around people who don't pay attention to the climate issue and don't want to hear it. . . . People on the operational side are more conservative." He also suggested that there might be some element of self-selection in terms of who is willing to be a corporate scientist. GM's former chief economist Marina Whitman discussed the pressure to adopt a bottom-line perspective: "There is a need for credibility with the line guys. We were the cost center, they were the profit center."

Managers in different functional areas generally adopted perspectives consistent with their departmental interests, demonstrating the interaction of technological and economic viewpoints. People responsible for advanced automotive technologies tended to see climate change as an opportunity and to accept that it was a serious cause for concern. According to GM's Frosch, "The spirit of the research labs is, we will show top management we can do it—we can change things." Although the R&D people could accept climate change as a problem because they had an interest in developing solutions, others in the organization took a more conservative approach. Managers responsible for product divisions and strategy, for example, were particularly concerned about the high cost of new technologies with little value to consumers.

The implication of this discussion is that corporate perspectives on science are not purely strategic, but are partly based on economic interests. More skeptical perspectives toward climate science became institutionalized within the American companies, which perceived climate change as more of an economic threat; in turn, the companies relied on these skeptical perspectives in anticipating a weak regulatory response and in formulating their R&D strategies. These institutionalized conceptions are not easy to change, and risk becoming an "iron cage" (DiMaggio and Powell, 1983) that constrains consideration of a full range of strategic options.

Perceptions of Market Viability for Low-Emission Technologies

Although the major auto companies are all multinationals and have been active in each other's markets for many years, the management of U.S.-based auto companies displayed a remarkably national orientation to their cognitive maps. In numerous interviews, corporate managers in Detroit, many with worldwide responsibilities, spoke about the difficulty of reducing emissions with gasoline near $1 a gallon, consumers who care little for fuel economy and desire larger vehicles, and a Senate unlikely to ratify Kyoto. These views are reinforced through membership in industry associations such as the GCC, which are dominated by U.S.-based companies. Ford's and GM's climate teams were both based in Detroit and comprised mainly U.S.-based personnel.

All the companies considered that consumer acceptance was the single biggest hurdle facing innovation efforts, though American companies tended to focus more on current consumption patterns and downplayed the potential for dramatic change. American companies were particularly critical of regulation such as the CAFE standards, which they saw as coming between the company and consumer requirements. Marina Whitman, GM's former chief economist, expressed the widely held view that consumer sovereignty would eventually triumph in the marketplace: "Consumers find a way around regulation. The shift from cars to trucks is an example, as consumers can find features on trucks that have been stripped out of cars."

The impact of low-emission technologies on price was seen as a problem even in Europe. A Ford Europe manager noted that "customers won't pay a premium for fuel economy. It's a mid-level concern for consumers, not in the top three, but not nine or ten as in the United States, where concern for fuel economy is fifteen years away." Companies related a number of experiences in which consumers reacted negatively to cars that pushed the environmental envelope, and these experiences appear to have become institutionalized as conventional wisdom. At GM, the decision to downsize luxury vehicles was commonly referred as the "Cadillac disaster." In Europe, Daimler, Opel, and Volkswagon all had introduced lightweight, fuel-efficient vehicles that had met limited demand.

The barrier to new technology was not just price. Hesse thought that there would need to be substantial changes in infrastructure, usage patterns, and attitudes for the small SMART car to sell in volume. European managers demonstrated a greater awareness that the success of new technologies was contingent on broader social and institutional change. A Volkswagon executive noted that "we are more active in trying to change consumers. You cannot force people to buy certain things, but what we are trying to do is just keep on presenting it to the market, and try to convince people to buy these type of products." U.S.-based companies, by contrast, tended to focus on consumer preferences and infrastructure as fixed constraints. One Ford Europe manager noted that diesel engines were increasingly seen as "hip and green" in Europe, whereas U.S. executives were convinced that American consumers would remember the noisy, dirty, shuddering diesels of the 1970s.

These different perspectives on consumer preferences explain, in part, the differences in innovation strategies. U.S.-based companies were planning a car of the future that would not require any change in transportation patterns, road infrastructure, or consumer behavior; rather, the burden of emissions reduction would be placed on advanced automotive technologies. This led to a focus on longer-term and more radical approaches to emission reduction, without sacrificing conventional car features. Such efforts were necessarily expensive, generating pessimism about the likely markets for such cars. European efforts, on the other hand, comprised more balanced, incremental investments in short- to medium-term emission reductions. For example, diesel-powered vehicles, which were much quieter, smoother, and cleaner than in the early 1980s, already accounted for 22 percent of family vehicles in Europe compared to only 2 percent in the United States (Bradsher, 1998b) and constituted more than 40 percent of new vehicle sales in 2001. Consumers were expected to play their part in adapting to new types of vehicles and to the changing role of private cars in the transportation system.

Historical experiences shaped company perspectives on the benefits of being a first mover in low-emission technologies. GM, for example, had invested more than $1 billion in its electric vehicle, of which fewer than 1000 had been sold (Lippert, 1997; Shnayerson, 1996). Although a few GM managers thought that the company had gained valuable expertise in electric drive chains, managers generally interpreted the experience as a commercial mistake. Similarly, GM managers felt that they had rushed too quickly to downsize their vehicles in response to earlier oil price shocks. Ford had invested an estimated $500 million in sodium-sulfur batteries, only to abandon the project because of safety concerns. With this shared experience, American companies did not appreciate the advantages of being a first mover.

European companies lacked this history of negative experiences with electric drive chains and viewed GHG emission controls as inevitable. Market prospects were viewed in a more optimistic light, and companies expressed willingness to take some risks to sustain market leadership during a period of technological upheaval. Daimler had taken a strategic decision to be a leader in fuel cell technology. The justification for this decision employed rhetorical strategies as much as any objective analytical framework. Hesse discussed "the need to stay in the driver's seat, to prepare for a future that is not the status quo."

DISCUSSION AND CONCLUSIONS

The case study applies institutional theory to explain the different responses of automobile companies to the challenge of climate change. We argue that strategic choices are based on assumptions and forecasts that arise from an organization's interactions with its institutional environment. Of particular importance to the climate issue are perceptions about climate science, anticipated regulatory responses, and the technological and market prospects for various low-emission options. These perceptions are formed in light of national environments, issue-specific context, and each company's corporate history and characteristics. Although institutional theory has traditionally been applied to account for conformity and isomorphism, here we provide a new perspective on organizational fields as complex, fragmented systems sustaining multiple discourses and practices in tension and contestation. These fields are intrinsically unstable and demonstrate heterogeneity instead of reaching a static isomorphic equilibrium.

Three explanations for divergent strategies were given. First, institutional pressures were transformed across organizational boundaries. Internal scientists played a critical role in how the climate issue was communicated and perceived within the organizations. Each firm's history influenced the degree to which future technological options were viewed as an opportunity or a threat. Managers in different functional areas generally adopted perspectives consistent with their departmental interests, and negotiation among these departments influenced the final position taken in relation to climate science and technology feasibility.

We also see that the automobile companies existed within multiple and nested fields. The American and European firms encountered the climate issue within institutional environments that varied in two key respects: the timing and context of the emergence of climate change as a strategic concern, and the political environment in each region. As discussed by Delmas and Terlaak (Chapter 15), national legal and political environments help to shape perceptions and expectations. The case illustrates how these perceptions guided political and technological strategies for addressing the challenge of climate change. American companies have, in general, expressed much more skepticism about climate science, have been much more aggressive in challenging the economic and scientific case for mandatory controls, and have been more cautious about the market for low-emission vehicles.

If this were the whole story, we would have a conventional institutional explanation for divergent strategies, based on the existence of two geographically distinct organizational fields. As discussed earlier, however, geographic boundaries are only one dimension of organizational fields. The international auto industry can, in many respects, be considered a single organizational field, which complicates this analysis. All the companies are active in each others' markets, and some of their subsidiaries, at least, are members of the same trade associations. The institutions and negotiations surrounding the climate change issue frequently bring personnel from the various companies together, suggesting that climate change constitutes an "issues arena" that itself has the characteristics of an organizational field. Within this broader field, there are competing discourses held by different country blocs, industry groupings, and NGOs.

The different national contexts discussed in this chapter can therefore be considered sources for competing normative and cognitive frames within the broader global automotive industry. Indeed, the existence of competing discourses can be observed *within* each region, as a result of the porous field boundaries and overlapping fields. For example, the win-win environmentalist discourse is already well established in U.S. industry (Levy, 1995) and has been adopted by the Pew Center on Global Climate Change, a U.S.-based group of companies that accepts the need for mandatory emission controls. This perspective competes with the more antagonistic view propounded by the GCC.

It would be easy to interpret company pronouncements on climate science as purely strategic behavior, aimed at delaying any regulation of emissions. The case clearly illustrates how actors strive to legitimize their positions by cloaking their arguments in the garb of scientific rationality (Frank, Chapter 2). Some lobbying and public relations activities can clearly be seen as strategic posturing, but the case strongly suggests that skeptical scientific perspectives came to be internalized, particularly in the U.S.-based companies. In turn, these perspectives informed assessments of markets for low-carbon vehicles and hence R&D strategies. Perceptions of science and of economic interests are thus mutually constitutive.

An important implication of the institutional approach developed here is that strategy is not based on a fixed, stable set of economic interests. Competing discourses and practices create field instability. Perceptions of economic interests will shift as companies are exposed to the changing pressures of their institutional environments. For example, companies do not just join particular industry associations in order to pursue a predetermined set of interests; rather, membership in these associations helps to frame and shape corporate perspectives. New organizations such as the Pew Center can therefore play an important role in shifting conceptions of economic interest, leading to a reevaluation of climate science and mitigation technologies.

There is evidence, in fact, that there is an ongoing process of substantial institutional change. By mid-1999 a number of writers had noted an apparent sea change in U.S. industry's stance on climate, as companies began to accept the scientific basis for emission controls and to invest significant sums in low carbon technologies (Houlder, 1998; Nauss, 1999; Newswire, 1999). No major scientific breakthroughs had occurred to explain this change. The Kyoto Protocol in 1997 was clearly a watershed event, but it is unlikely that the international treaty, by itself, affected corporate perspectives and strategies very much; after all, the treaty does not spell out regulatory mechanisms and is unlikely to gain ratification in the United States in its present form. Our research suggests that rather than looking for external shocks, one can explain these shifts in terms of endogenous contests concerning the science of climate change and markets for new technologies. Shifting discourses, competitive responses, and the emergence of new organizations generate a reconfiguration in the broader climate change issue arena. A detailed analysis of these changes is, however, beyond the scope of this chapter.

The study carries a number of implications for managers. The strategies of U.S. companies regarding the climate issue may have been overly conservative because of the institutionalization of skeptical perspectives on the science, a relatively narrow focus on domestic market and regulatory conditions, and a lack of appreciation of the potential for radical change in consumer behavior and the transportation system. Although early recognition of the climate issue in the United States allowed industry to organize effectively, the institutional vehicles created have tended to lock companies into an oppositional stance. In order to break out of this "iron cage" (DiMaggio and Powell, 1983), companies need to ensure that their strategy-making processes are open to a wider range of inputs. The globalization of top management can help ensure that a company is open to multiple perspectives and conditions, and the formation of top-level cross-functional climate teams can assist in this process. Indeed, such processes are already under way at several of the companies studied. Membership in a range of industry associations exposes a company to a broader diversity of perspectives.

The research also bears some important policy implications. If policy makers wish to steer the immense technological, financial, and organizational resources of the private sector toward GHG mitigation, then it is important that policy measures are developed such that they take account of the institutional embeddedness of corporate strategy. Relying on purely market mechanisms, such as taxes and emission trading systems, is likely to prove ineffective in the face of institutional inertia. Fiscal policies need to be combined with measures that address corporate expectations concerning regulation and market development. Engaging the private sector in integrated transportation planning initiatives could assist automobile companies in locating corporate innovation efforts within this broader framework, and provide greater predictability concerning the trajectory of technological evolution, emerging standards, and regulatory priorities.

REFERENCES

Alexander, Victoria. 1996. "Pictures at an Exhibition." *American Journal of Sociology,* 101(4), 797–839.

Anderson, Phillip, and Michael Tushman. 1990. "Technological Discontinuities and Dominant Designs: A Cyclical Model of Technological Change." *Administrative Science Quarterly,* 35, 604–633.

Boyle, Stewart. 1998. "Early Birds and Ostriches." *Energy Economist,* London, May: 12–17.

Bradsher, Keith. 1998a. "European Auto Division Calling for Improved Fuel Economy." *New York Times,* Apr. 26: 24.

Bradsher, Keith. 1998b. "New Rules Alter Plans for Diesel Engines." *New York Times,* Nov. 27: C2.

Callon, Michael. 1998. *The Laws of the Markets.* Oxford: Blackwell.

D'Aunno, Thomas, and Robert Sutton. 1991. "Isomorphism and External Support in Conflicting Institutional Environments: A Study of Drug Abuse Treatment Units." *Academy of Management Journal,* 34(3): 636–661.

DiMaggio, Paul J. 1988. "Interest and Agency in Institutional Theory." In L. Zucker, ed., *Institutional Patterns of Organization,* 3–21. Cambridge, MA: Ballinger.

DiMaggio, Paul J., and Walter W. Powell. 1983. "The Iron Cage Revisited: Institutional Isomorphism and Collective Rationality in Organizational Fields." *American Sociological Review,* 48(2): 147–160.

Dixit, Avinash, and Robert Pindyck. 1994. *Investment Under Uncertainty.* Princeton, NJ: Princeton University Press.

Edwards, Paul N., and Myanna H. Lahsen. Forthcoming. "Climate Science and Politics in the United States." In C. Miller and P. Edwards, eds., *Planetary Management and Political Culture: National Perspectives on Climate Science and Policy.* Cambridge, MA: MIT Press.

Edwards, Paul N., and Stephen H. Schneider. 1997. "Climate Change: Broad Consensus or Scientific Cleansing?" *Ecofables/Ecoscience,* 1(1): 3–9.

Eisenhardt, Kathleen M., and Shona L. Brown. 1996. "Environmental Embeddedness and the Constancy of Corporate Strategy." *Advances in Strategic Management,* 13: 187–214.

Fligstein, Neil. 1991. "The Structural Transformation of American Industry: An Institutional Account of the Causes of Diversification in the Largest Firms:

1919–1979." In W. Powell and P. DiMaggio, eds., *The New Institutionalism in Organizational Analysis,* 311–336. Chicago: University of Chicago Press.

Gelbspan, Ross. 1997. *The Heat Is On.* Reading, MA: Addison Wesley.

Granovetter, Mark. 1985. "Economic Action and Social Structure: The Problem of Embeddedness." *American Journal of Sociology,* 91: 481–510.

Greenwood, Royston, and C. R. Hinings. 1996. "Understanding Radical Organizational Change: Bringing Together the Old and the New Institutionalism." *Academy of Management Review,* 21(4): 1022–1054.

Hajer, Maarten A. 1995. *The Politics of Environmental Discourse: Ecological Modernization and the Policy Process.* Oxford: Clarendon Press.

Hoffman, Andrew J. 1999. "Institutional Evolution and Change: Environmentalism and the U.S. Chemical Industry." *Academy of Management Review,* 42(4): 351–371.

Hoffman, Peter. 1999. "DaimlerChrysler Unveils Liquid-Hydrogen NECAR 4 in U.S., Reaffirms 2004 Launch Date." *Hydrogen and Fuel Cell Letter,* April.

Holm, Peter. 1995. "The Dynamics of Institutionalization: Transformation Processes in Norwegian Fisheries." *Administrative Science Quarterly,* 40: 398–422.

Houlder, Venessa. 1998. "Business Grapples with Climate Changes." *Financial Times,* Nov. 11: 4.

Intergovernmental Panel on Climate Change (IPCC). 1995. *Climate Change 1995: The Science of Climate Change, Summary for Policy Makers.* Geneva: WMO, UNEP.

Jasanoff, Sheila. 1991. "Cross-National Differences in Policy Implementation." *Evaluation Review,* 15(1): 103–119.

Kempton, Willett, and Paul P. Craig. 1993. "European Perspectives on Global Climate Change." *Environment,* 35(3): 17–45.

Laraña, Enrique, Hank Johnston, and Joseph R. Gusfield. 1994. *New Social Movements: From Ideology to Identity.* Philadelphia: Temple University Press.

Leggett, Jeremy. 2000. *The Carbon War: Dispatches from the End of the Oil Century.* London: Penguin.

Levy, David. 1995. "The Environmental Practices and Performance of Transnational Corporations." *Transnational Corporations,* 4(1): 44–68.

Levy, David. 1997. "Environmental Management as Political Sustainability." *Organization and Environment,* 10(2): 126–147.

Levy, David, and D. Egan. 1998. "Capital Contests: National and Transnational Channels of Corporate Influence on the Climate Change Negotiations." *Politics and Society,* 26(3): 337–361.

Lippert, John. 1997. "New R&D Policy Powers GM Engine Quest." *Automotive News,* Apr. 14: 20.

Mansley, Mark. 1995. *Long-Term Financial Risks to the Carbon Fuel Industry from Climate Change.* London: The Delphi Group.

Montgomery, David W. 1995. "Toward an Economically Rational Response to the Berlin Mandate." Washington, DC: Charles River Associates.

Morgan, Granger M., and David W. Keith. 1995. "Subjective Judgments by Climate Experts." *Environmental Science and Technology,* 29(10): 468–476.

Nauss, Donald W. 1999. "Auto Makers Are Finding It's Not Easy Being 'Green'." *Los Angeles Times,* Jan.28: W6.

Newswire, U.S. 1999. "ABB, Intenergy, Shell International Join Growing Corporate Effort to Address Climate Change." *U.S.* Feb. 11.

Oliver, Christine. 1992. "The Antecedents of Deinstitutionalization." *Organization Studies,* 13(4): 563–588.

Oliver, Christine. 1996. "The Institutional Embeddedness of Economic Activity." *Advances in Strategic Management,* 13: 163–186.

Oliver, Christine. 1997. "The Influence of Institutional and Task Environment Relationships on Organizational Performance: The Canadian Construction Industry." *Journal of Management Studies,* 34(1): 99–124.

Powell, Walter W., and Paul J. DiMaggio. 1991. *The New Institutionalism in Organizational Analysis.* Chicago: University of Chicago Press.

Rothenberg, Sandra, and Stelios Zyglidopoulos. 2001. "The Move to Environmental Services: Understanding Environmental Strategy Through the Lens of Cognitive Dissonance." In the proceedings of *IABS Conference, 2001: Sustainable Scholarship.* Sedona, AZ, March 17.

Scott, W. Richard. 1994. "Institutions and Organizations: Toward a Theoretical Synthesis." In W. Richard Scott and John Meyer, eds., *Institutional Environments and Organizations.* Thousand Oaks, CA: Sage.

Scott, W. Richard, and John W. Meyer. 1991. "The Organization of Societal Actors: Propositions and Early Evidence." In W. W. Powell and P. J. DiMaggio, eds., *The New Institutionalism in Organizational Analysis,* 108–142. Chicago: University of Chicago Press.

Scott, W. Richard, and John W. Meyer. 1994. *Institutional Environments and Organizations.* Thousand Oaks, CA: Sage.

Shnayerson, Michael. 1996. *The Car That Could.* New York: Random House.

Stoffer, Harry. 1997. "Projected Fleet MPG Drops; Lowest Since '80." *Automotive News,* Apr. 7: 10.

8 | THE INSTITUTIONALIZATION OF VOLUNTARY ORGANIZATIONAL GREENING AND THE IDEALS OF ENVIRONMENTALISM: LESSONS ABOUT OFFICIAL CULTURE FROM SYMBOLIC ORGANIZATION THEORY

Linda C. Forbes and John M. Jermier

During the past two decades, the response of institutions and organizations to the alarming array of global environmental problems has been innovative. To address some of the problems, new international institutions and social practices have emerged (such as United Nations Conference on Environment and Development, Rio de Janeiro, 1992; United Nations Commission for Sustainable Development Conference, Toronto, 1999), giving rise to a new global environmental politics (see Paterson, 2000). Given the scope and magnitude of many environmental problems, such as climate change, toxic waste, and species extinction, it makes sense that transnational and other macro social and political forces would develop. At a more micro level, the response of the institutions of individual nation-states to environmental problems has been varied. In many cases, governments have maintained a command-and-control approach in regulating organizations whereas in other regions partnerships and voluntary initiatives have been encouraged. Where more latitude exists in how the state regulates organizations, the response of business institutions to the environmental movement has been complicated. Firms in some industries that have traditionally been seen as major offenders (such as chemical, gas and oil, and fast food) have seemingly taken leadership roles in championing voluntary proenvironmental initiatives. For example, the Chemical Manufacturers Association instituted the controversial Responsible Care Program both to improve the environmental and safety performance of firms in the industry and to improve their public image (King and Lenox, 2000). At the same time,

We would like to thank Andy Hoffman and Marc Ventresca, anonymous reviewers, and Ann Hironaka for their thoughtful comments on an earlier draft.

firms in industries that initially were ahead of the curve in greening their products and operations (such as the cosmetics industry) seem to have regressed from earlier aggressive campaigns that were seen as environmentally friendly.

Clearly, the natural environment has become a key strategic issue for many organizations even though there is wide variation in the types of greening that are practiced. Given the heightened public pressure on commercial and public organizations to play a positive role in environmental protection and restoration activities, it is not surprising that many organizations have developed some environmental management strategy that extends beyond mere compliance with legal requirements. Indeed, according to Schot and Fisher (1993: 12), during the 1990s "clear institutionalization of environmental concern" emerged, conveying substantial pressures on contemporary organizations to respond appropriately.

In the diverse academic fields that constitute organizational and management studies, scholars have written extensively on the greening of organizations, producing numerous conceptual models, empirical findings, prescriptive and advocacy statements, and other material related to the role of organizations in promoting sustainable development. Much of this literature is focused on strategy formulation and implementation with an emphasis on rational planning and top-down initiatives. A second component addresses environmental problems through the development and implementation of new technologies and comprehensive management structures and systems (such as the International Organization for Standardization's certification program, ISO 14001). In recent years, a third component has emerged as several scholars have argued that developing a green organizational culture is the essential ingredient in supporting sustainable development and in generating successful environmental performance (see Callenbach and others, 1993; Shrivastava and Hart, 1992; Throop, Starik, and Rands, 1993; Gladwin, 1993; Hoffman, 1993; Wehrmeyer, 1995; Jones and Welford, 1997; Fuchs and Mazmanian, 1998; Petts and others, 1999; Andersson and Bateman, 2000). They are optimistic that through the management and development of green cultures, organizations can be genuinely changed at the most fundamental of levels. Indeed, the nearly unbridled enthusiasm for creating greener organizations has spawned a reinvigorated interest in the concept of organizational culture (Fineman, 1996; Bazerman and Hoffman, 1999).

The contributions of organizational and management theorists to debates addressing global environmental problems are important despite their tendency to focus on microscopic organizational dynamics. Like studies of more transnational and other macro forces, studies of organizational systems have implications for understanding how institutional configurations affect the natural environment and, therefore, have policy and other political implications. The high ideals of many segments of the environmental movement challenge all contemporary institutions and organizations (as well as contemporary theorists) to recognize the seriousness of environmental destruction and degradation and to act accordingly to avert further crisis. One *critical question* facing organizational and management theorists has to do with how well contemporary organizational systems that are designed to protect and restore the natural environment match the ideals of environmental activists. A related question is how well contemporary theories and models of green organizational systems match the ideals of environmental activists. The primary purpose of this chapter is to address these questions by taking a closer look at the institutionalization of voluntary organizational greening.

We can't provide definitive answers to these questions in this chapter. But we do lay useful groundwork in three areas. First, we think it is useful simply to raise critical questions about the degree to which institutionalized organizational greening corresponds with authentic environmentalism and progressive politics. Second, we provide a critical, theoretical analysis of what seems to be a popular environmental management strategy being implemented by many organizations today —what can be seen as managing an organization's official culture through constructing a green ceremonial facade. Third, we reinforce Institutional Theory by bringing forward a core proposition from Symbolic Organization Theory (that formal organizations respond to pressures of legitimacy by attempting to project images of rationality to various stakeholders) and by building on important conceptual and empirical studies in the tradition of Symbolic Organization Theory. We think it is important to resurface some of this material, particularly empirical work that can inform analysis of symbolic organizational greening. We advocate tighter integration of institutional approaches to organizational analysis and Symbolic Organization Theory because, although some parallel arguments are being made, scholars in each tradition are often not aware of each other's work.

Our study is not the first to question the sincerity and meaningfulness of institutionalized organizational greening. For some time, students of corporate "greenwashing" (such as Tokar, 1997), operating from a well-rehearsed antibusiness stance, have warned against accepting surface-level greening as if it were a substantive contribution to environmental protection. They have been concerned that corporate environmentalism not be viewed as a substitute for more intensive environmental action. As far as we know, however, this chapter is the first source to construct a general theoretical and empirical foundation for examining voluntary organizational greening initiatives. By focusing on official culture and highlighting the concept of a green ceremonial facade, we offer an alternative new way of conceptualizing symbolic organizational greening. This contribution may support comparison and contrast with variations in environmental initiatives that might be more deep and abiding. Thus, we think this chapter may add both to studies of organizational greening and to Symbolic Organization Theory and Institutional Theory.

In the following section we discuss some selected models of organizational greening, emphasizing the institutionalized trend toward voluntary environmentalism. Later we provide a brief review of institutional approaches and selected research that spans some sixty years in order to begin a critical, theoretical analysis of contemporary organizational greening. Then we focus on the concept of a green ceremonial facade and raise critical questions about proactive environmental management, including formal environmental management systems. In concluding, we return to the theme of the ideals of environmentalism and caution against completely dismissing contemporary organizational greening as a deceptive facade.

THE INSTITUTIONAL TREND TOWARD VOLUNTARY ORGANIZATIONAL GREENING

The concept of organizational greening is potentially very powerful, but it has nearly as many definitions as there are scholars who use the term. Rasanen, Merilainen, and Lovio (1995) remarked that it remains unclear what greening actually has amounted to in organizational systems as opposed to what it could be. They pointed out that greening is a new "catch-phrase," covering a diverse set of organizational activities. Hoffman (1997: 14) made the point even more directly: ". . . there is no such thing as a 'green company.' The best one can do is describe the progression of how companies are 'going green'." From the theoretical perspective of institutional analysis, this makes sense because greening processes and activities are even more difficult to specify at the institutional level, where individual organizations are not seen as being in complete control of their own programs and other activities.

Most scholars favor a concept of organizational greening that includes a wide array of environmentally responsive, protective and restorative instruments, programs, and activities. They conceptualize greening as a *process* and imply that organizations vary in the degree to which they emphasize different components of greening (see Hunt and Auster, 1990; Pauchant and Fortier, 1990; Post and Altman, 1992; Shrivastava, 1992; Shrivastava and Hart, 1992; Roome, 1992; Smith, 1992; Schot, 1992; Rasanen, Merilainen, and Lovio, 1995; Hart, 1995; Halme, 1996;

Mercier and McGowan, 1996; Haas, 1996; Purser, 1997; Schaefer and Harvey, 1998; Berry and Rondinelli, 1998; Bansal and Roth, 2000; Winn and Angell, 2000). According to most organizational and management theorists, organizational greening, when relatively mature, is encompassing, permeating the system and anchoring its priorities. It infuses the organization's culture at all levels.

To provide a sense of what organizational factors are included in the process of greening, we briefly review several typologies of organizational greening that specify forms or stages of environmental sensitivity and responsiveness. We give special attention to Hunt and Auster's (1990) classic framework because it is one of the earliest studies of environmental management systems, because it is a prototype that is referred to by most other theorists, and because it is especially well developed. The other frameworks we consider were chosen because they were derived from contact with actual organizations and because they specify a wide range of approaches to environmental concern and action, including voluntary leadership. In combination, we think the typologies provide a useful illustration of how organizational researchers and management consultants conceptualize organizational greening. They also indicate how deep or superficial various attempts to green organizations can be, lending themselves well to our theoretical discussion of symbolic and substantive processes in organizations.

Hunt and Auster's (1990) model specifies a five-stage development continuum ranging from organizations that address environmental concerns with "band-aid solutions" ("beginners") to organizations that implement fully integrative systems ("proactivists"). The three main dimensions in their framework are the degree to which the program reduces environmental risk; commitment of the organization to environmentalism, including both resource allocations and degree of involvement of top managers; and the design characteristics of the program including its degree of integration and involvement with other key facets of the organization. Beginners handle environmental issues by avoidance or by adding responsibilities to existing positions. At the other end of the continuum, proactivist organizations have a well-resourced environmental staff with strong, motivated, and highly trained individuals, at least some of whom participate in the organization's dominant coalition. Environmentalism is a top priority for proactivist firms, and it is fully integrated throughout the organization as reflected in specific performance objectives, top-level reporting relationships, formalized monitoring and documentation, and daily involvement of legal counsels, public relations, manufacturing, and product design and marketing staff. What separates the proactivist organization from the next-highest stage of development in Hunt and Auster's framework, the "pragmatist," is that environmental management is not a top priority for the latter. Program funding may be tenuous and it is not as heavily structured and well integrated with the rest of the organization as in the proactivist organization. Hunt and Auster's (1990) "fire-fighter" and "concerned citizen" organizational types tend to pay lip service to environmental concerns and may represent the concerns with departments and other staff, but they fall far short on funding and other substantive commitments. Hunt and Auster make it clear that most firms fall in the first three stages of development, barely meeting demands for compliance but, in most cases, signaling an awareness of the importance of environmental problems.

Many of the more recent models of organizational greening resemble Hunt and Auster's (1990) approach in that they specify developmental stages through which organizations can progress, and they emphasize the contrast between relatively superficial environmentalism and a deeper, more encompassing approach that indicates proactiveness and voluntary leadership. This is reflected in Roome's (1992) model of environmental strategy that contrasts "compliance-oriented" with "compliance-plus" (leading-edge) organizations. The latter institute both cleaner technologies and more thorough greening of organizational structure and culture. Halme's (1996) case study of a Finnish container-manufacturing firm also illustrates this contrast, as she observed greening in terms of a radical paradigm shift from more "traditional management" to "environment-related management." The latter is based on an eco-sensitive world view consisting of shared values and underlying assumptions about the important role of business in solving environmental problems.

To continue the illustration, Hart's (1995) resource-based view of the firm specifies stages of development that begin with pollution prevention programs implemented with, for example, total quality environmental management and evolve into more encompassing sustainable development systems based in shared vision and a strong sense of social-environmental purpose. Similarly, Berry and Rondinelli (1998: 39) draw sharp contrasts among traditional firms that barely cope with environmental crises as they occur, slightly more progressive firms that practice pollution prevention, and "cutting-edge firms that are going beyond preventing pollution in their own operations and exploring new opportunities for developing green products, processes, and technologies."

Recent empirical research has continued the tradition of drawing contrasts between more and less environmentally progressive organizations and has begun to differentiate types with even greater currency. For example, in a study of organizations operating in diverse industries and nation-states, Bansal and Roth (2000) investigated the underlying motivations and contextual factors associated with adopting ecological initiatives. They identified three distinct types of firms: those motivated for ecological responsiveness by cost considerations and profit potential (competitiveness); those motivated to avoid legal sanctions, fines and penalties, bad publicity, clean-ups, and risk (legitimation); and those motivated by a concern for doing the right thing and promoting the social good (ecological responsibility). Although a number of firms in their study had mixed motives, it is clear that more ecologically responsive firms were proactive, whereas those focused on other considerations tended to be more reactive. As another example, Winn and Angell (2000) investigated internal processes associated with organizational greening in a sample of German firms. Like previous researchers cited earlier, they drew contrasts among firms on a continuum ranging from reactive to proactive implementation of environmental management activities and also contrasted firms based on the degree to which top management was committed to the environment and to sustainable development as reflected in their decision-making priorities. The four-cell typology that results displays some interesting approaches to organizational greening, including the "deliberate reactive" firm (that lags behind or even resists industry trends and that evinces no commitment to the environment), the "emergent active" firm (that seems to practice some environmental management activities through loose-coupling and from the bottom up, without formal policy commitments from top management), the "deliberate proactive" firm (that takes a leadership role in both policy advocacy on behalf of the environment and in the implementation of comprehensive environmental management systems), and the "unrealized" firm (that professes commitment to environmental goals and policies but does not implement anything but the most cursory environmental management).

It is clear from the research on the varieties of organizational greening that (1) the concept is multidimensional and unclear in its meaning, (2) the concept is used to represent a wide range of approaches that are believed to be possible, and (3) there is a strong trend noted in the literature toward voluntarism and proactivism that may or may not describe the actual approaches organizations take. As pointed out by Schaefer and Harvey (1998), the popular view of organizational greening that implies a linear, one-dimensional progression toward heightened environmental sensitivity and ecocentric practice may be an oversimplification and may even be misleading. Organizations may focus attention on one or a small number of highly visible green criteria and neglect all others, raising the difficult question about how this kind of approach corresponds with the high ideals of environmentalists and with progressive politics. As Hoffman (1997) noted, nearly all big corporations have moved beyond simple regulatory compliance as many have created pollution prevention or waste minimization programs, established environmental vice presidents and other key line and staff positions, formed board-level environmental management committees, and produced voluminous environmental annual reports. In addition, many organizations practice environmental auditing and reporting, have environmental affairs departments, use environmental themes in advertising and public relations, and even adopt green technologies and comprehensive environmental management systems. But to what degree do these green initiatives actually protect the natural environment from further destruction and degradation? In the spirit of critical inquiry, what do we know about the actual environmental effects of these initiatives? As suggested in the introductory section of this chapter, many organizational and management theorists believe that unless the culture of an organization is "greened" from the bottom up and deeply in the minds and hearts of employees, other seemingly environmentally friendly initiatives will be, at best, appurtenances. They may qualify the organization as "green" at the level of official culture but will fall far short of the ideals of environmentalists.

Unfortunately, empirical evidence is too limited to answer these critical questions. More research is needed that is focused on the relationship between environmental management programs or systems and environmental performance. We do have theoretical tools, however, that can be used to analyze these issues. Institutional Theory and a closely related intellectual approach, Symbolic Organization Theory, have been addressing questions similar to the ones raised here for several decades. In the next section, we employ them to frame some preliminary answers.

THE INSTITUTIONAL APPROACH TO ORGANIZATIONAL ANALYSIS AND SYMBOLIC PROCESSES

Excellent critical and integrative reviews of the new institutionalism in organizational analysis published relatively recently (Mizruchi and Fein, 1999; Hoffman, 1999; Tolbert and Zucker, 1996; Scott, 1995; DiMaggio and Powell, 1991) depict a wide range of perspectives on institutions within the school. Despite the heterogeneity in definitions, methods and measures characterizing the new institutionalism, there are some key ideas that most theorists in this tradition would accept. Scott's (1995: 33) definition of institutions might well be one idea that would garner wide support: "multifaceted systems incorporating symbolic systems—cognitive constructions and normative rules—and regulative processes carried out through and shaping social behavior." This definition calls attention to the symbolic and normative aspects of institutions and, therefore, to the cognitive processing of social and cultural environments. Perhaps more than any other feature, it is the focus on the cognitive aspect of institutionalist work that distinguishes it from other traditions in organizational analysis (DiMaggio and Powell, 1991; Scott, 1995). Influential exemplars in this tradition include Meyer and Rowan's (1977) classic study of organizations as symbolic systems and Zucker's (1977) seminal study of the role of language and symbols in the creation and transmission of institutions. Indeed, for at least some theorists in this tradition, the institutional approach might be seen as one way to elaborate the metaphor of organizational systems as cultural fields in which shared meanings and symbolic processes constitute the central reality. For example, Thomas and others (1987: 7) begin their book on Institutional Theory with the comment that "we have come to label the present perspective, for better or worse, as an institutional model, although we hope that 'culture' eventually can be reclaimed by macro-sociology." Thus the cultural perspective on organizations and the cognitive perspective on institutions are compatible, especially given the shared significance of symbolic processes.

Cultural analysis of organizational dynamics takes many forms but the most influential approach over the past two decades has been developed by Symbolic Organization Theorists who view organizations as sites of symbolic activity. They view organizations as symbol-processing systems wherein human action, values, beliefs, and attitudes are socially constructed, sustained, challenged, and sometimes changed (Pondy and Mitroff, 1979; Smircich, 1983; Jones, 1996). Symbols are tangible objects, events, and processes that represent or otherwise stand for deeper patterns of meaning and subjective experience. There is a correspondence between the surface-level manifestation and the psychic experience of the tangible entity that makes sense to actors knowledgeable about the group's history.

Symbolic Organization Theory distinguishes between an organization's official culture and its operative culture. The official culture can be defined as "the formal statements of an organization's mission and standards of conduct, as well as the corresponding formal structure and related physical objects" (Jermier and others, 1991: 171). The official culture is established in large part by top management and can be used instrumentally as a symbol to gain political favor or advantage. A core proposition in Symbolic Organization Theory is that formal organizations signal their intended purposiveness by projecting images of rationality to various stakeholders. Institutionalists have argued that this practice tends to produce political favor or advantage as key actors and agencies in the organization's institutional environment grant legitimacy and other resources according to adherence to institutionalized customs and rules (Zucker, 1987). The general theoretical point is that elements and characteristics of an organization's official culture may be shaped by normative expectations and pressures embedded in the relevant institutional environment. Oakes, Townley, and Cooper (1998: 257) recap the theme this way: "As changes occur in the institutional rules that define legitimacy, organizations respond by voluntarily adopting recommended changes or by giving the appearance of having adopted changes in order to appear legitimate."

Any feature of organizational life may be viewed symbolically, but analysis of the formal structure of an organization as a symbol is the most common referent. Whereas neo-institutional theorists trace the origins of their research tradition to the pieces by Meyer and Rowan (1977), Zucker (1977), and DiMaggio and Powell (1983), Symbolic Organization Theorists might note work published at least three decades earlier. To illustrate Symbolic Organization Theory's core proposition, we review some of the early research in this tradition and then summarize more recent research that we believe makes a continuing case for understanding organizations as symbolic realities.

In a little-known but brilliant study of the U.S. Navy, Page (1946) provides one of the first pictures of the inside of a symbolic bureaucracy. It reveals an informal system of organizing that is "shrouded in a group-imposed cloak of semi-mystery" (p. 90). The Navy, like other formal bureaucracies, is supposed to conform to "the book" (p. 89). But Page shows how several aspects of the formal structure are skirted to enhance efficiency or to serve the interests of various actors. The official status hierarchy symbolized in rank and rate; the official rules and procedures symbolized by "the book"; and the official impersonality symbolized in the salute, the uniform, and the language of subordination all are skirted routinely as the informal structure of the "inmate culture" (p. 89) emerges to produce solutions denied by the formal, institutionalized structure. And yet the "inmate culture" is no more important than the Navy's formal system of symbols and sacred traditions that legitimate the institution and its mission for, as Page (p. 90) pointed out, ". . . the bureaucratic structure requires *public* sanctification of the formal procedures and *private* sanctification of the informal."

A more familiar early work in this tradition is Gouldner's (1954) classic study of a gypsum factory. Focusing on the manner in which rules were initiated (either through unilateral pressure from management, unilateral pressure from workers, collateral pressure from both management and workers, or pressure from an external source), Gouldner identified three patterns of bureaucratic organization. Particularly relevant to this discussion is Gouldner's concept of the "mock bureaucracy," a form of rule-based organizing where the source of pressure comes from outside the firm. Gouldner argued that if rules are compatible with neither the preferences of managers nor workers, they will not be enforced except when under the scrutiny of the external source. He illustrated the concept of the mock bureaucracy by discussing the company's "no-smoking rule," as mandated by external authorities (insurance writers) concerned about fires in offices and production areas. Neither workers nor managers thought this rule was necessary in most settings and it was not enforced despite the fact that "no smoking" signs were posted everywhere. Only on those rare occasions when the fire inspector was present were the rules about smoking obeyed, but everyone was warned in advance of the inspector's arrival so that they would conform. According to Gouldner, "in the ordinary day-to-day conduct of work, this bureaucratic paraphernalia was ignored and inoperative" (p. 187). Thus, adherence to the rule was selective, showing its symbolic meaning as an instrument useful in fooling outsiders.

In this tradition's signature study, Jacobs (1969) examined the public impression projected by a social welfare agency compared with its behind-the-scenes operations. The agency Jacobs studied had, in appearance, all the defining features of an ideal-type bureaucracy—specialized positions, a hierarchical authority structure, written rules and codes, and impersonal processes. The agency was legitimated and funded based on how many community residents it helped who were experiencing temporary hardship and could not support themselves. Like most human service organizations, this agency had too many clients needing help, rendering caseworkers and support staff overloaded. In his ethnographic portrayal of how people in the system managed to accomplish their mandate while retaining their decorum, Jacobs emphasized both the desirability and the necessity of "unofficial change." For instance, caseworkers were required to aid clients with hospital appointments until such appointments had been completed, but this could be onerous and could interfere with the agency's official goal of clearing cases. Jacobs gives the impression that busy caseworkers often formally recorded clients who actually were scheduled for hospital visits as "healthy" if they did not have a written slip as proof of the appointment. Because clients were rarely organized enough to carry this documentation, and as they often did not want this type of assistance anyway, caseworkers and clients maneuvered around the constraints of the formal procedures. As Jacobs put it: "[t]he appearance is of meeting the rules and the reality is of beating them" (p. 418). According to Jacobs, each feature of the formal bureaucracy was routinely circumvented through "unofficial changes" which suggest that "it is possible for an organization to conform little or not at all to the conditions of bureaucracy, while maintaining an image of complete adherence to bureaucratic ideals" (p. 414)—the situation referred to as symbolic bureaucracy.

The notion that the formal structure of an organization can be a device that camouflages what actually goes on in the organization from an external public is well illustrated by these studies. It has been further documented and elaborated in a number of studies in both traditions published over the past three decades (among them, Meyer and Rowan, 1977; Kamens, 1977; Manning, 1977; Jermier and Berkes, 1979; Tolbert and Zucker, 1983; Baron, Dobbin, and Jennings, 1986; Jermier and others, 1991; Edelman, 1992; Westphal and Zajac, 1994; Oakes, Townley, and Cooper, 1998). This work suggests the more general proposition that organizations develop forms of "symbolic reassurance to achieve legitimacy from their influential constituents" (Mizruchi and Fein, 1999: 656).

THE CONCEPT OF A CEREMONIAL FACADE
AND ORGANIZATIONAL GREENING

A facade is the face or front part of something, especially an artificial or false front. Formal organizations present a facade that is usually crafted specifically to create a favorable impression. Goals, mission statements, programs, products, technologies, auditing and reporting systems, formal structure, and other elements of the organization's official culture can be crafted to correspond well with powerful forces in the institutional environment without much concern for how such elements enable or impede the organization's need for efficiency. When the elements are adopted and incorporated in the organization ceremoniously but are then decoupled in most practical ways from the technical core activities of the organization (see Meyer and Rowan, 1977; Hironaka and Schofer, Chapter 9), the conditions of symbolic bureaucracy exist. A ceremonial facade is instituted not to maximize technical performance and efficiency but to signal to relevant external publics and internal actors that society's expectations are now being met.

Earlier we focused primarily on the formal structuring of organizations. We argued that formal structures do not necessarily have much to do with coordinating and controlling work. Their elements can be designed and incorporated mostly to show that the organization is aware of what is expected by "rational" agents and agencies holding the power to grant legitimacy, deliver resources, and enhance prospects of survival. Often this institutional logic has more to do with modernist fad and fancy—keeping up with the latest technological and social engineering craze—than with establishing rational processes that are defensible in a more systematic sense. This is what makes the construction of a ceremonial facade exactly the right strategic ploy.

What relevance does this thesis have for interpreting the widespread enthusiasm for the varieties of organizational greening and environmental management? Through the lens of Symbolic Organization Theory, one can predict that organizations will respond to the institutionalized concern for the natural environment at least by managing public impressions so that an appearance of environmental stewardship is projected. There are, as Schot and Fisher (1993) suggest, indications that many firms are preoccupied with meeting regulatory demands. But normative pressures and expectations that go beyond regulatory compliance into the realm of proactive environmental management are pervasive, and many managers and board members perceive the need to align with these changing institutional norms (see Gladwin, 1993; Hoffman, 1997).

The institutional trend toward more proactive environmental management may lead to elaborate espousals and even formal programs and structures that symbolize deep greening of organizations. When viewed from the perspective of Symbolic Organization Theory, however, there is reason to be skeptical about the extent to which these initiatives match the ideals of environmentalism and evince a clear concern for the natural environment. As part of a green ceremonial facade, features such as revised mission statements, environmental auditing and reporting, creation of environmental affairs departments and appointment of high-ranking environmental officers, environmental themes in advertising and public relations, and even the adoption of comprehensive environmental management programs and green technologies might be no more than planned deceptions or well-meaning fictions that do not link substantively with technical performance. They may "green" the organization in its surface appearance but, due to a lack of grounding in the deeper layers of an organization's culture, they may have little effect on actual environmental performance.

This can be further illustrated by turning briefly to research on the ISO 14001 program. ISO 14001 is a comprehensive environmental management system that includes environmental policy, planning, implementation and operations, checking and corrective action, and management review. Organizations can become official, registered users of ISO 14001 if third-party auditors certify their implementation of the system. It is one of the fastest-growing trends in management. Worldwide registrations were predicted to exceed 20,000 by the end of 2000; nearly half a million certifications are reportedly in process (Hillary, 2000). ISO 14001 is now being championed even in conventional areas of business, such as the automotive industry (see Hasek, 1999). Currently, it is "the most acceptable badge of achievement on environmental management" (Hillary, 2000) and often passes as a bold move toward voluntary organizational greening and eco-leadership.

As a practical matter, however, the U.S. Environmental Protection Agency has not linked specific benefits to ISO 14001 registration (Hasek, 1998). This might be because of the myriad ways it can be and has been implemented (Hillary, 2000). More probably it is because ISO 14001, unlike the European Union's Eco-Management and Audit Scheme (EMAS), does not link certification to actual environmental performance. The empirical research on ISO 14001 is currently too limited to draw conclusions about its effects on environmental performance. Some scholars have observed both positive and negative outcomes (Steger, 1998; Hillary, 2000; Switzer, Ehrenfeld and Milledge, 2000; Mendel, Chapter 18), whereas others are convinced that ISO 14001 has more to do with conformance than with actual performance (Yap, 2000). In developing a key point about ISO 14001 from Krut and Gleckman (1998), Switzer, Ehrenfeld, and Milledge (2000) state: "[B]ecause the standard lacks minimum environmental performance requirements and does not [even] require full legal compliance as a condition of registration, some companies may use it to garner 'an easy A,' while continuing to operate in illegal or irresponsible ways."

CONCLUSION

In this chapter, we asked whether the current trend toward voluntary organizational greening should be seen more as an exercise in "greenwashing" or more as a genuine movement to protect the natural environment. We showed that organizational greening can mean many different things and that some of these have very little in common with authentic greening and progressive politics—ideals expressed by committed environmentalists. Even comprehensive programs and initiatives that require third-party auditing and external certification, like ISO 14001, can fail to produce more than impressions of conformance with a fad and fashions.

We argue that theoretical resources are needed to guide research helpful in sorting out more and less effective organizational greening initiatives. We need to move beyond categorical antibusiness sentiments in evaluating these initiatives. We used Symbolic Organization Theory and Institutional Theory to promote critical reflection on contemporary approaches to organizational greening. The concept of a green ceremonial facade was introduced to emphasize the symbolic maneuvering that can accompany organizational greening initiatives that manipulate elements of the official culture. Given the long history of research that demonstrates the importance of symbolic management through revision of the official culture, we contend that there are lessons that should be applied by organizational and management theorists in their attempts to assess critically the effectiveness of environmental management and other organizational greening initiatives.

At this point, our opinion about voluntary organizational greening is that there are good reasons to expect to find green ceremonial facades that are decoupled from actual operating concerns in many organizations. Our opinion on this issue is shaped more by theoretical analysis and empirical evidence about other organizational processes than by specific empirical evidence on organizational greening. The empirical evidence on organizational greening is too limited to be strongly persuasive, though it does suggest that many initiatives are undertaken tentatively, perhaps as a result of following the advice of some environmental management consultants (see Boiral and Sala, 1998).

We do not think, however, that all contemporary approaches to organizational greening should be completely dismissed as deceptive fads—mere empty symbols that mislead resource providers without mitigating environmental problems. In future research, we expect to find some more intensive initiatives. And as pointed out by Scott (1995), nothing is entirely symbolic to an institutionalist. Symbols can and do shape meaning that is dialectically interrelated with action. In their study of the introduction of business plans to museums and cultural heritage sites in Canada, Oakes, Townley, and Cooper (1998) persuasively illustrated the tangible effects of symbols. Despite its apparent political neutrality and paperweight character, they argued that business plans brought with them a language and taken-for-granted business logic that eventually subverted the traditional mission of the museums and historical sites. In the same way, organizational greening initiatives that begin with seemingly superficial symbols, such as the plans and policy statements of ISO 14001, might lead to further steps along the pathway to ecocentric organizing. Or, they might buttress the green ceremonial facade.

REFERENCES

Andersson, Lynne M., and Thomas Bateman. 2000. "Individual Environmental Initiatives: Championing Natural Environmental Issues in U.S. Business Organizations." *Academy of Management Journal,* 43: 548–570.

Bansal, Pratima, and Kendall Roth. 2000. "Why Companies Go Green: A Model of Ecological Responsiveness." *Academy of Management Journal,* 43: 717–736.

Baron, James N., Frank Dobbin, and P. Devereaux Jennings. 1986. "War and Peace: The Evolution of Modern Personnel Administration in U.S. Industry." *American Journal of Sociology,* 92: 350–383.

Bazerman, Max H., and Andrew J. Hoffman. 1999. "Sources of Environmentally Destructive Behavior: Individual, Organizational and Institutional Perspectives." *Research in Organizational Behavior,* 21: 39–79.

Berry, Michael A., and Dennis A. Rondinelli. 1998. "Proactive Corporate Environmental Management: A New Industrial Revolution." *Academy of Management Executive,* 12: 38–50.

Boiral, Oliver, and Jean-Marie Sala. 1998. "Environmental Management: Should Industry Adopt ISO 14001?" *Business Horizons,* 41: 57–64.

Callenbach, Ernest, Fritjof Capra, Lenore Goldman, Rudiger Lutz, and Sandra Marburg. 1993. *Ecomanagement.* San Francisco: Berrett Koehler.

DiMaggio, Paul J., and Walter W. Powell. 1983. "The Iron Cage Revisited: Institutional Isomorphism and Collective Rationality in Organizational Fields." *American Sociological Review,* 48: 147–160.

DiMaggio, Paul J., and Walter W. Powell. 1991. "Introduction." In Walter Powell and Paul DiMaggio, eds., *The New Institutionalism in Organizational Analysis,* 1–38. Chicago: University of Chicago Press.

Edelman, Lauren B. 1992. "Legal Ambiguity and Symbolic Structures: Organizational Mediation of Civil Rights Law." *American Journal of Sociology,* 97: 1531–1576.

Fineman, Stephen. 1996. "Emotional Subtexts in Corporate Greening." *Organization Studies,* 17: 479–500.

Fuchs, D. A., and D. A. Mazmanian. 1998. "The Greening of Industry: Needs of the Field." *Business Strategy and the Environment,* 7: 193–203.

Gladwin, Thomas N. 1993. "The Meaning of Greening: A Plea for Organizational Theory." In Kurt Fischer and Johan Schot, eds., *Environmental Strategies for*

Industry: International Perspectives and Research Needs and Policy Implications, 37–61. Washington, DC: Island Press.

Gouldner, Alvin W. 1954. *Patterns of Industrial Bureaucracy.* New York: Free Press.

Haas, Julie L. 1996. "Environmental ('Green') Management Typologies: An Evaluation, Operationalization and Empirical Development." *Business Strategy and Environment,* 5: 59–68.

Halme, Minna. 1996. "Shifting Environmental Management Paradigms in Two Finnish Paper Facilities: A Broader View of Institutional Theory." *Business Strategy and the Environment,* 5: 94–105.

Hart, Stuart L. 1995. "A Natural Resource-Based View of the Firm." *Academy of Management Review,* 20: 986–1014.

Hasek, Glenn. 1998. "ISO's Green Standard Takes Root: Non-U.S. Firms Are Most Aggressive in Adoption of ISO 14001." *Industry Week,* 247: 39–42.

Hasek, Glenn. 1999. "Automakers Issue New Mandate: Ford, GM Say Suppliers Must Be ISO 14001 Certified." *Industry Week,* 248: 19.

Hillary, Ruth. 2000. "Introduction to ISO 14001: Case Studies and Practical Experience." In Ruth Hillary, ed., *ISO 14001: Case Studies and Practical Experiences.* Sheffield, U. K.: Greenleaf Publishing.

Hoffman, Andrew J. 1997. *From Heresy to Dogma: An Institutional History of Corporate Environmentalism.* San Francisco: New Lexington Press.

Hoffman, Andrew J. 1999. "Institutional Evolution and Change: Environmentalism and the U.S. Chemical Industry." *Academy of Management Journal,* 42: 351–371.

Hoffman, Andrew J. 1993. "The Importance of Fit Between Individual Values and Organisational Culture in the Greening of Industry." *Business Strategy and the Environment,* 2: 10–18.

Hunt, Christopher B., and Ellen R. Auster. 1990. "Proactive Environmental Management: Avoiding the Toxic Trap." *Sloan Management Review,* 31: 7–18.

Jacobs, Jerry. 1969. "Symbolic Bureaucracy: A Case Study of a Social Welfare Agency." *Social Forces,* 47: 413–422.

Jermier, John M., and Leslie Berkes. 1979. "Leader Behavior in a Police Command Bureaucracy: A Closer Look at the Quasi-Military Model." *Administrative Science Quarterly,* 24: 1–23.

Jermier, John M., John W. Slocum Jr., Louis W. Fry, and Jeannie Gaines. 1991. "Organizational Subcultures in a Soft Bureaucracy: Resistance Behind the Myth and Façade of an Official Culture." *Organization Science,* 2: 170–194.

Jones, David, and Richard Welford. 1997. "Organizing for Sustainable Development: Structure, Culture, and Social Auditing." In Richard Welford, ed., *Hi-*

jacking Environmentalism: Corporate Responses to Sustainable Development,
157–178. London: Earthscan.

Jones, Michael Owen. 1996. *Studying Organizational Symbolism: What, How, Why?* Thousand Oaks, CA: Sage.

Kamens, David H. 1977. "Legitimating Myths and Educational Organizations: The Relationship Between Organizational Ideology and Formal Structure." *American Sociological Review,* 42: 208–219.

King, Andrew A., and Michael J. Lenox. 2000. "Industry Self-Regulation Without Sanctions: The Chemical Industry's Responsible Care Program." *Academy of Management Journal,* 43: 698–716.

Krut, Riva, and Harris Gleckman. 1998. *ISO 14001: A Missed Opportunity for Sustainable Global Industrial Development.* London: Earthscan.

Manning, Peter K. 1977. *Police Work.* Cambridge, MA: MIT Press.

Mercier, Jean, and Robert P. McGowan. 1996. "The Greening of Organizations." *Administration and Society,* 27: 459–482.

Meyer, John W., and Brian Rowan. 1977. "Institutionalized Organizations: Formal Structure as Myth and Ceremony." *American Journal of Sociology,* 83: 340–363.

Mizruchi, Mark S., and Lisa C. Fein. 1999. "The Social Construction of Organizational Knowledge: A Study of the Uses of Coercive, Mimetic, and Normative Isomorphism." *Administrative Science Quarterly,* 44: 653–683.

Oakes, Leslie S., Barbara Townley, and David J. Cooper. 1998. "Business Planning as Pedagogy: Language and Control in a Changing Institutional Field." *Administrative Science Quarterly,* 43: 257–292.

Page, Charles H. 1946. "Bureaucracy's Other Face." *Social Forces,* 24: 88–94.

Paterson, Matthew. 2000. *Understanding Global Environmental Politics.* New York: St. Martin's.

Pauchant, Thierry C., and I. Fortier. 1990. "Anthropocentric Ethics in Organizations, Strategic Management and the Environment: A Typology." *Advances in Strategic Management,* 6: 99–114.

Petts, Judith, Andrew Herd, Simon Gerrard, and Chris Horne. 1999. "The Climate and Culture of Environmental Compliance within SMEs." *Business Strategy and the Environment,* 8: 14–20.

Pondy, Louis R., and Ian I. Mitroff. 1979. "Beyond Open System Models of Organization." *Research in Organizational Behavior,* 1: 3–39.

Post, James E., and Barbara W. Altman. 1992. "Models of Corporate Greening: How Corporate Social Policy and Organizational Learning Inform Leading-Edge Environmental Management." *Research in Corporate Social Performance and Policy,* 13: 3–29.

Purser, Ronald E. 1997. "From Global Management to Global Appreciation: A Transformative Epistemology for Aperspectival Worlds." *Organization and Environment,* 10: 361–383.

Rasanen, Keijo, Susan Merilainen, and Raimo Lovio. 1995. "Pioneering Descriptions of Corporate Greening: Notes and Doubts About the Emerging Discussion." *Business Strategy and the Environment,* 3: 9–16.

Roome, Nigel. 1992. "Developing Environmental Management Strategies." *Business Strategy and the Environment,* 1: 11–24.

Schaefer, Anja, and Brian Harvey. 1998. "Stage Models of Corporate 'Greening': A Critical Evaluation." *Business Strategy and the Environment,* 7: 109–123.

Schot, Johan. 1992. "Credibility and Markets as Greening Forces for the Chemical Industry." *Business Strategy and the Environment* 1: 35–44.

Schot, Johan, and Kurt Fisher. 1993. "Introduction: The Greening of the Industrial Firm." In Kurt Fischer and Johan Schot, eds., *Environmental Strategies for Industry: International Perspectives and Research Needs and Policy Implications,* 3–33. Washington, DC: Island Press.

Scott, W. Richard. 1995. *Institutions and Organizations.* Thousand Oaks, CA: Sage.

Shrivastava, Paul. 1992. "Corporate Self-Greenewal: Strategic Responses to Environmentalism." *Business Strategy and the Environment,* 1: 9–21.

Shrivastava, Paul, and Stuart Hart. 1992. "Greening Organizations: 2000." *International Journal of Public Administration,* 17: 607–635.

Smircich, Linda. 1983. "Concepts of Culture and Organizational Analysis." *Administrative Science Quarterly,* 8: 339–358.

Smith, Dennis. 1992. "Strategic Management and the Business Environment: What Lies Beyond the Rhetoric of Greening?" *Business Strategy and the Environment,* 1: 1–9.

Steger, Ulrich. 1998. "Environmental Management Systems: Empirical Evidence and Further Perspectives." *European Management Journal,* 18: 23–37.

Switzer, Jason, John Ehrenfeld, and Vicki Milledge. 2000. "ISO 14001 and Environmental Performance: The Management Goal Link." In Ruth Hillary, ed., *ISO 14001: Case Studies and Practical Experiences.* Sheffield, U.K.: Greenleaf.

Thomas, George M., John W. Meyer, Francisco O. Ramirez, and John Boli, eds. 1987. *Institutional Structure: Constituting State, Society, and the Individual.* Newbury Park, CA: Sage.

Throop, Gary M., Mark Starik, and Gordon P. Rands. 1993. "Sustainable Strategy in a Greening World: Integrating the Natural Environment into Strategic Management." *Advances in Strategic Management,* 9: 63–92.

Tokar, Brian. 1997. *Earth for Sale: Reclaiming ecology in the Age of Corporate Greenwash.* Boston, MA: South End Press.

Tolbert, Pamela S., and Lynne G. Zucker. 1983. "Institutional Sources of Change in the Formal Structure of Organizations: The Diffusion of Civil Service Reform, 1880–1935." *Administrative Science Quarterly*, 28: 22–39.

Tolbert, Pamela S., and Lynne G. Zucker. 1996. "The Institutionalization of Institutional Theory." In Stewart C. Clegg, Cynthia Hardy, and Walter R. Nord, eds., *Handbook of Organization Studies*, 175–190. Thousand Oaks, CA: Sage.

Wehrmeyer, Walter. 1995. "Environmental Management Styles, Corporate Cultures and Change." *Greener Management International: The Journal of Corporate Environmental Strategy and Practice*, 12: 81–94.

Westphal, James D., and Edward J. Zajac. 1994. "Substance and Symbolism in CEOs' Long-Term Incentive Plans." *Administrative Science Quarterly*, 39: 367–390.

Winn, Monika, and Linda Angell. 2000. "Toward a Process Model of Corporate Greening." *Organization Studies*, 21: 1119–1147.

Yap, Nonita T. 2000. "Performance-Based ISO 14001: Case Studies from Taiwan." In Ruth Hillary, ed., *ISO 14001: Case Studies and Practical Experiences*. Sheffield, U.K.: Greenleaf.

Zucker, Lynne G. 1977. "The Role of Institutionalization in Cultural Persistence." *American Sociological Review*, 42: 726–743.

Zucker, Lynne G. 1987. "Institutional Theories of Organizations." *Annual Review of Sociology*, 13: 443–464.

9

DECOUPLING IN THE ENVIRONMENTAL ARENA: THE CASE OF ENVIRONMENTAL IMPACT ASSESSMENTS

Ann Hironaka and Evan Schofer

Several chapters in this book describe failures (or the incomplete success) of environmental policies in improving environmental conditions (see Jennings, Zandbergen, and Martens, Chapter 3; Forbes and Jermier, Chapter 8; and Sastry, Bernike, and Hart, Chapter 11). Indeed, research literature in both organizations and policy continually reminds us that policy failure is endemic. But to characterize a policy as a failure presumes a tight causal link between policy and outcome. Neo-institutionalism in organizational research suggests, however, that such presumptions are often simplistic. Policies and their outcomes are worked out within highly complex organizations embedded in equally complex institutional environments in which normative, cultural, and symbolic processes figure in as much as the rational and instrumental. By studying organizational environments, we can better understand the impacts of policies designed to protect the natural environment.

In this chapter we discuss the neo-institutional concept of "decoupling" to help reconceptualize policy impacts and move beyond the simple dichotomy of success and failure. Given the complexity of policy systems, success or failure of intended policy goals is only one of many outcomes, and perhaps not even the most important of them in the long term. We begin with a brief discussion of decoupling, highlighting some of the complex and indirect ways in which policies may have effects that extend beyond mere successful (versus decoupled or "failed") implementation. Then we turn to a case study of modern environmental impact assessment (EIA) laws, which exemplify some of the processes we discuss.

DECOUPLING IN ORGANIZATIONAL THEORY

Loose coupling refers to circumstances in which the relationship between linked organizational units becomes weak or disconnected (Weick, 1976; March and Olsen, 1976; Meyer and Rowan, 1977; Brunsson, 1993; see Orton and Weick, 1990, for a review). In its original conception, loose coupling is very broad. Weak or disconnected links may be horizontal or vertical and may take many forms, ranging from simple autonomy of organizational units to matters such as the disconnection between plan and implementation. Furthermore, the functional consequences of decoupling range from problematic to benign and even adaptive (see, for example, Weick, 1976).

Neo-institutional theorists first began to use the word "decoupling" as a near synonym to "loose coupling." However, the common usage of decoupling in organizational research is now decidedly more specific. Decoupling is most frequently used to describe the disconnection between high-level organizational decisions, plans, and policies with concrete implementation and efficacious organizational outcomes "on the ground" (Meyer and Rowan, 1977). Thus, decoupling in the context of policy is almost synonymous with policy failure. Many environmental policies, for instance, are designed to ameliorate actual environmental conditions. To the extent that they do not produce desired environmental outcomes, they could be labeled as decoupled.

One caveat: scholars increasingly equate decoupling (and failed implementation) with cynical action by organizations that desire the legitimacy of conformity but do not wish to bear costs of proper implementation (Krasner, 1999). Although some examples fit this pattern (such as Forbes and Jermier, Chapter 8), we resist this narrow meaning of decoupling and the actor-centric strategic presumptions that it implies. Neo-institutional theory and research have repeatedly pointed out the limits of organizational rationality and drawn attention to the importance of norms, the construction of organizational identities, and the ambiguity and complexity of organization action. In certain cases, decoupling may be the product of strategic action. However, it may also reflect altruistic or norms-based action, or even incompetence, accident, or chance (Meyer and Rowan, 1977; Orton and Weick, 1990). Whether or not strategic action is involved is an empirical question, not something that should be presumed.

Generally speaking, decoupling results from the complexities of modern organizations and their environments. Organizations are composed of multiple groups of actors with multiple, often conflicting goals that direct attention away from environmental policies. Moreover, organizations must also function in a complex environment, juggling different constituencies, interests, and norms (Meyer and Rowan, 1977). This lowers the likelihood that policy created in one part of an organization is effectively implemented in another. For example, strong external demands to address a specific issue, combined with severe resource constraints in an organization, can result in a total disconnection between organizational rules and actual practices "on the ground." This often occurs when poverty-stricken nations succumb to external pressure and introduce new environmental goals or legislation. Governments proceed to pass laws that have no hope of being implemented due to lack of resources.

Even in the wealthiest of nations, decoupling may occur when there is inherent complexity or ambiguity regarding core organizational tasks (Meyer and Rowan, 1977). In the case of environmental policies, the ambiguity shows up in the difficulty of defining what the best solution to environmental degradation would be. In the absence of a simple and straightforward solution to environmental problems, organizations commonly focus on policies and procedures that can be monitored and controlled; formal rationality supersedes substantive rationality of outcomes. Tight coupling is maintained over organizational procedures, which may become decoupled for the desired outcome of environmental amelioration.

POLICY IN A DECOUPLED WORLD

Research on decoupling has important implications for policy. First, decoupling provides a helpful framework for understanding the limited success of policy that is endemic in organizations. In doing so, it may help us create more realistic expectations about policy impacts.

More importantly, a major impact of decoupling is often overlooked: decoupling allows for policies to be *adopted* that would otherwise not be. Loosely coupled organizations can adopt policies that would be utterly unfeasible in a tightly coupled one. Decisive policies can be laid out and legislation passed despite lack of resources to implement them, despite ambiguity regarding solutions, and even despite the opposition of major constituencies. Thus, for example, even the most impoverished nations of the world can be environmental proponents, in some sense.

Policy adoption has powerful second-order consequences, even in the absence of implementation. Adoption is an important symbolic act that affects the identity and agenda of an organization. Through policy adoption an organization can define itself as "in a turnaround," as "family-friendly," or as "environmentalist."

Such formal policy statements determine the legitimate agenda of organizations and provide leverage or at least a foot in the door for internal and external constituencies to influence an organization. For example, when the government of Japan began to commit to proenvironment policies, it spurred a whole new set of proenvironmental protests. Citizens could legitimately make further environmental claims and criticize the government for failing to meet its existing commitments (Broadbent, 1998). So we argue that environmental impact assessment legislation opens up a node in which conflict over environmental issues can take place.

In addition, the symbolic act of policy adoption becomes part of the normative and cultural environment for other organizations in the same field (Scott and Meyer, 1994). As we discuss below, the adoption of environmental laws in the United States influenced the behavior of other governments—even while implementation in the United States remained uncertain. Interorganizational and international comparisons often do not attend to the details of implementation. Rather, it is *policies* that are copied and thus diffuse across organizational fields and the world system (Strang and Meyer, 1993).

In sum, decoupling facilitates adoption. Adoption, in turn, becomes a symbol that legitimates policy diffusion, and acts as a cultural resource for subunits and exogenous groups. This resource may be used to influence the organization itself, or brought to bear in struggles elsewhere.

The rise of environmental impact assessment legislation in the United States serves to illustrate both the processes that generate decoupling, as well as the broader effects to which we have alluded.

THE CASE OF ENVIRONMENTAL IMPACT ASSESSMENTS

With the rise of global environmental concerns have come various methods to aid in environmental protection. The Environmental Impact Assessment (EIA), also called an Environmental Impact Report (EIR), is one such method. EIAs are a widely used bureaucratic tool intended to forecast the environmental implications of new projects, usually involving some form of construction. The idea is to increase environmental awareness and minimize environmental degradation by providing information on environmental conditions to project planners and government officials making development decisions that might affect the local environment. Originating in the United States in 1969, EIA legislation has diffused to both industrialized and less-developed countries as part of attempts to prevent environmental degradation. There are usually three parts to an Environmental Impact Assessment (Gilpin, 1995; Ahmad, 1985). First, an Environmental Impact

Statement is written to describe the proposed project and its predicted environmental effects in the near- and long-term future. Second, the EIA lays out for decision makers the alternatives that might decrease environmental damage, and assesses the costs and benefits of each alternative. Third, the public and relevant interest groups are informed about the contents of the EIA and allowed to negotiate the details of the plan. The final decision on the project is usually made by a government agency.

At first glance EIAs appear to be an ideal instrument to avert environmental damage from corporate or government construction and industrial activity. Based on a rationalistic, scientific logic, EIAs provide the information needed to make sensible decisions and a decision process that results in decisions that can be justified as just and democratic.

But EIAs have proved disappointing in practice. They have been criticized for failing to produce the environmental awareness they were designed to. The bureaucratic nature of EIAs can obscure environmental awareness, rather than enhance it. Even when the proper procedures have been followed and the proper forms filled out, the result is often a mass of incomprehensible data and models—not clear indications of environmental impacts. For example, the Environmental Impact Statement for the Trans-Alaska Pipeline in the United States was reportedly more than two meters thick, filled with unnecessary verbiage and data, and impossible to read. This and other EIAs have been characterized as ". . . deadly, voluminous, and obscure and lack[ing] the necessary analysis and synthesis . . . inordinately long, with too much space devoted to unnecessary description rather than to analysis of impacts and alternatives" (Council on Environmental Quality, 1975: 632).

This is partly due to the litigious atmosphere within which many EIAs are conducted—particularly in the United States, where corporations and government agencies are frequently sued by environmental groups. EIAs are thus overly thorough and "court-proof," rather than serving the goal of promoting environmental awareness among decision makers (Wathern, 1988).

In other countries the problem is the opposite: EIAs are slipshod or not performed at all. In West Germany, the EIA process was not systematically implemented for years after it was legislated (Kennedy, 1981). Often the quality of EIAs is simply unknown because it is largely ignored. In France, virtually no studies have been done on the quality or effectiveness of the thousands of EIAs that have been performed (Sanchez, 1993). Under these circumstances, there is little incentive for developers to follow the procedures fully, much less provide useful analysis and data in their EIAs. One observer wearily notes, "It seems that [Environmental Impact Assessment] is more of a new bureaucratic procedure than a tool for challenging conventional wisdom and traditional practices of project preparations" (Sanchez, 1993: 263–64).

Some think the failure of environmental protection policies results from the organizational and institutional environments that led to the creation of EIAs and in which they are implemented. Ironically, although EIAs are sometimes perceived as failing to directly protect the environment, they may be succeeding in promoting broader institutional change. The modern EIA arose at a time when there was a growing demand for environmental solutions; tremendous ambiguity regarding what they might involve; a bureaucratic governmental environment (with strong commitments to "rational" procedures); and substantial commitment to democratic participation. Together these yielded a procedural solution that made, and continues to make, sense in its organizational context. But a variety of processes described by organizational and neo-institutional sociologists, such as decoupling and bureaucratic emphasis on procedural rather than substantive rationality, may help explain why EIAs do not always yield actual improvements in environmental conditions.

The Origins of the EIA: A Rationalistic, Procedural Solution

The factors that led to the creation of early EIA legislation induced decoupling in several ways. There was substantial pressure from various constituencies to address problems of environmental degradation. However, the goal is complex and difficult to define, and there are great uncertainties regarding the methods and technologies of achieving it. Strong environmental protection (such as severely limiting pollutants or development) can be incredibly costly to industry, and opposition from industry often makes legislation impossible to enact. The EIA "solution" is a procedural, rather than substantive, approach. Procedures like the EIA were created such that environmental protection would theoretically occur, even though the substantive issue of "environmental protection" was put into the background. In this decoupled solution, actual monitoring of environmental outcomes could be overlooked.

The history of the development of EIA legislation illustrates how pressure to address a problem, in combination with ambiguity over means and goals, can result in substantial decoupling of policy from practice. The political climate in the United States in the late 1960s reflected growing popular concern about environmental problems. EIAs were first legislated in the United States as part of the National Environmental Policy Act (NEPA) in 1969. In an attempt to unify existing environmental protection requirements into one agency and one document, the

NEPA created the U.S. Environmental Protection Agency (EPA) and included a provision that instituted EIA requirements for large federal and private-sector development projects. Previously, several federal agencies had jurisdiction over various aspects of the environment, but no one agency had oversight over the environment as a whole. Senator Edmund Muskie, author of the bill, believed that much environmental damage was caused simply because no single party was responsible for considering all of the possible environmental consequences before a road, a dam, or a building was constructed. He hoped that filing an EIA would at least allow decision makers to consider the environment while making development decisions.

The EIA in the United States showed that lawmakers wanted to do something to help protect the environment, even if they were unsure how go about it (Andrews, 1976; Anderson, 1973; Liroff, 1976). Where environmental threats were relatively well defined, substantive solutions were often possible—such as the Clean Air Act of 1972, which regulated specific sources of air pollution. However, the overall impact of new construction was complex and largely unknown. Congress felt pressured internationally and domestically to act on environmental problems without knowing how best to do so. It resorted to a classic technique: the creation of a bureaucratic procedure, the EIA, which was to be managed by the newly created EPA. The legislation was an exceptionally broad law that failed to describe specific procedures for carrying out EIAs, mostly because it was unclear even to the legislators what was to be done. Like many procedural solutions, the EIA reflected a sort of faith—that by following rational procedures, environmental protection would result.

It took many years to work out even the basic procedures of the EIA in the United States because the original legislation specified no details. The procedures were mostly clarified in the U.S. judicial system in a laborious and time-consuming manner (Anderson, 1973). The legislation left fundamental issues unspecified, such as who was required to perform EIAs, what the EIA should look like, and what the penalties were for failing to comply with EIA requirements. And there was no guarantee that the specifics of EIA procedures would have any relationship to actual environmental improvement. Moreover, bureaucratic focus emphasized the EIA itself, rather than substantive issues such as actual environmental outcomes. Operating within governmental agencies, a common form of decoupling occurred. The EIA was adapted to the bureaucratic concerns of the agency, rather than the original goal for which it was intended. In other words, a "proper" EIA was one that fulfilled all the bureaucratic requirements, not one that actually provided accurate and useful information to decision makers. In essence, the procedure substituted for the goal.

Institutionalized this way, the EIA could remain substantially decoupled from the actual substantive goal of environmental protection. One observer of the EIA system notes:

> Because [the EIA legislation] was not designed to control specific kinds or sources of pollution, its benefit to society is difficult to quantify. The act was designed primarily to institutionalize in the federal government an anticipatory concern for the quality of the human environment, that is, an attitude, a heightened state of awareness that, unlike pollution abatement, is measurable only subjectively and qualitatively. (Wood, 1995: 9).

Furthermore, as research on decoupling has frequently shown, there is little oversight or evaluation of actual outcomes. The effect of EIAs in protecting the environment has received little attention. Few studies have been carried out to evaluate EIAs in terms of the accuracy of the predictions of environmental impacts. One of those rare studies (Ginger and Mohai, 1993) shows large disparities between the predictions of the EIA and the actual consequences of the development project. The actual physical environment becomes thoroughly decoupled from the procedural enactment of environmental impact assessments.

Likewise, no single organization is responsible for evaluating and monitoring the quality of EIAs. Enforcement is left up to corporations, local, state and federal officials, and concerned citizens in the community, who vary considerably in their commitment to environmental issues. In the litigious United States, for instance, corporations are keenly aware that concerned citizens and domestic environmental groups might bring them to court for inadequate EIAs. This gives corporations an incentive to prepare procedurally correct EIAs. As there are no standards for evaluating an EIA on substantive environmental grounds, however, less attention is paid to this dimension. In many other countries, corporations are much less likely to be sued. Often this is because there is no mechanism for enforcement of EIA quality.

The International Environment Regime and the Worldwide Diffusion of the EIA

The decoupled nature of the EIA also made it a perfect candidate for diffusion worldwide. Unlike substantive laws specifying particular environmental protections, EIAs are relatively cheap, easy, and uncontroversial to enact, and they satisfy constituencies such as environmental groups. However, many Third World states lack the capacity to carry out procedures such as EIAs effectively. This is not necessarily due to a lack of motivation but to the difficulties of bureaucracy in countries torn by civil war or hampered by extreme poverty. The result can be even more extreme forms of decoupling surrounding the implementation of EIAs in these countries.

The same combination of pressing urgency to solve environmental problems and uncertainty of how to do it made the procedural solution of the EIA an ideal policy for rapid worldwide adoption. However, for most countries, both the urgent pressure and the procedural logic devolved from international rather than domestic sources. Over the past few decades, the problem of environmental degradation has become an increasingly urgent global concern. These concerns have become institutionalized through the creation of organizational and bureaucratic infrastructures intended to further the end of environmental protection—a world environmental regime. The expansion of this regime can be seen at the international level, particularly in the rapid increase in the number of international intergovernmental and nongovernmental environmental organizations (Meyer and others, 1997). All nation-states are expected to be concerned with and involved in issues such as climate change, biodiversity, and deforestation. Individuals are also supposed to do their part by recycling and resource conservation. Environmental protection has become an institutionalized norm at both the international and national level (Frank, Hironaka, and Schofer, 2000).

At the national level, an early sign of this trend was state adoption of bureaucratic forms such as environmental ministries and national environmental policies (Meyer and others, 1997; Frank and others, 2000). Legislative adoption of EIA programs parallels these trends (see Figure 9.1). The EIA is clearly spreading rapidly. Institutional theory would suggest that many countries adopted EIA legislation due to the influences of the institutional environment, rather than due to local interests or local perceptions of the effectiveness of EIAs. Procedures such as EIAs help nation-states to enhance their image in the international arena. EIAs allow corporations and nation-states to demonstrate their concern for environmental issues in a world in which such issues are high on the international political agenda. Thus, according to neo-institutional arguments, the adoption and performance of EIAs follows encouragement from the global environmental regime, rather than the actual functional efficacy of EIAs as a method of environmental protection.

International organizations have facilitated the spread of EIA legislation because the EIA fits well as a general solution to environmental problems. The ac-

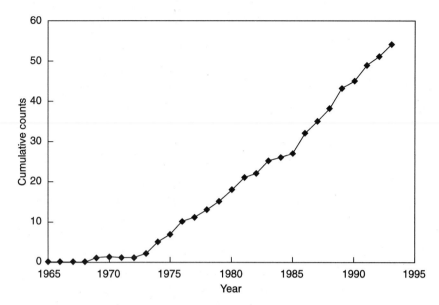

Figure 9.1   Country Adoption of National EIA Legislation

ceptability of the EIA is due to its basis in science and the neatness of procedural solutions over the complexity, cost, and impracticality of substantive ones. This makes the diffusion of the EIA easier, but also makes it less functional, because the universalized, standardized, and rationalized package of the EIA is not necessarily suited or well adapted to all political systems, ecosystems, and environmental problems.

The international environmental regime aids states in adopting EIA legislation by providing guidelines and advice—either directly or through large international conferences. For the 1992 Summit on the Environment and Development in Rio de Janeiro, participating states were required to write a book summarizing their environmental actions; one section was to be devoted to their EIA legislation or the prospects of adopting EIA legislation. Not surprisingly, many countries adopted EIA legislation in 1991 in preparation for the conference. UNEP, OECD, and the World Bank each have published guidelines for instituting EIA legislation and provide training and advisors to help, making it easy for nation-states to enact. International organizations find it easier to espouse a neat, standardized package such as the EIA rather than attempt the messy, expensive, and time-consuming process of tailoring an environmental protection program that would be appropriate to a given country (Horberry, 1985). Nations adopting EIAs score points in international opinion, even if they don't commit the resources and infrastructure necessary to make the policy effective (because of resource constraints or in a attempt to gain legitimacy without paying the costs). Thus the basic elements of an EIA are fairly standard worldwide.

Due to the influence of the international environmental regime, many countries in the Third World have EIA legislation. Some observers feel that, like their industrialized counterparts, these countries adopt EIA legislation mainly to appear environmentally responsible and in response to pressures from international environmental organizations and conferences such as the United Nations and the World Bank (Nor, 1991; Fowler and de Aguiar, 1993; Moreira, 1988).

However, the disjuncture between EIA goals and national institutional arrangement encourages decoupling. For example, EIAs were designed for implementation in democratic states with elaborate bureaucracies. In many cases, little effort was made to adapt EIA systems to the state structures of developing nations. Decoupling also results from the general lack of resources in developing countries. Additionally, many less-developed countries lack the ability to remediate their environmental problems even if they want to.

These problems have led to EIAs that appear hopelessly inadequate by Western standards. For instance, in some developing countries, EIAs have been classified as secret or subjected to corruption, and often are completely disregarded (Nor, 1991; Abracosa and Ortolano, 1987; Hirji and Ortolano, 1991). A particularly egregious case of the ineffective use of EIAs occurred in Kenya. The Kenyan water resources agency mocked the intent of an EIA by taking over the process in its own interests, defining the parameters of the study, selecting the consultants, and deciding whether to respond to the study recommendations at all (Hirji and Ortolano, 1991). Wood (1995: 305) describes the problems of implementing EIAs in developing nations:

> EIA reports are often confidential. Some EIA reports in developing countries are bound like Ph.D. theses, are about as indigestible, are produced with similarly limited numbers of copies and are not even available through inter-library loan. This is hardly an appropriate climate for peer and public review. . . . Too many examples exist in developing countries of mechanistic EIA reports being produced which have little or no effect on decisions.

Much of this stems from undemocratic political conditions. For a policy such as the EIA to function ideally, it helps for citizen participation to be familiar, comfortable, and even valued by both the state and the citizen. But in countries with authoritarian governments, in which citizens have few democratic privileges, it is not unusual for EIAs to be kept secret from the public or to have very limited dissemination. In Malaysia, for instance, Environmental Impact Statements are classified, making public participation impossible by law (Nor, 1991).

Additionally, where governments suffer from disorganization, corruption, and instability, EIAs reflect that. Many states lack the capability to provide basic civil order and governmental stability. Some lack the capacity and resources to effectively carry out quality EIAs. For instance, in the Philippines, EIA legislation was implemented in 1977 under an authoritarian government with a powerful but independent bureaucracy and a politically weak judiciary that could not stop industrial projects even if the project did not obtain EIA approval (Abracosa and Ortolano, 1987).

Finally, EIAs may be carried out according to local and divergent values of key decision makers. For example, decision makers may value development and economic priorities over environmental protection (Haeuber, 1992). This is not a flaw in the EIA system in these nations, but rather a difference in priorities. EIAs were meant to be an objective instrument that provided information by which to weigh development benefits against environmental costs. EIAs do not ensure environmental protection, particularly when decision makers are far more concerned with economic growth than with environmental protection.

Thus it is not surprising that EIA plan and implementation in some countries are frequently flawed. The top-down pressures for adoption from the international environmental regime discouraged developing states from designing unique environmental policy legislation tailored to their specific circumstances. Because developing countries often lack the state capacity, resources, and democratic systems that are taken for granted in the West, EIAs are typically ineffective.

Environmental Consequences Of EIAs

We have shown why EIA policies do not always have the beneficial effects on the environment that were originally intended. But this is not to say that EIAs have had no effects. Some are irrelevant to environmental protection—for instance, an increase in governmental bureaucracy and, in the United States, an added burden on the court system. However, some of those effects have indirectly led to increased environmental awareness and may have led to improvements on environmental conditions.

A big indirect effect of environmental policies such as EIAs is to reframe a nation's policy portfolio. By creating a national environmental policy, the government tacitly acknowledges that environmental protection is part of the purview and responsibilities of the state. This contrasts with the situation in the nineteenth century, when environmental pollution and resource scarcity was noticed but neither the state nor its citizens felt that these problems were the responsibility of the state to resolve (Hironaka, forthcoming).

EIAs and other environmental policies set a national agenda for environmental protection. They demonstrate at least a symbolic commitment to the environment and help to create a broader framework that makes it easier for states and citizen groups that want to help the environment. Thus there are both intended and unintended effects on environmental protection. So the creation of a national environmental agenda does increase activity on behalf of the environment.

In a more direct way, EIAs lead to an increase in environmental awareness. Developers who might not have otherwise thought about the environment are forced to consider it, even if their response is to try to hide how a new construction will affect the environment. Similarly, citizens who object to a new project may look to the EIA for environmental reasons to block it. This may not always be positive from an environmental policy maker's point of view, but it increases everyone's consideration of the environment, which was indeed one of the intended goals of EIAs.

Third, EIAs can and do provide a procedural mechanism that can be used by environmental groups as a means of forcing corporations and states to abide by environmental regulations. This use of the EIA was not foreseen by the original policy makers, who thought of the EIA as an informational tool rather than an excuse for litigation. However, domestic groups have seized on the EIA to stop development in the name of environmental protection. In some cases this is due to true environmental concern; sometimes it is only a convenient way to keep development out of one's backyard. The United States has had a large number of court cases involving EIAs, usually prosecuted by citizen groups against corporations. Today there are still about 100 court cases each year regarding EIAs, down from approximately 200 per year in the early 1970s (Wood, 1995). The most common cause of these legal actions is the absence or inadequacy of an EIA. Thus the EIA process provides an important way for groups to pursue environmental protection.

Domestic environmental groups in the United States have also used the EIA legislative act against the state itself. In 1975, domestic citizen groups sued the United States Agency for International Development (USAID) for failing to file EIAs on international projects. The U.S. Federal Court ruled against USAID, so USAID began requiring EIAs for all development projects (Gilpin, 1995). In this case the EIA law was used by citizens to force the state to conform to its own environmental requirements and, potentially, to increase environmental awareness internationally.

International pressures may also make EIAs more consequential, particularly in developing countries. Citizens in nondemocratic countries may have more difficulty in using EIAs against industry or the state than their counterparts in democracies. However, international pressures, particularly from international nongovernmental organizations, may aid domestic environmental groups in such countries. For instance, the threat of an international boycott, due in part to objections to inadequate EIA procedures, induced Scott Paper to withdraw from Indonesia (Stern, 1991). Also in Indonesia, a proposed dam project drew protest from local and international nongovernmental organizations on the grounds that the Environmental Impact Statement had been improperly performed. The result was a great deal of negative international attention that jeopardized foreign aid to Indonesia (Stern, 1991).

The mere threat that corporations might be brought to court on procedural challenges to their EIAs can lead to more environmentally sound development plans. Corporations writing EIA documents may consider environmental impacts more widely, or may even alter development plans preemptively, in an attempt to avoid environmental protests. EIA requirements have also improved state and community environmental knowledge, incorporated new actors into environmental debates, and improved the tools and quality of environmental planning (McDonald and Brown, 1995). These broad and indirect effects may occur regardless of the adequacy or accuracy with which EIA procedures are typically carried out.

Thus the institutionalization of environmental procedures as a routine part of bureaucratic proceedings allows increased intervention on behalf of the environment, even if EIAs in themselves are "failures." Increasingly, environmental considerations are becoming part of standard government operating procedures and are seen as the routine and standardized business of the state. In the long run, this is likely to lead to lasting environmental improvement.

CONCLUSION

Good-hearted environmentalists are often frustrated by the ineffectiveness of environmental policies. Even when well-designed legislation is enacted, it frequently fails to result in the improvement in the environment that was hoped for. But this chapter suggests that "failure" due to decoupling is predictable from a neo-institutional perspective. We also showed, however, that policies can have indirect and unanticipated consequences. Instead, policies may have broader consequences that benefit the environment through indirect mechanisms—as a symbolic and cultural resource that can lead to future environmental mobilization and change. This may not be comforting to environmental activists, because indirect effects are often visible only in hindsight. But they are real, and this perspective may comfort those who take a longer-term perspective on environmental protection.

REFERENCES

Abracosa, Ramon, and Leonard Ortolano. 1987. "Environmental Impact Assessment in the Philippines: 1977–1985." *Environmental Impact Assessment Review,* 7(4): 293–310.

Ahmad, Yusuf J. 1985. *Guidelines to Environmental Impact Assessment in Developing Countries.* London: Hodder and Stoughton.

Anderson, Frederick R. 1973. *NEPA in the Courts: a Legal Analysis of the National Environmental Policy Act.* Baltimore: Johns Hopkins University Press.

Andrews, Richard N. L. 1976. *Environmental Policy and Administrative Change.* Lexington, MA: Lexington Books.

Broadbent, Jeffrey. 1998. *Environmental Politics in Japan.* Cambridge, UK: Cambridge University Press.

Brunsson, Nils. 1993. "Ideas and Action: Justification and Hypocrisy as Alternatives to Control." *Accounting, Organizations and Society,* 18(6): 489–506.

Council on Environmental Quality. 1975. *Environmental Quality 1975: Sixth Annual Report.* Washington, DC: Government Printing Office.

Fowler, Harold G., and Ana Maria Dias de Aguiar. 1993. "Environmental Impact Assessment in Brazil." *Environmental Impact Assessment Review,* 13(3): 169–175.

Frank, David John. 1994. "Global Environmentalism: International Treaties in World Society." Ph.D. dissertation, Department of Sociology, Stanford University.

Frank, David John, Ann Hironaka, and Evan Schofer. 2000. "The Nation-State and the Natural Environment, 1900–1995." *American Sociological Review,* 65(Feb): 96–116.

Gilpin, Alan. 1995. *Environmental Impact Assessment: Cutting Edge for the Twenty-First Century.* Cambridge, UK: Cambridge University Press.

Ginger, Clare, and Paul Mohai. 1993. "The Role of Data in the EIS Process: Evidence from the BLM Wilderness Review." *Environmental Impact Assessment Review,* 13: 103–139.

Haeuber, Richard. 1992. "The World Bank and Environmental Assessment: The Role of Non-Governmental Organizations." *Environmental Impact Assessment Review,* 12: 331–347.

Hirji, Rafik, and Leonard Ortolano. 1991. "Strategies for Managing Uncertainties Imposed by Environmental Impact Assessment." *Environmental Impact Assessment Review,* 11: 203–230.

Hironaka, Ann. Forthcoming. "The Globalization of Environmental Protection: The Case of Environmental Impact Assessment." *Sociological Inquiry.*

Horberry, John. 1985. "International Organization and EIA in Developing Countries." *Environmental Impact Assessment Review,* 5: 207–222.

Kennedy, William V. 1981. "The West German Experience." In Timothy O'Riordan and W. R. Derrick Sewell, eds., *Project Appraisal and Policy Review,* 155–186. Chichester: Wiley.

Krasner, Stephen D. 1999. *Sovereignty: Organized Hypocrisy.* Princeton, NJ: Princeton University Press.

Liroff, Richard A. 1976. *A National Policy for the Environment: NEPA and Its Aftermath.* Bloomington: Indiana University Press.

March, James G., and Johan P. Olsen. 1976. *Ambiguity and Choice in Organizations.* Bergen, Norway: Universitetsforlaget.

McDonald, Geoffrey T., and Lex Brown. 1995. "Going Beyond Environmental Impact Assessment: Environmental Input to Planning and Design." *Environmental Impact Assessment Review,* 15: 483–495.

Meyer, John W., and Brian Rowan. 1977. "Institutionalized Organizations: Formal Structure as Myth and Ceremony." *American Journal of Sociology,* 83(2): 340–363.

Meyer, John W., John Boli, George M. Thomas, and Francisco O. Ramirez. 1997. "World Society and the Nation-State." *American Journal of Sociology,* 103(10): 144–181.

Moreira, I. Verocai. 1988. "EIA In Latin America." In Peter Wathern, ed., *Environmental Impact Assessment: Theory and Practice,* 239–254. London: Unwin Hyman.

Nor, Yahya M. 1991. "Problems and Perspectives in Malaysia." *Environmental Impact Assessment Review,* 11(2): 129–141.

Orton, J. Douglas, and Karl E. Weick. 1990. "Loosely Coupled Systems: A Reconceptualization." *Academy of Management Review,* 15(2): 203–223.

Sanchez, Luis Enrique. 1993. "Environmental Impact Assessment in France." *Environmental Impact Assessment Review,* 13(4): 255–265.

Scott, W. Richard, and John W. Meyer, eds. 1994. *Institutional Environments and Organizations.* Newbury Park, CA: Sage.

Strang, David, and John W. Meyer. 1993. "Institutional Conditions for Diffusion." *Theory and Society,* 22: 487–511.

Stern, Alissa J. 1991. "Using Environmental Impact Assessments for Dispute Management." *Environmental Impact Assessment Review,* 11: 81–87.

Wathern, Peter, ed. 1988. "The EIA Directive of the European Community." In Peter Wathern, ed. *Environmental Impact Assessment: Theory and Practice,* 192–209. London: Unwin Hyman.

Weick, Karl E. 1976. "Educational Organizations as Loosely Coupled Systems." *Administrative Science Quarterly,* 21: 1–19.

Wood, Christopher. 1995. *Environmental Impact Assessment: A Comparative Review.* New York: Wiley.

III INSTITUTIONAL PROCESSES OF NEGOTIATION AND NARRATIVE

10

INSTITUTIONS AS BARRIERS AND ENABLERS TO NEGOTIATED AGREEMENTS: INSTITUTIONAL ENTREPRENEURSHIP AND THE PLUM CREEK HABITAT CONSERVATION PLAN

John G. Troast Jr., Andrew J. Hoffman,
Hannah C. Riley, and Max H. Bazerman

In 1990, the spotted owl was formally listed as an endangered species. For Plum Creek Timber Company, the sixth-largest owner of private timberland in the country, this meant a fundamental change in its timber cutting practices. Under the aegis of the Endangered Species Act (ESA), federal agencies required the company to draw circles around each known nesting site and prohibited or severely limited its cutting practices within each circle to avoid owl "takes" (potential direct or indirect harm). Company loggers worked around a maze of migrating owl circles, each covering 2,523 acres (approximately four square miles). At one point, more than 70 percent of Plum Creek's acreage was tangled in 108 circles. The company spent $500,000 each summer to track shifting nest sites (Jostrom, 1999). Lorin Hicks, chief biologist at Plum Creek, recalled: "It was awful. We had to constantly change the circles as owls moved and add new circles as we found new owls, and we knew we were supporting a paradigm that biologists didn't feel was adequate. Owls don't necessarily use circles" (Durbin, 1997).

As an alternative to such costly and complex compliance programs, some private landowners have resorted to extreme measures to avoid the discovery of endangered species on their own properties. One classic illustration is the story of Ben Cone. For decades, Cone and his father had managed their land sustainably. In 1991, however, a wildlife biologist informed Cone that approximately twenty-

This paper was supported by the Dispute Resolution Research Center and the Kellogg Environmental Research Center at the Kellogg Graduate School of Management at Northwestern University and by the Faculty Research Fund at the Harvard Business School. In addition, we thank Michael Tushman, Marc Ventresca, and Peter Mendel for comments that have helped to improve this paper.

nine red-cockaded woodpeckers—members of an endangered species—were living on his property. Under the authority of the ESA, the government took control of the woodpecker's habitat, 1,560 acres, or about 15 percent of Cone's property (Baden, 1995). In fear of losing control of his remaining 85 percent, Cone drastically altered the way he forested his property. He harvested the oldest trees on the land remaining within his control, thus preventing the woodpeckers from expanding their habitat. In the process, he also put vast quantities of his forest out of commission, perhaps permanently. Both the government and Cone acted according to scripts influenced, if not defined, by the ESA. But in so doing, they created an outcome far worse than what was in the best interests of each.

During the 1980s, Habitat Conservation Plans (HCPs) were introduced as a way to avoid such economically and environmentally suboptimal outcomes. Conceptually, HCPs provide private landowners with a permit to violate specific aspects of the ESA, allowing the "incidental take" of listed species in the course of lawful development activities provided that the landowner follows certain steps to provide for conservation of that species as part of a larger habitat plan. HCPs are a call for negotiations between environmental and economic interests to improve upon the status quo. HCPs are intended to transform zero-sum conflicts over natural resource conservation and economic development into mutual gains (Raiffa, 1982; Bazerman, 1998; Hoffman and others, 1999).

In this chapter, we explore how existing institutions act as barriers to the adoption of an innovation in environmental policy (see also Levin and Espeland, Chapter 5). HCPs represent an attempt at pragmatic, context-based regulation (Mylonadis, Chapter 16), which seeks joint engagement of the government, regulated community, and other stakeholders (Fiorino, 1999). Unfortunately, such proposals clash with embedded beliefs held by many of these stakeholders.

Through analysis of the case of Plum Creek Timber's Native Fish HCP, we explore how an institutional entrepreneur promotes the adoption of a new regulatory form through cooperative negotiations.

To illustrate our analysis of the barriers to the adoption of HCPs at the institutional level, we present a case study of Plum Creek Timber's native fish HCP. We connect institutional analyses to the level of the individual organization by analyzing negotiations between the parties. In our view, institutional theory has become disembodied in recent years, moving away from the political aspects of early studies (Selznick, 1949), focusing disproportionately on the cognitive elements of institutions and the process of conformity (Zucker, 1983). Our intention is to bring together valuable aspects of both the old and the new institutionalism (Hirsch and Lounsbury, 1997). In particular, we highlight the entrepreneurial role that organizations can play in altering institutional beliefs and promoting new forms of interaction and debate. In doing so, we show how organizational action is both the product and the origin of social structures (Giddens, 1979).

Endangered species protection can be enhanced, we think, by exposing the underlying institutional tensions that impede the voluntary adoption of public-private sector collaboration. This allows the fashioning of new types of regulatory solutions that satisfy the interests and concerns of formerly adversarial parties.

LINKING INSTITUTIONAL AND NEGOTIATION FRAMEWORKS

In this chapter we apply theories of institutions and negotiations to explain policy debates as struggles between competing sets of interests and institutions. By linking the research disciplines, we can develop a multilevel, multiaspect framework that combines negotiation perspectives concerning individual decision making with institutional research on organizations, analyzing how these behaviors become institutionalized (Bazerman and Hoffman, 1999).

The Organizational Field as a Nexus for Issue-Based Negotiation

The locus of policy debates such as endangered species protection is the organizational field, "a community of organizations that partakes of a common meaning system and whose participants interact more frequently and fatefully with one another than with actors outside the field" (Scott, 1995: 56). The organizational field may include any constituent that imposes a coercive, normative or cognitive influence on the organization (Scott, 1991). In the case of HCPs, the field brings together interests such as government agencies (on the federal, state, and local level), commercial and noncommercial landowners, environmental activists, the local residents, and scientific, academic, professional communities (biologists, foresters, environmental engineers, economists, attorneys, consultants, financial managers), and others. Each of these interest groups enters the field with a diverse set of beliefs, techniques and professional guidelines.

Not just a collection of influential organizations, the field is the center of common channels of dialogue, discussion, and negotiation formed around a central issue (Hoffman, 1999). The concept of a defined "action arena" (Ostrom, 1999) or "arena of power relations" (Brint and Karabel, 1991: 335) is central to the diagnosis and explanation of the policy process where multiple field constituents compete over the definition of issues and the form of institutions which will guide organizational behavior (see Figure 10.1). The process may more resemble institutional war (White, 1992) than isomorphic dialogue, as is traditionally attributed

Influences of the Broader Social/Institutional Context

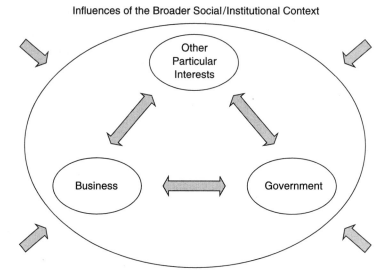

Figure 10.1   The Organizational Field as a Nexus of Issue-Based Negotiation

to field-level phenomena (DiMaggio and Powell, 1983). Institutional beliefs and perceptions are influenced by this field-level competition, but situated within individual organizations or populations of organizations. Therefore, to fully appreciate the complexity of institutional dynamics, one must analyze both the specific institutions that shape the nexus for an issue-based field and the competing institutions that may be promoted within the individual populations (or classes of constituencies) that inhabit that field.

Broadening the Negotiation Perspective

Negotiation frameworks can help us to model the interaction among these competing interests. In negotiations, parties seek to further their strategic interests through a balance of collaborative efforts to create value, and competitive efforts to claim it (Lax and Sebenius, 1986). Efficient negotiations maximize the value to be divided until neither party can do any better without leaving the other party worse off (Raiffa, 1982). In negotiations among ideological opposites, however, parties often miss valuable opportunities to expand the pie of resources to be divided because they are blinded by partisan biases (Keltner and Robinson, 1993) and win-lose assumptions about the negotiation process (Thompson, 1995). Seeking, sharing, and clarifying the interests of the various parties is crucial to the achievement of sustainable and efficient environmental agreements (Pruitt and Lewis, 1975; Thompson, 1991; Susskind, Levy, and Thomas-Larmer, 1999; Morrill and Owen-Smith, Chapter 4).

Although the behavioral decision and social psychological negotiation literature has offered important insights concerning the behavior of individual negotiators and their opponents, these do not extend to the behavior of organizations in their larger institutional context. Lax and Sebenius (1986: 322) hint at this connection, recognizing the complexity of large multiparty relationships and the need for negotiators to confront networks of "linked agreements" where effective action requires "extensive negotiation." They postulate that individual and organizational actors in the negotiation network act as both barriers to, and opportunities for, agreement. The premise that the social context acts as both a barrier and potential opportunity to negotiated agreement can be explored further using an institutional framework, and is linked to several important concepts about institutions and institutional change. By joining concepts and theories of negotiation dynamics with institutional dynamics observed at the organizational level, we can also attempt to explain institutions as both sources of constraint and opportunity.

Elements of Institutions

Institutions form the central context in which policy debates take place. They form structures where the conceptualizations of the relationship between economics and the environment become sources of both inertia and change by reconciling competing frames. Scott (1995) describes institutions as embodied in three foundational pillars: regulative, normative, and cognitive. Regulative aspects of institutions are based on legal sanction to which organizations accede for reasons of expedience. Normative aspects of institutions are morally grounded on, and organizations will comply with, these elements based on social obligation. Cognitive aspects of institutions are socially constituted assumptions or models of reality and refer to the collective constructions of social reality via language, meaning systems, and other rules of classification embodied in public activity. It is this cognitive aspect that emphasizes the taken-for-granted beliefs to which the organization will conform (Zucker, 1983).

These three pillars are depicted as analytically distinct (Scott, 1995), but they may be practically interconnected (Hoffman and Ventresca, 1999). Thus, the different institutional conceptions can be viewed as sources of tension in negotiations, rather than independent categories or alternative sources of pressure. Although HCPs may represent a shift in the regulative domain of institutions, they trigger many normative and cognitive elements that affect the decision-making negotiation dynamic, becoming sources of tension and resistance to change.

Institutional Change and the Role of the Institutional Entrepreneur

Few institutional analyses fully connect the influence of institutional fields to culture and practice on the level of the individual organization. Most researchers analyze the phenomena in terms of field-level change, not individual response, and thus create a theory that is oversocialized. In this context the field is seen as a homogenous collection of organizational actors, each behaving according to a social script dictated by the social environment (Granovetter, 1973). Further, the influence of the field tends to be depicted as unidirectional. There is little consideration of the role of individual actors in influencing the change process. Organizational actors have a role to play, but what is that role?

Some have attempted to address the issue of organizations as actors, arguing that firms can respond strategically to institutional pressures (Oliver, 1991), or that "institutional entrepreneurs" may strategically influence the process of institutional change (Hoffman, 1999; Lawrence, 1999). But in these cases the organization and the field are treated as separate and distinct. The firm responds to, or resists, institutional pressures rather than altering the bounds they create. But as integral members of the organizational field, certain organizations can influence the formation and evolution of the field and, as a result, affect change within the institutions that emerge. This role is often attributed to government (Fligstein, 1990; DiMaggio 1991). But where else is that power located within the broader constituency of the organizational field? Fligstein (1991) argues that the relative size and legitimacy of particular organizations creates differential power to dictate the actions of others and shape social fields. But we wonder how such power can be developed and nurtured through tactics and skills of negotiating within the political arena of the field (Fligstein, 1997; Morrill and Owen-Smith, Chapter 4).

In this chapter we depict the process of institutional interaction as recursive, such that social structure is both the medium and the outcome of practices within individual organizations and the broader field (Giddens, 1979). The government's HCP policy lets the private sector assume a leading role in the development of field-level policy. We show specific strategies an organization may adopt to influence this recursive process. Perhaps this will draw together elements of the "old" institutional conceptions of change, politics, and self-interested action (Selznick, 1949; 1957) into the "new" institutional conceptions of organizational fields, isomorphic conformity, and social change (Holm, 1995; Greenwood and Hinings, 1996; Kraatz and Zajac, 1996; Hirsch and Lounsbury, 1997). This chapter also demonstrates the dynamics by which the social structure changes to resolve important social challenges, such as protecting endangered species.

THE ENDANGERED SPECIES ACT AND
HABITAT CONSERVATION PLANS

Under the Endangered Species Act of 1973 (ESA), the U.S. government may designate any animal or plant species as endangered or threatened and prohibit its "take" (that is, any harm to a member of the species or its habitat). Some landowners think this is overly coercive and believe that environmental protection is at odds with economic interests (Hoffman and Ventresca, 1999). In 1982, Congress amended the ESA and introduced HCPs as a mechanism to encourage creative solutions that would balance conservation and economic imperatives. HCPs permit landowners to engage in the "incidental take" of protected species when pursuing otherwise lawful commercial activity. This means that landowners have greater regulatory flexibility and predictability in exchange for a commitment to beyond-compliance species protection on their property. Unless the species falls in jeopardy of extinction, the terms of the HCP agreement are guaranteed for the (sometimes decades-long) life of plan. In the timber industry, such long-term planning horizons are essential to commercial forest management. HCPs provide an opportunity to break the existing mold and to form creative public-private partnerships that loosen regulatory strangleholds, enhance long-term regulatory predictability and species protection, and improve conservation science and technology. HCPs also mitigate the perverse incentives to conceal or destroy evidence of listed species on private lands—in the words of one landowner to, "shoot, shovel, and shut up" (Crismon, 1998). In spite of the opportunities that voluntary programs such as HCPs present, many important economic and environmental stakeholders have been slow to adopt them (Hoffman and others, 2002).

In the first ten years of HCP's existence (from 1982 to 1991), only twelve HCP plans were approved (U.S. Fish and Wildlife Service, 1999). There are many reasons for this. The responsible federal agencies have been understaffed and constrained by limited resources (such as for site visits, scientific review, and program development). Most companies affected by the ESA know little about the HCP process, and many believe it is yet another costly web of government bureaucracy. Poised for battle with commercial interests, environmental activists have condemned HCPs as overly permissive and fundamentally flawed in their long-term design (Sabel, Fung, and Karkkainen, 1999). And all parties have a certain amount of historic distrust for others. In sum, HCPs have not emerged as an attractive mechanism for promoting environmental and development advocates to work collaboratively. Rather, they are seen as part of an idiosyncratic, bureaucratic process that is recreated on a case-by-case basis.

Hannan and Freeman (1989) suggest that first adopters of new institutional forms are vulnerable because participants are learning about each other and can only build trust over time through a history of reliability and accountability. More recent efforts by regulatory agencies have been focused on building that trust. In 1994, Interior Secretary Bruce Babbitt introduced the "No Surprises" policy, reassuring private landowners that the government would stand by the terms of any HCP negotiated. This policy stimulated growth in HCP adoption (see Figure 10.2). By the end of 1997, there were 243 HCP agreements in sixteen states, covering 6.2 million acres of land. The overwhelming majority of HCPs have involved small landholders and public or quasi-public organizations. The number of plans submitted by large timber companies was relatively small considering the total acreage likely affected by the Endangered Species Act.

Further, the long-term regulatory predictability of "No Surprises" heightened the long-term insecurity and resistance of conservationists. After an initial surge in

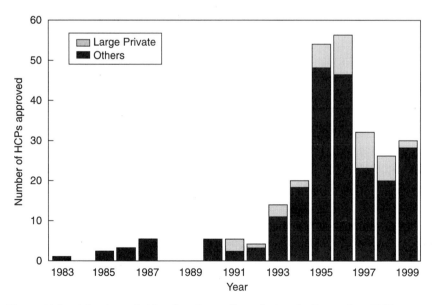

Figure 10.2   Adoption of a New Regulatory Form in Species Protection: HCP Approvals

project participation, a decline in the diffusion of HCPs followed. The decline can be attributed in part to renewed efforts within the environmental and scientific communities to resist perceived private-sector exploitation of the HCP process. For example, the Kareiva Report, a joint undertaking of the American Institute of Biological Sciences and the National Center for Ecological Analysis and Synthesis, examined 208 HCPs approved through August 1997 and found that a substantial number had not fulfilled the legally required standards for the "best available science" (Kareiva and others, 1999). On the basis of the Kareiva report and numerous other biological reviews of existing HCPs, the environmental community demanded stricter monitoring protocols and adaptive management plans that would be responsive over time to the welfare of affected species. Influenced by the threat of third-party lawsuits by environmental interests, federal regulators were forced to increase standards for applicants so as to meet these emerging criticisms (Sabel, Fung, and Karkkainen, 1999).

The adoption data on HCPs poses an interesting question because some timber companies use them and some do not. This is challenging for companies like Plum Creek. Now we examine both the underlying institutional tensions and the tactics employed by Plum Creek to influence change in the institutional field.

THE PLUM CREEK NATIVE FISH HCP: CONFRONTING INSTITUTIONAL TENSIONS TO NEGOTIATION

In 1997, Plum Creek owned, managed, and operated more than 2.4 million acres of timberland in Washington, Montana, Idaho, and Louisiana, ran twelve wood-product manufacturing facilities, and had 2,400 employees (Plum Creek Timber Company, 1997). Despite a controversial environmental past, the company had aggressively pursued a "green" reputation in more recent years. Beginning in 1991, Plum Creek formally amended its corporate mission by adopting a set of environmental principles to guide its timber business practices. Plum Creek's Cascades HCP was an example of what this new mission described as "environmental forestry." Completed in 1996, the plan was designed to protect northern spotted owls and 284 other species within the Cascades Region of the Pacific Northwest and allowed the company to log in areas formerly restricted by owl circles (Westneat, 1996).

In June 1997, Jim Kraft, vice president, general counsel, and secretary of Plum Creek, learned that four Montana environmental groups had won a lawsuit against the U.S. government for failing to act on their petition to list the bull trout as a threatened species on the endangered species list. The bull trout was the most litigated species in the history of the ESA; its designation as a threatened species had an effect on large tracts of territory stretching from the Pacific Ocean to the Continental Divide (Bader, 1998). Within this expanse of territory fell half of Plum Creek's entire land holdings. Due to the potential impact on the company's operations, Kraft and his colleagues had been following the progression of legal battles over bull trout protection. In anticipation of the species' listing, Lorin Hicks, chief biologist at Plum Creek, determined that the company was the largest known private landowner of bull trout habitat. Under the ESA, listing of the bull trout could substantially restrict the use of Plum Creek lands by banning new road construction, logging, grazing, or any other activity that might diminish the quality of the bull trout's stream habitat.

The dilemma faced by Plum Creek involved reconciling traditional regulative conceptions of the ESA with the unknown collaborative potential of HCPs. In deciding whether to pursue a second HCP, the company had to consider negotiation strategies. The decision to enter into an HCP negotiation was influenced by the institutional barriers embodied in regulations, litigation regimes, academic and professional repertoires, and social norms. Shifting these institutional barriers was complicated by those engaged in the field or negotiation nexus, whose "parallel cognitive conventions" (Douglas, 1986) sustained the existing regulative and normative institutions. The potential for a successful HCP outcome required an understanding of the organizational field and the potential for institutional change. Using the broader framework informed by the institutional literature and negotiation research, let us now explore four principal institutional tensions confronted by Plum Creek in its pursuit of a second HCP. These tensions demonstrate traditional conceptions of institutions as conforming elements as well as the opportunities for institutions to operate as enablers of change.

The Regulative Context: Contention and Ambiguity

American business and government have traditionally been viewed as adversarial (McGraw, 1984). The last century marked the growth and evolution of the central government as the principal regulatory body, whereas the courts emerged as the forum for "due process," providing legitimacy for many regulative institutions. The notion of command-and-control regulation suggests the role of government as the arbiter of the rules (Skocpol, 1985), dictating what is best for the environment, rather than as a facilitator of joint problem solving. Regulatory requirements are powerful scripts that the actors employ "to insure appropriate behaviors" (Powell and DiMaggio, 1991). But when the scripts change, the implications for organizational practice can be disruptive (Mylonadis, Chapter 16). Lorin Hicks described the response by timber companies to the listing of spotted owls in 1990: "It really required a huge paradigm shift on the part of the companies. An issue that we thought was a federal problem and a species that was thought to be peripheral . . . all of a sudden literally came home to roost on our lands. . . . Our job before we could do anything was to find them, learn about them, and understand them. . . . This was a huge regulatory and technical curve" (Hicks, 1999).

Furthermore, ESA enforcement has often been conflicting and ambiguous (Kostyack, 1997). Ambiguity in turn shapes compliance behaviors where rules in use replace rules in form (Ostrom, 1999), such that those who comply with the ESA can always resort to the courts for settlement. Yet this is not always in the corporation's best interests. Kraft offers his skepticism concerning a confrontational approach to ESA compliance:

> You could take a confrontational approach and say, "OK, go prove it." And, probably the government would have a tough time doing it. But . . . do we want to be in that mode of being in a confrontational approach, and often ending up in legal actions? . . . We believe that a collaborative approach—working out issues, and . . . giving us the kind of long-term predictability [we need]—is far more valuable than being in a constant war (Kraft, 1999).

Competing Belief Systems: Timber Companies and Environmentalists

Cognitive institutions are deeply held belief systems that can contribute to polarized views of business and environmental interests (Hoffman and Ventresca, 1999). They are influential in shaping the interests and values of the different actors in the HCP debate, particularly in the formulation of competing gains (Susskind and Field, 1996). The tension of cognitive institutions is magnified by the conflict between industry and special interest groups that have become increasingly political over time (McGraw, 1984; Ciglar and Loomis, 1986). The environmental groups pressured the government to list the bull trout as a threatened species through legal action. But the interests of these groups were much broader, and they interpret the listing of this "umbrella species" as a proxy, for more restrictive regulation of the large areas of affected habitat. Indeed, the bull trout was a favorite species among environmentalists because of its stringent habitat requirements— by protecting the bull trout, other stream life was sure to benefit. Arlene Montgomery spoke on behalf of Friends of the Wild Swan, one of the parties to the suit:

> We believe this is the biggest endangered-species listing ever. . . . It covers 32 national forests; the spotted owl only covered eight. And there's no single factor that has contributed to the bull trout's decline. It's probably part dams, part road

building, part logging, part grazing, and part development. It could affect a wide range of practices. It really puts everything on the table (*Omaha World-Herald*, 1997).

The notion of placing "everything on the table" obliquely refers to the environmentalists' hope for more stringent species-protection requirements. In this sense the environmental interests are seen as supporting the strictest principles of the ESA, expecting the government to respond in its traditional role of protector. The views of environmental groups are based on broadly held norms and values that reject the perceived exploitation of natural resources by corporations. As with Plum Creek, specific past behaviors contribute to these beliefs. In June 1990, the *Wall Street Journal* called into question the clear-cutting strategies employed by Plum Creek, which left large tracts of land visibly barren. U.S. Representative Rod Chandler (D-WA) characterized Plum Creek's reputation in the timber industry as the "Darth Vader of the State of Washington" (Farney, 1990: 1). To corporations, competition often reinforces the need to emphasize maximum profits over environmental protection. These values often operate at a deep cognitive level. Bob Jirsa, director of corporate and environmental affairs at Plum Creek, offered some insightful reflections when asked about the Darth Vader label:

> Our first reaction was to deny the allegations. We were, after all, operating well within the law, and we had already begun to change our harvest methods. Why should we be singled out from the other companies, the state, and federal government who were using the same practices as Plum Creek? But we gradually realized that this wasn't so much about us as it was about the general public's negative perception of our industry (Jirsa, 1999).

These competing perceptions held by environmentalists and Plum Creek executives reflect the subjective meaning actors apply to cognitive conceptions about the roles of business and government, views about environmental protection and perceptions of the varied particular interests (Levy and Rothenberg, Chapter 7). Attributions are shaped by deeply held preconscious belief systems that are often taken for granted (Zucker, 1983). And they are often reinforced by the regulative elements of the ESA.

Competing Tensions Between the ESA and HCPs

The shift from command-and-control implementation of the ESA to the negotiated implementation of HCPs highlights an underlying political tension in this debate and, therefore, resistance to adoption. The competing rule systems highlight the potential for institutions to serve as both barriers and enablers in the endangered-species debate. Environmental groups favor the strength of ESA regulations, with the government as arbiter of the rules and protector of the environment. However, enforcing the ESA is difficult, and private landowners can tie up the ESA process through protracted legal battles. But HCPs offer the opportunity to challenge the government in the debate over the best science, through negotiation.

The decision to pursue an HCP posed a dilemma for Plum Creek. It could continue to operate under the ESA, which could simplify its timber operation through compliance activities. The HCP would require a huge investment of time and money. The fact that Plum Creek had adopted very strict environmental principles in order to overcome the Darth Vader image minimized the risk of any violations under the ESA and thereby reduced future compliance costs in terms of protracted litigation (Kraft, 1999).

Although compliance with the ESA produces institutional tension it also creates an opportunity to explore other means to approaching these conflicting tensions. A successful HCP negotiation provides greater regulatory certainty than one could expect under the ESA. The success of the Cascades HCP offered Plum Creek hope that its working relationship with the government would prove more effective than the traditional forms of command-and-control regulatory confrontation.

The Normative Debate Over "Best Science"

The debate over the "best science" is at the core of the controversy over HCPs as an emerging institutional form. Under Section 10(a)(1)(B) of the ESA, the government is required to implement the "best science" when evaluating a proposed HCP. Environmental groups tend to favor the science that provides the most conservative and restrictive approach to the habitat. Private landowners seek to find scientific solutions that permit development activities. The government is left in the middle, relying on reports and evaluations performed by independent experts. But in this positioning of scientific opinions, science is often not free of the politics that govern the policy process, and opinions are often clouded by value judgments (Jasanoff, 1990).

The ultimate decision to pursue the Bull Trout HCP represented an institutional shift from the regulative premises of the ESA to a highly normative approach that included debates over science. Lorin Hicks described the scientific approach as one that produced a "technically credible plan that [was] legally defensible and operationally feasible" (Hicks, 1999). Following the "best science wins" principle, Plum Creek began producing technical papers to document the findings of its bull trout surveys and research. Plum Creek management recognized that strategies that were normatively sanctioned were more likely to be adopted (DiMaggio and Powell, 1983). The debate over the "best science" was shaped by the biologists, environmental attorneys, and policy makers who devised the ontological frameworks, developed typologies, and established guidelines (Scott and Backman, 1990).

The new normative framework of HCPs expanded the realm of debate considerably. According to Lorin Hicks, "We had to look at that decision from a legal standpoint, a business standpoint and a biology standpoint" (Hicks, 1999). By employing a team of its own biologists (led by Hicks), Plum Creek recognized the potential for change by engaging in these broader debates and thereby shaping the behaviors of timber companies and other private landowners affected by the Endangered Species Act. Thus science became the legitimating or framing device (Hirsch, 1986; Scott, 1995), and it served to both constrain and empower the behavior of the actors in the negotiation.

TACTICS OF THE INSTITUTIONAL ENTREPRENEUR

Neo-institutional conceptions of change are generally associated with "isomorphism" (DiMaggio and Powell, 1983). Organizations and other actors adapt to the environment through "co-optation," a coping mechanism (Selznick, 1949). Critics of the traditional view have argued that although the organization may adapt to the environment, the changes it makes in response may simply result in an environment shaped by the organization (Perrow, 1986). Furthermore, Powell and DiMaggio (1991) argue that we know little about how skillful entrepreneurs put multiple "institutional logics" to strategic use. The Plum Creek case study offers insights into the strategies employed by firms acting as institutional entrepreneurs. Organizations do not always conform to institutional pressures; sometimes they alter the institutional environment to reach their strategic objectives. Plum Creek's strategies for timber harvesting and bull trout protection were decided within the confines of the firm, but were also developed in concert with constituents outside the firm and within the organizational field.

Our conception of the institutional entrepreneur exhibits characteristics present in the economic view of the entrepreneur—a risk-taking and innovative firm seeking competitive advantage in a dynamic environment (Schumpeter, 1949). In this context, entrepreneurs represent a small number of firms who learn by doing and whose actions shape technology and policy cycles (Tushman, Anderson, and

O'Reilly, 1997). Further, in an effort to link behaviors to the individual firm, our notion of the institutional entrepreneur extends beyond industry-level perspectives such as risk and innovation to include management style and strategy. Stevenson (1983: 3) described the entrepreneur as an opportunistic promoter (in contrast to managers that act as administrators and trustees) seeking "opportunity without regard to resources currently controlled." HCPs offer an alternative to managing timber company resources and present a new set of risks and challenges. Only certain firms, entrepreneurial in nature, will "seek to differentiate through innovation and gain competitive advantage from opportunities in environmental strategies" (Hoffman and others, 2002). In this sense HCPs are a necessary but insufficient condition to enable institutional change, requiring the active support of the institutional entrepreneur (see Morrill and Owen-Smith, Chapter 4)—in this case, Plum Creek.

Plum Creek used four strategies in an effort to alter its institutional context: the greater exchange of information within the institutional field; the effective use of integrative solutions such as strategic partnerships; the active management of innovative alternatives in the development of a potentially new dominant designs; and the balancing of efforts to create and claim value.

Institutional Entrepreneurs: Building Networks and Managing Information

Institutional entrepreneurs recognize the institutional barriers to agreement and seek to carefully manage the prospects for change by engaging field-level debate. Plum Creek created a negotiation nexus within the institutional field in an effort to shape and reframe the dialogue with new types of information, and to foster development of collaborative partnerships and "winning coalitions" around its proposals (Lax and Sebenius, 1986). At the policy level, agency, industry, and environmental representatives engaged in a debate over how to balance the commercial management of forest resources with endangered species protection. At the project level, Plum Creek and the government negotiated specific agreements, such as the Cascades and Bull Trout HCPs. A tension exists between these two levels of activity and within the institutional context created by the ESA and HCPs. Plum Creek recognized that the parties in the policy debate—including environmentalists, politicians and government agents, industry representatives, and other particular interests—were essential to the legitimization of HCPs. This larger conception of the field highlights the importance of coalitions beyond the project level and confirms that the minimum winning coalition for a successful multiparty negotiation requires a broader consensus (Raiffa, 1982; Thompson, 2001).

Aldrich and Fiol (1994) suggest that entrepreneurs in emerging environments should pursue innovative strategies to gain legitimacy and transform institutional environments. Plum Creek actively engaged in a strategy to exchange information as part of a collective marketing and lobbying effort. It developed a CD-ROM that contained thirteen technical reports and four white papers providing research on the bull trout habitat. Labeled by some as "Plum Creek Science" (Koch, 1999), this research was habitat specific, peer reviewed and intended to form the building blocks of the HCP. During the negotiation, Plum Creek and the government contacted nearly seventy organizations (U.S. Fish and Wildlife Service and others, 2000), recognizing that any negotiation would also have to withstand the scrutiny of public input, including the well-coordinated efforts of multiple environmental groups. The government documented a total of 150 meetings, 110 letters and written communications, and 130 phone calls with agencies, tribes, and special interest groups (U.S. Fish and Wildlife Service and others, 2000). Infusing information into the network of actors increases opportunities for negotiated settlement in formalized environmental mediation (Morrill and Owen-Smith, Chapter 4).

Acting as an institutional entrepreneur, Plum Creek saw how it could enhance regulatory certainty by promoting a network of relationships in the broader institutional field rather than navigate a hierarchy characterized by old, complex, and conflicting rule regimes. The sharing of information in this network was guided by the norm of reciprocity rather than administrative fiat (Powell, 1990).

Institutional Entrepreneurs: Expanding the Opportunities for Agreement

Plum Creek actively sought a collaborative solution to overcome the deeply held belief that the interests of business and government were not compatible. Bazerman (1983) labels this assumption the "mythical fixed pie"—the inability of negotiators to find mutually beneficial trades when constrained by the myth that their interests are incompatible. The mythical fixed pie is particularly acute in an environmental context due to the historic mistrust and antagonism between parties (Bazerman and Hoffman, 1999).

Plum Creek viewed the opportunity to formalize an interorganizational relationship (IOR) with government as an integrating solution, rather than another complex layer of bureaucracy. Secretary of the Interior Bruce Babbitt described HCPs as "creative partnerships," but traditional conceptions of institutions may obscure such collaborative meaning. IORs typically describe strategic alliances, joint ventures, partnerships, and networks (Oliver, 1990). Whereas HCP agreements are delimited contractual agreements between business and government interests and involve specific monitoring and reporting requirements, these emerging regulatory forms take on the character of an IOR as distinguished from traditional regulative institutions. The HCP process also provides for public participation, enabling particular interests of citizens to provide comments during two distinct phases.

Ring and Van de Ven (1994) describe a process framework for cooperative IORs, where the goal is to establish and maintain continued interaction in an exchange relationship within the field where conditions for uncertainty are present. We believe these characteristics must be present in the ideal conception of an HCP. Jim Kraft described the philosophy behind adaptive management as a collaborative IOR: "We will use our best knowledge, models and best science and design experiments. . . . then you make feedback loops, you adjust your plan as you learn, so that the plan changes incrementally. Is there a leap of faith on both sides? Sure, but what's the alternative?" (Kraft, 1999).

The collaborative agreement or IOR available through HCPs represents a significant visible means that certain constituents within the field intend to challenge the fixed pie assumption. The "creative partnership" model enabled the Plum Creek HCP to become a forum for beneficial trades in which the parties can actively bargain over competing needs for regulatory certainty and environmental flexibility. This was evident in the conservation commitments agreed to by Plum Creek to address a range of challenges, including the number of species covered, the connectivity of impacted waterways, and adaptive monitoring needs (U.S. Fish and Wildlife Service and others, 2000). The Kareiva Report hinted at the potential for trades: "HCPs have economic, political, and scientific dimensions. Because HCPs represent negotiated compromises, it is essential to know what exactly is 'given up' in the process of arriving at a compromise" (Kareiva and others, 1999: 7).

Institutional Entrepreneurs: Managers of Innovation

Plum Creek demonstrated a willingness to move beyond the coercive influences of the regulative regime and shun isomorphic adaptation with respect to its timber management practices. Innovative firms must be "ambidextrous" in balancing existing and new technologies in order to influence dominant designs (Tushman, Anderson, and O'Reilly, 1997). Whereas the concept of dominant designs has been used to describe organizational evolution (Abernathy and Utterback,

1978; Tushman and Murman, 1998), most of the literature has focused on the design of product technologies and their relationship to organizational outcomes. But we see the extension of certain concepts of dominant designs to the HCP institutional context as a regulatory variant.

Tushman and Murman (1998) suggest that dominant designs evolve as a result of institutional forces moderated by both economic constraints and technological capabilities. These designs lie behind the technological frontier and emerge through a sequence of compromise and accommodation that occurs between powerful alliances. In this context, the HCP emerges as a potential new design incorporating "best science" through the process of negotiating mutual gains rather than the parties following the mimetic forces of promulgated science. If so, Plum Creek and the government can be seen as innovators building coalitions with particular interests to develop the best conservation technology for the habitat.

Anderson and Tushman (1990) demonstrated that dominant designs are influenced by technology cycles emerging more powerfully from eras of ferment rather than periods of incremental change. Given the dramatic rise of HCPs in recent years, this may signal that a current era of ferment will give rise to a new dominant design as standards and expectations converge. Thus dominant design and institutionalization merge. Although dominant designs can only be known in retrospect, understanding their potential may provide managers with opportunities to shape the character of new technological advances (Tushman and O'Reilly, 1997; Tushman and Murman, 1998). During negotiation, striving for a new dominant design offers both individual and organizational actors the perspective of an enduring, rather than an inertial, institution.

Institutional Entrepreneurs: Balancing
Efforts to Create and Claim Value

Plum Creek saw the Bull Trout HCP as an opportunity to lead the negotiation process by embracing the scientific norms supported by HCPs. Institutions can create barriers to a negotiated agreement, but they can also adapt to better serve the interests of actors in the organizational field. The creation of HCP agreements serves to diffuse the command-and-control approach, but their application also shifts institutional power among constituents within the field, particularly as actors assess what is considered the "best science" of endangered species protection. This power shift highlights the role of the government as a facilitator rather than the arbiter of rules. Because institutions are linked by the logic of appropriateness where promulgated rules are selected, matched, and interpreted within the demands of the position held by varied actors (March and Olsen, 1989), this shift has powerful implications for the actors within the field. It creates further dynamism when much of the policy debate is grounded in science, where "American regulatory decision-making highlights uncertainty, polarizes scientific opinion, and prevents efficient resolution of disputes about risk" (Jasanoff, 1990: 8).

By both responding to and influencing the institutional context, Plum Creek is simultaneously creating and claiming value (Lax and Sebenius, 1986). Its leadership efforts to promote the "best science" through an HCP provided an opportunity to create value by identifying alternatives that improved species protection and produced greater regulatory flexibility. Kraft (1999) offered the following observation on creating value: "There are a lot of win-win solutions here that don't necessarily cost you a lot of money. You can protect environmental values and still manage your business. That's what is attractive about an HCP: it creates a framework to do these kinds of things."

Although Plum Creek's leadership supported the creation of value by enlarging the pie of resources, the pursuit of "best science" may be seen as a threat by some government and environmental interests. Taking the lead and promoting best science risks creating a perceived asymmetry of information and thus being viewed as disproportionately distributive, an attempt to claim too much value. Cooperative efforts to create value often vie with competitive moves to claim value (Lax and Sebenius, 1986). In this context the debate over endangered species protection cannot be seen within the field as merely shifting power from government to industry. Rather, for institutional entrepreneurs like Plum Creek to succeed, it must demonstrate that collaborative designs such as HCPs are not unreasonably distributive but serve as better dispute resolution systems because reconciling interests is less costly and more effective than determining who is right (Ury, Brett, and Goldberg, 1993). Ultimately the evolution of an enhanced habitat and the recovery of the species will determine best science, but the legitimacy of HCPs will rely on institutional entrepreneurs that are skillful at balancing efforts to create and claim value.

CONCLUSION

This chapter highlights three themes: ideas that negotiation research brings to institutional theory, ideas that institutional theory brings to negotiation research, and ideas that social science brings to important societal problems such as endangered species protection.

The Study of Negotiation Can Contribute to Institutional Theory

Institutional change is both a source and a product of organizational action, and institutional entrepreneurs can alter the forums within which organizations may align and produce organizational action. The traditional focus on isomorphism within institutional analyses has drawn criticism for the theory's inability to explain the concept of organizational change (DiMaggio, 1988; Brint and Karabel, 1991; Hirsch, 1997; Hirsch and Lounsbury, 1997; Hoffman, 1999). But we argue that change is brought about by the concerted efforts of individual organizations that exercise strategic action. This fosters and shapes nascent institutions within the field. We explained one case study in which an organization challenged the prevailing rules of the game and employed political strategies to move from zero-sum conflict to mixed-motive collaboration. Organization-level action and institution-level analysis can be influenced by the institutional entrepreneur. Quoting other experts on the subject, we have highlighted specific tactics and strategies available broadly to the institutional entrepreneur who desires to effect change.

Institutional Theory as a Contribution to the Study of Negotiation

Traditional negotiation literature has tended to look at barriers to negotiation largely from psychological perspectives (Neale and Bazerman, 1991; Arrow and others, 1995; Ross and Ward, 1995; Thompson, 2001). The behavioral decision research in negotiation over the last twenty years has been dominated by a cognitive perspective focusing on how and why negotiation actors deviate from a rational model. But this has ignored key social and contextual variables (Bazerman, Curhan, and Moore, 2000). The Plum Creek HCP negotiation highlights the need to consider institutional barriers to negotiation. Behaviors in an environmental forum occur at multiple levels by engaging individual actors, organizations, interest groups, and the polity at large (Bazerman and Hoffman, 1999). As organizations are embedded in larger institutional environments, where social customs, practices, and beliefs influence organizational practices (Powell and DiMaggio, 1991), we argue that institutional analysis allows a better understanding of negotiation strategies. However, one of the strengths of the negotiation field over the last decade has been its ability to turn descriptive research into useful techniques. We think institutional analysis has primarily been a descriptive area of research; for it to have greater impact, it should shift in a prescriptively useful direction (Ehrenfeld, Chapter 19). We have suggested one way to do so in this chapter. We believe institutional theory can help players recognize the barriers to and enablers of change. This allows institutional theory to be used to reframe negotiations, because the players will better understand the underlying tensions and strategies.

Social Science as a Contributor to Understanding Environmental Issues

We have highlighted the importance of institutional and negotiations frameworks in analyzing social challenges such as endangered species protection. We have framed the debate around the concept of a negotiation nexus taking place within a field of actors, each presenting particular vested interests. Where the government has traditionally been viewed as the arbiter of rules within the economy (Skocpol, 1985), we suggest that the state and the economy are interdependent. The state is an actor within the organizational field, albeit usually a more powerful one than the companies it regulates. Given that all involved actors are constrained by the scientific and political uncertainties for managing environmental protection and endangered species protection, the government is subject to the same institutional forces as industry and environmental groups, and therefore must operate within the confines and limitations of field-level dynamics. This argues for a new image of the regulator, not as the dictator of standards based on data and analysis that it lacks (Mylonadis, Chapter 16), but as an actor that engages all other parties in collaboratively resolving social conflicts.

In this process, the role of the firm becomes transformed as well. Competitive and environmental strategy involves a co-alteration of the corporation's strategy and its institutional environment (Hoffman, 2000). The two are related. The organizational field may create restraints on organizational activity, but the individual agency creates opportunities for altering the form of those external pressures. Environmental strategy is driven by demands that emerge from within the organizational field and are embodied within the organizational structure and strategy of the firm. Similarly, a self-directed strategy may emerge from within the organization, but its success will require an alteration of the organizational field of which it is a part. The negotiation literature helps us illuminate ways to do this and describes the managerial skills needed.

REFERENCES

Abernathy, William, and James Utterback. 1978. "Patterns of Industrial Innovation." *Technology Review,* 80: 40–47.

Aldrich, Howard E., and C. Marlene Fiol. 1994. "Fools Rush In? The Institutional Context of Industry Creation." *Academy of Management Review,* 19(4): 645–670.

Anderson, Philip, and Michael L. Tushman. 1990. "Technological Discontinuities and Dominant Designs: A Cyclical Model of Technological Change." *Administrative Science Quarterly,* 35: 604–633.

Arrow, Kenneth, Robert Mnookin, Lee Ross, Amos Tversky, and Robert Wilson, eds., 1995. *Barriers to Conflict Resolution.* New York: Norton.

Baden, John. 1995, "The Adverse Consequences of the ESA." *Seattle Times,* Oct. 25: B5.

Bader, Mike. 1998. "Bull Trout Victory! Conservation Groups Win Bull Trout Listing as a Threatened Species Under the Endangered Species Act!" Press Release: June 11.

Bazerman, Max. 1983. "Negotiator Judgment: A Critical Look at the Rationality Assumption." *American Behavioral Scientist,* 27, 618–634.

Bazerman, Max. 1998. *Judgment in Managerial Decision Making.* New York: Wiley.

Bazerman, Max, and Andrew J. Hoffman. 1999. "Sources of Environmentally Destructive Behavior: Individual, Organizational and Institutional Perspectives." *Research in Organizational Behavior,* 21: 39–79.

Bazerman, Max, Jared Curhan, and Don Moore. 2000. "The Death and Rebirth of the Social Psychology of Negotiation." In Garth Fletcher and Margaret Clark, eds., *Blackwell Handbook of Social Psychology: Interpersonal Processes,* 196–228. Oxford, England: Blackwell.

Brint, Steven, and Jerome Karabel. 1991. "Institutional Origins and Transformations: The Case of American Community Colleges." In Walter W. Powell and Paul J. DiMaggio, eds., *The New Institutionalism in Organizational Analysis,* 337–360. Chicago: University of Chicago Press.

Ciglar, Alan J., and Burdett A. Loomis. 1986. "The Changing Nature of Interest Group Politics." In Alan J. Ciglar and Burdett A. Loomis, eds., *Interest Group Politics,* 1–26. Washington, DC: Congressional Quarterly.

Crismon, Sandra. 1998. "Pender County, North Carolina, Red-Cockaded Woodpecker Habitat Conservation Plan and Safe Harbor." In *Improving Integrated Natural Resource Planning: Habitat Conservation Plans,* National Center for Environmental Decision-Making Research.

DiMaggio, Paul. 1988. "Interest and Agency in Institutional Theory." In Lynne Zucker, ed. *Institutional Patterns and Organizations,* 3–21. Cambridge: Ballinger.

DiMaggio, Paul. 1991. "Constructing an Organizational Field as a Professional Project: US Art Museums, 1920–1940." In Walter W. Powell and Paul J. DiMaggio, eds., *The New Institutionalism in Organizational Analysis,* 267–292. Chicago: University of Chicago.

DiMaggio, Paul, and Walter W. Powell. 1983. "The Iron Cage Revisited: Institutional Isomorphism and Collective Rationality in Organizational Fields." *American Sociological Review,* 48: 147–160.

Douglas, Mary. 1986. *How Institutions Think.* Syracuse, NY: Syracuse University Press.

Durbin, Kathie. 1997. "Timber's Bad Boy Comes to the Table." *High Country,* 29(14): 15–17.

Farney, Dennis. 1990. "Unkindest Cut? Timber Firm Stirs Ire Felling Forests Faster Than They Can Regenerate." *Wall Street Journal,* June 18: A1.

Fiorino, Daniel. 1999. "Rethinking Environmental Regulation: Perspectives on Law and Governance." *Harvard Environmental Law Review,* 23(2), 441–469.

Fligstein, Neil. 1990. *The Transformation of Corporate Control.* Cambridge, MA: Harvard University Press.

Fligstein, Neil. 1991. "The Structural Transformation of American Industry: An Institutional Account of the Causes of Diversification in the Largest Firms: 1919–1979." In Walter W. Powell and Paul J. DiMaggio, eds., *The New Institutionalism in Organizational Analysis,* 311–336. Chicago: University of Chicago Press.

Fligstein, Neil. 1997. "Social Skill and Institutional Theory." *American Behavioral Scientist,* 40(4): 397–405.

Giddens, Anthony. 1979. *Central Problems in Social Theory: Action, Structure, and Contradiction in Social Analysis.* Berkeley: University of California Press.

Granovetter, Mark. 1973. "The Strength of Weak Ties." *American Journal of Sociology,* 78: 1360–1380.

Greenwood, Royston, and C. R. Hinings. 1996. "Understanding Radical Organizational Change: Bringing Together the Old and the New Institutionalism." *Academy of Management Review,* 21(4): 1022–1054.

Hannan, Michael T., and John Freeman. 1989. *Organizational Ecology.* Cambridge, MA: Harvard University Press.

Hicks, Lorin. 1999. Director of Fish and Wildlife Resources, Plum Creek Timber, May 13 Interview.

Hirsch, Paul. 1986. "From Ambushes to Golden Parachutes: Corporate Takeovers as an Instance of Cultural Framing and Institutional Integration." *American Journal of Sociology,* 91(4): 800–837.

Hirsch, Paul. 1997. "Sociology Without Social Structure: Neo-Institutional Theory Meets Brave New World." *American Journal of Sociology,* 102(6): 1702–1723.

Hirsch, Paul, and Michael Lounsbury. 1997. "Ending the Family Quarrel: Toward a Reconciliation of 'Old' and 'New' Institutionalisms." *American Behavioral Scientist,* 40(4): 406–418.

Hoffman, Andrew J. 1999. "Institutional Evolution and Change: Environmentalism and the U.S. Chemical Industry." *Academy of Management Journal,* 42(4): 351–371.

Hoffman, Andrew J. 2000. *Competitive Environmental Strategy: A Guide to the Changing Business Landscape.* Washington, DC: Island Press.

Hoffman, Andrew J., and Marc J. Ventresca. 1999. "The Institutional Framing of Policy Debates: Economics Versus the Environment." *American Behavioral Scientist,* 42(8): 1368–1392.

Hoffman, Andrew, Hannah Riley, John Troast, Jr., and Max Bazerman. 2002. "Cognitive and Institutional Barriers to New Forms of Cooperation on Environmental Protection: Insights from Project XL and Habitat Conservation Plans." *American Behavioral Scientist,* 45(5): 820–845.

Hoffman, Andrew, James Gillespie, Don Moore, Kimberly Wade-Benzoni, Leigh Thompson and Max Bazerman. 1999. "A Mixed-Motive Perspective on the Economics Versus Environment Debate." *American Behavioral Scientist,* 42(8): 1254–1276.

Holm, Petter. 1995. "The Dynamics of Institutionalization: Transformation Processes in Norwegian Fisheries." *Administrative Science Quarterly,* 40: 398–422.

Jasanoff, Sheila. 1990. *The Fifth Branch.* Cambridge, MA: Harvard University Press.

Jirsa, Bob. 1999. Director of corporate and environmental affairs, Plum Creek Timber, May 13 interview.

Jostrom, Mike. 1999. Bull Trout Project Manager, Plum Creek Timber, May 10 interview.

Kareiva, Peter, Sandy Andelman, Daniel Doak, Bret Elderd, Martha Groom, Jonathan Hoekstra, Laura Hook, Frances James, John Lamoreux, Gretchen LeBuhn, Charles McCulluch, James Regetz, Lisa Savage, Mary Ruckelshaus, David Skelly, Henry Wilbur, Kelly Zamudio, and the National Center for Ecological Analysis and Synthesis HCP Working Group. 1999. *Using Science in Habitat Conservation Plans.* Washington, DC: American Institute of Biological Studies.

Keltner, Dacher, and Robert Robinson. 1993. "Imagined Ideological Differences in Conflict Escalation and Resolution." *International Journal of Conflict Management,* 4: 249–262.

Koch, Ted. 1999. Lead negotiator, Fish & Wildlife Service in the Plum Creek NFHCP case. May 14 interview.

Kostyack, John. 1997. *Reshaping Habitat Conservation Plans for Species Recovery: An Introduction to a Series of Articles on Habitat Conservation Plans.* Symposium on Habitat Conservation Plans, Northwestern School of Law of Lewis and Clark College, Environmental Law.

Kraatz, Matthew, and Edward Zajac. 1996. "Exploring the Limits of the New Institutionalism: The Causes and Consequences of Illegitimate Organizational Change." *American Sociological Review,* 61: 812–836.

Kraft, Jim. 1999. General counsel and secretary, Plum Creek Timber, May 13 interview.

Lawrence, Thomas. 1999. "Institutional Strategy." *Journal of Management,* 25(2): 161–188.

Lax, David, and James Sebenius. 1986. *The Manager as Negotiator.* New York: Free Press.

March, James, and Johan Olsen. 1989. *Rediscovering Institutions: The Organizational Bias of Politics.* New York: Free Press.

McGraw, Thomas. 1984. "Business and Government: The Origins of the Adversary Relationship." *California Management Review,* 26(2): 33–52.

Neale, Margaret, and Max H. Bazerman. 1991. *Cognition and Rationality in Negotiation.* New York: Free Press.

Oliver, Christine. 1990. "Determinants of Interorganizational Relationships: Integration and Future Designs." *Academy of Management Review,* 15(2): 241–265.

Oliver, Christine. 1991. "Strategic Responses to Institutional Processes." *Academy of Management Review,* 16: 145–179.

Omaha World-Herald. December 29, 1997. "Bull Trout Highlights Difficulty of Getting 'Endangered' Status." Page 2.

Ostrom, Elinor. 1999. "Institutional Rational Choice: An Assessment of the Institutional Analysis and Development Framework." In P. A. Sabatier, ed. *Theories of the Policy Process,* 35–71. Boulder, CO: Westview Press.

Perrow, Charles. 1986. *Complex Organizations: A Critical Essay.* New York: Random House.

Plum Creek Timber Company. 1997. *Annual Report.*

Powell, Walter. 1990. "Neither Market Nor Hierarchy: Network Forms of Organization." *Research in Organizational Behavior,* 12: 295–336.

Powell, Walter, and Paul J. DiMaggio, eds. 1991. *The New Institutionalism in Organizational Analysis.* Chicago: University of Chicago Press.

Pruitt, Dean, and Steven A. Lewis. 1975. "Development of Integrative Solutions in Bilateral Negotiation." *Journal of Personality and Social Psychology,* 31: 621–630.

Raiffa, Howard. 1982. *The Art and Science of Negotiation.* Cambridge, MA: Harvard University Press.

Ring, Peter S., and Andrew H. Van de Ven. 1994. "Developmental Processes of Cooperative Interorganizational Relationships." *Academy of Management Journal,* 191: 90–118.

Ross, Lee, and Andrew Ward. 1995. "Psychological Barriers to Dispute Resolution." *Advances in Experimental Social Psychology,* 27: 255–303.

Sabel, Charles, Archon Fung, and Bradley Karkkainen. 1999. "Beyond Backyard Environmentalism: How Communities Are Quietly Refashioning Environmental Regulation." *Boston Review,* 24(5): 4–11.

Schumpeter, Joseph A. 1949. *The Theory of Economic Development.* Cambridge, MA: Harvard University Press.

Scott, W. Richard. 1991. "Unpacking Institutional Arguments." In Walter W. Powell and Paul J. DiMaggio, eds., *The New Institutionalism in Organizational Analysis,* 164–182. Chicago: University of Chicago Press.

Scott, W. Richard. 1995. *Institutions and Organizations.* London: Sage.

Scott, W. Richard, and Elaine Backman. 1990. "Institutional Theory and the Medical Care Sector." In Stephen Mick, ed., *Innovations in Health Care Delivery: Insights for Organizational Theory.* San Francisco: Jossey-Bass.

Selznick, Philip. 1949. *TVA and the Grass Roots.* Berkeley: University of California Press.

Selznick, Philip. 1957. *Leadership in Administration.* Berkeley: University of California Press.

Skocpol, Theda. 1985. "Bringing the State Back In: Strategies of Analysis in Current Research." In P. Evans, D. Rueschemeyer, and T. Skocpol, eds., *Strategies of Analysis in Current Research,* 3–43. New York: Cambridge University Press.

Stevenson, Howard. 1983. *A Perspective on Entrepreneurship.* Harvard Business School Note # 384–131. Revised August 23, 1988.

Susskind, Lawrence, and Patrick T. Field. 1996. *Dealing With an Angry Public: The Mutual Gains Approach to Resolving Disputes.* New York: Free Press.

Susskind, Lawrence, Paul Levy, and Jennifer Thomas-Larmer. 1999. *Negotiating Environmental Agreements: How to Avoid Escalating Confrontation, Needless Costs and Unnecessary Litigation.* Washington, DC: Island Press.

Thompson, Leigh. 1991. "Information Exchange in Negotiation." *Journal of Experimental Social Psychology,* 27: 161–179.

Thompson, Leigh. 1995. "'They Saw a Negotiation': Partisanship and Involvement in Negotiations." *Journal of Personality and Social Psychology,* 68: 839–853.

Thompson, Leigh. 2001. *The Mind and Heart of the Negotiator, 2nd ed.* Upper Saddle River, NJ: Prentice Hall.

Tushman, Michael, and Johann Peter Murman. 1998. "Dominant Designs, Technology Cycles, and Organizational Outcomes." *Research in Organizational Behavior,* 20: 231–266.

Tushman, Michael, and Charles O'Reilly. 1997. *Winning Through Innovation: A Practical Guide to Leading Organizational Change and Renewal.* Boston: Harvard Business School Press.

Tushman, Michael, Philip Anderson, and Charles O'Reilly. 1997. "Technology Cycles, Innovation Streams, and Ambidextrous Organizations: Organizational Renewal Through Innovation Streams and Strategic Change. In Michael Tushman and Philip Anderson, eds., *Managing Strategic Innovation Streams,* 3–23. New York: Oxford University Press.

U.S. Department of the Interior Fish and Wildlife Service. 1999. *Status of Habitat Conservation Plans.* Washington, DC: U.S. Government Printing Office.

U.S. Department of the Interior Fish and Wildlife Service, U.S. Department of Commerce National Marine Fisheries Service, Plum Creek Timber Company, Inc., and CH2M Hill. Sept. 2000. *Final Environmental Impact Statement and Native Fish Habitat Conservation Plan: Proposed Permit for Taking of Federally Listed Native Fish Species on Plum Creek Timber Company, Inc. Lands.*

Ury, William, Jeanne Brett, and Stephen Goldberg. 1993. *Getting Disputes Resolved: Designing Systems to Cut the Cost of Conflict.* 2nd ed. San Francisco: Jossey-Bass.

Westneat, Danny. June 26, 1996. "Logging That Will Protect Wildlife?" *The Seattle Times,* B1.

White, Harrison. 1992. *Identity and Control: A Structural Theory of Social Interaction.* Princeton, NJ: Princeton University Press.

Zucker, Lynne. 1983. "Organizations as Institutions." In S. Bacharach, ed., *Research in the Sociology of Organizations,* 1–47. Greenwich, CT: JAI.

11

CHANGING SHADES OF GREEN:
COUPLING AND DECOUPLING IN MONSANTO'S
ENVIRONMENTAL ORIENTATIONS, 1991–1997

M. Anjali Sastry, Jeffrey W. Bernicke, and Stuart L. Hart

Nowhere have organizations faced stronger pressures to adopt new behaviors or forms than in the ecological domain. Recent decades have seen industrial firms compelled, in one way or another, to appear "green" and to incorporate ecological considerations into their management. In the process, firms have had to address multiple stakeholders, uncertain science, potentially difficult organizational changes, and shifting performance standards. Such challenges offer an ideal situation in which to explore how organizations respond to institutional change in a complex arena. Widespread recognition that firms cannot become green overnight suggests that it can be difficult for them to respond to ecological imperatives. Yet little research has sought to understand the shift toward environmental management as an ongoing, evolving process in firms that seek legitimacy in the ecological domain.

Institutional theory provides us with an ideal starting point for such an endeavor. In particular, we look to four elements of the institutional approach to understanding organizations in the context of their settings. First, an emerging tradition of research into organizational responses to institutional pressures offers a typology that we draw on to classify observed behaviors. Second, institutional theorists' distinction between the task environment and the institutional domain provides us with ideas to explore and affords a lens for categorizing observations'. Third, institutional theorists recognize that symbolic acts and publicly used labels and language are important features of the organization's interaction with its institutional environment, which suggests that formal communications are valuable data sources. And fourth, the field's early history of longitudinal case studies (such as Zald and Denton, 1963; Selznick, 1966) points to the importance of studying change over time in the relationship between organization and environment.

Building on all four elements of institutional theory, in this chapter we explore evolution over time at the interface between one firm and its stakeholders. We define this interface as the firm's public reporting to its internal and external stakeholders. Our goal is to illuminate changes in the domains addressed at this interface and to suggest what these shifts might mean for both theory and practice. We show how one organization attempts to project an image into the institutional environment and how conflicts between that image and its task environment drive the evolution of that organization. Whereas Troast and others (Chapter 10) discuss the tactics used by one firm to influence the process elements of the field, in this chapter we focus on the image or reputation of one firm.

The firm we study is Monsanto, a Fortune 500 chemical company founded at the turn of the last century. Although the firm's roots were in the chemicals industry, like several of its competitors, Monsanto also had operations in biotechnology, agricultural products (such as seeds), and pharmaceuticals. By the late 1980s, the chemical industry as a whole faced increasing institutional pressure to publish Corporate Environmental Reports (CERs), public documents disclosing a firm's environmental performance and presenting its strategies to improve future performance. This led Monsanto and most of its competitors to begin producing CERs in the early 1990s. The adoption of CERs, however, tells only part of the story. As we show, the decision to publish the documents initiated an unfolding process that played out over time.

Through content analysis of Monsanto's published CERs, we investigate the firm's presentation of its environmental practices, performance, and goals over a seven-year period starting in 1991. Our goal is exploratory: to document and examine the changes that play out over time. In doing so, we examine institutional theory's predictions about firm responses to pressures to change. In particular, we draw on the distinction between the technical or task domain on the one hand and the institutional arena on the other. We assess the push toward green or environmental management in light of the theory, leading us to investigate decoupling—the notion that firms adopt new behaviors, practices, or forms ritually or ceremonially in order to stave off institutional pressures to change at a more fundamental level. Decoupling is not only a theoretical prediction: environmentalist critics have argued that chemical firms, oil companies, and others engaged in "greenwashing," particularly during the 1990s (Staubler and Rampton, 1995; Tokar, 1997; Beder, 1998; Greer and Bruno, 1998; Fagin, Lavelle, and Center for Public Integrity, 1999).

To explore both sets of ideas, we look for evidence of the decoupled response and explore and explain other responses we discover.

INSTITUTIONAL AND TECHNICAL DOMAINS
IN ORGANIZATIONAL RESPONSES TO PRESSURE

As the cognitive, normative, and regulative structures and activities that give stability and meaning to organizational actions (Scott 1992), institutions offer organizations "rationalized concepts of organizational work" that are instituted in society (Meyer and Rowan, 1977). Eventually these forms and practices become "infuse[d] with value beyond the technical requirements of the task at hand" (Selznick, 1957: 17). This symbolic value, institutional theory contends, explains the adoption of new practices that confer social legitimacy (Meyer and Rowan, 1977).

In contrast, practices that emerge in the technical or task domain are connected to the operations and activities central to the firm's business. In this domain, organizations rely on routines, norms, identities, and histories that are derived from and promote technical efficiency. Such routines make it easier for the organization to perform its work, signal reliability and continuity, and bolster technical effectiveness.

The differences between institutionally mandated behaviors and the demands of technical-economic rationality generate conflicting forces (DiMaggio and Powell, 1991; Palmer, Jennings, and Zhou, 1993). Organizations may struggle to adopt a legitimate but difficult-to-implement form or practice. One resolution is to undertake a symbolic adoption that involves separating structural elements from internal activities, mounting external displays of confidence, and inviting ceremonial inspection to protect core operations from external scrutiny (Thompson, 1967; Meyer and Rowan, 1977). Thus organizations buffer their cores by preventing new forms or practices from permeating the organization. The result is to decouple institutionally determined structures from the technical requirements of the task environment (Selznick, 1957; Thompson, 1967; Meyer and Rowan, 1977). Meyer and Rowan implied that decoupling is inevitable—that its converse, close alignment between institutionally demanded change and the organization's technical systems, harms organizations because it "merely makes public a record of inefficiency and inconsistency" (1977).

As institutional theorists have come to recognize (Scott, 1995), exploring the conflict between technical requirements and institutional pressures provides a fruitful starting point for examining organizational responses to shifts in external environments. For instance, Oliver added the notion of agency to explain that firms strategically choose to decouple when conditions are appropriate (1991). Building on this and other work, an emerging body of research sketches a complex picture of the determinants of organizational responses to institutional pressures. In some cases, differences in the adopted institutions or in the institutional field result in different patterns of institutionalization (such as Orrù, Biggart, and Hamilton, 1991; Davis and Greve, 1997). Even within the same institutional field and within a single institution, organizations differ in their adoptions because of imperfect copying (DiMaggio and Powell, 1983), varying interactions with local institutions and the public sphere (Selznick, 1966; Covaleski and Dirsmith, 1988; Edelman, 1990), or inherent organizational attributes such as size, embedded capabilities, and identity (Edelman, 1992; Goodstein, 1994; Westphal, Gulati, and Shortell, 1997; Fox-Wolfgramm, Boal, and Hunt, 1998).

Important questions remain, however. The notion that organizations shape institutions and the institutional setting even as they are shaped by them emerges as an important theme in recent work. Scott, for example, reminds us that the technical environment is itself grounded in the institutional, and so the two domains cannot be assumed to always conflict (1995: 130). Yet empirical work has shed little light on how the interactions between the technical and the institutional play out over time in organizations' responses to institutional pressures. Critics argue that one reason for the shortcoming is that existing models of institutionalization as a process are underdeveloped (Barley and Tolbert, 1997). Little research has focused on the dynamics of ongoing interactions between organization and institutional environment; rarely are organizational responses described as anything but reactions to external pressures in which there is variation among organizations but little variation over time. Exceptions include several recent longitudinal studies (Covaleski and Dirsmith, 1988; Edelman, 1992; Elsbach and Sutton, 1992; Westphal and Zajac, 1994; Fox-Wolfgramm, Boal, and Hunt, 1998). Yet even these studies fail to capture how the technical and institutional aspects of an organization might interact as its response to institutional pressures evolves over time. We argue that the evolution of the firm's self-presentation at its interface with internal and external stakeholders may offer a window into processes of institutionalization that looks beyond the sources used in most past studies.

In this sense, our case study allows us to go beyond a view of institutionalization in which external pressures produce one-time internal (or symbolic) changes in the organization. Instead, we account for ongoing processes by which organizations explore, present, interpret, and implement new practices. We argue that such processes are evident in the form and the content of the organization's formal communications with stakeholders, particularly in the ecological realm where the issues involved are complex and difficult to resolve (Clark and Jennings, 1997; Neu, Warsame, and Pedwell, 1998).

OUR DATA SOURCE: CORPORATE ENVIRONMENTAL REPORTS

A productive vein of research based on content analysis of annual reports recognizes that formal statements expose organizations' attempts to present themselves in the best possible light (such as Bettman and Weitz, 1983; Salancik and Meindl, 1984; Staw, McKechnie, and Puffer, 1993). Few studies have looked beyond attribution theory to make sense of the content of organizations' self-reports. Yet firm publications have also been shown to reveal cognitive maps and event interpretation (Fahey and Narayanan, 1989; Barr, Stimpert, and Huff, 1992; Barr, 1998). Notably, although little research examines other types of formal reporting by organizations, other documents may be less stylized and conventional than the annual report, and therefore reveal more about the organization.

Corporate environmental reports (CERs), first produced in the late 1980s, are voluntary, public documents designed to communicate a firm's environmental management programs, strategy, and performance to stakeholders. These reports have now become standard in many industries and typically detail not only a company's environmental management programs and performance but also its ideology and aspirations regarding the natural environment. Despite their rapid diffusion, CERs are far from standardized: each organization follows its own template in producing the report and the content of the reports varies greatly, within one organization over time and across organizations in an industry. This lack of standardization means that CERs may offer valuable insight into organizations.

Organizations use CERs to communicate with stakeholders as varied as environmentalists, customers, local communities, schoolchildren, regulators, competitors, suppliers, politicians, the media, and consumer activists. Employees are also a key audience for CERs (DeloitteToucheTohmatsu, IISD, and Sustainability Ltd., 1993). As public, voluntary reports, CERs commit the organization to social interaction (Goffman, 1967). The reports form part of the dialogue between an organization and its stakeholders, revealing how institutions are manifested in organizations and how they change over time (Clark and Jennings, 1997). Impression management may shape the dialogue between organization and stakeholders, but rather than concealing interaction, the "face work" central to impression management constitutes an essential part of the interaction between an organization and stakeholders (Goffman, 1967). Thus impression management shapes organizational members' attempts to make sense of their experiences. In addition, the importance of corporate communications is underscored by the observation that organizations come to "reside in the texts of specific persuasive campaigns" (Tompkins, Tompkins, and Cheney, 1989: 38). We assert that public corporate communications afford surprisingly rich sources of insight into organizations' attempts to make sense of and present institutional issues, at least in part *because* they reveal impression management, or the organization's attempt to conform to institutional requirements.

As we show, CERs depict the organization's own representation of the two forces it must address to survive: the technical and the institutional. CERs convey a sense of the organization's attempts to link the two when they report on the firm's own attributes and actions to match the demands of its environment. As we have noted, firms have faced uncertainty about what should be included in the environmental reports, what tone should be taken, and how problems—and advances—should be presented. Questions about the form and content of the reports may be linked to deeper questions about the meaning and implications of environmental management in general—questions that become important during the interpretation, decision making, and action that follow an initial decision to publish a CER.

OUR METHODS

We relied on two methods to characterize the firm's environmental stance and to tease out the ongoing processes reflected in CERs. First, we conducted a detailed content analysis of the seven Monsanto CERs published between 1991 and 1997, using a framework for classifying orientation to environmental issues. Second, we conducted a qualitative analysis of each CER in order to develop a holistic description of the key ideas and themes in the reports, as well as to confirm the trends in the content analysis and highlight examples of Monsanto's evolving environmental management orientation. The backdrop to both approaches was an extensive survey of published materials about Monsanto and environmental management during the 1990s. This context helped us to interpret the texts and served as a useful means of triangulating the data we obtained.

Structured Content Analysis

For the structured content analysis, coders (three graduate students) separately assessed each sentence in every CER from 1991 to 1997 according to the type of environmental management orientation it expressed. They also classified each sentence according to its type: attitude, action, or outcome. The resulting database allowed us to analyze the attitudes, actors, and actions within the organization and how these interrelate and change over time.

Table 11.1
Environmental Management Categories

	Institutional	Operational
Differentiated	Defense tactics	Pollution control
Integrated	Product stewardship	Pollution prevention
Anticipative	Sustainable leadership	Clean technology

Our framework for categorizing environmental management, described here, is based on notions central to the thinking on corporate environmental management during the 1990s. As such, it represents our attempt to capture the dominant macrolevel institutions that shaped the institutional field throughout that decade. We relied on academic research, practitioner publications, and our own expertise to construct the framework. It comprises six distinct orientations: defense tactics, pollution control, product stewardship, pollution prevention, sustainable leadership, and clean technology. These categories are differentiated along two dimensions. The first is the level at which the environmental management activity takes place, the *institutional* or the *technical*. The institutional level addresses the world of ideas, both within and outside the organization, whereas the operational level is more concerned with tasks and activity.

The second general dimension relates to the role that environmental management is perceived to play in the organization: whether it is *differentiated* from the operations of the firm, *integrated* into the firm's current activities as a part of doing business, or *anticipated* to be a valuable strategic resource in the future. (See Table 11.1.) The first orientation is reactive, whereas the latter two are proactive.

Several authors note the distinction between a reactive versus proactive approach to environmental management (such as Hunt and Auster, 1990; Smart, 1992; Walley and Whitehead, 1994). Firms with reactive orientations wait for regulation or public pressure to define what is required with regard to the environment. Defense tactics and pollution control are actions that reveal reactive orientations. Firms that use defense tactics respond reactively toward institutional actors. Specific defense tactics include liability set-asides, risk reduction, and specialized environmental staff. Defense tactics entail actions; their purpose is to buffer the organization's technical domain from external pressures. Thus we identify defense tactics with a reactive institutional orientation. Organizations that implement pollution control respond reactively to the technical demands of environmental management. Pollution control includes end-of-pipe treatment, compliance audits, and capital expenditure on mandated control technologies. Given their orientation toward dealing with problems after they have already been created, defense tactics and pollution control are *differentiated* from the operating aspects of the firm.

Firms with proactive environmental management orientations identify and implement solutions to environmental problems as a means of preempting regulation and public pressure and resolving issues before they become crises. Proactive approaches include pollution prevention, product stewardship, clean technology, and sustainable leadership (Hart, 1995; 1997). Product stewardship and sustainable leadership are institutionally oriented in that they involve ideas that relate the organization and its interactions with actors and institutions in its environment. Pollution prevention and clean technology are related to an organization's technical environment.

Proactive stances are further divided into two distinct orientations. Pollution prevention and product stewardship seek to improve existing products and processes in organizations embracing an *integrated* orientation. Specific technical practices that enact pollution prevention include waste reduction, energy efficiency, and materials management. Design for environment, life cycle analysis, and supply-chain management exemplify product stewardship, the institutional version of an integrated orientation.

Clean technology and sustainable leadership anticipate and invest in tomorrow's technologies and opportunities. Hence we label this the *anticipative* orientation. Resource allocation decisions to incorporate environmental factors into R&D and technology-development processes of firms represent clean technology in action. Sustainable leadership practices include stakeholder communication, management commitment, and articulation of future opportunities.

We also used a second, independent framework for our coding in order to develop as rich a picture as possible of the domains of the organization's presentation of itself. Here the goal was to differentiate between attitudes and actions. The first category captured ideas, beliefs, and institutions. The second category represented elements of the report related to the organization's task domain. We chose these terms as a natural approach to coding the firm's focus on the institutional versus the technical. If greenwashing and decoupling result in differences between the symbolic institutions embraced by the organization and what it does, we may see clues of this in self-reports of ideas, beliefs, and institutions on the one hand, versus its descriptions of concrete actions it has taken on the other hand. To round out this framework, we added "outcomes" to the coding list, as some results were neither actions nor attitudes.

For the textual coding, we randomized all sentences in a database and created an interface so that coders would see and assess only one sentence at a time. As each sentence appeared on the screen, the coders would first decide if the sentence was codable, to establish whether the sentence had anything to do with environmental management at Monsanto. We excluded uncodable sentences, such as those that were necessary only to maintain the flow of the report and those that said nothing substantive about Monsanto's orientation toward environmental management, as well as some that were relevant to Monsanto's environmental management but could not be understood in the limited context. (Our qualitative, thematic assessment of the CERs compensated for contextual losses here.)

Coders assigned one of the six environmental management orientations to each interpretable sentence. Next, they labeled the sentence as an attitude expressed, an action taken, or an outcome achieved by the firm. This allowed us to quantify the extent to which Monsanto discussed environmentalism, how much action based on those principles it reported, and how it discussed the success of those actions. The three coders for the CERs had a high level of agreement.[1]

Thematic Coding

In our qualitative assessment, the authors read the CERs, extracted themes, identified ideas that developed in multiple CERs, pinpointed notions that arose once and were then dropped, and looked for commitments, descriptions of action, statements of intent, and evaluations. As a double-check of the closed-ended coding, we compared our thematic analysis with the numerical analysis from the structured coding and found that they matched well. More importantly, we used the thematic analysis to extract information on the processes underlying the changes that the structured analysis revealed. What kinds of language did each report use? How were actions presented and justified? What institutions were invoked, and what was the rationale that accompanied each? A careful qualitative coding helped us to answer these questions.

RESULTS

Institutional Change

The content analysis of Monsanto's CERs depicts a shift in the content of Monsanto's corporate reporting over the seven years studied. Figure 11.1 shows that defensive and integrative orientations peak and then decline. At the same time, an anticipative orientation emerges, dominating the content of these reports by 1997.[2] The anticipative perspective appears to replace the defensive and integrative.

As Figures 11.2, 11.3, and 11.4 show, we see similar changes within each orientation. Recall that defense tactics, product stewardship, and sustainable leadership

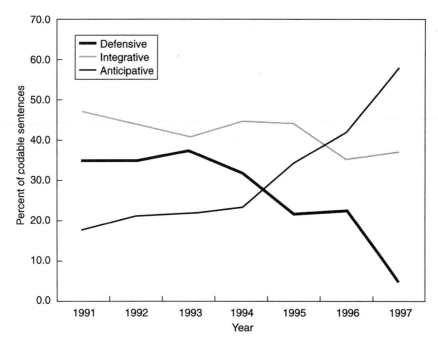

Figure 11.1   Overall Orientation Levels

address institutional domains, whereas pollution control, pollution prevention, and clean technology relate to the technical domain. The institutional and techni- cal domains of the defensive orientation move relatively closely with each other, whereas the differences are larger for the integrative and anticipative. Over time, the gaps between institutional and technical narrow for the integrative orientation. Yet for the anticipative orientation, the gap increases over time.

These trends within each orientation give rise to a notable pattern when the in- stitutional components of all three orientations are summed and plotted against the total for technical components of all three domains. Here we have plotted the total on a different scale, where each sentence that is coded defensive is weighted −1, each coded integrative is weighted 0, and each coded anticipative is weighted 1. We did this in order to recognize that each of these orientations puts the organi- zation at a different place on the spectrum of reactive to proactive responses. Fig- ure 11.5 shows that Monsanto always referred to institutions more than to tasks and the technical domain. In addition, the gap between the institutional and tech- nical grows over time, save for the last year.

From Figure 11.6, we also see an overall shift in the types of sentences in Mon- santo's CERs over the seven years. Our goal here was to see if the organization's

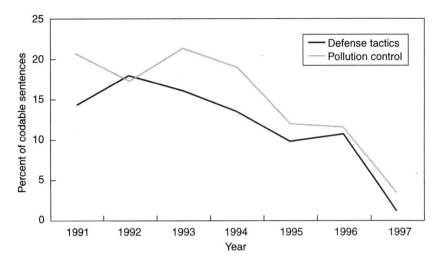

Figure 11.2   Defensive Orientation

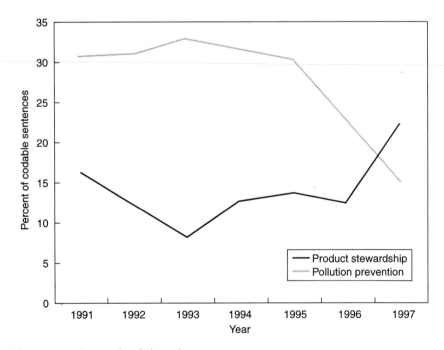

Figure 11.3   Integrative Orientation

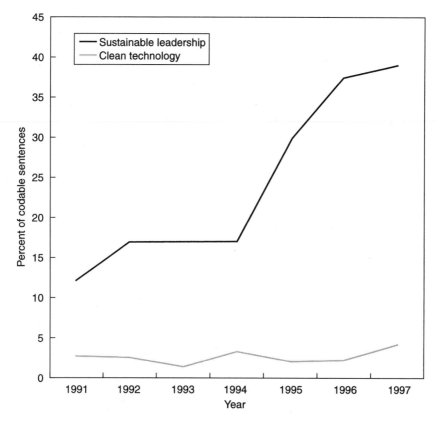

Figure 11.4   Anticipative Orientation

reporting about attitudes versus actions mirrored its reporting of the institutional versus the technical. In the years immediately following the first publication of a CER, we see that Monsanto focused primarily on actions. In these years, the majority of sentences related to some area of corporate environmental management. In this early era, approximately 40 percent of sentences were uncodable. In the later years we see attitudes, at 24 percent, dominating the sentence type in the reports. In all years, outcomes were consistently the least-used sentence type and peaked in 1996.

The number of uncodable sentences increased in the last three years, reaching 58 percent by the final year. Our check of uncodable sentences, in which we looked at them in context, reveals that they were almost never action statements and only occasionally attitude statements. The trend in codability suggests that in the later stages of CER development, Monsanto explored and presented the anticipative

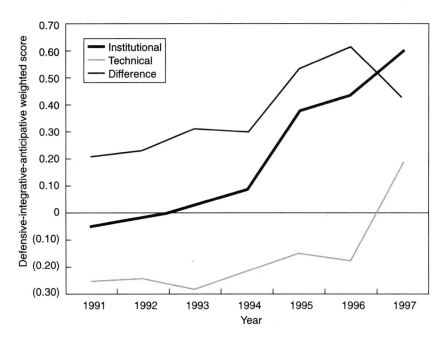

Figure 11.5   Institutional versus Technical Orientation

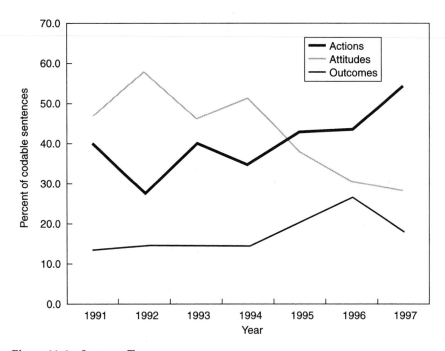

Figure 11.6   Sentence Types

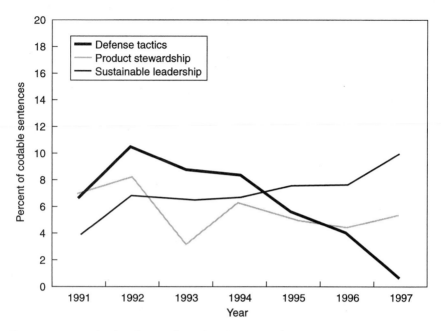

Figure 11.7 Institutional Focus in Action Statements by Orientation

orientation in such a way that it resulted in a less clear message regarding its environmental management orientation in the CER.

Thus Figure 11.6 suggests that the same broad pattern holds for both approaches to coding: actions and tasks appear more prevalent in early reports, and attitudes and institutions dominate in the later reports.

Despite the agreement between overall patterns in the two types of figures, we wondered whether action statements differed in terms of relating to actions aimed at the institutional environment (such as convening meetings with stakeholders or arranging to learn more about a new environmental management approach or adopting a new plan) versus actions aimed at the technical environment (such as implementing new technologies or putting into place new operational procedures or implementing a new plan). Hence we asked how this evolution plays out for action statements in terms of the three environmental orientations central to our study. Figures 11.7 and 11.8 show that institutionally oriented anticipative actions are relatively high and grow. The general trend is for both institutional and technical actions to fall over time in the other two domains (although integrative institutional actions vary more widely than others). As Figure 11.8 shows, in the technical domain anticipative actions are negligible throughout. Both defensive and integrative actions that are technically oriented fall over time.

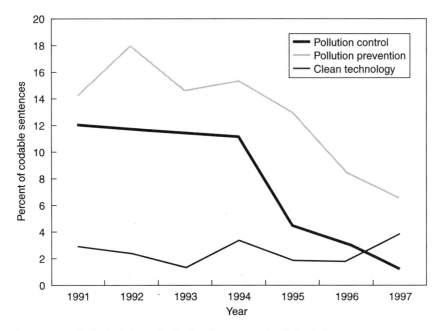

Figure 11.8   Technical Focus in Action Statements by Orientation

Taken together, the CERs reveal a significant change in Monsanto's environmental management orientation over time, particularly when the first four years are compared to the last three. In the initial years, we see a defensive and integrative orientation characterized by action. Over time, Monsanto develops a more anticipative orientation and attitudes dominate the content of CERs. It is noteworthy that even though Monsanto had been publishing CERs for several years by the late 1990s, its CERs had become less focused on firm-specific environmental management strategies and identifiable actions in the last few years we studied. Adding the thematic coding to our analysis helped to shed light on the changes we observed.

PROCESSES OF CHANGE: TWO ERAS

Drawing on our coding results, we interweave qualitative findings from the thematic coding with the quantitative results reported above to develop an integrated narrative of the evolution of corporate environmental reporting at Monsanto. The story falls into two key parts. First, processes of committing and expanding account for the content of Monsanto's early CERs between 1991 and 1995. Monsanto's second era, 1995–1997, is characterized by problems and uncertainty, and we see the organization engaging in a variety of processes aimed at exploration and dialogue.

The Early Era: Embarking on a Course of Action

Preparing a CER required management to explain past actions, interpret feedback from the environment and from within the organization, present new ideas, set goals, and explain what it means to be an environmentally responsible corporation. For Monsanto, the process began before the first CER. In 1988 the firm promised to reduce air emissions 90 percent worldwide by 1992. In the first CER, we learn of employees' efforts to meet this pledge by installing pollution control systems (Monsanto, 1991: 7), modifying systems (p. 9), introducing new materials into production (p. 13), redesigning products (p. 16), and increasing recycling (p. 16). Figure 11.6 illustrates the degree to which action dominated early CERs.

To Monsanto in the early 1990s, environmental management was synonymous with pollution prevention (see Figure 11.3). There was also emphasis on pollution control and defense tactics and some talk of product stewardship and sustainable leadership, but pollution prevention dominated the Monsanto mindset and the firm's actions reflected this. Expanding on its previous commitments, in the company's first CER Monsanto management issued a new "corporate-wide goal to achieve a 70 percent reduction by the end of 1995 of high-priority manufacturing waste" to all media (Monsanto, 1991: 22). Numerous anecdotes in early reports highlighted employee participation, demonstrated the value of these efforts, and acted as a reward system, serving to build employees' organizational commitment (O'Reilly and Chatman, 1996) as well as to tighten the coupling between the organization's institutional and technical orientations.

The content of early CERs suggests a growing dedication to the course of action the organization had already embarked on, signaling escalating commitment (see Staw and Ross, 1978). Language and vocabularies also reflected consistent thought, with the size of reports, number of sentences, and layout and design nearly identical for the first three years, with only minor changes in the fourth year.

As the 1990s progressed, Monsanto continued to develop its environmental stance, shifting its emphasis from a differentiated approach to an integrated orientation in which preventing rather than treating pollution was the operational focus, as Figures 11.2 and 11.3 show. During the early 1990s, the company's environmental performance improved steadily and it met its commitments; CEO letters from the 1991–1994 CERs chronicle progress toward emission goals and actions taken that showed how employees were keeping the "Monsanto Pledge," while chemical releases dropped dramatically. The institutional environment appeared to respond favorably: involvement on community advisory boards was presented as positive, and community members who sat on these boards offered favorable quotes in the CERs. Employees reportedly initiated a large number of improvement projects of all types. In 1992, as the company drew close to its 1993 deadline for cutting air pollution by 90 percent, Monsanto added a new goal: a 70 percent reduction in releases to all media by 1995 (Monsanto, 1992).

Later CERs: Dealing with Problems and Uncertainty

In 1993 Monsanto reached an important milestone: it met the goal it first set in 1988. Although the firm succeeded in reducing toxic air releases 90 percent by the deadline, its CER admitted that its success was not achieved solely by improving production processes but that the firm had closed down polluting plants, a tactic that would yield only short-lived improvements.

1994 marked a turning point in Monsanto's CERs. Although the cover was the same as each of the previous years, the internal format changed. Statistics on emissions, releases, transfers, spills, and so forth moved to the front of the CER, emphasizing the firm's first full year of operating with 90 percent fewer releases to air worldwide (Monsanto, 1994). Interaction with consultants was mentioned for the first time. This signaled the beginning of a trend of looking outward for answers to problems. Yet the public nature of Monsanto's commitment to pollution reduction goals meant that the firm would still have to report on its progress in this area.

The next year, results were not good. As the prior evidence foreshadowed, Monsanto could not meet its goal of reducing pollution to all media by 70 percent in 1995. Why not? The CEO invoked a dearth of technologies and a lack of appropriate rewards from the government and the marketplace by way of explaining that the firm, in a sense, got ahead of itself. A further explanation adds internal factors: surely Monsanto's century of existence as a chemicals business made it difficult for the company to undertake the massive changes in technology that would have enabled it to achieve the new goals. In mentioning the "old culture," (Monsanto, 1993: 2) management hinted that it recognized the importance of addressing organizational inertia, but little mention is made of such factors in subsequent CERs.

Although it is difficult to establish all the reasons for its failure, it is clear that Monsanto changed its actions in connection with its 1995 results. Around this time the firm issued two "million-dollar challenges" to the scientific community as rewards for cost-effective and practical solutions to water pollution control problems. (One prize was subsequently awarded for a technology that removes ammonia from organic waste streams, and Monsanto began its implementation [Monsanto, 1997]).

Indeed, 1995 brought an onslaught of changes to Monsanto's CERs. Robert Shapiro became the new chairman and CEO. After his letter at the front of the CER, in a break with past formats, two pages were devoted to quotes from environmentally oriented consultants and advisors working for and with the company (Monsanto, 1995). The cover changed from the standard dark green to beige and light green with a picture of plants and mottoes: "Assessing our performance" and "building our commitment to sustainability." Pages of external actors saying agreeable things about Monsanto and statistics showing Monsanto's improvement (but this time without numerical goals) moved to the front of the CER—pages 2–9. The number of sentences referring to actions dropped from 29 percent in 1994 to 17 percent. The percentage of sentences discussing pollution prevention and pollution control dropped as well, and talk of sustainable leadership rose (see Figure 11.4).

These dramatic changes in Monsanto's actions and in its presentation of itself suggest that a new CEO and the impending failure marked a change in course for the firm. We get the sense that Monsanto was exhausting its ideas for how to reduce emissions—at least within the range of its existing products and processes. The CERs depict a change in approach as Monsanto managers began to look to the outside world for solutions to their problems, hiring consultants, forming advisory boards, structuring dialogues with stakeholders, and even commissioning opinion surveys. Interactions with new institutional actors highlighted a potential solution to Monsanto's problems: sustainable development. The "principles of sustainability" (1995: 2) included moving environmental management even further upstream, so that not only is the manufacturing process clean, but so is the product itself.

Sustainable development represented a solution for Monsanto for three reasons. First, it was consistent with its emerging image and identity as an environmental company. While at the same time, thanks to widespread existing debates about the definition and operationalization of the concept and the absence of exemplary practicing organizations, it did not require immediate, specific changes in the organization's actions. The leeway afforded by the controversy of sustainable development meant that Monsanto could avoid further goal setting, and instead devote its energies to establishing what it would mean for the organization. Second, Monsanto's existing technology would serve as a starting point for developing clean and sustainable biotechnology products—products that fit with the firm's established competencies. Finally, sustainable development also allowed Monsanto to link its products and business mission to global problems in the form of growing populations coupled with decreasing water quality, land shortages, air quality concerns, and threats to other natural resources. Such links could elevate the social value of Monsanto, potentially enhancing its legitimacy. The 1996 CER describes Monsanto teams working in these areas.

A second change accompanied the shift to sustainability: the firm was split in two. Along with an admission of failure to achieve a 70 percent reduction in waste in 1996 came Monsanto's announcement that it would divest its chemical operations and become a life sciences company with sustainable development "a primary emphasis in everything we do" (Monsanto 1996: inside cover).[3]

Monsanto's 1996 CER exhibited other noteworthy changes. Sustainable leadership became the most common environmental management category mentioned in the CERs. The report itself grew in size to 940 sentences from 319 in 1994. The number of uncodable sentences also grew from 37 percent in 1994 to 56 percent in 1996. Our qualitative analysis shows that this growth in uncodable sentences reflects the amount of space that Monsanto devoted in its CER to publishing the views of external actors.

The diversity of external institutional actors also increased in 1996. The report lists and thanks some sixteen "distinguished outside experts" from a variety of disciplines and backgrounds who advised the firm (p. 21). The 1996 CER also presented a Monsanto-sponsored worldwide survey of teenagers on their environmental attitudes (pp. 11–13), as well as discussions from an international round table with heads of nongovernmental organizations, environmentalists, business consultants, corporate environmental officers, and journalists (pp. 14–19). Monsanto reported criticisms of its actions: for instance, it was chided for not drawing on opinions of a wide array of constituents in the development of its biotechnology products.

The 1996 CER represented Monsanto's attempt to act on ideas that emerged from the previous year's activities. In response to the thought leaders' injunctions, the 1997 CER presented multiple comments, many of them critical, about the European reaction to Monsanto's genetically enhanced soybeans (1997: 20–21). A second response to past criticisms was Monsanto's attempt to recognize the links between social problems and environmental problems, evident in the 1997 CER's inclusion of the firm's first annual review on corporate social responsibility. The 1997 report also mentions socially responsible initiatives, such as Monsanto's partnership with the Grameen Bank, an organization successful in combining social development and entrepreneurship.

The final obvious, but important, difference in the 1997 CER is its increased emphasis on clean technology. By 1997 Monsanto presented itself as creating products that helped the environment, rather than trying to minimize ill effects of conventional products (see Figure 11.3). Yet as Figure 11.8 indicates, its mentions of clean technology are associated with attitudes, not actions. Thus the gap between the institutions it discusses and the task-oriented actions it reports taking grew in the last years we studied. How can we interpret this development? What does institutional theory have to say about it? We turn now to consider the implications of our findings.

DISCUSSION

We began this chapter by asking whether institutional theory's prediction of decoupling would explain the shifts in form and content of Monsanto's environmental reports between 1991 and 1997. Our expectation that decoupling might prevail was informed by Oliver's (1991) specification of the conditions under which this response is likely. The situation Monsanto faced in the 1990s was consistent with ideal conditions for decoupling: the legitimacy and economic efficiency of the external pressure were relatively low, there were multiple constituents on which the organization was moderately dependent, demands were somewhat consistent with organizational goals but placed restrictive constraints on the organization, conformance was spreading, and uncertainty in the environment was high and the institutional setting was moderately interconnected (Oliver, 1991). Particularly at the outset of the era we studied, when chemical firms first adopted CERs the institutional field experienced much uncertainty about both CERs and environmental management and multiple stakeholders contributed to the public pressure on firms. Some of the sources of pressure to produce them—environmental watchdog groups, for instance—were not part of the mainstream of decision making on such issues, at least compared to today. Economic efficiency arguments for environmental management were mixed and the alignment between the firm's goals and environmental management was only partial, as the CERs themselves reveal. Some actors in the public arena at the time felt that there was only a limited set of opportunities for industrial greenness to pay off economically; beyond that point, environmental management was seen as a costly proposition. Yet the norm of publishing reports was spreading fast, and as the institution of the CER took hold in the industry it required firms like Monsanto to take a stance with respect to environmental management.

If institutional theory predicts that an organization facing such a situation would decouple its institutional and technical domains, invoking one set of ideas and practices ritualistically while minimizing changes to its operating or technical core, so too did critics of the chemical and biotech industries see the potential for greenwashing. By the second half of the 1990s, firms in these industries were accused of embracing ecological language and rhetoric while continuing to pollute, ignoring the needs of sustainable development and otherwise causing ecological problems with their actions (Staubler and Rampton, 1995; Tokar, 1997; Beder, 1998; Greer and Bruno, 1998; Fagin, Lavelle, and Center for Public Integrity, 1999).

Yet the Monsanto CERs reveal a different picture. Far from choosing one stance, and far from selecting a response that minimized required technical changes, Monsanto moved between orientations, at first deliberately making and expanding commitments that forced technical changes on the company, and then retreating from this approach in order to embrace an entirely new orientation. As our data reveal, Monsanto's early era of committing and expanding was accompanied by a tightening in the linkages between the institutional and the technical related to both defensive and integrative orientations. With respect to the anticipative orientation, the coupling between the institutional and technical was never great but was stronger in the early years than later.

The need for tight linkage between the technical and institutional in Monsanto's presentation of itself eventually posed problems for the organization. From our thematic coding, we learned that the initial underlying rhetoric was one of committing and expanding, with recent actions being presented in order to bolster the firm's appeals to its employees to enact the new orientation. As these early reports revealed, the same actions also served to demonstrate to outsiders that the organization was committed to environmental management. Yet this rhetoric of committing and expanding offered Monsanto no convenient rationale for slowing down or reducing the commitment—the coupling could not be easily broken.

In this sense, the tight coupling that characterized the first era was dysfunctional for the organization. The problem lay in Monsanto's technical domain: in trying to match actions and performance with commitments, eventually the technical could not match the institutional. The firm failed to keep its promises.

An obvious solution to this problem was to avoid making commitments that required the firm to change its technical domain in order to align with the institutional. Monsanto subsequently shifted focus, emphasizing the anticipative orientation at the expense of the other two. As we noted, the notion of sustainability is central to this orientation; yet its meaning for a firm like Monsanto was (and perhaps still is) unclear. Unlike the differentiated and integrated orientations, the anticipative orientation did not come with a set of defined organizational practices and yardsticks. Instead it was connected to vaguer notions of collective responsibility and collective effort, to thinking in longer time frames, and to developing new types of product that would be not only cleaner to manufacture but also benefit the environment in use. This was true of the orientation as presented by Monsanto, but it was also the case for the orientation as manifested at the macro-social level. As our thematic analysis revealed, underlying the firm's presentation of sustainability was a rhetoric that embraced exploration and dialogue.

In a sense, once Monsanto encountered difficulties in its attempts to align its technical domain with the institutional, it chose to reframe the institutional. The new focus did not entail quantitative targets and the firm no longer made promises that it could not keep in the form of specific performance goals. Yet this apparent solution—to loosen the coupling between the institutional and the technical—also turned out to be problematic for the firm. These problems are only hinted at in our data (recall that the last CER we studied reflected criticism of Monsanto's development of genetically modified seeds). As the subsequent history of the organization has revealed, they blossomed into crises of legitimacy (escalating criticism of genetic modification spread from Europe to North America; and the firm stopped development of some genetically modified seeds, containing the so-called "terminator gene," in an attempt to assuage critics). Was this problem originated by Monsanto's willingness to embrace the institutional dimension of the anticipative orientation without embarking on any technically related changes?

If this is the case, then the loose coupling evident in the later era of our study is also dysfunctional for the firm. Here there is a striking gap between the ideas and institutions presented in the reports and the specific technical actions mentioned. Interestingly, just as in the case with the committing and expanding rhetoric seen in the early era, the implications of the exploration and dialogue embraced by the firm when it espouses the anticipative orientation unfold only over the course of years. Exploration and dialogue by their very nature invite participation and hence scrutiny. Once the partners in the dialogue had access to the organization, the gap between the technical and the institutional may have been all the more apparent to these stakeholders.

The fact that problems are exposed only gradually underscores the unfolding nature of the reactions that the firm encounters when it embarks on a given response to institutional pressures. These consequences, as our case study dramatizes, may not be known in advance. Although external pressures and developments—shifts in the institutional and technical settings outside the organization—doubtless played a role in the changes we see in Monsanto's reports, the present study underscores the large extent to which the content of Monsanto's own past reports created the problems with which it struggled later.

Such a picture of shortsighted organizational responses to institutional pressures contrasts sharply with the strategic foresight credited to activist responding organizations (Oliver, 1991; Goodstein, 1994; Guthrie and Roth, 1999). It also contrasts with the institutionalist view that organizations actively seek the least onerous legitimate form of response to institutional pressure (Edelman, 1992; Davis and Greve, 1997). In the early era Monsanto appeared to go out of its way to choose a response strategy that would entail significant change for the organization, rather than the legal minimum. Perhaps most importantly, our picture of Monsanto exposes the limitations of taking a simplistic view of institutionalization in which external pressures produce a one-shot change in the organization. In its place, we propose that institutionalization should be viewed as an ongoing process that unfolds over time.

Thus our study helps to address a gap in existing knowledge: although institutional theory has helped us understand *why* organizational practices diffuse through a population of firms, it does not adequately explain *how* those practices evolve within adopting organizations (and, by extension, within the institutional environment). As we have noted, treating the adoption of an institutionally demanded practice is typically treated as a discrete event—the organization either adopts the practice or does not; the organization chooses one response or another—omits interacting processes by which organizations implement, interpret, and explore, and the implications of new practices and reshaping the practice, the organization, and institutions as they do so. As a result, to date we have had little understanding of the process by which organizations adopt these practices and the evolution of the subsequent form of that practice. Thus we have only limited understanding of how interactions between the organization's technical and task domains unfold over time.

Our findings reveal that institutionalization is an evolving—and potentially complicated—process for the organizations involved. Decoupling, adoption, adaptation, and abandonment together shape the trajectories of organizations struggling to contend with institutional demands and the technical requirements for efficient operations. Ongoing processes such as committing and expanding, as well as exploration and dialogue, both explain and enact the organization's orientations in its response to institutional pressures. What emerges from our case study is how early attempts to reconcile the competing forces of tasks and institutions generate apparent solutions, which in turn give rise to new challenges. Our analysis reveals that organizations do not always simply construct an "institutional face" when confronted with new demands from their external environments, without heeding their own histories, identities, and competencies. Instead, organizations may expend a great deal of effort to reconcile the institutional environment with the internal, organizational one—and even then, such reconciliation may be only fleeting, as the necessity for further changes ensues. The long-term result may be far from predictable. If Monsanto's 1997 spinning off of its chemicals business—formerly the technical core of the organization—is at least in part related to these ongoing processes, our case study provides a dramatic example of the unintended consequences that can emerge in a complex social system when an apparently simple new practice, corporate environmental reporting, is undertaken.

NOTES

1. For sentence type, Cohen's Kappa was 0.39 (that is, coders agreed on 39 percent more of the sentences than would be expected by chance), percent agreement was 48 percent, and $I_r = 0.766 \pm 0.071$ (interrater reliability where the underlying distribution is unknown with a 95 percent confidence interval). For environmental management orientation, Cohen's Kappa was 0.32, percent agreement was 41 percent, and $I_r = 0.737 \pm 0.073$. Because this is an exploratory study we do not report these reliability measures as statistical evidence. Instead, we provide them as evidence that these categories serve as a good starting ground for constructs that capture the vocabularies of environmental orientation.

2. For each orientation, when both components of each of the three orientations are added together, we find linear trends that are significantly different from zero with negative slope coefficients for both defensive and integrative orientations and a positive slope coefficient for the anticipative orientation.

Slope Coefficients: (standard errors in parentheses,

* indicates $p < 0.01$)

$\beta_{\text{Defensive}} = -0.033^* \ (0.0069);$

$\beta_{\text{Integrative}} = -0.023^* \ (0.0037);$

$\beta_{\text{Anticipative}} = 0.019^* \ (0.0040)$

3. In 1996, Monsanto announced that it would spin off its chemicals business. The spin-off took place in September 1997, creating Solutia, and making Monsanto a life sciences firm. Well before the divestiture, battle lines already existed. In a 1998 speech, a Solutia vice president claimed that for two decades Monsanto had experienced conflicts between the interests of its biotechnology faction and its chemicals faction: "Cultures and businesses within the corporation [Monsanto] had begun to diverge, and to diverge dramatically. To see the extent of the divergence, you have to go back to the late 1970s" (Cavner, 1998). Investments in biotechnology—which were dominated by acquisition rather than expansion—had begun in the late 1970s. By 1996, Cavner said, it was clear that "something would have to change" for Monsanto to survive these tensions. But even before the spin-off was considered, the natural divisions between the

engineering-oriented, more traditional chemicals segment and the life-sciences/biotechnology segment shaped internal debates at the company. According to this insider, rather than reaching a quick resolution this conflict played out over years. Thus differing opinions within the company may have contributed to arguments about environmental management.

Interestingly, CERs presented no detailed justifications for the spin-off; instead, the CEO's letter simply stated that "[we're] now organizing into two separate companies so that we and our shareholders can reap maximum value from our work" (Monsanto, 1996). As stock prices evidenced, Monsanto was worth more as two separate companies than it was as one. But it is also interesting to note that the life sciences company got the Monsanto name and the most lucrative products (including an important set of herbicides) whereas the chemical company made its start saddled with debt. Even so, Solutia's stock price rose in 1997 and the company's first CER pledged continuing commitment to pollution prevention. It did not mention sustainable development.

REFERENCES

Barley, Stephen R., and Pamela S. Tolbert. 1997. "Institutionalization and Structuration: Studying the Links Between Action and Institution." *Organization Studies,* 18(1): 93–117.

Barr, Pamela S. 1998. "Adapting to Unfamiliar Environmental Events: A Look at the Evolution of Interpretation and Its Role in Strategic Change." *Organization Science,* 9(6): 644–669.

Barr, Pamela S., J. L. Stimpert, and Anne S. Huff. 1992. "Cognitive Change, Strategic Action, and Organizational Renewal." *Strategic Management Journal,* 13: 15–36.

Beder, Sharon. 1998. *Global Spin: The Corporate Assault on Environmentalism.* White River Junction, VT: Chelsea Green.

Bettman, James R., and Barton A. Weitz. 1983. "Attributions in the Board Room: Causal Reasoning in Corporate Annual Reports." *Administrative Science Quarterly,* 28: 165–183.

Cavner, Dennis. 1998. "How Solutia Became Its Own Company: Remarks by Dennis Cavner, vice president of operations Excellence, Solutia, to Northwest Florida Engineers Meeting." See on the internet at http://www.solutia.com/Investor/SpeechesArticles/DennisCavner.html.

Clark, Vivien, and P. Devereaux Jennings. 1997. "Talking About the Natural Environment: A Means for Deinstitutionalization?" *American Behavioral Scientist,* 40: 454–464.

Covaleski, Mark A., and Mark W. Dirsmith. 1988. "An Institutional Perspective on the Rise, Social Transformation, and Fall of a University Budget Category." *Administrative Science Quarterly,* 33: 562–587.

Davis, Gerald F., and Henrich R. Greve. 1997. "Corporate Elite Networks and Governance Changes in the 1980s." *American Journal of Sociology,* 103: 1–37.

Deloitte Touche Tohmatsu, International Institute for Sustainable Development (IISD), and Sustainabilty Ltd. 1993. *Coming Clean: Corporate Environmental Reporting.* London: Deloitte Touche Tohmatsu.

DiMaggio, Paul J., and Walter W. Powell. 1983. "The Iron Cage Revisited: Institutional Isomorphism and Collective Rationality in Organizational Fields." *American Sociological Review,* 48: 147–160.

DiMaggio, Paul J., and Walter W. Powell. 1991. "Introduction." In Walter W. Powell and Paul J. DiMaggio, eds., *The New Institutionalism in Organizational Analysis*: 1–38. Chicago: University of Chicago.

Edelman, Lauren B. 1990. "Legal Environments and Organizational Governance: The Expansion of Due Process in the American Workplace." *American Journal of Sociology,* 95: 1401–1440.

Edelman, Lauren B. 1992. "Legal Ambiguity and Symbolic Structures: Organizational Mediation of Civil Rights Law." *American Journal of Sociology,* 97: 1531–1576.

Elsbach, Kimberly D., and Robert I. Sutton. 1992. "Acquiring Organizational Legitimacy Through Illegitimate Actions: A Marriage of Institutional and Impression Management Theories." *Academy of Management Journal,* 35: 699–738.

Fagin, Dan, Marianne Lavelle, and Center for Public Integrity. 1999. *Toxic Deception: How the Chemical Industry Manipulates Science, Bends the Law, and Endangers Your Health.* Monroe, ME: Common Courage Press.

Fahey, Liam, and V. K. Narayanan. 1989. "Linking Changes in Revealed Causal Maps and Environmental Change: An Empirical Study." *Journal of Management Studies,* 26(4): 361–679.

Fox-Wolfgramm, Susan J., Kimberly B. Boal, and James G. Hunt. 1998. "Organizational Adaptation to Institutional Change: A Comparative Study of First-Order Change in Prospector and Defender Banks." *Administrative Science Quarterly,* 43: 87–126.

Goffman, Erving. 1967. *Interaction Ritual.* New York: Doubleday, Anchor Books.

Goodstein, Jerry D. 1994. "Institutional Pressures and Strategic Responsiveness: Employer Involvement in Work-Family Issues." *Academy of Management Journal,* 37(2): 350–382.

Greer, Jed, and Kenny Bruno. 1998. *Greenwash: The Reality Behind Corporate Environmentalism.* New York: Apex Press.

Guthrie, Doug, and Louise Marie Roth. 1999. "The State, Courts, and Maternity Policies In U.S. Organizations: Specifying Institutional Mechanisms." *American Sociological Review,* 64(1): 41–63.

Hart, Stuart. 1995. "A Natural-Resource-Based View of the Firm." *Academy of Management Review,* 20: 986–1014.

Hart, Stuart. 1997. "Beyond Greening: Strategies for a Sustainable World." *Harvard Business Review,* Jan.–Feb.

Hunt, Christopher B., and Ellen R. Auster. 1990. "Proactive Environmental Management: Avoiding the Toxic Trap." *Sloan Management Review,* 31: 7–18.

Meyer, John W., and Brian Rowan. 1977. "Institutionalized Organizations: Formal Structure as Myth and Ceremony." *American Journal of Sociology,* 83(2): 340–363.

Monsanto. 1991. "Environmental Annual Review." St. Louis, MO: Monsanto.

Monsanto. 1992. "Environmental Annual Review." St. Louis, MO: Monsanto.

Monsanto. 1993. "Environmental Annual Review." St. Louis, MO: Monsanto.

Monsanto. 1994. "Environmental Annual Review." St. Louis, MO: Monsanto.

Monsanto. 1995. "Environmental Annual Review." St. Louis, MO: Monsanto.

Monsanto. 1996. "Environmental Annual Review." St. Louis, MO: Monsanto.

Monsanto. 1997. "Report on Sustainable Development Including Environmental, Safety and Health Performance." St. Louis, MO: Monsanto.

Neu, D., H. Warsame, and K. Pedwell. 1998. "Managing Public Impressions: Environmental Disclosures in Annual Reports." *Accounting, Organizations, and Society,* 23: 265–282.

Oliver, Christine. 1991. "Strategic Responses to Institutional Processes." *Academy of Management Review,* 16(1): 145–179.

O'Reilly, Charles A., and Jennifer A. Chatman. 1996. "Culture as Social Control: Corporations, Cults and Commitment." *Research in Organizational Behavior,* 18: 157–200.

Orrù, Marco, Nicole Woolsley Biggart, and Gary G. Hamilton. 1991. "Organizational Isomorphism in East Asia." In Walter W. Powell and Paul J DiMaggio, eds., *The New Institutionalism in Organizational Analysis,* 361–389. Chicago: University of Chicago.

Palmer, Donald A., P. Devereaux Jennings, and Xueguang Zhou. 1993. "Late Adoption of the Multidivisional Form by Large U.S. Corporations: Institutional, Political, and Economic Accounts." *Administrative Science Quarterly,* 38: 100–131.

Salancik, Gerald R., and James R. Meindl. 1984. "Corporate Attributions as Strategic Illusions of Management Control." *Administrative Science Quarterly,* 29: 238–254.

Scott, W. Richard. 1992. *Organizations: Rational, Natural, and Open Systems.* Englewood Cliffs, NJ: Prentice-Hall.

Scott, W. Richard. 1995. *Institutions and Organizations* (Vol. 32). Thousand Oaks, CA: Sage.

Selznick, Philip. 1957. *Leadership in Administration: A Sociological Interpretation.* New York: Harper and Row.

Selznick, Philip. 1966. *TVA and the Grass Roots.* New York: Harper.

Smart, Bruce, ed. 1992. *Beyond Compliance: A New Industry View of the Environment.* Washington, DC: World Resources Institute.

Staubler, John C., and Sheldon Rampton. 1995. *Toxic Sludge Is Good for You! Lies, Damn Lies, and the Public Relations Industry.* Monroe, ME: Common Courage Press.

Staw, Barry M., and Jerry Ross. 1978. "Commitment to a Policy Decision: A Multi-Theoretical Perspective." *Administrative Science Quarterly,* 23: 40–64.

Staw, Barry M., Pamela I. McKechnie, and Sheila M. Puffer. 1993. "The Justification of Organizational Performance." *Administrative Science Quarterly,* 28: 582–600.

Thompson, James D. 1967. *Organizations in Action.* New York: McGraw-Hill.

Tokar, Brian. 1997. *Earth for Sale: Reclaiming Ecology in the Age of Corporate Greenwash.* Boston: South End Press.

Tompkins, E.V.B., P. K. Tompkins, and G. Cheney. 1989. "Organizations as Arguments: Discovering, Expressing, and Analyzing the Premises for Decisions." *Journal of Management Systems,* 1: 35–48.

Walley, Noah, and Bradley Whitehead. 1994. "It's Not Easy Being Green." *Harvard Business Review,* 72: 46–52.

Westphal, James D., and Edward J. Zajac. 1994. "Substance and Symbolism in CEOs' Long-Term Incentive Plans." *Administrative Science Quarterly,* 39: 367–390.

Westphal, James D., Ranjay Gulati, and Stephen M. Shortell. 1997. "Customization or Conformity? An Institutional and Network Perspective on the Content and Consequences of TQM Adoption." *Administrative Science Quarterly,* 42: 366–394.

Zald, Mayer N., and Patricia Denton. 1963. "From Evangelism to General Service: The Transformation of the YMCA." *Administrative Science Quarterly,* 8: (214–234).

12 | INSTITUTIONAL EVOLUTION: THE CASE OF THE SEMICONDUCTOR INDUSTRY VOLUNTARY PFC EMISSIONS REDUCTION AGREEMENTS

Jennifer A. Howard-Grenville

In 1999 an international association of semiconductor manufacturers announced a voluntary commitment to reduce global warming gas emissions. Members of the World Semiconductor Council (WSC), who together produce 90 percent of the industry's output, committed to reduce emissions of PFCs, a class of potent global warmers, by 10 percent by 2010. Significantly, this reduction goal is absolute, not pegged to production volumes, in a notoriously fast-growing industry. The global market for semiconductor products—including microprocessors and memory chips used in computers, communications equipment, and other electronic devices—has grown at an average annual rate of 12 percent over the last decade and is forecasted to continue to grow at this rate for the next several years (SIA, 1999; SIA, 2000). To achieve the targeted reduction in PFC emissions, semiconductor manufacturers will have to more than halve PFC emissions per unit of production.

This is a formidable technical challenge, but the PFC reduction goal is also significant because neither regulatory nor public pressure played a central role in its development. Public concern over PFC emissions by the semiconductor manufacturing industry has never been high (Rand, 2000), perhaps because these emissions account for less than a tenth of 1 percent of global warming gas emissions in the United States (EPA, 2000). In 1999, regulatory mechanisms for the reduction of global warming gas emissions were largely nonexistent, and the 1997 Kyoto Protocol that established country goals for global warming gas emissions reduction had not been ratified by the majority of signatory countries (UNFCCC, 2000). In the absence of overt coercive pressures, why did the semiconductor manufacturing industry adopt an ambitious voluntary goal for the reduction of global warming gas emissions?

This chapter describes the complex chain of events that led to the adoption of the PFC reduction goal. A number of actors were involved and a number of different issues were under negotiation over a period of eight years. Technical, strategic, and environmental factors contributed to shifts in the core issues and to actors' interpretations of the core issues over time. As actors and their interpretations of the central issues evolved, the visible trappings of institutionalization—rules and structures—also evolved. Two distinct mechanisms operated between three stages of institutional evolution: first, a core idea—the environmental stewardship of global warming gases—was transferred from one industry to another; second, institutional rules and structures were broadened and deepened within a single industry.

By looking at what remained constant and what was subject to negotiation and reinterpretation during the development of the semiconductor industry's voluntary PFC emissions reduction agreements, this chapter illustrates the role of actors and context in the evolution of an institution for environmental protection. It supports the argument advanced by Troast and others (Chapter 10) that institutional change can be brought about by intentional, strategic action on the part of individual organizations. At the same time, it concurs with the observations of Sastry and others (Chapter 11) that institutional change is not a discrete event but an ongoing, possibly gradual, path-dependant evolution. Together these contributions highlight two key themes of the book: that institutions influence organizational action but are, at the same time, created and changed by organizational action, and that institutional fields are domains of conflict and change, centered around issues of debate.

INSTITUTIONAL EVOLUTION

Institutional theory has traditionally been invoked to explain why organizations develop similar practices in response to certain regulative, coercive, and normative pressures (Scott, 1995). Implicit in the idea of an institution is stability and persistence. Stability, however, need not suggest immutability. Institutions can and do change, and recent contributions to institutional theory have drawn attention to the role of individual actors and their interests in bringing about institutional change.

If we recognize that actors build and maintain institutions, whether by recreating norms (Scott, 1995) or actively intervening to change them (Oliver, 1991), the study of institutions enlarges to explicitly include the study of power relations between actors (Brint and Karabel, 1991). Institutional forms will reflect the fact that parties have competing interests, differing interpretations of the issues, and unequal capacity to influence outcomes (Hoffman, 1999; Greenwood and Hinings, 1996; Brint and Karabel, 1991).

When institutions are treated as "arenas of power relations, with some actors . . . occupying more advantaged positions than others" (Brint and Karabel, 1991: 355), institutional formation and change is seen as the outcome of a process of negotiation, in which less powerful actors are constrained by the interests and actions of the more powerful actors. The familiar coercive, mimetic, and normative processes that contribute to institutional isomorphism are "downstream processes" (Clarke, 1991: 143) that follow the co-construction of an institution by its participants. "Centers of authority" (Clarke, 1991: 144) may be created by powerful actors who enlist the support of others by translating and reconstructing their interests to mesh with their own.

Actors and issues are thus linked—the negotiation process that characterizes institutional formation is not merely a contest between players, but also a contest between ideas and interpretations of events. Focusing on the power of actors during the process of institutional evolution is only part of the picture; how actors construct events and frame their interests is also critical to understanding what approaches and solutions are adopted (Bansal and Penner, Chapter 13; Campbell, 1998; Dutton and Dukerich, 1991).

In the case described here, as in the analysis by Bansal and Penner in Chapter 13, attention is paid to how various actors interpreted core issues and enlisted support for their interpretations. In this case, the shifts in how actors framed the core issues, as well as shifts in the central actors themselves, define three stages of institutional evolution. The institutional change process is thus seen as directly linked to the actions of constituent organizations and their construction of the issues over time.

BACKGROUND

The case description that follows is based primarily on participant observation and interviews conducted by the author. A nine-month period of participant observation at one major semiconductor manufacturer was augmented by interviews with individuals from the semiconductor manufacturing industry, a PFC gas supplier (Chemco, a pseudonym), and the U.S. EPA. These interviews helped to fill in details about events that occurred before and after the participant observation period. Before describing the three stages of institutional evolution, it is necessary to give a short introduction to the issue of global warming and the contribution of PFC gases to it.

PFCs, or perfluorochlorines,[1] are one class of global warming gases. Global warming gases in the earth's atmosphere act like a one-way filter. They allow incoming solar radiation to reach the earth, but they absorb the radiation that is reflected off the earth's surface. As a result, heat is trapped near the earth's surface. Ubiquitous, naturally occurring substances such as carbon dioxide and water vapor are global warmers but the phenomenon of global warming has been intensified by the release of additional carbon dioxide as well as other gases to the atmosphere as a result of industrial activity. If current trends in global warming gas emissions go unchecked, some climate models predict that average global temperatures could rise by as much as 10° F over the next hundred years (EPA, 2001). This is thought to exceed any temperature change felt over the last 10,000 years, and it would likely bring about significant change in weather patterns, ocean levels, and ecosystems.

PFCs are particularly potent global warmers because they absorb much more radiation than an equivalent quantity of carbon dioxide, as measured by global warming potential (GWP). The GWP for carbon dioxide is 1, whereas the GWPs for PFCs used by the semiconductor industry range between 6,500 and 23,900 (EPA, 2000). PFCs are also some of the longest-lived global warming gases, meaning that the effect of even small quantities released to the atmosphere is felt for many thousands of years. The atmospheric lifetimes of PFCs used by the semiconductor industry range from several thousand to tens of thousands of years. Carbon dioxide, in contrast, has an atmospheric lifetime of between 50 and 200 years (EPA, 2000).

Those involved in the development of the semiconductor industry voluntary agreements had varying views about the extent and urgency of the problem of global warming, but they widely shared the view that it would be prudent to limit emissions of PFC gases to the atmosphere. One manager commented that getting rid of PFCs was "the right thing to do because it doesn't make sense to be using chemicals that have thousand-year atmospheric lifetimes, whether global warming is happening or not." Another commented that the concern over PFC emissions is "a force," and "whether it's real or not, it still has to be worked" (Howard-Grenville, 2000) The idea that PFC gases should not be released into the environment by industry carries through each stage of institutional evolution described below. This common thread, defined here as the institution itself, shows up in different ways at different stages. The actors at each stage and their interpretation of the key issues determine, to a large extent, how this common idea is treated and what institutional forms emerge.

THREE STAGES OF INSTITUTIONAL EVOLUTION

Stage 1: Stewardship (1992–1995)

The evolution of an institution for PFC emissions reduction began outside the semiconductor manufacturing industry itself. The key precipitating incident was an announcement made in 1992 by Chemco, the major supplier of PFC gases to the semiconductor manufacturing industry. Chemco's proposed new policy, formalized in 1993, was that any customer who emitted more than 20 percent of the quantity of C_2F_6 it purchased from Chemco would have its supply capped. C_2F_6, or perfluoroethane, was the PFC most used by semiconductor manufacturers, and Chemco was the sole supplier of the gas to many of those users.

Chemco, as one of the largest U.S. manufacturers of industrial chemicals, was acting in response to new concern about global warming. The 1992 Earth Summit and the adoption of the United Nations Framework Convention on Climate Change (UNFCCC) had given the issue of global warming a high public profile. Following these events, the Clinton administration announced the creation of a Climate Change Action Plan (C-CAP) and, through the EPA, launched a voluntary partnership with industry, called Climate Wise, to encourage reduction of greenhouse gas emissions. Chemco was one of the first members of Climate Wise and cited both the Earth Summit and C-CAP as factors that influenced the creation of its C_2F_6 business policy.

Another factor that almost certainly influenced Chemco's action was the development of product stewardship practices in the chemical industry. Product stewardship involves taking responsibility for products throughout their life cycle, that is, through distribution, customer use, and eventual disposal or recycling. Chemco and other chemical manufacturers were formally committed to developing product stewardship programs in accordance with their participation in the industry's voluntary code of environmental practice, called Responsible Care. The product stewardship code was the newest of Responsible Care's six codes of practice and was formally introduced in 1992, the year Chemco made its announcement regarding the use of C_2F_6.

The potential reputational benefits accrued by acting early on issues of environmental concern had been made clear to Chemco through its handling of another global problem, ozone depletion, several years earlier. In that case, a commitment to rapidly phase out CFCs had won public favor and advanced the development of the Montreal protocol for the elimination of CFCs and other ozone-depleting substances.

All this suggests that Chemco's main goal in developing its C_2F_6 business policy was to demonstrate environmental responsibility and possibly enhance its image as a leader in addressing the new environmental problem of global warming. It is not clear whether Chemco was consciously acting as an "institutional entrepreneur" (Chapter 10), that is, actively striving to export the idea of product stewardship to the semiconductor manufacturing industry. Evidence suggests that Chemco underestimated the impact its announcement would have on the semiconductor manufacturing industry. The fact that users of the gas were to be given only two years to ensure that their emissions of C_2F_6 did not exceed 20 percent of their purchased quantities implies that Chemco expected users to be able and willing to quickly adopt available technologies for reducing emissions.

In fact, U.S. semiconductor manufacturers responded to Chemco's business policy with alarm. Rather than viewing PFC emissions reduction simply as an opportunity for demonstrating environmental leadership, the semiconductor industry considered it a monumental challenge that struck at the heart of their manufacturing processes. One industry manager observed that Chemco's policy, if implemented, would have been "death to our industry."

There was good reason for this concern. The majority of PFCs used by the semiconductor industry are not consumed in the manufacturing process; when semiconductor manufacturers measured PFC emissions they found that as much as 80 percent of their purchased volumes were being emitted, far exceeding the limit Chemco sought to impose. Any solution to the problem would require significant changes in PFC use or treatment. Such changes, however, would have to come in the face of increasing demand for PFCs. Not only was forecasted growth in chip production expected to drive PFC use higher, but the greater complexity of chips being manufactured was expected to increase PFC use per chip. A potential cap on the availability of C_2F_6 threatened the capacity for growth in the industry. Furthermore, there was no known alternative to the use of PFCs in certain critical manufacturing steps. Even if alternatives had been available, their testing, development, and integration into the semiconductor manufacturing process likely would have taken longer than the two-year window Chemco had established for compliance with its policy.

Most agreed in principle with Chemco's position that it would be prudent to reduce PFC emissions, and that such reductions would likely gain public commendation, but the semiconductor manufacturers, individually and collectively, opposed the terms Chemco proposed. Rather than comply directly with Chemco's policy, the manufacturers began to recast the issue of stewardship of PFC gases in a way that fit the strategic and technical conditions of their industry. It was certainly Chemco's coercive power—by virtue of being the sole supplier of a critical process gas—that prompted the semiconductor industry to act, but the eventual outcome of this action was not dictated by Chemco. In this sense, Chemco can be seen as an "accidental" institutional entrepreneur. It planted the seed that compelled the semiconductor industry to develop rules and formal structures for the reduction of PFC emissions, but Chemco did not foresee nor direct these consequences. In fact, Chemco's early expectation was that its customers would likely abate any excess PFCs through high-temperature combustion; similar approaches were standard in chemical manufacturing.

Had abatement proved a feasible and attractive alternative to the semiconductor manufacturers, the story of institutional evolution would end here. But it did not. Many contextual factors made abatement of PFCs particularly unattractive to the semiconductor manufacturers. Air exhaust streams from semiconductor manufacturing are very dilute, so abatement of any gas is far less efficient than it might be for a more concentrated exhaust stream. This meant that abatement of PFCs would have significantly increased water use and nitrous oxide emissions[2] at facilities that were already attracting public attention for high water consumption. Furthermore, combustion of PFCs generates other species that are defined by the EPA as Hazardous Air Pollutants (HAPs). When a manufacturing facility's HAPs emissions exceed some threshold quantity, reporting requirements become more stringent and regulatory review may be required each time a process or chemical change is made. Exceeding this threshold was extremely unattractive to leading semiconductor manufacturers who can incur 35 to 40 chemical changes per year (EPA, 1999) as they hone manufacturing processes to produce state-of-the-art chips. The ability to carry out frequent process changes and avoid potential regulatory delays was considered critical to competitive success. Hence any technology that drove HAP emissions higher was resisted by the most powerful members of the semiconductor industry, as it interfered with manufacturing flexibility.

At the end of 1995, the original date for compliance with Chemco's C_2F_6 policy, few visible trappings of institutionalization had emerged within the semiconductor industry. A great deal had been done, however, to recast the issue of PFC stewardship in light of other issues critical to semiconductor manufacturers. The major U.S. semiconductor manufacturers had been working on several fronts—technical, commercial, and strategic—to ensure the continued supply of C_2F_6 and other PFCs as they searched for ways to reduce emissions. Through existing industry consortia and newly formed working groups they began to study and pilot PFC abatement and capture technologies, measure baseline PFC emissions, develop standard measurement techniques for evaluating emission levels, engage research organizations and universities in looking for non-PFC chemicals that would meet process requirements, and identify and qualify new commercial sources of PFCs. A key argument advanced by the semiconductor manufacturers was that Chemco's business policy forced them to adopt abatement, a solution low on the pollution prevention hierarchy, because insufficient time was available to research and develop alternatives such as recycling or chemical substitution. Because abatement of PFCs led to other undesirable environmental impacts, the manufacturers adopted the position that an approach higher on the pollution-prevention hierarchy, even one that took longer to develop and implement, would be better in the long run.

The semiconductor manufacturers engaged the U.S. Environmental Protection Agency to support their position. Representatives from the EPA were first involved when they were invited to a 1994 Global Warming Symposium organized by the semiconductor industry. Although the EPA was interested in reaching an agreement with the industry and had previously negotiated two voluntary agreements for PFC emissions reduction by other industries (Dutrow, 1997), it did not initiate this involvement. At the end of this stage of institutional evolution, when Chemco's policy was supposed to go into effect, the balance of power had already shifted considerably. Rather than complying outright with Chemco's policy, the semiconductor manufacturers were well on their way to redefining PFC gas stewardship, with the support of the key regulatory agency.

Stage 2: Voluntary Partnership (1996–1998)

The second stage of institutional evolution is distinguished by the creation of a voluntary agreement between the semiconductor manufacturers and the EPA. In 1996, the EPA announced that it had signed a Memorandum of Understanding (MOU) with fifteen semiconductor manufacturers operating in the United States.[3] MOU signatories included all of the major manufacturers and were together responsible for at least 75 percent of the industry's PFC emissions. They committed to "endeavor to reduce PFC emissions" relative to a 1995 baseline (EPA, 1996). Chemco was not a party to the MOU agreement, but it considered any semiconductor manufacturer who had signed the MOU to be complying with its business policy. The MOU had been designed to give the semiconductor manufacturers what they wanted—an assurance of a continued supply of needed quantities of PFCs and time to work on alternatives to abatement. But it did formalize within the industry a commitment to reduce PFC emissions over time.

The key players had shifted and the key issues had been redefined. Chemco was not a signatory to the MOU; the agreement had been reached voluntarily between semiconductor manufacturers and the EPA, albeit under the credible threat that Chemco could have capped (or could still cap) PFC supplies.

As the semiconductor manufacturers and the EPA emerged as the dominant players at this stage of institutional evolution, the central issues, reflected in the details of the MOU, also shifted. The MOU covered all PFCs and related gases used by the semiconductor industry, not just C_2F_6. Neither the semiconductor manufacturers, who needed a predictable supply of a number of PFCs, nor the EPA, which was interested in reducing overall global warming emissions, had an interest in an agreement covering only the gas (C_2F_6) governed by Chemco's business policy. Competitive interests also became important at this stage as semiconductor manufacturers feared that emissions quantities could be linked to confidential manufacturing or process details. As a result, the MOU called for the blind reporting of emissions estimates (both overall quantities and quantities normalized per unit of output) to the EPA.

The MOU also left open for negotiation some critical issues. It did not specify how PFC emissions reductions were to be obtained and it provided for a two-year period for research and development of alternative emissions reduction technologies or substitute chemicals. Furthermore, it did not specify target reductions nor timetables. The MOU only required that parties meet to discuss specific reduction targets after the two-year research and development period had passed. These provisions suggest strongly that, although working to find emissions reduction options that would be compatible with manufacturing priorities, the semiconductor manufacturers were also committed to protecting their own strategic interests in a highly competitive business. This became more clearly expressed in the third stage of institutional evolution where targets for emissions reduction were set with an explicit aim of creating a global "level playing field."

By 1998, when the EPA and the semiconductor manufacturers were due to come together and discuss targets for PFC emissions reduction, new developments had made the choice of technologies for emissions reduction less, rather than more, straightforward. One of the hallmarks of semiconductor manufacturing is continual incremental innovation that results in significant manufacturing process changes (enabling the production of significantly faster and more powerful chips) roughly every two years. By 1998 it was clear that a different mix of PFCs was expected to be used for future manufacturing processes, and that a higher proportion of relatively lower GWP gases would be used. These changes were being made primarily because they entailed manufacturing process improvements, but they also lowered anticipated global warming gas emissions. This good news was offset by the fact that considerable research and development time and money had been invested in certain technologies, like C_2F_6 recycling, that were optimized for the PFC mix soon to be made obsolete by manufacturing process changes. Even the powerful players in the industry could not fully predict nor direct the future state of technology for the manufacturing process, nor could they develop a PFC emissions reduction approach that would work for all manufacturing processes at all times. Events that might have seemed exogenous to the stewardship of PFC gases nonetheless were linked to how this issue was interpreted and how the interpretation changed over time.

Stage 3: Global Target (1998–1999)

The third stage in institutional evolution is marked by yet another shift in the actors and key issues around the stewardship of PFC gases. This time, the institutional field was broadened and deepened without fundamentally altering the arrangement of the previous period. The central issues shifted from those of technical alternatives and manufacturing implications to those more commonly associated with institutional field formation—standards and rules of inclusion.

The EPA had been negotiating the MOU with U.S. semiconductor manufacturers, and similar bodies in Japan and Europe had been negotiating voluntary agreements with manufacturers in those countries. These industry-government voluntary agreements were complemented in the third stage of institutional evolution by the creation of an industry-generated voluntary commitment. The WSC (World Semiconductor Council), an international association of semiconductor manufacturers, announced in 1998 that PFC emissions reduction was its highest environmental priority (Rand, 1999). The members of the WSC are responsible for manufacturing more than 90 percent of the semiconductors produced globally. In April of 1999, members of the WSC committed to an aggressive PFC emissions reduction goal—to reduce absolute emissions by 10 percent from a 1995 baseline by 2010. This goal was negotiated and agreed to by semiconductor manufacturers from the United States, Europe, Japan, and Korea.[4]

As mentioned earlier, one of the most significant aspects of the WSC goal is that it requires semiconductor manufacturers to reduce total emissions from their operations by 10 percent, rather than reduce emissions per unit of output. For an industry with historic growth rates of 12 percent over the last decade, and projected growth rates of 12 to 20 percent (SIA, 1999; 2000), even a small absolute reduction in overall emissions represents a large reduction in per-unit PFC emissions. New technologies for reducing PFC emissions enabled the setting of an absolute goal. Parties who were not central to the institutional field had played a part in developing technical alternatives. For example, one semiconductor equipment supplier worked in collaboration with a major semiconductor manufacturer to develop a technology expected to reduce PFC emissions from one manufacturing process by 99 percent (Motorola, 1999). In addition to the emergence of new technologies for emissions reduction, the changing mix in gases to be used meant overall global warming emissions for a typical manufacturing process would decrease over time even as output increased.

The fact that semiconductor manufacturers worked through their own trade association and not through individual government agencies to create the PFC emissions reduction goal demonstrates that the institutional field's power center had shifted more strongly, relative to earlier stages, to the manufacturers. An ongoing dialogue occurred between the EPA and the MOU signatories, but this was not the forum in which targets were created. Instead, U.S. semiconductor manufacturers were motivated by a strong competitive interest to try to create a single target that would be adopted worldwide. They spoke of creating a "global level playing field" in which semiconductor manufacturers operating in any country would face the same costs associated with PFC emissions control.

The EPA and other government agencies were indirectly powerful in this process. Although they were not at the negotiating table with WSC members, the threat remained that a government agency could take unilateral action to require PFC emissions reductions of a certain magnitude. This spurred the semiconductor manufacturers to set a goal that was at least as aggressive as existing goals under discussion. As a result, the 10 percent PFC emissions reduction target set by WSC members exceeds the targets negotiated between nation states in the 1997 Kyoto Global Warming Protocol.

The third stage of institutional evolution not only illustrates a growing interest among industry members in rules for inclusion (that is, a commitment to specific emission reductions) but also for participation in the new institutional field. To lay the ground rules for participation, WSC members took steps to develop standardized methods for measuring and reporting PFC emissions. For example, representatives from semiconductor manufacturers participated in a workshop organized by the United Nations Intergovernmental Panel on Climate Change (IPCC) to develop emission measurement techniques for high-GWP global warming gases. The earlier focus on technologies for reducing PFC emissions had been replaced with a focus on standard techniques to account for such reductions. As the technical and manufacturing challenges to PFC emissions reduction became relatively easier to meet, the core issue for the semiconductor manufacturers became the strategic matter of creating a workable framework and ensuring that it applied equally to all industry members.

This framework built upon the institutional foundations laid in the previous period. The MOU agreement between U.S. semiconductor manufacturers and the EPA, and similar industry-government agreements made in Europe and Japan, remained important. U.S. manufacturers still reported their emissions to the EPA in accordance with the MOU agreement. During negotiations to extend the MOU beyond its original expiration date (the end of 2000), the EPA sought to incorporate the semiconductor manufacturer's 10 percent reduction target (Rand, 2000) to make it a part of the industry-government agreement rather than simply an industry-wide goal.

At the end of this stage, it was unclear whether the voluntary structures that had emerged in the second and third stages of institutional evolution would become more strongly intertwined, or whether a different institutional form would eventually develop. Eight years after the initial event that triggered the formation of an institution around PFC emissions reduction for the semiconductor manufacturing industry, the institutional field remained in flux. But much change had taken place. By 2000, no major semiconductor manufacturer could operate legitimately without having made some sort of commitment to reduce PFC emissions, whether through industry-government partnerships or an industry-wide commitment or, most commonly, through both.

DISCUSSION

Early in this chapter, I asked why the semiconductor manufacturing industry committed to specific PFC emissions reduction targets in the absence of coercion from the usual sources, that is, public or regulatory pressure. The analysis of the three stages shows that the evolution of the institution followed a complex path that cannot be captured by looking at a single issue, a single time period, or a single group of actors. Table 12.1 summarizes the change in the central issues under negotiation at each stage.

Lessons can be drawn from this case about both the mechanisms of institutional evolution and the role of actors in the transformation of institutions. First, it is interesting to compare the mechanisms of institutional evolution that operated between each of the stages. Figure 12.1 summarizes each of these mechanisms.

Between stage 1 and stage 2, the evolution of the institution involved the transfer of the idea of PFC gas stewardship from one industry sector to another. Only the core idea remained intact through this transfer, however. The details of implementation were significantly recast by the semiconductor manufacturers as they rejected Chemco's limit and proposed ban. The focus on making PFC stewardship

Table 12.1
Central Issues in the Evolution of the Semiconductor Industry
Voluntary Agreements for PFC Emissions Reduction

Stage of Evolution	Central Issues
Stage 1: Stewardship	Leadership on global warming
	Product stewardship
Stage 2: Voluntary partnership	Stewardship consistent with competitive, strategic, and technical context of semiconductor manufacturing
	Development of alternatives to PFC abatement
Stage 3: Global target	Creation of global "level playing field" by setting single PFC reduction target
	Development of measurement and reporting standards

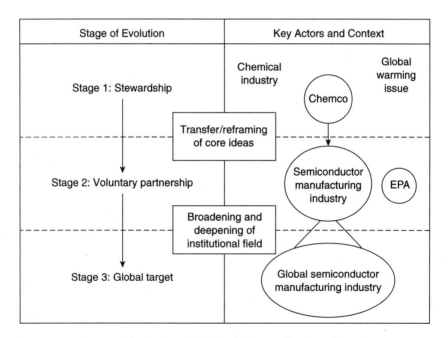

Figure 12.1 Stages of Evolution of PFC Emissions Reduction Efforts

compatible with the competitive, strategic, and technical context of semiconductor manufacturing gave rise to a new form, the voluntary industry-government agreement. The evolution of the institution between stage 2 and stage 3 was not so much a transfer of an idea from one set of actors to another but a further formalization of the rules and membership of the institutional field. By stage 3, the institutional field comprised primarily semiconductor manufacturers in partnership with their respective governments. The process that occurred between stages 2 and 3 was more consistent with "classical" ideas of institutional evolution, that is, with the broadening and deepening of the institutional field as new rules of inclusion were established and new members added.

To see the process of institutional evolution as only comprising stages 2 and 3, when semiconductor manufacturers were the dominant players, would be to miss the important precursors to the idea of PFC emissions reduction and the contextual factors that made the establishment of voluntary agreements and targets attractive. Yet there is danger in including everything in a story of institutional change. If every possible factor were to be considered endogenous to an institutional field, it would be impossible to define where any given field starts and ends. This case illustrates, however, that it is possible to trace a chain of events that clearly transfers an idea from one domain to another, and that certain actors play crucial roles in this transfer process. Chemco was an institutional entrepreneur (even if unintentionally) and acted as the conduit of the idea of PFC gas stewardship from the chemical industry to the semiconductor manufacturing industry. Chemco was influenced by its membership in the chemical manufacturing industry, but the issues salient to chemical manufacturers had only indirect influence over the semiconductor manufacturers; a single issue and single actor made the link.

This brings us to a discussion of power in the transformation of institutions. Rather than simply observing that different actors have more or less power to influence outcomes, this analysis suggests that the exercise of power during institutional evolution is contextual. A powerful player in one stage may become less powerful in a subsequent stage, or an actor's power may become greater because of another's interpretations of the issues at stake. Chemco was a powerful coercive force in the first stage and in the transition to the second stage, but by the third stage it was relatively peripheral. Chemco's power was dependent on a number of conditions. Had there been another source of PFCs, a technical alternative to abatement, or an anticipated decrease rather than increase in PFC use, the semiconductor industry might not have considered Chemco's initial announcement such a significant threat. The importance of PFCs in the manufacturing process turned Chemco's stewardship into a strategic issue, not just an environmental management choice for the semiconductor industry. This highlights the fact that power is not absolute but is contingent upon how different actors make sense of the issues at hand.

The contextualization of power is also illustrated by an interesting twist in traditional roles in this case. The semiconductor manufacturers responded to Chemco's coercive pressure by seeking collaboration with a regulatory agency. Traditionally, regulatory agencies exercise power through the rules they set. In this case, the agency was brought in to act as a broker between a supplier and its customers. The semiconductor manufacturers initiated the involvement with the EPA, not the other way around. Under different conditions, the relationship between the EPA and the semiconductor manufacturers may have been quite different.

IMPLICATIONS

This chapter makes it clear, as does much of this book, that the struggle to develop institutions for environmental protection is not just a struggle over environmental issues. Technical, strategic, and competitive issues are critical to understanding how each party interprets and constructs environmental issues. In this case, the actions taken and the rules established were as much a result of negotiation over related issues as they were a result of negotiation over environmental issues alone. It is interesting that at no time was the science behind global warming and PFCs called into question by the key actors.

Because institutional evolution can follow a complex and ever-changing course as issues and interests evolve and as the relative power of actors rises and falls, it may be difficult for outsiders to influence the development of voluntary institutions for environmental protection. To treat such institutions as entities with rich and unique histories, rather than the inevitable outcome of predictable actions, is to grapple with the reality of developing and influencing environmentally sound corporate practice.

No particular institutional outcome can be predetermined, but several factors contributed to the successful development of PFC emissions reduction targets. First, the fact that the environmental issue *was* linked closely to other core issues for semiconductor manufacturers gave it a sense of urgency and placed it in a class of problems—a threat to future manufacturing—that they could deal with. Second, the mechanisms that were eventually put in place were lodged in existing institutional forms. Voluntary industry-government partnerships for environmental protection are emerging but are not entirely new. The World Semiconductor Council, the body that developed the global target for PFC emissions reductions, had been formed to address trade issues as well as environment, health, and safety issues for the industry. Members had at least some shared history and had worked together in this and other international forums in the past. Finally, although in this case the contribution of PFCs to global warming had attracted very little public attention, the need to project a proactive image was felt by both Chemco and the semiconductor manufacturers. The potential for either regulatory action or public outcry to restrict PFC use made PFC stewardship an attractive alternative. This suggests that more generalized concern over environmental issues (such as, in this case, global warming) can spill over and influence institutional change around other specific issues.

CONCLUSION

The analysis in this chapter illustrates two core themes of this book. First, it has shown how an institutional field can evolve from its earliest stages through the intentional but not entirely predictable actions of its members. Specifically, the PFC case demonstrates that institutional evolution can occur either through the reframing of core ideas as they are transferred from one domain to another, or in the more traditional way as rules and membership are broadened and deepened. This chapter adds to the growing body of literature that focuses on the role of power and negotiation in institutional evolution, and expands it by suggesting that the power to influence institutional evolution is not absolute but is contingent on the role an actor occupies and the range of issues that are considered salient at any given time.

The second contribution of this chapter is not to institutional theory but to our understanding of environmental policy and practice. It is clear that the voluntary agreements to reduce PFC emissions did not come about solely in response to an environmental problem. Instead, they were created because the environmental issue took on particular meaning to organizational actors, and this meaning was derived from a particular technical, competitive, and strategic context. This suggests that environmental problems are fundamentally institutional, and that defining what constitutes an environmental hazard and, especially, defining appropriate ways to deal with such a hazard are not simply the domains of science or policy. As this entire book demonstrates, understanding organizational processes is critical to our understanding of environmental problems and their resolution.

NOTES

1. Examples of PFCs are C_2F_6, CF_4, and C_3F_8. The semiconductor manufacturing industry also uses two related compounds, NF_3 and SF_6, in similar applications. Although the latter two compounds are not strictly PFCs (because they do not contain chlorine), the semiconductor industry treats them as similar for the purposes of the voluntary agreement because they share similar global warming properties. In this chapter, the acronym PFC is similarly used to include NF_3 and SF_6.

2. Because air exhaust flows tend to be very dilute for semiconductor manufacturing facilities, the abatement of C_2F_6 and other process gases by combustion would have required heating large volumes of air to combust a relatively small volume of PFCs. In the process, a large quantity of cooling water would be used and high volumes of combustion by-products (such as NO_x, classified by the Clean Air Act as a criteria pollutant) generated. One source predicted that PFC abatement could have increased water consumption at a semiconductor facility by a factor of two.

3. By 1998, 23 semiconductor manufacturers had signed the MOU.

4. The baseline goal for Korean manufacturers is 1997, two years later than the baseline year for manufacturers from other countries. Taiwanese semiconductor manufacturers, also members of the WSC, intended to commit to the reduction goal in 2000 (Rand, 1999).

REFERENCES

Brint, Steven, and Jerome Karabel. 1991. "Institutional Origins and Transformations: The Case of American Community Colleges." In Walter W. Powell and Paul J. DiMaggio, eds., *The New Institutionalism in Organizational Analysis,* 337–360. Chicago: University of Chicago Press.

Campbell, John. 1998. "Institutional Analysis and the Role of Ideas in Political Economy." *Theory and Society,* 27: 377–409.

Clarke, Adele. 1991. "Social Worlds/Arenas Theory as Organizational Theory." In David Maines, ed., *Social Organization and Social Process: Essays in Honor of Anselm Strauss,* 119–158. New York: Aldine de Gruyter.

Dutrow, Elizabeth. 1997. EPA Negotiator for Semiconductor Industry PFC

MOU. Office of Atmospheric Programs, EPA. Personal communication (June 1997).

Dutton, Jane, and Janet Dukerich. 1991. Keeping an Eye on the Mirror: Image and Identity in Organizational Adaptation. *Academy of Management Journal*, 34: 517–554.

EPA. 1996. *Memorandum of Understanding Between the United States Environmental Protection Agency and (Semiconductor Company)*. Washington, DC: Environmental Protection Agency.

EPA. 1999. *XL Project Progress Report: Intel Corporation*. March 1999. Washington, DC: Environmental Protection Agency.

EPA. 2000. *Inventory of U.S. Greenhouse Gas Emissions and Sinks 1990–1998*. EPA Document no. 236-R-00-001, April. Washington, DC: Environmental Protection Agency.

EPA. 2001. "Global Warming: An Introduction." www.epa.gov/globalwarming/climate/index.html.

Greenwood, Royston, and C. R. Hinings. 1996. "Understanding Radical Organizational Change: Bringing Together the Old and New Institutionalism." *Academy of Management Review*, 21(4): 1022–1054.

Hoffman, Andrew J. 1999. "Institutional Evolution and Change: Environmentalism and the U.S. Chemical Industry." *Academy of Management Journal*, 42(4): 351–371.

Howard-Grenville, Jennifer A. 2000. "Inside Out: A Cultural Study of Environmental Work in Semiconductor Manufacturing." Unpublished doctoral dissertation. Cambridge, MA: Massachusetts Institute of Technology.

Motorola. 1999. "Motorola to Significantly Reduce Global Warming Gases." Motorola Press Release, April.

Oliver, Christine. 1991. "Strategic Responses to Institutional Processes." *Academy of Management Review*, 16: 145–179.

Rand, Sally. 1999. "The Semiconductor Industry's Model Strategy for Global Climate Protection." *Semiconductor Fabtech*, 10: 99–101.

Rand, Sally. 2000. Program manager for semiconductor industry partnership. Climate Protection Division, Environmental Protection Agency. Personal communication.

Scott, W. Richard. 1995. *Institutions and Organizations*. Thousand Oaks, CA: Sage.

SIA. 1999. "Semiconductor Forecast Summary," Semiconductor Industry Association. www.semichips.org/stats/.

SIA. 2000. "World Market Sales and Shares for 2000." Semiconductor Industry Association. www.semichips.org/stats/shares2.htm.

UNFCCC. 2000. "The Convention and Kyoto Protocol." *United Nations Framework Convention on Climate Change*. www.unfccc.int/resource/convkp.html.

IV

FIELD-LEVEL ANALYSES

13 INTERPRETATIONS OF INSTITUTIONS: THE CASE OF RECYCLED NEWSPRINT

Pratima Bansal and Wendy J. Penner

Institutional theory has provided important insights into understanding the processes and motivations of corporate environmental responsiveness (Bansal and Roth, 2000; Hoffman, 1997). It identifies the importance of institutional pressures in evoking corporate environmental responsiveness. Given that firms within the same organizational field experience similar pressures, institutional theory predicts that organizational practices will converge. This outcome is anticipated because of the bias of institutional theory toward explaining organizational similarities rather than differences (Greenwood and Hinings, 1996). At the core of institutional analysis is the assumption that institutional processes lead to a convergence of beliefs, values, structures, and actions.

But some researchers have started to recognize that institutional theory can also explain firm differences. Jennings, Martens, and Zandbergen (Chapter 3) demonstrate how differences in regulators' policies and resources lead to differential effects of coercive pressures, and Milstein, Hart, and York (Chapter 6) explain firm differences in an institutionalized environment by pointing to differences in firm skills and capabilities. Further, Levy and Rothenberg (Chapter 7) argue that the complex, porous, and fragmented nature of organizational fields can also lead to differences in firm responses. These studies apply a similar logic: the institutional

We thank the following people for their assistance in the development of this research project: Jane Dutton, Raymond De Young, Debra Meyerson, and Rick Price. Financial support was provided by the Rackham Interdisciplinary Committee on Organizational Studies at the University of Michigan. The data reported here were collected for the doctoral dissertation of Wendy Penner. The order of authorship was determined alphabetically.

environment acts on organizations, and organizations respond based on their internal dynamics, structures, and self-interests. These studies use firm-level or field-level attributes to explain firm-level differences.

Missing from the analysis is a discussion of how individual-level attributes can explain firm-level differences. Institutional theorists have widely recognized the opportunity to explain macrolevel outcomes by understanding microlevel processes. DiMaggio and Powell (1991: 16) claim that "there has been little effort to make neoinstitutionalism's microfoundations explicit." Zucker (1991: 105) goes further to say that "without a solid cognitive, microlevel foundation, we risk treating institutionalization as a black box at the organizational level, focusing on content at the exclusion of developing a systematic explanatory theory of process, conflating institutionalization with resource dependence, and neglecting institutional variation and persistence."

Microanalysis in institutional theory is not new, but it has focused primarily on institutionalization and convergence (Zucker, 1991; Suchman, 1995). In this chapter, we apply individual-level analysis, primarily the role of individual interpretations, to explain firm differences within the context of a specific issue. We argue that individual interpretations and institutionalization processes interact to influence organizational responses. People interpret their environment and, in doing so, enact that environment (Weick, 1995). Although regulative and normative structures may nudge firms in one direction, individual interpretations, we argue, can reveal underlying incongruities that accommodate variation in organizational responses.

In this study we investigate the use of recycled newsprint among newspaper publishers in Michigan. By analyzing data from interviews with twenty organizational members of four newspapers in Michigan, we identify the interpretations that discriminate among organizational responses to the recycled newsprint issue. In particular, we find that although all newspaper publishers operate within the same regulatory and normative context, organizational members perceive the issue and institutional pressures differently. As a result, we postulate that although the norms and regulations around a social issue may appear to be homogenous, cognitive heterogeneity may, as Zucker (1991) suggested, explain organizational differences.

In exploring the interaction between institutional processes and individual interpretations, this chapter makes two contributions. First, we discuss the possibility that there may be significant differences in individual interpretations of the cognitive context, even though there is general agreement about regulation norms, suggesting that the three pillars of institutional theory may operate at different degrees of institutionalization. Second, we identify three issue interpretations that are critical in explaining why four newspaper publishers in Michigan responded differently to the issue of recycled newsprint. We suggest that these three issue characteristics may explain different degrees of response to environmental issues.

ISSUE INTERPRETATIONS

According to cognitive categorization theory, individuals assign labels to issues to help remember and analyze them (Dutton and Jackson, 1987). How issues are labeled influences the response to them (Dutton, Fahey, and Narayanan, 1983). For example, issues labeled as urgent and feasible are more likely to receive a response than those that are not (Dutton and Duncan, 1987). Research into issue interpretations assumes that issues are constructed by organizational members to reflect the reality they inhabit (Berger and Luckman, 1967; Isabella, 1990; Weick, 1969). Although the reality they confront may be the same, individuals may construct issues in different ways. Because organizational members create the dominant reality in organizational life, their interpretations can give insights into organizational actions (Isabella, 1990).

Interpretations are formed based on individuals' cognitive categories (Rosch, 1978). Individuals use these categories as a mental shorthand to make sense of their environment (Simon and Kaplan, 1989). The cues used to define an environmental issue as a threat to one individual may be completely different from the cues used by another. After some time, the cues or rules used for assigning an issue to a cognitive category become more relevant in interpreting an issue than an unbiased evaluation of the stimulus (Gioia and Poole, 1984).

How an issue is identified, defined, and communicated can influence individual interpretations and, subsequently, organizational actions (Daft and Weick, 1984; Dutton and Duncan, 1987). For example, when organizational members view an issue as urgent and feasible, they will be more likely to work to mobilize organizational resources toward resolving the issue than if the issue is not so viewed (Dutton and Duncan, 1987). An issue that is interpreted as a threat versus an opportunity will also elicit different responses (Dutton and Jackson, 1987). However, these studies reveal little about how organizational members interpret their institutional context (Covaleski and Dirsmith, 1988). Ginsberg and Venkatraman (1992: 49) note that "previous research has neglected to show whether institutional contexts directly influence strategic responses or indirectly influence them through interpretation."

COGNITION IN INSTITUTIONAL THEORY

Institutional theory recognizes that the meanings or interpretations that members attach to organizational practices are central to understanding the process of institutionalization (DiMaggio and Powell, 1991). Shared cognitions define "what has meaning and what actions are possible" (Zucker, 1983: 2).

Three pillars support institutional processes: the regulative, normative, and cognitive (Scott, 1995). The regulative pillar represents the rules that constrain human behavior. These rules are represented not only as regulations, but also through contracts and membership guidelines. Coercive pressures are the primary means by which regulative institutions are distributed. The normative pillar is reflected in the norms, values, and beliefs of constituents. These provide stability to social order and facilitate communication and actions. Membership in clubs, the formalization of professions, and networks of individuals and firms serve to diffuse norms and values. Failing to respond to regulative and normative pressures can lead to punishment or alienation and threaten the resource base of the organization.

Whereas the regulative and normative pillars operate at the field and organizational level of analysis, the cognitive pillar operates also through the individual level of analysis. Members often share interpretations of an issue (Zucker, 1987). These constrain the way in which the world is perceived and what is considered to be acceptable or normal. As perceptions of what is considered right, acceptable, or legitimate guide an individual's actions, dialogue among organizational members will lead to the diffusion of these value systems (Suchman, 1995). Often the pressures are not overt but are diffused subliminally. Members of the field adopt the beliefs and values of their peers even as they influence those around them. A meaning system, then, is created that is more aligned among members of the same organization than with those outside of the organization.

INTERACTION BETWEEN ISSUE
INTERPRETATIONS AND INSTITUTIONAL THEORY

Research on issue interpretations explains how individuals categorize issues and why the categorization process influences action; institutional theory explains how individuals share these interpretations over time and why that leads to congruence in organizational actions. People pass on their perceptions and biases as they interact and, over time, they start to share cognitive rule structures and assign issues to similar categories. Institutionalization creates the routines by which issues are scripted and processed (Ashforth and Fried, 1988; Louis and Sutton, 1991). It provides the rules of the appropriateness of actions to determine how issues are ultimately interpreted and justified (Ginsberg and Venkatraman, 1992; Staw, 1980). Consequently, institutionalization influences both individual interpretations and subsequent actions. The collective interpretation of an issue determines the degree of cognitive institutionalization within the organizational field (Scott, 1995).

The intellectual map of the interactions between institutional contexts and issue interpretations, however, is incomplete. The degree to which the institutional context constrains or is constrained by issue interpretations is unknown. To see inside the "black box" of institutional processes requires insights not only into the direction of influence but the means by which institutional pressures influence organizational structures and actions. This chapter attempts to identify whether differences in organizational actions should be attributed to the interaction of institutional pressures and issue interpretations.

THE RECYCLED NEWSPRINT ISSUE

Issues refer to developments, events, or trends that organizational members collectively recognize as having some consequence for the organization (Dutton and Dukerich, 1991). Consequently, an issue provides an ideal opportunity to investigate individual interpretations. We apply this study to a specific issue, the use of recycled newsprint by newspapers. Using recycled newsprint helps reduce the pressures on landfills and reduces the destruction of forests. In 1991, old newsprint constituted between 6 and 18 percent of landfill space by volume (ANPA, 1990).

Institutional pressures to respond to the recycled newsprint issue were evident from the general public, national and state governments, and the largest newspaper publishing trade association, the American Newspaper Publishers Association (ANPA). The general public was well aware of the issue because of the very visible nature of accumulated old newsprint. Interviews with organizational members of the newspaper publishers had indicated that they received telephone calls and letters from readers. In addition, national and state governments had begun to encourage legislation mandating that newspapers meet quotas for recycled newsprint consumption. In September 1991, eleven states and two localities had passed legislation mandating newspapers use target percentages of recycled newsprint over time. Twelve states had gubernatorial voluntary recycled newsprint use agreements in place, and one state had a legislative voluntary agreement (ANPA, 1991). National legislation had not been imposed, but was being considered (Stein, 1990). Finally, ANPA had exerted pressure on newsprint mills to increase the production of recycled newsprint, advocated voluntary guidelines for recycled newsprint consumption, and advocated the need to do more to solve the recycled newsprint issues, such as the implementation of community recycling (ANPA, 1990).

The recycled newsprint issue was a particularly good one for studying the interaction of interpretations and institutionalization for two reasons. First, the normative and technical aspects of it suggested there were likely to be multiple interpretations of the issue. Corporate and social values of preserving the natural environment made it the "right thing to do." Newspaper publishers knew that they needed to respond to the recycled newsprint issue; however, they may not have agreed on the degree to which they should respond. Underpinning these normative expectations were technical considerations such as the costs and inefficiencies associated with recycled newsprint. Given the wide fluctuations in the price of recycled newsprint, the cost implications of this issue were indeterminate at the time of the study (Hilgartner and Bosk, 1988).

Second, this issue was defined narrowly. It was possible to pin down the potential responses to the recycled newsprint and the associated pressures. If we had chosen a more ambiguous issue, such as sustainable development, the responses and their commensurate interpretations would be too wide and too vague to build a good understanding of the relationship between institutional pressures, issue interpretations, and organizational responses.

The Sites

In-depth case studies were conducted at four Michigan-based daily newspapers. Newspapers with comparable circulation figures and membership in national chains were chosen to control for organizational-level differences. We selected the newspapers by choosing two that were very responsive to the recycled newsprint issue, the *College News* and the *State Journal,* and two that were not, the *City Press* and *Local Daily,* in order to contrast interpretations by organizational response. Pseudonyms are used in this chapter to preserve confidentiality. We determined the suitability of the newspapers by prescreening the organizational issue responses through an exploratory telephone call.

Interviews

Semi-structured interviews were conducted with five senior managers at each of the four newspapers. We chose these people because they appeared to be the key decision makers on the recycled newsprint issue. Also, multiple respondents were used in order to gather reliable data to determine whether issue interpretations were similar across respondents within the same firm. Interviewees were asked to define corporate social responsibility and to identify their competitors; how the newspaper competed; their newspaper's identity and image; their parents' identity and influence; adjectives that describe the recycled newsprint issue; the history of newspaper recycling at their paper; how the individual learned about the issue; issues similar to the recycled newsprint issue on which their newspaper has acted; their newspaper's response to the issue; and their reasons for the response. All interview questions were open-ended; clarification of the questions were provided only when requested. The interviews were conducted in person and typically lasted for approximately one hour. Excepting one, all of the interviews were audio recorded and fully transcribed. Detailed notes were taken of the excepted interview.

INTERPRETATIONS OF THE RECYCLED NEWSPRINT ISSUE

The four newspapers fell into two groups based on the amount of recycled newsprint content used and the response scope. These differences in issue response are paralleled by differences in issue interpretations, as described in this section.

Recycled Newsprint Issue Response

Recycled newsprint content. The percent of recycled newsprint that the newspapers used was considerably different between the *College News* and *State Journal* and the *City Press* and *Local Daily*. Although the *College News* used 12 percent and the *State Journal* used 11 percent, the *City Press* and *Local Daily* both used less than 1 percent. Interviewees were asked to rate their newspaper's response to the recycled newsprint issue on a scale of one to ten. Almost all respondents, independent of the newspaper for which they worked, indicated that they had a high degree of response to the recycled newsprint issue.

Response scope. Although recycled newsprint content provides a very direct measure of the response to the recycled newsprint issue, the data analysis revealed other types of responses that reflected greater response scope. For example, the *College News* and *State Journal* promoted their recycled newsprint content among their own employees and the local community. They advertised their recycled newsprint content in their newspapers and published articles dealing specifically with recycling in the community. In addition, the *College News* worked both with the local community recycling program to secure new markets for old newspapers and with a local recycling facility to recycle glossy paper, and its parent company acquired an interest in a recycling mill and expected to increase the recycled newsprint content. The *City Press* engaged in very little promotion, and the *Local Daily* in none.

Issue Interpretations

Issue importance. Issue importance refers to the members' beliefs about the potential loss involved in not acting on an issue or the potential gains from acting (Dutton, Stumpf, and Wagner, 1990). When the organizational loss incurred by not acting on an issue (or the gain from acting on it) is perceived to be high, organizational members are expected to interpret the issue as more important (Billings, Milburn, and Schaalman, 1980). Most managers of the *College News* and *State Journal* perceived the recycled newsprint issue as important for their newspapers. Specifically, they referred to a potential loss in public standing with community members or a loss in readership if the newspaper did not respond to the issue. A respondent from the *State Journal,* for example, said, "I'm surprised that we don't hear more about newsprint. I think we're living on borrowed time." All interviewees of the *College News* indicated that their readers were well informed about the recycled newsprint issue, and four of the five interviewed members of the State Journal indicated that the issue was important. Along with the importance attributed to the issue, interviewees at both papers said that environmental quality was personally important to their corporate leaders.

Managers of the *City Press* and *Local Daily* usually did not interpret the recycled newsprint issue as important to their readers. Although they thought the issue was generally important, reflecting the process of institutionalization, they did not believe it was important to their readers or their firm. They foresaw few associated losses with the issue given that the pressures from the local community were rather weak. Of the ten individuals interviewed at the *City Press* and *Local Daily,* nine did not indicate that the issue was important. The publisher of the *City Press,* for example, emphasized that the recycled newsprint issue is not really an environmental quality issue, but "a materials handling problem." A respondent from the *Local Daily,* which was mirrored by others there, said, "I think the public views the issue with complete apathy."

Issue responsibility. Issue responsibility refers to interviewees' assertions that their newspaper contributed to the issue and they must help resolve it. Interviewees at the *College News* and *State Journal* expressed concerns about landfill capacity, cutting down trees, making messes, and decomposition rates. They talked about "adequate supply of newsprint" and "scarcity." They viewed the issue as their responsibility and used language such as "social responsibility," "morally right actions," and "doing the right thing" when describing newspapers' responses to the issue. All five members of the *College News* and four members of the *State Journal* indicated that newspaper publishers were responsible for the issue.

Managers of the *City Press* and *Local Daily* thought otherwise. They argued that they were not "tearing down Sequoias to produce newsprint," that the forests being used were "completely sustainable," and that it was "only a matter of landfill space" and "the waste was not hazardous." They blamed politicians for bringing attention to the issue to discredit the media, or criticized the community's understanding of the issue. One respondent from the *City Press* said that "the function of newspapers gets exaggerated a little bit. . . . On average, newspapers are not more than 10 percent of landfill. In addition, they're not, you know, hazardous properties. They just take up space." Only two members of the *City Press* and one member of the *Local Daily* believed that they were responsible for the issue.

Issue feasibility. This refers to beliefs about the probability of successfully resolving the issue and includes two dimensions: issue understanding (the perception that actors know what is required to effectively solve an issue) and issue capability (the perception that actors have the means to solve an issue) (Dutton and Duncan, 1987). Issue capability reflects concerns about the cost of solving a problem and whether the organization can absorb it. Members of the *College News* and *State Journal* expressed a more complex understanding of how to resolve the recycled newsprint issue. For example, one member of the *State Journal* reflected on the cost implications of the de-inking process required to produce recycled newsprint and the needed capital expenditures. A member of *College News* spoke in detail about the mills that supplied recycled newsprint. Members of the *State Journal* and the *College News* also suggested a broader range of possible responses than the interviewees at the other newspapers did (such as promoting recycling to readers, implementing in-house recycling, and assisting with community recycling programs). A typical comment from these two publishers was made by someone at the *State Journal*: "There's nothing wrong with recycled newsprint. There are some that are better than others, but there is no reason not to use it." As with issue importance and responsibility, all five members of the *College News* and four of the five members interviewed at the *State Journal* indicated that it was feasible to respond to the issue.

Interviewees at the *City Press* and *Local Daily* did not seem to understand the recycled newsprint issue, and did not believe that they had the resources to solve the issue. They believed recycled newsprint was considerably more expensive than virgin newsprint and that it was of lesser quality. Further, they argued that there was an insufficient supply of recycled newsprint and that there was an adequate supply of virgin newsprint because it was being farmed from sustainable sources. Several members of the *City Press* and, to a lesser extent, the *Local Daily* believed that the only response to the recycled newsprint issue was to increase its content.

They did not indicate that other measures could or should be taken. Statements such as "We're doing all we can on the issue" and "I don't think, even with other resources, we could do anything more on the issue" reflect this limited range of response. Only one member of the *Local Daily* and *City Press* indicated that it was feasible to respond to the issue.

EXPLAINING FIRM-LEVEL DIFFERENCES

There was considerable similarity among the four newspapers. They all confronted the same issue regarding recycled newsprint and they all responded to the issue by including some recycled content. When asked to rate their organizational response to the issue, their perceptions of their organization's response were remarkably similar. The newspapers were also subject to similar regulative and normative institutions. They operated under the state of Michigan regulations; they belonged to the same trade association; and they confronted the same competitors. Superficially, these newspapers appeared to operate in similar institutional environments and were homogenous in their response to the recycled newsprint issue.

As we dug deeper into the data, differences emerged. In terms of issue response, two newspapers, the *College News* and *State Journal,* used considerably more recycled content than did the other two newspapers and engaged in peripheral recycling activities. In terms of cognitive institutions, there was considerable variation. Whereas members of the *College News* and *State Journal* agreed on the importance and feasibility of the issue and their responsibility toward it, the other two papers exhibited less consistency among their responses. In terms of perceptions of institutional pressures, the *College News* and *State Journal* respondents perceived high pressures, and the others perceived lower pressures.

Regulative, normative, and cognitive institutions can operate at different levels of analysis. The regulative and normative typically operate at the field or organizational level, but the cognitive could also apply to the individual. Institutional analysis has generally favored organizational and field-level analysis (Zucker, 1991).

Our data show that individual-level analysis permits microanalysis of the cognitive aspects of institutional processes. This analysis shows that organizational fields are not necessarily uniform. Pockets of differences in interpretations may exist in a sea of positive organizational responses. Our data show that there are distinguishable differences in the interpretations of the recycled newsprint issue, even though interviewees had similar beliefs about their organizational response to these pressures. In particular, we identify three characteristics that could lead to variation in organizational responses. We also show that although respondents interpreted the issue differently, they did not differ in their interpretations of their organization's response to the issue. So although entropy regarding the issue may exist within the organization field, disharmony about the organizational response may not.

Uncovering the interpretations of an issue may expose deeply embedded tensions in issue interpretations, which may be critical to the speed and direction of institutionalization. For example, Zucker (1991) shows that small changes in the degree of exteriority and objectivity of an issue can dramatically influence the degree to which it is institutionalized. A higher degree of accord among organizational members may lead to faster and fuller organizational response. Higher discord reflects greater entropy that may erode the regulative and normative aspects of institutionalization. A high level of discord within a pocket of an institutional field may be instrumental in later initiating regulative and normative institutional changes.

Regulative and normative institutions are associated with purposive action. DiMaggio and Powell (1991: 8) indicated that institutions are "the products of human design, the outcomes of purposive action by instrumentally oriented individuals." Lawrence (1999) identified two institutional strategies that may change these institutions: standardization and membership. Standardization strategies impose technical, legal, or informal standards on organizational processes, structures, and actions even as membership strategies dictate who can belong to the group. Although regulative and normative institutions can be imposed on firms through standardization and membership strategies that can lead to homogeneity, it is difficult to achieve conformity in individual interpretations. Normative and regulative mechanisms may accelerate the convergence of issue interpretations, but there is no indication that the convergence among interpretations is ever complete, even if it appears that the issue is taken for granted.

Prior research on organizational responses to environmental issues has emphasized its political and regulative aspects. Firm responses to environmental issues are often precipitated by pressures from outside the organization, such as from stakeholders or the anticipation of regulations. Our research shows that in spite of these pressures, differences in the interpretation of the issue's feasibility and importance and the firm's responsibility for causing the issue determined the type and degree of organizational response to the recycled newsprint issue. These characteristics may be specific to the issue of recycled newsprint, but we think they could apply to a wider array of environmental issues and warrant further investigation.

Issue feasibility speaks directly to economic versus environmental tensions (Hoffman and others, 1999). Differences in the interpretations of the feasibility of an issue suggest that the individuals on opposing sides differ in their interpretation of whether organizational benefits exceed the costs. This economic versus environmental debate has been articulated frequently in the popular and academic press (Miller, 1998; Porter and van der Linde, 1995; Walley and Whitehead, 1994). These discussions and disagreements are likely mirrored by individual members within organizations, leading to differences in issue interpretations.

Issue responsibility speaks to the diffuse aspects of environmental issues. The source of environmental emissions, whether they be to land, air, or water, are often undetectable. For example, carbon dioxide emissions, volatile organic compounds, and CFCs are virtually invisible. Because many firms contribute to these invisible emissions, it is easy for any one firm to duck responsibility by pointing to heavier polluters. Shared responsibility allows considerable discretion among organizational members to assume differing degrees of perceived responsibility in contributing to the issue.

Issue importance speaks to the uncertainty of the science pertaining to many environmental issues. In spite of the growing evidence of greenhouse gases, ozone depletion, the loss in biodiversity, there is still considerable uncertainty as to the impact of these effects on human life and welfare. Given the lack of "good science," individuals have considerable discretion in their interpretation of the importance of the issue.

Given the uncertainty regarding the economics, impacts, and outcomes, most environmental issues are subject to interpretation. Although institutional theory has been poised to address uncertain organizational environments by predicting that firms will seek to reduce that uncertainty by mimicking the structures and actions of successful peers (DiMaggio and Powell, 1991), uncertainty also permits firms considerably more discretion to pursue other organizational goals (Goodrick and Salancik, 1996). The uncertainty regarding environmental issues is primarily within the cognitive domain; that is, how issues are interpreted rather than in respect to norms and regulations. The commensuration of environmental metrics, standards, and regulations facilitates the convergence of issue interpretations (Levin and Espeland, Chapter 5); however, the persistence of a dominant economic rational and scientific paradigm hinders the processes of cognitive institutionalization and diffusion because of the difficulty in achieving consensus on the economics, impacts, and outcomes of environmental issues.

In this chapter we have delved into the cognitive dimension of institutional theory, applying notions of issue interpretations to the phenomena. The two literatures have quite different orientations: institutional theory emphasizes similarities, but issue interpretations recognize differences. Furthermore, both institutional theory and issue interpretations theory focus primarily on the organizational level of analysis, but the analysis of issue interpretations lends itself more easily to an individual level of analysis. By investigating individual interpretations of an issue to understand organizational responses, we have, to some extent, departed from the rubric of institutional theory. However, in doing so, we speak to a question that has increasingly occupied the agenda of institutional theorists: that of the processes of institutionalization and organizational change.

We also speak to the interests of environmentalists by highlighting the opportunities and challenges they might meet by effecting environmentally responsive organizational change. We outlined how individuals can frame the recycled newsprint issue. Some newspaper managers felt that their organization was responsible for the issue, that the issue was important, and that it was feasible to respond to the issue. To the extent that environmentalists can evoke the same frames of references in their dialogue, the more likely that they will effect change. However, changing the way in which an issue is interpreted is slow and arduous. Unlike changes to the regulative and normative institutional environments, which can be imposed from the top, changes to the cognitive environment need to be embraced by individuals. Effecting change among disparate individuals with varying interpretations of an issue is costly and time-consuming. In spite of this, efforts may be rewarded by changes that are significant and enduring.

REFERENCES

ANPA. 1990. "ANPA Sets Newsprint Goal." *Presstime,* May: 80.

ANPA. 1991. "Legislative Summary Sheet." Compiled Sept. 3. City Press: American Newspaper Publishers Association.

Ashforth, Blake E., and Yitzhak Fried. 1988. "The Mindlessness of Organizational Behaviors." *Human Relations,* 41(4): 305–329.

Bansal, Pratima, and Kendall Roth. 2000. "Why Companies Go Green: A Model of Corporate Ecological Responsiveness." *Academy of Management Journal,* 43(4): 717–736.

Berger, Peter L., and Thomas Luckman. 1967. *The Social Construction of Reality.* New York: Doubleday.

Billings, Robert S., Thomas W. Milburn, and Mary Lou Schaalman. 1980. "A Model of Crisis Perception: A Theoretical and Empirical Analysis." *Administrative Science Quarterly,* 25: 300–316.

Covaleski, Mark A., and Mark W. Dirsmith. 1988. "An Institutional Perspective on the Rise, Social Transformation, and Fall of a University Budget Category." *Administrative Science Quarterly,* 33(4): 562–587.

Daft, Richard L., and Karl E. Weick. 1984. "Toward a Model of Organizations as Interpretation Systems." *Academy of Management Review,* 9(2): 284–295.

DiMaggio, Paul J., and Walter W. Powell. 1991. "Introduction." In Walter W. Powell and Paul J. DiMaggio, eds., *The New Institutionalism in Organizational Analysis,* 1–40. Chicago: University of Chicago Press.

Dutton, Jane E., and Janet M. Dukerich. 1991. "Keeping an Eye on the Mirror: Image and Identity in Organizational Adaptation." *Academy of Management Journal,* 34(3): 517–554.

Dutton, Jane E., and Robert B. Duncan. 1987. "The Creation of Momentum for Change Through the Process of Strategic Issue Diagnosis." *Strategic Management Journal,* 8(3): 279–295.

Dutton, Jane E., and Susan E. Jackson. 1987. "Categorizing Strategic Issues: Links to Organizational Action." *Academy of Management Review,* 12(1): 76–90.

Dutton, Jane E., Liam Fahey, and V. K. Narayanan. 1983. "Toward Understanding Strategic Issue Diagnosis." *Strategic Management Journal,* 4(4): 307–323.

Dutton, Jane E., Stephen A. Stumpf, and David Wagner. 1990. "Diagnosing Strategic Issues and Managerial Investment of Resources." *Advances in Strategic Management,* 6: 143–167.

Ginsberg, Ari, and N. Venkatraman. 1992. "Investing in New Information Technology: The Role of Competitive Posture and Issue Diagnosis." *Strategic Management Journal,* 13 (special summer issue): 37–53.

Gioia, Dennis A., and Peter P. Poole. 1984. "Scripts in Organizational Behavior." *Academy of Management Review,* 9(3): 449–459.

Goodrick, Elizabeth, and Gerald R. Salancik. 1996. "Organizational Discretion in Responding to Institutional Practices: Hospitals and Cesarean Births." *Administrative Science Quarterly,* 14(1): 1–28.

Greenwood, Royston, and C. R. Hinings. 1996. "Understanding Radical Organizational Change: Bringing Together the Old and the New Institutionalism." *Academy of Management Review,* 21(4): 1022–1054.

Hilgartner, Stephen, and Charles L. Bosk. 1988. "The Rise and Fall of Social Problems: A Public Arenas Model." *American Journal of Sociology,* 94(1): 53–78.

Hoffman, Andrew J. 1997. *From Heresy to Dogma.* San Francisco: New Lexington Press.

Hoffman, Andrew J., James Gillespie, Don Moore, Kimberly A. Wade-Benzoni, Leigh L. Thompson, and Max H. Bazerman. 1999. "A Mixed-Motive Perspective on the Economics Versus Environment Debate." *American Behavioral Scientist,* 42(8): 1254–1276.

Isabella, Lynn A. 1990. "Evolving Interpretations as a Change Unfolds: How Managers Construe Key Organizational Events." *Academy of Management Journal,* 33(1): 7–41.

Lawrence, Thomas B. 1999. "Institutional Strategy." *Journal of Management,* 25(2): 161–188.

Louis, Meryl Reis, and Robert I. Sutton. 1991. "Switching Cognitive Gears: From Habits of Mind to Active Thinking." *Human Relations,* 44(1): 55–76.

Miller, William H. 1998. "Cracks in the Green Wall." *Industry Week,* 58 (Jan. 19): 58–68.

Porter, Michael E., and Claas van der Linde. 1995. "Green and Competitive: Ending the Stalemate." *Harvard Business Review,* 73(5): 120–134.

Rosch, Eleanor. 1978. "Principles of Categorization." In Eleanor Rosch and Barbara B. Lloyd, eds., *Cognition and Categorization,* 24–47. Hillsdale, NJ: Erlbaum.

Scott, W. Richard. 1995. *Institutions and Organizations.* Thousands Oaks, CA: Sage.

Simon, Herbert A., and C. A. Kaplan. 1989. "Foundations of Cognitive Science." In Michael I. Posner, ed., *Foundations of Cognitive Science.* Cambridge, MA: MIT Press.

Staw, Barry M. 1980. "Rationality and Justification in Organizational Life." *Research in Organizational Behavior,* 2: 45–80.

Stein, M. I. 1990. "Bennack: Promote Recycling or Face Regulation." *Editor & Publisher,* May 5: 25.

Suchman, Mark C. 1995. "Managing Legitimacy: Strategic and Institutional Approaches." *Academy of Management Review,* 20(3): 571–610.

Walley, Noah, and Bradley Whitehead. 1994. "It's Not Easy Being Green." *Harvard Business Review,* 72(3): 47–52.

Weick, Karl. 1969. *The Social Psychology of Organizing.* Reading, MA: Addison-Wesley.

Weick, Karl. 1995. *Sensemaking in Organizations.* Thousand Oaks, CA: Sage.

Zucker, Lynne G. 1983. "Organizations as Institutions." In Samuel B. Bacharach, ed., *Research in the Sociology of Organizations,* 1–47. Greenwich, CT: JAI Press.

Zucker, Lynne G. 1987. "Institutional Theories of Organization." *Annual Review of Sociology,* 13: 443–464.

Zucker, Lynne G. 1991. "The Role of Institutionalization in Cultural Persistence." In Walter W. Powell and Paul J. DiMaggio, eds., *The New Institutionalism in Organizational Analysis,* 83–107. Chicago: University of Chicago Press.

14

POLICY DISCOURSE, LOGICS, AND PRACTICE STANDARDS: CENTRALIZING THE SOLID-WASTE MANAGEMENT FIELD

Michael Lounsbury, Heather Geraci, and Ronit Waismel-Manor

In contrast to localized, strategic views of organizational action, institutional analyses in sociology have directed attention to how the definition of appropriate practices and behavior occur within systems of authority where the state, professions, or other actors set the rules (Block, 1990; Campbell, Hollingsworth, and Lindberg, 1990; DiMaggio and Powell, 1983; Hamilton and Biggart, 1988; Hollingsworth and Boyer, 1997; Meyer and Rowan, 1977). In developing this perspective, the concept of "field" has been used to guide analyses that aim to account for the interpenetration of cultural and social forces as well as dimensions of social similarity (horizontal relationships) and stratification (hierarchical relationships) (Bourdieu, 1984; DiMaggio, 1983; Grattet, 1997; Mohr and Duquenne, 1997; Scott, 1994). Even though institutionalists have been criticized for concentrating too much on social processes in relatively stable and established fields (see Hirsch and Lounsbury, 1997), a number of recent efforts try to redirect attention toward fields that are emerging or being transformed (such as Haveman and Rao, 1997; Lounsbury, 2002; Scott and others, 2000; Thornton and Ocasio, 1999). This chapter seeks to contribute to the debate about governance and policy-setting processes by focusing on how policy discourse shapes the development of practice standards in a transforming field (see also Mendel, Chapter 18).

We focus on the U.S. solid-waste crisis of the 1960s that led to the transformation of the field from a highly decentralized one to one that was much more hierarchical. Solid-waste management comprised a heterogeneous set of practices that

We would like to thank Rick Grannis, Andy Hoffman, Marc Ventresca, Dick Scott, and participants of the Organizations, Policy, and the Natural Environment conference for their helpful advice and comments.

were idiosyncratically defined at the town or municipality level until the 1960s, but by the early 1970s the federal government had held extensive hearings on the topic and created a new federal agency, the Environmental Protection Agency (EPA), which was to actively monitor and shape environmental practices including solid waste. As the federal government became increasingly involved in evaluating solid-waste problems and solutions, efforts were made to develop a standardized approach. To shed light on how practices were standardized in this field, we concentrate on conflicting claims about incineration and recycling that were resolved in the 1970s when elite players decided that incineration was better than recycling and provided a more appropriate complement to landfilling.

Through a detailed investigation of Congressional hearings on solid waste in 1969 and 1970, we show the wide diversity of expert opinions that were voiced about incineration and recycling. Congressional hearings provide a symbolic forum where views about policy, governance, and practice standards can be expressed. Also, field-level forums such as hearings or national meetings contribute to the consolidation of a heterogeneous set of views into shared meaning systems that guide actions such as field practices and governance (DiMaggio, 1991). Our analysis, consistent with recent arguments in economic sociology (such as McGuire, Granovetter, and Schwartz, 1993), organizational theory (such as Van de Ven and Garud, 1993), and science and technology studies (such as Bijker, Hughes, and Pinch, 1994; Jasanoff and others, 1995), demonstrates that practice standards do not always emerge as a result of natural or inevitable processes (Ventresca and Porac, forthcoming; see also Levin and Espeland, Chapter 5). In those hearings, no definitive evidence was presented, nor was there any clear consensus that incineration was more efficacious than recycling as a solid-waste solution. It may not be surprising that Congressional hearings contain widely diverse and conflicting views, but the degree of discord was striking given that the solid-waste field soon after converged on a set of practice standards in a relatively unproblematic way.

We show that despite the variety of kinds of claims made, especially about recycling and incineration, a *market-efficiency logic* that valorized for-profit actors over nonprofits such as citizen advocacy groups, informed much of the testimony and favored the subsequent adoption of incineration over recycling as a practice standard. Logics have been conceived of as organizing principles that govern the selection of technologies, define what kinds of actors are authorized to make claims, shape and constrain the behavioral possibilities of actors, and specify criteria of effectiveness and efficiency (Friedland and Alford, 1991). But contrary to the market-efficiency logic that favors short-term cost-benefit calculations, other claims about solid-waste practices were informed by a *central-governmental logic* that suggests that the federal government has a key role in shaping which practices became standard. Although these competing logics are evident in the hearings we analyze, the central-governmental logic was quite marginal.

We next provide a brief background on the emergence of a more hierarchically centralized solid-waste field, focusing on the role of the federal government in initiating a national dialogue on solid waste and fostering the development of standardized practices. We then present an analysis of the 1969–1970 Congressional hearings on solid-waste management that led to the passage of the 1970 Resource Recovery Act. Those hearings are particularly important because it was the first time that solid-waste practice alternatives were openly discussed and debated at the national level, enabling state institutions to shape standardization processes. Drawing on network analytic techniques, we derive witness clusters that guide our interpretation of the variety of views about the competing solid-waste practices of incineration and recycling and the logics that informed their claims. We conclude with a discussion of how our understanding of field dynamics and policy making can be expanded through analyses of discourse and processes by which dominant logics and practice standards emerge.

THE DYNAMICS OF THE SOLID-WASTE MANAGEMENT FIELD

In the first half of the twentieth century, the collection and disposal of solid waste was highly fragmented and unstandardized (Hays, 1979). After World War II, however, population growth and concomitant increases in consumption and discards led to a much more complicated situation for municipal solid-waste managers. The waste stream became much more diverse, the volume of waste increased dramatically, landfill space became scarce, and landfills began to pose health problems to nearby communities (Packard, 1960; U.S. Senate, 1964). In addition, urban growth led to highly fragmented trash collection and disposal arrangements with responsibility divided among many agencies, councils, and other groups (Melosi, 1981: 197). In the early 1960s, sanitation departments in many cities began to band together and seek help from state and federal governmental officials and agencies. In 1964, the federal government got involved in the issue of solid-waste management for the first time, sponsoring hearings that led to the passage of the 1965 Solid Waste Act.

Although the passage of the 1965 act marked the entrance of the federal government into debates about how solid-waste management activities should be organized, the act itself offered no concrete direction to municipalities. It mainly established national research and development programs for new and improved methods of waste disposal while also initiating a grant program to assist state and municipal governments in their efforts to experiment with new kinds of solid-waste technologies and methods. As part of this, the government undertook an extensive survey of how various communities organized their solid-waste management. This and related research and demonstration projects provided important information about U.S. solid-waste practices, making possible a more comprehensive understanding of how to bring more order and coherence to them by establishing national standards.

This signaled the need for a more centralized solid-waste management program, with the federal government playing a key role in developing solid-waste policy. Refuse was no longer an exclusively local issue. By the late 1960s, attention shifted toward open debate about what technological solutions for the management of solid waste could be developed to cope with problems such as the growing amount of consumer discards, landfill scarcity, and poor sanitation related to open dumping. In this milieu, large for-profit conglomerates such as *Waste Management* and *Browning-Ferris* emerged, as did manufacturers of solid-waste management equipment including those promoting new waste-to-energy incinerators. In essence, the entrance of the federal government into the solid-waste management field not only catalyzed a process of policy making, but also facilitated the creation of a nationwide solid-waste management industry and an increased concentration of control over solid-waste collection and hauling by large national conglomerates.

But although the 1965 Solid Waste Act set these processes of centralization in motion, there was little policy consensus about which solid-waste technologies could provide the best solutions to the multitude of problems raised in the 1964 hearings. In 1969 and 1970, Congress held hearings to have an open debate on the matter, resulting in the Resource Recovery Act of 1970. There was virtually unanimous consensus that unsanitary open dumps had to be shut down and that solid-waste management had to become much more standardized across the country. In addition, many experts testified in support of solid-waste practices such as sanitary landfills, waste-to-energy incineration (W-T-E), resource recycling, deep-sea disposal (ocean dumping), ocean incineration, composting, underground disposal, grinding, and disposal in sewers. There was great discord about which of these practices would be best.

Despite the wide variety of solid-waste practices discussed, as well as the conflict over which solutions were optimal, the solid-waste management field had converged on the practices of incineration and sanitary landfilling by the late 1970s. Sanitary landfills were relatively nonproblematic, as most experts viewed some amount of landfilling to be necessary, but there was great disagreement about incineration and recycling. Conflict over these practices was clearly evident in the 1969–1970 hearings, but was muzzled by the mid-1970s.

In the early 1970s, the pro-incinerator lobby, organized by the National Center for Resource Recovery, emerged and became a dominant force that successfully promoted its technology while helping to construct recycling as a costly, marginal activity promoted by radical environmental activists. In addition, in 1979, the EPA and the Department of Energy signed an agreement that endorsed W-T-E as a solid-waste solution, committing to the construction of 200–250 W-T-E facilities in the 1980s (Seldman, 1995). This seemed to imply the death of recycling, but subsequent Not-In-My-Backyard (NIMBY) movements halted the development of incineration facilities by the mid-1980s and recycling emerged as a legitimate solid-waste solution by the late 1980s (Lounsbury, Ventresca, and Hirsch, forthcoming; Schnaiberg and Gould, 1994).

In this chapter we bracket the dynamics of the solid-waste management field after 1970 to focus on the key debates about solid-waste practices in the 1969–1970 Congressional hearings. We do this not only to highlight the heterogeneity of social actors involved and the viewpoints expressed, but also their discord. Despite the apparent disagreement about solid-waste technologies, however, we show that testimony at the hearings was mainly informed by a market-efficiency logic, providing a symbolic framework that enabled elite actors in the field to construct a clear consensus about practice standards. Analyzing policy discourse in forums such as Congressional hearings is valuable because it can reveal logics that consequentially shape the development of fields.

DATA AND METHODS

The Congressional hearings leading to the passage of the Resource Recovery Act of 1970 were held before the Subcommittee on Air and Water Pollution of the Committee on Public Works of the Senate. The hearings began on April 10, 1969 and ended almost a year later. During that time, the subcommittee convened eighteen times. Fourteen of the hearings were held in Washington, D.C., but four were held in Boston, Jacksonville, Detroit, and San Francisco. Edmund S. Muskie, chairman of the subcommittee, opened the proceedings with a call to action: "We now think that the time has come to move beyond experimental research to the actual development of systems in our large metropolitan areas" (U.S. Senate, 1969–1970: 4/10/69, 1). It was clear that the federal government was interested in playing a much larger role in standardizing solid-waste practices across the country.

Although the solid-waste field had come to a consensus on the practices of incineration and sanitary landfilling by the mid- to late-1970s, these hearings provided an exceptional opportunity to identify the wide variety of potential techno-logical solutions considered just a few years earlier. The witnesses at the hearings represented a variety of federal, state, and municipal bodies and agencies, national trade associations, private industry, nonprofit organizations, academic institutions, environmental research groups, private citizens, and one consumer interest group. Private industry and governmental (federal, state, local) representatives, however, provided the majority of the testimony (close to 80 percent of all witnesses that testified). Approximately 32 percent of the witnesses represented private industry; 46 percent were from the government.

Through a detailed analysis of how these various actors made claims about solid-waste practices, we uncover the logics that undergirded testimony and shaped the development of practice standards in the solid-waste management field. We focus our attention on incineration and recycling, as these are of particular practi-cal and theoretical interest. We are particularly interested in the claims made for and against recycling and incineration and we investigate the extent to which tes-timony at these hearings indicated that incineration was the best solution for the solid-waste field.

Analytical Strategy

In analyzing Congressional hearing testimony, we were mainly interested in de-veloping a systematic understanding of the heterogeneity of views expressed about solid-waste solutions and their underlying logics. Recently researchers, drawing on a diverse range of theoretical perspectives including institutional analysis, the sociology of culture, and social theory, have begun to develop methods and ap-proaches to understand the social structures that underlie culture and discourse (Bourdieu, 1984; DiMaggio, 1986; Mische and Pattison, forthcoming; Mohr, 1998). One of the key insights and claims of this new line of work is that our understand-ing of institutional processes can be greatly enhanced by examining how the rela-tionship between material practices and symbolic constructions is mutually con-stitutive (Friedland and Alford, 1991). We draw on network analytic techniques (Knoke and Kuklinski, 1982) to evaluate similarities and differences in Congres-sional hearing testimony on solid-waste practices.

To do this, we analyzed the testimony of all witnesses in the hearings (n = 128) along several dimensions having to do with their views on various solid-waste practices (n = 38). The views were coded to provide as much detail as possible about solid-waste practices such as incineration, recycling, and landfilling (for example, we asked if incineration is or can be a suitable method for disposal of solid waste). Each witness was coded as either agreeing or disagreeing with each of thirty-eight views on the subject. Three coders analyzed over 2,500 pages of Congressional testimony.

Once all the testimonies were coded, we constructed a two-mode matrix of individuals providing testimony by views on solid-waste solutions (such as pro/anti recycling, recycling as the only solution, pro/anti incineration, and the like). This enabled us to draw on techniques to analyze what network analysts refer to as joint involvement or affiliation data (Breiger, 1974; Burt, 1991). These conventionally include data on director interlocks or cross-citations, but in this case we examined the extent to which witnesses share similar views on solid-waste solutions. We then performed cluster analyses and multidimensional scaling in UCINET (Borgatti, Everett, and Freeman, 1999) in an effort to understand how claims about different solid-waste practices are socially patterned. Our goal was not to develop a comprehensive understanding of the entire social structure of the hearings, but to help us interpret general views about recycling and incineration and the underlying logics that informed the claims of actors.

RESULTS

We report on five clusters that provide insight into the heterogeneity of views about the solid-waste practices of incineration and recycling. Recycling was the most frequently discussed solution, with 55 percent of the witnesses (71 individuals) supporting it. Of the 128 witnesses testifying at the hearings, 51 percent (65 people) thought that some form of recycling would be worthwhile; they based this on both technological feasibility and moral considerations, although many witnesses viewed it as something that would not provide a practical solution in the foreseeable future. For instance, the president of the Boston City Council argued that

> [Efforts] both national and local to recycle the ingredients of solid waste into innovative and novel byproducts is in my opinion an excellent and forward looking long range solution. But *we need not expend mental energy on these imaginative solutions* while the rubbish heap is encroaching on us (U.S. Senate, 1969–1970: 9/10/69, 5, emphasis added).

A representative from the Rhode Island Division of Air Pollution similarly claimed that

> [At] present, the two most satisfactory methods of disposing of this waste are by means of the sanitary landfill and by the reduction of combustible waste by incineration. . . . While waiting hopefully for the needed breakthrough in solid-waste

disposal, whether it be in recycling and reuse of material or a more efficient reduction process, we must meanwhile make a greater effort to improve conditions with the means we have in hand (U.S. Senate, 1969–1970: 4/10/69, 73–74).

Incineration was discussed as a solution to solid-waste management problems in 53 percent (sixty-eight witnesses) of the testimonies. These revealed widespread agreement that incineration is an effective solution to the problem of solid-waste management. More than 80 percent (forty-three witnesses) of the witnesses who discussed incineration considered it to be a satisfactory method. Among those who agreed, 93 percent (forty witnesses) suggested that incineration was not the complete answer but would work well in combination with other solutions such as recycling and/or landfilling.

Although support for both incineration and recycling was widespread, we derived clusters that highlight important variations in views about how well people think their solutions will work: "Gung-Ho Recyclers," "Goin' Green," "Green Cosmopolitans," "Red Cosmopolitans," and "Burn and Dumpers." Table 14.1 provides a summary of these witness clusters, highlighting differences in views about incineration and recycling, the underlying logics that guided arguments about technological solutions, and the kinds of organizations or groups that were represented in each of the clusters. Each offers a different position on the relative efficacy of incineration and recycling, but our analyses show that these views do not correlate in any obvious way with the organizations represented by cluster members. For instance, representatives of state and local governments and private solid-waste companies are dispersed across three clusters. This lack of correspondence between organizations represented and solid-waste solution views indicates that interest groups supporting particular solid-waste solutions had not emerged by the time of those hearings in any obvious way. We report on each of the clusters in turn.

Gung-Ho Recyclers

Although more than half of the witnesses at the hearings expressed some support for recycling, only four argued that it should be the *only* solution to the mounting problem of solid-waste management. Drawing on more ecocentric arguments that maintained that recycling was the only solution that would promote the ecological health of the planet by helping to restructure capitalistic production processes (Schnaiberg and Gould, 1994), members of this cluster advocated total and complete recycling. One of the witnesses, from the *Consumers Cooperative Society of Palo Alto,* issued a call for "100 percent recycling," arguing for the enactment of national legislation requiring that manufacturers of *all* products delivered to

Table 14.1

Discourse Clusters:

U.S. Congressional Hearings on Solid Waste, 1969–1970

Cluster Name	Technology Views	Logic	Cluster Membership
Gung-Ho Recyclers	Strong recycling advocates (anti-incineration)	Federal government as an important driver of recycling practices—it's the right thing to do!	Nonprofit advocacy group National trade associations Solid waste equipment manufacturer
Goin' Green	Moderate recycling advocates	Public-private partnerships as the way to facilitate the "efficient" development of recycling	National trade associations Private solid waste company State and local governments University professors
Green Cosmopolitans	Advocates of recycling in conjunction with incineration and landfilling	Create market incentives to encourage the private development of recycling	Environmental research groups Private solid waste company
Red Cosmopolitans	Incinerator advocates who view recycling and landfilling as complements	Let the market work no governmental involvement	National trade associations Private solid waste company State and local governments University professors Environmental engineers
Burn and Dumpers	Strong incinerator advocates (anti-recycling)	Let the market work, but government may want to facilitate development and diffusion of incineration technology	State and local governments Environmental engineers

consumers provide for and guarantee ". . . recycling of the container and any portion of the product not ordinarily used up by the buyer" (U.S. Senate, 1969–1970: 3/31/70, 2546).

Though witnesses constituting the Gung-Ho Recycling cluster commented on the many ecological benefits of recycling, arguments supporting recycling emphasized that the federal government had an important role to play in facilitating the widespread use of recycling as a major solid-waste solution. For instance, it was noted that technology related to recycling has been available since World War II, when the United States, Germany, and Japan relied on recycled material in order to replace strategic materials consumed by the war. The implication was that since the federal government was able to make recycling work in the 1940s, it could certainly do so again, though requiring the construction of a national infrastructure that would support the widespread adoption of recycling practices.

Goin' Green

Members of the Goin' Green cluster were recycling advocates who focused their arguments on how private, for-profit organizations could bring about an overall recycling infrastructure. Much of the discussion on the role of private industry in developing solid-waste solutions was fueled by concern about a section of law that awarded solid-waste construction grants only to public agencies. In an attempt to open such grants to private industry, a member of the American Paper Institute encouraged the government to embrace "the capacity, the ingenuity and the ability of the private sector in our economy to come up with answers" (U.S. Senate, 1969–1970: 2/26/70, 1876). A representative of Industrial Services of America echoed this sentiment by noting that a solid-waste solution that fails to take account of private enterprise deprives itself of "the greatest source of innovation in the field of solid wastes management . . . By stimulating investment in the private sector . . . we could greatly accelerate the program of private enterprise in the problem-solving process" (U.S. Senate, 1969–1970: 2/2/70, 2043). In contrast to the Gung-Ho Recyclers, who emphasize the importance of government action, members of the Goin' Green cluster argue that emphasizing the role of the private sector in recycling is an efficient solution.

Green Cosmopolitans

Green Cosmopolitans advocate recycling, but in a more restricted sense than Gung-Ho Recyclers or Goin' Green advocates. Green Cosmopolitans view recycling as only part of an overall solution to the problems of solid-waste management. Testimony by members of this cluster both criticized and offered support for all solid-waste solutions, although they concentrated their testimony on how recycling could be made efficient through the development of market incentives. For instance, a representative of the Metropolitan Waste Conversion Corporation argued that "the real secret to the program of recycling and reuse [is tied to] the opening up of markets for the consumption of the great volumes of material which we can reclaim" (U.S. Senate, 1969–1970: 6/23/69, 332).

Other witnesses argued that incentives needed to be designed to promote recycling at the household level and to promote the purchase of recycled materials over the use of raw materials. For example, a representative of Resources for the Future, Inc. proposed to "devise social and economic incentives that would make it worthwhile for [a] producer to design easy disposability and reuse [it] into [a] product" (U.S. Senate, 1969–1970: 2/23/70: 1522). It was argued that Congress should encourage the construction of recycling markets, as "the present mood of concern may be a unique occasion for modifying behavior, social customs, mechanisms and institutions" (U.S. Senate, 1969–1970: 2/23/70: 1519).

Red Cosmopolitans

Red Cosmopolitans actively supported incineration as a solution to solid-waste management, but emphasized the need for landfilling and, to a lesser extent, recycling. They acknowledge that incinerators have had problems in the past, but are technologically optimistic about how future innovations could deal with such problems. For instance, the Chairman of the *Ad Hoc Committee on Solid Waste Management, National Academy of Sciences/National Academy of Engineering* (NAS/NAE), argued that adequate technology was available to make possible the construction and operation of efficient incinerator facilities. It was argued that with advances in research on incineration, additional funds, and a trained management team to oversee operations, a high-quality incinerator could be created. A professor of environmental engineering at Stanford University contended that "[incineration] still holds the key to the reduction of volume of solid waste going to ultimate disposal" (U.S. Senate, 1969–1970: 2/25/70, 1801).

Though there was some support for recycling among Red Cosmopolitans, most witnesses highlighted its limitations. A representative from the Department of Environmental Health Sciences at the Harvard School of Public Health acknowledged the economic limits to recycling, which he saw as "likely to remain financially rewarding only for industrial waste products which often are substances of uniform composition, generated in pure form and in large quantities" (U.S. Senate, 1969–1970: 4/10/69, 28). Reservations about the economic feasibility of recycling were buttressed by the comments of a colonel from the Department of Defense, who considered the most feasible solid-waste disposal system to be the one that was the least expensive. "[If] it is going to cost more to reclaim [solid waste] than the salvage value, we feel that our obligation to the taxpayer is not to reclaim it. If it is a scarce material or one that is economically feasible to reclaim, we then try for reclamation" (U.S. Senate, 1969–1970: 10/2/69, 1013). Further, a representative of the Golden Gate Disposal Company, a private solid-waste disposal company, argued that the concept of recycling cannot be accomplished success-fully "where there is no market for salvaged materials" (U.S. Senate, 1969–1970: 3/31/70, 2527).

Burn and Dumpers

Burn and Dumpers are people who exclusively supported incineration over recy-cling. They argued, for instance, that "modern incineration equipment is the only immediate answer" (U.S. Senate, 1969–1970: 6/23/69, 251) to the country's solid-waste problems. Burn and Dumpers shared the technological optimism of Red Cosmopolitans who believed that engineering knowledge would be able to fix any inadequacies of incinerator technology. For instance, a professor from the school of engineering at the University of Florida suggested that with proper and thor-ough engineering and careful construction and operation, sanitary landfill, in-cinerators, and any number of other disposal methods could be made "safe, eco-nomical and acceptable" (U.S. Senate, 1969–1970: 10/28/69, 321). Witnesses in this cluster completely disregarded recycling as a potential solid-waste solution.

Figure 14.1 provides a multidimensional scaling plot of these five witness clus-ters, highlighting two key dimensions by which the overall discourse space of the solid-waste Congressional hearings can be understood. The horizontal axis shows how testimony varied in the extent that prorecycling versus proincineration views were espoused. The vertical axis highlights the competing logics that informed witnesses' arguments about how to develop solid-waste practice standards. Most of those who testified argued about potential solid-waste practices by emphasizing the role of private actors and the overall efficiency of their solutions. A few, includ-ing the Gung-Ho Recyclers, insisted on the importance of the federal government in actively constructing an infrastructure or somehow shaping practices in a more authoritative fashion.

While both logics were drawn on to make claims about the efficacy of recycl-ing and incineration technologies, our analysis indicates that it was the market-efficiency logic that dominated the hearings and, as the historical record has shown, came to inform how the solid-waste field was governed. Even though the federal government drove the centralization of the solid-waste management field by cre-ating the EPA, passing legislation, and encouraging the creation of solid-waste standards, it did not act authoritatively. Instead, it encouraged private industry to drive solid-waste field development. As a result, garbage collectors and haulers have merged so often that now there are only a handful of national solid-waste conglomerates that aim to standardize practices to make the solid-waste manage-ment field most profitable to them. In essence, the emergent market-efficiency

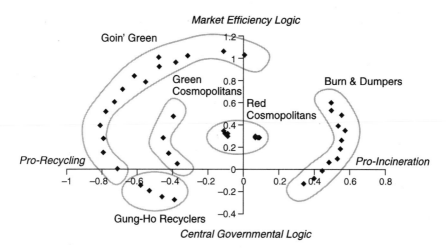

Figure 14.1 Multidimensional Scaling Plot of U.S. Congressional Hearings on Solid Waste, 1969–1970

logic valorized private, for-profit solid-waste conglomerates that were able to define which practices would become dominant. Voices in support of recycling became increasingly marginalized.

In the media as well as in solid-waste circles, incineration became favored over recycling, especially as initial experimentation with recycling in the early 1970s had been deemed a failure when many recycling programs that were created in the early 1970s ceased to exist within a few years. Often this was blamed on the inefficiency of recycling and the lack of recycling markets, although there were few concerted efforts to build a workable recycling market infrastructure. Incineration, on the other hand, came to be valorized because it was considered to be "efficient." It was supported by incineration vendors, engineers, consultants, law firms, the companies that were to manage the proposed incinerators and haul garbage to those facilities, as well as investment banking houses that stood to profit from issuing bonds to finance waste-to-energy facilities that cost as much as $100 million. In addition, new waste-to-energy incineration technology that converted waste into usable energy became particularly attractive in the 1970s when the country experienced an energy crisis. Overall, the market-efficiency logic favored incineration because it focused attention on near-term cost-benefit calculations that benefited a wide variety of for-profit interests, and neglected the more eco-centric arguments made by Gung-Ho Recyclers who maintained that recycling provides a solution that would be better for the environment than toxin-emitting incinerators.

DISCUSSION

In this chapter we argued that the U.S. solid-waste management field became more centralized and developed a reduced set of standardized practices because of the establishment of a market-efficiency logic in the 1970s. Even though incineration in combination with sanitary landfilling became accepted practice by the mid- to late-1970s, our analysis of Congressional hearings in 1969 and 1970 show that there was no definitive consensus about the relative efficacy of incineration over recycling. Both practices were argued for by approximately half of the witnesses who testified. In addition, our cluster analysis shows that the viewpoints expressed then were quite heterogeneous.

Knowing that incineration and sanitary landfilling became standard practices soon after the hearings gives us the chance to critically evaluate the role of those hearings in defining appropriate solid-waste solutions. A typical, realist interpretation of the role of Congressional hearings on waste management, for instance, would highlight the informational value of expert testimony. For example, during the course of the 1969–1970 hearings, Senator Edmund Muskie, chairman of the subcommittee running the hearings, stated:

> As in the past, this committee at the outset of hearings does not have a vested interest in any particular kind of legislation or any specific piece of legislation. We undertake always to respond to what we hear and learn in our hearings, and that will be our attribute this time. Even though we may have views as to what ought to be done on the basis of previous hearing and previous knowledge acquired by the committee, we do look forward with interest to being stimulated and educated and perhaps even led by the witnesses who appear before us. So it is in that mood that I open these hearings" (U.S. Senate, 1969–1970: 9/30/69, 498).

From an institutionalist lens, however, these solid-waste hearings must be understood in the context of the dynamics of the solid-waste management field that was being centralized. Field centralization is not a natural process but importantly involves the development of shared belief systems or logics that guide how decisions are made in fields. Logics are not necessarily supported by a consensus, however, but instead tend to be backed by powerful actors that are able to mute dissident voices. Under conditions where fields are emerging or experiencing transformation, there may be a great deal of ambiguity about the beliefs that provide meaning and order to actors that constitute fields. During such moments, actors, which are highly stratified, participate in field-level discourse in order to come to some sort of agreement about how the field should be organized or reorganized and what kinds of practices and interactions are appropriate. The analysis of discourse during such transformative or liminal periods is useful because it highlights the space of alternative logics and practices, and can illuminate hidden forms of power. We contend that a useful focal point for the analysis of emergent and transformative fields, therefore, has to do with tracking how the space of alternative logics and practices gets winnowed down into a dominant logic and a set of standardized practices.

In this chapter, we showed that much of the discourse at the hearings was informed by a market-efficiency logic, whereas a minority of the testimony reflected a competing central-governmental logic. We argued that this was important because the solid-waste field came to be informed by the market-efficiency logic that consequently shaped the development of solid-waste practices, favoring incineration over recycling by the mid-1970s. Even though our analysis shows that the market-efficiency logic dominated discourse at the hearings we analyzed, it is important to highlight the existence of other logics since different logics may lead to fundamentally different kinds of governance arrangements and practices. In the context of the solid-waste field, if the central-governmental logic became dominant, it is quite plausible to suggest that efforts to construct a comprehensive recycling infrastructure may have been undertaken as occurred in Germany and has developed in the United States over the past two decades.

We argue that recycling did not emerge as a mainstream solid-waste solution in the 1970s because private solid-waste conglomerates and incinerator manufacturers became empowered, as a result of the emergence of the market-efficiency logic, to define practices in ways that best suited their interests. At that time, recycling was not being promoted by any major for-profit actors. It was more of a locally supported social movement activity that would have required central-government backing in order to have been developed into a feasible solid-waste solution.

Theoretically, our study contributes to institutional analysis by highlighting the importance of studying the discursive and symbolic dimensions of social processes as a way to understand how institutional change occurs (Grattet, 1997; Mohr and Duquenne, 1997; see also Levy and Rothenberg, Chapter 7 and Morrill and Owen-Smith, Chapter 4). Though institutionalists have emphasized the importance of logics in providing order and meaning to field practices (Friedland and Alford, 1991; Scott, 1995), there has been very little effort to study how some logics become dominant over others or how they get transformed. To gain purchase on such questions, we believe that it is important to study claims-making processes during transformative periods when fields are emerging or being radically reorganized. Such research would not only expand the scope of institutional analysis but also contribute to a more complete understanding of policy making by highlighting how policy debates and discussions are field-level activities that involve the consolidation of meaning systems that shape policy decisions and the subsequent development of field practices (Hoffman, 1997; see also Hironaka and Schofer, Chapter 9, and Levin and Espeland, Chapter 5). Note that such discourse almost always involves political struggle that results in both winners and losers (Hirsch and Lounsbury, 1997).

Though the analysis of public testimony at Congressional hearings provides useful field-level discourse data, it would be useful to track changes in discourse over longer periods of time than analyzed in this chapter in order to better understand the temporal dynamics of logics and practices. The study of discourse dynamics is particularly important because it promises to bring elements of agency back into the study of institutional logics that have been mainly studied as abstract forces that are exogenous to the actions of field constituents. By studying the dynamics of discourse as an endogenous process, richer conceptualizations of the relationship of agency and institutions can be developed that account for the mutually constitutive relationship between culture and structure.

REFERENCES

Bijker, Wiebe E., Thomas P. Hughes, and Trevor Pinch. 1994. *The Social Construction of Technological Systems.* Cambridge, MA: MIT Press.

Block, Fred. 1990. *Postindustrial Possibilities: A Critique of Economic Discourse.* Berkeley: University of California Press.

Borgatti, Stephen P., Martin G. Everett, and Linton C. Freeman. 1999. *UCINET 5.0 Version 1.00.* Natick: Analytic Technologies.

Bourdieu, Pierre. 1984. *Distinction.* Cambridge, MA: Harvard University Press.

Breiger, Ronald L. 1974. "The Duality of Persons and Groups." *Social Forces,* 53: 181–190.

Burt, Ronald S. 1991. *Structure.* New York: Columbia University.

Campbell, John L., J. Rogers Hollingsworth, and Leon N. Lindberg. 1990. *Governance of the American Economy.* Cambridge, U.K.: Cambridge University Press.

DiMaggio, Paul. 1983. "State Expansion and Organizational Fields." In Richard H. Hall and Robert E. Quinn, eds., *Organizational Theory and Public Policy,* 147–161. Beverly Hills, CA: Sage.

DiMaggio, Paul. 1986. "Structural Analysis of Organizational Fields: A Blockmodel Approach." In Barry Staw and Larry Cummings, eds., *Research in Organizational Behavior,* 335–370. Greenwich, CT: JAI Press.

DiMaggio, Paul. 1991. "Constructing an Organizational Field as a Professional Project: U.S. Art Museums, 1920–1940." In Walter W. Powell and Paul J. DiMaggio, eds., *The New Institutionalism in Organizational Analysis,* 267–292. Chicago: University of Chicago Press.

DiMaggio, Paul, and Walter W. Powell. 1983. "The Iron Cage Revisited: Institutional Isomorphism and Collective Rationality in Organizational Fields." *American Sociological Review,* 48: 147–160.

Friedland, Roger, and Robert R. Alford. 1991. "Bringing Society Back In: Symbols, Practices, and Institutional Contradictions." In Walter W. Powell and Paul J. DiMaggio, eds., *The New Institutionalism in Organizational Analysis,* 232–263. Chicago: University of Chicago Press.

Grattet, Ryken. 1997. "Sociological Perspectives on Legal Change: The Role of the Legal Field in the Transformation of the Common Law of Industrial Accidents." *Social Science History,* 21: 359–397.

Hamilton, Gary G., and Nicole W. Biggart. 1988. "Market, Culture, and Authority: A Comparative Analysis of Management and Organization in the Far East." *American Journal of Sociology,* 94: S52–S94.

Haveman, Heather A., and Hayagreeva Rao. 1997. "Structuring a Theory of Moral Sentiments: Institutional and Organizational Coevolution in the Early Thrift Industry." *American Journal of Sociology,* 102: 1606–1651.

Hays, Samuel P. 1979. *Conservation and the Gospel of Efficiency.* New York: Atheneum.

Hirsch, Paul M., and Michael Lounsbury. 1997. "Ending the Family Quarrel: Toward a Reconciliation of 'Old' and 'New' Institutionalisms." *American Behavioral Scientist,* 40: 406–418.

Hoffman, Andrew J. 1997. *From Heresy to Dogma: An Institutional History of Corporate Environmentalism.* San Francisco: New Lexington Press.

Hollingsworth, J. Rogers, and Robert Boyer. 1997. *Contemporary Capitalism: The Embeddedness of Institutions.* Cambridge, U.K.: Cambridge University Press.

Jasanoff, Sheila, Gerald E. Markle, James C. Petersen, and Trevor Pinch, eds. 1995. *Handbook of Science and Technology Studies.* Thousand Oaks, CA: Sage.

Knoke, David, and James H. Kuklinski. 1982. *Network Analysis.* Beverly Hills, CA: Sage.

Lounsbury, Michael. 2002. "Institutional Transformation and Status Mobility: The Professionalization of the Field of Finance." *Academy of Management Journal,* 45.

Lounsbury, Michael, Marc J. Ventresca, and Paul M. Hirsch. Forthcoming. "Social Movements, Field Frames, and Industry Emergence: A Cultural-Political Perspective on U.S. Recycling." *Socio-Economics Review,* 1(1).

McGuire, Patrick, Mark Granovetter, and Michael Schwartz. 1993. "Thomas Edison and the Social Construction of the Early Electricity Industry in America." In Richard Swedberg, ed., *Explorations in Economic Sociology,* 213–246. New York: Russell Sage Foundation.

Melosi, Martin V. 1981. *Garbage in the Cities: Refuse, Reform and the Environment, 1880–1980.* College Station, TX: Texas A&M Press.

Meyer, John W., and Brian Rowan. 1977. "Institutionalized Organizations: Formal Structure as Myth and Ceremony." *American Journal of Sociology,* 83: 340–363.

Mische, Ann, and Philippa Pattison. Forthcoming. "Composing a Civic Arena: Publics, Projects, and Social Settings." *Poetics.*

Mohr, John W. 1998. "Measuring Meaning Structures." *Annual Review of Sociology,* 24: 345–370.

Mohr, John W., and Vincent Duquenne. 1997. "The Duality of Culture and Practice: Poverty Relief in New York City, 1888–1917." *Theory and Society,* 26: 305–356.

Packard, Vance. 1960. *The Waste Makers.* New York: D. McKay Co.

Schnaiberg, Allan, and Kenneth A. Gould. 1994. *Environment and Society.* New York: St. Martin's Press.

Scott, W. Richard. 1994. "Conceptualizing Organizational Fields." In Derlien Hans-Ulrich, Uta Gerhardt, and Fritz W. Scharpf, eds., *Systemrationalität und Partialinteresse,* 203–221. Baden, Germany: Nomos Verlagsgesellschaft.

Scott, W. Richard. 1995. *Institutions and Organizations.* Newbury Park, CA: Sage.

Scott, W. Richard, Martin Ruef, Peter Mendel, and Carol Caronna. 2000. *Institutional Change and Healthcare Organizations: From Professional Dominance to Managed Care.* Chicago: University of Chicago Press.

Seldman, Neil. 1995. "Recycling—History in the United States." In Attilio Bisio and Sharon Boots, eds., *Encyclopedia of Energy Technology and the Environment,* 2352–2367. New York: Wiley.

Thornton, Patricia H., and William Ocasio. 1999. "Institutional Logics and the Historical Contingency of Power in Organizations: Executive Succession in the Higher Education Publishing Industry, 1958–1990." *American Journal of Sociology,* 105: 801–843.

U.S. Senate. June 24–25, 30, July 1–2, 1964. "Technical hearings held on progress and programs relating to the abatement of air pollution." Committee on Public Works, special subcommittee on air and water pollution.

U.S. Senate. April 1969–March 1970. "Hearings on a bill to amend the Solid Waste Disposal Act." Committee on Public Works, subcommittee on air and water pollution.

Van de Ven, Andrew H., and Raghu Garud. 1993. "Innovation and Industry Development: The Case of Cochlear Implants." *Research on Technological Innovation, Management and Policy,* 5: 1–46.

Ventresca, Marc J., and Joseph Porac. Forthcoming. *Constructing Markets and Industries.* London: Elsevier Science.

15 | THE INSTITUTIONAL CONTEXT OF ENVIRONMENTAL VOLUNTARY AGREEMENTS

Magali Delmas and Ann Terlaak

One of the liveliest debates in contemporary social science surrounds the extent to which institutions matter (March and Olsen, 1989; Suchman and Edelman, 1997). Most of the literature in this context suggests that political and social institutions are crucial to explaining policy outcomes. A voluntary agreement (VA) is a new form of policy outcome that represents "an agreement between government and industry to facilitate voluntary action with a desirable social outcome, which is encouraged by the government, to be undertaken by the participant based on the participant's self interest" (Storey, Boyd, and Dowd, 1997: 3).

Since the 1990s, regulators in Europe and the United States increasingly use VAs to improve industry's environmental performance. They are now widespread and are seen as a response to the need for more flexible means to abate pollution and reduce the administrative burden of environmental regulation. A recent report remarks that "as a result, a pervasive use of VAs can be observed in OECD countries: over 300 Negotiated Agreements in the European Union . . . and over 40 voluntary programs managed by the U.S. government have been surveyed in recent years" (OECD, 2000). However, the types of VAs implemented in the different countries vary considerably.

In this chapter we focus on two types of voluntary agreements—negotiated agreements (NAs) and public voluntary programs (PVPs). In NAs, firms and regulators negotiate the targets of environmental performance that firms will have to reach and/or the means to reach these targets. These agreements are used as sub-

Financial support from the Institute on Global Conflict and Cooperation (IGCC) at the University of California San Diego is gratefully acknowledged.

stitutes to command-and-control regulation. In PVPs, participating firms voluntarily agree to adopt environmental standards that have been developed by regulatory agencies. In exchange the regulatory agency provides incentives such as R&D subsidies, technological assistance, or positive public relations. These programs complement existing regulation.

In the Netherlands, for instance, about 107 NAs were implemented by 1998 (Boerkey and Leveque, 1998), as compared to only two in the United States. (Mazurek, 1998). However, the U.S. Environmental Protection Agency (EPA) has implemented 31 Public Voluntary Programs (Mazurek, 1998), whereas these programs play a minor role in the Netherlands (Boerkey and Leveque, 1998).

Why are NAs used more often in the Netherlands and Public Voluntary Programs more in the United States? We propose that the legal, social, and cultural aspects of the institutional environment of each country facilitate or hamper the implementation of NAs and PVPs. As a result, the actual types of VAs implemented differ.

The body of literature on VAs, while small, is growing fast. Most studies assess VAs' environmental effectiveness (see EEA, 1997; Krarup and Ramesohl, 2000), analyze VAs' efficiency (such as Carraro and Siniscalco, 1996; Delmas and Terlaak, 2001; Glachant, 1999; Stranlund, 1995) or focus on firms' rationale to enter VAs (Amacher and Malik, 1996; Arora and Cason, 1995; Delmas and Terlaak, 2000; Hansen, 1999; Lyon and Maxwell, forthcoming; Segerson and Miceli, 1998). However, little research has been devoted to systematically explain national differences in the use of VAs.

Several chapters in this book discuss the evolution of voluntary arrangements as an institution for environmental protection. Our chapter provides further insight into the evolution of VAs. Rather than focusing on the role of firms' strategic behavior in determining VAs' implementation, we analyze the agreements from an institutional perspective and describe how institutional features (our "independent variables") facilitate or hamper the use of either negotiated agreements or public voluntary programs (our "binary dependent variable").

In the next section we identify the main attributes of NAs and PVPs and provide an institutional framework to analyze the factors that facilitate or hamper their implementation. In section three, we apply our framework to explain the implementation of the two types of VAs in the United States and the Netherlands. Section four is devoted to a concluding discussion. We explain how the framework can be useful for policy makers to analyze the factors hindering the diffusion of VAs. We also describe how our approach can help managers assess the risks and opportunities associated with VAs according to the institutional environment in which they are implemented.

INSTITUTIONAL FRAMEWORK

Although negotiated agreements and public voluntary programs are both labeled as environmental voluntary agreements, they differ in numerous ways and require distinctive institutional environment to arise.[1]

The Features of Negotiated Agreements

In negotiated agreements, regulatory agencies and firms negotiate the targets of the environmental performance that firms will have to reach and/or the means to reach regulatory targets. NAs can be concluded between regulatory agencies and industry or individual firms. By setting targets of environmental performance, they can be an alternative to command-and-control regulation. Alternatively, they can be used as a means to grant flexibility within the existing regulatory system.

A prominent example of an agreement implemented as an alternative to regulation is the German VA on Global Warming Prevention. In 1995, thirteen large German industry associations agreed to reduce their 1990 CO_2 emissions by 20 percent by the year 2005. In return, the government signaled that it would refrain from implementing an energy tax and/or heat ordinance as long as industry complies with the VA (BDI, 1996).

NAs that grant participants flexibility within the existing regulatory system are based on the idea that existing command-and-control systems stifle efficiency and innovation by declaring "one-size-fits-all" abatement strategies, rather than letting individual facilities decide how to control pollution. The EPA's Project XL (eXcellence and Leadership) is an example: in Project XL, firms define site-specific performance standards that are more stringent than current regulation, but benefit from some regulatory flexibility in how to meet them (Blackman and Mazurek, 2000).[2]

In NAs, the legitimacy of the negotiators from both sides is key for the success of the agreement. The regulatory agency must be credible in its ability to commit to its engagement. If the agreements negotiated between firms and regulatory agencies are easily challenged by other administrative bodies or by citizens, it is unlikely that firms will be willing to embark on uncertain ventures. For example, the execution of Project XL is hampered by uncertainties concerning EPA's authority to relax regulatory standards enacted by Congress (Boyd, Krupnik, and Mazurek, 1998). Once the VA is implemented, a credible threat of stricter regulation may also be useful to ensure compliance. This holds specifically true for legally non-binding agreements.

But industry negotiators must have the support of the entire industry to be credible in negotiation. Because negotiated agreements that replace regulations provide a collective benefit (the prevention of new legislation), free riding becomes a major concern. Regulatory agencies may therefore be concerned about the commitment of the individual firm. Industry negotiators are more likely to be credible representatives of the entire industry if the industry is organized through trade associations rather than fragmented. Also, negotiations are easier when the industry consists of a small number of large players.

Negotiated agreements that grant flexibility to existing regulators—unlike those used as an alternative to regulation—are usually negotiated between regulators and individual firms. In such a case, the legitimacy of the firm as a negotiator representing the rest of the industry is not an issue.

Negotiated agreements can conflict with third-party interests such as Non-Governmental Organizations (NGOs). If third parties have not been involved in the negotiations, they might view the agreements as exclusive decision processes that only involve the government and firms (Enevoldsen, 1998). The frequent exclusion of environmental groups and trade unions from VAs might be seen as incompatible with modern democratic regimes (Meadowcroft, 1998). In institutional environments where third parties have a strong voice, the emergence and implementation of such agreements is therefore likely to be challenged and rendered difficult. However, including third parties might not solve all problems, as the transaction costs of negotiating and finding an agreement can increase substantially (Blackman and Mazurek, 2000).

The Features of Public Voluntary Programs

In PVPs, regulatory agencies establish the frame and the basic requirements for participation. The program defines the preconditions of individual membership, the standards to be complied with by the firm, the monitoring criteria, and the evaluation of the results (OECD, 2000). In exchange, firms receive information on best environmental practices, R&D subsidies, technical assistance, or positive public reputation (for example, by being permitted to use an environmental logo) (OECD, 2000). Public voluntary programs are conceived as a complement to other policy instruments and thus do not result in a substitution or relaxation of existing regulation. PVP programs primarily focus on no-regret measures, that is, measures that are profitable for the firms to pursue. Theoretically, PVPs could engage individual firms or industry associations, however, practically most programs involve firms on an individual basis.

Examples of public voluntary programs include EPA's Climate Wise and Waste Wise Programs. For instance in Climate Wise, firms voluntarily pledge to reduce their CO_2 emissions. In return, the regulator provides or subsidizes an energy audit, software to track energy use, and public recognition (through award ceremonies or news press coverage). Another prominent example is EPA's 33/50 program in which firms agreed to reduce transfer and release of a number of toxic high priority chemicals.

Unlike in negotiated agreements, third-party involvement is less of an issue for PVPs because they do not replace or relax regulation. Similarly, most PVPs do not require congressional (or parliamentary) approval.

It may be difficult to monitor performance in PVPs, as these agreements are legally non-biding. Firms must honestly report their performance, and if they fear that information may be used against them, open communication and thorough monitoring may be hampered (Delmas, 2000).

In summary, negotiated agreements can replace regulations or grant flexibility of existing regulations, while public voluntary programs supplement regulations. In negotiated agreements, firms and regulators jointly negotiate the targets, as opposed to public voluntary programs where the regulatory agency unilaterally decides the frame and/or targets. To implement NAs, the regulator must be able to coordinate the agreement with other (potential or existing) regulations. If an NA serves as an alternative to regulation, it typically concerns and involves an entire industry. A credible regulatory threat of stricter regulation is important to ensure that industry complies with the arrangement. While third-party involvement may increase the legitimacy of NAs, it can also be an obstacle to the implementation of the agreements, as negotiations can be too costly and lengthy. As a supplement to existing regulation, third-party involvement and a regulatory threat become less important in PVPs. Firms most often enter PVPs on an individual basis, and the ability of firms to negotiate as one body therefore is not an issue.

We next draw on institutional theory to describe how different aspects of the institutional environment may result in the implementation of negotiated agreements or public voluntary programs as VAs to improve the environmental performance of firms.

LINKING THE INSTITUTIONAL
ENVIRONMENT TO VOLUNTARY AGREEMENTS

Institutional theory investigates how the institutional environment guides social choices (Hoffman, 1999). We describe how the institutional environment shapes the interplay of various organizational actors (the government, industry, and NGOs), and how this interplay creates a fertile (or unfertile) environment for the implementation of negotiated agreements and public voluntary programs.

The organizations that are part of our field of study are firms, regulatory agencies, and third parties such as NGOs. They represent the organizations that have a stake in the implementation of VAs. These organizations are embedded in a larger institutional environment, and the behavior of each is governed by regulative, normative, and cognitive aspects (Scott, 1995). Regulative aspects refer to the legal elements that govern the behavior of organizations. Normative aspects encompass the social elements—such as moral obligations—that shape action. Cognitive aspects refer to the cultural elements that govern choice, often without conscious thought (DiMaggio and Powell, 1983; Hoffman, 1999; Zucker, 1988).

The legal aspects of the institutional environment may impose constraints upon governmental action and, more specifically, government's ability to incorporate NAs in the existing regulatory system. The separation between legislative, executive, and judicial organs of the government is one factor constraining governmental behavior (Levy and Spiller, 1994; Vogel, 1993). For example, a strong and independent judiciary can limit administrative discretion by developing a body of administrative laws that constrain administrative action through administrative procedures. Also, a federal system limits central government authority through empowering state and local governments. This is in contrast with a centralized system in which authority of local governments is limited. Furthermore, fragmentation of power provides multiple access points for public interests, thereby controlling governmental behavior.

We argue that the government must be credible in its ability to negotiate and enforce negotiated agreements. Elements such as fragmentation of power and the ability of third parties to enter the game may provide uncertainty about governmental behavior and render more difficult the emergence and implementation of NAs. Therefore, the more the regulatory system is decentralized or fragmented, the more difficult it will be for the regulatory agency to commit credibly to the implementation of NAs. The implementation of PVPs, on the other hand, depends less on the regulator's ability to commit credibly to the arrangements, because the PVPs supplement regulation, are not legally binding, and primarily target profitable no-regret measures.

The legal aspects that affect industry's ability to be a credible negotiator and commit to NAs include the extent to which industry is organized as well as its bargaining power. The ability of industry to self-organize depends partly on the legal rules that facilitate or hamper cooperation. For example, antitrust regulation may be strictly enforced and as a result hamper firms to cooperate and negotiate as one body. Representatives of a loosely organized industry may not be a legitimate body to represent the interests of the entire industry.

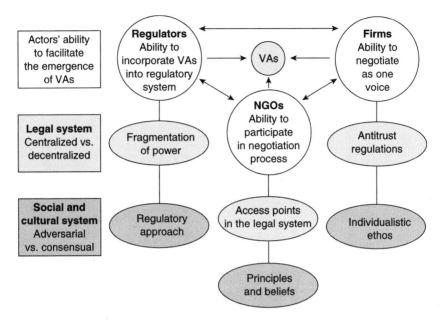

Figure 15.1 Institutions and Voluntary Agreements

The social and cultural aspects of the institutional environment also affect the implementation of voluntary agreements by guiding the actors' perception of reality and "how things are usually done." For example, if regulators are used to establish command-and-control regulation with little consultation with industry, most likely they will be reluctant to initiate an NA with industry. Indeed, such a negotiation would depart from their routine. If firms have an individualistic ethos, they might be less willing to cooperate with competitors and negotiate agreements with regulators at the industry level. And where NGOs take an adversarial stance and contest firms' initiatives with industry, their involvement may hamper the implementation of NAs.

Overall, if the social and cultural aspects of the institutional environment lead to adversarial relations among actors, the implementation of NAs is less likely than if a country is marked by consensual approaches to environmental problems. In such an adversarial environment the implementation of PVPs may be more feasible, as they do not require intensive negotiations among parties.

In Figure 15.1 we summarize the most important aspects of the institutional environment and how they influence the actors' ability to facilitate the emergence and implementation of VAs.

Figure 15.1 illustrates how the legal, social, and cultural aspects of the institutional environment shape the interplay of regulators, firms, and NGOs. These factors rarely influence the actors' behaviors independently. Rather, the potential emergence of NAs or PVPs will vary according to a combination of all these aspects. We suggest that an optimal institutional environment for negotiated agreements is marked by a centralized regulatory system and a consensual approach to environmental problems. An unfavorable institutional environment for NAs would be a decentralized regulatory system marked by adversarial relations among actors. In a mixed case where the legal organization of the institutional environment is marked by high decentralization but a culture of cooperation among actors, the emergence of VAs is likely.

We next discuss how the institutional aspects of the United States and the Netherlands shape the interaction of government, industry, and NGOs to provide a more or less fertile ground for the implementation of negotiated agreements and public voluntary programs.

THE USE OF PUBLIC VOLUNTARY PROGRAMS IN THE UNITED STATES

In the United States, VAs have been in use since the early 1990s. Today, approximately forty of them are in effect (Mazurek, 1998). Out of these, Project XL is one of two NAs that provide regulatory flexibility.[3] Most VAs are public voluntary programs. What explains the overwhelming use of PVPs rather than NAs in the United States?

Government

In the United States, environmental policy making is marked by fragmentation. Executive powers regarding environmental policy, for example, are granted to several players. The EPA, which is responsible for putting into effect most of the environmental statutes, shares responsibility for environmental protection with the Department of Energy, Interior, Agriculture, and State (Andrews, 1997; Kraft, 1996).

Fragmentation also results from dispersal of power in Congress. The House and Senate both have several committees that are responsible for environmental policy issues (Kraft, 1996). The presidential system additionally fuels fragmentation in the policy-making processes. This is because the separation of powers often produces divided governments with the president and the majority of Congress belonging to different political parties. As a result, the president and Congress often are at odds on any given policy issue (Rose-Ackerman, 1995; Kraft, 1999).

We mentioned earlier that a threat of stricter regulation might be required for the implementation of (and subsequent compliance with) negotiated agreements.

In the United States, the separation of power limits the credibility of such a threat, as the president and the majority of Congress might disagree on environmental issues. As a result, the bargaining position of regulators is restricted.

Congressional oversight over executive policy making may also be incompatible with NAs, which require administrative discretion. This causes uncertainties for firms participating in the XL Program, as it puts into question EPA's authority to provide flexibility within the existing regulatory system (Boyd, Krupnik, and Mazurek, 1998; Ginsberg and Cummis, 1996).

In the United States, extensive judicial review supplements Congressional oversight (Andrews, 1997; Melnick, 1983). Most environmental laws enable citizens to file suit against administrators for taking unauthorized action or for failing to perform their duties (Melnick, 1983). Furthermore, unlike in a two-sided fee-shifting system where losers pay all fees including the costs of the court, several U.S. environmental laws include provisions for the state to pay the victorious plaintiff's legal fees, and the losers to cover only their own legal costs (Rose-Ackerman, 1995).

This has often forced the EPA to follow inflexible procedures and has reduced the scope for negotiations between the agency and firms on the most cost-effective measures of pollution control (Wallace, 1995). Judicial overview can create an unfavorable environment for the implementation of NAs. Agreements that relax existing regulations are especially likely to be challenged by third parties that could sue the agency for failure to perform its duties.

The Public and NGOs

There are many diverse environmental groups in the United States. Their substantial staff capabilities and financial resources make them far more active and influential in policy advocacy than their counterparts in other countries (Andrews, 1997; Rose-Ackerman, 1995). Besides financial resources, they have access to information and formal rights for involvement in governmental decision processes, key elements that determine their influence on policy making.

Access to information is granted through a number of statutes. The Administrative Procedure Act requires public hearings and asks government agencies to publicly justify their regulatory proposals. The National Environmental Policy Act requires agencies to publish information about the environmental impacts of their proposals. The Freedom of Information Act and the Toxic Release Inventory guarantee the provision of further information (Kerwin, 1994). Overall, the weight of the judiciary, the transparency of the policy-making process, and its direct accountability to citizens turn environmental groups into important players in environmental policy making.

Problems with Project XL point out how legal aspects may impede a more wide-spread (and successful) implementation of NAs, and may favor the implementation of PVPs. As mentioned earlier, third parties can easily use lawsuits to object to the regulatory flexibility granted by Project XL. To avoid such opposition, third parties are often invited to be involved in the negotiation of the agreement. However, experience with Project XL suggests that such third-party involvement entails lengthy negotiations and results in costs outweighing benefits (Blackman and Mazurek, 2000). Because PVPs are not linked to existing or potential regulations, and because they focus on environmental performance beyond existing regulation, such programs are less vulnerable to legal actions from third parties.

Industry

In the United States, social and cultural aspects have limited the role of trade associations as a vehicle for industry self-regulation. More specifically, the notion of free capitalism and the individualistic ethos of American business culture may have hampered the association's role as a governing body (Vogel, 1986). American trade associations are historically "service associations" with lobbying as their primary activity (Galambos, 1966). Most U.S. industry associations thus service, rather than coordinate, their members. As a result, only very few American associations have adopted environmental codes of conduct (Nash, 1999). In the industries that did organize to collectively regulate their environmental performance—such as the chemical, oil, and forestry industries—organization might be interpreted as a response to a worsening of the industries' public images (King, Lenox, and Barnett, Chapter 17). However, when there is no such threat, and when the industry consists of numerous small and heterogeneous players, organization becomes less likely. The paint industry is an example: the lack of unity among its members made collective organization difficult and even resulted in the failure of an NA. In 1994, the EPA and the paint industry attempted to negotiate an agreement to control volatile organic compound emissions from coatings. They failed to reach consensus, as paint manufacturers were too heterogeneous and not able to agree on a common target (Piasecki, Fletcher, and Mendelson, 1999). Strict antitrust laws furthermore hamper the development of highly organized trade associations.

These cultural and legal features of the institutional environment impede the implementation of NAs, as the agreements require the support of the whole industry. This can best be achieved through negotiations with industry associations. However, as argued, American companies seem reluctant to subordinate themselves under trade associations. Yet the individualistic ethos of managers need not hamper the implementation of PVPs that are concluded between individual firms and regulators.

Overall, the implementation of any type of VA can be difficult given the deeply rooted adversarial attitudes of U.S. industry toward both labor and government. In such an adversarial setting—which is in contrast to the corporatist cooperative cultures more typical of Western Europe and Japan (Andrews, 1997; Vogel, 1986) —many companies might be reluctant to engage in collaborative actions with the government.

In conclusion, the U.S. institutional environment makes unlikely the implementation of negotiated agreements. Legal aspects (such as the fragmentation of the executive branch of government, the limited discretion of the EPA, the ability of third parties to enter the game, and antitrust laws) as well as social and cultural aspects (such as an individualistic ethos and adversarial attitudes of industry toward government) prevent the EPA from issuing a threat of regulation and from credibly committing to providing regulatory relief to participating firms. These also impede firms from negotiating as a unified body. The institutional environment seems to favor public voluntary programs that supplement existing regulations, are legally nonbinding (and thus do not need Congressional approval), allow firms to negotiate individually, and require comparably little commitment from regulators.

THE USE OF NEGOTIATED
AGREEMENTS IN THE NETHERLANDS

With the introduction of the first National Environmental Policy Plan (NEPP) in 1989, negotiated agreements, next to licenses, became the main element of Dutch environmental policy (OECD, 1995). Today the Netherlands have over 100 NAs in place (EEA, 1997).

NEPPs set strict long-term targets, but leave flexible the means to reach these targets. Overall targets are broken down by sectors. The government uses NAs (also called covenants in the Netherlands) to negotiate with industries how and at which pace to reach the targets of the NEPPS, as well as the evaluation and monitoring procedures. Regulatory authorities review these plans periodically.

NAs are binding on all parties. Both government—after receiving parliamentary approval—and industry sign the agreement (Zoeteman, 1998). The legal status of an NA is the same as an agreement under private law, which enables authorities to turn to civil courts for enforcement (OECD, 1995).

The Dutch agreements combine features of NAs that replace command-and-control regulations with those that grant flexibility within the regulatory system.

Policy makers use the agreements in tandem with licensing systems, and participants usually benefit from a relaxation of the licensing procedures (Wallace, 1995).

The implementation of Dutch VAs requires a high degree of coordination, stability, consensus, and credibility on the parts of all players. We next examine the aspects of the Dutch institutional environment that enable the Netherlands to successfully rely on these agreements.

Government

In the Netherlands, the national government plays a more significant role than in the United States (Lijphart, 1989; Shetter, 1987). More specifically, the Dutch democracy might be described as consensual-unitary, as opposed to the United States, which may be described as majoritarian-federal (Lijphart, 1989). Features such as executive power sharing in broad coalitions, a balanced executive-legislative relationship, a multiparty system, and parties that differ along many different issue dimensions describe the Dutch democracy as consensual. The Dutch parliament consists of two houses. Governments have historically had the support of the majority in both houses. There is no threshold for small-party representation, and the electoral system makes a coalition government almost inevitable. The Dutch system can also be characterized as unitary (or centralized if measured by the high share that the central government receives). It has a long tradition of central planning, which forecasts economic conditions and determines the most appropriate responses (Lijphart, 1989; Gladdish, 1991).

The Ministry of Housing, Spatial Planning and Environment (VROM) has great authority over environmental policy (OECD, 1995). However, VROM must coordinate its activities with other ministries. For example, NEPPs must be approved by the Cabinet of Ministers and Parliament. Once they are approved, a high degree of consensus and coordination makes credible the government's commitment to NEPPs and their implementation through NAs. Industry seems to face a closely-knit "governmental front" that agrees on environmental policy.

As compared to the United States, legal aspects clearly restrict the Dutch judiciary in its area of competence. Generally, the judiciary does not play any role in the formation of social legislation, as it has no power to review (or interpret the constitutionality of) decisions of the legislative and executive branches of government (Shetter, 1987).

An interesting cultural aspect of the Dutch institutional environment favors the implementation of NAs. Dutch environmental law enforcement had traditionally been lax. License issuers often refrained from legal action even where possible and pursued a policy of "talk, talk, and talk again" instead (Bressers and Plettenburg,

1997). In 1992, the judiciary started to play a more important enforcement role with the implementation of the National Enforcement System. Higher funding, improved governmental coordination, and judicial authorities that consolidated resources and designated specialized prosecutors induced a growing number of guilty verdicts (OECD, 1995).[4] Yet when compared to the United States, the role of courts in shaping environmental policy remains limited. As a result, firms and government can implement NAs without fearing that third parties will challenge their agreements in courts.

The Public and NGOs

The Dutch nature conservation movement has been marked by a culture of high expertise and formalized internal structures (Bressers and Plettenburg, 1997). Toward the end of the 1970s, the nature conservation groups started cooperating with the government. Since the implementation of the first NEPP, NGOs have evolved into respected professional negotiators that constructively criticize public action and seek concrete solutions (Timmer, 1997; Zoeteman, 1998). NGOs are increasingly responsible for monitoring the implementation of the NAs under NEPP (Timmer, 1997). The Dutch government considers some of the groups as important allies whom they subsidize, and they draw on their expertise for policymaking purposes (Bressers and Plettenburg, 1997; OECD, 1995).

Such culture of expertise facilitates the involvement of NGOs in negotiated agreements. Rather than automatically increasing transaction costs, their involvement can add expertise and increase public acceptance of the agreements.

Industry

The Dutch industry is highly organized (de Graeff, 1994). Two main national organizations (the Federation of Netherlands Industry and the Netherlands Christian Employers' Association) represent all sectors. These organizations address environmental concerns through a joint administrative committee that establishes and communicates the position of the associations on environmental issues.

Although the Netherlands has a strong culture of accommodation and consultation between government and industry (Daalder, 1989), industry originally opposed environmental policy. This position changed to a more cooperative attitude by the end of the 1980s, when, against the backdrop of rising (and united) political pressure and public environmental concerns, industry agreed to the first NEPP and cooperated on its implementation through Negotiated Agreements (Bressers and Plettenburg, 1997; Henselmans, 1998). Overall, the Dutch culture of consensual and trustful cooperation among all parties contrasts with the often hostile relationship between regulators, business, and NGOs in the United States (Timmer, 1997).

In conclusion, Dutch VAs benefit from the significant commitment of all parties, a willingness to cooperate and, at the very basis, trust that partners do not engage in opportunistic behaviors. Expertise, a tradition in central long-term planning, and consensus are a few of the themes that characterize the institutional environment in the Netherlands and that set the arena for NAs to be feasible. NEPPs and NAs are credible and stable: all parties that might create instability have bought into them, the executive is backed with the majority in both houses, court activities are limited, and all ministers are integrated, thereby making it unlikely that anyone will take opposing action.

The Dutch institutional environment allows the government to commit credibly to long-term NAs. The executive has enough authority to negotiate and coordinate the agreements with existing regulations. The system is centralized and NGOs are involved through consultation, rather than judicial activism. The good working relationship between the executive and industry furthermore facilitates negotiation processes.

CONCLUDING DISCUSSION

VAs have enjoyed widespread implementation throughout OECD countries, but the types of VAs implemented vary considerably among them. We argue that the institutional environment of each country has an impact on how easy it is to implement VAs. As far as these environments differ, different types of VAs are likely to emerge. We discussed the characteristics of the institutional environment in the United States that favor public voluntary programs, and the features of the Dutch institutional environment that lead to the development of negotiated agreements in the Netherlands. We primarily addressed the legal aspects of the institutional environments—that is, the laws and authority structures governing the interaction of players—but also captured underlying social and cultural aspects. We chose the United States and the Netherlands to illustrate our analysis, as these countries are similar in many ways but differ considerably in how they have implemented voluntary programs and negotiated agreements. Other nations differ even more greatly; for example, Germany uses a form of NAs at the federal level and PVPs at the state level.

We explained that the ability of a government to commit to NAs is key for their successful implementation. Elements such as the fragmentation of power and the ability of third parties to enter the game through the judiciary hamper the implementation of negotiated agreements. In the United States, high fragmentation of power and easy access for third parties to enter the game limits the EPA's discretion and therefore its credibility as a negotiator. In the Netherlands, NAs are embedded in a comprehensive plan that entails long-term targets and is approved by parliament. This enforces the ability of the regulator to commit credibly to the agreements.

In terms of the access of third parties to the negotiation process, the U.S. environment offers more access to NGOs through easy court standing and a strong judiciary. The institutional environment of the Netherlands also provides access to third parties. However, the mode of third-party involvement in the two countries differs substantially. In the United States, third parties enter the game through the judiciary. In the Netherlands, a strong tradition of accommodation and consensual decision making involves third parties through expertise-driven consultations. We described that the ability of companies to coordinate their action is a key factor in implementing NAs that serve as an alternative to regulation. In the United States, trade associations play a lesser role than in the Netherlands to coordinate firms' responses to environmental regulation that renders more difficult the implementation of NAs.

Cooperation and consensus can only flourish if the process involves trust among partners. It seems that a culture of collaboration between regulatory agencies and firms is an important factor that requires consideration when discussing the implementation of different types of VAs. In the United States, an adversarial relationship between the EPA and industry has hampered most of the efforts in the 1990s to implement NAs. In the Netherlands, the relationship between regulators and industry has traditionally been more cooperative. A trustful relationship between firms and government is particularly important for the success of agreements in which firms exchange sensitive information. We suggested that in the United States, easy citizen standing in courts might hamper open communication and thorough monitoring, as firms fear disclosing information that can be used against them in courts.

In summary, the institutional environment of the United States makes difficult the implementation of negotiated agreements. Project XL nicely illustrates these difficulties. When XL started, the EPA had originally hoped to approve fifty firms into Project XL. By 1998, however, the EPA only had approved two XL plans (Boyd, Krupnik, and Mazurek, 1998). The U.S. environment allows for a widespread implementation of public voluntary programs. These invite individual firms to participate, and thus do not require industry-wide organization or consensus. Because the regulatory agency sets the basic requirements for participation, and participating firms then set their own pollution reduction targets, these programs require no negotiations. They supplement existing regulation and as such do not require congressional or third-party approval, which makes them less vulnerable to third-party objections.

Like the other chapters of this book, our work draws attention to the institutional elements that shape policy outcomes in the form of new forms of coordination and cooperation. We depart from the "top-to-bottom" view that regulatory processes are external and regulatees are obliged to either resist or conform. We propose a multidirectional perspective where all organizations within the field of study are subject to institutional pressures and are shaping policy outcomes. Our main contribution is to identify the legal as well as social and cultural elements that govern the interplay between regulatory agencies, firms, and NGOs, and that favor or hamper the implementation of voluntary agreements between these organizations. It is possible that noninstitutional factors also drive the use of public voluntary programs in the United States and of negotiated agreements in the Netherlands. For example, it might be that strict environmental regulations in the United States already have forced firms there to considerably improve their environmental performance. As a result, the United States might find it harder to implement NAs that would require industry to undertake measures that go beyond no-regret activities. If so, NAs in the Netherlands could be the outcome of the pursuit of the low-hanging fruit that the United States has already picked up through conventional regulation.

Our analysis can provide guidance to firms about whether or when to enter VAs. From the perspective of business, participation in NAs can allow firms to have a say in the negotiation of the targets or the implementation of environmental regulation. However, participation in negotiated agreements can be risky. The benefits of participating can easily be outweighed by their associated costs if the agreements are implemented in an institutional setting that limits the agreements' stability. Managers must be aware of such institutional limitations.

We have described the main aspects of institutional environments that favor or disfavor the implementation of NAs and PVPs in the United States and the Netherlands. It would be interesting to look at other European and Asian cases. Further research should also assess the possibility of implementing VAs in countries with political instability. Would it be possible to implement agreements in developing countries that have almost no regulatory systems in place? What type of VA would be feasible there? We hope future research will provide insights into these issues.

NOTES

1. Some classifications have also included unilateral commitments or self-regulation (such as Responsible Care or ISO 14001) as VAs. These unilateral commitments include firms that self-organize without soliciting regulatory approval or involvement. We do not consider them as voluntary "agreements" between firms and regulatory agencies. For a definition of unilateral commitments see OECD, 2000: 8.

2. In a sense, the regulatory agency is replacing command and control standards by performance-based standards.

3. The second negotiated agreement is the common-sense Initiative in which regulators, industry, and third parties attempted to review and revise inefficient and ineffective regulations. However, the project failed to produce any tangible products (Mazurek, 1998).

4. These enforcement activities reduced the rate of operations that required licenses but were operating without any from 78 percent in 1990 to 41 percent in 1992 (OECD, 1995).

REFERENCES

Amacher, Gregory S., and Arun S. Malik. 1996. "Bargaining in Environmental Regulation and the Ideal Regulator." *Journal of Environmental Economics and Management,* 30: 233–253.

Andrews, Richard N. L. 1997. "United States." In Martin Jaenicke and Helmut Weidner, eds., *National Environmental Policies,* 25–44. New York: Springer.

Arora, Seema, and Timothy N. Cason. 1995. "An Experiment in Voluntary Environmental Regulation: Participation in EPA's 33/50 Program." *Journal of Environmental Economics and Management,* 28: 271–286.

BDI (Bundesverband der Deutschen Industrie). 1996. *Updated and Extended Declaration by German Industry and Trade on Global Warming Prevention.* March. Cologne, Germany: BDI.

Blackman, Allen, and Janice Mazurek. 2000. "The Cost of Developing Site-Specific Environmental Regulations: Evidence from EPA's Project XL." *Discussion paper 99-35-REV,* Washington, DC: Resources for the Futures.

Boerkey, Peter, and Francois Leveque. 1998. *Voluntary Approaches for Environmental Protection in the European Union.* ENV/EPOC/GEEI(98)29/FINAL. Paris: Organization for Economic Co-Operation and Development.

Boyd, Jim, Alan J. Krupnik, and Janice Mazurek. 1998. *Intel's XL Permit: A Framework for Evaluation.* Washington, DC: Resources for the Future.

Bressers, Hans Th. A., and Loret A. Plettenburg. 1997. "The Netherlands." In Martin Jaenicke and Helmut Weidner, eds., *National Environmental Policies.* New York: Springer.

Carraro, Carlo, and Domenico Siniscalco. 1996. "Voluntary Agreements in Environmental Policy: A Theoretical Appraisal." In Anastasios Xepapadeas, ed., *Economic Policy for the Environment and Natural Resources: Techniques for the Management and Control of Pollution,* Chapter 5. Cheltenham, UK: Edward Elgar.

Daalder, Hans. 1989. "The Mould of Dutch Policies: Themes for Comparative Inquiry." In Hans Daalder and Galen Irwin, eds., *Politics in the Netherlands. How Much Change?,* 1–20. London: Frank Cass.

de Graeff, Jan Jaap. 1994. "Environmental Cooperation Between Government and Industry in the Netherlands." Speech by the director of the Environment and Spatial Planning Office of the Federation of Dutch Enterprises (VNO) and the Dutch Christian Federation of Employees (NCW), presented at the Resource Renewal Institute, California. See http://www.rri.org/gparchive/iidegraeff.html.

Delmas, Magali. Fall, 2000. "Barriers and Incentives to the adoption of ISO 14001 in the United States." In *Duke Environmental Law and Policy Forum,* 1–38.

Delmas, Magali, and Ann Terlaak. 2000. "Voluntary Agreements for the Environment: Institutional Constraints and Potential for Innovation." In Kurt Deketelaere and Eric Orts, eds., *Environmental Contracts,* 349–369. Boston: Kluwer Academic.

Delmas, Magali, and Ann Terlaak. 2001. "A Framework for Analyzing Voluntary Agreements." *California Management Review,* 43 (Spring): 44–64.

DiMaggio, Paul, and Walter W. Powell. 1983. "The Iron Cage Revisited: Institutional Isomorphism and Collective Rationality in Organizational Fields." *American Sociology Review,* 48: 147–160.

EEA (European Environmental Agency). 1997. "Environmental Agreements." In Environmental Issues Series, vol. 3. Copenhagen: European Environmental Agency.

Enevoldsen, Martin. 1998. "Democracy and Environmental Agreements." In Peter Glasbergen, ed., *Co-operative Environmental Governance: Public-Private Agreements as a Policy Strategy,* 201–226. Boston: Kluwer Academic.

Galambos, Louis. 1966. *Competition and Cooperation: The Emergence of a National Trade Association.* Baltimore: Johns Hopkins University Press.

Ginsberg, Beth S., and Cynthia Cummis. 1996. "EPA's Project XL: A Paradigm for Promising Regulatory Reform." *Environmental Law Reporter,* 26: 10057–10064.

Glachant, Mathieu. 1999. "The Cost Efficiency of Voluntary Agreements for Regulating Industrial Pollution." In Carlo Carraro and Francois Leveque, eds., *Voluntary Approaches in Environmental Policy,* Chapter 5. Boston: Kluwer Academic Publishers.

Gladdish, Ken. 1991. *Governing from the Center. Politics and Policy-Making in the Netherlands.* London: Northern Illinois University Press.

Hansen, Lars Garn. 1999. "Environmental Regulation Through Voluntary Agreements." In Carlo Carraro and Francois Leveque, eds., *Voluntary Approaches in Environmental Policy.* Boston: Kluwer Academic.

Henselmans, Jan. 1998. *Green Planning in the Netherlands.* "The Role of Nongovernmental Organizations." Paper presented at the conference on Green Plan Leadership, Resource Renewal Institute, Dec. 10, 1998, San Francisco.

Hoffman, Andrew J. 1999. "Institutional Evolution and Change: Environmentalism and the U.S. Chemical Industry." *Academy of Management Journal,* 42: 351–371.

Kerwin, Cornelius. 1994. *Rulemaking: How Government Agencies Write and Make Policy.* Washington, DC: CQ Press.

Kraft, Michael E. 1996. *Environmental Policy and Politics: Toward the Twenty-First Century.* New York: Harper Collins College.

Kraft, Michael E. 1999. "Environmental Policy in Congress: Consensus or Gridlock?" In Norman J. Vig and Michael E. Kraft, eds., *Environmental Policy: New Directions for the Twenty-First Century,* 97–120. Washington, DC: CQ Press.

Krarup, Signe, and Stefan Ramesohl. 2000. *Voluntary Agreements in Energy Policy. Final Report from the Project "Voluntary Agreements—Implementation and Efficiency" (VAIE).* Copenhavn: AKF.

Levy, Brian, and Pablo Spiller. 1994. "The Institutional Foundations of Regulatory Commitment: A Comparative Analysis of Telecommunications Regulation." *Journal of Law Economics and Organization,* 10: 201–246.

Lijphart, Arend. 1989. "From the Politics of Accommodation to Adversarial Politics in the Netherlands: A Reassessment." In Hans Daalder and Galden Irwin, eds., *Politics in the Netherlands: How Much Change?,* 139–153. London: Frank Cass.

Lyon, Thomas P., and John W. Maxwell. Forthcoming. "Self-Regulation, Taxation and Public Voluntary Environmental Agreements." *Journal of Public Economics.*

March, James G., and Johan P. Olsen. 1989. *Rediscovering Institutions.* New York: Free Press.

Mazurek, Janice. 1998. *The Use of Voluntary Agreements in the United States: An Initial Survey.* ENV/EPOC/GEEI(98)27/FINAL. Paris: Organization for Economic Co-Operation and Development.

Meadowcroft, James. 1998. "Co-operative Management Regimes: A Way Forward?" In Pieter Glasbergen, ed., *Co-operative Environmental Governance: Public-Private Agreements as a Policy Strategy,* 21–42. Boston: Kluwer Academic.

Melnick, R. Shep. 1983. *Regulation and the Courts: The Case of the Clean Air Act.* Washington, DC: Brookings Institution.

Nash, Jennifer. 1999. "The Emergence of Trade Associations as Agents of Environmental Performance Improvement." Presented at the Eighth International Greening of Industry Network Conference. University of North Carolina, Chapel Hill, Nov. 14–17.

OECD. 1995. *Netherlands.* OECD Environmental Performance Reviews. Paris: Organization for Economic Co-Operation and Development.

OECD. 2000. *Voluntary Approaches for Environmental Policy in OECD countries: An Assessment.* Paris: Organization for Economic Co-operation and Development.

Piasecki, Bruce, Kathleen Fletcher, and Frank Mendelson. 1999. *Environmental Management and Business Strategy.* New York: Wiley.

Rose-Ackerman, Susan. 1995. *Controlling Environmental Policy. The Limits of Public Law in Germany and the United States.* New Haven, CT: Yale University Press.

Scott, W. Richard. 1995. *Institutions and Organizations.* Thousand Oaks, CA: Sage Publications.

Segerson, Kathleen, and Thomas J. Miceli. 1998. "Voluntary Environmental Agreements: Good or Bad News for Environmental Protection?" *Journal of Environmental Economics and Management,* 36: 109–130.

Shetter, William Z. 1987. *The Netherlands in Perspective.* Leiden: Martinus Nijhoff.

Storey, Mark, Gale Boyd, and Jeff Dowd. 1997. *Voluntary Agreements with Industry.* Paris: Organization for Economic Co-operation and Development.

Stranlund, John. K. 1995. "Public Mechanisms to Support Compliance to an Environmental Norm." *Journal of Environmental Economics and Management,* 28: 205–222.

Suchman, Mark C., and Lauren B. Edelman. 1997. "Legal Rational Myths: The New Institutionalism and the Law and Society Tradition." *Law and Social Inquiry,* 21: 903–941.

Timmer, Dagmar. 1997. "Strategic Cooperation. The Role of NGOs in the Netherlands' National Environmental Policy Plan." Paper presented at the seminar series "Private Sector Innovation in Environmental Management: The Dutch Green Plan Story" of the Resource Renewal Institute in Minnesota, Oregon, and California, February 1997.

Vogel, David. 1986. *National Styles of Regulation: Environmental Policy in Great Britain and the United States.* Ithaca, NY: Cornell University Press.

Vogel, David. 1993. "Representing Diffuse Interests in Environmental Policy Making." In R. Kent Weaver and Bert A. Rockman, eds., *Do Institutions Matter? Government Capabilities in the United States and Abroad.* Washington, D.C.: Brookings Institution.

Wallace, David. 1995. *Environmental Policy and Industrial Innovation, Strategies in Europe, the US and Japan.* London: Earthscan Publications.

Zoeteman, Kees. 1998. "Green Planning in the Netherlands. The Government Point of View." Paper presented at the conference on Green Plan Leadership, Resource Renewal Institute, December 9–11, 1998, San Francisco.

Zucker, Lynne. 1988. "Where Do Institutions Come From? Organizations as Actors in Social Systems." In Lynne Zucker, ed., *Institutional Patterns and Organizations: Culture and Environment,* 23–49. Cambridge, MA: Ballinger.

V

GOVERNANCE AND

REGULATORY STRUCTURES

16 OPEN-SOURCING ENVIRONMENTAL REGULATION: HOW TO MAKE FIRMS COMPETE FOR THE NATURAL ENVIRONMENT

Yiorgos Mylonadis

The natural environment has improved markedly in countries where environmental regulation has been stepped up. Of course, there is always room for improvement and much of the focus of current research is about fine-tuning the existing regulatory regime to improve the coordination between government and regulated firms (Orts and Deketelaere, 2001). Nevertheless, many of these successes in ongoing environmental issues have been overshadowed by moments of regulatory breakdown of the kind encountered in the disposal of the Brent Spar oil platform (Pope and Sullivan, 1995), the building of the Three Gorges Dam (*Economist*, 2000b), or the marketing of Monsanto's genetically modified corn (Magretta, 1997). Beyond their symbolic significance, breakdowns are of interest because they may help generate insights about how the existing regulatory regime can be improved (Winograd and Flores, 1986).

THE PROBLEM WITH EXTANT REGULATORY APPROACHES

In general, regulation has been successful in cases where environmental objectives are well defined and when regulators can clearly pinpoint the business activities that cause them.[1] Either of these conditions are not always easy to achieve. Most environmental objectives are defined not in terms of environmental well-being (such as an increase in biodiversity) but in terms of pollution avoidance (such as

I would like to acknowledge the financial support of the Athens Laboratory of Business Administration (ALBA) for this research project. Marc Ventresca, Peter Levin, and Wendy Espeland provided helpful comments. The usual disclaimer applies.

protection of nearly extinct species). And pollution is avoided, in turn, when the business activity that is apparently causing it (for example, a land-use change) is held in check. As a result, environmental objectives relating to new business models or new technologies often cannot be set unless companies pursue a potentially polluting business activity and a link can be drawn between the particular activity and pollution. This puts managers and regulators equally at a disadvantage. Monsanto managers who decided to pursue genetic engineering as the overarching focus of the firm (Magretta, 1997), for example, were surprised to discover that their products were perceived as polluting (Stip, 2000). This must have been embarrassing to regulators as well, as the product passed all relevant government regulatory hurdles.

So when it comes to nonconventional issues, it seems regulators are in an unfavorable position, often in a fire-fighting role. To the extent that managers' actions have a sizeable environmental impact, regulators discover that impact after it has taken place, react by formalizing the environmental objective, and seek to establish compliance activities to accomplish it. The considerable lag that exists between the managers' actions and the regulators' reactions is the fertile ground for the activist undertakings of Non-Governmental Organizations (NGOs) with an environmental focus. Environmental advocates regulate in an ad hoc manner, defining environmental issues of concern and selectively identifying business activities as the culprits. The irony is that the regulatory system suffers from an embarrassment of riches: each of its various constituencies possesses knowledge and the ability to mobilize resources. Yet despite their resources and capabilities, the system as it stands cannot coordinate them when the opportunity arises to undertake innovative or nonroutine activities, and does not help them join forces to provide guidance to firms seeking to invest in activities with a potentially novel environmental impact.

The cost of this failure is heavy, both in terms of environmental protection lost and in economic benefits not accomplished. The loss in economic benefit occurs because the regulatory regime fails to guide entrepreneurs in an environmentally responsible fashion, whether in the context of major economic development decisions (such as Three Gorges Dam in China) or in the context of a technological breakthrough (such as genetically engineered food). Managers who lack guidance can pursue several paths, all of which are problematic. Ritualistic compliance with elaborate but largely irrelevant regulatory processes (DiMaggio and Powell, 1983) is one possibility. As was the case with genetically engineered products, producers may adhere to the letter of the law, running the risk that customers will disapprove of the legitimacy managers have strived for in their products. Or they might seek to coopt regulatory authorities (Selznick, 1966) by lobbying or other means (Pfeffer and Salancik, 1978). For example, in their attempt to divert and dam part of the river Acheloos in Greece, like their counterparts in China, managers for the state electric company lobbied for a customized law that rationalized their choices and in the process steamrolled over any environmental issues that arose (http://www-penelope.et.ic.ac.uk/penelope/About.htm, 2000). Failure is also an option. For example, in Massachusetts in the mid-1980s, in response to intense activist protests, the company IT, a large waste treatment firm, called off a plan to build a hazardous waste commercial treatment, storage, and disposal facility (Mylonadis, 1993). As a result, wastes were hauled to other states for treatment and disposal, thus generating new risks associated with transport.

A related problem with most existing regulatory approaches is that they do not foster innovation. Regulation assesses projects with an environmental impact from the standpoint of the damage they might cause to the extant natural environment but leaves out the potential benefits to humanity and the positive environmental externalities that may result from improvements to welfare that a project is likely to bring about; these are much harder to calculate. This practice has been formalized as the "Precautionary Principle," which seeks to avoid undertaking projects that might harm the environment (Ruhl, 2000). The practical implication of the Precautionary Principle is that environmental assessments of major projects are likely to support a conservative development path that favors the pursuit of alternatives. These have known consequences over the pursuit of unconventional albeit potentially more environmentally benign alternatives (such as dismantling the decommissioned Brent Spar oil-drilling platform on shore rather than disposing of it in the deep sea, or conventional farming versus farming based on genetically modified products).

This is the policy paradox. On the one hand, environmental regulation is called upon to tackle increasingly complex problems. These problems require the mobilization of firms, nongovernmental organizations, and other organizations with the ability to develop innovative responses. On the other hand, in coming of age, the regulatory frameworks we deploy seem to rely on outdated theories about the responsiveness of firms. Not surprisingly, firms behave quite consistently with the way these theories expect them to. They shun innovation, although they are capable of undertaking it to pursue environmental objectives, and instead comply with often grossly inefficient regulatory mandates. This is puzzling, in light of recent scholarship that argues that individuals are reflexive in the face of ambiguity (Giddens, 1976) and that firms are capable of innovation, which helps them create and exploit business opportunities (Chandler, 1977). Is it possible that the existing regulatory regimes do such a good job of removing ambiguity for regulated firms that the sterilized environment in which firms often operate deprives them of any impetus for innovation? If so, perhaps regulatory regimes should be viewed as instruments for facilitating the mobilization of societal resources in the presence of ambiguity. Such regimes could encourage innovation by regulated firms that address pressing environmental issues and avoid breakdowns of the kind previously discussed.

NAVIGATING AMIDST A SEA OF AMBIGUITY

The concept of environmental regulation is based on the idea that regulators[2] articulate the socially desired objectives of environmental protection, specify the activities to be regulated, and specify the means of achieving these objectives. In this regard, environmental regulation is driven by the ideology of environmental protection. Much of this is tempered by the rhetoric of "public comment," in which regulators invite firms and interest groups to submit their counterarguments for proposed regulation. This is essentially a form of institutionalized lobbying where each of the invited parties tries to advance its interests against the others. Ultimately, the government regulator, as the arbiter of social values, sets the standards that economic activity should adhere to. Ideology in disregard of economic trade-offs has successfully driven social policy in the past. It helped eradicate smallpox (Radetsky, 1999) and abolish slavery (Miller, 1996). More recently it helped legislators to pass laws that ensure the protection of the lives of workers on the job (McEvoy, 1995).

But the nature of environmental issues makes addressing them in an ideologically pure way problematic. Almost all human activity involves "pollution" of some kind. Unlike smallpox or slavery, it is virtually impossible to regulate economic activity to achieve zero pollution (or, at the very least, we don't know how to do it). Even if corporations have a general idea how to help improve the environment, the concrete definition of that idea requires knowledge that remains to be discovered. Polaroid's experience in developing a waste-reduction framework illustrates the point. The fundamental logic about achieving waste reduction at the source had been imagined by its engineers and outside academics long before the company developed a full-fledged waste-reduction program (Mylonadis, 1993). But not until Polaroid's engineers embarked on a drawn-out test of the feasibility of the idea was the actual knowledge about how to do it developed. The case of lead-free paint demonstrates a related point. Even if a known win-win possibility exists, inertia or superstition can ensure that some key actors will discover it much later. Despite the existence of related experience in Europe, it took U.S. paint manufacturers many decades to acknowledge that paints could be produced lead-free with no adverse implications for quality or cost (Warren, 2000). Thus, in general, the question regulators confront is not how to *entirely* avoid pollution. Instead, they seek to identify the cost to welfare of a particular amount of pollution avoided and—based on this assessment—decide on *how much* pollution to avoid.

The ambiguity inherent in these tradeoffs between material and environmental well-being manifest themselves in choices confronting the regulator about both *how* to regulate and *what* to regulate. The problem in choosing *how* to regulate occurs because firms know better than the regulator the most cost-efficient way of reducing a given pollutant. A celebrated example of this information asymmetry is the case of benzene air pollution at Amoco's plant in Yorktown, Virginia (Goodstein, 1995: 193). Amoco proved to the EPA that the process the EPA sought in order to control benzene emissions polluted much less than fugitive emissions at the loading dock, which were not regulated. If the regulator could measure the full environmental impact of the business activities of the regulated firm, it could afford to be agnostic about the pollution control methodology the regulated firm adopted. However, measuring full environmental impact would be extremely costly and difficult. This may explain why, in the case of most air regulation, government regulators rely on models of pollution and on known pollution control technologies. In the case of water pollution and accidental ground pollution, government regulators rely on self-reported sampling and self-reports. Finally, in the case of solid-waste disposal, regulators rely on transport manifests. With no overall knowledge of the environmental performance of the regulated firm, the regulator is tempted to prescribe an approach to pollution reduction. The dilemma of the regulator is that the prescriptive approaches restrict firm discretion in seeking the most efficient path to pollution reduction and thus may result in greater losses of material well-being. Conversely, more flexibility to the regulated firm to allow them to reduce pollution in a more efficient way may reduce the ability of the regulator to monitor the performance of the regulated firm.

An analogous problem involves the choice of *what* business activity to regulate. The regulators' struggle to continuously catch up with the impact of the activities undertaken by businesses is compounded by the fact that final products are a composite of a variety of activities and that they affect the environment in a variety of ways. The role of the regulator is to decide which product is preferable from an environmental standpoint. The more obvious the link between corporate activity and environmental improvement, the more tempting it is for the regulator to attempt to control the activity directly.

Contrast this with the approach of manufacturers themselves. Rather than directly control the behavior of their product development and production engineers to reduce the environmental impact of the firm, leading firms develop tools that enable engineers to assess the environmental impact of each of their activities. Engineers are given the freedom to choose the activities and raw materials as long as the total environmental impact of the product is within set limits. For example, Volvo, the automobile manufacturer, has developed a database that ranks, for the benefit of its designers, materials according to their environmental friendliness (Rowledge, Brady, and Barton, 1999). Volvo emphasizes that the ranking of the materials should be used only as a heuristic because contextual considerations upstream and downstream in the supply chain of the component make the task of life cycle analysis for each material an inexact science. For that reason Volvo allows its users to alter assumptions underlying the environmental friendliness of a particular component (Rothenberg and Maxwell, 1995). It is possible to develop finer tools the narrower the definition of the problem becomes. For example, by focusing on prioritizing waste management activities for chemicals classified according to their degree of toxicity, Polaroid developed a highly structured methodology for waste reduction (Mylonadis, 1993). As in the case of Volvo, Polaroid's methodology also enabled its engineers to exercise their professional judgment. Indeed, by being offered as a guide rather than a prescribed set of activities, such mechanisms reinforce the need to exercise judgment rather than remove that need.

A similar toolkit that allowed firms to choose technologies and activities as long as these combinations produced socially desired environmental results could enable the use of judgment at the societal level. The advantage of this approach over the existing ones is that it actively encourages activities that accomplish environmental goals as opposed to establishing environmentally related constraints on existing activities. Although sophisticated control and monitoring mechanisms such as Environmental Impact Statements (Hironaka and Schofer, Chapter 9) exist widely within the existing institutional regimes, these regulate negative environmental spillovers that are by-products of an otherwise valuable economic activity, rather than systematically seek out initiatives that deliver environmentally valuable goods. For example, rather than utilize the Federal Drug Administration approval mechanism to formally ask whether the production of genetically modified food is an environmentally benign activity, the question would be to motivate firms to compete in defining what *is* an environmentally benign food production activity.

Because of these considerations, it is very hard to pursue environmental regulation on ideological grounds. Still, even in the case of the protection of humans, ideological grounds for regulation become less important when definitional issues surface and when the causality between the practice and the objective is not clear. For example, ideology-based regulation is less applicable in the more complicated issue of child labor where corporate initiatives, local legal frameworks, and generalized frameworks of social justice stand at odds with each other (Diller, 1999). The same occurs in the introduction of safety features in automobiles: although some safety features are required by law following Ralph Nader's ideological campaign (Nader, 1965), many of the most innovative safety features found on automobiles today are the prerogative of individual automobile manufacturers. In general, if the link between the outcome sought and the range of activities that may affect it is tenuous, the answer to the question "What is a right outcome?" is likely to be found in the question "What activity should be developed?" These concerns in the environmental context have motivated legal scholars to make a case for "pragmatic" environmental regulation. The pragmatic approach recognizes the complexity and ambiguity related to environmental issues and seeks to establish a middle ground between environmental ideology and utilitarianism (Farber, 1999, 2000).

An important realization given these considerations is that society does not possess ex ante the knowledge for protecting the environment, nor has it clear preferences about one bundle of polluting activities over another. Rather society develops its options for protecting the natural environment and its revealed preference structure as it goes along. In sociological parlance, the practices for the protection of the natural environment are socially constructed. Individuals are always open to the possibility of acting reflexively (Giddens, 1984) and when they do so they construct their social world. However, individuals often act mindlessly or heedlessly (Weick and Roberts, 1993). In general, Giddens argues, individuals are likely to act reflexively when routinized behavior does not produce the results they intend (Giddens, 1984). In the face of such "breakdown" and armed with a distinctly human quality—the intention to "go on" with life—individuals negotiate novel practices. Because these breakdowns and the associated reflexivity are more likely to be present in contexts that are high in ambiguity, social construction is more pronounced in these cases. Practically, this means that regulators are unlikely to know what activities to regulate or how to regulate them. It also means that the knowledge to tackle such problems is dispersed in society. A wide range of stakeholders, including advocates, consultants, regulators, legislators, consumers, and managers, need to volunteer their knowledge to resolve the inconsistencies and forge choices out of the dilemmas that arise. The problem that arises is to envision a framework that would guide the collective effort of these constituencies.

REGULATING KNOWLEDGE-
INTENSIVE COLLECTIVE ACTIVITIES

The natural environment is not the only context in which ambiguities emerge. Any organizing activity that is driven not by routine but by the need to structure knowledge is rife with ambiguity. It follows that the analysis of the regimes that govern the mobilization of collective activity in these contexts may offer valuable insights for regulatory regimes in the environmental context. It is helpful here to draw a distinction between two kinds of ambiguity present in knowledge-intensive collective activities, which result in two kinds of choices for managers: a choice about means and a choice about ends (Thompson and Tyden, 1959).

With regard to means, managers may agree or disagree about the causal process by which outcomes may be realized (Scott, 1998). If they agree on causality, it also means that they know *how* to organize. From the perspective of the individual decision maker who controls resource deployment, this implies that he or she possesses knowledge about the best way for resources allocated to a particular task to carry it through. Conversely, from the standpoint of an individual decision maker, organizational disagreement implies he or she does not possess the organizational technology that will enable the organization to achieve a given objective.

The same problem arises with respect to ends, as organizational participants may agree or disagree about the organizational outcomes they would like to pursue (Scott, 1998). If they agree, they share an understanding of *what* is to be accomplished. From the perspective of the individual decision maker who controls resource deployment, this implies that he or she can designate the area that will ensure the best use of resources and set a target to be achieved. Conversely, disagreement about desired objectives for the organization means that the decision maker is agnostic about the best uses of the resources he or she has control over or about the outcome that the deployment of resources can be expected to produce.

Figure 16.1 suggests a number of decision contexts as illustrations of the possibilities that the cross-classification of this simple means-ends distinction produces.

When decision makers know what objective to pursue and how to organize this pursuit, it is rational for them to maintain control over the way resources are used and the objective that their utilization accomplishes. This includes a choice about the domain in which they are deployed and whether they can perform well in that domain. For example, a phone directory rarely arouses doubt about how it is organized or the desired outcome of somebody who looks up a number in it. Similarly, the publishers of encyclopedias and dictionaries usually relinquish control to the author of a particular lemma over the way an entry is written, although the

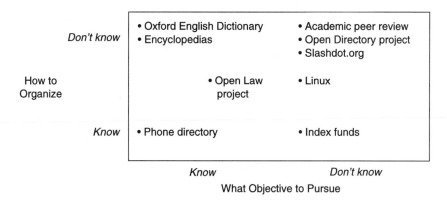

Figure 16.1   Organizing Knowledge-Intensive Collective Activities

publisher still retains control over what lemmas will be analyzed (*Economist,* 1999a). At the other extreme, ambiguity may exist over the direction of resource deployment but not over method. For example, investors who utilize index funds fully subscribe to a methodology for choosing stocks while remaining largely agnostic about the firms in which they intend to invest.

The examples in the northeast corner of the matrix in Figure 16.1 are the most challenging because managers can exercise the least amount of direct control over resources—be these human or physical. In the case of academic journals, for example, the nominal decision makers, the editors, share much of the decision making with the reviewers over whether a particular article is relevant to the audience of the journal (that is, the question of what areas to focus on) even though they have discretion over the final decision. In addition, the choice about the way in which a submission will be assessed is fully the province of the reviewers.

The interactive possibilities made available through the Internet extend even further the notion of peer review. The Open Directory project is an Internet directory similar in appearance to Yahoo! but radically different in the organizational logic that sustains it. The difference lies in the fact that the development of individual categories in Open Directory is decentralized to tens of thousands of editors who have considerable discretion over the content of their sections and the way they go about developing this content (*Economist,* 1999a; http://dmoz.org/about .html, 2000). Because the managers of the site cannot directly control the editors, they have developed an indirect disciplining mechanism that allows site users to vote on the effectiveness of each editor. Slashdot.org (http://slashdot.org/about .shtml, 2000), another news site, employs a more sophisticated voting method that weights more heavily the votes of more involved users of the site. If the users consistently agree that a particular editor does not perform well, the editor is removed. It is important to note here that users do not have predetermined criteria for judging the performance of editors. They judge this performance in context, and it is reasonable to believe that because they are familiar with the context they will know what constitutes "good" versus "bad" editorial activity.

This approach to collective development has come to be known as open-source development. Not all open-source projects are necessarily that open-ended. Open Law is a project intended to challenge the U.S. Term Extension Act by inviting contributions to its legal strategy from legal experts and the public at large (*Economist*, 1999a). Contributions are mediated by a core group of other contributors. In this case, the objective of the project is defined with some degree of specificity and the intermediation of the legal experts suggests that the same is true of the method employed for selecting strategy proposals. The development of the Linux operating system has proceeded along similar principles. Each contributor to the system chooses the approach he or she deems best, although a panel of experts approves of the robustness of the solution proposed before it is incorporated into Linux. Contributors also choose what area to focus on—always within the relatively limited confines of the functionality of an operating system (Raymond, 1999).

These examples indicate that managers have recourse to alternatives when they realize that they do not possess all the knowledge necessary about either means or ends to make an informed decision. The alternative to directly controlling resources is to develop processes for appointing qualified "experts," to delegate the responsibility for decisions to these experts, and to develop mechanisms that empower informed users to approve or disapprove of the choices experts make. In such a regime, managers exercise their discretion and judgment by making choices about the range of activities to focus on and about the range of contributors who could qualify as experts.

Open sourcing has some distinct advantages over more traditional ways of controlling resources. For one, the approach is more democratic because it involves a wide variety of stakeholders (Freeman, 1984). Also, it has the potential to solve problems better because it recognizes that knowledge is distributed (Tsoukas, 1996). Moreover, this knowledge can be relied upon to not only solve a particular problem but also to establish criteria for desirable performance. In contrast to mainstream organizational theories that hypothesize that external monitors and enforcers are a necessary ingredient of an efficient productive system, Ostrom and her colleagues have shown that it is possible to arrive at a similar outcome via endogenously derived performance criteria and even endogenous performance monitoring (Ostrom 1990, 1992; Ostrom, Schroeder, and Wynne, 1993). If performance

metrics are impossible to establish (as in the case of peer review in scientific journals) peers exercise their best judgment of what constitutes "best" performance. If
metrics can be developed, peers establish a methodology for calculating performance and participants strive to perform to the best of their abilities. In either
case, performance assessment is the result of continual monitoring by a network
of peers so that decision makers systematically reexamine the efficacy of resource
allocation. I have argued earlier that social construction is more pronounced the
more ambiguous the context is in which actors operate. Regulators, often inadver-
tently, remove much of this ambiguity and in so doing reduce the discretion managers have over *how* they mobilize their resources. It becomes clear to managers
that initiatives which could lead to the attainment of particular societal objectives
will not be rewarded unless they conform to a *format* that the regulator has predetermined. An open-sourcing regime can be designed so that actors maintain
discretion over both of these kinds of choices and in so doing give them an incentive to act reflexively as they consider initiatives that are related to the natural
environment.

An obvious disadvantage of open sourcing is that the invitation of contributions runs the risk of revealing to competitors the objectives of the organization
and the method it adopts to accomplish them. This could make the organization
vulnerable to competitors or others who might seek to undermine its success. Organizations that rely on open sourcing counter this threat by making the best use
of the distributed contributions to their project. For example, the Open Law project acknowledges the threat but believes that "what we lose in secrecy, we expect to
regain in depth of sources and breadth of argument" (http://eon.law.harvard.edu/
openlaw/faq.html, 2000). Similarly, a business columnist for the *San Jose Mercury
News,* who has embarked on an experiment in "open-source journalism," contends that despite the threat of competitors relying on his material, the "eventual
column on the topic will be much better if I hear from smart people like you before I write it" (http://weblog.mercurycenter.com/ejournal/faq, 2000).

ADOPTING OPEN-SOURCING IN THE
ENVIRONMENTAL REGULATORY CONTEXT

The recognition that the achievement of improved environmental performance is
a socially constructed process means that this field is fraught with ambiguity. Managers are faced with the same kind of choices as in other knowledge-intensive organizational contexts. In the environmental context, managers and regulators
could agree or disagree over ways to reduce pollution (means) as well as the pol-

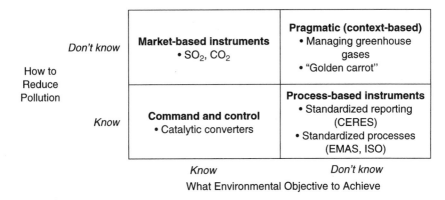

Figure 16.2   Organizing Knowledge-Intensive Environmental Regulation

luting activities to target and the level of control necessary (objectives). From the perspective of the regulator, to agree over means is to assert that the regulator knows the best way to reduce pollution, and to agree over ends means that the regulator knows what polluting activities to control and how much. The cross-classification of these options gives rise to four possibilities that correspond to four broad approaches to environmental regulation: (a) command-and-control regulation, (b) market-based instruments, (c) process-based instruments, and (d) pragmatic (context-based) approaches. These possibilities are depicted in Figure 16.2.

In what has come to be known as the "command-and-control" approach, the regulator knows what polluting activities to target and by how much to reduce pollution in order to achieve a particular environmental objective. She also knows what is the best way to reduce pollution. Under these conditions, it is very efficient to designate the particular methodology for that end and require it of polluters who engage in these activities. This is particularly true when it is hard for the regulator to monitor actual environmental performance of the polluters (Goodstein, 1995). The requirement to fit catalytic converters to gasoline-consuming automobiles illustrates the first set of conditions. The case of pleasure speedboats illustrates the second condition as well, in that it is difficult to monitor their environmental performance. An advantage of this approach is the low monitoring cost. A key disadvantage is that it discourages innovation because environmental overperformers are not rewarded in any way.

In other instances, regulators know well what polluting activities they intend to regulate, how much pollution ought to be reduced by so as to achieve a particular environmental objective, and are able to measure the environmental performance of these activities. However, they also recognize that polluters may know the best way to reduce pollution. In these cases they can reward over-performers by allow-ing them to sell the right to pollute to under-performers so that the aggregate en-vironmental objective is achieved (Hockenstein, Stavins, and Whitehead, 1997). Such marketor "incentive"-based instruments have been adopted in the United States for SO_2 emissions and are being proposed internationally for CO_2 emissions under the Kyoto protocol. The key to the success of this approach is not only the ability to identify the polluting activities and measure their impact but also the ability to "commensurate," or "compare and integrate different objects according to a common metric" such as CO_2 or SO_2 (Levin and Espeland, Chapter 5). The major benefit of this approach is that it encourages polluters to innovate on ways to improve their environmental performance. However, if business activities have much impact upon a number of environmental objectives, commensuration might be hard to achieve, and trade among polluters will not take place.

Another approach to environmental regulation is exemplified in process-based instruments. These attempt to standardize the organizational response of a pol-luter along the lines of a specific methodology. But because these methodologies are applied in a wide range of contexts, it is extremely hard to measure and ag-gregate the environmental outcome they produce. It is not surprising, therefore, that most of these frameworks have no performance requirements. For that reason they are also often referred to as "self-regulation" (Nash and Ehrenfeld, 1996) or "incentive-based" regulation (Goodstein, 1995: 278). Examples of this approach include frameworks for standardized reporting, such as the CERES protocol or frameworks for the adoption of standardized processes such as EMAS or ISO 14000. The major advantage of this approach is its versatility. However, that ver-satility comes at the cost of monitoring environmental performance. It has been argued that the process of committing firms to self-review their performance will generate a reflexive process that makes opportunities for improvement self-evident to them (Orts, 1995). Still, performance is an integral aspect of theories of reflexive action (Giddens, 1984; Habermas, 1990). Individuals realize the new op-portunities available to them only when there is a breakdown in their routine that alerts them to the need to think reflexively. Individuals are motivated to innovate in these moments because this will allow them to go on in the context they oper-ate. Individuals can go on when their peers approve of their social performance. Unless the polluters stand to benefit from comparing their performance to that of a peer group of polluters, it is unlikely that the decontextualized review of their en-vironmental impact will generate the impetus required to make them act reflex-ively. This is consistent with the criticism that environmental advocacy groups have often raised against process-based regulation, when it is devoid of outcome-based performance measures.

It is when regulators do not know the best way to achieve environmental objectives and when they do not know the activities that need to be regulated or the extent to which they need to be regulated that the impetus arises for open-sourcing environmental regulation. The request for contributions here concerns the best methodology for addressing an environmental issue. In addition, contributors also help identify which business activities ought to be controlled and by how much their environmental impact ought to be reduced.

Who are the players most ideally suited to define the activities that need to be regulated? Economic constituencies, including incumbents and potential entrants, are relevant here because they have intimate knowledge about the impact of the current or proposed business activities on the natural environment. The technical knowledge of scientists, whether they are part of the academic community, part of the advocacy community, or part of the regulatory community, is another valuable source of input. Finally, environmental advocates possess knowledge about the environmental desires and preferences of citizens. The contributions of these players serve to frame the context for regulation—that is, to define the business activities whose environmental improvement will be sought and the maximum level of pollution that society is willing to accept.

Of all of these players, firms are best suited to contribute to the question of how much pollution reduction is enough over and beyond the minimum reduction threshold that regulators require. Firms can do this because they can assess the material tradeoffs and the cost (or benefit) to consumers involved in improving their environmental performance. Most importantly, they can do this because they relate "how much" to "what activity" rather than regarding these two questions as being independent of each other. The U.S. and North American responses to the need to reduce ambient CO_2 illustrate this point. In the United Kingdom, the Royal Commission on Environmental Pollution sought to regulate gross CO_2 emissions by drastic measures such as the doubling of fuel prices over a decade (*Economist*, 1998). In the United States and Canada, utilities had embraced a wider definition of the problem, shifting the emphasis from reducing CO_2 emissions to the management of ambient carbon dioxide. This involved a much more varied range of activities such as understanding how to minimize the damage caused to nonharvested trees in the Malaysian rainforest (PR Newswire, 1996), motivating Iowa farmers to inject seeds into their soil without tilling it, or preserving a forest in Bolivia (*Economist*, 1999b; *Economist*, 2000a). The objective of each of these activities is to improve the carbon sequestration capacity of the soil or plants, thus arriving at the same environmental outcome (reduction of the environmental impact of this particular greenhouse gas) via the regulation of a wide variety of activities that affect that objective.

There is a subtle but important difference between context-based regulation and market-based regulation. To achieve market-based regulation, the regulator needs to know the class of activities that have an impact on the environmental objectives she would like to achieve. This helps commensurate any activity as long as it belongs to this class. For example, all electric utilities that are considered to contribute to the problem of SO_2-related pollution in the Northeast United States are regulated under the SO_2 trading scheme. This standardization of measures helps aggregate a large and well-defined number of firms with potentially diverse activities among them. Large numbers of participants and standardization on a measure that they all aspire to improve are conditions conducive for market exchange. In contrast, context-based regulation occurs when the regulator does not know which activities (or firms) to regulate or how much is enough environmental improvement. This makes it harder to agree on a measure to be improved on. Even if the regulator devises such a measure, she is likely to come up with a measure that is specific to a small subset of firms whose particular contribution is likely to help achieve a particular objective. The more specific the measure, the more meaningful it will be to these firms and the less meaningful to other firms whose contribution is not relevant for the particular objective. The effect of such discrimination mobilizes selected firms who can utilize their resources to achieve the aims set by the regulator and leaves everyone else indifferent. The smaller numbers involved and the fact that measures of environmental impact are likely to vary according to the way each player defines the problem reduces the likelihood that exchange can take place. Thus a market-based regime is a special case of a context-based regime.

An example of a context-specific regulation was the "Golden Carrot." The Golden Carrot was a voluntary incentive scheme initiated by a group of utilities in the United States in the mid-1990s. The utilities benefit from financing ways to conserve energy that are more inexpensive than their earnings from selling this energy to their customers. In this case they were willing to share some of the profit that arose with firms that helped produce more energy-efficient refrigerators. Golden Carrot had many similarities with market-based regulation. Regulators defined ex ante product development and early sales of energy efficient refrigerators as the activities they intended to reward. Because these efforts were monetized in an explicit formula, they were commensurate just as in the case of trading schemes the pollution reduction efforts of utilities are commensurate via the reference to the common metric of SO_2 tons. However, an important difference was that regulators left open the amount of environmental improvement that producers could bring about in order to get their reward. The fact that a reward was tied to this particular accomplishment open-sourced to all major refrigerator manufacturers the method for energy efficiency and level of efficiency that each participant in this race aspired toward. Another difference from a market-based scheme was the small number of players participating. The race was set to target only refrigerator producers and therefore only the refrigerator divisions of three major white goods manufacturers participated. This approach did not enable the facilitation of market exchanges but did focus the attention and energies of each producer on coming up with a highly efficient refrigerator. The regulators admitted that the winning proposal delivered energy efficiency that far surpassed their expectations.

This discussion so far has elaborated on the conditions that would favor the adoption of open-source environmental regulation. We now turn to examine the key design decisions that the construction of such a system would involve.

DESIGNING AN OPEN-SOURCE ENVIRONMENTAL REGULATORY FRAMEWORK

Such a system would have to reward individual firm excellence, ensure the participation of all the players who could make a difference, establish a mechanism for arriving at criteria for choosing a winner, and establish a clear reward for the winner.

Rewarding Individual Excellence

Unlike command-and-control and procedure-based approaches to environmental regulation, open-source regulation is based on the assumption that firms' efforts will be greater the more they are rewarded. This suggests that differential performance should be rewarded, just as in the case of market-based regulation. Unlike market-based regulation, however, in this framework there is no need to limit the extent of improvement in the environmental impact firms are willing to undertake. Therefore better performers can reap the full reward—not just the part that is proportional to their performance compared to their peers. The ability of this system to deliver results beyond the expectations of regulators depends precisely on its ability to engage competitors in a race to emulate each other's best efforts.

Bringing in All the Important Players

A crucial moment in this approach is when the context for the race is set. So who should be involved in setting the context and who could initiate such context-setting (Farber, 2000)? Starting from the latter question, it is to the advantage of the regulator to enable any bona fide participant to initiate the process. Those most likely to be willing are firms, especially when they see an opportunity to frame a race in a way that will reward their contribution. For example, Ecover, the European detergent manufacturer, had often alleged that established firms had successfully lobbied regulators against tightening the environmental standards for this class of products. The regulator should discourage such initiatives to the extent they are merely preemptive moves intended to crowd out potentially superior environmental performance initiatives by competitors.

Because incumbent firms are likely to be important contributors to the race, they should have a say in defining it so that it is meaningful to them. However, incumbent firms are also likely to benefit from the presence of commercially successful legacy products in the market and this might minimize their incentive to innovate along the lines the regulators intend them to. Potential new entrants do not carry these liabilities and could introduce new technologies or new ways of doing business that would advance the environmental objectives of the regulators. The problem is that firms may be created purely as a result of the race announcement. Even if they already exist, they are likely to be small and lack the resources to participate fully. But this problem can be overcome. Venture capitalists, consultants, academics, recruiters, and related professionals who populate the particular field the race will be set in can serve as ad hoc speakers for potential new entrants. Other key contributors who can help define the context are environmental advocates. Government regulators can act as final arbiters in this process. This process might resemble the one currently adopted by U.S. regulators when inviting public comment for a proposed regulation. The difference is that the current process has to be initiated by government regulators, primarily seeks to involve incumbent firms, and is framed as zero-sum negotiation where, predictably, advocates argue for more regulation and incumbent firms for less.

Arriving at Criteria for Choosing a Winner

In the case of the Golden Carrot, the criteria for choosing a winner were established up front as the race was defined. Adopting this practice presents a paradox, because the criteria for what constitutes a "best" environmental performance are established before competing firms have a chance to define these on the basis of their own attempts to improve their impact. This is clearly the wrong order if one subscribes to the notion that environmental knowledge is socially constructed. This means that knowledge of what objectives to achieve and how to achieve them evolves together with regulation-induced, managerial attempts to address environmental issues. There are alternative ways of arriving at criteria instead of their outright establishment at the outset of the race. Firms that contribute techniques for improving their environmental impact can propose and justify criteria on the basis of which experts ought to evaluate their proposed activities, just as trial lawyers invoke precedents to establish the relevance of their arguments. To carry the legal analogy further, just as judges and the jury decide whether to ultimately accept the lawyers' arguments, the decision about what criteria to adopt will have to rely with the ultimate arbiters, a panel of experts in the particular context in which the race takes place. The interactive practice established by the adoption of open-sourcing on the Internet suggests that these reviewers are not only assessors but their judgments can in turn also be assessed by the broader community of experts in the field.

Establishing Clear Rewards

This system hinges upon its ability to motivate participating firms to exert unusual effort so that they contribute and achieve results that are better than the ones that could be achieved under alternative regulatory regimes. So a crucial component is the reward it can offer to participating companies. The nature of the reward will differ depending on the power of the initiator of the race. For example, a government authority can confer statutory privileges or preferential access to government controlled resources, whereas an industry association or a nonprofit organization can reward based on the resources that its members have control over. Accordingly, the reward will take different forms. In the case of the Golden Carrot, it was a portion of the dead weight loss that the actions of the refrigerator companies helped recoup. Another way of rewarding participants is to endorse the result of their efforts in the spirit of the Energy Star programs in the United States or CERES reporting principles. If a governmental regulator set up such a regime, she could motivate participants by committing to adopt the environmental impact they achieve as the floor for environmental objectives in the future. This commitment would provide a first-mover advantage to the companies that are most successful in bringing about environmental improvements and offer them the ability to benefit from their efforts in a regime where there is a penalty associated with performing at levels lower than the ones they have achieved.

DISCUSSION

Open-source regulation is a regime based on the notion that firms can act as reflexively in the context of environmental goods (Orts, 1995) as they do in the context of their core productive activities. But actors tend to act reflexively when confronted with "breakdowns" in the course of ongoing pursuits. The general problem with existing regulatory regimes is that they remove much of the ambiguity that produces such breakdowns in the early stages of product development. One negative consequence of this is that regulatory prescriptions are often inefficient. Another potentially more harmful consequence is that regulated firms are lured into procedural compliance with the letter of the regulation and are as surprised as regulators are when such compliance does not result in wider legitimacy for their operations. The breakdowns that occur after firms have expended significant efforts and made irreversible asset-specific investments in complying with regulations are debilitating and are more likely to result in organizational failure than in reflexive action. Open-sourcing is intended to anticipate the eventual occurrence of such breakdowns and intentionally design them in the regulatory regime to motivate actors to act reflexively. These designed-in breakdowns take the form of competitive races among firms who seek to emulate their peers and stand out among them in contests that regulators set.

Open-sourcing invites the participation of firms, nongovernmental organizations, proxies for potential entrants, and others in the definition of the contests, in the establishment of the rewards, and in the assessment of the competitive entries. This broad inclusion is in the spirit of stakeholder approaches to corporate governance (Freeman, 1984) that seek to identify and maximize joint gains among groups with diverse interests (Troast and others, Chapter 10). But these approaches are often hampered by unclear motivations on the part of firms about who to include in the decision-making process (that is, how broadly should "stakeholders" be defined?) and the motivation for including them (utilitarian or idealistic motives for inclusion). A particular advantage of open-sourcing is that it allows for competitive contests even in contexts that are not well defined and thus contexts not particularly amenable to commensuration and market-based initiatives. The regulator empowers firms who choose to participate in an open-sourcing regime to go beyond predetermined outcomes or activities and provides them with incentives to discover new uses of resources they control and reach for the pursuit of environmental objectives over and beyond what was considered achievable in advance of the competition. This context-based regime is a recursive system where performance definition and monitoring is endogenized. This regime can be restricted to the special case of market-based regulation if performance standards are set exogenously and specified so that they refer to specific activities and firms (Levin and Espeland, Chapter 5).

The challenge for open-sourcing in a specific context lies in setting the parameters of the competitive race. Because the terms of the race are likely to favor participants with a certain resource endowment more than others, these terms are likely to be contested. The contest is likely to mirror the existing debates with participants driven either by ideological posturing or the pursuit of utilitarian interests (Emirbayer and Mische, 1998). The challenge in the design of such a regime is to promote the recursive aspects of the system. This is likely if competitors are focused as much on immediate gains from the contest prize as on the skills and know-how they will derive for use in related business pursuits.

NOTES

1. Goodstein (1995: 232–233) points out that during the twenty-five years or so since environmental legislation appeared in the United States "in spite of the fact that economic activity almost doubled . . . emissions of some waterborne pollutants have dropped dramatically." In addition, firms have started to focus on "reducing pollution through pollution prevention," and "particularly nasty new pesticides are not likely to make it through the EPA's initial screen. . . . In other words, the fact that regulation has managed to hold the line against economic growth is itself an impressive accomplishment." Achievements have been most notable in areas where the objective is well defined and the culprit is well known, such as airborne lead concentrations.

2. "Regulator" here is defined more broadly to include a wide variety of institutional actors who seek to modify the environmental performance of firms (Bendell, 2000). The definition includes government regulators who specify how environmental laws will be interpreted, specify outcomes or processes, and monitor regulation implementation. But nongovernmental organizations who advocate for the environment also act as ad hoc regulators. A third type of regulation involves codes and standards developed by industry associations, or independent associations with which firms voluntarily comply (Goodstein, 1995). Thus firms too can be considered regulators.

REFERENCES

Bendell, Jem. 2000. "Civil Regulation: A New Form of Democratic Governance for the Global Economy?" In Jem Bendell, ed., *Terms for Endearment: Business, NGOs and Sustainable Development*, 237–254. Sheffield: Greenleaf.

Chandler, Alfred Dupont. 1977. *The Visible Hand: The Managerial Revolution in American Business*. Cambridge, MA: Belknap Press.

Diller, Janelle. 1999. "A Social Conscience in the Global Marketplace? Labour Dimensions of Codes of Conduct, Social Labelling and Investor Initiatives." *International Labour Review*, 138(2): 99–130.

DiMaggio, Paul J., and Walter W. Powell. 1983. "The Iron Cage Revisited: Institutional Isomorphism and Collective Rationality in Organizational Fields." *American Sociological Review*, 48(2): 147–160.

Economist. 1998. "Climate Change: A Taxing Issue." 344(8025): 34.

Economist. 1999a. "The Internet: Hacker Journalism." 353(8148): 66.

Economist. 1999b. "Emissions: Seeing Green." 353(8143): 73.

Economist. 2000a. "Cultivating Carbon." 354(8163): Special Section: 12.

Economist. 2000b. "Power Clash." 355(8170): 43–44.

Emirbayer, M., and A. Mische. 1998. "What Is Agency?" *American Journal of Sociology,* 103(4): 962–1023.

Farber, Daniel A. 1999. *Eco-Pragmatism: Making Sensible Environmental Decisions in an Uncertain World.* Chicago: University of Chicago Press.

Farber, Daniel A. 2000. "Triangulating the Future of Reinvention: Three Emerging Models of Environmental Protection." *University of Illinois Law Review,* (1): 61–81.

Freeman, R. Edward. 1984. *Strategic Management: A Stakeholder Approach.* Boston: Pitman.

Giddens, Anthony. 1976. *New Rules of Sociological Method.* Stanford, CA: Stanford University Press.

Giddens, Anthony. 1984. *The Constitution of Society: Outline of the Theory of Structuration.* Berkeley: University of California Press.

Goodstein, Eban. 1995. *Economics and Environment.* Upper Saddle River, NJ: Prentice Hall.

Habermas, Jurgen. 1990. *Moral Consciousness and Communicative Action.* Cambridge, MA: MIT Press.

Hockenstein, Jeremy B., Robert N. Stavins, and Bradley W. Whitehead. 1997. "Crafting the Next Generation of Market-Based Environmental Tools." *Environment,* 39(4): 12–22.

http://dmoz.org/about.html. 2000. Accessed October 20, 2001.

http://eon.law.harvard.edu/openlaw/faq.html. 2000. Accessed October 20, 2001.

http://www.penelope.et.ic.ac.uk/penelope/About.htm. 2000

http://slashdot.org/about.shtml. 2000. Accessed October 20, 2001.

http://weblog.mercurycenter.com/ejournal/faq. 2000. Accessed October 20, 2001.

Magretta, Joan. 1997. "Growth Through Global Sustainability: An Interview with Monsanto's CEO Robert B. Shapiro." *Harvard Business Review,* 75(1): 78–88.

McEvoy, Arthur F. 1995. "The Triangle-Shirtwaist-Factory Fire of 1911: Social-Change, Industrial-Accidents, and the Evolution of Common-Sense Causality." *Law and Social Inquiry,* 20(2): 621–651.

Miller, William Lee. 1996. *Arguing About Slavery: The Great Battle in the United States Congress.* New York: Knopf.

Mylonadis, Yiorgos. 1993. *The "Green" Challenge to the Industrial Enterprise Mindset: Survival Threat or Strategic Opportunity?* Unpublished doctoral dissertation. Cambridge, MA: Massachusetts Institute of Technology.

Nader, Ralph. 1965. *Unsafe at Any Speed: The Designed-in Dangers of the American Automobile.* New York: Grossman.

Nash, Jennifer, and John Ehrenfeld. 1996. "Code Green: Buisness Adopts Voluntary Environmental Standards." *Environment,* 38(1): 16–20.

Orts, Eric W. 1995. "Reflexive Environmental Law." *Northwestern University Law Review,* 89(1227): 1241–1242.

Orts, Eric W., and Kurt Deketelaere. 2001. "Introduction: Environmental Contracts and Regulatory Innovation." In Eric W. Orts and Kurt Deketelaere, eds., *Environmental Contracts: Comparative Approaches to Regulatory Innovation in the United States and Europe.* Boston: Kluwer Law International.

Ostrom, Elinor. 1990. *Governing the Commons: The Evolution of Institutions for Collective Action.* Cambridge, UK: Cambridge University Press.

Ostrom, Elinor. 1992. *Crafting Institutions for Self-Governing Irrigation Systems.* San Francisco: ICS Press.

Ostrom, Elinor, Larry D. Schroeder, and Susan G. Wynne. 1993. *Institutional Incentives and Sustainable Development: Infrastructure Policies in Perspective.* Boulder, CO: Westview Press.

Pfeffer, Jeffrey, and Gerald R. Salancik. 1978. *The External Control of Organizations: A Resource Dependence Perspective.* New York: Harper & Row.

Pope, Kyle, and Allana Sullivan. 1995. "Offshore Oil-Rig Quandary: Sink or Spend." *Wall Street Journal—Eastern Edition,* 121 ed. A12.

PR Newswire. December, 4, 1996. "U.S. Electric Utility Companies Are Now Waiting to Reduce Greenhouse Gas Emissions."

Radetsky, Michael. 1999. "Smallpox: A History of Its Rise and Fall." *Pediatric Infectious Disease Journal,* 18(2): 85–93.

Raymond, Eric S. 1999. *The Cathedral and the Bazaar: Musings on Linux and Open Source by an Accidental Revolutionary.* Beijing: O'Reilly.

Rothenberg, Sandra, and James Maxwell. 1995. "Extending the Umbrella of Social Concern: Volvo's Strategic Approach to Environmental Management." *Corporate Environmental Strategy,* 3(2): 5–15.

Rowledge, Lorinda Rae, Kevin S. Brady, and Russell Scott Barton. 1999. *Mapping the Journey: Case Studies in Strategy and Action Toward Sustainable Development.* Sheffield, U.K.: Greenleaf.

Ruhl, J. B. 2000. "Working Both (Positivist) Ends Toward a New (Pragmatist) Middle in Environmental Law." *George Washington University Law Review,* 68: 522.

Scott, W. Richard. 1998. *Organizations: Rational, Natural, and Open Systems* (4th ed.). Upper Saddle River, NJ: Prentice Hall.

Selznick, Phillip. 1966. *TVA and the Grass Roots: A Study in the Sociology of Formal Organization.* New York: Harper & Row.

Stip, David. 2000. "Is Monsanto's Biotech Worth Less Than a Hill of Beans?" *Fortune,* 141(4): 79–81.

Thompson, James D., and Arthur Tyden. 1959. "Strategies, Structures, and Processes of Organizational Decision." In James D. Thompson et al., eds., *Comparative Studies in Administration*: 195–216. Pittsburgh: University of Pittsburgh Press.

Tsoukas, Haridimos. 1996. "The Firm as a Distributed Knowledge System: A Constructionist Approach." *Strategic Management Journal,* 17(10): 11–25.

Warren, Christian. 2000. *Brush with Death: A Social History of Lead Poisoning.* Baltimore, MD: Johns Hopkins University Press.

Weick, Karl, and Karlene Roberts. 1993. "Collective Mind in Organizations: Heedful Interrelating on Flight Decks." *Administrative Science Quarterly,* 38: 357–381.

Winograd, Terry, and Fernando Flores. 1986. *Understanding Computers and Cognition.* Reading, MA: Addison-Wesley.

STRATEGIC RESPONSES TO THE REPUTATION COMMONS PROBLEM

Andrew A. King, Michael J. Lenox, and Michael L. Barnett

Firms within an industry often find themselves "tarred by the same brush." When accidents occur, stakeholders often punish both the offending firm and the entire industry as well. For example, the Union Carbide accident in Bhopal, India, damaged public perception of the entire chemical industry (Rees, 1997). Similarly, the Exxon Valdez oil spill affected all members of the petroleum industry (Hoffman and Ocasio, 2001). Likewise, the Three Mile Island incident was caused by the missteps of a single firm at a single facility, but the reputation of the entire nuclear power industry was harmed (Rees, 1997). As these examples illustrate, a firm's reputation may be tied to other firms, and so reputation may be a common resource shared by all members of an industry.

As with many shared resources, an industry's reputation may be overexploited. A firm can benefit from the favorable reputation of an industry even as it takes individual actions that may harm this shared reputation. In other words, industry reputation can suffer from the "tragedy of the commons" often observed for natural resources such as fisheries and oil fields (Hardin, 1968). Collectively firms wish to maintain a positive reputation; privately they have incentives to overexploit that reputation. Thus firms must strategically manage the *reputation commons.*

In the following pages, we explore when a reputation commons is likely to occur and discuss how firms individually and collectively respond to the problems associated with it. We review traditional commons problems and discuss the special conditions under which reputation commons problems arise. In particular, we propose that when stakeholders cannot differentiate the individual performance of firms but can sanction them, a reputation commons is likely. Thereafter, we discuss strategies for resolving the reputation commons problem. We propose that firms can solve the reputation commons problem by reducing the sanctioning ability of stakeholders and by "privatizing" reputation.

THE REPUTATION COMMONS PROBLEM

As scholars have long observed, "rational, self-interested individuals will not act to achieve their common or group interest . . . unless there is coercion or some other special device to make individuals act in their common interest" (Olson, 1965: 2). As a result, when many individuals share a scarce resource, that resource is subject to "the tragedy of the commons" (Hardin, 1968). The tragedy ensues when the cost of overexploiting the common resource is distributed among all members of the group while the benefit accrues only to the exploiter. Each user tends to maximize personal welfare at the expense of collective welfare by extracting too much and returning too little. In such a "game," each player has a dominant strategy to deplete the commons (Dawes, 1980).

Although commons problems are pervasive and take many varied forms, scholars have tended to focus on only a narrow class often referred to as common pool resources (Ostrom, 1990; Ostrom, Gardner, and Walker, 1994). In a common pool resource (CPR) problem, firms directly affect a common resource and suffer directly from the depletion of this resource. For example, fishermen are directly harmed if they overfish a particular area. In contrast, many environmental problems relate to cases where users harm a common physical resource but are not directly affected by that resource's degradation. For example, a manufacturing facility may emit pollutants that damage a common resource (such as the atmosphere) yet be unaffected by or even profit from the damage they cause. The harm caused to the common resource is only passed to the polluter if stakeholders act to sanction the firm. For example, consumers may boycott the firm's products or suppliers may refuse to provide goods and services.

Traditionally, scholars have assumed that such stakeholder-mediated situations did not pose a commons problem (Pearce and Turner, 1989). Pollution, for example, is generally thought of as a pure externality—a by-product of one's action that has an impact on others. In the classic Coasian argument, one-to-one negotiation can efficiently resolve externality problems (Coase, 1960). For example, if one neighbor offends another by playing loud music, the offended neighbor may pay the other to reduce the noise. In doing so, the neighbors may maximize joint welfare.

However, such direct solutions to externalities require that the marginal impact of each polluter can be determined and affected parties can impose sanctions (or rewards). Determining the marginal impact of each polluting firm requires massive amounts of information. When such information is not available or is costly to acquire, stakeholders may simply identify a group of firms that may have harmed a resource and distribute the responsibility for any damage equally among them. For example, the U.S. Superfund legislation does not allocate the cost of cleaning up a hazardous waste dump in proportion to the contribution to the dump. Rather each and every contributor is held responsible for the full cost (Hoffman, 1997). In such cases, a unique type of commons problem exists. Because stakeholders do not differentiate between firms, all users (polluters) of a resource share a common threat of sanction. In essence, because stakeholders cannot distinguish the relative performance or effect of each user, all users share a common stakeholder assessment of their character. Consequently, the action of one firm affects the reputation of another.

In the presence of externalities where stakeholders do not differentiate among firms, we say that a *reputation commons* exists. A reputation commons becomes a *reputation commons problem* when stakeholders are able to act against firms. Consider, for example, the chemical industry. Union Carbide's accident in Bhopal, India, affected public support for every chemical company (Rees, 1997). This single accident damaged the financial performance of the entire industry. In this case, the chemical industry faced a reputation commons problem because stakeholders did not fully distinguish the relative quality or performance of each firm but could reward or sanction each firm. Not all industries suffer the common fate inherent in a reputation commons problem. In the following sections, we analyze when these two conditions may arise.

Ability to Differentiate

If stakeholders possess ample information on the relative performance of individual firms within an industry, then no reputation commons exists. Each firm's impact can be individually and distinctly measured, and stakeholders can directly influence each firm (Coase, 1960). Each firm possesses a unique reputation and can take unilateral action to effectively shape its reputation. In short, though reputation still remains a concern of the firm, it is not a *commons* problem.

However, in many instances stakeholders do not possess sufficient information to distinguish an individual firm's performance. At the extreme, stakeholders may not be able to distinguish which industry is responsible for damage to a resource. For example, a community may recognize that its river is polluted but may be unable to determine if this damage is caused by industrial activity or agriculture. More often, stakeholders can distinguish which industry is responsible but cannot differentiate the relative effect of individual firms. For example, environmental activists may note that dolphins are being killed in tuna nets without knowing the relative rate of dolphin fatalities for each tuna supplier.

When stakeholders know which industry is responsible for damage to a resource but cannot differentiate the relative effect of individual firms, they may collectively sanction *all* firms that they think might have damaged the resource. They may, for example, lobby for regulation that restricts access to important resources for the entire industry, or they may organize a boycott of the entire industry's products. In some cases, lacking the ability to distinguish among firms, stakeholders may choose to demonstrate their power by penalizing a single visible firm. This firm need not have below-average performance. Indeed, it may be chosen almost at random or simply because it is more vulnerable to stakeholder pressure. For example, Nike was attacked for its third-world labor practices, though many others in the athletic shoe industry employed similar practices (Lee and Bernstein, 2000). Along the same lines, Kathy Lee Gifford, the television personality, was singled out for attack because her Wal-Mart clothing line was manufactured in sweatshops (Greenhouse, 1997). However, many other popular clothing lines have similar practices.

This shared fate due to the inability of stakeholders to differentiate is the result of several factors. First, simply creating a worthwhile measure of impact is complicated. Consider the difficulties stakeholders face in determining the relative effect of firms in the chemical industry on cancer rates. Such firms manufacture or emit numerous chemicals. Some of these chemicals are toxic and some are not. Those that are vary greatly in their toxicity. In addition, how and where the firm releases each chemical also determines the probability that it will cause cancer. To determine the relative impact of each firm, a stakeholder would have to know about each chemical, its toxicity, the nature of its releases, and the state of the environment in which it was released. As demonstrated by recent tort cases, such a calculation can be both complicated and costly (Harr, 1996). Wealthier stakeholders may be better able to acquire the information and processing capabilities needed to perform such analysis. Indeed, in part for these reasons, scholars propose that firms choose to locate polluting facilities in less wealthy and less politically active areas (Lesbirel, 1998; McAvoy, 1998).

Determining the effect of firms' actions is even more difficult when those actions are combined. Physical resources may integrate the combined impact of firms over previous periods. As a result, the current inputs to the resource may not reflect the resource's condition. Physical systems can delay the effect of inputs, making it more difficult to infer the source of changes to the physical resource. Many simple resources, such as oceans and lakes, can have extremely complicated, even chaotic, dynamic properties. As a result, stakeholders may have great difficulty in inferring each firm's influence on the common resource.

As the chemical industry example illustrates, the externalities of industrial action are frequently unclear (Hironaka and Schofer, Chapter 9). Even with objective information, stakeholders may remain unable to properly differentiate firm-level cause and effect, and thus a reputation commons may still exist. Commensuration is a social process wherein unique entities (such as heterogeneous chemical manufacturers) are measured according to a common metric (Espeland and Stevens, 1998). Often simply knowing the absolute impact of each firm is insufficient. Stakeholders must be able to determine the *relative* performance of each firm. To do this they must consider how each firm's characteristics may affect its performance. It makes no sense, for example, to compare firms of widely different sizes. It may also make no sense to compare firms that make even slightly different products, or that differ in the amount of the process they perform. Heterogeneity among firms in an industry can make such performance appraisal more difficult. Heterogeneity in reporting can also impede the analysis of firm performance. In the absence of reporting standards, firms may release widely differing information about their activities. Such nonstandardized reporting requires analysts to untangle each firm's effect out of a snarl of differing measures. In short, because individual firm impact is difficult to parcel out in a complex world with limited information, stakeholders often judge all firms within an industry to be equally culpable. This tarring by the same brush produces a reputation commons.

Ability to Sanction or Reward

Though firms may share a common reputation, it need not be a reputation commons *problem*. To become a reputation commons problem, stakeholders must possess a credible threat to sanction or reward firms. The degree to which stakeholders can sanction or reward firms in an industry is determined by stakeholder attributes, industry properties, and the institutional environment. Foremost are the attributes of stakeholders. More numerous, distant, and heterogeneous stakeholders are less likely to coordinate their influence, and thus less likely to build into a sufficiently powerful political force to sway firm actions. For example, Ford's recent introduction of the Excursion, the world's largest and most inefficient sports utility vehicle, received only muted condemnation from stakeholders. The Excursion affects both the safety of fellow drivers and the state of the environment, but consumer safety and environmental groups are very different and have little experience with coordinating joint action. Thus, despite dubbing it the "Ford Valdez," outraged but disparate stakeholder groups "proved no more worrisome to boat-towing Excursion owners than the Miatas they picked out of their grilles" (Ahrens, 2000: W14). Simply forming a common language and common measure to allow engagement presents a significant barrier. On the same day the Union of Concerned Scientists rated Ford as "one of the dirtiest auto companies on the planet," Calstart's Green Index rated Ford as the cleanest (O'Dell, 2000: G1).

Industry properties also may affect the degree to which stakeholders can reward or sanction firms. Concentrated industries may be able to use their market power to offset stakeholder action. Industries in the early stages of the value chain may be less vulnerable to boycotts or other manifestations of stakeholder pressure, as their products and services are less visible and thus less subject to scrutiny.

Institutional conditions strongly influence the degree to which stakeholders can sanction users of common resources. In some nations, stakeholders face the burden of proving the negligence of polluters. In other nations, stakeholders need only show that damage has occurred. Institutions also differ in the extent to which they require disclosure of business information (Delmas and Terlaak, Chapter 15). In the United States, the government requires firms to report toxic emissions, accidents, and the transfer of material waste. The U.S. government also collects and processes information on each industry. If stakeholders file suit against a company, they can access information about the company's production process. The litigious nature of U.S. society reduces informal social pressure against taking such legal action (Delmas and Terlaak, Chapter 15). Once legal precedents are established, stakeholders can routinize sanction procedures (Jennings, Martens, and Zandbergen, Chapter 3). These institutional conditions make it relatively easy for stakeholders to sanction firms in the United States.

STRATEGIC RESPONSES TO THE REPUTATION COMMONS PROBLEMS

In general, scholars have proposed two main solutions to the commons problem: regulation and privatization. Some scholars argue that in many cases regulation by a central authority or "Leviathan" (Hobbes, [1668] 1960) is the only means of avoiding the tragedy of the commons (Hardin, 1968). It is difficult to make physical boundaries across common resources such as fisheries, underground water, oil fields, and the atmosphere. For example, due to the difficulty of portioning bodies of water, governments often issue limited fishing permits and enforce size and quantity limits on harvests. Of course, government regulation can be inefficient and burdensome, and so privatization remains the preferred solution to most com-

Table 17.1
Strategic Responses to the Reputation Commons Problem

Reducing the Threat of Stakeholder Sanction	"Privatizing" the Reputation Commons
Improve collective performance	Reveal individual performance
Manage stakeholder perceptions	Team with credible stakeholders
Lobby government	Make credible investments
Co-opt threatening stakeholders	Adopt standardized reporting
	Form an elite club

mons dilemmas. In the classic example of privatization, sheepherders who share a pasture erect fences to establish private property (Hardin, 1968). Today airwaves are auctioned and even air pollution has been divided into "pollution rights" and traded.

Unlike a physical resource that is privatized by physical barriers, a reputation commons may be privatized through differentiation. Privatizing such a resource requires firms to enact supporting institutional structures. Whereas building fences around parcels of land may subdivide a pasture, privatizing a reputation commons requires the building of "mental fences" in the minds of stakeholders to distinguish the reputation of individual or groups of firms.

As such, novel solutions are available for reputation commons problems that are not applicable to common pool resource problems. Given the sapient nature of stakeholders, firms can solve the reputations commons problem by "reasoning with the resource." For example, firms may placate stakeholders by improving the reputation of the entire industry. Firms may improve their collective performance or manage the perceptions of stakeholders. Alternatively, firms may "privatize" the reputation commons by actively differentiating themselves from others. Firms may ally with credible stakeholders, join standards for reporting, or form elite clubs of superior performers. Table 17.1 summarizes the strategies available to firms in coping with a reputation commons. We next consider each of these strategies in detail.

Reducing the Threat of Stakeholder Sanction

The most obvious strategy, yet perhaps most difficult to achieve, is for firms to reduce the threat of sanctions by collectively improving their performance and thus placating stakeholders. Firms may solve the reputation commons problem by actually reducing damage to the underlying physical commons of concern. To this end, firms may share information on best practices with each other to raise aggregate performance. Firms also may economize on improvement costs by collectively investing in research and development. Both of these solutions, though, suffer from the normal pitfalls of collective action. Some firms may try to free ride off the efforts of others by refusing to improve performance, reveal practices, or to invest in collective efforts.

To overcome free riding, firms have formed quasi-governmental bodies that create standards of conduct and penalize violations of these standards. Trade associations increasingly perform this function through the establishment of "codes of conduct." In one of the most publicized examples, the Chemical Manufacturers' Association established the Responsible Care program (Hoffman, 1997; King and Lenox, 2000). Firms agree to a set of principles and practices that purportedly minimize the environmental impact of chemical manufacturing. However, due to antitrust concerns, trade associations cannot force participation in codes of conduct. Thus such programs will likely still suffer from free riding, making it very difficult for them to improve the overall performance of the industry (King and Lenox, 2000).

Instead, firms may find it easier to manage perceptions rather than actually improve performance. To improve the overall reputation of the industry, firms may promote symbolic efforts to meet or exceed stakeholder demands (King and Baerwald, 1998). Trade associations often attempt to raise the image of the entire industry by coordinating public relations campaigns. For example, trade associations frequently purchase commercial media time to tout the improvements in quality of life due to plastics, the health benefits of milk, or the public service endeavors of tobacco companies.

In addition to managing perceptions, firms may erect institutional barriers that prevent stakeholders from sanctioning firms. Firms may form alliances with each other to form a more powerful political force. For example, members of the tobacco industry formed agreements for how to respond to stakeholder pressure to change cigarette legislation (Miles, 1982). Likewise, the American Medical Association provides a strong single political voice for medical doctors. In general, one of the primary activities of trade associations is lobbying government on their members' behalf.

Erecting institutional barriers need not be done collectively. Individual firms may attempt to prevent sanctions by forming alliances with important stakeholder groups. For example, companies may support local community action panels and even include representatives of these panels on their corporate boards. Once "co-opted," stakeholders may be less willing to impose sanctions (Pfeffer and Salancik, 1978; Selznick, 1949). For example, Shell Oil hired Sustainability Inc. to create a strategy for the company and a plan for measuring the company's social performance (Harrison, 1998). Similarly, Mitsubishi Motors formed an alliance with the Rainforest Action Network (RAN) to diffuse RAN's demonstrations about Mitsubishi's logging practices (Hayes, 1999).

"Privatizing" the Reputation Commons

Firms may engage in a number of strategies to privatize the reputation commons. Companies may take unilateral action to differentiate themselves from other companies. For example, they may provide information to stakeholders to differentiate their performance. Unfortunately, the complicated and subjective nature of environmental problems may encourage some firms simply to engage in empty propaganda. King and Baerwald (1998) argue that firms can manipulate the information that they reveal about their environmental impact to confuse or mislead stakeholders. Given this complexity and potential for misleading behavior, stakeholders may reject information provided by a firm unilaterally.

To add credibility to claims of superior performance, firms may choose to work with a reputable stakeholder. For example, McDonald's formed an alliance with the Environmental Defense Fund (EDF) to develop new packaging for its products. Although it was difficult to communicate the relative merits of the new packaging, EDF's participation lent credence to claims that the new design had lower environmental impact (Rayport and Lodge, 1990). However, the participation of an environmental organization may not always provide credibility. Stakeholders' interests may differ from those of the allied environmental organization, or stakeholders may fear that the organization has been "captured" by the cooperating company (Selznick, 1949). For example, following the EDF/McDonald's cooperative effort some stakeholders pointed out that the new design only provided superior performance in locations without established recycling programs. Others argued that better designs existed, but EDF sought to gain financial and reputation benefit from an amicable completion of the design effort (Rayport and Lodge, 1990).

In some cases firms may make a visible investment to demonstrate their superior quality. For example, a company might invest in waste treatment equipment to show commitment to a clean operation. Applied Energy Services (AES) invested in a tree farm in Guatemala to demonstrate to its stakeholders that it was serious about trying to be socially responsible (Shabecoff, 1988). These visible investments provide credible information to stakeholders only to the extent that superior companies adopt such actions and lower-quality companies do not. Unfortunately, determining if this is the case can be very complicated. To interpret the meaning of investments, stakeholders need rich information about costs and benefits of the action. For example, to determine the real meaning of the AES tree investment, stakeholders needed to know how much money was spent, the length of the contract, the effect of the trees, and what other companies had done.

Ironically, firms may simplify the information processing required to differentiate firms by banding together. For example, firms may agree to standards for reporting environmental impact that allow better comparison among themselves. Existing examples of standards of reporting differ substantially in their scope and fidelity. At one extreme, an industry may agree on simple labels to communicate basic information to stakeholders. For example, firms in the tuna industry created a simple label that informed the stakeholder whether or not the product was produced in a way that was "dolphin safe." At the other extreme, the Global Reporting Initiative (GRI) is creating worldwide standards for reporting the combined social and environmental effect of companies. The goal is to provide comprehensive and comparable information about companies' overall social performance.

Both types of reporting systems have their limitations. The "dolphin-safe" label does not provide information on damage to turtles and other endangered species. More complicated systems may provide more complete information but may provide so much information that it is too costly to process. For example, the Toxic Release Inventory in the United States takes more than a year to compile and still longer for analysts to interpret.

As an alternative, companies may band together to reveal information about industry subgroups. This can reduce the information processing costs for both firms and stakeholders. Interestingly, trade-association-sponsored codes of conduct have been used to distinguish the performance of members versus nonmembers. For example, by publicizing Responsible Care (RC) and providing reports about RC activities and the aggregate performance of firms in RC, the Chemical Manufacturers' Association helps to distinguish RC members from the rest of the industry. This does not differentiate individual members, but it may help elevate the reputation of member firms above that of nonmembers.

Of course, membership in such an elite subgroup must be carefully controlled. If membership elevates a firm's performance, all firms in the industry have an incentive to join. Indeed, the worst performing firms may gain the most from joining. If too many low-performing firms join, the aggregate performance of the subgroup may fall below that of the industry average. In anticipation of this problem, a successful industry subgroup must set entrance criteria that are sufficient to prevent adverse selection and moral hazard (King and Lenox, 2000).

CONCLUSION

Most research on commons problems investigates examples where users of a common resource are directly affected by the depletion of that resource. However, in many cases damage to a common resource does not automatically and directly affect the firms that cause the damage. Firms internalize the impact of the damage to the common resource only when individuals or groups that hold a stake in the common resource (that is, stakeholders) place pressure on these firms.

By recognizing that stakeholders act as a mitigating force between the actions of a firm and the consequences to the firm, we alter the commons paradigm considerably. Stakeholders must make sense of a firm's actions and assess sanctions in an environment where the impacts of industrial action are often unclear (Jennings, Martens, and Zandbergen, Chapter 3; Hironaka and Schofer, Chapter 9) and the common language necessary to make sense of outcomes is often lacking (Frank, Chapter 2; Levin and Espeland, Chapter 5). Under such conditions, stakeholders often cluster firms together when making assessments—imposing one common reputation on the group of firms.

When stakeholders can sanction firms but do not differentiate between the actions of individual firms, we say that a *reputation commons problem* exists. Because the "resource" in a reputation commons problem is the perceptions of mindful agents (the stakeholders), novel solutions are possible. Because stakeholders have the power of sanction and reward, managing the perceptions that form reputation is critical (Fombrun, 1996). Firms may attend to issues of symbolism and procedure as they engage in a dialogue with stakeholders in order to influence the perceptions that ultimately shape their reputation (Forbes and Jermier, Chapter 8; Lounsbury, Geraci, and Waismel-Manor, Chapter 14).

Information is the central and critical element of any solution to the reputation commons problem. Firms must communicate any improvements in individual and collective performance to stakeholders. To subdivide the common reputation, firms must help stakeholders to distinguish among firms with varying levels of performance. When it is costly to provide information to differentiate each firm's performance, groups of firms will form to privatize part of the common reputation. When both differentiation costs and economies of scale are minimal, firms may try to perfectly privatize the reputation commons by reporting information to stakeholders in a manner that allows stakeholders to distinguish each firm's performance.

It seems remarkable that information costs should create such problems in this emerging information age. But we must remember that raw data rarely has value and separate facts rarely provide understanding. To be useful, facts must be collected and organized so that they can be compared. Understanding the performance of firms in an industry requires that each firm disclose information about its own performance. When many strategic actors each hold a piece of a larger puzzle, we cannot assume that the full picture will be revealed. Instead, we must consider how each actor will use the possession of its piece to its best advantage. In some cases, the efforts of enough actors may prevent any part of the image from emerging. In other cases, a few clear regions of the puzzle may emerge. Finally, under just the right circumstances each actor may cooperate so that the entire puzzle can be solved.

REFERENCES

Ahrens, Frank. Oct. 1, 2000. "$88 a Fill-Up." *The Washington Post:* W14.

Coase, Ronald H. 1960. "The Problem of Social Cost." *Journal of Law and Economics,* 3:1–44.

Dawes, Robyn M. 1980. "Social Dilemmas." *Annual Review of Psychology,* 31: 169–193.

Espeland, Wendy N., and Mitchell L. Stevens. 1998. "Commensuration as a Social Process." *Annual Review of Sociology,* 24: 313–343.

Fombrun, Charles J. 1996. *Reputation: Realizing Value from the Corporate Image.* Boston: Harvard Business School Press.

Greenhouse, Steven. 1997. "Accord to Combat Sweatshop Labor Faces Obstacles." *New York Times,* April 13: 1.

Hardin, Garrett. 1968. "The Tragedy of the Commons." *Science,* 162: 1243–1248.

Harr, Jonathan. 1996. *A Civil Action.* New York: Vintage Books.

Harrison, Michael. 1998. "We Looked in the Mirror and We Didn't Like What We Saw." *The Independent,* April 22: 19.

Hayes, Randy. 1999. Speech given at Multi-Stakeholder Consultative Meeting to Identify the Key Elements of a Review of Voluntary Initiatives and Agreements. Toronto, Canada, March 12.

Hobbes, Thomas. [1668] 1960. *Leviathan.* Oxford: Basil Blackwell.

Hoffman, Andrew J. 1997. *From Heresy to Dogma: An Institutional History of Corporate Environmentalism.* San Francisco: New Lexington Press.

Hoffman, Andrew J., and William Ocasio. 2001. "Not All Events Are Attended Equally: Toward a Middle-Range Theory of Industry Attention to External Events." *Organization Science,* 12(4): 414–434.

King, Andrew, and Sara Baerwald. 1998. "Using the Court of Public Opinion to Encourage Better Business Decisions," in Ken Sexton, Alfred Marcus, K. William Easter, and Timothy D. Burkhardt, eds., *Better Environmental Decisions: Strategies for Governments, Businesses and Communities,* 309–330. Washington, DC: Island Press.

King, Andrew, and Michael Lenox. 2000. "Industry Self-Regulation Without Sanctions: The Chemical Industry's Responsible Care Program." *Academy of Management Journal,* 43: 698–716.

Lee, Louise, and Aaron Bernstein. 2000. "Who Says Student Protests Don't Matter?" *Business Week,* June 12: 94.

Lesbirel, S. Hayden. 1998. *NIMBY Politics in Japan: Energy Siting and the Management of Environmental Conflict.* Ithaca, NY: Cornell University Press.

McAvoy, Gregory E. 1998. "Partisan Probing and Democratic Decision-Making: Rethinking the NIMBY Syndrome." *Policy Studies Journal,* 26: 274–292.

Miles, Robert H. 1982. *Coffin Nails and Corporate Strategies.* Englewood Cliffs, NJ: Prentice-Hall.

O'Dell, John. 2000. "So Who's the Greenest of Them All?" *Los Angeles Times,* March 29: G1.

Olson, Mancur. 1965. *The Logic of Collective Action: Public Goods and the Theory of Groups.* Cambridge, MA: Harvard University Press.

Ostrom, Elinor. 1990. *Governing the Commons: The Evolution of Institutions for Collective Action.* Cambridge, UK: Cambridge University Press.

Ostrom, Elinor, Roy Gardner, and James Walker. 1994. *Rules, Games, and Common-Pool Resources.* Ann Arbor: University of Michigan Press.

Pearce, David W., and R. Kerry Turner. 1989. *Economics of Natural Resources and the Environment.* Baltimore: Johns Hopkins University Press.

Pfeffer, Jeffrey, and Gerald R. Salancik. 1978. *The External Control of Organizations: A Resource Dependence Perspective.* New York: Harper & Row.

Rayport, Jeffrey F., and George C. Lodge. 1990. "The Perils of Going 'Green.'" *St. Petersburg Times,* December 9: 7D.

Rees, Joseph. 1997. "Development of Communitarian Regulation in the Chemical Industry." *Law and Policy,* 19: 477–528.

Selznick, Phillip. 1949. *TVA and the Grass Roots.* Berkeley: University of California Press.

Shabecoff, Philip. 1988. "U.S. Utility Turns to Guatemala to Aid Air." *New York Times,* October 12: A14.

18 INTERNATIONAL STANDARDIZATION AND GLOBAL GOVERNANCE: THE SPREAD OF QUALITY AND ENVIRONMENTAL MANAGEMENT STANDARDS

Peter J. Mendel

The international standardization sector consists of a set of voluntary organizations that rely on consensus among technical experts and other professionals to generate common rules and frameworks. In an expanding global society characterized by fragmented regulatory authority, international standardization is an increasingly prevalent hybrid form of social coordination and governance. Two series of standards introduced by the International Organization for Standardization (ISO)—ISO 9000 and ISO 14000—exemplify these processes.

The ISO 9000 series for quality management systems evolved from standards originally implemented by Western military procurers in the 1960s. Such schemes involving audits of supplier operations, in addition to inspection of products, became increasingly common in both the public and private sectors as customers tended toward deeper integration within a more delimited supply chain (Hutchins, 1993a). Beginning in 1977 the ISO strove to "[refine] all the most practical and generally applicable principles of quality systems" of various existing industry and national level quality control systems into a single global standard (Rothery, 1993: 19). Since the introduction of ISO 9000 in 1987 and its incorporation into European Union (EU) trade directives in 1992, over 270,000 certificates have been issued in 143 countries. To date, it is the most popular set of standards ever developed by the ISO.

The research for this paper was supported by a MacArthur Fellowship from Stanford University's Center for International Security and Cooperation and staff development funds from RAND. The author would also like to thank Andrew Hoffman, Marc Ventresca, and Magali Delmas for their helpful comments.

Following the success of this model, the ISO developed a concomitant series of standards for environmental management systems (EMS), the ISO 14000 program. Similar to its predecessor, it coincided with the intensification of a broader international movement, in this case the Rio de Janeiro Global Environment summit in 1992 (which petitioned the ISO to adopt its cause) and the "Decision on Trade and the Environment" at the Uruguay Round of GATT in 1994 (Kirschner, 1995). Although not yet explicitly incorporated into trade directives, it has gained recognition from a variety of international regulatory powers, including the EU and international lenders (Henderson, 1995). And despite pertaining to a more sensitive public issue than quality, the series has already garnered a substantial following. Since its inception in 1996, over 7,800 certificates and counting have been issued worldwide.

The objective of this chapter is to outline the key mechanisms behind the explosive popularity of these international environmental- and quality-management systems. Many common arguments for the rise of the standards, including those professed by standards producers themselves, center on the benefits to adopting organizations in terms of operational efficiency (ISO, 1992) and functional competencies (Delmas, 2000). Regardless of the veracity of these benefits, the functions of an organizational form do not substitute as an explanation for its adoption (Scott, 1992). The spread of management reform programs in particular often take on the character of fads or fashions (Abrahamson, 1996), relying on general perceptions of appropriateness, adoption by influential peers and opinion leaders, and other social processes of diffusion (Strang and Soule, 1998).

We first describe the relevant features of the institutional and market contexts from which the standards originated and that encourage their adoption. Distinct attention is paid to standardization sectors at the global and national levels. Second we examine the content and substance of the ISO standards. What exactly is being diffused, and how might this bear on where, when, and by whom adoption occurs? The nature of the standards is also relevant to policy makers for understanding *how* these programs can help sustain organizational improvement on socially desirable values, such as environmental or quality performance.

In fact, ISO 9000 and 14000 are relatively novel for the international standards sector in that they offer accreditation regimes for organizational actors—or "soft" standards—as opposed to conventional product or technical requirements. Such systems tend to standardize procedures, rights, and roles rather than goals or outcomes. For example, the ISO 9000 standards, unlike conventional quality initiatives, do not signify that an organization's output is "fit for its intended use." As with the ISO 14000 standards, they primarily ensure that an organization has a documented set of procedures in place to which it adheres. Although this kind of content-free, formal rationalization does not emphasize specific organizational outcomes, these programs have great potential to mobilize and structure efforts around highly salient strategic issues.

Taking the institutional context and nature of the standards into account, most of the rest of this chapter is devoted to explicating the specific mechanisms that have led to the worldwide diffusion of ISO 9000 and 14000. Current organizational research typically groups institutional pressures for isomorphism, or the tendency for organizations to adopt similar forms, into three broad categories: *coercive* mechanisms in which social actors are mandated to conform to structures and policies; *normative* pressures in which actors follow out of a sense of moral obligation or what is expected as "best practice"; and *cognitive* factors in which actors are predisposed toward adoption based on taken for granted assumptions of the social landscape and their roles and positions within it (DiMaggio and Powell, 1991, Scott, 1994; see also Delmas and Terlaak, Chapter 15, for similar use of this framework). In practice, all three elements tend to be present in any given institutional process (Scott, 1995). This has been especially the case with the diffusion of the ISO environmental and quality systems, as the authorizing effect of regulative mechanisms has shaded and mixed with even more prominent normative and cognitive pressures (Mendel, 2001). Indeed, in an expanding world context in which it is difficult to legislate or enforce "hard" criteria, international standards regimes are increasingly attractive to organizations across a variety of countries and industries.

GLOBAL CONTEXT AND ORGANIZATIONAL FIELDS

During the past several decades, many organizational fields have become "globalized," a much acclaimed phenomenon that compels organizations of all sorts to be "world class" (even those with a solely domestic audience) and suscepts them to management fashions legitimated at the international level. In the commercial sphere, processes of globalization are evident in the proliferation of multinational enterprises as well as the substantial internationalization of the management profession itself (Engwall, 1998; Kipping, Furusten, and Gammelsaeter, 1998).

Nonprofit sectors at the world level have experienced equally remarkable growth since the end of World War II (Boli and Thomas, 1999). These comprised a wide range of international nongovernmental organizations (INGOs), including the global environmental movement (Frank, Chapter 2; Frank and others, 2000). INGOs frequently interact with international governmental organizations and the nation-state system, which is virtually devoid of a centralized authority capable of government-like control on a global scale (Meyer and others, 1997).

Within the nongovernmental domain are a host of organizations focusing on scientific knowledge and technique that represent a "peculiarly invisible" rationalizing pillar of world culture—setting guidelines, disseminating information, writing codes of ethics, and a number of other seemingly mundane activities (Boli and Thomas, 1997). One of these most vigorous sectors consists of standardization bodies specifically dedicated to the production of standards under a "voluntary" process. These standards-developing organizations (SDOs) have acted as behind-the-scenes "institutional entrepreneurs," building standards into international structures and promoting them as solutions for facilitating integration, exchange, and trust across global markets.

STANDARDIZATION PROCESSES

Broadly speaking, standardization refers to attempts to explicitly formulate general rules defining and regulating activity (Brunsson and Jacobsson, 2000). It is generally easier to rationalize technical and physical entities than social and economic actors, which in modern times are more apt to be construed as unique and autonomous. As a result, standardization of the latter generally involves procedures, rights, and roles rather than goals and outcomes. Such "content-free" rationalization (Meyer, 1997: 10) imparts a procedural nature to standards. When applied to the activities and structures of organizational actors, this produces a formal managerial reform program. Combined with a monitoring mechanism—or conformity assessment, in standardization parlance—the end result is an accreditation or certification regime.

Standards can be generated as a result of de facto processes (such as a product specification gaining predominant market share), by formal regulatory processes (such as government procurement or safety requirements), or through a voluntary consensus process (Zuckerman, 1997; NRC, 1995). A consensus standard arises through the coordinated efforts of key parties in a market or issue area. These may include technical experts, designers, and producers, but also consumers, corporate and government purchasing officials, and regulatory authorities who are brought together in designated standards-development organizations (SDOs) or forums. Brunsson (2000) considers this type of standardization a distinct social form of co-ordination, especially suited to domains in which markets and hierarchies are weak or fragmented.

Consensus standards may become de facto in use or referenced in government regulations or procurement policies, yet standards makers typically insist on their voluntary identity. In fact, producers of consensus standards are very sensitive to real and perceived conflicts of interest. Standards-setting processes can be inherently political, with decisions representing material consequences of potential significance to various interests. As self-intended arbiters of the public good, SDOs rest their authority on neutrality, primarily relying on the role of the objective technical expert (Loya and Boli, 1999). To the degree that the influence of sectoral interests cannot be entirely discounted, SDOs buttress their neutrality through democratic representativeness (Tamm-Hallstrom, 1998). Being fair and open to all affected parties is a noted concern, especially among those from liberal polities that place a high value on plurality of interests (Healy and Pope, 1996; Stuurman, 1996).

National Standardization Sectors

Variations in national standards systems closely follow differences in styles of rationality and forms of collective action. In polities with statist traditions, standardization is centralized into a national standards body with relatively strong authority over standards development and prescribed relations to state agencies, in some cases operating directly as governmental units. In associational, pluralist contexts, standardization tends to be private and decentralized.

Standards development in the United States is at the extreme of the latter, having been "to a large extent . . . private, voluntary, consensus-driven, and bottom-up" (Hutchins, 1993a: 53). Close to half of the active standards in the country were created by over 400 private bodies (Toth, 1991), whereas government procurement and regulatory standards are distributed across a variety of fragmented agencies and jurisdictions at the federal, state, and local levels (Breitenberg, 1987).

The International Standardization Sector

The first permanent example of international cooperation in standards development was the International Electrotechnical Congress (IEC), founded in 1906. Twenty years later, national standards bodies from European and several other countries established the short-lived International Standards Association. After World War II, the association was reconstituted as the International Organization for Standardization (or ISO), generally confining itself to nonelectrical standards. The ISO, like the IEC, designates as a member only one national standards body per country, which is required to represent all standardizing interests (such as firms, the sciences, consumers, and government).

Regional standardization began in Europe with the founding of the Comité Européen de Normalisation (CEN) and CENELEC, the European version of the IEC. Other bodies have followed, including the pan-American COPANT, the Arab Organization for Standardization (AOSM), the pan-African ARSO, and the Pacific

Rim's PASC. These organizations tend to concentrate on promoting regional trade and coordinating with larger markets, rather than developing standards per se (Loya and Boli, 1999).

Europeans are well represented in the global standards sector, both in number of regional organizations and involvement in the international standardization bodies (Zuckerman, 1997). The prominence of standardization in Europe in great part has arisen from its usefulness in promoting European integration. As mutual recognition of national policies or direct negotiation of common regulations have proven difficult, this onerous task increasingly has been delegated through a "new approach" (Fligstein and Mara-Drita, 1996) to standards-making organizations. The deliberations of these bodies of experts are then incorporated or referenced in European Union (EU) directives. This reliance on standardization has led to a unique contribution of the EU to global governance—explicitly fusing the professional authority of conventional nongovernmental organizations with its gradually evolving regulatory powers.

Standardization also has gained notice among institutions of international political economy as world trade regimes, such as the World Trade Organization, concentrate more intensely on dismantling nontariff barriers to trade. As a consequence, the trend in recent years has been toward the use of international standards in place of national and proprietary codes. From a European perspective, these processes of international standardization present a means of obliging American de facto standards to become open and compatible (Zuckerman, 1997: 19). Other regions are equally concerned with balancing the traditional dominance of European bodies in global standards-making processes (Loya and Boli, 1999: 175). Industrialized countries, moreover, have taken a clear interest in integrating developing countries into the global regime. Western powers, including the United States, provide technical and financial assistance to encourage centralized national standards infrastructures consistent with international systems (NRC, 1995).

THE NATURE OF ISO
INTERNATIONAL MANAGEMENT STANDARDS

Here we take a closer look at the substance of the ISO 9000 and 14000 standards and compare them to other types of management reform programs. How do they relate to conventional managerial thinking and discourse on organizational improvement? What exactly is being diffused when organizations become certified to the standards, and how are they used within and across organizational settings?

Unlike other quality initiatives, the ISO 9000 standards do not attempt to evaluate a finished product, a delivered service, an organization's operational effectiveness, or its competitive performance in providing customer value or meeting market requirements (Lamprecht, 1991; Reimann and Hertz, 1994). Hence a company's certification to ISO 9000 standards is not a sign of product quality in the conventional sense that a firm's output is "fit for its intended purpose." ISO 14000 shares this formal, procedural spirit and does not call for specific emission reductions or performance levels (Kirschner, 1995). As the chairman for the U.S. advisory group to ISO 14000 stated, "It will make no statement regarding what is desirable for the environment. Neither will it lay out environmental goals, performance levels, or technology specifications" (House, 1995).

Registration merely ensures, through third-party verification and internal audits, that an organization has a documented "management system"—a written set of rules and procedure—in place to which it adheres (Hagigh, 1992). To achieve and retain certification, organizations are evaluated for conformance according to the standards' "model" (Lamprecht, 1993: 24) or "template" (Rothery, 1993: 16) of a quality or environmental management system. In other words, the standards serve as an accreditation regime similar to those for educational or health institutions but are generally applicable to any type of organization: commercial, public, or otherwise.

The ISO Model and Certification Process

The ISO 9000 standards are actually a series of five documents separated into two "guidance standards" intended as interpretive references and three "contractual standards" from which an organization may choose to become certified depending on the scope of system elements to be considered (Lamprecht, 1993).[1] ISO 14000 was designed for compatibility with ISO 9000 and adheres to the same basic structure (House, 1995), although currently only one contractual standard is offered, ISO 14001, consisting of five basic system elements.[2] The contractual standards and their system elements cover a broad range of operational features (Hutchins, 1993a) and are intended to be extremely generic, as reflected in their brevity (ISO 9001, for example, is only seven pages long).

Registration rests on documentation of the organization's quality or environmental "management system," ultimately codified into a comprehensive manual. During initial certification and periodic "surveillance" audits thereafter, the third-party auditors (termed registrars or notifying bodies) focus on verifying that organizational operations conform to the documented procedures. Likewise, internal audits attempt to keep the system documentation and actual processes in alignment (Lamprecht, 1993).

Preparing and continually referring to such an overarching manual requires an organization to review, outline, and integrate procedures across varied departments according to the ISO-developed framework (Mullin, 1992). This systematization occurs predominantly at the conceptual level in extracting and codifying the essential elements of a quality- or environmental-management system from a forest of current procedures (Rothery, 1993: 16).[3] Where procedures have not been formalized and documented, the process acts to increase the rationalization of operations along a set of standard categories. In this way, certification acts as a shorthand means of communicating internal systems to customers and other constituents, as well as providing a common procedural language across organizations and subunits (Kagan, 1992).[4]

At the same time, the standards readily serve as a way to justify desired organizational action, available to members at many levels. Not only does certification externally validate mechanisms of technocratic control, such as the structuring of work procedures and the auditing of operations (Walgenbach, 1997), its authority may also be employed overtly in everyday battles of organizational contestation. Framing demands and decisions as required by the ISO system documentation enhances their status as rationally produced or at least not wholly arbitrary procedures. And in the end, no one wants to be blamed as the party responsible for losing or endangering certification. This especially reflects the power and value of the ISO credential apart from any direct effects on operational performance.

Efficiency and Operational Effectiveness

Although, as noted, improvements in technical efficiency and product quality are not a requirement of the standards, the certification process can provide "occasions for structuring" (Barley, 1986) and help identify potential organizational enhancements (Dichter, 1993). Even though they are only partial and somewhat biased, many beneficial claims of ISO 9000 certification in particular take this form, such as reduced scrap, fewer rejects, better on-time delivery, and elimination of operational and product deficiencies (Valenti, 1993; Hagigh, 1992).[5]

However, those most critical of the ISO model have feared that the heavy reliance on conformance to documented procedures stifles innovation (Port, 1993). For firms in fast-paced environments, such as high-technology sectors, inconsistencies are likely to develop between the technical requirements for rapid organizational change and the procedural requirements of the standards. A primary mechanism of resolving such incongruities is to "decouple" elements of structure from core production activities (Meyer and Rowan, 1977). This may entail, for instance, maintaining formal elements and rituals of the regime, such as the system manual and periodic audits, even though actual operations may vary significantly from the documented procedures at any given point in time.

ISO 9000 and the Quality Movement

The distinctions noted above between the ISO 9000 model and conventional definitions of quality have been reflected as well in the practical constitution of the quality assurance field. The contemporary quality movement primarily emerged out of ideas from a number of management gurus working in the milieu of competitive rivalry between Japanese and American firms. Currently labeled Total Quality Management (TQM), it encompasses a variety of techniques that share a vision of results-oriented productive activity, including employee participation, continuous improvement, statistical process control, competitive benchmarking, and innovation (Cole, 1999; Hackman and Wageman, 1995; Westphal, Gulati, and Shortell, 1997).

Europeans initially were seen as lagging behind both Japan and the United States in these developments (Levine, 1991). In particular, the quick acceptance of ISO 9000 in Europe was considered by many American quality professionals as an overly formal, if not wholly misdirected, response to industrial quality concerns (Stratton, 1993; Juran, 1993). However, despite disparate origins, contrasting styles of rationality, and initial antagonism, there has been a surprising degree of accommodation and mutualism as ISO 9000 has acquired international popularity. At present, both approaches share a substantial degree of support from professional consultants and associations, with many viewing ISO 9000 as a foundation for more advanced TQM practices (Kochan, 1993; Port, 1993).[6]

ISO 14000 and the Environmental Management Movement

Similar to its cousin, ISO 14000 has had to contend with a variety of preexisting professional groups and rival environmental management systems (EMS). Some national EMS schemes served as models for the ISO program, such as Britain's BS 7750,[7] and folded quite readily into the international scheme. However, a recognizable environmental audit profession dates back at least to the 1970s (Cahill and Schomer, 1995), and its traditional approach can differ noticeably from that of ISO 14000 in terms of both a process-versus-outcomes and a voluntary-versus-regulatory perspective (Reverdy, 1996). Likewise, there have been a host of competing EMS systems and protocols since ISO 14000 was in development, such as the American Society for Testing and Materials (ASTM) Environmental Site Assessment Standard, World Bank Environmental Guidelines for international lenders, and, most significantly, the EU's Eco-Management and Audit Scheme (EMAS) system (Apsan, 1995; Reverdy, 1996).

ISO 14000 seems to have won many of these initial battles, as evidenced by its popularity particularly after 1997. The continuing success of the ISO 9000 program is a likely contributing factor. This predecessor series greatly increased the public visibility of the ISO and its programs (ISO, 1997: 9), providing added boosts of momentum with each revision (Daniels, 2000). But as with ISO 9000, ISO 14000 is not necessarily incompatible with other approaches. For example, ISO 14000 principles include a commitment to legal environmental requirements. French authorities have even considered an EMS program that would combine the ISO and EMAS systems (Henderson, 1995).

THE GLOBAL DIFFUSION OF INTERNATIONAL STANDARDS

Figures 18.1 and 18.2 display the growth in numbers of certificates by region and suggest a similar pattern of diffusion for ISO 9000 and ISO 14000. Europe leads the way in adoption of both standards, with Asia/Pacific second and North America a distant third.

However, a breakdown of certificates by industry yields several differences. Table 18.1 lists the ten industries with the highest prevalence of certificates for both standards programs in 1998. Although there is substantial overlap, ISO 14000 shows less concentration of certificates in any given industry. In addition, electricity supply and pulp and paper—two industries with strong environmental concerns and public scrutiny—do not appear on the ISO 9000 list. Though this may be partly due to comparing the two standards at different points in their development,[8] it also underscores the political sensitivity of environmental issues as the major and most consequential contrast between the two standards regimes (Delmas, 2000; Apsan, 1995). Although quality as a corporate buzzword has entered the general lexicon over the past few decades, it certainly does not command the public attention or passion of subjects such as biodiversity and eco-sustainability.

Mechanisms of Diffusion

Given the similarities and differences in the spread of the ISO 9000 and ISO 14000 standards, what factors explain their adoption across countries and industries? Both standards have been regularly justified as an efficient collective solution that replaces a plethora of incommensurate or redundant national, industry, and customer requirements with a single international system (Heller, 1993; Hagigh, 1992). Thus organizations facing a multitude of separate standards and verifications would

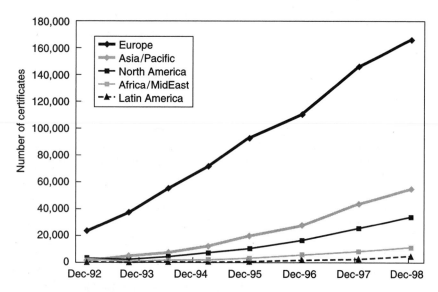

Figure 18.1   ISO 9000 International Quality Management Certificates by World
Region

SOURCE: The ISO Survey of ISO 9000 and ISO 14000 Certificates (ISO, 1999)

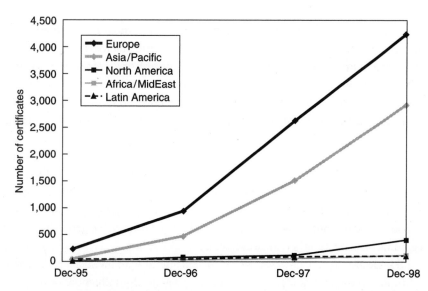

Figure 18.2   ISO 14000 International Environmental Management Certificates by
World Region

SOURCE: The ISO Survey of ISO 9000 and ISO 14000 Certificates (ISO, 1999)

Table 18.1

Industries with Highest Prevalence of ISO International Environmental
and Quality Management Certificates, Worldwide 1998

ISO 9000	ISO 14000
Electrical equipment (15.9%)	Chemicals (9.7%)
Metals (12.6%)	Machinery equipment (8.0%)
Machinery equipment (8.8%)	Other transport equipment (4.4%)
Construction (8.6%)	Electricity supply (4.2%)
Wholesale and retail trade (7.2%)	Construction (4.2%)
Other services (5.7%)	Metals (4.1%)
Chemicals (5.1%)	Food products (3.8%)
Transport and communications (5.1%)	Electrical equipment (3.0%)
Engineering services (3.5%)	Pulp and paper products (2.9%)
Food products (3.2%)	Other services (2.9%)

SOURCE: The ISO Survey of ISO 9000 and ISO 14000 Certificates (ISO, 1999)

be expected to adopt most quickly. But this fails to account for the prior development of customer, industry, and national standards systems; also, case research suggests that the ISO model has augmented, rather than reduced, the number of costly audits by validating their use as a social control mechanism (Walgenbach, 1996).

Alternatively, the standards may yield operational efficiencies for organizations facing particular technical conditions. Advocates of the standards and others argue that the emphasis on consistency is a basic aspect of performance (ISO, 1992; NRC, 1995), which may be especially beneficial for firms utilizing process technologies such as chemical or steel production. Other organizations in fields employing "uncertain" or "pre-paradigmatic" (Kimberly, 1984: 99) technologies not amenable to precise measurement of outcomes—such as software development, mental health, education, and public administration—may rely extensively on procedurally oriented assessments (Meyer and Scott, 1983; Wilson, 1989). This reasoning is similar to Mylonadis' arguments (Chapter 16) advocating either process-based or "pragmatic, context"-based environmental regulation when it is unclear which polluting activities should be targeted, but would allow for greater variation across industries and technological processes depending on how much is generally known regarding how they could reduce emissions.

All these arguments, however, lack sufficient attention to the social processes of diffusion (Strang and Soule, 1998). Collective agents and influential others help define salient issues and provide proper solutions (Meyer and Rowan, 1977). What problems are most pressing, which methods are considered rational, how should criteria be derived—for that matter, how is "uncertainty" to be gauged? Organizations and other actors rely on management gurus, issue activists, public officials, various media, and the like to answer these questions and lend support to organizational activities and survival. As a result, the spread of such "solutions" and models, including ISO 14000 and 9000, is strongly conditioned by the institutional and cultural contexts in which organizations find themselves and their locations and relationships with respect to other actors. These processes can be delineated into three broad categories—coercive, normative, and cognitive mechanisms (Scott, 1995; DiMaggio and Powell, 1991).

Coercive Mechanisms

Coercive mechanisms refer to the effects of actors having the power to establish rules and manipulate sanctions. Organizations feel pressure to conform to these demands because they are compelled or mandated through regulation or exchange. As described previously, the ISO 9000 standards owe much of their notoriety to inclusion in legal rules related to the formation of the Single Market in Europe. In 1989 the EU published a "Global Approach to Conformity Assessment" that advised companies to adopt a certified quality-management system based on ISO 9000. In 1992 a series of EU trade directives directly mandated conformity assessment of both products and production processes for a limited set of regulated product categories with particular health and safety issues, including construction products, pressure vessels, medical devices, and telecommunications equipment among others (European Commission, 1997). ISO 9000 registration for these categories is technically neither mandatory nor sufficient—there are alternate means to certify production processes, and it usually must be combined with product testing in order to obtain the necessary "CE mark" product certification (Saunders, 1992). However, because of the complexity of regulations and expense of alternatives, ISO 9000 certification is in practice a de facto requirement for regulated products in EU member countries (Byrnes, 1992).

These legal rules in turn become marketing requirements for supplier organizations (Rothery, 1993), which generate a pyramiding diffusion down the supply chain (Brokaw, 1993). Moreover, markets tend to develop prestige hierarchies (Kimberly, 1984) or status orders reflecting cost, revenue, and quality profiles of producers (Podolny, 1993). ISO 9000 certification is frequently used as such a visible, although relatively blunt, marketing tool to distinguish among suppliers (Brokaw, 1993).

Market-induced requirements have had strong effects. Soon after the introduction of ISO 9000, adoption appeared driven more by market and customer pressure than government regulation (Hagigh, 1992), spreading rapidly outside of European regulated product sectors. For example, ISO 9000 certifications in the

United States now rival the number in Germany, even though only a fraction, approximately 19 percent, of the $103 billion worth of American goods exported to Europe in 1992 fell into regulated categories (Kochan, 1993). These processes illustrate how regulative rules operate by both "imposition"—complying to avoid or induce sanctions, and "authorization"—conforming to gain legitimacy (Scott, 1991). They also demonstrate how coercive legal and market requirements frequently shade into normative pressures.

Normative Mechanisms

Normative mechanisms refer to the effects of authoritative and influential others who profess values and prescriptions that organizations follow out of a sense of moral obligation or what is expected as "best practice." The normative strength of the ISO standards is reflected in its perception as a "method of demonstrating the kind of careful management" that can "protect one from product liability or charges of negligence" in European courts (Rothery, 1993: 4). Although the appeal is probably strongest in Europe, ISO 9000 has also become a "premier standard for optimal customer-supplier relationships" (Zaciewski, 1993) in the world marketplace (Tattum, 1992). Prominent carriers of these norms include regulatory agents, professional communities, and multinational enterprises.

Regulatory agents influence organizations not only through imposition and authorization, but also by educational activities and incentive programs promoting "best practices." Authorities have mounted major national campaigns for ISO 9000 registration in developed countries ranging from the United Kingdom (NAO, 1990; Dale and Oakland, 1991) to Japan (Marquardt, 1992). The EU itself has encouraged adoption of the standards through a variety of programs, including subsidies to small- and medium-sized enterprises (Walgenbach, 1996). In many developing countries, such as those in the Association of Southeast Asian Nations (ASEAN), the standards are at the heart of industry efforts to become competitive and are "aided by promotional campaigns launched by government and business leaders" (Coeyman, 1993).

Professional and scientific communities can greatly catalyze diffusion by their acceptance and promulgation of a standard. As described earlier, professionals working through a variety of standardization and other organizations have played an instrumental role in developing and institutionalizing the ISO standards. In many countries, both quality and environmental professional associations join with standards bodies in coordinating registration activities. At the European level, similar bodies primarily focus on professional coordination—for example, the European Organization for Quality Control (EOQC) and the European Organization for Testing and Certification (EOTC). The growth in ISO certifications has itself spawned additional professional groups and occupations directly related to certification activities, such as registrars, notifying bodies, and registration consultants who further disseminate standards models while providing their services.

These processes are amplified by the span and influence of these professional fields. As a consequence, rates of diffusion have increased with overall growth in the standardization and environmental and quality sectors, both at the national and international levels. Likewise, the secular expansion in professional management fields, typically represented by management consultancy, intensifies the diffusion of all types of managerial reforms. Although mainstream strategic consulting firms typically leave ISO certification services to more specialized auditing companies, the use of such services may indicate a susceptibility to external managerial norms.

Last, multinational enterprises are increasingly recognized as models of organizational form and conduits for the transfer of management knowledge across borders (Arias and Guillen, 1998). A foreign subsidiary interacts with its foreign peers as well as local organizations, importing management forms into the host country and exporting ideas and practices back to other parts of the parent organization and the broader global fields in which it operates. Transmission is generally considered strongest within units of the multinational corporation, and organizations with foreign subsidiaries in Europe are thus especially likely to adopt both the ISO 14000 and 9000 standards.

Cognitive Mechanisms

Cognitive mechanisms refer to the fundamental effects of mental maps and definitions of the world in shaping the roles and perceptions of social actors (Meyer and Rowan, 1977; Scott, 1994). The regulative and normative arguments above rely heavily on relational links between actors, that is, the transfer of models through direct contacts and interactions among organizations and individuals. Cognitive pressures operate more diffusely through shared cultural frames and taken-for-granted cognitive orders (Strang and Meyer, 1993). "Theorization" of abstract conceptions and categories, a central activity of academics, consultants, and other professionals, allows for easier access of models through common cultural links. Under these processes, the more general and abstract a model, the more rapid and universal its diffusion becomes. Many observers, including the Secretary-General of the ISO, have attributed the popularity of the standards to their breadth and generic character (Byrnes, 1992; Lamprecht, 1991).

Nonrelational or broadcast patterns of diffusion are evident as the ISO 9000 and 14000 models become institutionalized in managerial culture more broadly and spread to organizational fields outside the customer-supplier, professional, and exchange networks described earlier. For example, explicit application of ISO 9000 has already been observed in such localized sectors as public utilities (Hutchins, 1993b), training and education (Elliot, 1993; Berthelot, 1993; De La Salle University, 1997) and hospitals (Quality Systems Update, 1996). Specific cognitive mechanisms relevant to the ISO standards include the prevalence of the models, predispositions for formal organizational solutions, and social roles and positions in relation to others who have already adopted.

Prevalence. Both institutional and organizational ecology theorists have associated the taken-for-grantedness of a social form with its prevalence or density within a relevant population or field of organizations (Hannan and Freeman, 1977; Scott, 1995). Consequently, accelerated rates of adoption will be associated with the total number or proportion of registered organizations within a field, and not merely the immediate customers or competitors of a focal organization.

Formal predispositions and mentalities. Some organizations, sectors, and even countries may exhibit proclivities for formal managerial solutions, such as the ISO standards. At the organizational level, these predispositions are reflected in greater degrees of general bureaucratization, such as use of codified procedures, organizational charts, and other accreditations. At the country level, the "mentalities" of professional, state, and other institutional elites have been shown to decidedly shape the diffusion of management ideas (Guillen, 1994). As argued earlier, one important dimension of national polities is the pattern of authority, such as those based on a formal style of rationality. Thus countries with statist orientations, such as France and many Latin American countries, will also show proportionately higher rates of adoption. Within the standardization sector specifically, these orientations are reflected by a strong state role in standards-making activities.

Social roles and system position. Finally, organizations are much more likely to model the behavior of those considered similar (or in network terminology, occupying structurally equivalent positions) and those recognized as successful or advanced. Diffusion research has frequently emphasized the impact of initial adoption by "opinion leaders" and "high prestige" organizations (Kimberly, 1984). Peripheral organizations may be among the first to try a new, unproven innovation, but adoption by core organizations will increase rates of diffusion throughout a network or industry (Pastor, Meindl, and Hunt, 1998).

Similar processes of reference and comparison based on roles within a social system occur among nation-states as well (Meyer and others, 1997). Paths of socioeconomic development situate countries in differing world-historical or geopolitical positions in systems of cultural and economic exchange. Developed countries located in core positions tend to act as referent societies, supplying and demonstrating organizational models (Guillen, 1998). Conditions of perceived national crises or performance lags increase the likelihood that elites in a specific country will search for and adopt putatively effective archetypes.

One problem with using development as a simple predictor for adoption of organizational models is that it poorly distinguishes between countries. Both core and peripheral nation-states engage in emulation, the former in order to catch up and the latter to achieve or maintain supremacy (Arias and Guillen, 1998: 121–122). However, core countries that had once been or are close to becoming world leaders are particularly sensitive to declining economic competitiveness and geopolitical status. Developed countries spared this experience or who have been disavowed of ambitions for world dominance appear generally relieved of these pressures (Djelic, 1998).

CONCLUSION

The international standardization sector provides a unique combination of professional and regulatory authority at the world level. The standards systems it produces, particularly those for organizational actors such as ISO 9000 and ISO 14000, are an increasingly prevalent and useful form of governance in an expanding yet fragmented global political economy.

ISO 9000 may not approach quality with the same results-oriented focus as the conventional quality movement, and ISO 14000 may not target environmental emissions as directly as traditional environmental management and regulation regimes. However, compared to the multitude of programs hyped by private consultants in both fields, the codified and formal character of the ISO standards offers greater assurance of what blueprint for rationalizing organizational operations has been implemented. In addition, the accreditations' general seal of approval in global circles acts as a strong inducement for large numbers of organizations, even in countries such as the United States that are not usually predisposed to formal social and managerial solutions.

Some organizations that seek to distinguish themselves as "entrepreneurs" in terms of environmental or quality competence may be most critical of the ISO standards in not rewarding outstanding performance or innovative, "context-based" solutions (see also Mylonadis, Chapter 16). But for many other organizations, perhaps innovative in other areas, the standards represent an effective device for internally emphasizing and externally demonstrating commitment to quality and environmental issues.

As a consequence, the ISO standards have great potential to shape organizational processes and ultimate outcomes. Although management fads and fashions may be difficult to discern from pure imitative behavior, organizational learning and the translation of ideas can occur (Cole, 1999). Likewise, the ISO 9000 and 14000 programs serve to standardize practices and terminology, mobilize resources, and structure organizational efforts. For ISO 14000 especially, the standards can help integrate environmental issues into routine administrative decision-making and mainstream managerial values.

NOTES AND REFERENCES

NOTES

1. The ISO 9000 document is primarily a guide for deciding which of the contractual standards (ISO 9001, 9002, or 9003) to apply to an organization. ISO 9004 provides further guidelines for implementing and using the standards. ISO 9001, the most comprehensive assurance model, specifies twenty quality-system elements, from product design and production to installation and servicing; ISO 9002 focuses on production and installation; and ISO 9003 encompasses a limited number of elements related to final inspection and testing (Tamm-Hallstrom, 1996: 68–69; Lamprecht, 1993: 4–7).

2. In addition, ISO 14001 was expected during its design to cost from between a half to a third less to implement than ISO 9000 (House, 1995).

3. It should be noted that the commitment to become and remain certified is not trivial. A survey of ISO 9000–certified companies in the United States (Dun & Bradstreet, 1996) reported that it takes approximately fifteen months on average to achieve registration, with average internal costs of between $51,000 to $321,000 depending on the size of the organizational unit, not including costs of consultants, initial registration, and required semiannual audits. Although approximately 85 percent of companies are registered on their first attempt, losing certification may be more costly in terms of reputation than if an organization had never been certified in the first place (Lamprecht, 1993: 88).

4. Improving the transparency of work processes and communication between departments have been ranked among the highest benefits of ISO 9000 by adopters in the United States and Germany (Dun & Bradstreet, 1996; Walgenbach, 1997).

5. The British Standards Institute estimated that registered firms reduce operating costs by 10 percent on average (Marquardt, 1992), and a U.S. survey reported rather rough and subjective annual savings of $77,000 during the first year of registration (Dun & Bradstreet, 1996). However, only 29 percent of respondents had systems in place to accurately track internal costs. To further keep such claims in perspective, "increased operational efficiency/productivity" was ranked as only the fourth frequently cited internal benefit of achieving ISO 9000 registration (40 percent), below "better documentation" (88 percent), "greater quality awareness" (83 percent), and "enhanced intercompany communications" (53 percent).

6. In fact, the ISO 9000 guidance standards discuss concepts such as customer satisfaction and continuous quality improvement at length (Tamm-Hallstrom, 1996; Kochan, 1993), but of course the contractual standards do not evaluate the choice of techniques or the effectiveness of outcomes.

7. France, Spain, and Ireland had also developed their own national EMS programs (Roberts, 1995).

8. Although the chemical industry, which leads the ISO 14000 list and has played an active role in its development (Kirschner, 1995), is further down the rankings for ISO 9000 in 1998, it was similarly prominent in the initial diffusion of the quality standards.

REFERENCES

Abrahamson, Eric. 1996. "Management Fashion." *Academy of Management Review*, 21: 254–285.

Apsan, Howard N. 1995. "ISO 14000: Standardizing Environmental Management Beyond ASTM." *Total Quality Environmental Management*, Summer: 115–118.

Arias, Maria Eugenia, and Mauro Guillen. 1998. "The Transfer of Organizational Techniques Across Borders: Combining Neo-Institutional and Comparative Perspectives." In Jose Luis Alvarez, ed., *Diffusion and Consumption of Business Knowledge*, 110–137. New York: St. Martin's Press.

Barley, Stephen R. 1986. "Technology as an Occasion for Structuring: Evidence from Observations of CT Scanners and the Social Order of Radiology Departments." *Administrative Science Quarterly*, 31: 78–108.

Berthelot, Ron. 1993. "Making the Most of ISO 9000." *Training and Development*, 47(2): 9.

Boli, John, and George M. Thomas. 1997. "World Culture in the World Polity: A Century of International Non-Governmental Organization." *American Sociological Review*, 62: 171–190.

Boli, John, and George M. Thomas. 1999. *Constructing World Culture: International Nongovernmental Organizations Since 1875*. Stanford, CA: Stanford University Press.

Breitenberg, Maureen, ed. 1987. *Index of Products Regulated by Each State*. NBSIR 87-3608. Gaithersburg, MD: National Bureau of Standards, U.S. Department of Commerce.

Brokaw, Leslie. 1993. "ISO 9000: Making the Grade." *INC*, 15(6): 98–99.

Brunsson, Nils. 2000. "Standardization as a Social Form." In Nils Brunsson and Bengt Jacobsson, eds., *A World of Standards*, 52–70. Oxford: Oxford University Press.

Brunsson, Nils, and Bengt Jacobsson. 2000. "Standardization." In Nils Brunsson and Bengt Jacobsson, eds., *A World of Standards,* 1–23. Oxford: Oxford University Press.

Byrnes, Daniel. 1992. "Exploring the World of ISO 9000." *Quality,* 31(10): 19–31.

Cahill, Lawrence B., and Dawne P. Schomer. 1995. "The Potential Effect of ISO 14000 Standards on Environmental Audit Training in the United States." *Total Quality Environmental Management,* Spring: 5–14.

Coeyman, Marjorie. 1993. "Gaining Ground in Asia/Pacific: ISO 9000 as the Standard." *Chemical Week,* 152(16): 54.

Cole, Robert E. 1999. *Managing Quality Fads.* New York: Oxford University Press.

Dale, Barrie G., and John S. Oakland. 1991. *Quality Improvement Through Standards.* Cheltenham, U.K.: Stanley Thorne.

Daniels, Susan E. 2000. "Management System Standards Poised for Momentum Boost." *Quality Progress,* 33(3): 31–39.

De La Salle University. 1997. "De La Salle University Aspires for ISO-9000 Seal." *Abut-Tanaw: Institutional Publication of the De La Salle University System,* Manila, Phillipines, 25(2): 20.

Delmas, Magali A. Fall, 2000. "Barriers and Incentives to the Adoption of ISO 14001 in the United States." *Duke Environmental Law and Policy Forum,* 1–38.

Dichter, Carl. 1993. "Software Audits." *Unix Review,* 11(10): 42–49.

DiMaggio, Paul J., and Walter W. Powell. 1991. "The Iron Cage Revisited: Institutional Isomorphism and Collective Rationality in Organization Fields." In Walter W. Powell and Paul J. DiMaggio, eds., *The New Institutionalism in Organizational Analysis,* 63–82. Chicago: University of Chicago Press.

Djelic, Marie-Laure. 1998. *Exporting the American Model: The Postwar Transformation of European Business.* Oxford: Oxford University Press.

Dun & Bradstreet. 1996. *ISO 9000 Survey: Comprehensive Data and Analysis of U.S. Registered Companies, 1996.* Chicago: Irwin Professional Publishing.

Elliot, Steven. 1993. "Management of Quality in Computing Systems Education: ISO 9000 Series Quality Standards Applied." *Journal of Systems Management,* 44(9): 6–11.

Engwall, Lars. 1998. "The Standardisation of Management." Paper for the CEMP Workshop in Lausanne, Switzerland, November 20–21.

European Commission. 1997. *The European Quality Assurance Standards (EN ISO 9000 and EN 45000) in the Community's New Approach Legislation.* Brussels: EC Directorate General III—Industry.

Fligstein, Neil, and Iona Mara-Drita. 1996. "How to Make a Market: Reflections on the Attempt to Create a Single Market in the European Community." *American Journal of Sociology,* 102(1): 1–33.

Frank, David J., and others. 2000. "The Nation-State and the Natural Environment over the Twentieth Century." *American Sociological Review,* 65: 96–116.

Guillen, Mauro F. 1994. *Models of Management: Work, Authority, and Organization in a Comparative Perspective.* Chicago: University of Chicago Press.

Guillen, Mauro F. 1998. "International Management and the Circulation of Ideas." In Cary L. Cooper and Denise M. Rousseau, eds., *Trends in Organizational Behavior,* Vol. 5, 47–63. New York: Wiley.

Hackman, J. Richard, and Ruth Wageman. 1995. "Total Quality Management: Empirical, Conceptual and Practical Issues." *Administrative Science Quarterly,* 40: 309–342.

Hagigh, Sara E. 1992. "Obtaining EC Product Approvals After 1992: What American Manufacturers Need to Know." *Business America,* 113(4): 30–33.

Hannan, Michael T., and J. Freeman. 1977. "The Population Ecology of Organizations." *American Journal of Sociology,* 82: 929–964.

Healy, Maurice, and Nicholas Pope. 1996. "Consumer Representation in Standards-Making." Paper presented at the Third Annual European Academy of Standardization Conference, Stockholm, May 3–5.

Heller, Karen. 1993. "ISO 9000: A Framework for Continuous Improvement." *Chemical Week,* 153(10): 30–32.

Henderson, Douglas A. 1995. "Lending Abroad: The Role of Voluntary International Environmental Management Standards." *Journal of Commercial Lending,* July: 47–52.

House, Geoff. 1995. "Raising a Green Standard." *Industry Week,* 244(14): 73–74.

Hutchins, Greg. 1993a. *ISO 9000: A Comprehensive Guide to Registration, Audit Guidelines, and Successful Certification.* Essex Junction, VT: Oliver Wright.

Hutchins, Greg. 1993b. "ISO 9000 Offers a Global 'Mark of Excellence.'" *Public Utilities Fortnightly,* 131(8): 35–36.

ISO (International Organization for Standardization). 1992. *International Standards for Quality Management—Compendium.* 2nd edition. Geneva: ISO 9000 Central Secretariat.

ISO. 1997. *Friendship Among Equals: Recollections from ISO's First Fifty Years.* Geneva: ISO Central Secretariat.

ISO. 1999. *The ISO Survey of ISO 9000 and ISO 14000 Certificates—Eighth Cycle.* Paris: ISO Central Secretariat.

Juran, J. M. 1993. "Assessing Quality Growth in the US." *Quality,* 32(10): 48–49.

Kagan, Andrew. 1992. "ISO 9000: Transport Engineering Sectors Move Toward Registration." *Chemical Week,* 151(19): 48–52.

Kimberly, John R. 1984. "Managerial Innovation." In Paul C. Nystrom and William H. Starbuck, eds., *Handbook of Organizational Design*, 84–104. New York: Oxford University Press.

Kipping, Matthias, Staffan Furusten, and Hallgeir Gammelsaeter. 1998. "Converging Towards American Dominance? Developments and Structures of the Consultancy Fields in Western Europe." Paper presented for the EGOS 14th Colloquium, Theme Group on "The Creation and Diffusion of Management Practices," Maastricht, Netherlands, July 9–11, 1998.

Kirschner, Elisabeth. 1995. "Environmental Management Systems Get Worldwide Benchmark." *Chemical and Engineering News*, April 3: 13.

Kochan, Anna. 1993. "ISO 9000: Creating a Global Standardization Process." *Quality*, 32(10): 26–34.

Lamprecht, James L. 1991. "ISO 9000 Implementation Strategies." *Quality*, 30(11): 14–17.

Lamprecht, James L. 1993. *Implementing the ISO 9000 Series*. New York: Marcel Dekker.

Levine, Jonathan B. 1991. "It's an Old World in More Ways Than One." *Business Week*, special edition on quality: 26–28.

Loya, Thomas, and John Boli. 1999. "Standardization in the World Polity: Technical Rationality over Power." In John Boli and George M. Thomas, eds., *Constructing World Culture: International Nongovernmental Organizations Since 1875*, 169–197. Stanford, CA: Stanford University Press.

Marquardt, Donald W. 1992. "ISO 9000: A Universal Standard of Quality." *Management Review*, 81(1): 50–52.

Mendel, Peter J. 2001. *Global Models of Organization: International Management Standards, Reforms, and Movements*. Unpublished doctoral dissertation, Department of Sociology, Stanford University.

Meyer, John W. 1997. "Contextual Conditions of Standardization." Paper presented at the SCANCOR/SCORE Seminar on Standardization, Lund, Sweden, September 18–20.

Meyer, John W., and Brian Rowan. 1977. "Institutionalized Organizations: Formal Structure as Myth and Ceremony." *American Journal of Sociology*, 83: 340–363.

Meyer, John W., and W. Richard Scott. 1983. *Organizational Environments: Ritual and Rationality*. Beverly Hills, CA: Sage.

Meyer, John W., John Boli, George M. Thomas, and Francisco O. Ramirez. 1997. "World Society and the Nation-State." *American Journal of Sociology*, 103(1): 144–181.

Mullin, Rick. 1992. "Service Sector Gets in Line: Still No Rush to Register." *Chemical Week*, 150(17): 46.

NAO (National Audit Office). 1990. *Department of Trade and Industry: Promotion of Quality and Standards.* House of Commons paper HC157 (1989–90). London: HMSO.

NRC (National Research Council). 1995. *Standards, Conformity Assessment, and Trade into the 21st Century.* Washington, DC: National Academy Press.

Pastor, Juan C., James Meindl, and Raymond Hunt. 1998. "The Quality Virus: Interorganizational Contagion in the Adoption of Total Quality Management." In Jose Luis Alvarez, ed., *Diffusion and Consumption of Business Knowledge,* 201–218. New York: St. Martin's Press.

Podolny, Joel M. 1993. "A Status-Based Model of Market Competition." *American Journal of Sociology,* 98(4): 829–872.

Port, Otis. 1993. "More Than a Passport to European Business." *Business Week,* 3343: 146H–146J.

Quality Systems Update. 1996. "Hospital's Quality System Gets Clean Bill of Health." *Quality Systems Update: A Global ISO 9000 & ISO 14000 Information Service,* 6(3): 1, 6.

Reimann, Curt W., and Harry S. Hertz. 1994. "The Malcolm Baldrige National Quality Award and ISO 9000 Registration: Understanding Their Many Important Differences." Report from the Office of Quality Programs, National Institute of Standards and Technology, Gaithersburg, MD.

Reverdy, Thomas. 1996. "The Invention of the Environmental Management System: New Standards and Voluntary Schemes in the Field of Environment Regulation." Paper presented at the Third Annual European Academy for Standardization conference, "Standards and Society," Stockholm, May 3–5.

Roberts, Michael. 1995. "BS7750 First to Leap into the Fray: Which Environmental Standard to Choose?" *Chemical Week,* April 5: 48.

Rothery, Brian. 1993. *ISO 9000,* 2nd ed. Brookfield, VT: Gower.

Saunders, Mary. 1992. "ISO 9000 and Marketing in Europe: Should U.S. Manufacturers Be Concerned?" *Business America,* 113(8): 24–25.

Scott, W. Richard. 1991. "Unpacking Institutional Arguments." In Walter W. Powell and Paul J. DiMaggio, eds., *The New Institutionalism in Organizational Analysis,* 164–182. Chicago: University of Chicago Press.

Scott, W. Richard. 1992. *Organizations: Rational, Natural, and Open Systems.* 3rd ed. Englewood Cliffs, NJ: Prentice Hall.

Scott, W. Richard. 1994. "Institutions and Organizations: An Attempt at Theoretical Synthesis." In W. Richard Scott and John W. Meyer, eds., *Institutional Environments and Organizations,* 55–80. London: Sage.

Scott, W. Richard. 1995. *Institutions and Organizations: Theories and Research.* London: Sage.

Strang, David, and John W. Meyer. 1993. "Institutional Conditions for Diffusion," *Theory and Society*, 22: 487–511.

Strang, David, and Sarah A. Soule. 1998. "Diffusion in Organizations and Social Movements: From Hybrid Corn to Poison Pill." *Annual Review of Sociology*, 24: 265–290.

Stratton, Brad. 1993. "A Few Words About the Last Word." *Quality Progress*, 26(10): 63–65.

Stuurman, Kees. 1996. "Standards, Democracy and Legislation." Paper presented at the Third Annual European Academy of Standardization Conference, Stockholm, May 3–5.

Tamm-Hallstrom, Kristina. 1996. "The Production of Management Standards." *Revue D'Economie Industrielle*, 75(1): 61–76.

Tamm-Hallstrom, Kristina. 1998. "Construction of authority in two international standardization bodies." Paper presented at the SCANCOR Conference on Organizations Research, Stanford University, Stanford, CA, Sept. 20–22.

Tattum, Lyn. 1992. "ISO 9000 in Europe: The Competitive Edge Is Dulled." *Chemical Week*, 151(19): 37–38.

Toth, Robert B., ed. 1991. *Standards Activities of Organizations in the United States*. National Institute of Standards and Technology (NIST) Special Publication 806. Washington, DC: Government Printing Office.

Valenti, Michael. 1993. "In Search of Quality . . . American Firms Turn to ISO 9000." *Mechanical Engineering*, 115(4): 42–46.

Walgenbach, Peter. 1996. "The Institutionalization of Total Quality Management." Presentation to the Stanford Workshop on Comparative Systems, Stanford, CA.

Walgenbach, Peter. 1997. "Show Biz Hype or Rowing on the Galley." Working paper. Department of Business Administration and Organization Theory, University of Mannheim.

Westphal, James D., Ranjay Gulati, and Stephen M. Shortell. 1997. "Customization or Conformity? An Institutional and Network Perspective on the Content and Consequences of TQM Adoption." *Administrative Science Quarterly*, 42: 366–394.

Wilson, James Q. 1989. *Bureaucracy: What Government Agencies Do and Why They Do It.* New York: Basic Books.

Zaciewski, Robert. 1993. "Shifting the Process Control Paradigm—Automotive Standards to ISO 9000." *Quality*, 32(4): 38–39.

Zuckerman, Amy. 1997. *International Standards Desk Reference.* New York: AMACOM.

VI CLOSING COMMENTARY

19 ENVIRONMENTAL MANAGEMENT: NEW OPPORTUNITIES FOR INSTITUTIONAL THEORY

John R. Ehrenfeld

Let me begin with a few words about myself, so you can get a clearer picture of where I come from. I am an engineer at heart. I have a Ph.D. in chemical engineering and for a good part of my professional career I worked in that field. This pursuit took me over a long and somewhat checkered pathway but one always concerned with environment and, more recently, sustainability.

So how did I come to be providing commentary on a book titled, "Organizations, Policy, and the Natural Environment?" What is an engineer doing in this scene dominated by scholars of organizational theory and, in particular, institutional theory? I think it is a reasonably logical step for one with my background and interests. Early in my career I worked in the study and design of environmental technology; later, the study and design of policy was the focus of my work and teaching at MIT. All these areas rest on two particular streams of organizational design, artifactual structures and institutional structures. As the institutional model I hold dearest—Giddens's (1984) structuration theory—points out, there is no real difference between the two. They both make up the structure from which cultural or routine organizational behavior arises. Any distinctions are an analytic convenience.

Like any good designer or planner, I will use anything that works if it achieves the objectives of the design. For a variety of unrelated reasons, I drifted into the field of institutional theory, with its connections to agency and language, and found a great set of tools to apply to design tasks. And so, I have fallen into the domain to which many of the authors of this book are devoting their academic careers. This background provides me a different point of view on what's happening, even though I have little formal training in organizational or institutional theory.

The new point of view I bring to my research is largely the result of learning from my students and of my own reading.

This chapter first examines a question of importance to all scholars who are interested in environmental issues and who are also working in a business school: Are studies of environment and business distinct from other "standard" areas within the structure of schools of business? This question is even more important as "environment" is giving way to "sustainability" as a strategic concern of businesses. I then will turn to some comments on the theories that thread through the chapters presented in this volume and will suggest that standard models of institutional theory may not illuminate all of the phenomena being observed by these and other scholars. I will offer a framework for exploring power relations in firms that builds on the prior discussion, and, finally, I will make a few suggestions for a research agenda aimed at elevating the position of business and environment work in both the intellectual spectrum and the career ladder.

WHY IS ENVIRONMENT DIFFERENT?

"Why is the environment different from all other broad social norms?" If it were not, then it would be difficult to argue that the study of environmental management in firms is special and deserves treatment that is distinct from other strategic pressures. I suggest that there are four possible answers.

1. All other norms are purely anthropomorphic. Environment or sustainability invokes nature in some form. Further, making environment an explicit factor should force an awareness of the connectedness of business to the surrounding not-so-natural-anymore world.

2. Economic measures are largely reified and object-like. Consensus metrics for analyzing and managing the environment are in an early evolutionary phase. This makes the conventional wisdom about the relationship between measurement and management problematic and requires new approaches.

3. Other social norms in the business school agenda relate mainly to the satisfaction of the rights or needs and wants of autonomous individuals. The environment relates to survival, and sustainability relates to flourishing beyond mere satisfaction, including concerns about equity and justice, which are collective, not individual, social criteria.

4. Other management issues can often be reduced to two-by-two matrices. Environment and sustainability are complex notions with extremely complex institutional fields.

The disciplines on which standard business pedagogy and practice rests all have solid anthropomorphic roots that limit the extent to which they take stock of the natural environment. Neoclassical economics holding a hegemonic position in faculties assume that materials will magically show up in and disappear from economic activities without regard to the real state of the world. By contrast, institutional theory can be said to rest on consequences of the power of the voices that constitute an institutional field. Here too Mother Nature is voiceless, represented only by human spokespersons. Are these ventriloquists an adequate substitute for the interests of nature, which must be served ultimately in the business world? Probably not. The population-ecology framework for studying organizational dynamics perches lifelessly on an analogy to nature. It too fails to realistically and adequately represent the forces of nature that more and more are seen to have very significant implications for business strategy and management.

The second point is more practical. Even if one accepts that environment and sustainability should be made an explicit part of business practice theory, there is little or no consensus as to how one should measure their significance or determine how one is performing with respect to them. Consensus metrics, following from the idea that commensuration is important (Levin and Espeland, Chapter 5), are still in a very early stage of evolution. We do not know how to measure much of what we do in firms. The connections between what flows in and out of a firm's boundaries or along the life cycle of its products and the state of the world are complex and still poorly understood.

Some chapters in this book mention the Global Reporting Initiative (GRI) being developed under the aegis of CERES. This effort has arisen over questions about both what aspects of environmental performance to measure and how, and about how to present this kind of data to stakeholders. A diverse group of stakeholders has been involved in the process of developing the GRI, but this does not guarantee a consensus of the breadth and solidity to parallel that which exists in the field of financial accounting. Although profit is nothing more than a socially constructed and highly reified distinction, very powerful institutional stakeholders back it. No such legitimation process has occurred for measures related to environmental or sustainable performance, nor is there likely to be one for some time as the institutional field is diverse and incoherent and the phenomena involved are far more complicated than those of financial accounting.

Institutional theory, in particular, is concerned with norms, the set of "shoulds" from which all members of the institutional field derive their positions. The most important economic norms, in a policy or strategic sense, relate in some way to the satisfaction of human desires, whether they are deemed needs or wants. In the corporate world, these often come down to ensuring that the customer gets what he or she wants. By contrast, emergent environmental and sustainability norms, as implicitly or explicitly held by actors in this field, contain a large dose of survival concerns at a minimum. This shift in norms poses a fundamentally different basis for strategic design criteria. It suggests a shift in emphasis from private goods of production and consumption to public goods that make up the life-support system for human beings and others. The policy thrust of the Rio Summit of 1992 reflects this change in norms with its shift in focus away from traditional pollution control and waste management themes that reflect the standard economic paradigm to a focus on equity and the future. Both concepts are tied to the idea of flourishing instead of some other socially constructed norm, such as Pareto optimality.

I have come to define "sustainability" as the possibility that humans and other forms of life flourish forever. The Greeks had a word for this type of sustainability: "aephoria," which is derived from *ae,* meaning forever, and *phoria,* meaning to bear fruit or to flourish. This is very different from the prevailing environmentalist goals of sustainable development or environmental eco-efficiency. Such normative targets have dominated the corporate strategy field in both practice and pedagogy. But my definition reflects an understanding of the limits of the natural system and human concerns that transcend those reified in neoclassical economics.

The last point in my list of ways that business and environmental sustainability is distinct from other parts of the business curriculum may be the weakest part of my argument, but it deserves consideration. Sustainability is a far more complex and difficult concept than anything modern societies have had to mull about and build into strategic and policy thinking. If one believes that sustainability is merely a possibility, then we cannot have tools and measures to tell us where we stand toward maintaining that possibility. Sustainability, if it is to be, will show up in the future, but we can only act in the present and we can only guess about the sustainability of current practices. Perhaps for some time, the tools and measures we are developing now will be sufficient to drive business strategies toward this goal.

The institutional field is large and contains stakeholders from every domain of societal concern. Dick Scott (Chapter 20) and many other authors in this book have observed the consequences of such a complex field for both theory and practice. For example, even the carefully drawn framework of Christine Oliver (1991) would be stretched to fit the competing demands of the many voices a firm must respond to continuously these days. In any case, environmental management and, even more so, sustainability cannot be treated as just two more external threats to a firm.

CRITICAL THEMES OF SOCIAL
THEORY AND THE ENVIRONMENT

I would now like to turn my attention to a summary of the theoretical points made in the papers in this book and to provide my own conclusions. My first observation is that the strategic notion of sustainability is changing quickly. To understand and design organizations and strategies in response, one needs both static and dynamic models. My favorite theory for handling both these aspects of institutional behavior is, as I already noted, Giddens's structuration theory (1984). Like so many institutional models that deal with both agency and collective behavior, Giddens's theory rests strongly on context, history, and individual contingency. That makes it a powerful and robust tool for explanation, although perhaps it is too general for those whose standards are Popperian (Popper, 1962) and demand falsifiability in their theories. In one sense, because it is contextual and historical, structuration theory is a poor generic design tool. But it offers a powerful way to think about firm behavior toward the environment and sustainability.

For those not familiar with Giddens's theory, he claims that cultural (or organizational) behavioral reproduction arises from four elements of structure. The structure constitutes, and is in turn constituted by, the action that takes place. The four categories of structure are

1. Codes of signification (a form of rule) or, in other words, the filters that give ontological meaning to the phenomenological world surrounding a group of actors.
2. Normative rules that prescribe the right thing to do under specific circumstances or worlds as interpreted by the actors through the filters.
3. Allocative resources, or the tools, technology, and other means that empower the actors in the world.
4. Authoritative resources, or the structure of domination (power) that establish who has the authority to allocate artifactual and human resources.

Giddens's model makes no distinction between these last two types of resources. Perhaps this is one of the reasons that the "flourishing" sought in sustainability has become so distant; human workers cannot always distinguish themselves from the technologies they are embedded within. As an aside, Giddens and others have written extensively on this "problematique" of modernity (Giddens, 1990).

As in the societal application of Giddens, this structure constitutes a business organization; that is, it grants "firmness." The two most important categories of structure relative to thinking about the environment today seem to be the normative and ontological (signification) rules. This follows from the newness and strangeness of environment and sustainability as concerns of contemporary managers. Even though environment may now be considered to be a standard element for business concern, its place in the belief and normative structure of most firms is low. (Howard-Grenville, Chapter 12) Thus, when considering environment and sustainability, these two categories are the more important levers of change and represent significant departures from the case of business as usual where resources, both allocative and authoritative, are more important. Businesses and academic scholars within the same school of strategic thinking are quite fixed on the meaning of things and on standard normative procedures to follow. About the only problems to be faced by strategists are the choices among the myriad of books that promise to show the right way to tomorrow's success.

Barley (1986) and others (for example, Orlikowsky, 1992) who build directly on Giddens look at what happens to organizational structure when you introduce a change in technology (allocative resource). They point to the slow but often profound consequences. Barley's (1986) studies of medical technology exemplify Giddens's notion of the duality of structure. Changes in allocative resources lead to changes in meaning structures and norms that in turn affect the routines in an organization. My own studies of environmental management indicate that routine behavioral changes follow shifts in the two rule categories faster than changes in authority or technology (Ehrenfeld, 1998). Organizational learning theory—even the basic notion of learning—ties very closely to these categories and how they change and mutate. Double-loop learning, as discussed in the early works of Argyris and Schön (1978), involves shifts in rule categories as critical to allowing for deep-seated change in routine behavior. This is not to say that one can ignore resources. Authoritative resources play a very important part in the diffusion of the idea of a firm. One eventually has to know who has the power to do what.

The firm as a whole is usually the focus of institutional theory. Most of the research presented in this book looks at the firm (the organization) as the target of the empirical work. But the collapse of the structures into a single set is problematic. Firms, like societies, have subcultures that should also be the target of empirical research. The "firmness" of an organization—that is, the reified object described by an outside observer—is manifest through the subcultural elements shared by all, or at least those that possess the dominant authoritative resources. The forces that produce institutional change are first recognized by one of the subcultural units. In the case of environment, the unit is often outside the central culture and is weak in authoritative resources.

Giddens's structuration theory is useful in this context, tying the internal set of subcultures to the forces that push the firm in the larger institutional context. His societal model (Giddens, 1984) can be construed to mean that organizations are power containers, sites where wider societal rules and norms are taken in and modified to fit the local culture. His core concern is with the interplay of authority and the allocation of resources that make that authority meaningful and consequential. Organization theories of power, authority, and meaning since Weber (1978; 1981) have focused on parts of this. Giddens, in particular, emphasizes the constituting aspects of resources and rules, a point of view also developed by institutionalists from Goffman (1967) to Meyer and Rowan (1977), who make meaning central in their analyses.

Jennifer Howard-Grenville, in her recent ethnographic study of "Chipco," a leader in the semiconductor industry, looked at the mainline culture and the environmental part of the firm (Howard-Grenville, 2000). "Chipco" has one of the strongest monocultures of any company, and her work explored barriers to the diffusion of the cognitive parts of structure, from the weak part of the firm to the stronger core. Her work completes a long cycle at MIT that began almost ten years ago with the dissertation of another contributor to this volume, Yiorgos Mylonadis, who in 1993 studied the formation of meaning in the environmental area and showed the critical importance of boundary-spanning individuals. Unlike "Chipco," where the core proved to be refractory to diffusion of a new cultural structure, the individual boundary spanner in the firm Mylonadis studied developed sufficient authority to introduce a new language of environmental management and helped to establish new norms that were infused into the organization-wide culture.

What makes an organization a "firm" is the signification and normative structure that is shared. But the firm's resources are almost always allocated to the sub-organizations within the firm, such as divisions, departments, or other subcultural entities. Thus, if one wishes to use structuration or other culture-based theories, one must pay close attention to the subcultures that constitute the firm. One should expect to find common cognitive or normative views, but also to find a distribution of resources among the subcultures.

In designing policy or in taking stakeholder action, it is important to recognize this dynamic structuration process. As Andy Hoffman showed in his MIT dissertation (1995), it is important not to see it as a unidirectional, outside-to-inside process. In his book *From Heresy to Dogma* (1997), Hoffman points out that the interactions of a firm with the institutional field in which it is embedded are two-way, with the firm influencing outside stakeholders and vice versa.

Most often, environment enters the organization as an issue somewhere down in the subcultures and follows a diffusion process until the cause gets taken up by actors with sufficient authority to allocate resources. Nothing is going to happen until resources are allocated. No amount of clear understanding or normative exhortations is going to show up in action until the resources that move the world are allocated. Our recent work at MIT on the adoption of ISO 14001 shows this quite clearly (Switzer, Ehrenfeld, and Milledge, 2001). Firms that have made commitments to environmental management systems but fail to allocate resources to the effort demonstrate little change in behavior following the implementation of ISO 14001 or some other environmental management system (EMS).

Figure 19.1 depicts this. Michael Lenox (1998), in his doctoral work, suggested this simple presentation. It is much more difficult to move into the upper right quadrant horizontally than vertically. I have added arrows to this effect to reflect some of the findings of our work on EMSs (Nash and Ehrenfeld, 2001). Firms that first invest in resources without changing understandings or normative structures hit a barrier when they attempt to move to the right. Firms that lead with commitments will most often eventually find the right arrangements of resources to achieve the new goals or vision. The duality theory of structuration (structure creates action and is, in turn, constituted by it) implies that changes in any of Giddens's four categories will cause changes in the others. Our findings suggest that introducing new resources leads to slower changes in the underlying codes of signification of norms than does the opposite process. As an aside, rationalization strategies such as those proposed by Michael Porter—resource productivity (Porter and van der Linde, 1995) or the World Business Council for Sustainable Development—eco-efficiency (WBCSD, undated) are not likely to produce the kind of leadership needed to transform firms from "green" to "sustainable."

As a way to close these observations about institutional theory and environment, I would like to add that some sort of reflexive breakdown is an essential part of the dynamic culture change process. Because cultures are defined by routines or transparent (unreflected) sets of actions, change can only come about through an interruption that makes the actors involved aware that something is different. It could be a new green or sustainability policy statement from the top echelon or a new piece of equipment that forces routine activity to pause while the players contemplate a new action strategy. In my experience, the staying power of the interruption and new patterns of structure that emerge depends on the relative power of the authority perceived to have caused the breakdown.

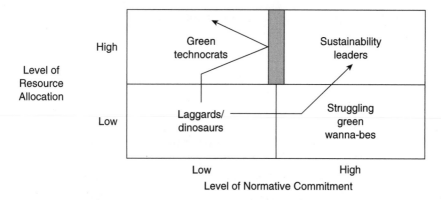

Figure 19.1 Pathways to Environmental Leadership

SOURCE: Adapted from Lenox, 1998

A TAXONOMY OF AUTHORITATIVE RESOURCES

Power comes up in many of the chapters in this volume and always lurks in the background of any study of action. All institutionalists would agree on the importance of authority, but few have developed empirical ways of examining it. We know that looking at formal organizational charts is only a start and rarely represents the actual structure of domination as Giddens terms it. Let me complete my discussion of situations in which institutional theories are important in the study of firms and the natural environment by suggesting a taxonomy of authoritative resources that can be used empirically. This taxonomy fits into the structuration model of Giddens. Its other intellectual roots lie with Jurgen Habermas's *Theory of Communicative Action* (1981) and more directly with the "speech act" theorists, John Austin (1962) and John Searle (1989).

There are some semantic differences between Austin and Searle, but their categories are more or less equivalent. Searle's categories are used in the following discussion. He names four types of speech acts that are important in understanding action (he adds a fifth that is not relevant to this discussion): declarations, assertives, directives, and commissives. *Assertives* are those speech acts that bring "words to world." They are simply my assertion that what I am talking about exists in the world. They are ontological in nature. Assertions have no direct power to bring about change, as there is no agency attached to them. They just sort of lie there on the table. The outcome eventually does depend on whether the assertive claim is accepted by an actor, but there is no power in the assertion itself. It is simply a statement of what is.

Directives, various forms of requests, initiate the action-producing process. Searle says that they bring "world to words." Every act starts with a request, perhaps even in the conversation always going on in our heads. Directives are universal to every language. They are often tacit, but action always starts with an actor hearing that a request has been uttered. Directives are only half of the action context, however. The other half is some promise or *commissive* uttered by the actor. The simplest form of an action-producing conversation goes something like this: A says "Please do X by Y," and B follows by saying "I will do X by Y"—X being some output. Both of these speech acts bring world to words. If B actually follows through (people do break their promises at times), then there will be something new in the world. If you are a policy maker, that is what you want. If you are a boss, you want changes in the world. From an environmental point of view, concerned stakeholders want very specific changes in the world. To be most effective in realizing these changes, policy makers and strategic designers must take into account the way that action actually gets produced in the "real" world.

To understand how new behaviors are produced, one must look at the fourth type of speech act, *declarations.* Declarations bring world to words like assertives do, but they have one added attraction. They create new worlds. Declarations differ from assertives in that they have enough authority behind them to change worlds simply in the act of speaking. A canonical example is a judge rendering a verdict. When a judge says you are guilty, it changes your world. The judge has the authority to make that transformation. In structuration theory, this act corresponds to creating new codes of signification.

Table 19.1 summarizes this discussion so far. Levels of power in organizations can be measured by the type of speech act different actors use and by watching the response. "Executives" have sufficient power to make declarations and create new meaning for the actors with whom they interact. They can create what a company is, merely by saying so. We hear such statement frequently in corporate public relations materials; for example, Ford's statement that "Quality is Job One."

"Managers" have the power to utter directives and enforce commissives. Managers manage commitments. Basically, they are empowered to say "in," "out," "do this," "bring me that," or "We have to do something now!" Managers also have the declarative authority to allocate resources.

"Workers" are actors who do whatever has been directed. Workers are empowered only to make promises and actually do something tangible. The words of executives and managers are only linguistic utterances; nothing changes in the world until their promises become translated into action. Workers will not routinely make promises, however, unless they think they have adequate resources.

Table 19.1
Speech Act Framework for Identifying Authoritative Resources (Power)

Class	Input	Structuration Category	Output	Primary Speech Act
Executives	World	Signification	Vision/mission/policy	Declarations
Designers/strategists	Mission/vision	Normative	Strategies	Assertives
Managers (principals)	Strategies	Allocative	Commitments (intentions)	Directives
Workers (agents)	Requests	Allocative	Actions/outcomes	Commissives

"Designers/strategists" convert new world visions into actionable strategies (norms) by applying their models of how the world works. They are the ones who say, "Boss, if you say that Quality is Job One, then I will create strategies that make it so." The models they use are always merely assertive, although they may be quite complex.

In most institutional models, these roles are fixed. Accepting that is a mistaken assumption in a lot of organizational theory literature. An executive is not always an executive. Executives are only executives when they are making declarations. Executives are also managers at times; they may even be workers. Managers are also workers. One shifts from moment to moment. When looking at the interaction of a field and a firm, it is important to identify players not by their formal place in the organization, but by the role they are taking within the conversation that has been created by that interaction. Such conversations are always going on in institutional processes. They may be implicit conversations with a perception of an institution that is made up by the listener, or they may be explicit. The linguistic nature of institutional processes is muted in theories that reify the roles of the participants. The intersection of the firm and outside actors is only linguistic in nature.

Searle and Austin point out that speech acts form a taxonomy that can be tied to real actions that produce changes in the material world, the concern of all business. Searle limits his discussion of power to the argument that authority derived from contextual norms is needed to make declarations effective in the world. Habermas (1979) goes further and notes that speech acts and the power hierarchy implicit in the taxonomy are useful tools to identify where and how domination shows up among actors. He creates an ideal construction of "undistorted communication" in which a collection of agents consensually (that is, in an undominated manner) agree to coordinate their actions. Giddens recognizes the centrality of domination in the structures that constitute cultural activities, but fails to provide a scheme for identifying who has what dominating power. One must infer the power structure by looking at activity. The utility of the explicit structure of domination or authoritative power I suggest in Table 19.1 and in the text lies in its potential use in empirical studies such as those described in many of the chapters of this book.

Simple isomorphic models lack distinctiveness to make such differentiation. For example, the reified concepts of coercive, mimetic, or normative forces are only loosely connected to specific actors in a firm. Over long periods, such concepts certainly have been helpful in explaining organizational behavior. But in periods of very dynamic change when organizations face new institutional challenges, these theories are significantly limited in their ability to explain how firms adapt to the new conversations within which they have become embedded. Much research now examines the early responses of firms to new demands from customers, regulators, NGOs, and others. The results should be helpful to business strategists and public policy makers, among others. They are still in the early stages of formulating strategies and policies and need guidance about how firms react to new challenges and internalize changes in behavior. Structuration theory coupled to this taxonomy of power offers a way to build theories that can inform them in their design efforts.

I have found this to be a useful framework for studying the intersection between the external institutional field and companies located in it under a variety of circumstances: under policy regimes, under negotiating regimes, in the face of stakeholder interests, and the like. As noted earlier, we used this framework in studying how the ISO 14001 EMS is being adopted (Switzer, Ehrenfeld, and Milledge, 2001). It is interesting to look at who is involved in the process and where in the organization they sit. Adoption happens in different ways from firm to firm. In some cases, the plant manager acting as an executive says, "We're going to adopt ISO. We will be an ISO facility." In other cases, someone at corporate headquarters many miles away says, "We'll be an ISO company." It matters considerably, in terms of consequences and implementation, which of these people issues the mandate.

The explicit application of structuration theory to much of the work in this volume is problematic because the empirical focus of most authors was on the field level and often followed a comparative research design. In the most general interpretation of Giddens's work at the societal level, changing norms are expected to show up as changed patterns of action in the constituent parts of the society. The idea of an institutional field could be construed as a miniature society with the similar implications for the process of institutionalizing. In this sense, changes in routine among the target members of a field could be seen as the result of structuration. The potential advantage of structuration theory is that it offers analytic categories on which to base empirical research. Giddens, himself, noted, however, that there is a danger in this construction of the theory, in that structuration is not categorical in essence and that compartmentalization is only a convenience.

Chapter 8, by Forbes and Jermier, might be examined in the light of structuration theory. They point to the four-cell matrix that Winn and Angell (2000) developed to explain differences among firms undergoing the "greening" institutionalization process. The cells are very similar to those in Figure 19.1, which is derived in part from a structuration model. They argue that firms may develop "facades as strategic ploys to signal to important actors in the institutional field that the firm is paying attention to their concerns." This may be so, but it does not consider the potential that even this response to the institutional field may ultimately produce more substantive and perhaps isomorphic change. Giddens's model is dualistic in that new practices, for whatever reasons they are instituted, produce changes in the underlying structure, which in turn produce other new practices. In this case the strategic adoption of voluntary standards, for whatever reasons, may, and I believe does, produce behavior consistent with that sought by the members of the field in the first place (Nash and Ehrenfeld, 2001; Howard, Nash, and Ehrenfeld, 2000).

THE NEED FOR AN ARTICULATED RESEARCH AGENDA

Calling attention to one of the themes of this book, let me address a concern that has cropped up recurrently in formal and informal discussions. Why has it been so difficult to have our work accepted as legitimate in our home institutions? When we are together as a group of researchers looking at environmental management or the development of sustainability strategies in firms, the authors of this book have no trouble finding significance in each other's work, while still being appropriately critical. I will not attempt to answer my own question in depth and will only make a few comments related to the possible role of institutional theory in understanding this situation.

Perhaps it is because so much is new in the environmental and sustainability areas and so many stakeholders are demanding the floor that we no longer know who the "usual suspects" are. There is little consensus these days on which groups to keep in the studies and which to omit. This situation differs from the historical context for some of the key early institutional research that looked at highly evolved areas, for example, the Tennessee Valley Authority long after it had been established. The key players in the field then were quite distinct.

But the number and variety of actors expressing an interest in the environment and sustainability today is very large. Table 19.2, for example, lists a sample of various members of the institutional field who are noted in the literature as desiring to influence the behavior of firms. Using conventional notions of isomorphism—coercive (C), mimetic (M), and normative (N)—this table estimates which of the factors contribute to increased reflexivity in a firm. Reflexivity may produce changes in the belief or normative structure of the firm if powerful actors inside the firm deem new requests and new norms incident on the firm meaningful to the continued success of the current set of routine practices.

The conventional wisdom at most schools of business today about environment and sustainable development (only a few schools refer to sustainability) is that these areas of concern are not distinctive from those already covered in other courses and subspecialties. Attention to relevant actors is already part of the standard curriculum, goes the argument, so nothing special needs to be done. I disagree. The presence of so many institutional factors makes these areas distinctively interesting from an academic point of view. The dynamic and complex context confounds many if not most strategic models. It also makes their study more problematic, a condition that may scare off less adventuresome researchers. The most popular strategic models for studying environmental management and sustainability are variants of standard economic rational models, building on concepts such as resource productivity and eco-efficiency. These may reflect the interests of many, but they are not likely to satisfy Mother Nature and other voiceless interests.

Another key question that bears on the permanence of the papers in this book is whether the models we develop are descriptive or prescriptive. Are we or should we be normative? Is the environment a green and fuzzy thing? Should we study it because we think the world needs to be greener or not? This distinction poses a conflict in most business schools.

I have been fortunate, as my position is not in the MIT Sloan School of Management, although many of my Ph.D. students have come from there. I teach mostly in the Technology and Policy Program in the School of Engineering. In engineering, it is customary to do research to develop descriptive models that can and will be used prescriptively for design. By contrast, management students, however, often follow norm-driven pursuits. Action research programs followed by some may seem "squishy" and not up to the same objective standards demanded by analytic research. But is there anything wrong with doing good, high-quality research that

Table 19.2
Institutional Field Factors That Increase Reflexivity

Element in the Institutional Field	Isomorphic Categories[a]
Stakeholder pressures	C
Bad press/events	C, M
EMS implementation	N
Costly, inflexible regulations	C, M
Customer demands	C
Green employees	N
Sustainability financial indicators	C, M
Voluntary processes	N, C, M
Sectoral peer pressure	M
Mother Nature	C, N

[a] C, coercive; M, mimetic; N, normative

leaves something different in place? I don't think so, but I would be hesitant to suggest this to my younger colleagues as a route to tenure.

There is, however, a critical need in the study of environment and sustainability for large data sets. Without them we cannot explicate finer structure in the institutional context of environmental or sustainability behaviors of firms. We must have larger, richer sets of data than are now available. Scholars in this field often run out of things to say, not because they ran out of theory but because they ran out of data.

Thus we must argue for institutional change across faculties and within the NSF to support such data collection and to reward related scholarship. One example of the power of large data sets comes from our work at MIT on voluntary codes of practice. Although I believe the earlier, more qualitative research we did was important, the project had more impact and became more legitimate since Andy King and Mike Lenox built a very large data set based on the EPA TRI report, other EPA data, and DUNS business information at the facility level (King and Lenox, 2000).

As a group we do have much to say, not only to our peers and colleagues, but also to the subjects of our research in business, government, and civil society. We need to make a better case to level the playing field for our kind of institutional models for policy design. It is hard for academics to get to the policy-making table in the first place, but we might do better if we could begin to agree on a few issues among ourselves. For example, What are the best prescriptive models from among the many that constitute institutional theory? This does not mean we all have to think alike, but I do not think we will get very far if every little subgenre within this thing called institutional theory or policy theory argues that it should rule the roost. We do need some form of convergence such as has occurred over many years in economics. Note that this does not mean we must lose the variability we see in the institutional behavior in the environmental domain.

Variations are part of what makes this empirical area interesting. And recognizing variability in behavior is important in making policy. Although much institutional theory has been devoted to the study of convergence and applied to the construction of efficient policies, perhaps the key to designing future effective policies for managing environmental issues and sustainability is to accept variability. A shift from process to product and to the resource implications of economic activity should respect the uniqueness of firms. New policy and strategic management regimes can depart from the traditional risk-based models that could tolerate little or no departure from standards. Although innovation was important, errors could lead to unacceptable consequences. Where one more microgram of sulfur dioxide posed health threats, we probably can tolerate products that are 20 percent recyclable instead of 22 percent. There will be more slack in the future. Innovation can be the cornerstone of policy. Porter and van der Linde (1995) argued quite persuasively about the benefit of regulatory schemes that promote product and process.

Environmental and sustainability policy and the strategies being adopted by firms to comply are changing. The European model of extended producer responsibility is slowly being expanded around the globe in one form or another. This policy model is fundamentally different from the economic models used to design earlier strategies. It is much more institutional in nature and more concerned with change, relationships with stakeholders, life along the product life cycle including the supply chain, and the like. This is a great opening for those committed to institutional theory building and application. But I believe we have to pick our targets carefully. The hegemony of standard economic, rational models is strong. The very existence of this book signals that the process of building a common base and coalescence around a smaller set of models shows that the process has begun.

REFERENCES

Argyris, Chris, and Donald Schön. 1978. *Organizational Learning: A Theory of Action Perspective.* Reading, MA: Addison-Wesley.

Austin, John. L. 1962. *How to Do Things with Words.* Cambridge, MA: Harvard University Press.

Barley, Steven R. 1986. "Technology as an Occasion for Structuring: Evidence from Observations of CT Scanners and the Social Order of Radiology Departments." *Administrative Science Quarterly* 31: 78–108.

Ehrenfeld, John R. 1998. "Cultural Structure and the Challenge of Sustainability." In Ken Sexton, Alfred Marcus, K. William Easter, and Timothy D. Burkhardt, eds., *Better Environmental Decisions,* 223–244. Washington, DC: Island Press.

Giddens, Anthony. 1984. *The Constitution of Society.* Berkeley: University of California Press.

Giddens, Anthony. 1990. *The Consequences of Modernity.* Stanford, CA: Stanford University Press.

Goffman, Irving. 1967. *Interaction Ritual.* Garden City, NY: Anchor.

Habermas, Jurgen. 1979. *Communication and the Evolution of Society.* Boston, MA: Beacon Press.

Habermas, Jurgen. 1981. *The Theory of Communicative Action, Vol. 1: Reason and the Rationalization of Society.* Boston: Beacon Press.

Hoffman, Andrew J. 1995. "The Environmental Transformation of American Industry: An Institutional Account of Organizational Evolution in the Chemical and Petroleum Industries." Ph.D. dissertation. Cambridge, MA: Massachusetts Institute of Technology.

Hoffman, Andrew J. 1997. *From Heresy to Dogma: An Institutional History of Corporate Environmentalism.* San Francisco: New Lexington Press.

Howard-Grenville, Jennifer. A. 2000. "Inside Out: A Cultural Study of Environmental Work in Semiconductor Manufacturing." Ph.D. dissertation. Cambridge, MA: Massachusetts Institute of Technology.

Howard, Jennifer, Jennifer Nash, and John R. Ehrenfeld. 2000. "Standard or Smokescreen? Implementation of a Non-regulatory Environmental Code," *California Management Review,* 42(2): 63–71.

King, Andrew, and Michael J. Lenox. 2000. "Industry Self-Regulation Without Sanctions: The Chemical Industry's Responsible Care Program." *Academy of Management Journal,* 43(4): 698–711.

Lenox, Michael. 1998. "Agency and Information Costs in the Intra-firm Diffusion of Practice." Ph.D. dissertation. Cambridge, MA: Massachusetts Institute of Technology.

Meyer, John W., and Brian Rowan. 1977. "Institutionalized Organizations: Formal Structure as Myth and Ceremony." *American Journal of Sociology,* 83: 340–363.

Mylonadis, Yiorgos. 1993. "The 'Green' Challenge to the Industrial Enterprise Mindset: Survival Threat or Strategic Opportunity." Ph.D. dissertation. Cambridge, MA: Massachusetts Institute of Technology.

Nash, Jennifer, and John R. Ehrenfeld. 2001. "Factors That Shape EMS Outcomes in Firms." In Cary Coglianese and Jennifer Nash, eds., *Regulating from the Inside: Can Environmental Management Systems Achieve Policy Goals?* Washington, DC: PFF Press.

Oliver, Christine. 1991. "Strategic Responses to Institutional Processes." *Academy of Management Review,* 16: 145–179.

Orlikowsky, Wanda J. 1992. "The Duality of Technology: Rethinking the Concept of Technology in Organizations." *Organizational Science,* 3(3): 398–427.

Popper, Karl R. 1962. *Conjectures and Refutations: The Growth of Scientific Knowledge.* New York: Basic Books.

Porter, Michael E., and Claas van der Linde. 1995. "Green and Competitive: Ending the Stalemate." *Harvard Business Review* (September–October): 120–134.

Scott, W. Richard. 1995. *Institutions and Organizations.* Thousand Oaks, CA: Sage Publications.

Searle, John. 1989. *Speech Acts.* Cambridge, UK: Cambridge University Press.

Switzer, Jason, John R. Ehrenfeld, and Vicki Milledge. 2001. "ISO 14001 and Environmental Performance: The Management Goal Link." In Ruth Hillary, ed., *ISO 14001 Case Studies and Practical Experience.* London: Greenleaf Publishing.

WBCSD. (Undated). "Eco-efficient Leadership for Improved Economic and Environmental Performance." Geneva: World Business Council for Sustainable Development.

Weber, Max. 1978. *Economy and Society.* Berkeley: University of California Press.

Weber, Max. 1981. "Bureaucracy." In Oscar Brusky and George Miller, eds., *The Sociology of Organizations: Basic Studies,* 196–244. New York: Free Press.

Winn, Monika, and Linda Angell. 2000. "Toward a Process Model of Corporate Greening." *Organization Studies,* 21, forthcoming.

20 ORGANIZATIONS AND THE NATURAL ENVIRONMENT: EVOLVING MODELS

W. Richard Scott

A special issue of the *Academy of Management Journal* (Starik, Marcus, and Ilinitch, 2000), along with this volume, the conference that spawned it, and other recent events signals the rise of a new field of academic study. It calls attention to the growing level of concern and associated activity worldwide with the condition of the natural environment and to the important roles played by organizations both as despoiler and potential savior. These are starring roles, but there are many supporting parts: organizations as record keeper, referee, scientific association, interest group, regulator, and international watchdog agency, among others. Our project is predicated on the assumption that enhanced knowledge of organizational structures and processes as they relate to the natural environment is vital to its long-term protection and enhancement. But benefits should flow in both directions: examining the interface of organizations and natural environments is also expected to raise new issues and pose challenges to our theories and methods, enabling us to grow the science.

ORIGINS

In most of the social sciences until recently, the term "environment" has been used to refer to social and cultural influences on behavior, not to the natural environment. When interest in the latter did develop, it tended to do so first in the applied branches of the sciences. In sociology, for example, the first general recognition of the natural environment was in rural sociology during the 1960s, then in the Society for the Study of Social Problems in the early 1970s. A section (a formally organized interest group) dedicated to it was created by the American Sociological

Association in 1976 (Dunlap and Catton, 1979). The comparable unit in the Academy of Management, the interest group on Organizations and the Natural Environment, did not exist until 1994.

By contrast to most social science, in the area of organizational sociology early references to the environment were primarily to the natural environment, but with an important difference to the current emphasis. With the coming of open systems theory in the 1960s, organizational scholars were sensitized to the importance of the environment as the source of inputs and the market for outputs. The *task environment* took center stage as analysts examined the nature and source of material resources, technologies, and information essential to the transformation of inputs into outputs (Dill, 1958; Thompson, 1967). Not until the mid-1970s did researchers begin to theorize effects associated with the social, political, and cultural environments of organization (Meyer and Rowan, 1977; Pfeffer and Salancik, 1978). This chapter concentrates on this later work, but note that early attention to the task environment did not enable organizational students to focus on the natural environment in the sense represented here. In most earlier works the organization's interests were privileged and there was little if any awareness that it might be in an organization's interest to promote the quality of the natural environment, whether locally or more generally. The environment was of consequence only to the extent that it could do something to or for some particular organization immediately or in the short-term future.

An important general shift in the framing of environmental and social processes began to occur in the social sciences during the late 1970s. Early work embodied an assumption of "human exceptionalism" (or "exemptionalism"), a view that culture, technology, language, and other distinguishing features somehow render human actors exempt from ecological principles and from environmental influences and constraints. This was challenged by a "new ecological paradigm" that stressed the "ecosystem-dependence of human societies" (Catton and Dunlap, 1978). Social structures and processes are not above or separate from those of the natural environment but inextricably intertwined with them. This new perspective has been increasingly embraced by organizational scholars and has resulted in more illuminating, subtle, and useful models, as elucidated in this chapter.

THE REGULATORY ENVIRONMENT

The onset of public awareness in the United States of troubles besetting the natural environment over the last few decades can be dated rather precisely, coinciding with the publication of Rachel Carson's eye-opening expose *Silent Spring* (1962).[1]

As chronicled by Hoffman (1997), this best-selling book raised public consciousness about the destructive side effects of scientific advances—in this case, agricultural technologies. It "forever changed how industrial activity and technology were viewed in the context of balancing improvements in our standard of living against degradation of our national environment" (Hoffman, 1997: 57). This helped spur a series of steps by the federal government to regulate the behavior of industrial and commercial organizations in the public interest.

Regulatory policy is a distinctive arena of governmental oversight. Its characteristic features were laid down by Theodore Lowi (1972), who distinguished three principal areas of domestic policy: *distributive,* aimed at promoting private activities thought to be desirable for all (for example, public lands and agricultural subsidies); *redistributive,* involving attempts to manipulate the allocation of wealth and property rights to secure greater equity of opportunities or outcomes (for example, welfare programs and income taxes); and *regulative,* seeking to protect the general public by setting the conditions under which private activities can be undertaken (for example, oversight of banks and control of pollution).[2] Lowi argued that "policies determine politics": each type of policy is associated with a distinctive kind of politics, activating different interest groups and political actors.

In contrast with other types of policy, the setting and implementation of regulatory policy is frequently marked by inattention and passivity on the one hand coupled with intense involvement on the other. Often benefits tend to be widely distributed while costs are concentrated (see Stigler, 1971). For example, the benefits of reduced pollution from a factory will be enjoyed by all the residents of the local area, whereas the costs of reducing pollution will be borne primarily by companies in the offending industry. The politics are complex. Because benefits are widely distributed and may not be highly visible, recipients have little incentive to organize to protect their interests. If policies are to materialize, it often takes a visible and well-publicized incident and skilled policy entrepreneurs. If they are successful and new programs and agencies are created, social activists may be recruited to lead them, creating what Wilson (1989) has termed an "entrepreneurial agency." But, says Wilson:

> [S]uch an agency will be very much at risk: when the zeal of their early allies flags, it will find itself confronting an environment where much of the information it needs and many of the political resources to which it must respond will be in the hands of an interest fundamentally hostile to its purposes (p. 78).

Because costs are concentrated, the affected special interests—typically lodged in organizations—will have a strong incentive to resist the reforms required or the controls imposed. Resistance can take many forms, but one of the most commonly described is that of cooptation: agency capture. For the reasons suggested by Wilson, and perhaps also in response to not only political but material incentives, agency officials may come more and more to see the situation through the eyes of the regulated industry. It is not uncommon for agency officials to "desert" or "go native," joining the industry after completing their apprenticeship in the public sector (see Noll, 1971; Wilson, 1980).

This portrait of the problems attending regulative policy, developed by political scientists and economists during the 1970s, has come to be widely accepted (Noll, 1985). Many of its themes are reflected in the early stages of neo-institutional analysis in organizational sociology.

EARLY CONCEPTIONS OF THE
INSTITUTIONAL ENVIRONMENT

Advances

From its conceptualization in the 1980s, the institutional environment was defined so as to encompass the regulatory environment. An important advantage the institutionalists provided was their broader conception of both the environment and the organizations affected. Rather than restricting attention to a single organization or type (population) of organization, the scope of study was quickly broadened to the *organizational field* (DiMaggio and Powell, 1983; Scott and Meyer, 1983; Hirsch, 1985). As defined by DiMaggio and Powell (1983: 148), the field refers to:

> those organizations that, in the aggregate, constitute a recognized area of institutionalized life: key suppliers, resource and product consumers, regulatory agencies, and other organizations that produce similar services and products.

This has numerous advantages when it comes to analyzing arenas within which regulatory processes occur. First, rather than isolating a single organization or organizational form for examination, an enriched social world is depicted, including competitors, partners, and various types of funding and governance units. The decisions and actions of both regulators and regulatees are recognized to be supported and constrained by a variety of other intersecting, competing, and complementary relations. In short, the dyadic relation linking regulatory agency and target organization is shown to be embedded in a broader social environment. This has many implications, including the notion that a regulator's influence may be affected by the extent to which governance structures within the field are unitary or fragmented (Scott and Meyer, 1983; Powell, 1988); that a target organization's response could be affected by the response of comparable organizations (DiMaggio and Powell, 1983); and that regulatory controls aimed at one type of organization may have unanticipated effects on other types. For example, regulations designed to affect the behavior of hospitals may have unexpected effects on the behavior of home health agencies or extended-care facilities (Scott and others, 2000).

A second advantage of the institutionalist perspective is that it recognizes the broad array of control mechanisms at work in all fields. In addition to regulatory processes, organizations are variously subject to competitive or market forces, normative constraints, and cultural-cognitive controls (Scott, 2001). Many governance structures and mechanisms are at play in most organizational fields (Schmitter, 1990; Campbell, Hollingsworth, and Lindberg, 1991); regulators do not enjoy a monopoly over influence and control. Early researchers recognized that organizations attend to industrywide practices and are responsive to localized network norms. They also realized the importance of shared beliefs and conceptions.

Limitations

These advances were tempered by numerous shortcomings and the use of overly simplified models of the relation between regulators and target organizations. Early institutionalists tended to embrace a "top-down" model in which governance bodies, including regulators, were viewed as imposing controls on subject organizations. Regulators were seen as part of an institutional environment that was *external* or exogenous to the field and capable of exercising *determinant* influence over its members. The language employed was that of institutional "pressures," "controls," and "constraints." The predicted response was that of passive "conformity," "compliance," and "structural isomorphism." Note that although students of regulation assumed that the natural response of organizations to regulatory pressure would be resistance followed by attempts to neutralize regulators by capture and cooptation, early institutionalists presumed that organizations would normally respond to the demands of institutional authorities by acquiescent conformity (Meyer and Rowan, 1977; DiMaggio and Powell, 1983). Both positions were oversimplifications.

Both regulation theorists and early institutionalists embraced what Suchman and Edelman (1997: 929) describe as "legal formalism," a view that presumes that "laws are explicit, authoritative, and coercive—at least until proven otherwise." In early conceptions, regulatory processes were external and regulatees were obliged to either resist or conform.

EVOLVING MODELS OF INSTITUTIONAL
ENVIRONMENTS: FROM INSTITUTIONAL
EFFECTS TO INSTITUTIONAL PROCESSES

Recent theorizing and research move well beyond some of these early simplifications and distortions. They depict a more nuanced and complex world that allows for many possible actions and reactions on the part of all parties. Current scholars are more likely to speak of institutional "processes" rather than institutional "effects." The latter connotes the operation of an external agent acting in a unilateral manner. It tends to presume one-way causality and determinant outcomes. The current process conception enables receptivity to multiple processes, levels, directions of influence, and institutional regimes.

Regulative and Normative Processes

As noted, early studies of institutional effects focused on a limited range of organizational responses: compliance, conformity, and structural isomorphism. Indeed, such responses were regarded as prima facie evidence that institutional processes were at work. Drawing on the insights of resource dependence theorists, Oliver (1991) was among the first to argue that organizations might respond in other, more strategic ways. She pointed out that in addition to "acquiescence," organizations might well seek compromise, attempt avoidance, exercise manipulation, or express defiance. In addition to these individual-level responses, organizations may seek to join with like others to pursue a variety of related collective strategies (Scott, 2001). Of course, not all of these responses are available to all organizations at all times. As Goodrick and Salancik (1996) explain, sometimes strategic responses are inappropriate. Theorists and researchers are now examining the conditions under which one or another response is likely.

Similarly, scholars increasingly recognize that governance systems, including regulatory agencies, behave in various ways. Sometimes laws and rulings are clear and unambiguous, enforcement machinery is strong, and sanctions sure. In other cases, rather than being explicit, laws are "obscure, fragmented and highly ambiguous" (Suchman and Edelman, 1997: 929). Laws are passed, particularly in contested arenas that are vague in intent and ambiguous in meaning. Surveillance may be rare and enforcement lax, sometimes by design. Participants in organizations subject to these laws resort to collective sense-making activities (Weick, 1995), attempting to discover what the law is and what kinds of responses will be regarded as evidence of compliance. For example, in the case of civil rights legislation passed during the 1960s in the United States, personnel managers exchanged information and floated a variety of proposals at professional meetings and in their journals seeking to learn what "equal opportunity" or "affirmative action" required. Legislators worked to clarify the meaning of these statutes, and the federal courts weighed in with their own interpretations and rulings. Participants proposed interpretations of what it meant to be in compliance, and judges examined the merits of varied responses as they collectively built legal precedence (Dobbin and others, 1993; Edelman, 1992). Such circumstances "render law endogenous: the content and meaning of law is determined within the social field that it was designed to regulate" (Edelman, Uggen, and Erlanger, 1999: 407). Moreover, in such circumstances, organizations become more responsive to the normative pressures constructed in professional networks than to the coercive machinery of the state, and managers seek to invent efficiency rationales to justify their responses (Dobbin and Sutton, 1998). Sense making and negotiating activities take place at numerous levels within the field: within individual organizations as teams and committees meet to consider alternative interpretations and responses; in networks linking organizations as managers and professionals seek advice and information from a wider set of colleagues; among field-level associations (for example, trade and professional associations) where conferences are convened and position papers crafted; and between representatives of regulatory agencies, judicial bodies, and "client" organizations and associations. Compromises are hammered out and common understandings constructed. A nested set of interacting parties stretches from the nation-state down to the level of the individual organizational participant, with broader systems and forums both constraining and being informed by more localized networks.

In some circumstances, then, more coercive regulative processes are joined and/or replaced by normative processes, and unilateral directives give way to bidirectional, reciprocal interactions between various interested parties. Here, a "top-down" image of institutional pressures is supplemented by a recognition of "bottom-up" influences. A unidirectional causal model needs to be replaced by a Giddens-type "structuration" model in which structures and actors are recursively constrained, empowered—and constituted (Giddens, 1984).

Constitutive Processes

Institutional processes do not simply influence and attempt to control the behavior of existing actors; they also create new types of actors with new ways of acting in the pursuit of new interests. The operation of such constitutive processes is, in fact, the main story of recent developments in environmental policy and politics. Professionals of various types—chemists, biologists, engineers—paved the way by developing new conceptual models requiring new kinds of information assessing the state of our natural environment. Aided by the persistent efforts of a wide variety of nonprofits and advocacy groups who transform scientific evidence into normative prescriptions, these professionals have transformed our conceptions of what the natural environment is and how we relate to it. At the industry and firm levels, responsible managers have begun to recognize that pollution and other forms of environmental degradation are not simply externalities to be borne by someone else, but factors adversely affecting their own interests. There is increasing awareness that the old practices "foul our own nest." Professionals and environmental social movement organizations have successfully reframed our conception of the natural environment.

In so doing, new actors have been created. New types and categories of environmental scientists have emerged. Regulatory agencies that began as small, limited operations staffed by inspectors and lawyers have expanded to cover numerous and diverse arenas and host many of the new scientists and engineers. Organizations immersed in these changing environments respond by mapping the new complexity into their own structures. They develop their own environmental departments and their own experts in the areas in which they work. The pressures to attend to the broader needs of the environment are not only external, but increasingly internal to organizations.

Working from inside brings many advantages. Environmental concerns are less likely to be considered an alien agenda to be resisted or grudgingly pursued. Environmental concerns are more likely to be introduced early in planning stages rather than tacked on to meet a required environmental impact report. Environmental concerns are more likely to benefit, rather than be cut off, from insider knowledge. Environmental concerns are more likely to be incorporated into the standards—such as "green accounting"—employed by a firm or industry to measure its own effectiveness (Anderson and Bateman, 2000; Cairncross, 1993; Hoffman, 1997; Streeck and Schmitter, 1985; Taylor, 1984).

Such assertions may well be overstated as we view the scene at the beginning of a new millennium, but there seems little doubt that they provide a foundation for a basic change in the ways the natural environment are regarded and treated. Cultural-cognitive transformations that give rise to and empower new actors and new ways of acting, once set in motion, are powerful forces capable of engendering fundamental social change.

CONCLUSION

An institutional perspective supports a broader and longer view of organizational and social change. It encourages us not to restrict our attention to the legal or regulatory aspects of environmental controls, but to consider also the changing normative systems and cultural-cognitive frames. It also reminds us to be reflexive and put ourselves in the picture.

The structuration perspective outlined in this chapter will not be complete if we do not include ourselves among the actors and schemas at play in current development. Scholars with organizational interests can choose to either advance or suppress attention to the natural environment. Until recently, we have done little to advance attention to and analysis of this broader view of organizational-environment interdependence. But efforts are now under way. Landmark studies have been carried out that provide the underpinnings of a necessary scholarly base. Interest groups and sections have been established in mainstream professional associations affording contacts among scholars sharing these interests and providing beacons to attract and nurture fledging scholars. Conferences have been convened and papers published. If all goes well, these early efforts will spawn additional research, generate public and corporate funding, devise courses and training aids, and, eventually, produce specialists who will devote their careers to enhancing our knowledge of organizations and the natural environment.

NOTES

1. This development has been characterized as the second wave of environmentalism in the United States, the first wave having occurred during the latter part of the nineteenth century when conservation and wilderness protection movements led to such developments as the creation of the national park and forest systems (Egri and Herman, 2000).

2. A fourth policy arena identified by Lowi was "constituent policy," which was primarily concerned with the infrastructure mediating the relation between representatives and the electorate (such as reapportionment or setting up a new agency). Two broad dimensions underlie the typology: whether the likelihood of coercion is immediate or remote, and whether policies are directed at the conduct of specific actors (including corporate actors) or at the broader environment of conduct. Regulative policy is characterized by immediate coercion directed at specific actors (Lowi, 1972: 299–300).

REFERENCES

Anderson, Lynne M., and Thomas S. Bateman. 2000. "Individual Environmental Initiative: Championing Natural Environmental Issues in U.S. Business Organizations." *Academy of Management Journal,* 43: 548–570.

Cairncross, Frances. 1993. *Costing the Earth.* Boston: Harvard Business School Press.

Campbell, John L., J. Rodgers Hollingsworth, and Leon N. Lindberg, eds. 1991. *Governance of the American Economy.* New York: Cambridge University Press.

Carson, Rachel. 1962. *Silent Spring.* Boston: Houghton Mifflin.

Catton, William R., and Riley E. Dunlap. 1978. "Environmental Sociology: A New Paradigm." *American Sociologist,* 13: 41–49.

Dill, William R. 1958. "Environment as an Influence on Managerial Autonomy." *Administrative Science Quarterly,* 2: 409–443.

DiMaggio, Paul J., and Walter W. Powell. 1983. "The Iron Cage Revisited: Institutional Isomorphism and Collective Rationality in Organizational Fields." *American Sociological Review,* 48: 147–160.

Dobbin, Frank R., and John R. Sutton. 1998. "The Strength of a Weak State: The Rights Revolution and the Rise of Human Resources Management Divisions," *American Journal of Sociology,* 104: 441–476.

Dobbin, Frank R., John R. Sutton, John W. Meyer, and W. Richard Scott. 1993. "Equal Opportunity Law and the Construction of Internal Labor Markets." *American Journal of Sociology,* 99(2): 396–427.

Dunlap, Riley E., and William R. Catton, Jr. 1979. "Environmental Sociology." *Annual Review of Sociology,* 5: 243–273.

Edelman, Lauren B. 1992. "Legal Ambiguity and Symbolic Structures: Organizational Mediation of Civil Rights Law." *American Journal of Sociology,* 97: 1531–1576.

Edelman, Lauren B., Christopher Uggen, and Howard S. Erlanger. 1999. "The Endogeneity of Legal Regulation: Grievance Procedures as Rational Myth." *American Journal of Sociology,* 105: 406–454.

Egri, Carolyn, and Susan Herman. 2000. "Leadership in the North American Environmental Sector: Values, Leadership Styles and Contexts of Environmental Leaders and Their Organizations." *Academy of Management Journal,* 43: 571–604.

Giddens, Anthony. 1984. *The Constitution of Society.* Berkeley: University of California Press.

Goodrick, Elizabeth, and Gerald R. Salancik. 1996. "Organizational Discretion in Responding to Institutional Practices: Hospitals and Casarean Births." *Administration Science Quarterly,* 41: 1–28.

Hirsch, Paul M. 1985. "The Study of Industries." In Samuel B. Bacharach and Stephen M. Mitchell, eds., *Research in the Sociology of Organizations,* 4, 217–309. Greenwich, CT: JAI Press.

Hoffman, Andrew J. 1997. *From Heresy to Dogma: An Institutional History of Corporate Environmentalism.* San Francisco: New Lexington Press.

Lowi, Theodore. 1972. "Four Systems of Policy, Politics, and Choice." *Public Administrative Review,* 32: 298–310.

Meyer, John W., and Brian Rowan. 1977. "Institutionalized Organizations: Formal Structure as Myth and Ceremony." *American Journal of Sociology,* 83: 340–363.

Noll, Roger G. 1971. *Reforming Regulation.* Washington, DC: Brookings Institution.

Noll, Roger G., ed. 1985. *Regulatory Policy and the Social Sciences.* Berkeley: University of California Press.

Oliver, Christine. 1991. "Strategic Responses to Institutional Processes." *Academy of Management Review,* 16: 145–179.

Pfeffer, Jeffrey, and Gerald Salancik. 1978. *The External Control of Organizations*. New York: Harper & Row.

Powell, Walter W. 1988. "Institutional Effects on Organizational Structure and Performance." In Lynne G. Zucker, ed., *Institutional Patterns and Organizations: Culture and Environment*, 115–136. Cambridge, MA: Ballinger.

Schmitter, Philippe. 1990. "Sectors in Modern Capitalism: Models of Governance and Variations in Performance." In Renato Brunetta and Carlo Dell'Arginga, eds., *Labour Relations and Economic Performance*, 3–39. Houndmills, UK: Macmillan.

Scott, W. Richard. 2001. *Institutions and Organizations*. 2nd ed. Thousand Oaks, CA: Sage.

Scott, W. Richard, and John W. Meyer. 1983. "The Organization of Societal Sectors." In John W. Meyer and W. Richard Scott, eds., *Organizational Environments: Ritual and Rationality*, 129–153. Beverly Hills, CA: Sage.

Scott, W. Richard, Martin Ruef, Peter J. Mendel, and Carol A. Caronna. 2000. *Institutional Change and Healthcare Organizations: From Professional Dominance to Managed Care*. Chicago: University of Chicago Press.

Starik, Mark, Alfred A. Marcus, and Anne Y. Ilinitch, eds. 2000. "Special Research Forum: The Management of Organizations in the Natural Environment." *Academy of Management Journal*, 43: 539–736.

Stigler, George. 1971. "The Theory of Economic Regulation." *Bell Journal of Economics and Management Science*, 2: 3–21.

Streeck, Wolfgang, and Philippe C. Schmitter, eds. 1985. *Private Interest Government: Beyond Market and State*. Beverly Hills, CA: Sage.

Suchman, Mark C., and Lauren B. Edelman. 1997. "Legal Rational Myths: The New Institutionalism and the Law and Society Tradition." *Law and Social Inquiry*, 21: 903–941.

Taylor, Serge. 1984. *Making Bureaucracies Think: The Environmental Impact Statement Strategy of Administrative Reform*. Stanford, CA: Stanford University Press.

Thompson, James D. 1967. *Organizations in Action*. New York: McGraw-Hill.

Weick, Karl E. 1995. *Sensemaking in Organizations*. Thousand Oaks, CA: Sage.

Wilson, James Q. 1980. "The Politics of Regulation." In James Q. Wilson, ed., *The Politics of Regulation*, 357–394. New York: Basic Books.

Wilson, James Q. 1989. *Bureaucracy: What Government Agencies Do and Why They Do It*. New York: Basic Books.

States and European political environment and, 182–83
Automobile safety, 375

Babbitt, Bruce, 242, 250
Bansal, Pratima, 200, 293
Barley, Steven, xxi, 440
Bartels, Carlton, 119, 141
Bazerman, Max, 250
Beck, Ulrich: *Risk Society*, 18–19
Behavioral changes: organizational theory and, 440
Belief systems, *see* Cognitive institutions
Bellman, Howard, 104
Benefits: vs. costs, 322
Berer, Johannes, 123
Berry, Michael A., 199
Best practice, 409, 420
"Best science" debate: HCPs and, 247–48, 253
Birds: study and protection of, 43
Black-Eye effect: of Soderstrom, Ilinitch, and Thomas, 160, 161
Boston City Council: solid-waste disposal, 333
Bottom-up process: of subversive storytellers, 96
Boundary-spanning individuals, 441
Branch plants: enforcement rates for, 69–70, 73–74
Britain: CO_2 regulation in, 382
British Columbia: effect of political regimes and enforcement districts on environmental enforcement, 64–66, 75–80; environment enforcement in Lower Fraser Basin, 57–83; environmental charges in (1985–1996), 63; methodology for assessing enforcement variation, 71–75
British Columbia Ministry of Environment, Lands, and Parks (BCMOELP), 61
Bull trout: protection of, 244

Bureaucracy: EIAs and, 225; Gouldner's patterns of organization for, 204; Jacobs' study of, 204–5; Navy as symbolic, 203; unofficial changes in, 204–5
Business: corporate environmentalism and, 2; environment and sustainability as part of, 437; government regulation and enforcement and, 244–45; and natural environment, 12; regulation applied to, 373–74. *See also* Industry

California: Arco and clean air regulation in, 165
Canada: CO_2 regulation in, 382; water regulation enforcement in, 64. *See also* British Columbia
"Cap-and-trade" solutions: to air quality regulation, 120
Capital: as entity, 126
Carbon dioxide (CO_2), 178–79, 182, 382
Carson, Rachel, 90, 454
Catalytic converters, 181–82, 380
CE mark product certification, 419
CEMS, *see* Continuous emissions monitoring system (CEMS)
Centers of authority, 293
Central-government logic: about solid-waste management, 329, 330, 340–41
CERCLA, *see* Superfund
CERES, 437
CERs, *see* Corporate Environmental Reports (CERs)
Certification (ISO): commitment to, 425n3; ISO 9000 process and, 413–14; for ISO programs, 416; pressure to meet ISO standards and, 421
CFCs: ozone depletion and, 295
Chambliss, Elizabeth, 58
Change processes: collective action/movements literature and, 93; cultural, 442–43; heterogeneity and, 178; institutional, 11

Chemco (pseud.): EPA memorandum of understanding and, 298–99; PFC emissions reduction and, 295–302, 304

Chemical Manufacturers' Association (CMA): Responsible Care Program of, 4–5, 166, 194, 400, 402

Chemicals industry: ISO 14000, ISO 9000, and, 426n8; PFC gases and, 295; reputation commons in, 393, 397; study of coercive pressures on environmental strategies in, 157–61, 162. *See also* Monsanto

Chicago Board of Trade: pollution permit trading and, 119, 134

City Press, see Recycled newsprint in Michigan

Clean Air Act (1972), 220

Clean Air Act Amendments (1990), 120; Title IV of, 120, 124, 131

Clean air regulation: Arco and, 165

Clean Seas, 104

Clean technology, 269; at Monsanto, 280–81

Climate change: automobile industry strategic responses in United States and Europe, 178–90; timing and context of, as strategic concern, 180–82

Climate science: auto industry perspectives on, 184–85, 188–89

CMA, *see* Chemical Manufacturers' Association (CMA)

CO$_2$ emissions: German VA on Global Warming Prevention and, 348

Coalitions: grassroots ECR, 108

Codes of conduct: environmental, 355; from trade associations, 402

Codes of signification, 439

Coercive pressures, 409; in chemicals and computer industries, 157–61, 162; for conforming to ISO standards, 419–20; exploratory study of pressure on environmental strategies, 156–61, 162; im-

plications of study for theory development, 162–68; isomorphism and, 151, 152, 153–56

Cognition: in institutional theory, 314

Cognitive categorization theory: issue interpretations and, 313, 320, 322

Cognitive commensuration, 126; for pollution permits trading, 135–37

Cognitive features, 409; of VAs, 351

Cognitive institutions: in HCP debate, 245–46

Cognitive pressures: for conforming to ISO standards, 421–22

Cognitive processes, 264, 314, 320, 322

Cognitive reality: in new institutionalism, 202

Cohen's Kappa, 286n1

Collaborative agreement: HCPs and, 250–51

Collective action frames, 93–94; ECR practice and, 104–9; narrative perspective and, 93; social psychology of, 93; subversive stories and, 96–97

Collective activities: regulation of knowledge-intensive, 376–79

Collective good: natural resources and, 48

Collective rationality, xxiii; field-level institutions and, xx, 5–12; vs. individual rationality, 8; institutional processes and, 7; of organizational fields, 7–8; process of, 11; social network approach and, 10–12

Collective responsibility: for common problems, 395–96

College News, see Recycled newsprint in Michigan

Command-and-control approach: to air pollution control, 120; institutional bases for, 122; vs. market-based regulation, 131; to regulation, 380

Commensuration: cognitive, 126, 135–37; core dimensions of, 126–27; definition

(EMAS), 2, 381, 416; vs. ISO 14001 program, 207
Economic conceptions of firm, 16
Economics: value of environment and, 123
Ecosystem: as model, 51; national parks and, 52–53; nation-state responsibility for, 49; nature as universal system, 47; regional, 61, 66–67. *See also* Scientific model of nature protection
ECR, *see* Environmental conflict resolution (ECR)
Edelman, Lauren B., 58, 457
Ehrenfeld, John, 207
EIAs, *see* Environmental Impact Assessment (EIA)
Electric vehicles, 181, 187
EMAS system, *see* Eco-Management and Audit Scheme (EMAS)
Emergency Planning and Community Right to Know Act (EPCRA), 156
Emerson, Kirk, 108
Emissions controls: global automobile industry and, 178–90; Monsanto efforts at, 277–80; semiconductor industry voluntary PFC emissions reduction agreements and, 291–305
EMP, *see* Environmental Mediation Project (EMP)
Employee groups: as field-level constituency, 14
Employees: corporate environmental reports and, 266
Endangered Species Act (ESA): competing tensions with HCPs, 246–247; conflicting and ambiguous enforcement of, 245; Habitat Conservation Plans and, 241–43; spotted owl and, 235
Endangered species protection: as organizational field, 237–38. *See also* Habitat Conservation Plans (HCPs)
Energy Department: and W-T-E as solid-waste solution, 331

Enforcement: in British Columbia's Lower Fraser Basin, 58; and compliance, 58, 80–83; domain of, 59, 61–63; environmental, 60–61; institutional perspective on, 58–61; in local domains, 61; methodology for assessing variation in, 71–75; organizational characteristics and context of, 77–79; policy issues in, 66–67; rate variations in, 66–71; regulatory system and organizational changes and, 60; types of variations in, 64–71
Enforcement agency: treatment of companies by, 80
Enforcement districts: effect on environmental enforcement, 75–80
Engineering concerns, 15–16
England (Britain), *see* Britain
Entrepreneurs: institutional, 93, 104, 248–53
Environment: use of term for natural environment, 453–54. *See also* Natural environment
Environmental associations: enforcement rates against members and, 70, 79
Environmental awareness: EIAs and, 225–27
Environmental conflict resolution (ECR), 90–113; collective action and, 104–9; internal disagreements over, 106, 107–8; narrative perspective on institutional change and, 92–97; Santa Barbara and, 102–4; Snoqualmie and, 100–102; Storm King and, 97–100
Environmental conflicts: federal resolution assistance, 107–9
Environmental Defense (group), 4
Environmental Defense Fund (EDF): McDonald's and, 401
Environmental economics: allocation and, 123
Environmental enforcement: in British Columbia, 57–83; methodology for assess-

strategies and practices, 163–68; environmental litigation and, 99; as externality, 394; from human activity, 372; marginal impact of, 394–95; Monsanto goals for controlling, 277–81; as negative externality, 123–24; open sourcing and regulation of, 379–84; permits for, 119–41; polluter knowledge of controlling, 381; regulation of, 67–68; remediation of, 130–32; reputation commons and, 393–404; selling futures in, 119–41; tradable pollution as regulation, 130–41. *See also* Enforcement; Regulation; specific types

Pollution prevention, 269; at Monsanto, 277

Porter, Michael, 442

Powell, Walter W., 7, 152, 203, 248, 312, 321, 456

Power: contextualization of, 304–5; in institutional transformation, 304; organizational levels of, 444, 445; speech acts and, 444–46

Pragmatist organizations, 199

Precautionary Principle, 371

President's Science Advisory Committee, 181

Pressures: impact of external on organization, 265–66; on industry (*see* specific pressures); institutional and technical domains in organizational responses to, 264–66

Prices: value commensuration for pollution and, 134

Primary manufacturing: enforcement rates against, 69

Privatization: of reputation commons, 401–2

Proactive organizations, 198–99; Chemco, semiconductor manufacturers, and, 305–6; environmental management orientations of, 269

Process-based instruments: for environmental regulation, 381

Product markets: elimination of, 15

Product stewardship, 269; in chemical industry, 295

Production processes, 15

Professional community: and pressure to meet ISO standards, 420–21

Progress politics: correlation with institutionalized organizational greening, 196

Project XL (EPA), 348, 355, 360

Propaganda: privatization of reputation commons and, 401

Protection of nature, 42–43

Public: NGOs and (Netherlands), 358; NGOs and (U.S.), 354–55

Public information: commensuration and, 127

Public perception: of industries, 159–60

Public policy: commensuration and, 125; market-based theories of, 121–24

Public voluntary programs (PVPs), 346, 347; features of, 349–50; in United States, 347

PVPs, *see* Public voluntary programs (PVPs)

Quality movement: ISO 9000 and, 415

Quality standards, 407–24

Quasi-governmental bodies: standards from, 400

Radon, xxi

Rasanen, Keijo, 197

Rates of enforcement: methodology for assessing variation and sources, 71–75; types of variations in, 66–71

Rationalization: in world culture, 47–48

Raw materials, 15

RCRA corrective actions, 159

Reactive firm orientation, 268–69

Recycled newsprint in Michigan, 315–23;